D1207564

Traffic Engineering and QoS Optimization of Integrated Voice & Data Networks

The Morgan Kaufmann Series in Networking
Series Editor, David Clark, M.I.T.

For further information on these books and for a list of forthcoming titles, please visit our Web site at http://www.mkp.com.

Traffic Engineering and QoS Optimization of Integrated Voice & Data Networks

GERALD R. ASH
Fellow and Senior Technical Consultant, AT&T Labs

AMSTERDAM • BOSTON • HEIDELBERG • LONDON
NEW YORK • OXFORD • PARIS • SAN DIEGO
SAN FRANCISCO • SINGAPORE • SYDNEY • TOKYO
Morgan Kaufmann Publishers is an imprint of Elsevier

ELSEVIER

MORGAN KAUFMANN PUBLISHERS

Acquisitions Editor	Rick Adams
Publishing Services Manager	George Morrison
Production Editor	Dawnmarie Simpson
Associate Acquisitions Editor	Rachel Roumeliotis
Production Assistant	Melinda Ritchie
Cover Design	Eric DeCicco
Composition	Integra Software Services, Pvt Ltd.
Technical Illustration	Integra Software Services, Pvt Ltd.
Copyeditor	Melissa Revelle
Proofreader	Phyllis Coyne et al. Proofreading
Indexer	Broccoli Information Management
Interior Printer	The Maple-Vail Book Manufacturing Group
Cover Printer	Phoenix Color Corporation

Morgan Kaufmann Publishers is an imprint of Elsevier.
500 Sansome Street, Suite 400, San Francisco, CA 94111

This book is printed on acid-free paper.

Library of Congress Cataloging-in-Publication Data
Ash, Gerald R.
Traffic engineering and Qos optimization of integrated voice & data networks/Gerald R. Ash.
    p.   cm.
  Includes bibliographical references and index.
  ISBN-13: 978-0-12-370625-6 (hardcover : alk. paper)
  ISBN-10: 0-12-370625-4 (hardcover : alk. paper)
1. Telecommunication—Traffic—Management.   2. Computer networks—Quality control.
3. Internet telephony—Quality control.   I. Title.
TK5105.8865.A84 2006
621.382′1—dc22

                                                                          2006020078

ISBN 13: 978-0-12-370625-6
ISBN 10: 0-12-370625-4

For information on all Morgan Kaufmann publications, visit our Web site at www.mkp.com or www.books.elsevier.com

Printed in the United States of America
06 07 08 09 10   5 4 3 2 1

Working together to grow
libraries in developing countries

www.elsevier.com | www.bookaid.org | www.sabre.org

ELSEVIER   BOOK AID International   Sabre Foundation

In memory of my parents,
who gave me life and shaped who I am.
And dedicated to my wife, children, and grandchildren,
who gave my life meaning, fulfillment, and joy.

Contents

Foreword

There is no question that there has been a radical shift in the type of services carried over the Internet. Changes in technology and bandwidth availability have been leveraged by new Internet protocols to realize new services, all of which are implemented over the same core network. This is truly a widening of the functions available to a customer, as the simple data delivery mechanisms have been extended down the food-chain to offer virtual private networks, virtual LANs, and pseudowires to carry transport circuits over the connectionless infrastructure of the Internet. At the same time, the convergence of voice, video, and data has become a reality, with many millions of individuals using voice over IP connections, telecoms companies migrating their telephony to IP, video being streamed point-to-point and point-to-multipoint across the Internet, and the more established data services like Web access continuing to grow. All of these different service types place very different demands for Quality of Service (QoS) and result in the network operator needing to make widely different contractual Service Level Agreements (SLAs) with the customers.

The term *Traffic Engineering* has come to mean very different things to different people. Some view it as a relatively static, off-line, planning activity that is used to dimension capacity planning within a transport network. Others see it as a dynamic mechanism for placing traffic within a network. In either case the objective is the same: to optimize the use of the network resources so that maximum revenue is derived from minimum expenditure. Clearly this objective is met by avoiding congestion, placing existing traffic so that capacity is available to meet further services, providing adequate QoS so that differentiated services can be sold to the customers, and planning capacity so that resources will be available in good time to meet the demands.

Historically, some of the division in the interpretation of traffic engineering stems from the separation between a transport-centric view of networks where long-term circuits are provisioned only after a rigorous planning exercise, and a data-centric view of networking where data are dynamically directed to the available bandwidth, and around network hot-spots. But the networking world is converging, and those who are not willing to embrace both concepts of traffic engineering will be left behind.

Network engineers must be willing to accept the necessity both of careful capacity planning and on-line, dynamic traffic engineering. Modern networks must be able to adapt flexibly to rapid variations in traffic demand, and must be able to offer significant discrimination between service types by meeting substantially different SLAs for each service's traffic.

This flexibility critically includes the ability to perform network planning and traffic engineering across multiple network layers. When we consider that connections within one network layer provide capacity within a higher network layer (for example, a

TDM circuit may realize a TE link in an MPLS network), it should be clear that capacity planning in the higher layer requires network engineering in the lower layer. Thus, as capacity planning becomes more dynamic in response to flexible service demands, the network engineering of lower layers develops into dynamic traffic engineering. Fully coupling these processes across layer boundaries enables multi-layer traffic engineering that can make optimal use of network resources at all layers, and can ensure that multiple client layers can be integrated over a single, lower, server layer.

All of this demands that considerably more attention be paid to the techniques of traffic engineering. We need a formal understanding of the issues within the network and the mechanisms available to provide adequate QoS. We need a thorough analysis of the various possible approaches to traffic management and capacity planning, and we need to tie these methods to our many years of experience with network optimization and the latest operational techniques for predicting traffic behavior, including forecasting, performance monitoring, and fault analysis. With access to this information and the full toolset, we will be ready to take our networks forward to meet the demands of convergence between network layers, as well as the demands of convergence of services onto a common network infrastructure.

Adrian Farrel
Llangollen
Old Dog Consulting
Co-chair of the IETF's CCAMP, PCE, and L1VPN working groups
June 2006

Preface

Why This Book?

About a decade ago AT&T completed its worldwide evolution/revolution to dynamic routing in its global circuit-switched voice/ISDN network. It had taken nearly 2 decades to make that all happen. The first implementation began on July 14, 1984, Bastille Day, which celebrates the French Revolution and itself represented a major revolution in network technology. Both revolutions aimed at introducing more freedom and fairness, but fortunately, the revolution that occurred in 1984 did not result in any chopped-off heads, as did the first revolution: the scientists and engineers responsible for the routing revolution only were subjected to hats-off treatment! Dynamic routing was big news on cutover day, and the national news in the United States covered the event. Over the next 2 decades, the transition to a fully deployed global dynamic routing network was enormous, and the payoff was dramatic. There was much celebrating, backslapping, and crowing along the way. Eventually I published a very large book on the technology, but at about the same time, and as it continuously does, the world was changing fundamentally: the Internet was rising on the horizon.

Astounding breakthroughs by the NetHeads (who we suppose come from Geekia) gave us the Internet: intelligent end-user devices that communicate with packet switching and can define new services, an automated, distributed, and self-organizing network, protocols that are end to end and open, but where quality of service (QoS) is not assured. This Internet revolution trumped 100 years of crown-jewel technological innovation by the BellHeads (who we suppose come from Telephonia), which yielded the greatest machine ever devised: a global, intelligent telephone network, densely connected by circuit switching, protocols that are often proprietary, and where QoS is assured by careful engineering and management.

This Internet technology revolution fully eclipsed the voice/ISDN dynamic routing revolution, and also my book, and over time these were gradually forgotten. But while one door closed, another door opened: constant and unchangeable through the changing world were the traffic engineering and QoS optimization (TQO) principles used to design dynamic routing protocols. TQO controls a network's response to traffic demands and other stimuli, such as network failures, and encompasses traffic management through optimization and control of routing functions, and capacity management through optimization and control of network design. TQO principles have been used to design the revolutionary dynamic routing implementations worldwide and can be used to design integrated voice/data dynamic routing networks in any technology, particularly Internet technology.

This book explains, illustrates, and applies these design principles, which include class-of-service routing, connection admission control, source-based dynamic path selection, dynamic resource allocation/protection, dynamic transport routing, queuing priority mechanisms, integrated services performance realization, and others. I have been deeply involved in applying these principles to AT&T's network evolution, where I lead the internal routing/addressing/traffic-engineering strategy ("RATS") team that spear-headed the evolution studies. RATS conducted detailed modeling/analysis and case studies for a wide range of alternative architectures under consideration, which are presented throughout this book for both intranetwork and internetwork TQO/dynamic routing design. Network evolution stemming from the RATS effort revolutionized the reliability, performance, traffic handling efficiency, and revenue generation capability of the integrated voice/ISDN network and inspired a worldwide migration to TQO/dynamic routing by many other carriers. We provide detailed case studies of the optimization of multiprotocol label switching (MPLS)/generalized MPLS (GMPLS)-based integrated voice/data dynamic routing networks. These studies illustrate the application of the TQO design principles and provide a basis for generic TQO (GTQO) protocol requirements for MPLS/GMPLS-enabled technologies.

Approach

TQO is important because networks are subject to overloads and failures, no matter how big or how fat ("overprovisioned") we build them and/or how sophisticated we design their management and control technology. We've all experienced communication network overloads and failures, they happen all the time. Web sites go down and congest, terrorist attacks and hurricanes knock out data centers and server farms, and cellular networks are unusable during events such as 9/11 and the devastating 2005 hurricanes. Overload/failure events are typical and unavoidable in all types of networks, no matter what the technology, size, etc. These negative effects of overloads and failures can be greatly mitigated by TQO methods, which have been used in data networks since Morse's invention of the telegraph in 1835 and in voice networks since Bell's invention of the telephone in 1876. There is of course proof for the benefits of TQO, and we show that. TQO/dynamic networks achieve essentially zero traffic loss performance under normal traffic/network conditions, capital savings from efficient network design/optimization, new services revenue, and operational cost efficiencies through automation and real-time network control. New services can be designed and introduced based on the class-of-service routing concept, enabling services to be defined through provisioning of tables and parameters in the traffic router nodes rather than through new software/hardware development.

We describe analysis, design, and simulation models developed by the author and his colleagues over the past 2 decades and use these to analyze the various components of TQO, to conduct large-scale case studies of converged networks, to design the GTQO protocol, and to quantify the benefits. We use a layered model of TQO [traffic/application layer, MPLS label switched path (LSP)/connection layer, GMPLS LSP/logical link layer, physical network layer, and operations/management layer] and formulate the TQO design problem and discuss its solution at each layer. A comprehensive coherent vision is analyzed at each layer of a converged network architecture, which considers the deep technical issues as well as the impact of the divergent BellHead/NetHead views. As to the latter, a cultural dynamic that became apparent in RATS was the large gap between the BellHead culture, representing the voice/ISDN circuit-switching technologies, and NetHead culture, representing the IP-, ATM-, and frame-relay-based technologies. NetHeads live and build computer data networks and have their geek culture and beliefs, while BellHeads live and build telephone voice networks and have their rather square culture and beliefs. These two worlds have been at war for nigh-on to 40 years, and this "war of two worlds" is the battlefront setting for this book.

Regarding TQO, NetHeads believe that networks should be very fat and designed to carry any traffic the network might encounter—careful engineering is neither desired nor required. BellHeads believe that networks should be carefully engineered to carry the expected traffic—they have sophisticated theories to do careful engineering to assure QoS. NetHeads are scornful of BellHeads' careful engineering and QoS assurance, "capacity is free," just put in an infinite amount and stop worrying! BellHeads counter that those who proclaim "capacity is free" aren't the ones paying for it, and that 100 years of careful traffic engineering have proven successful and wise! This book reflects the lessons and wisdom of both worlds, and in RATS these cultures did work well together, despite the gap, and reached consensus on innovative architecture directions. NetHeads will see a lot of BellHead philosophy in this book, and perhaps declare this a "BellHead book," but BellHeads will see much NetHead thinking as well, and perhaps declare this a "NetHead book."

In the end, we speak of truce and focus on the convergence of these two disparate worlds, bridging the gap between BellHeads and NetHeads in TQO space. Both Geekian and Telephonian views are taken into account since both are right. If indeed GTQO methods are developed and implemented, NetHeads should be happy to see that their ingenious protocols, particularly MPLS, GMPLS, and others, are central to the GTQO requirements. BellHeads will recognize that their time-honored and successful networking principles—bandwidth reservation, dynamic alternate routing, traffic management, capacity management, and others—are included as well. So everyone will be happy at least some of the time and no one will be unhappy all of the time with this approach.

A main avenue to realize requirements is through the standards process, and needed standards extensions are discussed, including end-to-end QoS signaling with NSIS (next steps in signaling), PCE (path computation element), DSTE (DiffServ-aware MPLS traffic engineering), MPLS crankback, and others. Alternatives to the GTQO approach, including distributed virtual network approaches, flow-aware networking, centralized TQO approaches, and game theoretic approaches, are presented for thoughtful comparisons and discussion.

Audience

This book is targeted at practitioners, network designers, and software engineers who want an in-depth understanding of TQO of converged IP/MPLS/GMPLS networks and provides an excellent supplementary text for academic courses at the graduate or undergraduate level in computer networking, network design, network routing, optimization, and emerging standards. Practitioners will find descriptions of current TQO trends and solutions and will find answers to many of their everyday questions and problems. This book also provides a comprehensive resource for researchers in traffic engineering, optimization, network design, network routing, voice/data network technology, and network convergence standards.

This book assumes a working knowledge of networks, protocols (particularly Internet protocols), and optimization techniques. The reader should be fully familiar with the concepts of Internet protocol (IP), IP routing, and MPLS/GMPLS signaling basics. These topics are reviewed briefly, and references are provided for more information; however, there is no intent to provide an exhaustive treatment of these topics.

Content

Chapter 1 begins with a general model for TQO functions at each network layer, as well as traffic management and capacity management operational functions. Network layers include the traffic/application layer, connection/MPLS LSP layer, logical link/GMPLS LSP layer, physical network layer, and operations/management layer. We formulate the TQO design problem addressed at each layer and outline the solution approach, where the latter includes an analysis of TQO design and operational experience, as well as design/analysis studies. The analysis of TQO design and operational experience traces the evolution and benefits of TQO methods using ARPANET to illustrate TQO evolution in data networks and the AT&T network to illustrate TQO evolution in voice networks. TQO design principles are identified, and TQO benefits are quantified based on the operational experience. We present the key results and conclusions of the modeling and analysis studies, case studies, and GTQO protocol design.

In Chapter 2, we present models for call/session routing, which entails number/name translation to a routing address associated with service requests, and also compare various connection (bearer-path) routing methods. We introduce a full-scale, 135-node national network model and a multiservice traffic demand model, which are used throughout the book to study various TQO scenarios and trade-offs in TQO optimization, including (a) fixed routing, time-dependent routing, state-dependent routing (SDR), and event-dependent routing (EDR) path selection, (b) two-link and multilink path selection, (c) resource management and connection admission control methods, (d) service priority differentiation of key services, normal services, and best-effort services, and (e) single-area flat topologies versus multiarea hierarchical topologies. The TQO modeling shows that (a) multilink routing in sparse topology networks provides better overall performance under overload than meshed topology networks, but performance under failure may favor the meshed topology options with more alternate routing choices, and (b) EDR path selection methods exhibit comparable or better network performance compared to SDR methods.

In Chapter 3, we examine QoS resource management methods and illustrate per-flow versus per-virtual-network (VNET) resource management and multiservice integration with priority routing services. QoS resource management includes class-of-service routing, connection admission control, priority routing, bandwidth allocation/protection/reservation, priority queuing, and other related functions. Class-of-service routing provides a means to define network services through table-driven concepts rather than software development and new network deployment. The conclusions reached include (a) bandwidth reservation is critical to stable and efficient network performance and for multiservice bandwidth allocation, protection, and priority treatment and (b) per-VNET bandwidth allocation is essentially equivalent to per-flow bandwidth allocation in network performance and efficiency.

In Chapter 4, we discuss routing table management approaches and provide information exchange requirements needed for interworking across network types. Routing table management entails the automatic generation of routing tables based on information such as topology update, status update, and routing recommendations. This information is used in applying routing table design rules to determine path choices in the routing table. Link-state routing protocols such as open shortest path first (OSPF) use topology-state update mechanisms to build the topology database at each node, typically conveying the topology status through flooding of control messages containing link, node, and reachable-address information. Congestion in link-state protocols can result in widespread loss of topology database information and overload in flooding of topology database information. These and other routing table management information exchange issues are examined in this chapter. Results show that per-VNET QoS resource management, sparse, single-area flat topology, multilink routing, and EDR path selection methods lead to dramatically lower routing table management overhead.

In Chapter 5 we describe methods for dynamic transport routing, which can be realized by the capabilities of GMPLS and optical cross-connect devices to dynamically rearrange transport network capacity. GMPLS technology enables a revolutionary new approach to integrated control of the layer 3 dynamic connection routing and layer 2 dynamic transport routing to shift transport bandwidth among node pairs and services. This allows simplicity of design and robustness to load variations and network failures and provides automatic link provisioning, diverse link routing, and rapid link restoration for improved transport capacity utilization and performance under stress. We conclude that GMPLS-based dynamic transport routing provides greater network throughput and, consequently, enhanced revenue, achieves efficient network design and capital savings, and greatly enhances network performance under failure and overload.

In Chapter 6 we discuss optimization methods and principles for routing design optimization, including shortest path models and discrete event simulation models.

We also discuss optimization methods and principles for capacity design optimization, including (a) discrete event flow optimization (DEFO), (b) traffic load flow optimization, (c) virtual trunk flow optimization, and (d) dynamic transport routing capacity design. We quantify the impacts of traffic variations on network capacity design, including minute-to-minute, hour-to-hour, day-to-day, and forecast uncertainty/reserve capacity design impacts. We illustrate the use of the DEFO model for various comparative analyses, including (a) per-flow versus per-VNET design, (b) multilink versus two-link routing design, (c) single-area flat topologies versus two-level hierarchical topology design, (d) EDR versus SDR design, and (e) dynamic transport routing versus fixed transport routing network design. The conclusions show that (a) sparse topologies with multilink dynamic routing lead to capital cost advantages compared with two-link routing in meshed topologies, (b) EDR methods exhibit comparable design efficiencies to SDR, and (c) dynamic transport routing achieves capital savings by concentrating capacity on fewer, high-capacity physical fiber links. DEFO design models are shown to be extremely flexible and successful in the design of complex routing algorithms and as a basis for network capacity design methods.

In Chapter 7 we present TQO operational requirements for traffic management and capacity management functions in both data and voice networks, including (a) performance management, which collects and analyzes real-time network status and performance data and detects and corrects abnormal network conditions, (b) fault management, which deals with problems and emergencies, such as router failures and power losses, and (c) capacity management, which gathers statistics on equipment and facility use and analyzes trends to project required network upgrades and capacity augments. Traffic management controls are described, including code blocks, connection request gapping, and reroute controls, and we illustrate the conditions that warrant activation of these controls. Capacity management processes are described, including capacity forecasting, daily and weekly performance monitoring, and short-term network adjustment. We illustrate these functions with examples, and in particular we illustrate an MPLS network management implementation by taking an example from AT&T's MPLS operations architecture.

In Chapters 8 and 9 we present several case studies of TQO protocol design in operational networks: (a) circuit-switched integrated voice/ISDN dynamic routing network design for intranetwork applications, (b) circuit-switched integrated voice/ISDN dynamic routing network design for access and internetwork applications, (c) two case studies where TQO designs went astray, but which provide valuable lessons for future designs, and (d) MPLS/GMPLS-based integrated voice/data dynamic routing network design. In the final case study, we develop a 71-node national network model and multiservice traffic demand model for the TQO protocol design and again use the DEFO model for the design and optimization. We illustrate the optimization of an EDR-based path selection protocol from among a large set of candidates, show that a separate emergency-services queue is needed to assure emergency-services performance for scenarios where the normal priority queue congests, and quantify the significant benefits attainable in loss/delay performance for both voice and data traffic. These case studies provide an important basis for the GTQO protocol requirements.

Chapter 10 summarizes the results of studies presented in this book and, based on the results of these studies and operational experience, a GTQO protocol is described for application to MPLS/GMPLS-enabled technologies. Some of the important conclusions derived from the analysis models are (a) EDR path selection is preferred to SDR path selection and (b) aggregated per-VNET bandwidth allocation is preferred to per-flow bandwidth allocation. These design choices reduce control overhead, thereby increasing scalability, whereas the GMPLS-based dynamic transport routing capabilities provide greater network reliability, throughput, revenue, and capital savings. The GTQO requirements apply to access, core, intranetwork, and internetwork architectures and include end-to-end QoS signaling, class-of-service routing, per-VNET QoS resource management, dynamic bandwidth reservation, DSTE bandwidth allocation, EDR path selection, differentiated services (DiffServ) queuing priority, separate high-priority queue for emergency services, and GMPLS-based dynamic transport routing. In addition to the GTQO protocol, we present several other TQO approaches that may well be deployed and identify various standards extensions needed to accommodate the GTQO requirements and capabilities, including end-to-end QoS signaling, path computation element, DiffServ-enabled traffic engineering, MPLS crankback, and others.

Appendix A reviews some of the key TQO technologies: MPLS, GMPLS, QoS mechanisms, integrated services (IntServ), resource reservation protocol (RSVP), DiffServ, and MPLS-based QoS mechanisms. This is intended as a quick refresher and/or a brief introduction for those unfamiliar with these technologies. Ample references are provided for more detailed coverage of these important topics.

Acknowledgments

There are a large number of people I wish to acknowledge and profusely thank for assistance, collaboration, help, encouragement, great ideas, and fun over the past 15 years or so.

Very helpful comments and suggestions were made on the book proposal by Adrian Farrel, Luyuan Fang, Bur Goode, Michal Pioro, Ragu Raghuram, and JP Vasseur. Their review and suggestions definitely improved the presentation and I'm indebted to them for their help and encouragement in the course of developing this work. Thanks to Bur Goode for providing some wake-up-call-type comments on preliminary drafts of the manuscript. Bur's comments helped inspire the book's NetHead/BellHead themes and quest to seek "this is a NetHead book"-type reactions in the final manuscript.

Adrian Farrel, Lorne Mason, and Michal Pioro reviewed the draft manuscript and made extensive comments and suggestions. I feel their candid evaluations and inputs have definitely helped improve this book, and I sincerely appreciate their time and effort. Special thanks to Adrian for all his help and encouragement, from beginning to end, and for writing the Foreword. Rick Adams, Rachel Roumeliotis, and Dawnmarie Simpson provided support, encouragement, helpful suggestions, and patience throughout the course of producing the book, and for that I'm sincerely thankful.

Within AT&T I'd like to especially thank the following people for their excellent contributions, collaborations, support, and on-going discussions: Bruce Blake, Deborah Brungard, Chris Chase, Jin-Shi Chen, Angela Chiu, Suching Chou, Gagan Choudhury, Li Chung, Martin Dolly, Kevin D'Souza, Chuck Dvorak, Jerry Ezrol, Luyuan Fang, Saul Fishman, Tom Frost, Liza Fung, Bur Goode, Mohammed Hamami, Jim Hand, Chuck Kalmanek, Christopher Kwan, Wai Sum Lai, Chin Lee, Yoni Levy, Clayton Lockhart, Joyce Migdall, John Mulligan, Al Morton, Quynh Nguyen, John Oetting, Ragu Raghuram, Scott Sayers, Mostafa Hashem Sherif, Percy Tarapore, Diana Woo, Yung Yu, and David Zerling.

In the IETF I'd like to extend warmest thanks to the following people for all their collaboration, helpful comments, assistance, and encouragement: Arthi Ayyangar, Dan Awduche, Attila Bader, Lou Berger, Nabil Bitar, David Black, Jim Boyle, Igor Bryskin, Anna Charny, Dean Cheng, Yacine El Mghazli, Adrian Farrel, Matthias Friedrich, Xiaoming Fu, Durga Gangisetti, Robert Hancock, Atsushi Iwata, Lars-Erik Jonsson, Cornelia Kappler, Georgios Karagiannis, Kenji Kumaki, Chris Lang, Francois Le Faucheur, Jean-Louis Le Roux, Andy Malis, Andrew McDonald, Thomas Morin, Eiji Oki, Dave Oran, Dimitri Papadimitriou, Tom Phelan, Hal Sandick, Tom Scott,

Hannes Tschofenig, Sven van den Bosch, JP Vasseur, Lars Westberg, and Raymond Zhang.

In the ITU I'd like to particularly thank the following people for their many contributions, insights, discussions, and comments in the course of this work: Mikael Ahman, Anne Elvidge, Davide Grillo, Tommy Petersen, Bruce Pettitt, Jim Roberts, Michael Tuxen, and Manuel Villèn-Altamirano.

Within the ATM Forum I'm indebted to the following people for their significant input and valuable help throughout the course of this work: Carl Rajsic, Peter Roberts, John Ruttmiller, and Mickey Spiegel.

I owe a debt of gratitude to the many other esteemed colleagues for their pioneering, creative work over the past 15 years and who were kind enough to provide information contained in this book: Dave Allan, Joyce Bradley, Terry Brown, Kenneth Chan, Fu Chang, Prosper Chemouil, Jiayu Chen, Joshua Dayanim, Joachim Dressler, Jack Dudash, Victoria Fineberg, Alan Frey, Lindsay Hiebert, BaoSheng Huang, Frank Kelly, Peter Key, K. R. Krishnan, John Labourdette, Kenichi Mase, Lorne Mason, Jerry McCurdy, David McGuigan, Deep Medhi, Chris Metz, Arne Oestlie, Jennifer Rexford, Steven Schwartz, Harmen Van der Linde, and Ben Vos.

I'm deeply indebted to all of these people for their collaborations over the past 15 or more years. It's been my privilege to work with these talented individuals, and to all these people, my heartfelt thanks.

About the Author

Gerald R. Ash is from Glen Rock, New Jersey. He graduated from grammar school, high school, Rutgers, and Caltech, but got sent to Vietnam instead of being able to attend his Caltech graduation. He spent the first 20 years of his AT&T career as "the consummate BellHead" (as one colleague put it) but for the next 15 years sought to be a blossoming NetHead (although he never attempted the standard ponytail, beard, tee-shirt, shorts, and sandals). He does not claim to be a NetHead, but over the last 15 years has advanced to become perhaps 50% NetHead. He is happily married for over 40 years, has three children and four grandchildren. He is interested in your reaction to the book. He can be contacted at gash@att.com.

Chapter 1
Traffic Engineering and QoS Optimization Models

1.1 Introduction

Dear reader, the setting for this book is the "war of two worlds," so different that we imagine they exist on separate planets. Let's call these planets Geekia, where the NetHeads dwell, and Telephonia, where the BellHeads dwell. In his classic paper "NetHeads versus BellHeads," Steve Steinberg [STEINBERG96] described these two worlds, which have been at war for nigh-on to 40 years. The NetHeads are those who live and build computer data networks and have their geek culture and beliefs. The BellHeads are those who live and build telephone voice networks and have their rather square culture and beliefs. NetHead culture requires a ponytail, beard, tee-shirt, shorts, and sandals (no socks). BellHead culture requires a neat haircut, clean shaven, suit, and tie.

Fundamental NetHead beliefs, which led to the astounding breakthroughs that gave us the Internet, are that data networks should be sparsely connected and very fat; they should be designed to be large enough to carry any traffic the network might encounter—careful engineering is neither desired nor required. Telephony is just another Internet service, the network ends in intelligent end-user devices that can define new services, while the network itself is automated and self-organizing, yet not where the primary intelligence resides; protocols are end to end and open (e.g., TCP/IP).

Fundamental BellHead beliefs, which fueled 100 years of crown-jewel technological innovation and yielded the greatest machine ever devised, are that networks should be densely connected and carefully engineered to carry the expected traffic—they have sophisticated theories to do careful engineering. Quality of service (QoS) is assured, networks are intelligent, end devices are not, and protocols are often proprietary. NetHeads are scornful of BellHeads' careful engineering and QoS assurance, "capacity is free," just put in an infinite amount and stop worrying! BellHeads counter that those who proclaim "capacity is free" aren't the ones paying for it, and that 100 years of careful traffic engineering has proved successful and wise!

This book is focused on the convergence of these two disparate worlds and is trying to bridge the gap between the NetHeads and the BellHeads in the traffic engineering

(TE) and QoS optimization (TQO) space. I hope to motivate people to read the book and more importantly to apply it. As such, the requirements put forth are for consideration by network architects and developers alike. Ultimately, I believe, network directions along this line will eventually emerge and/or perhaps be reinvented. For example, technologies such as the generalized multiprotocol label switching (GMPLS)-based directions discussed in Chapter 5 have emerged, i.e., have been reinvented, if you will. But we'll get to that more in Chapter 5.

So any means by which the requirements proclaimed in this book emerge into real network applications and capabilities would be just fine with me and represent an expected outcome as well as a great step forward for converged networks in general. That end result is really the essential motivation and perhaps lasting value of the book. So let's bridge this gap between the BellHead and the NetHead worlds using the TQO ether to communicate between them; in a nutshell that's what the book is all about folks.

I spent the first 20 years of my career as "the consummate BellHead," as one well-respected colleague put it, but for the next 15 years I sought to be a blossoming NetHead (although I never attempted a ponytail, beard, tee-shirt, shorts, and sandals). I do not claim to be a NetHead, but over the last 15 years I've become perhaps 50% NetHead. The book reflects the lessons and wisdom of both worlds and the hope is that both Geekia and Telephonia will adopt a convergence treaty based on these important lessons. I promise that it will be worthwhile for both NetHeads and BellHeads to pay attention to these lessons. NetHeads may see a lot of BellHead philosophy in this book and perhaps declare this a "BellHead book," but BellHeads will see much NetHead thinking as well and perhaps declare this a "NetHead book."

We'll return to Geekia and Telephonia from time to time in the book because these worlds have much to teach us. We'll show a little later how very differently they are in building network standards. Where in Geekia they hold Internet Engineering Task Force (IETF) meetings with hoards of bearded, highly intelligent, and innovative geeks flopping on the floors, glued to their computers, and ravaging the cookies and food between inventions. There is no way to overstate the impact of their output, however. While in Telephonia they hold International Telecommunication Union (ITU) meetings where everyone dresses formally, sits politely, speaks in turn, and are perhaps a little boring, yet may quietly cut your throat if the need arises. They have set the global standards for decades and still make maybe a bit slow but steady progress. We'll get into all these standards development aspects much more later, but for now, let's get right to the heart of the matter, and the convergence of two worlds.

TQO is an indispensable network function that controls a network's response to traffic demands and other stimuli, such as network failures. The TQO methods encompassed in this book include the following:

- Traffic management through optimization and control of routing functions, which include call/session routing (number/name translation to routing address), connection routing, QoS resource management, routing table management, and dynamic transport routing.

- Capacity management through optimization and control of network design.
- TQO operational requirements for traffic management and capacity management, including forecasting, performance monitoring, and short-term network adjustment.

The book describes and analyzes TQO methods for integrated voice/data dynamic routing networks. These functions control a network's response to traffic demands and other stimuli, such as link failures or node failures. The functions discussed are consistent with the definition of TE employed by the Traffic Engineering Working Group (TEWG) within the IETF:

> Internet "traffic engineering" is concerned with the performance optimization of operational networks. It encompasses the measurement, modeling, characterization, and control of Internet traffic and the application of techniques to achieve specific performance objectives, including the reliable and expeditious movement of traffic through the network, the efficient utilization of network resources, and the planning of network capacity.

This definition of TE methods is somewhat inconsistent with the ITU-T usage of the term "traffic engineering," which has more to do with network dimensioning and capacity planning. While these functions are encompassed by the definition of TE, the scope of the analysis in the book goes well beyond dimensioning and includes call/session and connection routing, QoS resource management, routing table management, dynamic transport routing, and operational requirements.

Current and future networks are evolving rapidly to converged networks that carry a multitude of both voice/ISDN and packet data services. Historically, these services have been provided on Internet protocol (IP)-based, asynchronous transfer mode (ATM)-based, and time division multiplexing (TDM)-based networks. Within networks and services supported by IP, ATM, and TDM protocols have evolved various TQO methods. The TQO mechanisms are covered in the book, and a comparative analysis and performance evaluation of various TQO alternatives are presented, as are the operational requirements for TQO implementation.

Although the telecommunications industry is in turmoil, the direction it is headed is clear: networks will evolve to a converged, integrated voice/data/video, IP-based, multiprotocol label switching (MPLS) network layer carrying legacy and emerging services, running over a high-capacity optical transport infrastructure. These converged networks promise to deliver lower operating costs and easier service deployment. Such infrastructures enable service providers to offer a "triple play" suite of voice, data, and video services. In migrating to the converged architecture, service providers will replace obsolete network elements with services-over-IP/MPLS network elements, which will enable them to deploy new services, thereby increasing revenue and average revenue per user.

The Internet technology revolution fully eclipsed the voice/ISDN dynamic routing revolution, but the TQO principles used to design dynamic routing protocols were constant and unchangeable through the changing world. This book explains, illustrates, and applies these TQO design principles that have been applied before, and will be applied again. They are timeless and unchangeable through the technological paradigm shifts that occur, such as from the voice TDM world to the integrated voice/data MPLS world. They are applied again in this book to draw our conclusions.

A focus of the book is on TQO protocol design for MPLS- and GMPLS-based networks. MPLS and GMPLS are revolutionary new network control capabilities designed and standardized in the IETF. Given that networks are evolving rapidly toward converged MPLS/GMPLS-based technologies, we present analysis studies and examples of MPLS/GMPLS network design and TQO protocol optimization. Results of these analysis models illustrate the trade-offs between various TQO approaches. We provide detailed case studies of TQO protocol design, including the optimization of MPLS/GMPLS-based integrated voice/data dynamic routing networks.

Furthermore, a generic TQO (GTQO) protocol is described for IP-based, MPLS/GMPLS-enabled technologies, where both Geekian and Telephonian views are taken into account in the GTQO approach, as both are right. If indeed these GTQO methods are developed and implemented, NetHeads should be happy to see that their venerable and ingenious protocols, particularly MPLS, GMPLS, and others, are central to the GTQO requirements. BellHeads will recognize that their time-honored and highly successful networking principles—bandwidth reservation, dynamic alternate routing, traffic management, capacity management and planning, and others—are included as well. So everyone will be happy at least some of the time and no one will be unhappy all of the time with this approach.

We begin this chapter with a general model for TQO functions, which include traffic management and capacity management functions responding to traffic demands on the network. We introduce the TQO functions at each network layer, formulate the TQO design problem addressed in the book, and outline the solution approach followed in the book. The latter includes an analysis of TQO design and operational experience, as well as design/analysis studies presented throughout the book. We present key results and conclusions of the GTQO design based on TQO design/operational experience in voice and data networks, modeling and analysis studies, and detailed case studies.

Chapter 2 presents models for call/session routing, which entails number/name translation to a routing address associated with service requests, and also compare various connection (bearer-path) routing methods. Chapter 3 examines QoS resource management methods in detail and illustrates per-flow versus per-virtual-network (VNET) (or per-class-type, per-traffic-trunk, or per-bandwidth-pipe) resource management and the realization of multiservice integration with priority routing services. In particular, Chapter 3 examines TQO protocol design requirements for MPLS-based dynamic routing networks. Chapter 4 identifies and discusses routing table management approaches. This includes a discussion of TQO signaling and information exchange requirements needed for interworking across network types so that the information exchange at the interface is compatible across network types. Chapter 5 describes methods for dynamic transport routing, which is enabled by the capabilities of GMPLS and optical cross-connect devices, to dynamically rearrange transport network capacity. In particular, Chapter 5 examines TQO protocol design requirements for GMPLS-based dynamic routing networks. Chapter 6 describes optimization methods for routing design and capacity management, and Chapter 7 presents TQO operational requirements.

Chapter 8 presents four case studies for TQO protocol design in operational networks: (a) two case studies for circuit-switched integrated voice/ISDN dynamic routing networks for both intranetwork and internetwork applications, respectively, and (b) two case studies where designs went astray, but at the same time provided valuable lessons for future design. Chapter 9 presents a fifth case study for TQO protocol design in operational networks, which provides a detailed optimization study of MPLS/GMPLS-based integrated voice/data dynamic routing networks. This case study provides a basis for the GTQO protocol presented in Chapter 10.

The principal conclusions and study results presented in the book are summarized in Chapter 10. Based on the results of these studies, as well as established practice and experience, a GTQO protocol is described and the IP/MPLS/GMPLS standards developments needed to accommodate the GTQO protocol requirements and capabilities are summarized. Clearly the GTQO protocol is one of many possibilities; Chapter 10 also presents several other TQO approaches that may well be deployed in some form, including (a) distributed virtual network-based TQO approaches, some analogous to the GTQO approach, and flow-aware networking, (b) centralized TQO approaches, such as TQO processor (TQOP), resource and admission control function, intelligent routing service control point, DiffServ bandwidth broker, and network-aware resource broker, and (c) competitive and cooperative game theoretic models.

Appendix A reviews some of the key TQO technologies: MPLS, GMPLS, QoS mechanisms, IntServ, resource reservation protocol (RSVP), DiffServ, and MPLS-based QoS mechanisms. This is intended as a quick refresher and/or a brief introduction for those unfamiliar with these technologies. Ample references are provided for more detailed coverage of these important topics.

1.2 Terminology and Definitions

This section defines some key terminology used in the book. It is a good idea to go through these definitions quickly, especially as Geekians and Telephonians sometimes use the same terms in different ways. It also might be necessary for you to return to these definitions now and then to refresh this terminology state information periodically as you go through the book so that it does not get corrupted or deleted.

Let's start with some of the most basic terms in the book: link, path, and route. Note in particular that the NetHead and BellHead definitions and pronunciation of "route" and "routing" are quite different. NetHead (data network) "routing" is the process of making the longest prefix match [RFC1812] and, based on that match, then looking up the "NextHop" for that prefix. The NextHop is determined by a constrained shortest path first (CSPF) computation, which can be made synchronously, asynchronously, or hop by hop with the longest prefix match. Paths normally consist of multiple links in a data network.

BellHead (voice network) "routing," on the other hand, begins with "address translation" (normally an E.164 address) in place of "longest prefix match," and the outcome is to determine a routing table. The routing table is a set of paths connecting the same originating node-destination node pair, where the "set of paths" may consist of a single path or multiple paths. This set of path may be computed in real time along with the address translation or be predetermined by some off-line calculation and downloaded to the network. Paths normally consist of multiple links in voice networks, but paths in voice networks employing dynamic routing are often constrained to one- or two-link paths.

Note that both NetHead routing and BellHead routing typically use some type of "dynamic routing" for route computation, and we say much more about different forms of dynamic routing for voice, data, and integrated voice/data networks in Chapter 2 and in Section 1.6.

Note also that we provide no guidance on pronunciation. One issue I always had with "NetHead routing" was that the NetHeads changed the pronunciation of "route" and "routing": it is the ancient BellHead "rooooting" pronunciation versus the much more recent NetHead "rowting." I know that folks in the United Kingdom still pronounce it correctly, but personally I feel a bit embarrassed to pronounce it the BellHead way so I reluctantly use the NetHead pronunciation. Curiously, "rowting" is the original correct pronunciation, and "routeing" was the correct spelling. As with many issues of pronunciation and spelling, the United States is still locked into the 17th century and is historically correct. NetHeads typically populate the IETF and always use "rowting," whereas BellHeads are historically in the ITU, which uses United Kingdom spelling and pronunciation (even spells "routeing" in some older recommendations). The good news about a book is that no one can tell how you pronounce it, unless of course you tell everyone as I just did.

Terminology for link, path, and route, as used in the book, is illustrated in Figure 1.1. A link is a transmission medium (logical or physical) that connects two nodes, a path is a sequence of links connecting an origin and destination node, and a route is the set of different paths between the origin and the destination that a call/session might be routed on within a particular routing discipline. Here a call/session is a generic term used to describe the establishment and release, at the application layer, of a connection or data flow at the bearer layer. More generally, call/session routing refers to the path that signaling messages take through the infrastructure during call/session setup. In this context, a call/session can refer to a voice call established perhaps using the SS7 signaling protocol or to a web-based data flow session, established perhaps by SIP, HTTP, or other IP-based signaling protocol. Call/session routing and various implementations of routing tables are discussed in Chapter 2.

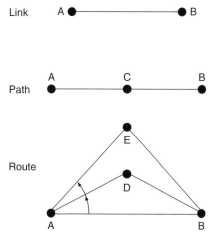

Figure 1.1 Terminology.

Alternate path routing:	A routing technique where multiple paths rather than just the shortest path between a source node and a destination node are utilized to route traffic, which is used to distribute load among multiple paths in the network.
Autonomous system (AS):	A routing domain that has a common administrative authority and consistent internal routing policy. An AS may employ multiple intranetwork routing protocols and interfaces to other ASs via a common internetwork routing protocol.
Blocking:	The denial or nonadmission of a call/session or connection request based, e.g., on the lack of available resources (e.g., link bandwidth, queuing resources, call processing resources, application server resources, or media server resources).
Call:	Generic term to describe the association between end points and key transit points (such as domain boundaries) and involves coordinating the establishment, utilization, and release of connections (bearer paths) or data flows in support of a requested end-to-end service.
Call/session routing:	Number (or name) translation to routing address(es), perhaps involving use of network servers or intelligent network (IN) databases for service processing.
Circuit switching:	Transfer of an individual set of bits within a TDM time slot over a connection between an input port and an output port within a given circuit-switching node through the circuit-switching fabric (see Switching).

Class of service:	Characteristics of a service such as described by service identity, virtual network, link capability requirements, QoS, and traffic threshold parameters.
Class type:	DiffServ-aware MPLS traffic engineering (DSTE) term equivalent to VNET (see VNET).
Connection:	Bearer path, label switched path, virtual circuit, and/or virtual path established by call/session signaling, routing, and connection routing.
Connection admission control (CAC):	Process by which it is determined whether a link or a node has sufficient resources to satisfy the QoS required for connection or flow. CAC is typically applied by each node in the path of a connection or flow during setup to check local resource availability.
Connection routing:	Connection establishment through selection of one path from path choices governed by the routing table.
Crankback:	A technique where a connection or flow setup is back-tracked along the call/connection/flow path up to the first node that can determine an alternative path to the destination node.
Destination node:	Terminating node within a given network.
Event dependent routing (EDR):	A dynamic routing strategy in which traffic/topology status data are kept locally; infrequent exchange between nodes; paths hunted according to various rules, e.g., select primary path then currently successful alternate path, randomly select new alternate path if QoS/traffic parameters cannot be realized; success-to-the-top (STT) method allows up to N crankbacks to find successful via path.
Fixed routing (FXR):	A static routing strategy in which an off-line processor predetermines paths, e.g., based on hierarchical routing rules; path selection order is fixed in time and is independent of traffic patterns; paths hunted according to various rules (e.g., hierarchical routing rules); call/session lost is blocked at via node, crankback from via node not normally used.
Flow:	Bearer traffic associated with a given connection or connectionless stream having the same originating node, destination node, class of service, and session identification.
Dynamic routing:	Flexible, nonfixed routing methods encompassing time-dependent routing (TDR), state-dependent routing (SDR), and event-dependent routing (EDR); encompasses network optimization methods involving traffic engineering and QoS functions; used interchangeably with traffic engineering and QoS optimization (TQO) methods.

Grade of service (GoS):	A number of network design variables used to provide a measure of adequacy of a group of resources under specified conditions (e.g., GoS variables may be probability of loss, dial tone delay).
Grade of service standards:	Parameter values assigned as objectives for GoS variables.
Host:	A computer that communicates using Internet protocols. A host may implement routing functions (i.e., operate at the IP layer) and may implement additional functions, including higher-layer protocols (e.g., TCP in a source or destination host) and lower-layer protocols (e.g., ATM).
Integrated services:	A model that allows for integration of services with various QoS classes, such as key-priority, normal-priority, and best-effort priority services.
Link:	A bandwidth transmission medium between nodes that is engineered as a unit.
Logical link:	A bandwidth transmission medium of fixed bandwidth (e.g., T1, DS3, OC3) at the link layer (layer 2) between two nodes, established on a path consisting of (possibly several) physical transport links (at layer 1), which are switched, for example, through several optical cross-connect devices.
Multiservice network:	A network in which various classes of service share transmission, switching, queuing, management, and other resources of the network.
Node:	A network element (switch, router, exchange) providing switching and routing capabilities or an aggregation of such network elements representing a network.
O-D pair:	An originating node to destination node pair for a given connection/bandwidth-allocation request.
Originating node:	Originating node within a given network.
Packet switching:	Transfer of an individual packet over a connection between an input port and an output port within a given packet-switching node through the packet-switching fabric (see Switching).
Path:	A concatenation of links providing a connection/bandwidth-allocation between an O-D pair.
Physical transport link:	A bandwidth transmission medium at the physical layer (layer 1) between two nodes, such as on an optical fiber system between terminal equipment used for the transmission of bits or packets (see Transport).
Policy-based routing:	Network function that involves the application of rules applied to input parameters to derive a routing table and its associated parameters.

Quality of service (QoS):	A set of service requirements to be met by the network while transporting a connection or flow; the collective effect of service performance that determines the degree of satisfaction of a user of the service; typically encompasses packet classification, scheduling, policing, and queuing treatment.
QoS class:	See Class of service.
QoS resource management:	Network functions that include class-of-service identification, routing table derivation, connection admission, bandwidth allocation, bandwidth protection, bandwidth reservation, priority routing, and priority queuing.
QoS routing:	See QoS resource management.
QoS variable:	Any performance variable (such as congestion, delay) that is perceivable by a user.
Route:	A set of paths connecting the same originating node-destination node pair (note that the "set of paths" may consist of a single path and may be computed in real time).
Router:	A host that implements routing functions, which enables communication between other hosts by forwarding IP packets based on the content of their IP destination address field.
Routing:	Process of determination, establishment, and use of routing tables to select paths between an input port at the ingress network edge and output port at the egress network edge; includes the process of performing both call/session routing and connection routing (see Call/session routing and Connection routing).
Routing table:	Describes the path choices and selection rules to select one path out of the route for a connection/bandwidth-allocation request.
Session:	Lasting connection between a user and a peer (typically a server) involving exchange of packets; e.g., initiated by the session initiation protocol (SIP) and session description protocol (SDP).
State-dependent routing (SDR):	A dynamic routing strategy in which traffic/topology status data are exchanged by (a) distributed method by flooding or node-to-node query and paths computed locally or (b) centralized by status updates to TQO processor; recommended paths periodically requested by or sent to nodes; paths hunted according to various rules, e.g., originating node selects primary path and then least-loaded alternate path; crankback from via node to originating node if QoS/traffic parameters cannot be realized.

Switching:	Connection of an input port to an output port within a given node through the switching fabric.
Time dependent routing (TDR):	A dynamic routing strategy in which an off-line processor predetermines paths based on measured/predicted traffic; path selection order changes with time according to traffic patterns and paths hunted according to various rules (e.g., cyclic, sequential); crankback from via node to originating node if QoS/traffic parameters cannot be realized.
Traffic engineering:	Encompasses traffic management, capacity management, traffic measurement and modeling, network modeling, and performance analysis.
Traffic engineering methods:	Network functions that support traffic engineering and include call/session routing, connection routing, QoS resource management, routing table management, and capacity management.
Traffic engineering and QoS optimization (TQO):	Network optimization methods encompassing traffic engineering and QoS functions; used interchangeably with dynamic routing methods.
Traffic stream:	A class of connection requests with the same traffic characteristics.
Traffic trunk:	An aggregation of traffic flows of the same class routed on the same path (see Logical link).
Transport:	Transmission of bits or packets on the physical layer (layer 1) between two nodes, such as on an optical fiber system between terminal equipment [note that this definition is distinct from the IP protocol terminology of transport as end-to-end connectivity at layer 4, such as with the transmission control protocol (TCP)].
Via node:	An intermediate node in a path within a given network.
Virtual network (VNET):	Formed by MPLS LSPs routed on layer 2 logical links between nodes, which are allocated bandwidth to meet performance requirements; traffic routers dynamically route connections in response to call/session requests that fall within classes of service assigned to VNETs; e.g., real-time voice traffic may form one VNET and premium private data traffic may form another VNET.

Note that "TQO methods" and "dynamic routing methods" are used somewhat interchangeably. As in the above definitions, TQO encompasses network optimization of TE and QoS functions, and dynamic routing encompasses network optimization of flexible TDR, SDR, and EDR TE, as well as QoS functions. TDR, SDR, and EDR methods are defined above and are described in Chapter 2. Example implementations of TDR, SDR, and EDR are given in Section 1.6.

The following terms encompassing TQO standards and technologies are defined and described in Chapter 10, Section 10.6, and Appendix A:

- assured services requirements and architecture [ASSURED-SERVICES-RQMTS, ASSURED-SERVICES-ARCH]
- broadband remote access server (BRAS) [DSLFORUM-TR-059]
- crankback routing extensions for alternate routing during MPLS LSP setup or modification [CRANKBACK]
- differentiated services (DiffServ) [RFC2475]
- DiffServ-aware MPLS traffic engineering (DSTE) mechanisms [RFC3564, RFC4124]
- dynamic quality of service (DQOS) [CABLELABS-DQOS-05]
- emergency telecommunications service (ETS)/government emergency telecommunications service (GETS) support in IP networks [ETS1, ETS2, ETS3]
- generalized multiprotocol label switching (GMPLS) [RFC3945]
- header compression over MPLS [RFC4247, HC-OVER-MPLS-PROTOCOL]
- IP multimedia subsystem (IMS) [3GPP-TS.22.228]
- maximum allocation with reservation (MAR) bandwidth constraints model for DSTE application [RFC4126, PRIORITY1, PRIORITY2]
- multiprotocol label switching (MPLS) [RFC3031]
- MPLS-based QoS standards [RFC3270]
- MPLS proxy admission control [MPLS-PROXY1, MPLS-PROXY2]
- next steps in signaling (NSIS) and end-to-end QoS signaling protocol [QOS-SIG-NTLP, QOS-SIG-NSLP, QOS-SIG-QSPEC, QOS-SIG-Y1541-QOSM]
- open shortest path first (OSPF) congestion control mechanisms [RFC4222]
- path computation element (PCE) capability for interarea, inter-AS, and interservice provider optimal, diverse, and MPLS fast reroute (FRR) path computation [PCE-ARCHITECTURE, PCE-REQUIREMENTS, PCE-PROTOCOL]
- protection/restoration mechanisms to support fast restoration capabilities [GMPLS-RECOVERY-SPEC, GMPLS-RECOVERY-PROTOCOL]
- PseudoWire (PW) [RFC3985]
- QoS specification (QSPEC) signaling of QoS parameters [QOS-SIG-QSPEC]
- resource reservation protocol (RSVP) [RFC2205]
- RSVP aggregation extensions over DSTE tunnels [DSTE-AGGREGATION]
- session border controller (SBC) [CAMARILLO05]
- session initiation protocol (SIP) [RFC3261, RFC3312]
- SIP resource priority header (RPH) [RFC4412]
- Y.1541 admission control priority service classes [PRIORITY3, PRIORITY4]

1.3 TQO Background and Motivation

TQO is important because networks are subject to overloads and failures, no matter how big or how fat we build them and/or how sophisticated their management and control technology. Familiar to us all are road networks, which exasperate us with their constant overloading and failing, mass transportation networks (trains, buses, etc.), which are subject to all-too-frequent overloads and failures. Too many cars/vehicles lead to road "congestion," while a road "failure" might be from a traffic accident (lanes closed), bridge collapse (road completely blocked), or dense fog (closes road).

Likewise, we've all experienced communication network overloads and failures, they happen all the time. Web sites go down and congest (e.g., "web site unavailable," "try again later," "World Wide Wait"), terrorist attacks and hurricanes knock out data centers and server farms, hacker attacks overwhelm web sites, and cellular networks are unusable during events such as 9/11/2001 and the devastating 2005 hurricanes in New Orleans and other places. On 9/11/2001 I was in Geneva and completely unable to call my wife in New Jersey, as the international and domestic telephone networks were too jammed on a global scale. However, we could exchange email on the Internet, and thank God for that! Certain congestion events are predictable, such as a global Christmas day traffic overload of the worldwide telephone network, but many are not. I monitor daily network performance reports for large data networks and voice networks, where it is completely normal to see daily hot spots, localized failures, and overloads clearly identified by data. I claim that such overload/failure events are typical and unavoidable in all types of networks, no matter what the technology, size, etc. At the same time, I'm quite familiar with those who try to claim that some types of networks "never" overload or congest, no matter what. It's just not so, TQO is important and needed when that inevitably happens.

This book reflects the lessons and wisdom of both Geekia and Telephonia worlds, and the GTQO protocol requirements presented in this book are based on these important lessons. We'll demonstrate that these cultures have worked well together, despite the gap, and reached consensus on innovative architecture directions. NetHeads will see a lot of BellHead philosophy in this book and perhaps declare this a "BellHead book," but BellHeads will see much NetHead thinking as well and perhaps declare this a "NetHead book." In the end, we speak of truce and focus on the convergence of these two disparate worlds, where bridging the gap between BellHeads and NetHeads in TQO space is one goal of this book.

So what are these lessons and wisdom? Mainly, these negative effects of overloads and failures can be mitigated greatly by TQO methods in the form of traffic management, capacity management, and control technology. TQO has been used in data networks since Morse's invention of the telegraph in 1835 and in voice networks since Bell's invention of the telephone in 1876. There is, of course, proof for the benefits of TQO, and at this juncture I crow about the glowing success of TQO in voice/ISDN networks to make the main point of the book that TQO can be highly beneficial in any network, particularly in converged MPLS-based voice/data dynamic routing networks. Right now the sophistication of TQO in TDM networks is virtually unknown to NetHeads, who often perceive TDM voice networks as using ancient 100-year-old telephone network technology and repeatedly describe such networks as if they used tin cans connected by strings.

One experience I had was at an MPLS conference in 2003, where I gave an invited talk describing the lessons learned from the voice/ISDN TQO implementations and how they could be evolved into IP/MPLS-based TQO. A Cisco vice president, who was also a speaker at the conference, summed up my talk with something like "to the BellHeads everything looks like a telephone call" (i.e., "when all you have is a hammer, everything looks like a nail"). There is a great deal more to be learned from the TQO experience in voice/ISDN dynamic routing networks than what the VP took away. BellHeads can be faulted too for a woeful lack of understanding of the sophistication of Geekia protocols and networks and for blithely dismissing same as irrelevant, for decades, that is, until the Internet revolution completely took over in the 1990s.

This book describes a comprehensive coherent vision of a converged network infrastructure, architecture, and protocols for the Next Generation Network (NGN), along with large-scale case studies of converged networks using analysis and optimization tools that colleagues and I have developed over the past two decades. Having pioneered the implementation of dynamic routing methods on a worldwide scale and widely contributed to a number of standards bodies (IETF, ITU-T, ATM Forum, MFA Forum) over the past two decades, I believe this direct experience places me in a position to assess the challenges of network convergence and to extend these highly successful techniques to the converged NGN infrastructure. Indeed some potential obstacles to this NGN vision have been removed by participating in the necessary TQO extensions to standards such as (G)MPLS, RSVP, DSTE, NSIS, and others. Various proposals have been advanced for providing end-to-end QoS, including variations of the GTQO protocol, flow-aware networking, game theoretic-based models, and others. These other approaches are compared in Chapter 10 to the GTQO approach to a converged NGN infrastructure.

This book advances the evolution possibilities for an IP/GMPLS/DWDM protocol stack in greater depth and scope than other proposals made to date. This is important, as there is a growing consensus in the networking community that IP/(G)MPLS/DWDM should be the target protocol stack for the NGN. It is timely in that we are now at a crossroads where there are various alternative visions of how the Internet could or should evolve. The articulation of a comprehensive coherent vision of the NGN and its evaluation is made difficult not only because of technical challenges, but also because of the divergent BellHead/NetHead cultures. Also, the business model is fundamentally different for the global Internet, where the planning procedures have not kept up with the vast changes in technology. Traffic measurement and planning have become more decentralized, and no one administration has global topology information, traffic data, or control.

The competitive structure of the access and core networks means that traffic forecasting is more challenging as the volume of traffic produced depends on the pricing strategy and cross technology impacts. For example, competitive pricing models, such as for wireless services, make the demand harder to predict, and cross technology impacts such as VoIP services impact on PSTN traffic demand have a large range of uncertainty. However, such econometric and competitive factors have been incorporated in the decentralized forecasting and planning in the telecom world and such approaches can be extended to the decentralized global Internet structure. In addition, the fact that an end-to-end connection may span several domains operated by different administrations makes QoS delivery a challenging issue. However, that property also has applied since day 1 in voice and data networking, where a large number of independent, interconnected network operators must together operate the "global network" in a cooperative, coherent way. An administrative model is discussed in Chapter 7 that is centralized within a given administrative domain, and such approaches are used today across multiple, decentralized, interconnected domains. This model can be extended in an analogous way to the multioperator global Internet, wherein a federated approach is still necessary for security and national autonomy.

We use analysis and simulation to analyze the various components of TQO, to carry out detailed case studies, to design the GTQO protocol, and to quantify the benefits. To do this, we use a layered model of TQO that we now present and then formulate the TQO design problem and discuss its solution.

1.4   TQO Functional Model

Figure 1.2 illustrates a model for TQO functions in data, voice, and converged networks. The central box represents the network, which can have various architectures and configurations, and the TE and QoS optimization methods used within the network. Network configurations include metropolitan area networks, national intercity

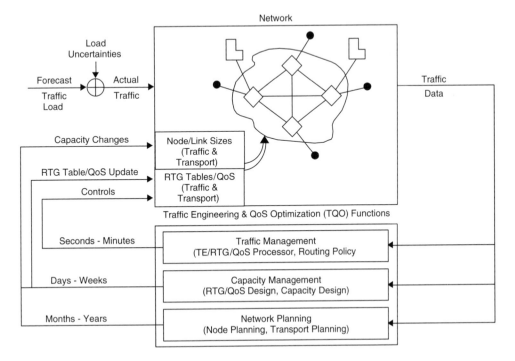

Figure 1.2   Traffic engineering and QoS optimization (TQO) model for voice, data, and converged networks.

networks, and global international networks, which support both hierarchical and nonhierarchical structures and combinations of the two. Routing tables describe the path choices from an originating node to a terminating node for a connection request for a particular service. Hierarchical and nonhierarchical traffic routing tables are possible, as are fixed routing tables and dynamic routing tables. Routing tables are used for a multiplicity of traffic and transport services on the telecommunications network. QoS optimization methods are applied in the network, which encompass the classification, scheduling, policing, and queuing treatment of packets within the queuing functions implemented in the network.

TQO functions include traffic management, capacity management, and network planning. Traffic management ensures that network performance is maximized under all conditions, including load shifts and failures. Capacity management ensures that the network is designed and provisioned with sufficient capacity to meet performance objectives for network demands at minimum cost. Network planning ensures that node and transport capacity is planned and deployed in advance of forecasted traffic growth. Figure 1.2 illustrates traffic management, capacity management, and network planning as three interacting feedback loops around the network.

The input driving the network ("system") is a noisy traffic load ("signal"), consisting of predictable average demand components added to unknown forecast error and load variation components. The load variation components have different time constants ranging from instantaneous variations, hour-to-hour variations, day-to-day variations, and week-to-week or seasonal variations. Accordingly, the time constants of the feedback controls are matched to the load variations and function to regulate the service provided by the network through capacity, routing, and QoS resource management adjustments. It has long been known that feedback control systems, such as illustrated in Figure 1.2, reduce sensitivity to random and unknown inputs [BLACK34, BODE40, KUO95, NYQUIST32]. The degree of sensitivity reduction is directly related to the "gain" of the feedback loop or to how closely the system is monitored and the level of feedback correction applied to drown out the noise entering the system. That is, the traffic management and capacity management functions are geared to provide sufficient feedback to cancel the effects of the noisy traffic inputs to the system that would tend to otherwise disrupt the system. These noisy inputs and their effects on the network are discussed later in this section.

Traffic management functions include (a) call/session routing, which entails number/name translation to routing address, (b) connection or bearer-path routing methods, (c) QoS resource management, (d) routing table management, and (e) dynamic transport routing. These functions can be (a) decentralized and distributed to the network nodes, (b) centralized and allocated to a centralized controller such as a TQO processor, or (c) performed by a hybrid combination of these approaches.

Capacity management plans, schedules, and provisions needed capacity over a time horizon of several months to 1 year or more. Under exceptional circumstances, capacity can be added on a shorter term basis, perhaps one to several weeks, to alleviate service problems. Network design embedded in capacity management encompasses routing design, bandwidth allocation, and capacity design. Routing design takes account of the capacity provided by capacity management, and on a weekly or possibly real-time basis adjusts routing tables and QoS resource management bandwidth allocations, as necessary, to correct service problems. The updated routing tables/bandwidth allocations are provisioned (configured) in the nodes either directly or via an automated system. Network planning includes node planning and transport planning, operates over a multiyear forecast interval, and drives network capacity expansion over a multiyear period based on network forecasts.

The scope of the TQO methods includes the establishment of connections for narrowband, wideband, and broadband multimedia services within multiservice networks and between multiservice networks. Here a multiservice network refers to one in which various classes of voice/data/video services share the transmission, node processing, management, and other resources of the network. These services include constant-bit-rate (CBR) services, variable bit rate (VBR) services, and unassigned bit rate (UBR) best-effort services. There are quantitative performance requirements that the various services are required to meet, such as end-to-end traffic loss, delay, and/or delay-jitter objectives. These objectives are met through the application of TQO methods, traffic management, and capacity management.

Figure 1.3 illustrates the four network layers considered in the TQO model analyzed and designed in this book. These layers correspond to the central network box in Figure 1.2. An additional layer considered in the analysis and design is the TQO operational/management layer, which is shown in the feedback loops around the central network box in Figure 1.2 (not shown in Figure 1.3).

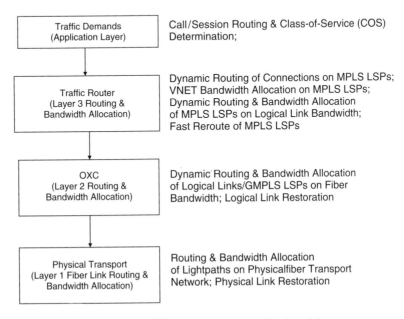

Figure 1.3 TQO network layers functional model.

The relevant functions performed at each layer are summarized in the following sections.

1.4.1 Traffic/Application Layer

At this layer call/session routing takes place, for example, using the session initiation protocol (SIP) [RFC3261, RFC3312], as discussed in Chapter 2. Call/session routing involves the translation of a number or name to a routing address. Number (or name) translation results in the IP address, E.164 ATM end-system addresses (AESA), or network routing addresses (NRAs), which are used for routing purposes and therefore must be carried in the connection–setup information element. Class of service (COS) of a call/session is also determined, which can include service identity, transport requirements, routing parameters, and link capabilities, as described in Chapter 3.

Table 1.1 summarizes examples of traffic models used to represent the different traffic variations under consideration. Traffic models for both voice and data traffic are reflected. These traffic load variation models drive all the TQO functions illustrated in Figure 1.2, including the network TQO protocols, traffic management, capacity management, and network planning.

For instantaneous traffic load variations, the load is typically modeled as a stationary random process over a given period (normally within each hourly period) characterized by a fixed mean and variance. From hour to hour, mean traffic loads are modeled as changing deterministically; e.g., according to their 20-day average values. From day to day, for a fixed hour, the mean load can be modeled, for example, as a random variable having a gamma distribution with a mean equal to the 20-day average load. From week to week, the load variation is modeled as a random process in the network design procedure. The random component of the realized week-to-week load is the forecast error, which is equal to the forecast load minus the realized load. Forecast error is accounted for in short-term capacity management.

In traffic management, traffic load variations such as instantaneous variations, hour-to-hour variations, day-to-day traffic variations, and week-to-week variations are responded to in traffic management by appropriately controlling call/session and connection routing, path selection, routing table management, and/or QoS resource management. Traffic management provides monitoring of network performance through collection and display of traffic and performance data and allows traffic management controls, such as destination-address per-connection blocking, per-connection gapping, routing table modification, and path selection/reroute controls, to be inserted when circumstances warrant. For example, a focused overload might lead to application of call/session gapping controls in which a connection request to a particular destination address or set of addresses is admitted only once every x seconds, and connections arriving after an accepted call/session are rejected for the next x seconds. In that way call/session gapping throttles the call/sessions and prevents overloading the network to a particular focal point. The capacity management impacts identified in the right-hand column of Table 1.1 are discussed in Chapter 6.

Table 1.1 Traffic Load Variation Models for Call/Session Arrival Processes

Traffic Variations Time constant	Load variation examples for traffic management	Illustrative traffic model for capacity management	Capacity impacts
Minute to minute	Real-time random traffic fluctuations; bursty overflow traffic; Focused overloads (e.g., caused by radio/TV call-ins, natural disasters); general overloads (e.g., caused by peak-day calling); traffic congestion caused by network failure (e.g., fiber cut or node failure); traffic shifts due to price variations for transit traffic, arbitrage, and bulk resale	Stochastic model; normally with two parameters (mean and variance); focused and general overload traffic excluded; network failure traffic excluded	Busy-hour traffic load capacity (excludes focused overload, general overload, and network failure traffic)
Hour to hour	Business traffic day peak; web-based (consumer) traffic evening peak; mobile traffic (consumer) weekend/evening peak	Deterministic model; 20-day average time-varying mean; multihour design	Hour-to-hour capacity
Day to day	Monday morning busiest for business day traffic compared to average morning; Sunday evening busiest for web-based traffic compared to average evening; Friday evening busiest for mobile traffic compared to average evening	Stochastic model; normally with two parameters (mean and variance); several levels of variance modeled for low/medium/high day-to-day variations	Day-to-day capacity
Week to week	Winter/summer seasonal variations; forecast errors	Stochastic model; normally with two parameters (mean and variance); maximum flow routing and capacity design	Reserve capacity

Here we characterize traffic parameters for connections, flows, and packet streams. Recall from the terminology defined in Section 1.2 that a connection is a bearer path, LSP, virtual circuit, and/or virtual path established by call/session signaling and connection routing. A flow is defined as bearer traffic associated with a given connection or connectionless stream having the same originating node, destination node, class of service, and session identification. Connection and flow arrivals occur, for example, with call/session setups using call/session signaling protocols such as SS7 and SIP. Flows can also be established with control protocols such as TCP [RFC793] and user datagram protocol (UDP) [RFC768].

Each connection or flow contains a set of source traffic parameters that describe the traffic characteristics of the source as follows:

Peak packet rate (PPR): PPR is the maximum allowable rate at which packets can be transported along a connection; PPR is the determining factor in how many packets are sent per unit time to minimize jitter and is coupled with packet delay variation (PDV), defined later, to indicate how much jitter is allowable.

Sustainable packet rate (SPR): SPR is the average allowable, long-term packet transfer rate on a specific connection.

Maximum burst size (MBS): MBS is the maximum allowable burst size of packets that can be transmitted contiguously on a particular connection.

Minimum packet rate (MPR): MPR is the minimum allowable rate at which packets can be transported along a connection.

Work has been done on measurement and characterization of data traffic, such as web-based traffic [FELDMAN00, FELDMAN99, LELAND94]. Some of the analysis suggests that web-based traffic can be self-similar, or fractal, with very large variability and extremely long tails of the associated traffic distributions. Characterization studies of such data traffic have investigated various traditional models, such as the Markov-modulated Poisson process (MMPP), in which it is shown that MMPP with two parameters can suitably capture the essential nature of the data traffic [HEYMAN99, BOLOTIN99, MEIER-HELLSTERN89].

Modeling work has been done to investigate the causes of the extreme variability of web-based traffic. As shown in [HEYMAN00], the congestion-control mechanisms for web-based traffic, such as window flow control for TCP traffic, appear to be at the root cause of its extreme variability over small timescales. It has also been shown [FELDMAN99] that the variability over small timescales is impacted in a major way by the presence of TCP-like flow control algorithms, which give rise to burstiness and clustering of IP packets. However, it has also been found [FELDMAN99] that the self-similar behavior over long timescales is almost exclusively due to user-related variability and is not dependent on the underlying network-specific aspects.

Regarding the modeling of voice and data traffic in a multiservice model, it has been suggested [HEYMAN00] that regular flow control dynamics are more useful to model than the self-similar traffic itself. Much of the traffic to be modeled is VBR traffic subject to service level agreements (SLAs), which is subject to admission control based on equivalent bandwidth resource requirements and also to traffic shaping in which out-of-contract packets are marked for dropping in the network queues if congestion arises. Other VBR traffic, such as best-effort Internet traffic, is not allocated any bandwidth in the admission of session flows, and all of its packets would be subject to dropping ahead of the CBR and VBR-SLA traffic. Hence, think of the traffic model as consisting of two components:

• The CBR and VBR-SLA traffic that is not marked for dropping constitutes less variable traffic subject to more traditional models.
• The VBR best-effort traffic and the VBR-SLA traffic packets that are marked and subject to dropping constitute a much more variable, self-similar traffic component.

Considerable work has been done on the modeling of broadband and other data traffic, in which two-parameter models that capture the mean and burstiness of the connection and flow arrival processes have proven to be quite adequate. A good reference on this is [E.716]. Much work has also been done on measurement and characterization of voice traffic, and two-parameter models reflecting mean and variance (the ratio of the variance to the mean is sometimes called the peakedness parameter) of traffic have proven to be accurate models. The large variability in packet arrival processes is modeled in an attempt to capture the extreme variability of the traffic.

Chapter 2 introduces models used in this book for variability in the packet arrival processes and a two-parameter, multiservice traffic model for connection and flow arrival processes. These models are manageable from a modeling and analysis aspect and attempt to capture essential aspects of data and voice traffic variability for purposes of analysis of TQO methods.

1.4.2 MPLS LSPs/Layer 3

Traffic routers are typically used to perform the functions at this layer, where dynamic routing of connections takes place in response to traffic demands in the form of calls/sessions. See Section 1.6 for an overview of dynamic routing technology in both data networks and voice networks. Calls/sessions fall within classes of service, and COSs are assigned to virtual networks at this layer. A VNET is allocated bandwidth on layer 2 logical links, and the bandwidth allocation is managed to meet performance requirements. As illustrated in Figure 1.4, high-priority, real-time voice traffic may form one VNET made up of MPLS label switched paths (LSPs) between the network nodes. See Appendix A for a review of MPLS technology. Normal priority voice and virtual private network data traffic may form other VNETs made up of separate and additional MPLS LSPs between the nodes, as illustrated in Figure 1.4.

A TQO design analyzed in the book optimizes the routing and bandwidth allocation of the LSP mesh forming the VNETs, with traffic for various classes of service (also known as QoS classes) carried on the VNET bandwidth so as to satisfy various performance objectives. As described in the next section, this mesh of MPLS LSPs forming the VNETs is carried in turn by GMPLS LSPs forming the layer 2 logical link network; these GMPLS LSPs are optimally routed and allocated bandwidth so

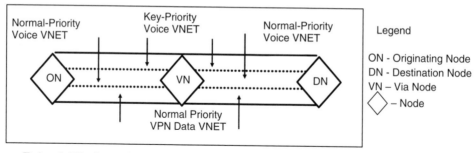

□ bandwidth allocated on a per-virtual-network (per-VNET) basis

□ ON allocates bandwidth to each VNET based on demand

   ❖ VNET bandwidth increase when more bandwidth needed

   ❖ VNET bandwidth decrease periodically when bandwidth becomes idle

□ VNs keep local link state & compare link state to bandwidth requests

   ❖ send crankback/bandwidth-not-available message to ON if bandwidth request not met

Figure 1.4 Per-virtual network (VNET) bandwidth management.

as to satisfy various performance objectives. Bandwidth allocated to VNETs can be shared with other VNETs when relatively idle, but is protected for exclusive use by traffic assigned to the particular VNET when necessary. This is accomplished through dynamic bandwidth reservation mechanisms explained in Chapter 3. VNET designs are modeled and analyzed extensively in this book, and it is shown that aggregated per-VNET bandwidth allocation is preferred to per-flow bandwidth allocation, with lower routing table management overhead and thereby increasing scalability. Alternatives to VNET architectures are considered as well, e.g., in Chapter 3 and in the case studies presented in Chapter 9. It is shown in these studies that the VNET approach is superior to other alternatives and the basis for the GTQO protocol presented in Chapter 10.

Capacity design of VNET architectures considers all VNETs at once in an integrated network design, in which all the complex dynamic functions are considered together, including per-VNET dynamic routing, per-VNET dynamic bandwidth allocation, bandwidth sharing, bandwidth reservation, and per-VNET queuing. In short, the integrated VNET design takes into account the complex dynamics, and efficiencies, of statistical multiplexing in packet networks where bandwidth is maximally shared. This full sharing approach avoids the network inefficiencies that would result from designing separate VNETs in which bandwidth is not shared and statistical multiplexing is not realized. All of these dynamics are considered at once in the capacity design while meeting multidimensional QoS/GoS performance objectives identified in Section 1.7.1.3. An extremely effective approach to dimensioning these VNET-based networks is the discrete event flow optimization (DEFO) method discussed in Chapter 6.

A to E MPLS LSP Routing (Layer 3)

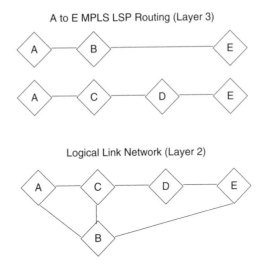

Logical Link Network (Layer 2)

Figure 1.5 A-E MPLS LSPs (layer 3) routed over logical link network (layer 2).

Figure 1.5 illustrates traffic router nodes, the logical link layer 2 network, and the MPLS LSPs routed at layer 3 from node A to E overlaid on the layer 2 network. The logical link network is relatively sparse, which means that many nodes are not connected directly by layer 2 logical links. On the other hand, as we shall see later, the nodes are more densely interconnected by MPLS LSPs forming the VNETs, but these are not all shown in Figure 1.5 to keep it uncluttered. Only the two LSPs routed from node A to node E are shown. The TQO design pursued optimizes the routing and bandwidth allocation of the LSP mesh forming the VNETs, with traffic for various classes of service carried on the VNET bandwidth so as to satisfy various performance objectives.

MPLS LSPs are dynamically routed at this layer over the logical links on the layer 2 network. The logical links on the layer 2 network are formed by routing GMPLS LSPs over the physical transport network as described in the next section. Bandwidth is allocated on the MPLS LSPs comprising the VNETs, and the bandwidth allocation is managed to meet performance requirements. Fast rerouting of MPLS LSPs takes place at this layer, should an LSP fail on the network. Calls/sessions are routed over connections on the LSPs. For example, a voice call/session from node A to E in Figure 1.5 may route either on LSP A-B-E or on LSP A-C-D-E.

Connection or bearer-path routing design at this layer is considered in Chapter 2 and involves the selection of a path from the originating node to the destination node in a network. Connection/bearer-path routing methods are categorized into the following four types: fixed routing, time-dependent routing, state-dependent routing, and event-dependent routing. These methods are associated with routing tables, which consist of a route and rules to select one path from the route for a given connection or bandwidth-allocation request.

FXR is a static routing strategy in which an off-line processor predetermines paths, for example, based on hierarchical routing rules. Path selection order is fixed in time and is independent of traffic patterns, and paths are hunted according to various rules, such as hierarchical routing rules. Calls/sessions are lost if blocked at a via node, and crankback from a via node is not normally used.

TDR is a dynamic routing strategy in which an off-line processor predetermines paths based on measured/predicted traffic. Path selection order changes with time according to traffic patterns, and paths are hunted according to various rules (e.g., cyclic, sequential). Crankback from a via node to the originating node can be used if QoS/traffic parameters cannot be realized at the via node.

SDR is a dynamic routing strategy in which traffic/topology status data are exchanged by (a) a distributed method by flooding or node-to-node query, where paths are computed locally by a node, or (b) centralized by status updates to a TQO processor; where recommended paths are periodically requested by or sent to nodes. Paths are hunted according to various rules, e.g., an originating node selects the primary path and then the least-loaded alternate path. Crankback from a via node to the originating node can be used if QoS/traffic parameters cannot be realized at the via node.

EDR is a dynamic routing strategy in which traffic/topology status data are kept locally, with infrequent exchange between nodes. Paths are hunted according to various rules, e.g., select primary path, then select the currently successful alternate path, and randomly select a new alternate path if QoS/traffic parameters cannot be realized. The success to the top (STT) method allows up to N crankbacks to find a successful via path.

MPLS LSP dynamic routing design is considered in Chapters 2 and 3 and involves QoS resource management functions, which include class-of-service derivation, policy-based routing table derivation, connection admission control, bandwidth allocation, bandwidth protection, bandwidth reservation, priority routing, priority queuing, and other related resource management functions.

Routing table management design at this layer is considered in Chapter 4 and involves optimal management of routing table information, such as topology update, status information, or routing recommendations. Such routing table management information is used for purposes of applying routing table design rules for determining path choices in the routing table. This information is exchanged between one node and another node, such as between an originating and destination node, for example, or between a node and a network element such as a TQO processor. This information is used to generate the routing table, and then the routing table is used to determine the path choices used in the selection of a path.

1.4.3 Logical Links/GMPLS LSPs/Layer 2

Optical cross-connect (OXC) and other optical transport switching devices are typically used at this layer to perform dynamic routing of logical links using GMPLS LSPs on the physical fiber transport network. An overview of GMPLS technology is given in Appendix A. GMPLS LSPs are allocated bandwidth on the physical fiber transport network, and the bandwidth allocation is managed to meet performance requirements. Fast restoration of GMPLS LSPs takes place at this layer should a logical link/GMPLS LSP fail on the network.

Logical links are designed by routing GMPLS LSPs over the physical transport network, as illustrated in Figure 1.6, and the TQO design includes the choice of paths and bandwidth allocation for the GMPLS LSPs. Figure 1.7 illustrates traffic router nodes and the physical fiber transport network for a national network model. The physical fiber network is relatively sparse, which means that many nodes are not connected directly by physical links. On the other hand, the nodes are more densely interconnected by GMPLS LSPs forming the layer 2 logical links, but these are not shown in Figure 1.7 to keep it uncluttered.

Figure 1.8 illustrates the layer 3/2 traffic/connection switching nodes (traffic router nodes) and the layer 2/1 logical/physical link OXC transport switching nodes. Figure 1.8 illustrates the routing of the logical links in Figure 1.6 through the connection switching nodes and transport switching nodes. As illustrated in Figure 1.8, the layer 2 logical links are multiplexed onto the higher capacity physical fiber links. Logical links are established through use of the OXC transport switching nodes.

Figures 1.6, 1.7, and 1.8 illustrate the mapping of layer 2 logical links onto the layer 1 physical transport network of Figure 1.7. Some logical links overlay two or more fiber-backbone links. For example, in Figure 1.7, logical link AD traverses fiber-backbone links AB, BC, and CD. One TQO design considered in this book optimizes the routing and bandwidth allocation of the GMPLS LSPs forming the layer 2 logical link network. This logical link network then carries the traffic for the various classes

Logical Link Network View (Layer 3/2)

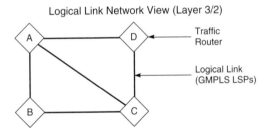

Physical Fiber Transport Network View (Layer 2/1)

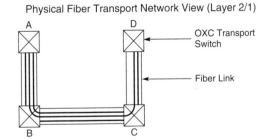

Figure 1.6 Logical links (layer 2) and physical transport network links (layer 1).

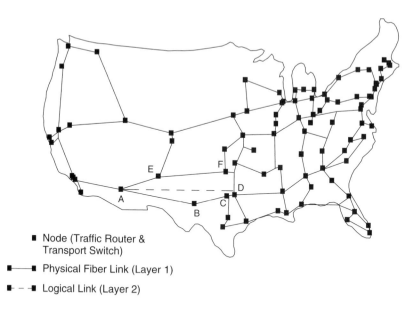

■ Node (Traffic Router & Transport Switch)

■——■ Physical Fiber Link (Layer 1)

■– –■ Logical Link (Layer 2)

Figure 1.7 Traffic router nodes and physical fiber transport network.

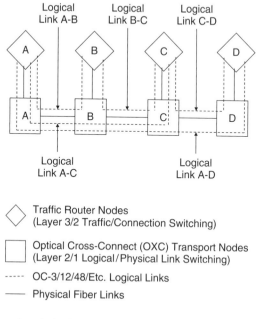

◇ Traffic Router Nodes
(Layer 3/2 Traffic/Connection Switching)

☐ Optical Cross-Connect (OXC) Transport Nodes
(Layer 2/1 Logical/Physical Link Switching)

----- OC-3/12/48/Etc. Logical Links

—— Physical Fiber Links

Figure 1.8 Logical network and physical network topology showing layer 3 connection switching and layer 2 logical link switching.

of service on the VNET bandwidth formed by the mesh of MPLS LSPs, which in turn are optimally routed and allocated bandwidth so as to satisfy various performance objectives. As shown in Chapter 2, voice networks are typically highly interconnected by logical links (perhaps $>70\%$ connected), whereas data networks are typically more sparsely interconnected (perhaps $<20\%$ connected). GMPLS technology allows integrated control of the MPLS LSP VNET layer, GMPLS LSP logical link layer, and physical fiber transport layer dynamic routing networks and can realize the capabilities now illustrated in connection with Figure 1.6.

Figure 1.6 indicates that a "direct" logical link is obtained by cross-connecting through an OXC transport node location under GMPLS control. Thus, the logical link network is overlaid on a sparse physical one. An OXC cross-connect device is traversed at each network node on a given logical link path, as illustrated in Figure 1.6. It is clear from Figures 1.6 and 1.7 that in the logical layer 2 network, many node pairs may have a "direct" logical link connection where none exists in the physical transport network. In this case a direct logical link is obtained by cross-connecting through an OXC transport-switching node. This is distinct from the call/session connection switching situation, in which a bearer connection is actually switched at an intermediate node location. This distinction between layer 2 transport switching (cross-connecting) and layer 3 connection switching is a bit subtle, but it is fundamental to call/session routing of connections at layer 3 and transport routing of logical links at layer 2.

Referring to Figures 1.6 and 1.8, we illustrate one of the logical inconsistencies encountered when the logical link network is designed to be essentially separate from the physical transport link network. On the alternative path for connection setups from node B to nodes C through A, two logical links are involved: the logical link from B to A and the logical link from A to C. On this alternate path, layer 3 connection switching is performed at node A to set up the B to C connection. However, observe from Figures 1.6 and 1.8 that the physical link path for this connection is, in fact, B to A to B to C, i.e., up and back from B to A (a phenomenon known as "backhauling") and then across from B to C. The sharing of capacity by various traffic loads in this way actually increases the efficiency of the network because the backhauled capacity to and from B and A is only used when no direct A to B or A to C traffic wants to use it. It is conceivable that under certain conditions, capacity could be put to more efficient use, which is studied much further in Chapter 5.

GMPLS LSP dynamic routing design at this layer is considered in Chapter 5 and involves dynamic transport routing at layer 2 enabled by GMPLS technology, which combines with dynamic call/session routing of layer 3 connections to shift bandwidth among node pairs and services through the use of flexible transport switching technology, such as OXCs. Layer 2 dynamic transport routing offers advantages of simplicity of design and robustness to real-time load variations and network failures and can provide automatic link provisioning, diverse link routing, and rapid link restoration for improved transport capacity utilization and performance under stress. OXCs can reconfigure logical link capacity on demand and in real time, such as for peak-day traffic, weekly redesign of link capacity, or emergency restoration of capacity under node or transport failure.

1.4.4 Physical Fiber Transport/Layer 1

At this layer, light paths are routed and allocated bandwidth on the physical fiber transport network. GMPLS LSPs can be used, for example, in a hierarchical fashion to provision high bandwidth "express links" between nodes, using perhaps fiber cross-connect devices. The express links appear as layer 1 physical links and are used to route layer 2 logical links, as described in the previous section. Chapter 5 and Appendix A further discuss such GMPLS capabilities. The bandwidth allocation is managed to meet performance requirements, and fast restoration of physical links and express links takes place at this layer should a physical link or logical express link/GMPLS LSP fail on the network. Physical transport network design and bandwidth allocation at this layer, as well as fast restoration under failure, are considered in Chapters 5 and 6.

1.4.5 Operational/Management Layer

The TQO operational/management layer is shown in the feedback loops around the central network box in Figure 1.2. This is the final layer considered in TQO analysis and design, and the design of the TQO operational and management functions performed at this layer are considered in Chapter 7. TQO functions to be designed at this layer include the following (see Figure 1.2):

- Traffic management. This includes real-time performance monitoring, network control, and work center functions. Network controls include code controls, cancel controls, and reroute controls.
- Capacity management—Forecasting. This includes load forecasting, including configuration database functions, load aggregation, basing, and projection functions, and load adjustment cycle and view of business adjustment cycle.
- Capacity management—Daily and weekly performance monitoring. This includes daily congestion analysis, study-week congestion analysis, and study-period congestion analysis.
- Capacity management—Short-term network adjustment. This includes network design to respond to congestion identified by daily and weekly performance monitoring.

Note that there are critical operational and management functions that are not directly TQO related, but are essential to the operation of an MPLS network, such as service ordering, provisioning, and maintenance, as well as fault monitoring, analysis, troubleshooting, and repair. These operational functions are also considered in Chapter 7.

Capacity management optimization is considered in Chapter 6, and three models are described, including (a) discrete event flow optimization models, (b) traffic load flow optimization models, and (c) virtual trunk flow optimization models. DEFO models have the advantage of being able to model traffic and routing methods of arbitrary complexity. Capacity management must provide sufficient capacity to carry the expected traffic variations, such as those detailed in Table 1.1, so as to meet end-to-end traffic performance objectives, such as loss/delayed probability objective levels. Traffic load variations lead in direct measure to capacity increments and can be categorized as (a) minute-to-minute instantaneous variations and associated busy-hour traffic load capacity, (b) hour-to-hour variations and associated "hour-to-hour ("multihour") capacity," (c) day-to-day variations and associated "day-to-day capacity," and (d) week-to-week variations and associated "reserve capacity." These factors are analyzed in Chapter 6, and it is shown that capacity management optimization can save on the order of 30–50% of the network cost.

1.5 TQO Design

This section formulates the TQO design problem addressed in this book associated with each TQO layer and identifies the TQO design solution approach. The latter includes evaluating TQO design and operational experience and modeling, analysis, and case studies. We highlight the key results and conclusions.

1.5.1 TQO Design Problem Statement

The following sections provide a brief problem statement for TQO design at each TQO layer and refer to the chapters in the book where the problem solution is addressed.

1.5.1.1 Traffic/Application Layer Design

Problem Statement: Find an optimal call/session routing design, class-of-service routing strategy, and routing information exchange management approach for arbitrary traffic loads and network topology, which yields maximum-flow/revenue and minimum-cost capacity, with minimal control overhead, subject to meeting performance constraints.

Call/session routing design and class-of-service routing design are considered in Chapter 2 and Chapter 3, respectively. Routing information exchange management design is addressed in Chapter 4. SIP with preconditions for purposes of call/session bandwidth negotiation and allocation is considered in the case study in Chapter 9.

1.5.1.2 MPLS LSP Dynamic Routing and Bandwidth Allocation Layer 3 Design

Problem Statement: Find an optimal layer 3 connection/bearer-path routing design, MPLS LSP dynamic routing and bandwidth allocation strategy, routing table management procedure, and fast MPLS LSP restoration design for arbitrary traffic loads and network topology that yield maximum flow/revenue and minimum cost capacity, with minimal control overhead, subject to meeting performance constraints.

Connection/bearer-path routing design and MPLS LSP dynamic routing and bandwidth allocation design are considered in Chapters 2 and 3, routing table management design is addressed in Chapter 4, and fast restoration under failure is considered in Chapter 5.

1.5.1.3 GMPLS LSP (Logical Link) Routing and Bandwidth Allocation Layer 2 Design

Problem Statement: Find an optimal layer 2 GMPLS LSP dynamic routing and bandwidth allocation design and fast GMPLS LSP restoration strategy for arbitrary traffic loads and network topology that yield maximum flow/revenue and minimum cost capacity, with minimal control overhead, subject to meeting performance constraints.

GMPLS LSP dynamic routing and bandwidth allocation design, as well as fast restoration design under failure, are considered in Chapter 5.

1.5.1.4 Physical Fiber Transport/Layer 1 Design

Problem Statement: Find an optimal layer 1 physical transport network design, bandwidth allocation strategy, and fast physical link restoration procedure for arbitrary traffic loads and network topology that yield maximum flow/revenue and minimum cost capacity, with minimal control overhead, subject to meeting performance constraints.

Physical transport network design and bandwidth allocation at this layer, as well as fast restoration under failure, are considered in Chapters 5 and 6.

1.5.1.5 Operational/Management Layer Design

Operations/Management Design Problem Statement: Find an optimal TQO operations and management design, including traffic management and capacity management functions identified earlier, for arbitrary traffic loads and network topology that yields maximum flow/revenue and minimum cost capacity, with minimal control overhead, subject to meeting performance constraints.

Minimum Cost Capacity Design Problem Statement: Given traffic loads and node locations, find the minimum cost link topology, link capacity, and dynamic routing/TQO design, subject to meeting performance constraints.

Maximum Flow/Revenue Dynamic Routing/TQO Design Problem Statement: Given traffic loads and network topology/capacity, find the maximum flow/revenue dynamic routing/TQO design.

TQO operations/management design and capacity design are considered in Chapters 6 and 7.

1.5.2 TQO Design Approach

Two main avenues are followed to solve the TQO design problem formulated in Section 1.5.1:

- TQO design/operational experience in voice, data, and integrated voice/data networks.
- Results of analysis, modeling, and case studies.

In both cases, the Geekian and Telephonian views of the avenue are taken into account. We all know very well that both BellHeads and NetHeads have the best solution to most any problem, not just the TQO problem of interest in this book. These are usually very different solutions, but both are always right.

We also admit that the optimal solution to this problem presented in this book is not the one and only optimal solution. To the contrary, in addition to the GTQO approach, Chapter 10 presents several other excellent solution approaches that may well be deployed in some form. Goodness knows that there will always be multiple optimal solutions deployed out there, and never just one.

So now let's briefly examine both avenues in our solution approach.

1.5.2.1 Design and Operational Experience

We relate TQO design experience in Section 1.6 using ARPANET and AT&T's dynamic routing voice network as examples of the TQO design/operational experience. Note that all other voice dynamic routing network deployments worldwide are summarized in Section 1.6. TQO has been used in data networks since about 1835, when Morse invented the telegraph, and in voice networks since about 1876, when Bell invented the telephone. These experiences teach us about design principles that can be applied to TQO design of any network, particularly to converged (G)MPLS-based voice/data dynamic routing networks.

Furthermore, TQO design and operational experience clearly illustrate the benefits of TQO, and based on these experiences there is proof that deployed TQO designs have huge benefits. To show this, we crow about the glowing success of TQO in voice/ISDN networks, with which I have long-term and detailed design and implementation experience. We illustrate the benefits of dynamic nonhierarchical routing (DNHR) implementation in 1984, real-time network routing (RTNR) in 1991, and real-time internetwork routing (RINR) in 1995, which revolutionized AT&T's national, international, and access networks [ASH98]. The dynamic network achieved (a) dramatically increased throughput, traffic handling efficiency, reliability, and performance, (b) automated operations, (c) large capital savings with efficient network design/optimization methodology, and (d) new services revenue based on the class-of-service routing concept, including 800 Gold, Emergency Services Priority Routing, International Services Priority Routing, and Software Defined Network Priority Routing. This migration inspired a worldwide migration to TQO/dynamic routing by many other carriers.

We reiterate that "TQO methods" and "dynamic routing methods" are used somewhat interchangeably. As in the definitions given in Section 1.2, TQO encompasses network optimization of TE and QoS functions, whereas dynamic routing encompasses network optimization of flexible time-dependent routing, state-dependent routing, and event-dependent routing TE, as well as QoS functions. DNHR is an example of TDR, and RTNR/RINR are examples of SDR, whereas the GTQO method is an example of EDR. TDR, SDR, and EDR methods are defined and described in Chapter 2.

1.5.2.2 Modeling, Analysis, and Case Studies

Section 1.5.4 discusses the modeling/analysis and case studies presented throughout this book for both intranetwork and internetwork TQO design. I have been deeply involved over a long period of time in applying TQO design principles to AT&T's network evolution, where I led the internal routing/addressing/traffic-engineering strategy (RATS) team that spearheaded the evolution studies. RATS conducted detailed modeling/analysis studies for a wide range of alternative architectures under consideration. This was first done with the migration of AT&T's global voice/ISDN network to real-time, adaptive TQO (DNHR, RTNR, and RINR described earlier) through the 1980s and 1990s.

In the mid-1990s RATS began working on the evolution to an all packet-based, converged voice/data TQO/dynamic routing architecture. BellHead RATS, representing the voice/ISDN circuit-switching technologies, felt that a Telephonian-type solution was optimal (e.g., RTNR/RINR), whereas the NetHead RATS, representing the ATM, frame-relay, IP-based technologies, felt that a Geekian solution was optimal (e.g., PNNI). In the end, both were right, and having the two cultures work together to close the gap proved to be a huge benefit. An initial emphasis to migrate to an ATM-based integrated network technology soon refocused to an IP/MPLS-based architecture. In the early 2000s, RATS completed its comprehensive case study of architecture evolution to a converged IP/MPLS voice/data network architecture.

These modeling, analysis, and case studies are the basis for evaluating a wide range of alternatives presented in Chapters 2–6, 8, and 9 and support the GTQO protocol in Chapter 10. GTQO encompasses many ingenious NetHead protocols—MPLS, GMPLS, DiffServ, DSTE, RSVP, NSIS, SIP, and others—and highly successful, time-honored BellHead networking principles are included as well—bandwidth reservation, dynamic alternate routing, traffic management, capacity management and planning, and others. So the cultural gap is filled up and overflowing with everyone's best ideas, NIH is out of the picture here, and everyone is happy!

1.6 TQO Design and Operational Experience

There is a long history to TQO: data networks came first with Morse's invention of the telegraph in 1835 and later came voice networks with Bell's invention of the telephone in 1876. This section starts with TQO design/operational experience in data networks using ARPANET as an example, when computer control and automation began to evolve in the late 1960s. We then summarize TQO design/operational experience in voice networks using the AT&T network as an example from manual operation in the 1920s to today's automation.

In both cases of data and voice network TQO design/operational experience, we focus first on the network layers described in Section 1.3, primarily layer 3/2 routing design and operational experience. We then discuss the management layer design and operational experience, and focus on traffic management. Finally, we highlight the TQO principles that evolved and the benefits derived from the TQO design/operational experiences.

1.6.1 Design and Operational Experience in Data Networks

In 1968 the Defense Advanced Research Projects Agency (DARPA) contracted with Bolt, Beranek & Newman (BBN) to create the ARPANET, and in 1970 the first five nodes were in place: UCLA, Stanford, UC Santa Barbara, University of Utah, and BBN. Vint Cerf and Robert Kahn specified the basis for the transmission control protocol/Internet protocol (TCP/IP) in 1974, and in 1984 the Internet with its 1000 hosts converted to TCP/IP for its messaging. TCP provides application programs with access to the network using a reliable, connection-oriented transport layer service. IP receives datagrams from the upper-layer software and transmits them to the destination host based on a best-effort, connection-less delivery service.

1.6.1.1 Data Network Routing Layer Design/Operational Experience

Packet-switched data networks typically use link-state, or shortest path first, dynamic routing protocols. Such protocols are distributed database protocols and are classified as SDR protocols as defined in Chapter 2. The functions of the link-state dynamic routing protocol include the following:

- Discovery of neighbors and link status
- Synchronization of topology databases
- Flooding of topology state information
- Election of peer group or area leaders
- Summarization of topology state information
- Construction of the routing hierarchy

The first link-state dynamic routing protocol was developed for use in the ARPANET [McQUILLAN80], which formed the basis for all other link-state protocols. The OSPF [RFC2328] protocol was later developed for use in IP-based networks and the PNNI [ATMFORUM-0055.002] routing protocol for use in ATM-based networks. In a link-state routing protocol, each node maintains a link-state database describing the network topology. Each participating node has an identical database that includes each node's usable interfaces and reachable neighbors. Each node distributes its local state throughout the network by flooding and constructs a tree of shortest paths with itself as the root. This shortest-path tree gives the route to each destination in the node.

Each node bundles its topology state information, which is reliably flooded throughout the peer group or area. Topology state parameters can include relatively static parameters such as link metrics (or administrative weights), and dynamic information, such as available link bandwidth. Reachability information consists of routing addresses and address prefixes, which describe the destinations to which connections may be routed. Hello packets are sent periodically by each node on interconnecting links, and in this way the Hello protocol makes the two neighboring nodes known to each other. The Hello protocol runs as long as the link is operational. It can therefore act as a link failure detector when other mechanisms fail. Each node exchanges Hello packets with its immediate neighbors and thereby determines its local state information. This state information includes the node identity and peer group or area membership of the node's immediate neighbors and the status of its links to the neighbors. Link-state protocols implement a hierarchy mechanism to ensure that the protocol scales for large networks. The hierarchy begins at the lowest level where the lowest-level nodes are organized into peer groups or areas.

TQO and routing in the ARPANET evolved with a new routing algorithm introduced in ARPANET in 1980 [McQUILLAN80]. The new algorithm used shortest path first routing trees with various precautions to ensure that the routing databases in all nodes are consistent. Deficiencies of the old algorithm were remedied by the new one, and the new algorithm formed the basis for OSPF routing, which is widely deployed in the Internet today. The new approach resolved problems with the older algorithm, which included the following:

- entire routing tables were transmitted; these long packets slowed other traffic
- each node used local information (e.g., delay estimates based on queue length) to make routing decisions so inconsistencies in routing tables might develop
- lack of stability: sometimes too slow to respond to connectivity changes, sometimes overreacts for minor changes
- queue length is a poor indicator of line delay and a poor predictor of packet latency

The new algorithm builds stable routing trees as follows:

- updates based on 10-s average packet delay measurements (upper bound on update frequency)

- updates only if the newly measured average delay differs from the previous value by some threshold T; if not, T is reduced by d (initially $T = 64$ ms, $d = 12.8$ ms)
- ensures all nodes have the same routing information database
- allows system to react quickly to large changes and slowly to small ones
- each node must generate at least 1 update per minute
- new node cannot come up until it has heard updates from all other nodes
- new node additions/removals recognized as connectivity changes
- updates sent by "flooding," i.e., transmit on all links except the one on which it was received
- transient loops possible, but short lived in practice

The increase in the size of the Internet also challenged the capabilities of the routers. Originally, there was the single distributed algorithm, as described above, for routing that was implemented uniformly by all the routers in the Internet. As the number of networks in the Internet exploded, this initial design could not expand as necessary so it was replaced by a hierarchical model of routing, with an interior gateway protocol (IGP) used inside each region of the Internet and an exterior gateway protocol (EGP) used to tie the regions together. This design permitted different regions to use a different IGP so that different requirements for cost, rapid reconfiguration, robustness, and scale could be accommodated.

Not only the routing algorithm, but the size of the addressing tables, stressed the capacity of the routers. Routing and addressing therefore evolved to make it easy for people to use the network: hosts were assigned names so that it was not necessary to remember the numeric addresses and a table was used to translate the names to routing addresses. Originally, there were a fairly limited number of hosts so it was feasible to maintain a single table of all the hosts and their associated names and addresses. However, given the scale of the Internet and the shift to having a large number of independently managed networks (e.g., LANs) meant that having a single table of hosts was no longer feasible, and the domain name system was invented [RFC882, RFC883] to permit a scalable distributed mechanism for resolving hierarchical host names (e.g., www.acm.org) into an Internet address. New approaches for address aggregation, in particular classless interdomain routing [RFC1519], were introduced to control the size of router tables.

Some general observations on packet-switching technology and data network optimization implications are now discussed. In contrast to circuit-switching technology, packet switching tends to have lower switching node cost relative to transport, which leads to sparse logical topologies and relatively high-capacity logical links. Sparsely connected networks tend to minimize transport cost. Having few links tends to concentrate the network load, raising the load per link and the link capacity requirement. When doing minimum cost capacity design for these sparsely connected networks, dynamic routing protocols do not tend to have significant design cost advantages over FXR protocols because the high-capacity links have low (or zero) levels of traffic loss and overflow (alternate routed) traffic, which precludes the need for alternate routes. The lack of alternate routed traffic tends to give dynamic routing little optimization advantage over FXR for minimum cost design. That is, carrying all the design load on the shortest path without alternate routing tends to minimize cost. However, under scenarios where links are overloaded, congest, and give rise to alternate routed traffic, maximum flow routing design for sparse packet-switched networks tends to favor a dynamic routing solution in order to take advantage of a large number of route choices to access available link capacity.

1.6.1.2 Data Network Management Layer Design/Operational Experience

In the beginning of the Internet, the emphasis on TQO traffic management and capacity management aspects (also known as "network management" in data networks) was on defining and implementing protocols that achieved interoperation of the functional areas of data network management, as follows:

- Performance management—focus on smooth network performance and ability to handle current workload; monitor real-time network status and performance, packets dropped, timeouts, collisions, CRC errors, etc.
- Fault management—deal with network problems and emergencies (e.g., router failures, power losses); entails both reactive and proactive network fault management
- Capacity management—gather statistics on equipment and facility use; analyze trends to determine required bandwidth increases and/or network upgrades
- Configuration management—track device settings, inventory, configuration, provisioning, and make adjustments as needed

Early on in the ARPANET, network management was fairly straightforward. For example, by 1970 the network control center (NCC) at the ARPANET BBN node began operation, and all the other network nodes had to report to the NCC every minute to confirm they were alive. As the network grew larger, it became clear that the sometimes ad hoc procedures used to manage the network would not scale. Manual configuration of tables was replaced by distributed automated algorithms, and better tools were devised to isolate faults. By 1987 it became clear that a protocol was needed that would permit network elements such as routers to be remotely managed in a uniform way. Several protocols for this purpose were proposed, including the simple network management protocol (SNMP) [RFC1157], along with management information bases (MIBs) containing configurable parameter data, traffic data, and other management information, and are now widely used for data network management. Operational use of SNMP and MIBs within an MPLS network architecture is discussed further in Chapter 7.

Various TQO mechanisms later evolved in data networks, including integrated services (IntServ), RSVP, DiffServ, MPLS-based QoS capabilities, and others. These technologies and standards are reviewed in Chapter 10, Section 10.6, and Appendix A.

1.6.2 Design and Operational Experience in Voice Networks

Voice network TQO started to evolve as early as the 1920s, with TE and layer 3 routing methods progressing steadily from manual routing methods to fully automated dynamic routing methods used today, with management layer procedures making very significant advances as well. These experiences are reviewed here using the AT&T network as an example.

1.6.2.1 Voice Network Routing Layer Design/Operational Experience

In 1930 a hierarchy of connection switching nodes was established [OSBORN30], and that network routing architecture limited the number of nodes in a "long-distance" voice call to six in any connection. Routing was handled manually by operators at specialized switchboards following rather involved operating procedures. During the late 1940s, a new plan [PILLIOD52] established 10 regions and a five-level hierarchy of connection-switching nodes centering on the 10 regional nodes at the top of the hierarchy. Crossbar connection switching technology was deployed in the 1950s and enabled direct distance dialing, automatic alternate routing, automatic message accounting, and efficient network design techniques for the five-level alternate routing network. The hierarchical routing network with electromechanical connection switching nodes evolved through the 1960s, and in the 1970s, electronic, computer-controlled connection switching and common channel signaling began to evolve. Significantly, the planning for direct distance dialing and the five-level hierarchical network was of such quality that only minor refinements were necessary until it was replaced by dynamic routing starting in the early 1980s.

By taking advantage of computer-controlled node processing and common channel signaling, dynamic routing networks then began to emerge. I have been deeply involved in the evolution of the AT&T global network to a dynamic routing architecture, the first commercial dynamic routing network in the world, and the fundamentally changed traffic management, capacity management, and planning operations that went with this dynamic routing architecture [ASH98]. I have also witnessed the subsequent worldwide evolution of many metropolitan, national, international, and private networks to similar architectures.

Results of studies spanning conception, theoretical development, economic/feasibility analysis, system development specification, implementation, planning, and overall project management led to the implementation of DNHR, beginning in July 1984. By October 1987, DNHR was implemented throughout the AT&T network and was followed by a major upgrade to RTNR in 1991, to RINR in the global international network in 1995, and to RINR in the local exchange carrier access networks in 1998. This DNHR, RTNR, and RINR deployment represents a major departure from the traditional design, engineering, and management of telecommunications networks and revolutionized the routing/TE capabilities, design, traffic management, capacity management, and planning operations of the entire global AT&T network. Over the implementation period of dynamic routing from 1984 to 1999, a number of new operations systems supporting TQO were specified, designed, developed, tested, and put into operation. In all, over 140 connection switching nodes serving domestic, international, and access traffic were converted to dynamic routing.

As detailed in [ASH98], the dynamic network provides vastly improved performance quality for customers, new services, increased revenue, and greatly reduced capital and operations costs. Dynamic routing achieved essentially zero traffic loss network performance under normal traffic and network conditions, flexibility afforded by instant traffic data, efficient network design/optimization methodology, and operational techniques enabling real-time network control. New services were designed and introduced based on the class of service routing concept, which enabled new services to be defined through provisioning of tables and parameters in the nodes rather than with software and hardware development (class of service routing is described further in Chapter 3). New services introduced with the class of service routing concept included 800 Gold, Emergency Services Priority Routing, International Services Priority Routing, and Software Defined Network Priority Routing.

AT&T's successful deployment of dynamic routing inspired many other network providers to plan and implement dynamic routing of their own design, which achieved similar benefits. These worldwide dynamic routing implementations and their current status are summarized in Table 1.2 [ASH04]. References are also provided in Table 1.2 on the various systems for readers interested in more details.

Further details on the benefits of TE/dynamic routing are given below, following a discussion of the experiences with traffic management and capacity management TQO experience in voice networks.

Some general observations on TDM circuit-switching technology and dynamic routing network optimization implications are now discussed. TDM connection switching tends to be expensive relative to transport, which leads to highly connected, meshed logical topologies and relatively low-capacity logical links. Highly connected, meshed networks tend to minimize connection switching cost. Having many links tends to distribute the network load, lowering the load per link and the link capacity requirement. When doing minimum cost capacity design for these meshed networks, dynamic routing protocols tend to have significant design cost advantages over FXR protocols because the large number of alternate route choices affords dynamic routing an optimization advantage. In addition, low-capacity links need to have higher levels of traffic blocking and overflow (alternate routed) traffic in order to achieve high occupancy and run efficiently. More alternate routed traffic tends to give dynamic routing an optimization advantage over FXR. Finally, maximum flow routing design for meshed TDM networks tends to favor a dynamic routing solution for the same reasons: a large number of route choices and the benefit of driving low-capacity links to high occupancy and more alternate routed traffic.

Table 1.2 Operational Circuit-Switched Dynamic Routing Systems

Routing type	Dynamic routing systems	Network	Start year	End year	Comments
TDR	Dynamic nonhierarchical routing (DNHR) [ASH81, ASH98]	AT&T US National Network	1984	1991	DNHR replaced by RTNR in 1991
		AT&T FTS-2000 Network	1987	2002	DNHR replaced by RTNR in 2002
SDR centralized periodic	GTAI (GTAI is an Italian acronym: Management of the Traffic Transit Italcable switches) [DiBENEDETTO89]	Italcable	1984	1985?	This routing mechanism was implemented between the three intercontinental switches operated by Italcable
	Dynamically controlled routing (DCR) [REGNIER90]	Stentor Canada National Network	1991	In operation	Also known as high-performance routing (HPR)
		Bell Canada Network	1992	In operation	Consists of one DCR network local to the Toronto area and one local to the Montreal area
		Sprint National Network	1994	In operation	
		MCI US National Network	1995	In operation	
		Qwest Communications National Network	1999	In operation	
SDR distributed periodic	Worldwide intelligent network routing (WIN) [ASH89]	Worldwide Intelligent Network	1993	In operation	WIN data are currently exchanged among AT&T/US, CHT-I/Taiwan, and Alestra/Mexico
SDR Distributed call-by-call	Real-time network routing (RTNR) [ASH91, ASH98]	AT&T US National Network	1991	In operation	

(Continued)

Table 1.2 Operational Circuit-Switched Dynamic Routing Systems—cont'd

Routing type	Dynamic routing systems	Network	Start year	End year	Comments
	Real-time internetwork routing (RINR) [ASH98]	AT&T FTS-2000 Network	2002	In operation	
		AT&T Global International Network	1995	In operation	
EDR	State- and time-dependent routing (STR) [MASE89]	NTT Japan National Network	1992	2002	The deployment of STR started in 1992, but operation stopped in 2002 when D60 switches were replaced by new switches
	Dynamic alternative routing (DAR) [GIBBENS88]	British Telecom UK National Network	1993	?	
	Success-To-the-Top network routing (STT) [ASH98]	AT&T US National Network	1995	1999	STT is a method used to route calls with voice enhancement devices in the path
	Lastabehängige Automatische Wegesuche (LAW) (in English, automatic last choice routing)	Deutsche Telecom National Network	1995	In operation	LAW is implemented in the transit network as well as regional and international access networks
	Acheminement multiple intelligent (AMI) [in English, multiple intelligent routing (MIR)]	France Telecom Long Distance Network	1998	In operation	AMI/MIR is an EDR system with multiple overflow routes and crankback

1.6.2.2   Voice Network Management Layer Design/Operational Experience

Voice network traffic management and capacity management TQO aspects began in the AT&T network with the establishment of regional traffic control centers in Chicago, Cleveland, and New York, which processed information affecting traffic in their region and communicated with each other and regional nodes via teletype. Manually operated wall displays showed the condition of network routes, and network managers implemented plans for coping with unusual calling patterns by instructing manually operated nodes to reroute connection requests or temporarily reassign bandwidth. Voice network traffic and capacity management were designed to meet demands for efficient service during the peak periods of a normal business day. Unusual events, such as overloads and failures, could cause delays and required active, coordinated management of the network as a whole.

Voice traffic management (also known as "network management" in voice networks) encompasses all of the activities necessary to identify conditions that may adversely affect network performance and service to the customer, and the application of network controls to minimize their impact. This includes the following functions:

- Monitor real-time network status and performance; collect and analyze relevant data
- Detect abnormal network conditions
- Investigate and identify the reasons for abnormal network conditions
- Initiate corrective action and/or control
- Coordinate actions with other network management centers and work areas (e.g., maintenance) on matters that affect service
- Issue reports of abnormal network situations, actions taken, and results obtained
- Provide advance planning for known or predictable network situations

By the 1960s, connection switching technology had evolved to allow sending real-time network status information to status boards in a centralized network management center in New York plus three regional centers in Chicago, Rockdale, Georgia, and White Plains, New York. This automation enabled network managers to respond more quickly to unusual situations and to instruct nodes to reject connection requests with little chance of completion or send connection requests over alternate routes with available bandwidth resources.

Network overloads early in the 1960s, particularly on Christmas day, led to severe node processing congestion in electromechanical, crossbar nodes. A large increase in connection setup attempts resulted in node processing congestion when the processing capacity of connection setup elements called "senders" was exceeded. In this case the node processing congestion spread to connected nodes and throughout the network and caused significant degradation of network performance. An analogous phenomenon most of us have experienced is grid lock on city streets. This arises, for example, when cars enter intersections and cannot move because they are blocked by other cars and these cars then block other cars from passing through the intersection.

This grid-lock situation spreads quickly to other intersections and locks up a whole city's road network. This Christmas overload experience illustrated the problems of automated routing in causing congestion to arise and spread and the need for congestion control and that traffic management controls were vitally needed to inhibit node processing congestion by removing attempts from the congested node that have a low chance of resulting in a successful connection.

The Cuban missile crisis of October 1962 provided an early test for these network management centers and traffic management controls. As President Kennedy addressed the nation, network managers placed controls throughout the network to prevent the volume of Miami-bound connection attempts from overwhelming nodes and bandwidth resources throughout the southeast. This real-life test demonstrated the effectiveness of the voice network TQO methods that had emerged.

Computer-controlled node processing and common channel signaling in the late 1970s enabled the ability to actively manage the network—both with automatic traffic management controls and by management intervention with manually activated traffic management controls. The centralized network management center moved to Bedminster, New Jersey, and included domestic and international network status boards automatically updated every 12 s and databases to instantly provide managers with the information needed to reroute connections. Managers used computer systems and terminals to find detailed information on any node or route in the network and to implement controls anywhere in the network. Along with the implementation of dynamic routing throughout the global network in the 1980s and 1990s, traffic management automation continued to evolve into the new millennium, with the introduction of the Global Network Operations Center to monitor all voice and data network services and operations.

Automatic traffic management controls include dynamic overload control (DOC), which responds to node congestion, and dynamic bandwidth reservation (DBR), which responds to link congestion. DOC and DBR are fully automatic controls and selective in the sense that they control traffic destined for hard-to-reach points in the network more stringently than other traffic. When a node detects hard-to-reach address codes, these codes are immediately communicated to other nodes. DBR is automatically enabled by nodes when congestion is detected, which is particularly important in minimizing the use of less efficient alternate path connections when necessary.

Code-blocking controls block connection requests to particular destination addresses or groups of addresses. These controls are particularly useful in the case of focused overloads, such as sometimes occurs with radio call-in give-away contests, especially if the connection requests are blocked at or near their origination. Code-blocking controls need not block all connections unless the destination node is completely disabled, such as through a natural disaster or equipment failure. Rather, code-blocking controls can typically control a percentage of the connection requests to a particular code.

A connection-gapping control, illustrated in Figure 1.9, is typically used by network managers in a focused overload. Connection gapping allows one connection request for a controlled code or set of codes to be accepted into the network, by each node,

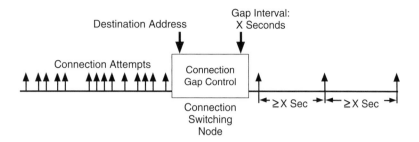

Figure 1.9   Connection gap control benefits derived from TQO design/operational experience in voice networks.

once every x seconds, and connection requests arriving after the accepted connection request are rejected for the next x seconds. In this way, connection gapping throttles the connection requests and reduces the overload to the particular focal point.

Expansive reroute controls are able to modify routes by inserting additional paths at the beginning, middle, or end of a path sequence. Such reroutes can be inserted manually or automatically.

1.6.2.3   Benefits Derived from TQO Design/Operational Experience in Voice Networks

The TQO design and operational experience have clearly demonstrated the benefits to customers in terms of new service flexibility and improved service quality and reliability, at reduced cost. We illustrate these benefits through examples from the dynamic routing experience [ASH98], where the following improvements are achieved over fixed hierarchical routing that preceded the conversion to dynamic routing:

- essentially zero traffic loss performance under normal traffic conditions
- improved performance under network overloads and failures
- increased revenue and network throughput through maximum flow/revenue routing design
- increased revenue from new services deployment through class-of-service routing capabilities
- lower operational expense costs through centralization and automation of network operations
- lower operational expense costs through automation with class-of-service routing capabilities
- lower capital costs through minimum cost network design and voice/data integration
- overall higher quality service for customers as a competitive advantage

Peak days such as Christmas, Mother's Day, and Thanksgiving, in addition to unpredictable events such as earthquakes, hurricanes, and failures, demonstrate the

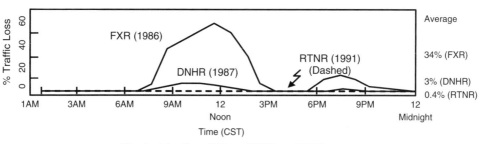

Thanksgiving Day, FXR vs. DNHR vs. RTNR

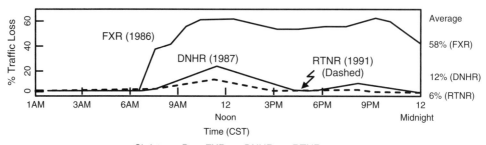

Christmas Day, FXR vs. DNHR vs. RTNR

Legend
FXR – Fixed Hierarchical Routing
DNHR – Dynamic Nonhierarchical Routing (Time Dependent Dynamic Routing Strategy)
RTNR – Real-Time Network Routing (State-Dependent Dynamic Routing Strategy)

Figure 1.10 TQO/dynamic routing performance with peak-day traffic loads.

benefit of dynamic routing in responding to traffic load patterns that deviate severely from normal day traffic for which the network is designed. Peak-day traffic loss probability results show that the performance improvements of DNHR (a time-dependent dynamic routing strategy) over FXR and RTNR (a state-dependent dynamic routing strategy) over DNHR are dramatic. As illustrated in Figure 1.10, in the case of Thanksgiving day traffic overload, as routing evolved from FXR to DNHR to RTNR, average network traffic loss probability, which is about 34% for FXR, is down to 3% with DNHR and then down to 0.4% with RTNR, which is nearly a factor of 100 improvement. The average traffic loss probability for Christmas day traffic overload is down from 58% for the FXR network, to 12% for the DNHR network, to 6% for the RTNR network, which is almost a factor of 10 improvement. Also, there is significantly less network capacity relative to demand in the RTNR network versus the FXR network because of the efficiencies of dynamic network design, and there is more traffic load as the network evolved from FXR to DNHR to RTNR.

Higher completion rates and greater network throughput are good both for customers and for service providers. Significantly increased revenue and throughput were observed, for example, with RINR implementation in the international, interdomain network. The addition of more alternate paths and dynamic selection of paths with

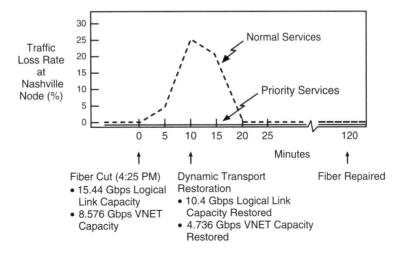

Figure 1.11   TQO/dynamic routing performance with fiber cut.

most likely completion dramatically increased minutes of revenue producing traffic on the network. Peak days on the international network, such as Chinese New Year, had significantly increased throughput after RINR was introduced (see discussion of Tables 8.7, 8.8, and 8.9 in Chapter 8).

Dynamic routing provides a self-healing network capability to ensure a network-wide path selection and immediate adaptation to failure. As illustrated in Figure 1.11, a fiber cut near the Nashville node severed 8.576 Gbps of logical link/VNET capacity in the RTNR connection switching network (private-line transport capacity was also lost in the fiber cut). In the example, dynamic transport restoration is implemented by centralized automatic control of transport cross-connect devices [CHAO91] to quickly restore service following a transport failure, such as caused by the cable cut. After dynamic transport restoration of 4.736 Gbps of logical link/VNET capacity, a total of 3.84 Gbps of logical link/VNET capacity was still out of service in the connection switching network. Traffic connection loss rate is shown at 5 min intervals, corresponding to network traffic data received every 5 min. At time 0 (the fiber cut), many connections are disconnected instantly and customers begin redialing to restore their connections. RTNR dynamic connection routing is able to complete these redialed connections on idle network logical link/VNET capacity. However, connections can be completed only up to a certain point because a large amount of logical link/VNET bandwidth capacity has been temporarily lost. Traffic loss rate therefore builds up after a few minutes as available logical link/VNET capacity is filled by redialed/reestablished connections and additional redialed and/or new connections cannot be completed.

However, at the same time dynamic transport routing is restoring the logical link capacity on backup physical transport capacity, which causes the traffic loss rate to start to fall again. Over the duration of this event, more than 12,000 connections were lost in the connection-switching network, almost all of them originating or terminating at the Nashville node, and it is noteworthy that the traffic loss rate in the network returned to zero after the 4.736 Gbps of logical link/VNET capacity was restored, even though there was still 3.84 Gbps of logical link/VNET capacity still out of service. RTNR was able to find paths on which to complete traffic even though there was far less logical link/VNET capacity than normal even after the dynamic transport restoration.

Hence dynamic connection routing in combination with dynamic transport restoration provides a self-healing network capability, and even though the cable was repaired 2 h after the fiber cut, degradation of service was minimal. In this example, dynamic connection routing also provided priority routing for selected customers and services, which permits priority connections to be routed in preference to other connections, and traffic loss rate of the priority services is essentially zero throughout the whole event. Over the duration of an event, connections are lost until sufficient capacity is restored for the network to return to zero traffic loss rate. That is, both dynamic connection routing and dynamic transport routing are able to find available paths on which to restore the failed connections. This improved network performance provides additional service revenues as formerly lost connections are completed and it improves service quality to the customer, thus providing a competitive advantage.

Combining dynamic transport routing with dynamic connection routing using GMPLS control capabilities is discussed much more in Chapter 5.

Dynamic routing lowers capital costs through improved network design in the range of 10 to 30% of FXR network cost over a range of network configurations and applications, as shown in Chapter 6. In particular, studies have shown that dynamic network design and optimization techniques lower transmission and switching costs by 10% or more savings in metropolitan area networks [FIELD83, CHEMOUIL86, GAUTHIER87, KRISHNAN88], 15% or more in domestic long-distance networks [CAMERON82, GIBBENS86, STACEY87, CARON88, MITRA91, LANGLOIS91, WATANABE87, ASH81, ASH81a, ASH83, ASH85, ASH88, ASH89a, ASH91, ASH92], and 25% or more in international networks [ASH89, ASH94a].

Results show that voice and data services integration through class-of-service routing, discussed further in Chapter 3, enables more efficient and robust network performance with independent traffic control for each voice or data class of service. It also provides efficient sharing of integrated transport network capacity and implements an integrated class-of-service routing feature for extending dynamic routing to new and emerging services. Several new services were enabled and introduced with RTNR/RINR class-of-service routing, such as 800 Gold Service, International Priority Routing, Emergency Services Priority Routing, and others. These services remain in operation, providing new service revenue for the provider and service quality and features for customers. These service features can also be (and have been) used to differentiate service providers from their competitors and as incentives for customer retention in the highly competitive communications industry.

Dynamic routing lowers operations expense through centralized and automated network management/design, as illustrated in Chapter 7.

1.6.3   TQO Design Principles and Benefits Derived from Experience

These design and operational experiences have provided lessons learned and dynamic routing/TQO protocol design principles applicable to MPLS/GMPLS network evolution (these appear again in the case studies presented in Chapters 8 and 9):

- COS routing capabilities for service flexibility and multiservice VNET bandwidth allocation
- CAC, source-based path selection, crankback, for bandwidth allocation to COSs/VNETs
- load state mapping, bandwidth reservation techniques for stable performance, and bandwidth sharing
- dynamic connection routing, priority routing, EDR path selection for efficient utilization, and reduced routing overhead
- dynamic transport routing for fast restoration and efficient utilization
- queuing priority mechanisms for COS differentiation
- meet performance objectives for integrated COSs

Also from these experiences in data and voice network TQO evolution, several network management/traffic management TQO principles evolved to ensure efficient network operation, as follows:

- performance and traffic data collection for (a) network surveillance for real-time traffic management and (b) network engineering
- controls to ensure network performance under congestion and failure
- traffic management principles: (a) utilize all available bandwidth; redirect overflow traffic to idle capacity on alternate routes, (b) keep available bandwidth filled with high probability of completion traffic by identifying and reducing likely ineffective connection attempts close to their source, (c) under congestion, give priority to connections requiring fewer links; avoid long multilink connections from blocking several shortest path connections, and (d) inhibit node processing congestion and prevent its spread; remove low probability of completion connection attempts from congested nodes

Many years ago I attended AT&T's "network management school" in Morristown, New Jersey, to learn how to apply these principles. A near real-world experience was created by having each student operate a simulated traffic management center (i.e., a little booth with simulated control panel, displays, communication media to other little booths). In response to network congestion arising from a simulated Christmas day overload situation based on real traffic data, the student was expected to analyze traffic data, recognize the network condition requiring manager intervention, coordinate with other network managers (in their own little booths), and apply controls based on the traffic management principles taught in the course. If node processing congestion arose in the simulated Christmas day network, and, worse, if it spread, the student probably failed the course! This was an excellent way to learn how the traffic management principles worked and should be applied.

As illustrated in the previous section, the benefits from implementing these TQO/dynamic routing principles are as follows:

- essentially zero traffic loss performance under normal traffic patterns
- improved performance under network overloads and failures
- increased revenue and network throughput through maximum flow/revenue routing design
- increased revenue from new services deployment through COS routing capabilities
- lower operational expense costs through automation with COS routing capabilities
- lower operational expense costs through centralization and automation of network management/design
- lower capital costs through minimum cost network design and voice/data integration
- overall higher quality service for customers to achieve a competitive advantage

1.7 Modeling, Analysis, and Case Studies

Chapters 2–9 use network models to illustrate the traffic engineering methods developed in this book. Details of the models are presented in each chapter in accordance with the TQO functions being illustrated.

A full-scale 135-node national network model is used together with a multiservice voice/data traffic demand model to study various TQO scenarios and trade-offs. A 71-node model is developed in Chapter 9 for a case study of TQO protocol design for MPLS/GMPLS-based integrated voice/data dynamic routing networks. Typical data and voice traffic loads are used to model the various network alternatives. The variable bit rate data services traffic model incorporates typical data traffic load patterns and includes (a) variable bit rate real-time traffic, representing services such as IP-telephony, (b) variable bit rate nonreal-time traffic, representing services such as WWW multimedia and credit card check, and (c) unassigned bit rate traffic, representing best-effort services such as email, voice mail, and file transfer multimedia applications. Voice/ISDN traffic loads are segmented in the model into constant-bit-rate services, including business voice, consumer voice, international voice, high-priority voice, normal- and high-priority 64-Kbps ISDN data, and 384-Kbps ISDN data. The cost model represents typical node costs and transport costs and illustrates the economies of scale for costs of high-capacity network elements.

We pause here to consider whether Geekia NetHeads might say at this point: "As I expected, this is a BellHead book, look at all the voice emphasis in the model!" Well, to the contrary, as we show in Chapter 2, most of the traffic load volume in the model represents, by far, data services. A second important point is the modeling assumption that PSTN legacy voice and ISDN data services currently offered on service provider networks must be migrated to the converged IP/MPLS network. That is, legacy PSTN services will not disappear, but will be carried on the converged IP/MPLS network along with legacy packet data services, legacy private line services, new voice/data services, etc. Therefore the model includes legacy PSTN services, emulated on an IP/MPLS network, as well as traditional packet data services. This view in the model is consistent with the next-generation network (NGN) concept [CARUGI05], which proposes to have PSTN services emulated on the NGN architecture. Continuity of service offerings is seen as a critical element in successful migration to a converged voice/data network.

Many different alternatives and trade-offs are examined in the analysis models, including the following:

- centralized routing table control versus distributed control
- off-line, preplanned (e.g., TDR-based) routing table control versus on-line routing table control (e.g., SDR or EDR based)
- per-flow traffic management versus per-virtual-network (or per-traffic trunk or per-bandwidth pipe) traffic management
- sparse logical topology versus meshed logical topology
- FXR versus TDR versus SDR versus EDR path selection
- multilink path selection versus two-link path selection
- path selection using local status information versus global status information
- global status dissemination alternatives, including status flooding, distributed query for status, and centralized status in a TQO processor

Table 10.1 in Chapter 10 summarizes comparisons and observations based on the modeling in each of these alternatives and trade-offs (further details of these results are contained in Chapters 2–9). Also presented in Chapter 10 is a summary of the main conclusions reached in the book based on the modeling and analysis presented in each chapter, as well as on TQO design/operations experience.

1.7.1   Analysis, Design, and Optimization Methods Used in Modeling Studies

This section highlights the analysis, design, and optimization techniques used, which include (a) routing design and optimization methods, (b) capacity design and optimization methods, and (c) QoS and GoS performance measures.

1.7.1.1   *Routing Design and Optimization Methods*

The techniques used for routing design and optimization are, among others, shortest path optimization and discrete event simulation modeling. The Bellman–Ford algorithm is a good general method for shortest path optimization [BELLMAN57] and is presented in Chapter 6. Sparse multilink shortest path (MSPR) network topologies with relatively low layer 2 logical link connectivity lend themselves to shortest path optimization techniques, and the Bellman–Ford algorithm is used in many of the MSPR designs presented in this book.

Discrete event simulation models provide performance analysis, routing design, and capacity design and are a versatile method to study and optimize TQO performance. Such models can accurately capture nonlinear and complex network behavior and are used, for example, in the design of very complex routing and bandwidth allocation algorithms, as well as in capacity design. We apply these techniques to MSPR, SDR, and EDR routing designs and to two-link SDR and EDR routing designs analyzed in Chapters 2–6, case studies presented in Chapters 8 and 9, and to the GTQO protocol design in Chapter 10.

Simulation techniques are used in the detailed case study of two-link SDR design presented in Chapter 8 to optimize routing design parameters, such as (a) number of link occupancy states (compare three-, four-, five-, and six-state models) and (b) triggering mechanism for automatic bandwidth reservation. A detailed case study of integrated voice/data MSPR EDR design is presented in Chapter 9, where routing design parameters are optimized by using simulation models, such as (a) level of reserved capacity (varied from 0 to 10% of link capacity), (b) number of allowed primary and alternate paths (varied from 2 to 10 paths), and (c) algorithm for increasing and decreasing VNET bandwidth allocation, where various models are studied and compared. Simulation models are used in Chapters 2–6.

1.7.1.2 Capacity Design and Optimization Methods

Several capacity design optimization techniques are used in the book and described in Chapter 6. One such optimization technique that is perhaps little known but that has proved to be versatile and accurate is the DEFO technique. The DEFO model is used for many of the network capacity design studies presented in Chapter 6. DEFO models optimize the routing of discrete event flows, as measured in units of individual connection requests, and the associated link capacities. The greatest advantage of the DEFO model is its ability to capture very complex network behavior through the equivalent of a simulation model provided in the design modules. By this means, very complex routing networks have been designed by the model, which include all of the MSPR, SDR, and EDR routing methods discussed in Chapter 2, the multiservice VNET resource allocation models discussed in Chapter 3, and the complex multiservice dynamic routing design case studies presented in Chapters 8 and 9. Sparse and meshed topologies, as well as hierarchical and flat topologies, are designed by the DEFO model. Examples of DEFO capacity design are given in Chapter 6, which include the following:

- per-VNET versus per-flow network capacity design
- integrated versus separate voice/ISDN and data network capacity designs
- MSPR versus two-link network capacity design
- single-area flat versus two-level hierarchical network capacity design
- EDR versus SDR network capacity design
- dynamic transport routing versus fixed transport routing network capacity design

The reader is encouraged to take a good look at the DEFO model for possible application to routing/TQO protocol design and capacity design studies.

1.7.1.3 QoS and GoS Performance Measures

QoS and GoS performance measures are essential to describing the performance of a network. The following measures evaluated in the modeling studies are important to both circuit-switched and packet-switched networks:

Grade of service:	A number of network design variables used to provide a measure of adequacy of a group of resources under specified conditions (e.g., GoS variables may be probability of loss, dial tone delay).
Blocking:	Denial or nonadmission of a call/session or connection request based, for example, on the lack of available resources, such as link bandwidth, queuing resources, node processing resources, application server resources, or media server resources.
Loss/delayed probability:	Denial or nonadmission of a call/session or connection request or packet loss/delay within the queuing functions based, for example, on the lack of available resources, such as link bandwidth, queuing resources, node processing resources, application server resources, or media server resources.

QoS measures relevant to a given channel in packet-switched networks are as follows [Y.1540]:

Packet transfer delay (PTD):	PTD is defined for all successful and errored packet outcomes and is the time $(t_2 - t_1)$ between the occurrence of two corresponding packet reference events, ingress event at time t_1 and egress event at time t_2, where $(t_2 > t_1)$ and $(t_2 - t_1) \leq T_{\max}$. If the packet is fragmented, t_2 is the time of the final corresponding egress event. The end-to-end packet transfer delay is the one-way delay between the measurement points at the source and destination.
Packet delay variation (PDV):	Variations in packet transfer delay are also important. Streaming applications might use information about the total range of packet delay variation to avoid buffer underflow and overflow. Variations in packet delay will cause retransmission timer thresholds to grow and may also cause packet retransmissions to be delayed or cause packets to be retransmitted unnecessarily. PDV is defined based on the observations of corresponding packet arrivals at ingress and egress measurement points. Packet delay variation (v_k) for a packet k between source and destination is the difference between the absolute packet transfer delay (x_k) of the packet and a defined reference packet transfer delay, $d_{1,2}$, between those same measurement points: $v_k = x_k - d_{1,2}$.

The reference packet transfer delay, $d_{1,2}$, between source and destination is the absolute packet transfer delay experienced by the first packet between those two measurement points. Positive values of PDV correspond to packet transfer delays greater than those experienced by the reference packet; negative values of PDV correspond to packet transfer delays less than those experienced by the reference packet. The distribution of PDVs is identical to the distribution of absolute packet transfer delays displaced by a constant value equal to $d_{1,2}$.

Packet error ratio:	Ratio of total errored packet outcomes to the total of successful packet transfer outcomes plus errored packet outcomes in a population of interest.
Packet loss ratio:	Ratio of total lost packet outcomes to total transmitted packets in a population of interest.

1.7.2 Key Results from Modeling Studies

We now summarize the main results of the analysis models, as well as conclusions derived from the analysis. We do this now to provide the NetHead or BellHead reader, as the case may be, an early capsule of what is to come. My intent is to trigger some early reflection (controversy?) regarding the validity, usefulness, practicality, and applicability of the results. In addition, I'd like to draw the reader's attention to some of the most interesting, and perhaps least known, conclusions (they should not be missed!):

- EDR path selection is preferred to SDR path selection (Chapter 2) and could dramatically reduce IGP flooding needed, thereby increasing IGP scalability (Chapter 4)
- aggregated per-VNET bandwidth allocation is preferred to per-flow bandwidth allocation and provides the same or better performance (Chapter 3)
- bandwidth reservation techniques are critical to stable network operation and efficient use of resources (Chapter 3)
- GMPLS-based dynamic transport routing provides greater network reliability, throughput, revenue, and capital savings (Chapter 5)
- DEFO design models are extremely flexible and successful in the design of very complex routing algorithms and as a basis for network capacity design methods (Chapter 6)

1.8 Generic TQO (GTQO) Protocol and Benefits

Based on TQO design/operational experience, modeling results, and case studies, a GTQO protocol is summarized here and details are covered in Chapter 10 for consideration in network evolution. The GTQO protocol is applicable to core networks, access networks, and internetwork applications. It incorporates distributed,

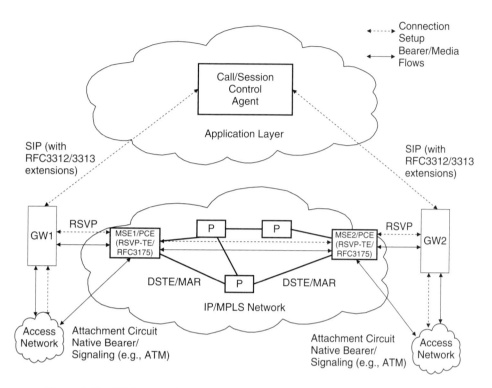

Figure 1.12   GTQO protocol model for MPLS/GMPLS-based dynamic routing networks.

on-line processing, aggregated, per-VNET (versus per-flow) bandwidth allocation, and dynamic transport routing capabilities. It is based on the analysis and findings in this book and on the results of the case studies presented in Chapters 8 and 9, as well as TQO design and operational experience.

Figure 1.12 illustrates the GTQO protocol model, details are given in Chapter 10, and here is a summary of the key elements:

- class-of-service routing to define service elements in terms of component application/network capabilities to avoid software development or network element development for new service deployment (Chapter 3)
- alternate routing use and control to ensure efficient and stable network performance (Chapters 2, 3, and 9)
- per-VNET QoS resource management, bandwidth allocation, dynamic bandwidth reservation, and DiffServ-aware MPLS TE (DSTE) methods for multiservice networking and lower routing table management overhead (Chapters 2, 3, and 9)
- MPLS-based explicit routing and alternate routing (Chapters 2, 3, and 9)
- success to the top event-dependent routing (STT-EDR) path selection methods for better performance and lower overhead (Chapters 2, 3, and 4)

- MPLS/DiffServ functionality for packet scheduling and priority queuing (Chapters 2, 3, 4, and 9)
- separate emergency-services queue to assure emergency-services performance when normal priority queue congests (Chapter 9)
- sparse, single-area flat topology (while retaining edge-core architecture) and multi-link routing for better performance and design efficiency (Chapters 2–6, and 9)
- GMPLS-based dynamic transport routing, fast reroute, and transport restoration for better reliability, performance, and design efficiency (Chapters 5 and 6)
- traffic and performance monitoring for traffic management and capacity management; implement traffic management controls such as code blocks, connection gapping, and reroute controls (Chapter 7)
- DEFO models for capacity design of multiservice GTQO networks to capture complex routing behavior and design (Chapters 6 and 9)

These GTQO requirements are based on:

- TQO design and operational experience in voice, data, and integrated voice/data networks (Chapter 7)
- analysis and modeling studies, which illustrate the trade-offs between various TQO approaches (Chapters 2–6)
- case studies, which provide the GTQO protocol comparison studies and requirements (Chapters 8 and 9)

The benefits of the GTQO protocol are as follows:

- class-of-service routing saves software, hardware, and new network development for new service deployment (Chapter 3)
- STT-EDR path selection and per-VNET bandwidth allocation reduce IGP flooding and control overhead dramatically, thereby increasing scalability (Chapters 3 and 4)
- GMPLS-based dynamic transport routing increases network reliability, throughput, revenue, and capital savings (Chapter 5)
- DEFO design models are able to handle very complex routing/bandwidth allocation algorithms for capacity design (Chapter 6)
- lower operations and capital cost on the order of 30–50% of network cost (Chapters 6 and 7)
- improved performance and greatly increased network throughput (Chapters 2–9)
- simplified and automated network operations/management (Chapters 5 and 7)

Simplified network operations and management come about because of the following impacts of the GTQO methods:

- distributed control (Chapter 2)
- eliminate available link bandwidth flooding (Chapter 4)

- larger/fewer areas (Chapter 4)
- automatic provisioning of topology database (Chapter 3)
- fewer links/sparse network to provision (Chapter 2)

1.9 Standards Needs to Realize GTQO Protocol Requirements

Various IP/MPLS/GMPLS standards are needed to realize GTQO protocol model requirements and capabilities, which include the following:

- DiffServ-aware MPLS traffic engineering (DSTE) mechanisms [RFC3564, RFC4124]
- MAR bandwidth constraints model for DSTE application [RFC4126, PRIORITY1, PRIORITY2]
- path computation element (PCE) capability for interarea, inter-AS, and interservice provider optimal, diverse, and FRR path computation [PCE-ARCHITECTURE, PCE-REQUIREMENTS, PCE-PROTOCOL]
- RSVP aggregation extensions over DSTE tunnels [DSTE-AGGREGATION]
- header compression over MPLS [RFC4247, HC-OVER-MPLS-PROTOCOL]
- QoS signaling protocol and signaling of QoS parameters [QOS-SIG-NTLP, QOS-SIG-NSLP, QOS-SIG-QSPEC, QOS-SIG-Y1541-QOSM]
- admission control priority service classes [PRIORITY3, PRIORITY4]
- service priority signaling requirements [TRQ-QOS-SIG, PRIORITY5]
- emergency telecommunications service (ETS) support in IP networks [ETS1, ETS2, ETS3]
- SIP resource priority header [RPH]
- crankback routing extensions for alternate routing during MPLS LSP setup or modification [CRANKBACK]
- protection/restoration mechanisms to support fast restoration capabilities [GMPLS-RECOVERY-SPEC, GMPLS-RECOVERY-PROTOCOL]
- OSPF congestion control mechanisms [RFC4222]
- assured services requirements and architecture [ASSURED-SERVICES-RQMTS, ASSURED-SERVICES-ARCH]
- MPLS proxy admission control [MPLS-PROXY1, MPLS-PROXY2]

Chapter 10 provides further details and status regarding these GTQO protocol standards developments. Standards will need to play a major role in the realization of the results and conclusions presented in this book. In my experience, the breakup of the Bell System in 1984 and the ultimate spin-off of the manufacturing arm of AT&T in the mid-1990s had a profound impact on how network architecture requirements were realized after the breakup. AT&T was no longer a "vertically integrated" monopoly where systems engineers gave architecture requirements to development engineers, and the architecture became reality. Quite the opposite, vendors, now in separate corporations, took the driver's seat and became both network architects and developers. Vendor/developers now told the service-provider/system engineers what architecture they needed and what was actually available to purchase. This was not always what systems engineers had in mind.

The main avenue on how to realize system engineers' requirements then became through the standards process. This of course had always been the case: most service providers do not have their own manufacturing arm, and vendors are usually obligated to implement and offer standards-based solutions to service providers. So along with the internal RATS-team effort, I became heavily involved in the external standards-based requirements and solutions.

Highly successful and well-received TQO/routing standardization efforts ensued in the ITU-T, primarily in the Routing Question in Study Group 2 (Network Operations), where a significant series of TQO/routing standards emerged. In particular, the [E.360.x] series of 7 standards laid the groundwork for vendor requirements for TQO/routing. I also pursued standardization efforts in the IETF, where the initial thrust was to bring the [E.360.x] series of recommendations into the IETF standardization effort and ultimately influence emerging Traffic Engineering Working Group (TEWG), MPLS, routing, and other IETF standards. But once again there was much learning to be had in the IETF NetHead culture. A well-known and well-respected IETFer met my original foray on the IETF mailing lists with a stern lecture: "this is not the way we do things in the IETF and in the Internet!" A browser search still brings up this original email lecture from Curtis Villamizar.

While the E.360.x-based RFCs never came to fruition, I had significant input to several RFCs that introduced some of the basic E.360.x concepts. This is ongoing and will continue, and eventually . . . well, who knows what will eventually happen.

1.10 Conclusion and Applicability of Requirements

Sophisticated, on-line TQO routing methods have been widely deployed in TDM voice networks, but have yet to be extended to IP-based and integrated voice/data MPLS-based networks. The worldwide marketing success of these TQO solutions and products could provide some basis for vendors to pay more attention to needed TQO capabilities for converged networks and their market potential. We've shown in this chapter how service providers and their customers would benefit from these capabilities in terms of network performance and profitability and further demonstrate this with analysis and case studies throughout this book. Service provider interest in adopting such TQO features also leads to vendor profitability.

Application of the TQO design principles developed in this chapter, as well as the modeling/analysis studies, case studies, design/operational experience, and standards efforts, lead us to the GTQO protocol requirements and conclusions presented in this book. These GTQO requirements are for consideration by network architects and developers alike, who will hopefully be motivated to apply these requirements.

Both Geekian and Telephonian views are taken into account, which guarantees the excellence of the solution. I believe that ultimately network directions along this line will emerge, and/or perhaps just be reinvented. In either case, the result would be a good step forward.

When such "optimal solutions" are presented to colleagues, technical reviewers, upper management, and especially to you, inevitably the questions come: "did you try this or consider that?" One is forced to show global optimality across all solutions, and this book examines a wide swath of the solution space, which, if nothing else, stimulates broad thinking on the topic. I'm tempted to say that all possibilities are examined but that might be a small exaggeration. Several independently derived TQO solutions are presented and thrown into the mix, including distributed, centralized, and game theoretic and pricing-based TQO approaches. Be you NetHead or BellHead, you will surely question the same way—"did you try this or consider that?"—so read more chapters, gather your evidence, make your judgments, confirm your biases, and, most especially, do your broad thinking on the topic. In the end, you're the judge, so take aim and shoot. And please let me know what you think (gash@att.com).

Dear reader, I've set the stage for the "war of the worlds" encompassing Geekia and Telephonia, where we seek convergence of these disparate worlds and try to bridge the enormous gap between the NetHeads and the BellHeads in TQO space. We have already proven that such unity is possible in a limited context: the existence proof is the GTQO protocol case studies and requirements presented in this book. We have illustrated the TQO design principles that have been applied before and that we apply again in Chapters 2–9:

- COS routing capabilities for service flexibility and multiservice VNET bandwidth allocation
- CAC, source-based path selection, and crankback for bandwidth allocation to COSs/VNETs
- load state mapping, bandwidth reservation techniques for stable performance, and bandwidth sharing
- dynamic connection routing, priority routing, EDR path selection for efficient utilization, and reduced routing overhead
- dynamic transport routing for fast restoration and efficient utilization
- queuing priority mechanisms for COS differentiation
- meet performance objectives for integrated COSs
- performance and traffic data collection for network surveillance/design
- controls to ensure network performance under congestion and failure
- traffic management to efficiently utilize available bandwidth and inhibit node processing congestion

We show that these principles are constant and unchangeable through the major technological changes now taking place from TDM voice networks to integrated voice/data MPLS networks. We examine in detail the TQO layers and optimization problems formulated in this chapter and apply the TQO design principles in the process of solving these problems. Along the way many TQO alternatives are examined, and problems solved. Together these will allow you the reader to understand TQO design principles and apply them yourself.

Chapter 2
Call/Session Routing and Connection Routing Methods

2.1 Introduction

As we discussed in Chapter 1, there is much experience with voice, data, and integrated voice/data TQO design. I have been deeply involved over the past three decades in the migration of AT&T's worldwide network to real-time, adaptive, TQO, which is also known as "dynamic routing." The initial migration, based on voice/ISDN technology, took place through the 1980s and 1990s and revolutionized the reliability, performance, traffic handling efficiency, and revenue generation capability of the integrated voice/ISDN network. These breakthroughs also inspired a worldwide migration to TQO/dynamic routing among many carriers (see Table 1.2 in Chapter 1) and are still widely implemented, highly successful, and very much in operation.

Over this period I led the RATS team that performed in-depth analysis of integrated voice/data TQO design. Work on the evolution to an all-packet-based, converged network architecture began at AT&T in the early 1990s. Detailed modeling and analysis studies considered a wide range of alternative architectures. At the outset the primary thrust was to migrate all voice/ISDN and data services to an integrated, ATM-based technology. However, other possible migrations, such as to an all IP-based architecture, hybrid TDM/packet architectures and others, were also on the table. The RATS team consisted of both voice/ISDN network specialists and data network specialists, who worked together toward a consensus on an architecture direction for this migration. What became immediately apparent was the large gap, internally to AT&T as well as externally, between the Telephonia BellHead culture (representing the voice/ISDN circuit-switching technologies) and Geekia NetHead culture (representing the ATM/frame-relay/IP packet-switching technologies). Early on I was informed of my obvious BellHead status and limitation by a well-respected (by the author and throughout AT&T) NetHead representative on the team.

While the gap persists to this day, the cultures did work well together, despite the gap, and reached consensus on innovative architecture directions that incorporated the best ideas of both worlds. The work on these studies of TQO protocol design and conclusions reached start now and continue to the end of the book, including multiple case studies in Chapters 8 and 9.

From these experiences and studies have emerged TQO protocol design principles, as follows:

- COS routing mechanisms for multiservice bandwidth allocation
- aggregated bandwidth allocation to VNETs
- CAC and priority mechanisms for bandwidth allocation to COSs/VNETs
- dynamic routing capabilities, including source-based path selection, crankback, load state mapping, and EDR path selection
- bandwidth reservation techniques for stable performance and bandwidth sharing
- dynamic transport routing for fast restoration and efficient utilization
- queuing priority mechanisms for COS differentiation
- meet performance objectives for integrated COSs with TQO principles
- performance and traffic data collection for network surveillance/design
- controls to ensure network performance under congestion and failure
- traffic management to efficiently utilize available bandwidth; inhibit node processing congestion

There is much to be learned from applications of these TQO protocol design principles, which is the focus of this chapter. As outlined in Chapter 1, the problem statement for TQO design in this chapter includes the following:

- Traffic/application layer design: Find an optimal call/session routing design and class-of-service routing strategy for arbitrary traffic loads and network topology, which yields minimum cost capacity design and maximum flow/revenue, subject to meeting performance constraints.
- MPLS LSP dynamic routing and bandwidth allocation layer 3 design: Find an optimal connection/bearer-path routing design and MPLS LSP dynamic routing and bandwidth allocation strategy for arbitrary traffic loads and network topology, which yields minimum cost capacity and maximum flow/revenue, subject to meeting performance constraints.

In this book we assume the separation of call/session routing and signaling for call/session establishment from connection (or bearer-path) routing and signaling for bearer-channel establishment. Call/session routing protocols primarily translate a number or a name, which is given to the network as part of a call/session setup, to a routing address needed for the connection (bearer-path) establishment. Call/session routing/signaling protocols include, for example, the session initiation protocol (SIP) [RFC3261], H.323 [H.323], media gateway control [RFC2805], and the ISDN user part (ISUP) [Q.761]. Connection routing/signaling protocols include, for example, the resource reservation protocol (RSVP) [RFC2205], next steps in signaling (NSIS) [RFC4080], PNNI [ATMFORUM-0055.0025], UNI [ATMFORUM-0061.000], and ISUP [Q.761] signaling.

A specific connection or bearer-path routing method is characterized by the routing table used in the method. The routing table consists of a set of paths and rules to select one path from the route for a given connection request. When a connection request arrives at its originating node (ON), the ON implementing the routing method executes the path selection rules associated with the routing table for the connection to determine a selected path from among the path candidates in the route for the connection request. In a particular routing method, the path selected for the connection request is governed by the connection routing, or path selection, rules. Various path selection methods are discussed: fixed routing path selection, time-dependent routing path selection, state-dependent routing path selection, and event-dependent routing path selection.

We introduce a full-scale, 135-node national network model and a multiservice traffic demand model, which is used throughout to study various TQO scenarios and trade-offs in TQO optimization. The models are used in this chapter to illustrate TQO network design, including integrated voice and data designs based on MPLS technology. Various performance analyses are presented for network overloads and failures, which illustrate the benefits of TE and QoS optimization on network performance. These models provide in-depth studies of the trade-offs between various TQO approaches, including:

- FXR, TDR, SDR, and EDR path selection methods
- two-link and multilink path selection methods
- resource management and connection admission control methods
- service priority differentiation of key services, normal services, and best-effort services
- single-area flat topologies versus multiarea hierarchical topologies

Performance comparisons are presented for various TQO methods and a baseline case of no TQO methods is applied. The TQO modeling conclusions include the following: (a) in all cases of the TQO methods being applied, network performance is always better and usually substantially better than when no TQO methods are applied, (b) sparse topology multilink-routing networks provide better overall performance under overload than meshed topology networks, but performance under failure may favor the meshed topology options with more alternate routing choices, (c) single-area flat topologies exhibit better network performance and greater design efficiencies in comparison with multiarea hierarchical topologies, (d) EDR path selection methods exhibit comparable or better network performance compared to SDR methods, (e) state information in SDR provides only a small network capital cost advantage and essentially equivalent performance to EDR options, and (f) voice and data integration can provide capital cost advantages, as well as operational simplicity and expense cost reduction.

2.2   Call/Session Routing Methods

Call/session routing entails number (or name) translation to a routing address, which is then used for connection establishment. Routing addresses can consist, for example, of (a) E.164 numbers [E.164], (b) E.164 ATM end system addresses (AESAs) [E.191], and/or (c) IP addresses [RFC1518, STEVENS94]. As discussed in Chapter 4, a TQO requirement is the need for carrying E.164 addresses, E.164-AESA addresses, and IP addresses in the connection-setup information element (IE). In that case, E.164 addresses, E.164-AESA addresses, and IP addresses become the standard addressing method for interworking across IP-, ATM-, and TDM-based networks. Another TQO requirement is that a call/session identification code (CIC) be carried in the call/session-control and bearer-control connection-setup IEs in order to correlate the call/session–control setup with the bearer-control setup [Q.1901]. Carrying these additional parameters in the Signaling System 7 (SS7) ISDN User Part (ISUP) connection-setup IEs is referred to as the bearer-independent call control (BICC) protocol.

Number (or name) translation, then, should result in E.164, E.164-AESA, and/or IP routing addresses. E.164 formats are covered in [E.164] and IP-address formats in [RFC1518]. The AESA address has a 20-byte format as shown in Figure 2.1 [E.191].

The IDP is the initial domain part and the DSP is the domain-specific part. The IDP is further subdivided into the AFI and IDI. The IDI is the initial domain identifier and can contain the 15-digit E.164 address if the AFI is set to 45. AFI is the authority and format identifier and determines what kind of addressing method is followed; based on the 1 octet AFI value, the length of the IDI and DSP fields can change. The E.164-AESA address is used to determine the path to the destination end point. E.164-AESA addressing for B-ISDN services is supported in ATM networks using PNNI through use of the AESA format. In this case the E.164 part of the AESA address occupies the 8 octet IDI, and the 11 octet DSP can be used at the discretion of the network operator (perhaps for subaddresses). The AESA structure also supports AESA DCC (data country code) and AESA ICD (international code designator) addressing formats.

Voice network call/session routing begins with address translation of the E.164 address, and the outcome is to determine a routing table. The routing table is a set of paths connecting the same originating node-destination node pair, where the set of paths may consist of a single path or multiple paths. This set of paths may be computed in real time along with the address translation or be predetermined by some off-line calculation and downloaded to the network. Paths normally consist of multiple links in voice networks, but paths in voice networks employing dynamic routing are often constrained to one- or two-link paths.

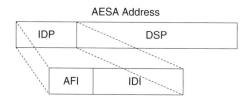

Figure 2.1 AESA address structure.

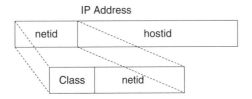

Figure 2.2 IP address structure.

Within the IP network, routing is performed using IP addresses, illustrated in Figure 2.2. Translation databases, such as based on domain name system (DNS) technology [RFC3271], are used to translate the E.164 numbers/names for call/sessions to IP addresses for routing over the IP network. The IP address is a 4-byte address structure as shown in Figure 2.2.

There are five classes of IP addresses. Different classes have different field lengths for the network identification field. Classless interdomain routing (CIDR) [RFC1518] allows blocks of addresses to be given to service providers in such a manner as to provide efficient address aggregation. This is accompanied by capabilities in the BGP4.0 protocol for efficient address advertisements [RFC4271, STEVENS94]. IP data network call/session routing is the process of making the longest prefix match [RFC1812] and, based on that match, to then look up the NextHop for that prefix. The NextHop is determined by a constrained shortest path first (CSPF) computation, which can be made synchronously, asynchronously, or hop by hop with the longest prefix match. Paths normally consist of multiple links in a data network.

2.3 Connection (Bearer-Path) Routing Methods

Connection routing is characterized by the routing table used in the method and rules to select one path from the route for a given connection or bandwidth-allocation request. When a connection/bandwidth-allocation request is initiated by an ON, the ON implementing the routing method executes the path selection rules associated with the routing table for the connection/bandwidth allocation to find an admissible path from among the paths in the route that satisfies the connection/bandwidth-allocation request. In a particular routing method, the selected path is determined according to the rules associated with the routing table. In a network with originating connection/bandwidth-allocation control, the ON maintains control of the connection/bandwidth-allocation request. If crankback (CBK)/bandwidth not available (BNA) is used, for example, at a via node (VN), the preceding node maintains control of the connection/bandwidth-allocation request even if the request is blocked on all the links outgoing from the VN.

Here we are discussing network-layer connection routing (sometimes referred to as "layer 3" routing), as opposed to link-layer logical-link ("layer 2") routing or physical-layer ("layer 1") routing. The term "link" normally means "logical link." Chapter 5 addresses logical-link routing.

The network-layer (layer 3) connection routing methods addressed include those discussed in:

- Open Shortest Path First (OSPF) [RFC2328], Border Gateway Protocol (BGP) [RFC4271], and Multiprotocol Label Switching (MPLS) [RFC3031] for IP-based routing methods
- User-to-Network Interface (UNI) [ATMFORUM-0061.000], Private Network-to-Network Interface (PNNI) [ATMFORUM-0055.002], ATM Inter-Network Interface (AINI) [ATMFORUM-0025.001], and Bandwidth Modify [ATMFORUM-0148.001] for ATM-based routing methods
- Recommendations [E.170], [E.350], and [E.351] for TDM-based routing methods

In an IP network, logical links called traffic trunks can be defined that consist of MPLS label switched paths (LSPs) between the IP nodes. Traffic trunks are used to allocate the bandwidth of the logical links to various node pairs. In an ATM network, logical links called virtual paths (VPs) (the equivalent of traffic trunks) can be defined between the ATM nodes, and VPs can be used to allocate the bandwidth of the logical links to various node pairs. In a TDM network, the logical links consist of trunk groups between the TDM nodes.

A sparse logical link network is typically used with IP and ATM technology, as illustrated in Figure 2.3, and FXR, TDR, SDR, and EDR can be used in combination with multilink shortest path selection.

A meshed logical-link network is typically used with TDM technology, but can also be used with IP or ATM technology as well, and selected paths are normally limited to one or two logical links, or trunk groups, as illustrated in Figure 2.4.

Paths may be set up on individual connections (or "per flow") for each call/session request, such as on a switched virtual circuit (SVC). Paths may also be set up for

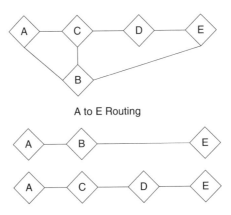

A to E Routing

Figure 2.3 Sparse logical network topology with connections routed on multilink paths.

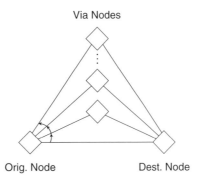

Figure 2.4 Mesh logical network topology with connections routed on one- and two-link paths.

bandwidth-allocation requests associated with "bandwidth pipes" or traffic trunks, such as on switched virtual paths (SVPs) in ATM-based networks or constraint-based routing label switched paths (CRLSPs) in IP/MPLS-based networks. Paths are determined by (normally proprietary) algorithms based on the network topology and reachable address information. These paths can cross multiple peer groups in ATM-based networks and multiple autonomous systems (ASs) in IP-based networks. An ON may select a path from the routing table based on the routing rules and the QoS resource management criteria, described in Chapter 3, which must be satisfied on each logical link in the path. If a link is not allowed based on QoS criteria, then a release with the CBK/BNA parameter is used to signal that condition to the ON in order to return the connection/bandwidth-allocation request to the ON, which may then select an alternate path. In addition to controlling bandwidth allocation, the QoS resource management procedures can check end-to-end transfer delay, delay variation, transmission quality considerations, such as loss, echo, and noise, and other criteria for path selection.

When source routing is used, setup of a connection/bandwidth-allocation request is achieved by having the ON identify the entire selected path, including all VNs and DN in the path in a designated-transit-list (DTL) or explicit-route (ER) parameter in the connection-setup IE. If the QoS or traffic parameters cannot be realized at any of the VNs in the connection-setup request, then the VN generates a CBK/BNA parameter in the connection-release IE, which allows a VN to return control of the connection request to the ON for further alternate routing. In Chapter 4, the DTL/ER and CBK/BNA elements are identified as being required for interworking across IP-, ATM-, and TDM-based networks.

As noted earlier, connection routing, or path selection, methods are categorized into the following four types: FXR, TDR, SDR, and EDR. We discuss each of these methods in the following paragraphs. Examples of each of these path selection methods are illustrated in Figures 2.5, 2.6, and 2.7 and are discussed in the following sections.

It is important to note that all these routing methods are applicable to voice networks, data networks, and integrated voice/data networks. This is illustrated by examples in

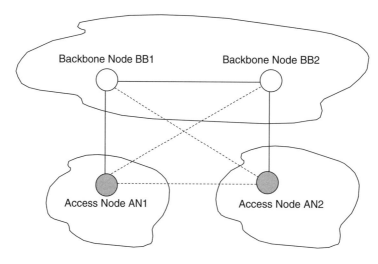

Figure 2.5 Hierarchical fixed routing path selection methods (two-level multidomain hierarchical network).

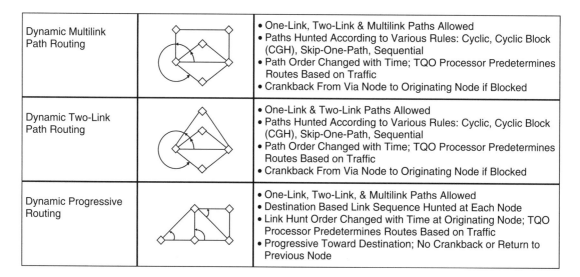

Dynamic Multilink Path Routing		• One-Link, Two-Link & Multilink Paths Allowed • Paths Hunted According to Various Rules: Cyclic, Cyclic Block (CGH), Skip-One-Path, Sequential • Path Order Changed with Time; TQO Processor Predetermines Routes Based on Traffic • Crankback From Via Node to Originating Node if Blocked
Dynamic Two-Link Path Routing		• One-Link & Two-Link Paths Allowed • Paths Hunted According to Various Rules: Cyclic, Cyclic Block (CGH), Skip-One-Path, Sequential • Path Order Changed with Time; TQO Processor Predetermines Routes Based on Traffic • Crankback From Via Node to Originating Node if Blocked
Dynamic Progressive Routing		• One-Link, Two-Link, & Multilink Paths Allowed • Destination Based Link Sequence Hunted at Each Node • Link Hunt Order Changed with Time at Originating Node; TQO Processor Predetermines Routes Based on Traffic • Progressive Toward Destination; No Crankback or Return to Previous Node

Figure 2.6 TDR dynamic path selection methods.

this section and also by the analysis, modeling, and case studies presented throughout the book. Geekians can rest assured that Telephonians are not pulling a fast one here.

In particular, the TQO methods based on the EDR and SDR dynamic routing protocols illustrated in Figure 2.7 are shown in the analysis, modeling, and case studies to be extensible to integrated voice/data TQO networks, particularly to IP/MPLS technology. In the analysis of integrated voice/data TQO protocol design and optimization, we illustrate the trade-offs between these various approaches and show

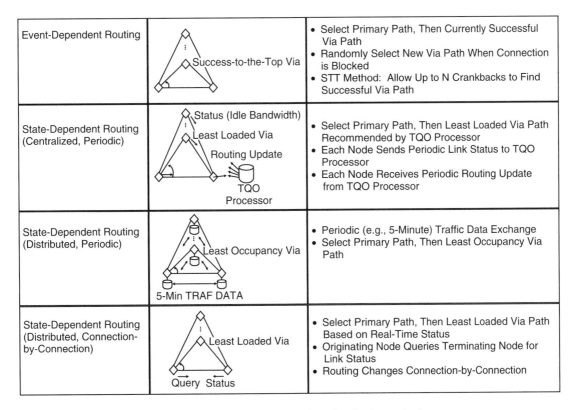

Event-Dependent Routing	Success-to-the-Top Via	• Select Primary Path, Then Currently Successful Via Path • Randomly Select New Via Path When Connection is Blocked • STT Method: Allow Up to N Crankbacks to Find Successful Via Path
State-Dependent Routing (Centralized, Periodic)	Status (Idle Bandwidth) Least Loaded Via Routing Update TQO Processor	• Select Primary Path, Then Least Loaded Via Path Recommended by TQO Processor • Each Node Sends Periodic Link Status to TQO Processor • Each Node Receives Periodic Routing Update from TQO Processor
State-Dependent Routing (Distributed, Periodic)	Least Occupancy Via 5-Min TRAF DATA	• Periodic (e.g., 5-Minute) Traffic Data Exchange • Select Primary Path, Then Least Occupancy Via Path
State-Dependent Routing (Distributed, Connection-by-Connection)	Least Loaded Via Query Status	• Select Primary Path, Then Least Loaded Via Path Based on Real-Time Status • Originating Node Queries Terminating Node for Link Status • Routing Changes Connection-by-Connection

Figure 2.7 EDR and SDR dynamic path selection methods.

that (a) aggregated per-VNET network bandwidth allocation compares favorably with per-flow allocation and (b) EDR methods perform just as well or better than SDR methods with flooding, which means that EDR path selection has potential to significantly enhance network scalability. These conclusions and results are directly applied to the GTQO protocol requirements presented in Chapter 10.

Vendors have yet to announce such GTQO capabilities in their products, however. Current practice often involves overprovisioning of IP networks, thereby avoiding the need for more efficient TQO capabilities, but with concomitant low utilization and efficiency [ODLYZKO03]. Consistent with Odlyzko's analysis, Meddeb [MEDDEB05] concludes that in order to support QoS in IP networks, "average network utilization should be kept low, typically less than 30 percent." There is therefore an opportunity for increased profitability and performance in IP/MPLS-based networks through application of the GTQO protocol.

There is not an extensive literature on this emerging topic as yet, which is still under development. Awduche [AWDUCHE99, RFC3272] gives excellent overviews of TQO approaches for IP-based networks and also provides traffic engineering requirements [RFC2702]. Crawley [RFC2386] and Xiao [XIAO99] provide good background and context for TQO in the Internet. A few early implementations of off-line, network management-based TQO approaches have been published, such as in the Global Crossing network [XIAO00a], Level3 network [LEVEL3-TE], and Cable & Wireless network [CABLE-WIRELESS-TE]. Some studies have proposed more elaborate TQO approaches in IP networks [APOSTOLOPOULOS99, ELWALID01, MA98, XIAO00b], as well as in ATM networks [AHMADI92].

2.3.1 Hierarchical Fixed Routing Path Selection

FXR is an important routing topology employed in all types of networks, including IP-, ATM-, and TDM-based networks. In IP-based networks, there is often a hierarchical relationship among different "areas," or subnetworks. Hierarchical multidomain (or multiarea or multiautonomous-system) topologies are normally used with IP routing protocols (OSPF, BGP) and ATM routing protocols (PNNI), as well as within almost all TDM-based network routing topologies.

For example, in Figure 2.5, BB1 and BB2 could be backbone nodes in a "backbone area" and AN1 and AN2 could be access nodes in separate "access areas" distinct from the backbone area. Routing between the areas follows a hierarchical routing pattern, whereas routing within an area follows an interior gateway protocol (IGP), such as OSPF plus MPLS. Similarly, in ATM-based networks the same concept exists, but here the "areas" are called "peer groups," and, for example, the IGP used within peer groups could be PNNI. In TDM-based networks, the routing between subnetworks, for example, metropolitan area networks and long-distance networks, is normally hierarchical, as in IP- and ATM-based networks, and the IGP in TDM-based networks could be either hierarchical or dynamic routing. We now discuss more specific attributes and methods for hierarchical FXR path selection.

In an FXR method, a routing pattern is fixed for a connection request. A typical example of fixed routing is a conventional, TDM-based, hierarchical alternate routing pattern where the route and route selection sequence are determined on a preplanned basis and maintained over a long period of time. Hierarchical FXR is illustrated later in this section. FXR is applied more efficiently, however, when the network is non-hierarchical, or flat, as compared to the hierarchical structure [ASH98].

The aim of hierarchical fixed routing is to carry as much traffic as is economically feasible over direct links between pairs of nodes low in the hierarchy. This is accomplished by application of routing procedures to determine where sufficient load exists to justify high-usage logical links and then by application of alternate-routing principles that effectively pool the capacities of high-usage links with those of final links, to the end that all traffic is carried efficiently.

The routing of connection requests in a hierarchical network involves an originating ladder, a terminating ladder, and links interconnecting the two ladders. In a two-level network, for example, the originating ladder is the final link from lower level 1 node to the upper level 2 node, and the terminating ladder is the final link from upper level 2 node to the lower level 1 node. Links AN1–BB2, AN2–BB1, and BB1–BB2 in Figure 2.5 are examples of interladder links.

The identification of the proper interladder link for the routing of a given connection request identifies the originating ladder "exit" point and the terminating ladder "entry" point. Once these exit and entry points are identified and the intraladder links are known, a first-choice path from originating to terminating location can be determined.

Various levels of traffic concentration are used to achieve an appropriate balance between transport and connection switching. The generally preferred routing sequence for the AN1 to AN2 connections is as follows:

- A connection request involving no via nodes: path AN1–AN2.
- A connection request involving one via node: path AN1–BB2–AN2, AN1–BB1–AN2, in that order.
- A connection request involving two via nodes: path AN1–BB1–BB2–AN2.

This procedure provides only the first-choice interladder link from AN1 to AN2. Connection requests from AN2 to AN1 often route differently. To determine the AN2-to-AN1 route requires reversing the diagram, making AN2–BB2 the originating ladder and AN1–BB1 the terminating ladder. In Figure 2.5 the preferred path from AN2 to AN1 is AN2–AN1, AN2–BB1–AN1, AN2–BB2–AN1, and AN2–BB2–BB1–AN1, in that order. The alternate path for any high-usage link is the path the node-to-node traffic load between the nodes would follow if the high-usage link did not exist. In Figure 2.5, this is AN2–BB1–AN1.

2.3.2   Time-Dependent Routing Path Selection

Dynamic routing allows routing tables to be changed dynamically, either in an off-line, preplanned, time-varying manner, as in TDR, or on-line, in real time, as in SDR or EDR. With off-line, preplanned TDR path selection methods, routing patterns contained in routing tables might change every hour or at least several times a day to respond to measured hourly shifts in traffic loads, and in general TDR routing tables change with a time constant normally greater than a call/session holding time. A typical TDR routing method may change routing tables every hour, which is longer than a typical voice call/session holding time of a few minutes. Three implementations of TDR dynamic path selection are illustrated in Figure 2.6, which shows multilink path routing, two-link path routing, and progressive routing.

TDR routing tables are preplanned, preconfigured, and recalculated perhaps each week within the capacity management network design function. Real-time dynamic path selection does not depend on precalculated routing tables. Rather, the node or centralized TQO processor senses the immediate traffic load and, if necessary, searches out new paths through the network possibly on a per-traffic-flow basis. With real-time path selection methods, routing tables change with a time constant on the order of or less than a call/session holding time. As illustrated in Figure 2.7, on-line, real-time path selection methods include EDR and SDR.

TDR methods are a type of dynamic routing in which the routing tables are altered at a fixed point in time during the day or week. TDR routing tables are determined on an off-line, preplanned basis and are implemented consistently over a time period. The TDR routing tables are determined considering the time variation of traffic load in the network, e.g., based on measured hourly load patterns. Several TDR time periods are used to divide up the hours on an average business day and weekend into contiguous routing intervals sometimes called load set periods. Typically, the TDR routing tables used in the network are coordinated by taking advantage of noncoincidence of busy hours among the traffic loads.

In TDR, the routing tables are preplanned and designed off-line using a centralized TQO processor, which employs a TDR network design model. Such models include the TLFO model discussed in Chapter 6, which has been used for many years for DNHR network design. The off-line computation determines the optimal routes from a very large number of possible alternatives in order to maximize network throughput and/or minimize the network cost. The designed routing tables are loaded and stored in the various nodes in the TDR network and are recomputed and updated periodically (e.g., every week) by the TQO processor. In this way an ON does not require additional network information to construct TDR routing tables once the routing tables have been loaded. This is in contrast to the design of routing tables on-line in real time, such as in the SDR and EDR methods described later in this section. Paths in the TDR routing table may consist of time-varying routing choices and use a subset of the available paths. Paths used in various time periods need not be the same.

Paths in the TDR routing table may consist of the direct link, a two-link path through a single VN, or a multiple-link path through multiple VNs. Path routing implies selection of an entire path between originating and terminating nodes before a connection is actually attempted on that path. If a connection on one link in a path is congested (e.g., because of insufficient bandwidth), the connection request then attempts another complete path. Implementation of such a routing method can be done through control from the originating node, plus a multiple-link crankback capability to allow paths of two, three, or more links to be used. Crankback is an information-exchange message capability that allows a connection request rejected on a link in a path to return to the originating node, or upstream VN, for further alternate routing on other paths. Path-to-path routing is nonhierarchical and allows the choice of the most economical paths rather than being restricted to hierarchical paths.

Path selection rules employed in TDR routing tables, for example, may consist of simple sequential routing. In the sequential method all traffic in a given time period is offered to a single route and lets the first path in the route overflow to the second path, which overflows to the third path, and so on. Thus, traffic is routed sequentially from path to path, and the route is allowed to change from hour to hour to achieve the preplanned dynamic, or time-varying, nature of the TDR method.

Other TDR path selection rules can employ probabilistic techniques to select each path in the route and thus influence the realized flows. One such method of implementing TDR multilink path selection is to allocate fractions of the traffic to routes and to allow the fractions to vary as a function of time. One approach is cyclic path selection, illustrated in Figure 2.6, which has as its first route (1, 2, . . . , M), where the notation (i, j, k) means that all traffic is offered first to path i, which overflows to path j, which overflows to path k. The second route of a cyclic route choice is a cyclic permutation of the first route: (2, 3, . . . , M, 1). The third route is likewise (3, 4, . . . , M, 1, 2) and so on. This approach has computational advantages because its cyclic structure requires considerably fewer calculations in the design model than a general collection of paths. The route congestion level of cyclic routes is identical; what varies from route to route is the proportion of flow on the various links.

Two-link TDR path selection is illustrated in Figure 2.6. An example implementation is two-link sequential TDR (2S-TDR) path selection. By using the crankback signal, 2S-TDR limits path connections to at most two links, and, in meshed network topologies, such TDR two-link sequential path selection allows nearly as much network utilization and performance improvement as TDR multilink path selection. This is because in the design of multilink path routing in meshed networks, about 98% of the traffic is routed on one- and two-link paths, even though paths of greater length are allowed. Because of connection switching costs, paths with one or two links are usually less expensive than paths with more links. Therefore, as illustrated in Figure 2.6, two-link path routing uses the simplifying restriction that paths can have only one or two links, which requires only single-link crankback to implement and uses no common links as is possible with multilink path routing. Alternative two-link path selection methods include the cyclic routing method described above and sequential routing.

DNHR, implemented in the AT&T national network from 1984 until 1991, when it was replaced by RTNR, is an example of a TDR method. Its successful implementation demonstrated all the benefits of dynamic routing discussed in Section 1.6.2 (Chapter 1); see, for example, Figure 1.10 and discussion, which illustrates peak Christmas day performance for DNHR compared to FXR compared to RTNR. TDR draws its benefits from the variation of traffic patterns due to time of day, business/residence, seasonal, and other traffic variations. These traffic patterns are somewhat predictable and the routing patterns and network capacity can be optimized by taking advantage of these traffic variations. Extensive treatment of DNHR design, implementation experience, and benefits is discussed in [ASH98].

In sequential routing, all traffic in a given hour is offered to a single route, and the first path is allowed to overflow to the second path, which overflows to the third path, and so on. Thus, traffic is routed sequentially from path to path with no probabilistic methods being used to influence the realized flows. The reason that sequential routing works well is that permuting path order provides sufficient flexibility to achieve desired flows without the need for probabilistic routing. In 2S-TDR, the sequential route is allowed to change from hour to hour. The TDR nature of the dynamic path selection method is achieved by introducing several route choices, which consist of different sequences of paths, and each path has one or, at most, two links in tandem.

Paths in the routing table are subject to depth-of-search (DEPTH) restrictions for QoS resource management, which is discussed in Chapter 3. DEPTH requires that the bandwidth capacity available on each link in the path be sufficient to meet a DEPTH bandwidth threshold level, which is passed to each node in the path in the setup message. DEPTH restrictions prevent connections that route on the first-choice or primary (often the shortest) ON-DN path, for example, from being swamped by alternate routed multiple-link connections.

A TDR connection setup example is now given. The first step is for the ON to identify the DN and routing table information to the DN. The ON then tests for spare capacity on the first or shortest path, and in doing this supplies the VNs and DN on this path, along with the DEPTH parameter, to all nodes in the path. Each VN tests the available bandwidth capacity on each link in the path against the DEPTH threshold. If there is sufficient capacity, the VN forwards the connection setup to the next node, which performs a similar function. If there is insufficient capacity, the VN sends a release message with crankback/bandwidth-not-available parameter back to the ON, at which point the ON tries the next path in the route as determined by the routing table rules. As described above, the TDR routes are preplanned off-line and then loaded and stored in each ON.

Allocating traffic to the optimum path choice during each time period leads to design benefits due to the noncoincidence of loads. Because traffic demands change with time in a reasonably predictable manner in many network applications, the routing also changes with time to achieve maximum link utilization and minimum network cost. Several TDR routing time periods are used to divide up the hours on an average business day and weekend into contiguous routing intervals. The network design is performed in an off-line, centralized computation in the TQO processor that determines the optimal routing tables from a very large number of possible alternatives in order to minimize the network cost. In TDR path selection, rather than determine the optimal routing tables based on real-time information, a centralized TQO processor design system employs a design model, such as the TLFO model described in Chapter 6. The effectiveness of the design depends on how accurately we can estimate the traffic load on the network. Forecast errors are corrected in the short-term capacity management process, which allows routing table updates to replace link augments whenever possible, as described in Chapter 7.

2.3.3 State-Dependent Routing Path Selection

In SDR, the routing tables are altered automatically according to the state of the network. For a given SDR method, the routing table rules are implemented to determine the path choices in response to changing network status and are used over a relatively short time period. Information on network status may be collected at a central TQO processor or distributed to nodes in the network. The information exchange may be performed on a periodic or on-demand basis. SDR methods use the principle of routing connections on the best available path on the basis of network state information. For example, in the least loaded routing (LLR) method, the residual capacity of candidate paths is calculated, and the path having the largest residual capacity is selected for the connection. Various relative levels of link occupancy can be used to define link load states, such as lightly loaded, heavily loaded, or bandwidth-not-available states. Methods of defining these link load states are discussed in Chapter 3. In general, SDR methods calculate a path cost for each connection request based on various factors, such as the load state or congestion state of the links in the network.

In SDR, the routing tables are designed on-line by the ON or a central TQO processor through the use of network status and topology information obtained through information exchange with other nodes and/or a centralized TQO processor. There are various implementations of SDR distinguished by (a) whether the computation of the routing tables is distributed among the network nodes or centralized and done in a centralized TQO processor and (b) whether the computation of the routing tables is done periodically or connection by connection.

This leads to three different implementations of SDR:

- centralized periodic SDR (CP-SDR)—here the centralized TQO processor obtains link status and traffic status information from the various nodes on a periodic basis (e.g., every 10 s) and performs a computation of the optimal routing table on a periodic basis. To determine the optimal routing table, the TQO processor executes a particular routing table optimization procedure such as LLR and transmits the routing tables to the network nodes on a periodic basis (e.g., every 10 s).
- distributed periodic SDR (DP-SDR)—here each node in the SDR network obtains link status and traffic status information from all the other nodes, either triggered by a state change (e.g., through flooding of state changes throughout the network) or on a periodic basis (e.g., every 5 min) and performs a computation of the optimal routing table on a periodic basis (e.g., every 5 min). To determine the optimal routing table, the ON executes a particular routing table optimization procedure such as LLR.
- distributed connection-by-connection (DC-SDR) SDR—here an ON in the SDR network obtains link status and traffic status information from the DN, and perhaps from selected VNs, on a connection-by-connection basis and performs a computation of the optimal routing table for each connection. To determine the optimal routing table, the ON executes a particular routing table optimization procedure such as LLR.

In DP-SDR path selection, nodes may exchange status and traffic data, for example, every 5 min, between traffic management processors, and based on analysis of these data, the traffic management processors can dynamically select alternate paths to optimize network performance. This method is illustrated in Figure 2.7. Flooding is a common technique for distributing the status and traffic data; however, other techniques with less overhead are also available, such as a query-for-status method, as discussed in Chapter 4.

Figure 2.7 illustrates a CP-SDR path selection method with periodic updates based on periodic network status. CP-SDR path selection provides near-real-time routing decisions by having an update of the idle bandwidth on each link sent to a network database every 5 s. Routing tables are determined from analysis of the status data using a path selection method that provides that the shortest path choice is used if the bandwidth is available. If the shortest path is busy (e.g., bandwidth is unavailable on one or more links), the second path is selected from the list of feasible paths on the basis of having the greatest level of idle bandwidth at the time; the current second path choice becomes the third and so on. This path update is performed, for example, every 5 s. The CP-SDR model uses dynamically activated bandwidth reservation and other controls to automatically modify routing tables during network overloads and failures. CP-SDR requires the use of network status and routing recommendation information-exchange messages.

Figure 2.7 also illustrates an example of a DC-SDR path selection method. In DC-SDR, the routing computations are distributed among all the nodes in the network. DC-SDR uses real-time exchange of network status information, such as with query and status messages, to determine an optimal path from a very large number of possible choices. With DC-SDR, the originating node first tries the primary path and if it is not available finds an optimal alternate path by querying the destination node and perhaps several via nodes through query-for-status network signaling for the busy-idle load status of all links connected on the alternate paths to the destination node. The originating node then finds the least loaded alternate path to route the connection request. DC-SDR computes required bandwidth allocations by virtual network from node-measured traffic flows and uses this capacity allocation to reserve capacity when needed for each virtual network. Any excess traffic above the expected flow is routed to temporarily idle capacity borrowed from capacity reserved for other loads that happen to be below their expected levels. Idle link capacity is communicated to other nodes via the query-status information-exchange messages, as illustrated in Figure 2.7, and the excess traffic is dynamically allocated to the set of allowed paths that are identified as having temporarily idle capacity. DC-SDR controls the sharing of available capacity by using dynamic bandwidth reservation, as described in Chapter 3, to protect the capacity required to meet expected loads and to minimize the loss of traffic for classes of service that exceed their expected load and allocated capacity.

Paths in the SDR routing table may consist of the direct link, a two-link path through a single VN, or a multiple-link path through multiple VNs. Paths in the routing table are subject to DEPTH restrictions on each link.

OSPF and PNNI are examples of widely deployed DP-SDR methods in data networks. Several other examples of SDR implementations are given in Chapter 1, Table 1.2. Nortel's dynamically controlled routing (DCR) is an example of a CP-SDR method and is in current operation in five major networks. AT&T's real-time network routing (RTNR) is an example of a DC-SDR method and has been in operation since 1991. The worldwide intelligent network is an example of a DP-SDR method and has been in operation since 1993. These SDR implementations demonstrated all the benefits of dynamic routing as discussed in Section 1.6.2 (Chapter 1); see, for example, Figure 1.10 and discussion, which illustrates peak Christmas day performance for RTNR compared to DNHR compared to FXR. Extensive treatment of RTNR design, implementation experience, and benefits is discussed in [ASH98].

2.3.4 Event-Dependent Routing Path Selection

In EDR, the routing tables are updated locally on the basis of whether connections succeed or fail on a given path choice. In EDR learning approaches, the path last tried, which is also successful, is tried again until congested, at which time another path is selected at random and tried on the next connection request. EDR path choices can also be changed with time in accordance with changes in traffic load patterns. Success-to-the-top (STT) EDR path selection, illustrated in Figure 2.7, is a decentralized, on-line path selection method with updates based on random routing. STT-EDR uses a simplified decentralized learning method to achieve flexible adaptive routing. The primary path, path-p, is used first if available, and a currently successful alternate path, path-s, is used until it is congested. In the case that path-s is congested (e.g., bandwidth is not available on one or more links), a new alternate path, path-n, is selected at random as the alternate path choice for the next connection request overflow from the primary path. As described in Chapter 3, dynamically activated bandwidth reservation is used under congestion conditions to protect traffic on the primary path. STT-EDR uses crankback when an alternate path is congested at a via node, and the connection request advances to a new random path choice. In STT-EDR, many path choices can be tried by a given connection request before the request is rejected. An interesting comparative analysis of various learning algorithms, including STT-EDR, is given in [HEIDARI06].

In the EDR learning approaches, the current alternate path choice can be updated randomly, cyclically, or by some other means and may be maintained as long as a connection can be established successfully on the path. Hence the routing table is constructed with the information determined during connection setup, and no additional information is required by the ON. Paths in the EDR routing table may consist of the direct link, a two-link path through a single VN, or a multiple-link path through multiple VNs. Paths in the routing table are subject to DEPTH restrictions on each link. Note that for either SDR or EDR, as in TDR, the alternate path for a connection request may be changed in a time-dependent manner considering the time variation of the traffic load.

Examples of current EDR implementations are given in Chapter 1, Table 1.2. Current implementations of EDR are in operation in France Telecom's national network and Deutsche Telecom's national network. The GTQO protocol described in Chapter 10, and the subject of a detailed case study presented in Chapter 9, is an example of an EDR method applicable to integrated voice/data GMPLS-based dynamic routing networks.

2.4 Internetwork Routing

In current practice, internetwork routing protocols generally do not incorporate standardized path selection or per class-of-service resource management. For example, in IP-based networks, BGP [RFC4271] is used for internetwork routing but does not incorporate per class-of-service resource allocation as described in this section. Also, MPLS-based techniques have not yet been fully addressed for internetwork applications [see Chapter 10 for discussion of standards extensions, such as path computation element (PCE), which are in progress]. Extensions to internetwork routing methods discussed in this section therefore can be considered to extend the call/session routing and connection routing concepts to routing between networks.

Many of the principles described for intranetwork routing can be extended to internetwork routing. As illustrated in Figure 2.8, internetwork routing paths can be divided into three types: (a) a primary shortest path between the originating network and destination network, (b) alternate paths with all nodes in the origination network and destination network, and (c) alternate paths through other networks.

Internetwork routing can support a multiple ingress/egress capability, as illustrated in Figure 2.8 in which a connection request is routed either on the shortest path or, if not available, via an alternate path through any one of the other nodes from an originating node to a border node.

Within an originating network, a destination network could be served by more than one border node, such as OBN1 and OBN2 in Figure 2.8, in which case multiple ingress/egress routing is used. As illustrated in Figure 2.8, with multiple ingress/egress routing, a connection request from the originating node ON1 destined for the destination border node DBN1 tries first to access the links from originating border node OBN2 to DBN1. In doing this it is possible that the connection request could be routed from ON1 to OBN2 directly or via VN2. If no bandwidth is available from OBN2 to DBN1, the control of the connection request can be returned to

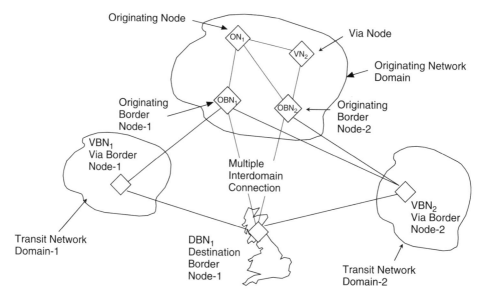

Figure 2.8 Multiple ingress/egress internetwork routing.

ON1 with a crankback/bandwidth-not-available indicator, after which the connection request is routed to OBN1 to access the OBN1-to-DBN1 bandwidth. If the connection request cannot be completed on the link connecting border node OBN1 to DBN1, the connection request can return to the originating node ON1 through use of a crankback/band-not-available indicator for possible further routing to another border node (not shown). In this manner all ingress/egress connectivity is utilized to a connecting network, maximizing connection request completion and reliability.

Once the connection request reaches an originating border node (such as OBN1 or OBN2), this node determines the routing to the destination border node DBN1 and routes the connection request accordingly. In completing the connection request to DBN1, an originating border node can dynamically select a primary shortest path, an alternate path through an alternate node in the destination network, or perhaps an alternate path through an alternate node in another network. Hence, with internetwork routing, connection requests are routed first to a shortest primary path between the originating and destination network, then to a list of alternate paths through alternate nodes in the terminating network, then to a list of alternate paths through alternate nodes in the originating network (e.g., OBN1 and OBN2 in Figure 2.8), and finally to a list of alternate paths through nodes in other networks.

Examples of alternate paths that might be selected through a via network are ON1–OBN1–VBN1–DBN1, ON1–OBN1–VBN2–DBN1, or ON1–VN2–OBN2–VBN2–DBN1 in Figure 2.8. Such paths through via networks may be tried last in the example network configuration shown in Figure 2.8. For example, flexible internetwork routing may try to find an available alternate path based on link load states, where known, and connection request completion performance, where it can be inferred. That is, the originating border node (e.g., node OBN1 in Figure 2.8) may use its link status to a via node in a via (e.g., links OBN1–VBN1 and OBN1–VBN2) in combination with the connection request completion performance from the candidate via node to the destination node in the destination network in order to find the most available path to route the connection request over. For each path, a load state and a completion state can be tracked. The load state indicates whether the link bandwidth from the border node to the via node is lightly loaded, heavily loaded, reserved, or busy. The completion state indicates whether a path is achieving above-average completion, average completion, or below-average completion. The selection of a via path, then, is based on the load state and completion state. Alternate paths in the same destination network and in a via network are each considered separately. During times of congestion, the link bandwidth to a candidate via node may be in a reserved state, in which case the remaining link bandwidth is reserved for traffic routing directly to the candidate via node. During periods of no congestion, capacity not needed by one virtual network is made available to other virtual networks that are experiencing loads above their allocation.

Similar to intranetwork routing, internetwork routing can use discrete load states for internetwork links terminating in the originating border node (e.g., links OBN1–VBN1, OBN1–DBN1, OBN2–DBN1). As described in Chapter 3, these link load states could include lightly loaded, heavily loaded, reserved, and busy/bandwidth not available, in which the idle link bandwidth is compared with the load state thresholds for the link to determine its load condition. Completion rate is tracked on the various via paths (such as the path through via node VBN1 or VBN2 to destination node DBN1 in Figure 2.8) by taking account of the information relating either successful completion or noncompletion of a connection request through the via node. A noncompletion, or failure, is scored for the connection request if a signaling release message is received from the far end after the connection request seizes an egress link, indicating a network in-completion cause value. If no such signaling release message is received after the connection request seizes capacity on the egress link, then the connection request is scored as a success. Each border node keeps a connection request completion history of the success or failure, for example, of the last 10 connection requests using a particular via path, and it drops the oldest record and adds the connection request completion for the newest connection request on that path. Based on the number of connection request completions relative to the total number of connection requests, a completion state is computed.

Based on the completion states, connection requests are normally routed on the first path with a high completion state with a lightly loaded egress link. If such a path does not exist, then a path having an average completion state with a lightly loaded egress link is selected, followed by a path having a low completion state with a lightly loaded egress link. If no path with a lightly loaded egress link is available, and if the search depth permits the use of a heavily loaded egress link, the paths with heavily loaded egress links are searched in the order of high completion, average completion, and low completion. If no such paths are available, paths with reserved egress links are searched in the same order, based on the connection request completion state, if the search depth permits the use of a reserved egress link.

The rules for selecting primary shortest paths and alternate paths for a connection request are governed by the availability of shortest path bandwidth and node-to-node congestion. The path sequence consists of the primary shortest path, lightly loaded alternate paths, heavily loaded alternate paths, and reserved alternate paths. Alternate paths are first selected, that include nodes only in the originating and destination networks, and then selected through via networks if necessary.

Thus, as illustrated, internetwork routing methods can be considered to extend the intranetwork call/session routing and connection routing concepts, such as flexible path selection and per-class-of-service bandwidth selection, to routing between networks.

2.5 Modeling of TQO Methods

This book uses full-scale national network node models together with multiservice traffic demand models to study various TQO scenarios and trade-offs. The 135-node national model is illustrated in Figure 2.9. A 71-node model is developed in Chapter 9 for a case study of TQO protocol design for MPLS/GMPLS-based integrated voice/data dynamic routing networks. Figure 2.9 illustrates the placement of the traffic router

Figure 2.9 The 135-node national network model.

nodes in the model. *However, it is important to note that to keep Figure 2.9 uncluttered, the logical link layer 2 network and the MPLS LSPs overlaid on the layer 2 network are not shown. See Section 1.4 and Figure 1.3 in Chapter 1 for a discussion of the TQO layers functional model.*

For some of the topologies investigated in this chapter (e.g., packet-switched data network-oriented topologies), the logical link network is relatively sparse, which means that many nodes are not directly connected by logical layer 2 links. On the other hand, for other topologies investigated in this chapter (e.g., circuit-switched voice network-oriented topologies), the logical link network is relatively dense (or meshed), which means that many nodes are directly connected by logical layer 2 links. However, as shown later, all the topologies are densely interconnected by MPLS LSPs forming the VNETs, but again these are not all shown in Figure 2.9 to keep it uncluttered.

VNETs are formed by MPLS LSPs routed on layer 2 logical links between nodes. Traffic routers dynamically route connections in response to call/session requests that fall within classes of service assigned to VNETs. A VNET is allocated bandwidth on layer 2 logical links, and the bandwidth allocation is managed to meet performance requirements. For example, real-time voice traffic may form one VNET made up of MPLS label switched paths (LSPs) between the network nodes. Premium private data traffic may form another VNET made up of separate and additional MPLS LSPs between the nodes. The TQO design pursued here optimizes the routing and bandwidth allocation of the LSP mesh forming the VNETs, with traffic for various classes of service (also known as QoS classes) carried on the VNET bandwidth so as to satisfy various performance objectives. This mesh of MPLS LSPs forming the VNETs is carried in turn by GMPLS LSPs forming the layer 2 logical link network; these GMPLS LSPs are optimally routed and allocated bandwidth so as to satisfy various performance objectives. As shown later, circuit-switched voice network-oriented network topologies are typically highly interconnected by logical links (perhaps >70% connected), whereas packet-switched data network-oriented topologies are typically interconnected more sparsely (perhaps <20% connected). GMPLS technology allows integrated control of the MPLS LSP layer, GMPLS LSP logical link layer, and physical fiber transport layer dynamic routing networks.

Bandwidth allocated to VNETs can be shared with other VNETs when relatively idle, but is protected for exclusive use by traffic assigned to the particular VNET when necessary. This is accomplished through dynamic bandwidth reservation mechanisms to be explained in Chapter 3. VNET designs are modeled and analyzed extensively, and it is shown that aggregated per-VNET bandwidth allocation is preferred to per-flow bandwidth allocation and lowers routing table management overhead, thereby increasing scalability. STT-EDR path selection combined with per-VNET bandwidth allocation dramatically reduces flooding of network status changes and control overhead, such as used in SDR approaches (e.g., OSPF). Alternatives to VNET architectures are considered as well, e.g., in Chapter 3 and in the case studies presented in Chapter 9, cases are considered where (a) no VNETs exist but rather all traffic is combined on available bandwidth, (b) services are differentiated only by queuing mechanisms such as DiffServ, and (c) other architecture alternatives. As shown in these studies, the VNET approach is superior to other alternatives and is the basis for the GTQO protocol presented in Chapter 10.

The capacity design of VNET architectures considers all VNETs at once in an integrated network design, in which all the complex dynamic functions are considered together, including per-VNET dynamic routing, per-VNET dynamic bandwidth allocation, bandwidth sharing, bandwidth reservation, and per-VNET queuing. In short, the integrated VNET design takes into account the complex dynamics, and efficiencies, of statistical multiplexing in packet networks where bandwidth is maximally shared. This full sharing approach avoids the network inefficiencies that would result from designing separate VNETs, one at a time, in which bandwidth is not shared and statistical multiplexing is not realized. All of these dynamics are considered at once in the capacity design while meeting multidimensional performance objectives (see Section 1.7.1 in Chapter 1 for a discussion of QoS and GoS performance measures). An extremely effective approach to dimensioning such networks is the DEFO method summarized in Chapter 1 and discussed in detail in Chapter 6. Several other examples of integrated network designs using the DEFO model are illustrated in Chapter 6, including GMPLS-based combined layer 2 and layer 3 network designs.

Typical data and voice traffic loads are used to model the various network alternatives. The variable bit rate data services traffic model incorporates typical traffic load patterns and includes (a) variable bit rate real-time traffic, representing services such as IP-telephony, (b) variable bit rate nonreal-time traffic, representing services such as WWW multimedia and credit card check, and (c) unassigned bit rate traffic, representing best-effort services such as email, voice mail, and file transfer multimedia applications. Voice/ISDN traffic loads are segmented in the model into constant-bit-rate services, including business voice, consumer voice, international voice, high-priority voice, normal- and high-priority 64-Kbps ISDN data, and 384-Kbps ISDN data. Typical voice/ISDN traffic loads are based on 72 h of a full-scale national network loading. Three levels of traffic priority—key, normal, and best effort—are given to the various class-of-service categories, or VNETs, as illustrated in Tables 2.1a–2.1c. Class-of-service, traffic priority, and QoS resource management are all discussed further in Chapter 3. The cost model represents typical connection switching and transport costs and illustrates the economies of scale for costs of high-capacity network elements.

Table 2.1a Virtual Network (VNET) Traffic Model Used for TQO Studies

Virtual network index	Virtual network name	Service identity examples	Virtual network traffic priority and traffic characteristics
VNET-1 (CBR)	Business voice	Virtual private network (VPN), direct connect 800, 800 service, 900 service	Normal priority; 64-Kbps CBR; 72-h traffic load data (Saturday, Sunday, Monday, 1998)
VNET-2 (CBR)	Consumer voice	CBR voice service (CVS)	Normal priority; 64-Kbps CBR; 72-h traffic load data (Saturday, Sunday, Monday, 1998)
VNET-3 (CBR)	INTL voice outbound	INTL CVS outbound, INTL 800 outbound, global VPN outbound, INTL transit	Normal priority; 64-Kbps CBR; 72-h traffic load data (Saturday, Sunday, Monday, 1998)
VNET-4 (CBR)	INTL voice inbound (key)	INTL CVS inbound, INTL 800 inbound, global VPN inbound, INTL transit inbound	Key priority; 64-Kbps CBR; 72-h traffic load data (Saturday, Sunday, Monday, 1998)
VNET-5 (CBR)	800-gold (key)	Direct connect 800 gold, 800 gold, VPN-key	Key priority; 64-Kbps CBR; 72-h traffic load data (Saturday, Sunday, Monday, 1998)
VNET-6 (CBR)	64-Kbps ISDN	64-Kbps switched digital service (SDS), 64-Kbps switched digital INTL (SDI)	Normal priority; 64-Kbps CBR; 72-h traffic load data (Saturday, Sunday, Monday, 1998)
VNET-7 (CBR)	64-Kbps ISDN (key)	64-Kbps SDS and SDI (key)	Key priority; 64-Kbps CBR; 72-h traffic load data (Saturday, Sunday, Monday, 1998)
VNET-8 (CBR)	384-Kbps ISDN	384-Kbps SDS, 384-Kbps SDI	Normal priority; 384-Kbps CBR; 72-h traffic load data (Saturday, Sunday, Monday, 1998)

(Continued)

Table 2.1a Virtual Network (VNET) Traffic Model Used for TQO Studies—cont'd

Virtual network index	Virtual network name	Service identity examples	Virtual network traffic priority and traffic characteristics
VNET-9 (VBR-RT)	IP-telephony variable rate, EQUIV-BW allocation, interactive, and delay sensitive	IP-telephony, compressed voice	Normal priority; variable rate, EQUIV-BW allocation, interactive, and delay sensitive; VBR-RT: 10% of VNET1 + VNET2 + VNET3 + VNET4 + VNET5 traffic load, connection data rate varies from 6.4 to 51.2-Kbps (25.6-Kbps mean)
VNET-10 (VBR-NRT)	IP multimedia variable rate, EQUIV-BW allocation, noninteractive, and not delay sensitive	IP multimedia, WWW, credit card check	Normal priority; variable rate, EQUIV-BW allocation, noninteractive, and not delay sensitive; VBR-NRT: 30% of VNET2 traffic load, connection data rate varies from 38.4 to 64-Kbps (51.2-Kbps mean)
VNET-11 (UBR)	UBR best effort variable rate, no BW allocation, noninteractive, and not delay sensitive	Voice mail, email, file transfer	Best-effort priority; variable rate, no BW allocation, noninteractive, and not delay sensitive; UBR: 30% of VNET1 traffic load, connection data rate varies from 6.4 to 3072-Kbps (1536-Kbps mean)

Geekia NetHeads might get very concerned at this point that "this is just a Bell-Head model, look at all the voice emphasis in the model!" Well, as shown in Tables 2.1a, 2.1b, and 2.1c, most of the traffic load volume in the 135-node multiservice traffic model represents, by far, packet-based data services. Second, an underlying assumption in the model is that PSTN legacy services, such as 64-Kbps voice and ISDN services currently offered on service provider networks, would be emulated on the converged IP/MPLS network. That is, legacy PSTN services would not disappear, but would be migrated to a converged IP/MPLS network carrying all new voice/data services, legacy packet data services, legacy voice services, private line services, etc. Therefore the model includes legacy PSTN services, which are assumed to be emulated on an IP/MPLS network, as well as traditional packet-based data services. This view in the model is consistent with the next generation network (NGN) concept, as described in [CARUGI05], which proposes to have PSTN services emulated on the MPLS-based NGN architecture. Continuity of service offerings is seen to be a critical element in successful migration to a converged voice/data network. There is no

Table 2.1b Virtual Network (VNET) Traffic Model Used for TQO Studies Average Number of Flows by Network Busy Hours (CST)

Virtual network index	Virtual network name	Sunday 8:00 PM	Monday 10:00 AM	Monday 11:00 AM	Monday 2:00 PM	Monday 3:00 PM	Monday 4:00 PM	Monday 8:00 PM	Monday 9:00 PM
VNET-1 (CBR)	Business voice	108,459.3	616,190.8	678,423.2	672,853.4	676,348.1	661,489.9	232,997.4	193,837.5
VNET-2 (CBR)	Consumer voice	457,580.8	247,198.4	269,968.7	258,178.2	263,387.9	280,522.8	465,911.6	484,810.9
VNET-3 (CBR)	INTL voice outbound	28,124.5	25,976.3	27,276.2	22,417.6	23,079.2	23,053.9	21,939.3	22,064.3
VNET-4 (CBR)	INTL voice inbound (key)	11,725.8	23,969.9	25,098.4	18,491.8	18,034.8	17,382.3	12,112.0	12,239.6
VNET-5 (CBR)	800-gold (key)	1,506.5	6,672.7	7,489.9	7,457.3	7,611.5	7,408.6	3,211.4	2,741.6
VNET-6 (CBR)	64-Kbps ISDN	908.1	3,306.7	3,587.7	3,922.3	3,515.7	3,161.6	1,677.5	1,390.6
VNET-7 (CBR)	64-Kbps ISDN (key)	77.2	454.8	419.2	181.2	168.6	168.8	162.5	116.8
VNET-8 (CBR)	384-Kbps ISDN	1.0	21.0	18.0	29.2	33.2	26.8	2.2	2.0
VNET-9 (VBR-RT)	IP-telephony	60,739.8	92,000.8	100,825.9	97,940.1	98,846.3	98,986.0	73,616.9	71,567.2
VNET-10 (VBR-NRT)	IP multimedia	137,274.5	74,159.5	80,990.6	77,453.5	79,016.2	84,156.8	139,773.5	145,443.2
VNET-11 (UBR)	UBR best effort	27,154.7	166,574.9	184,626.4	183,204.2	183,602.5	179,601.3	60,477.9	49,866.7
Total		833,552.2	1,256,525.8	1,378,724.2	1,342,128.8	1,353,644.0	1,355,958.8	1,011,882.2	984,080.4

Table 2.1c Virtual Network (VNET) Traffic Model Used for TQO Studies Average Data Volume (Mbps) by Network Busy Hours (CST)

Virtual network index	Virtual network name	Sunday 8:00 PM	Monday 10:00 AM	Monday 11:00 AM	Monday 2:00 PM	Monday 3:00 PM	Monday 4:00 PM	Monday 8:00 PM	Monday 9:00 PM
VNET-1 (CBR)	Business voice	6,941.3	39,436.3	43,419.0	43,062.7	43,286.3	42,335.4	14,911.7	12,405.5
VNET-2 (CBR)	Consumer voice	29,285.2	15,820.7	17,278.0	16,523.5	16,856.8	17,953.4	29,818.3	31,028.0
VNET-3 (CBR)	INTL voice outbound	1,800.0	1,662.5	1,745.7	1,434.7	1,477.1	1,475.4	1,404.1	1,412.1
VNET-4 (CBR)	INTL voice inbound (key)	750.4	1,534.1	1,606.3	1,434.7	1,477.1	1,1112.5	775.2	783.3
VNET-5 (CBR)	800-gold (key)	96.4	427.1	479.4	477.3	487.1	474.2	205.5	175.5
VNET-6 (CBR)	64-Kbps ISDN	58.1	211.6	229.6	251.0	225.0	202.3	107.4	89.0
VNET-7 (CBR)	64-Kbps ISDN (key)	4.9	29.1	26.8	11.6	10.8	10.8	10.4	7.5
VNET-8 (CBR)	384-Kbps ISDN	0.4	8.1	6.9	11.2	12.8	10.3	0.9	0.8
VNET-9 (VBR-RT)	IP-telephony	1,554.9	2,355.2	2,581.1	2,507.3	2,530.5	2,534.0	1,884.6	1,832.2
VNET-10 (VBR-NRT)	IP multimedia	7,028.5	3,797.0	4,146.7	3,965.6	4,045.6	4,308.8	7,156.4	7,446.7
VNET-11 (UBR)	UBR best effort	41,709.7	255,858.8	283,585.9	281,401.8	282,012.7	275,867.7	92,894.2	76,595.1
Total		89,229.8	321,140.5	355,105.4	351,081.4	352,421.8	346,283.5	149,168.7	131,775.7

Telephonia BellHead plot here to replicate the PSTN using MPLS/GMPLS-based TQO methods, rather the intent is to emphasize realistic migration to an IP/MPLS-based converged network technology.

The voice/ISDN loads are segmented in the model into eight constant-bit-rate (CBR) VNETs, including business voice, consumer voice, international voice in and out, key-service voice, normal- and key-service 64-Kbps ISDN data, and 384-Kbps ISDN data. For the CBR voice services, the mean data rate is assumed to be 64 Kbps for all VNETs, except the 384-Kbps ISDN data VNET-8, for which the mean data rate is 384 Kbps. Note that the overhead for each traffic flow is also included. For example, the packetized 64-Kbps voice is assumed to have a CBR of 86.8 Kbps, which includes a G.711 voice payload (20-ms packets) of 160 bytes, RTP/UDP/IP headers of 40 bytes, PPP header with 4-byte FCS of 9 bytes, and MPLS labels of 8 bytes. Similar overhead considerations are included for the other traffic streams.

Equivalent bandwidth is considered for the variable rate connections. An equivalent bandwidth considers an inflation of the mean data rate, and typically the more the statistical variation and burstiness of the source traffic, the larger the inflation factor. The equivalent bandwidth allocation then provides a performance guarantee in terms of mean delay, jitter, and packet loss probability. For example, an equivalent bandwidth model allocates the equivalent source bandwidth to each queue, and the queues then deliver the required performance guarantees by limiting the number of equivalent sources served so that their equivalent bandwidths sum to less than the capacity of the queue.

There is a huge literature on equivalent bandwidth models [e.g., ASH87, DZIONG97, KELLY91]. Although I cannot prove it, in fact I [ASH87] may have been the first paper (or at least one of the first) on the equivalent bandwidth concept. I don't blatantly claim that "I invented it" as Al Gore did of the Internet, I'll just quietly imply that I invented it and await someone out there to quickly prove me wrong. It took quite a while for colleagues at AT&T to grasp the essential idea, but finally one rather amazed colleague declared that "you've converted a packet network design problem to a circuit network design problem!," recognizing that there that was a wealth of knowledge and methodology to solve circuit-network design problems and now those techniques could be applied to packet network design problems. In addition, Janusz Filipiak, who was then a professor at Krakow University, privately endorsed the idea that I invented equivalent bandwidth, but he probably doesn't remember that so it won't stand up in court.

The data services traffic model incorporates typical traffic load patterns and comprises three additional VNET load patterns. These data services VNETs include the following:

- variable bit rate real-time (VBR-RT) VNET-9, representing services such as IP-telephony and compressed voice,
- variable bit rate nonreal-time (VBR-NRT) VNET-10, representing services such as WWW multimedia and credit card check, and
- unassigned bit rate (UBR) VNET-11, representing services such as email, voice mail, and file transfer multimedia applications.

For VBR-RT connections, the data rate varies from 6.4 to 51.2 Kbps with a mean of 25.6 Kbps. The VBR-RT connections are assumed to be interactive and delay sensitive. For the VBR-NRT connections, the data rate varies from 38.4 to 64 Kbps with a mean of 51.2 Kbps, and the VBR-NRT flows are assumed to be non-delay sensitive. For UBR connections, the data rate varies from 6.4 to 3072 Kbps with a mean of 1536 Kbps. The UBR flows are assumed to be best-effort priority and non-delay sensitive. For modeling purposes, the service and link bandwidth is segmented into 6.4-Kbps slots, i.e., 10 slots per 64-Kbps channel.

Here the traffic loads are dynamically varying and tracked by the exponential smoothing models discussed in Chapter 3. Table 2.1b gives the average number of flows for each VNET (class of service) in various network busy hours, and Table 2.1c gives the average data volume in Mbps for each VNET (class of service) in various network busy hours. We can see that the voice/ISDN traffic (i.e., VNETs 1–8 in Tables 2.1a–2.1c) has a majority of the flows (approximately 75%) of the total in Monday busy hours compared to the various "data" traffic sources (i.e., VNETs 9–11 in Tables 2.1a–2.1c). However, the voice/ISDN traffic represents a minority of the total traffic data volume (approximately 20–30%) of the total Mbps demand compared to the various "data" traffic sources (i.e., VNETs 9–11 in Tables 2.1a–2.1c). The model is based on traffic projections for "data" traffic and actual voice/ISDN traffic levels, wherein the data traffic dominating the voice/ISDN traffic is a realistic scenario under many traffic projections.

Note also the time variation of the various classes of service. The business voice traffic (VNET-1) peaks in the Monday daytime busy hours and is considerably lower in intensity in the Sunday and Monday evening hours. The consumer voice traffic (VNET-2) follows an opposite pattern. The best-effort traffic (VNET-11) follows a pattern similar to business voice, peaking in the Monday daytime hours, but of course is much larger in data volume (Mbps) compared to the voice traffic. On the other hand, the IP multimedia traffic (VNET-10) follows a pattern similar to the consumer voice traffic. These noncoincident traffic patterns make it more efficient to carry them on the same multiservice network, wherein capacity can be used more efficiently because it is shared across different time periods. There are classes of service with large data volumes and small data volumes, which all must be combined in the multiservice network, and meet their QoS requirements.

The cost model represents typical connection switching and transport costs and illustrates the economies of scale for costs projected for high-capacity network elements in the future. Average allocated costs are derived by considering the costs of connection switching network elements and transport network elements and then allocating these costs over the supported bandwidth of the associated network elements. This is a typical approach used in cost modeling, as described and recommended in the Bell System "Green Book" Table 2.2 gives the model used for average allocated connection switching and transport costs allocated per 64-Kbps unit of bandwidth.

The DEFO design model, described in Chapter 6, is used in the design and analysis of five connection routing methods with TQO methods applied: two-link STT-EDR path routing in a meshed logical network, two-link DC-SDR routing in a meshed

Table 2.2 Cost Assumptions (Average Allocated Cost per Equivalent 64-Kbps Bandwidth)

Data rate	Average allocated transport cost	Average allocated connection switching/cross-connect cost
DS3	$0.19 \times$ miles $+ 8.81$	26.12
OC3	$0.17 \times$ miles $+ 9.76$	19.28
OC12	$0.15 \times$ miles $+ 7.03$	9.64
OC48	$0.05 \times$ miles $+ 2.77$	3.92

logical network, and multilink STT-EDR, DC-SDR, and DP-SDR routing, as might be supported, for example, by MPLS TE in a sparse logical network. We also model the case where no TQO call/session and connection routing methods are applied.

In the model, call/sessions are routed by the originating node, for example, using E.164 numbers for voice call/sessions, where ENUM and DNS [RFC3271] concepts are typically incorporated, as described in Chapter 4. Through case studies, Chapters 8 and 9 illustrate the combining of SIP call/session setup, connection setup, class-of-service routing, and bandwidth reservation techniques in both the access network and the core network. Connection-level routing is now described for each considered option.

Network models for the two-link STT-EDR/DC-SDR and multilink STT-EDR/DC-SDR/DP-SDR networks are now described. In the two-link STT-EDR and DC-SDR models, we assume 135 packet-switched-nodes (MPLS or PNNI based). Synchronous-to-asynchronous conversion (SAC) is assumed to occur at packet-switched nodes for link connections from circuit-switched nodes. Links in these two-link STT-EDR/DC-SDR models are assumed to provide more fine-grained (1.536-Mbps T1 level) logical link bandwidth allocation, and a meshed network topology design results among the nodes, i.e., links exist between most (90% or more) of the nodes. In the two-link STT-EDR/DC-SDR models, one- and two-link routing with crankback is used throughout the network. Two-link path selection is modeled with both STT path selection and distributed connection-by-connection SDR (DC-SDR) path selection. Packet-switched nodes use two-link STT-EDR or two-link DC-SDR routing to all other nodes. Quality-of-service priority queuing is modeled in the performance analyses, in which the key services are given the highest priority, normal services the middle priority, and best-effort services the lowest priority in the queuing model. This queuing model quantifies the level of delayed traffic for each virtual network. In routing a connection with two-link STT-EDR routing, the ON checks the equivalent bandwidth and allowed DEPTH first on the direct path, then on the current successful two-link via path, and then sequentially on all candidate two-link paths. In routing a connection with two-link DC-SDR, the ON checks the equivalent bandwidth and allowed DEPTH first on the direct path and then on the least-loaded path that meets the equivalent bandwidth and DEPTH requirements. Each VN checks the equivalent bandwidth and allowed

DEPTH provided in the setup message and uses crankback to the ON if the equivalent bandwidth or DEPTH is not met.

In the multilink STT-EDR/DC-SDR/DP-SDR model, we assume 135 packet-switched nodes. Because high rate OC3/12/48 links provide highly aggregated link bandwidth allocation, a sparse network topology design results among the packet-switched nodes, i.e., high rate OC3/12/48 links exist between relatively few (10 to 20%) of the packet-switched nodes. Second, multilink shortest path selection with crankback is used throughout the network. For example, the STT EDR TQO algorithm used is adaptive and distributed in nature and uses learning models to find good TQO paths. With STT EDR, if the LSR-A to LSR-B bandwidth needs to be modified, say increased by delta-BW, the primary LSP-p is tried first. If delta-BW is not available on one or more links of LSP-p, then the currently successful LSP-s is tried next. If delta-BW is not available on one or more links of LSP-s, then a new LSP is searched by trying additional candidate paths until a new successful LSP-n is found or the candidate paths are exhausted. LSP-n is then marked as the currently successful path for the next time bandwidth needs to be modified.

Quality-of-service priority queuing is modeled in the performance analyses, in which the key services are given the highest priority, normal services the middle priority, and best-effort services the lowest priority in the queuing model. This queuing model quantifies the level of delayed traffic for each virtual network. The multilink path selection options are modeled with STT path selection, DC-SDR path selection, and distributed periodic path selection (DP-SDR). In the model of DP-SDR, the status updates are modeled with flooding of link status updates every 10 s. Note that the multilink DP-SDR performance results should also be comparable to the performance of multilink centralized periodic SDR (CP-SDR), in which status updates and path selection updates are made every 10 s, respectively, to and from a TQO processor.

In routing a connection with multilink shortest path selection with two-link STT-EDR routing, for example, the ON checks the equivalent bandwidth and allowed DEPTH first on the first choice path, then on a current successful alternate path, and then sequentially on all candidate alternate paths. Again, each VN checks the equivalent bandwidth and allowed DEPTH provided in the setup message and uses crankback to the ON if the equivalent bandwidth or DEPTH is not met.

In the models the logical network design is optimized for each routing alternative, while the physical transport links and node locations are held fixed. We examine the performance and network design trade-offs of logical topology design (sparse or mesh) and routing method (two-link, multilink, fixed, dynamic, SDR, EDR, hierarchical, nonhierarchical, etc.).

Generally the meshed logical topologies are optimized by one- and two-link routing, whereas the sparse logical topologies are optimized by multilink shortest path routing (MSPR). Modeling results include the following:

- Designs for dynamic two-link routing (SDR, EDR) and multilink routing (SDR, EDR)
- Designs for voice/ISDN-only traffic (VNETs 1–8 in Table 2.1) and data-only traffic (VNETs 9–11)

- Designs for integrated voice/ISDN and data traffic (VNETs 1–11)
- Designs for fixed hierarchical routing
- Designs where all voice traffic is compressed (VNETs 1–5 and VNET 9 all use the IP-telephony traffic characteristics of VNET 9)
- Performance analyses for overloads and failures

Generally the routing and capacity designs for the meshed logical topologies are optimized by using the DEFO algorithms presented in Chapter 6, whereas the routing and capacity designs for the sparse logical topologies are optimized by using the shortest path optimization and DEFO algorithms presented in Chapter 6.

2.5.1   Network Design Comparisons

Illustrative network design costs for voice/ISDN-only designs (VNETs 1–8 in Table 2.1), for data-only designs (VNETs 9–11 in Table 2.1), and for integrated voice/ISDN and data designs (VNETs 1–11 in Table 2.1) are given in Figures 2.10, 2.11, and 2.12, respectively. These design costs and details are discussed further in Chapter 6.

Design results show that the two-link STT-EDR and two-link DC-SDR logical mesh networks are highly connected (90% +), whereas the multilink MPLS-based and PNNI-based networks are connected sparsely (10–20%). The network cost comparisons illustrate that the sparse MPLS and PNNI networks achieve a small cost advantage, as they take advantage of the greater cost efficiencies of high bandwidth logical links (up to OC48), as reflected in Table 2.2. However, these differences in cost may not be significant and can change as equipment costs evolve and as the relative cost of connection switching and transport equipment changes. Sensitivities of the results to different cost assumptions were investigated. For example, if the relative cost of transport increases relative to connection switching, then the two-link meshed

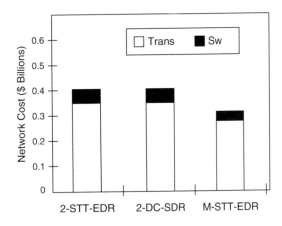

Figure 2.10   Voice/ISDN network design cost (includes traffic for VNET-1 to VNET-8 in Table 2.1).

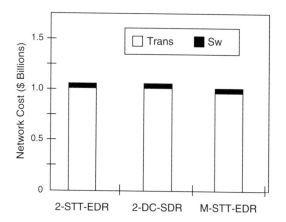

Figure 2.11 Data network design cost (includes traffic for VNET-9 to VNET-11 in Table 2.1).

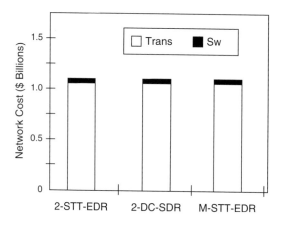

Figure 2.12 Integrated voice/ISDN and data network design cost (includes traffic for VNET-1 to VNET-11 in Table 2.1).

networks can appear to be more efficient than the sparse multilink networks. These results are consistent with those presented in other studies of meshed and sparse logical networks as a function of relative connection switching and transport costs [e.g., see ASH98].

Comparing the results of separate voice/ISDN and data designs and integrated voice/ISDN and data designs shows that integration does achieve some capital cost advantage of about 5 to 20%. The larger range of integration design efficiencies is achieved as a result of the economies of scale of larger capacity network elements, as reflected in cost assumptions given in Table 2.2. However, probably more significant are the operational savings of integration that result from operating a single network rather than two or more networks. In addition, the performance of an integrated voice and data network leads to advantages in capacity sharing, especially when different traffic classes having different routing priorities, such as key service and best-effort service, are integrated and share capacity on the same network. These performance results are reported later in this section. A study of voice compression for all voice traffic, such as might occur if IP-telephony is widely deployed, shows that network capital costs might be reduced by as much as 10% if this evolutionary direction is followed. An analysis of fixed hierarchical routing versus dynamic routing illustrates that more than a 20% reduction in network capital costs can be achieved with dynamic routing. In addition, operation savings also result from simpler provisioning of the dynamic routing options.

2.5.2   Network Performance Comparisons

Performance analyses for overloads and failures include connection admission control with QoS resource management. As we discuss in Chapter 3, in the example QoS resource management approach, we distinguish key services, normal services, and best-effort services. Performance comparisons are presented in Tables 2.3, 2.4, and 2.5 for various TQO methods, including two-link and multilink EDR and SDR approaches, and a baseline case of no TQO methods applied. Table 2.3 gives performance results for a 30% general overload, Table 2.4 gives performance results for a six times overload on a single network node, and Table 2.5 gives performance results for a single logical-link failure. Numbers in the tables indicate the percentage of total network traffic lost

Table 2.3 Performance Comparison for Various Connection-Routing TQO Methods and No TQO Methods; 30% General Overload (% Lost/Delayed Traffic) (135-Node Multiservice Network Model)

Virtual network	Two-link STT-EDR	Two-link DC-SDR	Multilink STT-EDR	Multilink DC-SDR	Multi-link DP-SDR	No TQO methods applied
Business voice	0.00	0.00	0.00	0.00	0.00	3.18
Consumer voice	0.03	0.02	0.00	0.00	0.00	2.61
INTL-out	5.40	4.82	0.00	0.00	0.00	3.62
INTL-in (key)	0.00	0.00	0.00	0.00	0.00	3.63
Key voice	0.00	0.00	0.00	0.00	0.00	3.27
64-Kbps ISDN data	1.27	1.21	0.00	0.00	0.00	3.18
64-Kbps ISDN data (key)	0.00	0.00	0.00	0.00	0.00	2.58
384-Kbps ISDN data	0.00	0.00	0.00	0.00	0.00	6.51
VBR-RT voice	0.28	0.20	0.00	0.00	0.00	3.07
VBR-NRT MM	0.04	0.02	0.00	0.00	0.00	2.54
UBR MM	21.8	23.2	4.16	4.16	4.15	3.37

Table 2.4 Performance Comparison for Various Connection-Routing TQO Methods and No TQO Methods; 6× Focused Overload on OKBK (% Lost/Delayed Traffic) (135-Node Multiservice Network Model)

Virtual network	Two-link STT-EDR	Two-link DC-SDR	Multilink STT-EDR	Multilink DC-SDR	Multi-link DP-SDR	No TQO methods applied
Business voice	5.27	2.28	0.00	0.06	0.08	9.42
Consumer voice	7.29	3.50	0.00	0.20	0.23	13.21
INTL-out	3.43	3.36	0.00	0.00	0.04	6.03
INTL-in (key)	2.19	4.21	0.00	0.00	0.00	6.55
Key voice	0.81	1.77	0.00	0.00	0.00	8.47
64-Kbps ISDN data	0.84	0.33	0.00	0.00	0.00	2.33
64-Kbps ISDN data (key)	0.00	0.00	0.00	0.00	0.00	0.46
384-Kbps ISDN data	0.00	0.00	0.00	0.00	0.00	0.00
VBR-RT voice	5.42	2.59	0.00	0.39	0.49	9.87
VBR-NRT MM	7.12	3.49	0.00	2.75	3.18	12.88
UBR MM	14.07	14.68	12.46	12.39	12.32	9.75

Table 2.5 Performance Comparison for Various Connection-Routing TQO Methods and No TQO Methods; Failure on CHCG-NYCM Link (% Lost/Delayed Traffic) (135-Node Multiservice Network Model)

Virtual network	Two-link STT-EDR	Two-link DC-SDR	Multilink STT-EDR	Multilink DC-SDR	Multilink DP-SDR	No TQO methods applied
Business voice	0.00	0.00	0.00	0.64	0.64	0.72
Consumer voice	0.00	0.00	0.00	0.44	0.43	0.52
INTL-out	0.00	0.00	0.00	0.00	0.00	0.00
INTL-in (key)	0.00	0.00	0.00	0.18	0.19	0.23
Key voice	0.00	0.00	0.00	0.46	0.51	0.58
64-Kbps ISDN data	0.00	0.00	0.00	0.95	0.89	0.94
64-Kbps ISDN data (key)	0.00	0.00	0.00	0.00	0.00	0.00
384-Kbps ISDN data	0.00	0.00	0.00	0.00	0.00	0.00
VBR-RT voice	0.00	0.00	0.00	0.55	0.55	0.62
VBR-NRT MM	0.00	0.00	0.00	0.44	0.42	0.51
UBR MM	2.06	1.65	0.17	0.64	0.64	0.72

(blocked) in the admission control, in which case all paths have insufficient capacity, plus the percentage of traffic delayed in the queues. Note that on high rate links, traffic delayed in the queues will almost always be dropped/lost, as shown in the case of a "bufferless" model [BONALD02].

In all cases of the TQO methods being applied, the performance is always better and usually substantially better than when no TQO methods are applied. Performance analysis results show that the multilink STT-EDR/DC-SDR/DP-SDR options (in sparse topologies) perform somewhat better under overloads than the two-link STT-EDR/DC-SDR options (in meshed topologies) because of greater sharing of network capacity. Under failure, the two-link STT-EDR/DC-SDR options perform better for many of the virtual network categories than the multilink STT-EDR/DC-SDR/CP-SDR options because they have a richer choice of alternate routing paths and are much more highly connected than the multilink STT-EDR/DC-SDR/DP-SDR networks. Loss of a link in a sparsely connected multilink STT-EDR/DC-SDR/DP-SDR network can have more serious consequences than in more highly connected logical networks. Performance results illustrate that capacity sharing of CBR, VBR, and UBR traffic classes, when combined with QoS resource management and priority queuing, leads to efficient use of bandwidth with minimal traffic delay and loss impact, even under overload and failure scenarios. These QoS resource management trends are examined further in Chapter 3.

The STT and SDR path selection methods are quite comparable for the two-link, meshed-topology network scenarios. However, the STT path selection method performs somewhat better than the SDR options in the multilink, sparse-topology case. In addition, the DC-SDR path selection option performs somewhat better than the CP-DCR option in the multilink case, which is a result of the 10-s-old status information causing misdirected paths in some cases. Hence, it can be concluded that (a) frequently updated, available link bandwidth (ALB) state information does not necessarily improve performance in all cases and (b) if ALB state information is used, it is sometimes better that it is very recent status information.

2.5.3 Single-Area Flat Topology vs Multiarea Two-Level Hierarchical Network Topology

We also investigated the performance of hierarchical network designs, which represent the topological configuration to be expected with multiarea [or multiautonomous system (multi-AS), or multidomain] networks. Figure 2.13 shows the model considered, which consists of 135 edge nodes each homed onto 1 of 21 backbone nodes. Typically, the edge nodes may be grouped into separate areas and the backbone nodes into another area. Within each area a flat routing topology exists; however, between edge areas and the backbone area a hierarchical routing relationship exists. This routing hierarchy is modeled in Chapter 3 for both per-flow and per-virtual-network bandwidth allocation examples; here the results are given for the per-flow allocation case in Tables 2.6 to 2.8 for the 30% general overload, six times focused overload, and link failure examples, respectively. We can see that the performance of the hierarchical network case is substantially worse than the flat network model, which models a single area or autonomous system consisting of 135 nodes.

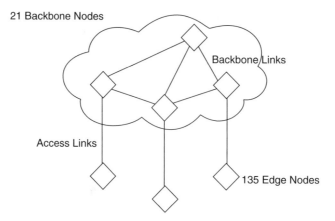

21 Backbone Nodes

Backbone Links

Access Links

135 Edge Nodes

Figure 2.13 Hierarchical network model.

Table 2.6 Performance of Single-Area Flat vs Multiarea Two-Level Hierarchical Network Topology; Percentage Lost/Delayed Traffic under 30% General Overload (Multilink STT-EDR Routing; 135-Node Network Model)

Virtual network	Single-area flat topology	Multiarea two-level hierarchical topology
Business voice	0.00	0.00
Consumer voice	0.00	0.00
INTL-out	0.00	0.00
INTL-in (key)	0.00	0.00
Key voice	0.00	0.00
64 SDS	0.00	0.00
64-Kbps ISDN data (key)	0.00	0.00
384-Kbps ISDN data	0.00	0.00
VBR-RT voice	0.00	0.00
VBR-NRT MM	0.00	0.00
UBR MM	4.16	9.06

Some of the reasons for the better performance of the flat network model compared to the hierarchical network case are as follows:

- Path selection is more constrained in a hierarchical network because some shortest paths between nodes are excluded by the hierarchical rules imposed (see Figure 1.10 in Chapter 1 and explanation)
- Limited visibility in selecting paths in a hierarchical network is caused by the aggregation of TE data between domains

Table 2.7 Performance of Single-Area Flat vs Multiarea Two-Level Hierarchical Network Topology; Percentage Lost/Delayed Traffic under 6× Focused Overload on OKBK (Multilink STT-EDR Routing; 135-Node Network Model)

Virtual network	Single-area flat topology	Multiarea two-level hierarchical topology
Business voice	0.00	1.70
Consumer voice	0.00	2.22
INTL-out	0.00	0.89
INTL-in (key)	0.00	0.00
Key voice	0.00	0.00
64-Kbps ISDN data	0.00	0.27
64-Kbps ISDN data (key)	0.00	0.00
384-Kbps ISDN data	0.00	0.00
VBR-RT voice	0.00	0.93
VBR-NRT MM	0.00	1.80
UBR MM	12.46	12.88

Table 2.8 Performance of Single-Area Flat vs Multiarea Two-Level Hierarchical Network Topology; Percentage Lost/Delayed Traffic under Failure on CHCG-NYCM Link (Multilink STT-EDR Routing; 135-Node Network Model)

Virtual network	Single-area flat topology	Multiarea two-level hierarchical topology
Business voice	0.00	0.00
Consumer voice	0.00	0.00
INTL-out	0.00	0.00
INTL-in (key)	0.00	0.00
Key voice	0.00	0.00
64-Kbps ISDN data	0.00	0.00
64-Kbps ISDN data (key)	0.00	0.00
384-Kbps ISDN data	0.00	0.00
VBR-RT voice	0.00	0.00
VBR-NRT MM	0.00	0.00
UBR MM	0.17	1.38

2.5.4 Network Modeling Conclusions

The TQO modeling conclusions are summarized as follows:

- Capital cost advantages may be attributed to the sparse topology options, such as the multilink STT-EDR/DC-SDR/DP-SDR options, but may not be significant compared to operational costs, and are subject to the particular connection switching and transport cost assumptions. Capacity design models are detailed further in Chapter 6 and operational issues in Chapter 7.

- In all cases of the TQO methods being applied, the performance is always better and usually substantially better than when no TQO methods are applied
- The sparse topology multilink-routing networks provide better overall performance under overload, but performance under failure may favor the two-link STT-EDR/DC-SDR options with more alternate routing choices. One item of concern in the sparse topology multilink-routing networks is with postdial delay, in which perhaps five or more links may need to be connected for an individual connection request.
- Single-area flat topologies exhibit better network performance and, as discussed and modeled in Chapter 6, greater design efficiencies in comparison with multiarea hierarchical topologies. As illustrated in Chapter 4, larger administrative areas can be achieved through the use of EDR-based TQO methods as compared to SDR-based TQO methods.
- State information as used by two-link and multilink SDR options provides only a small network capital cost advantage and essentially equivalent performance to the two-link STT-EDR options, as illustrated in the network performance results.
- Various path selection methods can interwork with each other in the same network, which is required for multivendor network operation.
- QoS resource management, as described further in Chapter 3, is shown to be effective in achieving key service, normal service, and best-effort service differentiation.
- Voice and data integration can provide capital cost advantages, but may be more important in achieving operational simplicity and expense cost reduction.
- If IP-telephony takes hold and a significant portion of voice call/sessions use voice compression technology, this could lead to more efficient networks.

Overall the packet-based (e.g., MPLS/TE) multilink, sparse topology routing strategies offer several advantages. Sparse logical topology with high-speed connection switching and transport links may have economic benefit due to lower cost network designs achieved by the economies of scale of higher rate network elements. The sparse, high-bandwidth, logical-link networks have been shown to have better response to overload conditions than logical mesh networks due to greater sharing of network capacity. The packet-based routing protocols have capabilities for automatic provisioning of links, nodes, and reachable addresses, which provide operational advantages for such networks. Because the sparse high-bandwidth-link network designs have dramatically fewer links to provision compared to mesh network designs (10–20% connected versus 90% or more connected for mesh networks), there is less provisioning work to perform. In addition to having fewer links to provision, sparse high-bandwidth-link network designs use larger increments of capacity on individual links and therefore capacity additions would need to occur less frequently than in highly connected mesh networks, which would have much smaller increments of capacity on the individual links. The sparse-topology, multilink-routing methods are synergistic with the evolution of data network services that implement these protocols, and such routing methods have been in place for many years in data networks. Should a service provider pursue integration of the voice/ISDN and data services networks, these factors will help support such an integration direction.

2.6 Summary and Conclusions

We have discussed call/session routing and connection routing methods employed in TQO functions. Several connection routing alternatives were discussed, which include FXR, TDR, EDR, and SDR methods. Models were presented to illustrate the network design and performance trade-offs between the many TQO approaches explained in the chapter, and conclusions were drawn on the advantages of various routing and topology options in network operation. Overall the packet-based (e.g., MPLS/TE) multilink, sparse topology-routing strategies were found to offer several advantages.

The following conclusions are reached:

1. In all cases of the TQO methods being applied, network performance is always better and usually substantially better than when no TQO methods are applied.
2. Sparse topology multilink-routing networks provide better overall performance under overload than meshed topology networks, but performance under failure may favor the two-link STT-EDR/DC-SDR meshed topology options with more alternate routing choices.
3. Single-area flat topologies exhibit better network performance and, as discussed and modeled in Chapter 6, greater design efficiencies in comparison with multiarea hierarchical topologies. As illustrated in Chapter 4, larger administrative areas can be achieved through the use of EDR-based TQO methods as compared to SDR-based TQO methods.
4. EDR TQO path selection methods exhibit comparable or better network performance compared to state-dependent-routing methods.
   a. EDR TQO methods are shown to an important class of TQO algorithms. EDR TQO methods are distinct from the TDR and SDR TQO methods in how the paths (e.g., MPLS label switched paths, or LSPs) are selected. In the SDR TQO case, the available link bandwidth (based on LSA flooding of ALB information) is typically used to compute the path. In the EDR TQO case, because the ALB information is not needed to compute the path, ALB flooding does not need to take place (reducing the overhead).
   b. EDR TQO algorithms are adaptive and distributed in nature and typically use learning models to find good TQO paths. For example, in an STT EDR TQO method, if the LSR-A to LSR-B bandwidth needs to be modified, say increased by delta-BW, the primary LSP-p is tried first. If delta-BW is not available on one or more links of LSP-p, then the currently successful LSP-s is tried next. If delta-BW is not available on one or more links of LSP-s, then a new LSP is searched by trying additional candidate paths until a new successful LSP-n is found or the candidate paths are exhausted. LSP-n is then marked as the

currently successful path for the next time the bandwidth needs to be modified. The performance of distributed EDR TQO methods is shown to be equal to or better than SDR methods, centralized or distributed.

c. While SDR TQO models typically use ALB flooding for TQO path selection, EDR TQO methods do not require ALB flooding. Rather, EDR TQO methods typically search out capacity by learning models, as in the STT method described above. ALB flooding can be very resource intensive, as it requires link bandwidth to carry LSAs, processor capacity to process LSAs, and the overhead can limit area/autonomous system size. Modeling results show that EDR TQO methods can lead to a large reduction in ALB flooding overhead without loss of network throughput performance (as shown in Chapter 4).

d. State information as used by SDR options (such as with link-state flooding) provides essentially equivalent performance to the EDR options, which typically used distributed routing with crankback and no flooding.

e. Various path selection methods can interwork with each other in the same network, as required for multivendor network operation.

5. Internetwork routing methods extend the intranetwork call/session routing and connection routing concepts, such as flexible path selection and per-class-of-service bandwidth selection, to routing between networks.

2.7 Applicability of Requirements

EDR TQO path selection methods are already in widespread use in TDM-based dynamic routing networks, as discussed in Chapter 1. These methods are generally simple, efficient, and have the distinct advantage of reducing the control overhead, leading to more scalable TQO solutions. Such EDR TQO methods are also applied currently to both intranetwork and internetwork dynamic routing networks and are clearly of interest to service providers.

Scalability of networks is a major concern, and TQO methods used to enhance network scalability are certainly of interest to service providers. Scalable TQO methods allow migration to flatter network topologies, which are simpler to manage than hierarchical topologies. TQO methods that respond automatically to network conditions are most desirable to service providers rather than the manual or semiautomatic methods currently available in typical packet-switched data network operation.

Vendors have yet to announce such TQO capabilities in their products. Successful TQO methods have been widely deployed in TDM networks, which could provide some basis for vendors to take note of these TQO requirements and capabilities and their potential marketability. Service providers and their customers would surely benefit from these capabilities in terms of network performance and profitability, as demonstrated in this chapter and throughout the book. Service provider interest in adopting such TQO features also leads to vendor profitability.

Chapter 3
Traffic Engineering and QoS Optimization of MPLS-Based Integrated Voice/Data Dynamic Routing Networks

3.1 Introduction

This chapter continues the TQO evolution discussion and focuses on QoS resource management in an IP/MPLS-based, converged voice/data network architecture. As discussed in Chapter 1, AT&T's internal RATS team performed evolution studies of an IP/MPLS-based architecture. In the course of this work, a wide range of alternative architectures were considered, and the modeling and analysis studies and conclusions reached are described in this chapter, with an emphasis on the analysis of QoS resource management approaches.

Figures 3.1–3.5 give a pictorial summary of the RATS activity. Telephonia BellHead RATS and Geekia NetHead RATS had widely divergent opinions as to the right architectural approach. Some participants came from the TDM voice world and thought in terms of highly successful voice/ISDN network dynamic routing strategies such as RTNR and STT-EDR. Some participants came from the IP data world, where dynamic routing strategies such as OSPF and MPLS were fast becoming the de facto technologies of choice for networks worldwide. Some participants came from an ATM world, where PNNI was proving to be a revolutionary dynamic routing technology and some NetHead RATS pushed hard on ATM SVP overlays using ATM data switching and cross-connect technology. Spirited (should I say heated?) arguments were the norm, with the TDM, IP, and ATM technology RATS all feeling confident on the basis of representing highly successful, well-entrenched technologies that were already the basis for lucrative service offerings.

In the end, the analysis and detailed case studies proved to be the vehicle for Telephonia BellHead RATS and Geekia NetHead RATS to reach consensus on innovative architecture directions that incorporated the best ideas of both worlds. Need

Do Careful Engineering with
Intelligent Design Algorithms; Meet
GoS with Minimum Cost

Install Infinite Bandwidth &
Stop Worrying; Bandwidth is
Free!

Figure 3.1 BellHeads and NetHeads have different ideas on TQO network optimization . . .

Figure 3.2 . . . so the BellHeads and NetHeads got together on the RATS team to optimize the MPLS/GMPLS converged network design . . .

I say that what emerged as a GTQO design looked more coherent than Figure 3.5—that's supposed to be a joke depicting the "elephant designed by committee" pitfall.

This chapter captures the wide range and diversity of ideas, architectures, alternatives, and technologies that were considered by RATS. While the range considered is not exhaustive, it is certainly comprehensive.

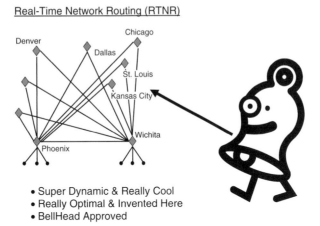

Figure 3.3   . . . great BellHead ideas flowed . . . "let's use RTNR, it's really cool and really optimal . . . "

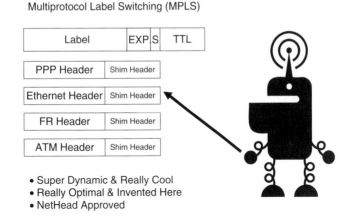

Figure 3.4   . . . and great NetHead ideas flowed . . . "let's use MPLS, it's really cool and really optimal . . . "

As outlined in Chapter 1, the problem statement for TQO design in this chapter includes the following:

- Traffic/application layer design: Find an optimal class-of-service routing design for arbitrary traffic loads and network topology, which yields minimum cost capacity and maximum flow/revenue, subject to meeting performance constraints.

Figure 3.5 . . . and in the end the BellHead RATs and NetHead RATs came up with a GTQO design incorporating the best ideas of both worlds.

- MPLS LSP dynamic routing and bandwidth allocation layer 3 design: Find an optimal connection/bearer-path routing design and MPLS LSP dynamic routing and bandwidth allocation strategy for arbitrary traffic loads and network topology, which yields minimum cost capacity and maximum flow/revenue, subject to meeting performance constraints.

QoS resource management (sometimes called QoS routing) functions include class-of-service identification, routing table derivation, connection admission control, bandwidth allocation, bandwidth protection, bandwidth reservation, priority routing, priority queuing, and other related resource management functions. QoS resource management methods have been applied successfully in circuit-switched networks [ASH98] and are being extended to packet-switched, IP/(G)MPLS-based networks. In this chapter we define and analyze a wide variety of MPLS-based QoS resource management methods, in which bandwidth is allocated to each of several virtual networks (VNETs) and VNETs are assigned a priority corresponding to either high-priority key services, normal-priority services, or best-effort low-priority services. VNETs are formed by MPLS LSPs routed on layer 2 logical links between nodes. Traffic routers dynamically route connections in response to call/session requests that fall within classes of service assigned to VNETs. A VNET is allocated bandwidth on layer 2 logical links, and the bandwidth allocation is managed to meet performance requirements. For example, real-time voice traffic may form one VNET made up of MPLS (LSPs) between the network nodes. Premium private data traffic may form another VNET made up of separate and additional MPLS LSPs between the nodes. The TQO design analyzed in this chapter optimizes the routing and bandwidth allocation of the LSP mesh forming the VNETs, with traffic for various classes of service (also known as QoS classes) carried on the VNET bandwidth so as to satisfy various performance objectives. This mesh of MPLS LSPs forming the VNETs is carried in turn by GMPLS LSPs forming the layer 2 logical link network. Bandwidth allocated to VNETs can be shared with other VNETs when relatively idle, but is protected for exclusive use by traffic assigned to the particular VNET when necessary. This is accomplished through dynamic bandwidth reservation mechanisms explained in this chapter. Changes in VNET bandwidth capacity can be determined by edge nodes on a per-flow (per-connection) basis or based on an overall aggregated bandwidth demand for VNET capacity (not on a per-connection demand basis). In the latter case of per-VNET bandwidth allocation, based on the aggregated bandwidth demand, edge nodes make periodic discrete changes in bandwidth allocation, i.e., either increase or decrease bandwidth, such as on the constraint-based routing label switched paths (CRLSPs) constituting the VNET bandwidth capacity. It is shown that aggregated per-VNET bandwidth allocation is preferred to per-flow bandwidth allocation lower routing table management overhead, thereby increasing scalability. STT-EDR path selection combined with per-VNET bandwidth allocation dramatically reduce flooding of network status changes and control overhead, such as used in SDR approaches (e.g., OSPF). Alternatives to VNET architectures are considered as well, for example, where (a) no VNETs exist but rather all traffic is combined on available bandwidth, (b) services are differentiated only by queuing mechanisms such as DiffServ, and (c) other architecture alternatives. It is shown in these studies that the VNET approach is superior to other alternatives and is the basis for the GTQO protocol presented in Chapter 10.

Capacity design of VNET architectures considers all VNETs at once in an integrated network design, in which all the complex dynamic functions are considered together, including per-VNET dynamic routing, per-VNET dynamic bandwidth allocation, bandwidth sharing, bandwidth reservation, and per-VNET queuing. In short, the integrated VNET design takes into account the complex dynamics, and efficiencies, of statistical multiplexing in packet networks where bandwidth is maximally shared. This full sharing approach avoids the network inefficiencies that would result from designing separate VNETs, one at a time, in which bandwidth is not shared and statistical multiplexing is not realized. All of these dynamics are considered at once in the capacity design while meeting multidimensional performance objectives using the discrete event flow optimization (DEFO) method discussed in Chapter 6.

QoS resource management therefore can be applied on a per-flow (or per-call/session request or per-connection-request) basis or can be applied beneficially to traffic trunks (also known as "bandwidth pipes" or "virtual trunks") in the form of CRLSPs in IP/(G)MPLS-based networks.

QoS resource management provides integration of services on a shared network for many classes of service such as the following:

- Constant bit rate real-time services, including voice, 64-, 384-, and 1536-Kbps ISDN switched digital data, international transit, priority defense communication, virtual private network, 800/FreePhone, fiber preferred, and other services.
- Variable bit rate real-time services, including IP-telephony, compressed video, and other services.
- Variable bit rate nonreal-time services, including WWW file transfer, credit card check, and other services.
- Unassigned bit rate best-effort services, including voice mail, email, file transfer, and other services.

Examples of service priorities within these VNET categories include the following:

- High-priority key services such as constant/variable rate real-time emergency and defense voice communication
- Normal-priority services such as constant/variable rate real-time voice; variable rate non-delay-sensitive WWW file transfer
- Low-priority best-effort services such as variable rate non-delay-sensitive voice mail, email, and file transfer

GTQO protocol requirements for QoS resource management are given in Chapter 10 for intranetwork, access, and internetwork applications. These requirements are based on the results in this chapter and other analysis in the book, as well as operational considerations and case studies presented in Chapters 8 and 9.

A key requirement of the GTQO QoS resource management function is class-of-service identification/routing. Class-of-service identification/routing provides a means to define network services through table-driven concepts rather than software development and new network deployment. Whereas the historical model of new service development always led to a "stovepipe" approach with specialized software development to implement the service and hardware development to build a new network and network elements, class-of-service routing defines service and network capabilities in tables within the network nodes. That is, definitions of new services capabilities are table driven and require no software development or network element development.

Bandwidth allocation control in the GTQO method is based on estimated bandwidth needs, bandwidth use, and status of links in the VNET. The edge node, or originating node (ON), determines when VNET bandwidth needs to be increased or decreased on a CRLSP and uses an illustrative MPLS CRLSP bandwidth modification procedure to execute needed bandwidth allocation changes on VNET CRLSPs. In the bandwidth allocation procedure the resource reservation protocol (e.g., RSVP-TE [RFC3209]) could be used, for example, to specify appropriate parameters in the resource reservation message (a) to request bandwidth allocation changes on each link in the CRLSP and (b) to determine if link bandwidth can be allocated on each link in the CRLSP. If a link bandwidth allocation is not allowed, a crankback notification message allows the ON to search out possible bandwidth allocation on another CRLSP. In particular we illustrate a depth-of-search (DEPTH) parameter in the resource reservation message to control the bandwidth allocation on individual links in a CRLSP. In addition, we illustrate a modify parameter in the resource reservation message to allow dynamic modification of the assigned traffic parameters (such as peak data rate, committed data rate, etc.) of an already existing CRLSP. Finally, we illustrate the crankback notification message to allow an edge node to search out additional alternate CRLSPs when a given CRLSP cannot accommodate a bandwidth request.

As shown in this chapter and the case studies in Chapters 8 and 9, dynamic bandwidth reservation, a network capability that enables preferential treatment for "preferred" traffic over "nonpreferred" traffic, is an essential GTQO capability for a converged MPLS-based network. Two case studies in Chapter 8 illustrate the essential need for bandwidth reservation methods to guard against excessive alternate routing.

We again use the full-scale national network model developed in Chapter 2 to study various TQO scenarios and trade-offs. As discussed in Chapter 2, the overhead for each traffic flow is included in the model (e.g., packetized 64-Kbps voice with constant bit rate of 86.8 Kbps, which includes the G.711 voice payload, RTP/UDP/IP headers, PPP header, and MPLS labels). Also, an assumption in the model is that PSTN legacy services, such as 64-Kbps voice and ISDN services, are emulated when moved to an IP/MPLS network, which is consistent with the next generation network (NGN) requirement to have emulated PSTN services carried on the MPLS-based NGN architecture [CARUGI05]. We reiterate that there is no BellHead Telephonia plot to replicate the PSTN using MPLS-based TQO methods, rather the intent is to emphasize a realistic migration to an IP/MPLS-converged network technology.

The conclusions reached in this chapter are that (a) class-of-service routing is an important capability of converged TQO networks to define table-driven service elements and component application/network capabilities to avoid software development, network element development, and new network implementation for new service deployment, (b) bandwidth reservation is critical to the stable and efficient performance of TQO methods in a network and to ensure the proper operation of multiservice bandwidth allocation, protection, and priority treatment, (c) per-VNET bandwidth allocation is essentially equivalent to per-flow bandwidth allocation in network performance and efficiency, with much lower routing table management overhead requirements compared to per-flow allocation, (d) QoS resource management is shown to be effective in achieving key-service, normal-service, and best-effort service differentiation, and (e) both MPLS QoS and bandwidth management and DiffServ priority queuing management are important for ensuring that multiservice network performance objectives are met under a range of network conditions.

We now illustrate the principles of QoS resource management, identify many alternative approaches to QoS resource management, and finally analyze the trade-offs in the various approaches.

3.2 Class-of-Service Routing

QoS resource management functions include class-of-service routing, routing table derivation, connection admission, bandwidth allocation, bandwidth protection, bandwidth reservation, priority routing, and priority queuing. In this section we discuss class-of-service identification and routing table derivation.

Class-of-service routing provides a means to define network services through table-driven concepts rather than software development and new network deployment. In the class-of-service routing model, tables are installed in network elements, such as edge routers, and updated through provisioning of the tables through automated management systems. The historical model of new service development always led to the latter, i.e., specialized software had to be developed to implement the service and network features particular to the service usually required a new network to be built with new network elements and capabilities being required. This process was slow and expensive and led to a proliferation of networks—"stovepipes" as they are sometimes called.

Class-of-service routing is the antithesis of the historical stovepipe approach and is fully consistent with converged network evolution and deployment. Class-of-service routing defines elements of a service in terms of application and network capabilities, which can then be specified and provisioned in tables within the network nodes. That is, definition of new services capabilities are table driven and require no software development or network element development. An illustration of table-driven class-of-service routing capabilities is given in the following sections. Such capabilities have been in operation in AT&T's network for about 15 years, with great success. New services have been defined along the way, including 800 Gold Service, International Priority Routing, Emergency Services Priority Routing, and others. Class-of-service routing should be an important element of future converged TQO network capabilities.

3.2.1 Class-of-Service Identification

QoS routing and resource management entails first identifying the required class of service (or QoS class) and determining the class-of-service parameters, which may include, for example, service identity (SI), virtual network (VNET), link capability (LC), and QoS and traffic threshold parameters.

The SI describes the actual service associated with the connection. The VNET describes the bandwidth allocation and routing table parameters to be used by the connection. The LC describes the link hardware capabilities, such as fiber, radio, satellite, and digital circuit multiplexing equipment (DCME), that the connection should require, prefer, or avoid. The combination of SI, VNET, and LC constitutes the class of service, which together with the network node number is used to access routing table data.

In addition to controlling bandwidth allocation, the QoS resource management procedures can check end-to-end transfer delay, delay variation, and transmission quality considerations such as loss, echo, and noise.

Determination of class of service begins with translation at the originating node. The number or name is translated to determine the routing address of the destination node. If multiple ingress/egress routing is used, multiple destination node addresses are derived for the connection. Other data derived from connection information, such as link characteristics, Q.931 message information elements, and service control point routing information, are used to derive the class of service for the connection.

3.2.2 Routing Table Derivation

Class of service is identified at the network edge, and it is important that the identification be uniform at all edge points throughout the network in order to avoid inconsistent treatment within the network. Inconsistent treatment, for example, could lead to some services hogging bandwidth to the detriment of other services in the network. Class-of-service parameters are derived through application of policy-based routing. Policy-based routing involves the application of rules applied to input parameters to derive a routing table and its associated parameters. Input parameters for applying policy-based rules to derive SI, VNET, and LC could include numbering plan, type of origination/destination network, and type of service. Policy-based routing rules may then be applied to the derived SI, VNET, and LC to derive the routing table and associated parameters.

Hence policy-based routing rules are used in SI derivation, which, for example, uses the type of origin, type of destination, signaling service type, and dialed number/name service type to derive the SI. The type of origin can be derived normally from the type of incoming link to the connected network domain, connecting to a directly connected (also known as nodal) customer equipment location, an access node within a local exchange carrier domain, or an international carrier location. Similarly, based on the dialed numbering plan, the type of destination network is derived and can be a directly connected customer location if a private numbering plan is used (e.g., within a VPN), a domestic access node within a local exchange carrier domain location if a domestic E.164 number is used to the destination, or an international access node location if the international E.164 numbering plan is used. Signaling service type is derived based on bearer capability within signaling messages, information digits in dialed digit codes, numbering plan, or other signaling information and can indicate constant-bit-rate voice service (CVS), virtual private network (VPN) service, ISDN switched digital service (SDS), and other service types. Finally, dialed number service type is derived based on special dialed number codes such as 800 numbers or 900 numbers and can indicate 800 (FreePhone) service, 900 (mass announcement) service, and other service types. Type of origin, type of destination, signaling service type, and dialed number service type are then all used to derive the SI.

The following examples use policy-based routing rules to derive class-of-service parameters. A CVS SI, for example, is derived from the following information:

- The type of origination network is a domestic access node within a local exchange carrier domain because the connection originates from a domestic local exchange carrier node.
- The type of destination network is a domestic access node within a local exchange carrier domain, based on the domestic E.164 dialed number.
- The signaling service type is long-distance service, based on the numbering plan (domestic E.164).
- The dialed number service type is not used to distinguish the CVS SI.

An 800 (FreePhone) service SI, for example, is derived from similar information, except that the dialed number service type is based on the 800 dialed "FreePhone" number to distinguish the 800 service SI.

A VPN service SI, for example, is derived from similar information, except that the signaling service type is based on the originating customer having access to VPN-based services to derive the VPN service SI.

A service identity mapping table uses the four inputs listed above to derive the service identity. This policy-based routing table is changeable by administrative updates, in which new service information can be defined without software modifications to the node processing. From the SI and bearer service capability the SI/bearer-service-to-virtual network mapping table is used to derive the VNET.

Table 2.1a in Chapter 2 illustrates the VNET mapping table. Here the SIs are mapped to individual virtual networks. Routing parameters for priority or key services are discussed further later in this section.

Link capability selection allows connections to be routed on links that have the particular characteristics required by these connections. A connection can require, prefer, or avoid a set of link characteristics such as fiber transmission, radio transmission, satellite transmission, or compressed voice transmission. LC requirements for the connection can be determined by the SI of the connection or by other information derived from the signaling message or from the routing number. Routing logic allows the connection to skip those links that have undesired characteristics and to seek a best match for the requirements of the connection. For any SI, a set of LC selection preferences is specified for the connection request. LC selection preferences can override the normal order of selection of paths. If an LC characteristic is required, then any path with a link that does not have that characteristic is skipped. If a characteristic is preferred, paths having all links with that characteristic are used first. Paths having links without the preferred characteristic will be used next. An LC preference is set for the presence or absence of a characteristic. For example, if fiber-optic transmission is required, then only paths with links having *Fiberoptic = Yes* are used. If we prefer the presence of fiber-optic transmission, then paths having all links with *Fiberoptic = Yes* are used first, followed by paths having some links with *Fiberoptic = No*.

3.2.3 Class-of-Service Routing Steps

The class-of-service routing method consists of the following steps:

- At the ON, the destination node (DN), SI, VNET, and QoS resource management parameters are determined through the number/name translation database and other service information available at the ON.
- The DN and QoS resource management parameters are used to access the appropriate VNET and routing table between the ON and the DN.
- The connection request is set up over the first available path in the routing table with the required transmission resource selected based on QoS resource management data.

In the first step, the ON translates the dialed digits to determine the address of the DN. If multiple ingress/egress routing is used, multiple destination node addresses are derived for the connection request. Other data derived from connection request information include link characteristics, Q.931 message information elements, information interchange (II) digits, and service control point (SCP) routing information and are used to derive the QoS resource management parameters (SI, VNET, LC, and QoS/traffic thresholds). Each connection request is classified by its SI. A connection request for an individual service is allocated an equivalent bandwidth equal to EQBW and routed on a particular VNET. For CBR services the equivalent bandwidth EQBW is equal to the average or sustained bit rate. For VBR services the equivalent bandwidth EQBW is a function of the sustained bit rate, peak bit rate, and perhaps other parameters. For example, EQBW equals 86.8 Kbps of bandwidth for CBR voice service (CVS) connections, which includes the G.711 voice payload, RTP/UDP/IP headers, PPP header, and MPLS labels.

In the second step, the SI value is used to derive the VNET. In the multiservice, QoS resource management network, bandwidth is allocated to individual VNETs, which is protected as needed but otherwise shared. Under normal nontraffic-lost/delayed network conditions, all services fully share all available bandwidth. When traffic loss/delay occurs for VNET i, bandwidth reservation acts to prohibit alternate-routed traffic and traffic from other VNETs from seizing the allocated capacity for VNET i. Associated with each VNET are average bandwidth (*BWavg*) and maximum bandwidth (*BWmax*) parameters to govern bandwidth allocation and protection, which are discussed further in the next section. As discussed, LC selection allows connection requests to be routed on specific transmission links that have the particular characteristics required by a connection request.

In the third step, the VNET routing table determines which network capacity is allowed to be selected for each connection request. In using the VNET routing table to select network capacity, the ON selects a first choice path based on the routing table selection rules. Whether or not bandwidth can be allocated to the connection request on the first choice path is determined by the QoS resource management rules given later in this section. If a first-choice path cannot be accessed, the ON may then try alternate paths determined by FXR, TDR, SDR, or EDR path selection rules described in Chapter 2. Whether or not bandwidth can be allocated to the connection request on the alternate path again is determined by the QoS resource management rules now described.

3.3 Dynamic Bandwidth Allocation, Protection, and Reservation Principles

As mentioned earlier, QoS resource management functions include class-of-service identification, routing table derivation, connection admission, bandwidth allocation, bandwidth protection, bandwidth reservation, priority routing, and priority queuing. In this section we discuss connection admission, bandwidth allocation, bandwidth protection, and bandwidth reservation. Note that other QoS routing constraints are taken into account in the QoS resource management and route selection methods, including end-to-end transfer delay, delay variation, and transmission quality considerations such as loss, echo, and noise [Y.1541].

This section specifies the resource allocation controls and priority mechanisms, and the information needed to support them. In the illustrative QoS resource management method, the connection/bandwidth-allocation admission control for each link in the path is performed based on the status of the link. The ON may select any path for which the first link is allowed according to QoS resource management criteria. If a subsequent link is not allowed, then a release with crankback (bandwidth not available) is used to return to the ON and select an alternate path. This use of EDR path selection, which entails the use of the release with crankback/bandwidth-not-available mechanism to search for an available path, is an alternative to SDR path selection, which may entail flooding of frequently changing link state parameters, such as available bandwidth. The trade-offs between EDR with crankback and SDR with link-state flooding are discussed further in Chapter 6. In particular, when EDR path selection with crankback is used in lieu of SDR path selection with link-state flooding, the reduction in the frequency of such link-state parameter flooding allows for larger domain (area, peer group, etc.) sizes. This is because link-state flooding can consume substantial processor and link resources in terms of message processing by the processors and link bandwidth consumed by messages on the links.

Two cases of QoS resource management are considered in this chapter: per-virtual-network (per-VNET) management and per-flow management. In the per-VNET method, such as for IP-based MPLS networks, aggregated LSP bandwidth is managed to meet the overall bandwidth requirements of VNET service needs. Individual flows are allocated bandwidth within the CRLSPs accordingly, as CRLSP bandwidth is available. In the per-flow method, bandwidth is allocated to each individual flow, such as in SVC setup in an ATM-based network, from the overall pool of bandwidth, as the total pool bandwidth is available. A fundamental principle applied in these bandwidth allocation methods is the use of bandwidth reservation techniques. We first review bandwidth reservation principles and then discuss per-VNET and per-flow QoS resource allocations.

Bandwidth reservation (called "trunk reservation" in TDM network terminology) gives preference to the preferred traffic by allowing it to seize any idle bandwidth in a link, while allowing nonpreferred traffic to only seize bandwidth if there is a minimum level of idle bandwidth available, where the minimum bandwidth threshold is called the reservation level. P. J. Burke [BURKE61] first analyzed bandwidth reservation behavior from the solution of the birth–death equations for the bandwidth reservation model. Burke's model showed the relative lost-traffic level for preferred traffic, which is not subject to bandwidth reservation restrictions, as compared to nonpreferred traffic, which is subject to the restrictions. Figure 3.6 illustrates the percentage lost traffic of preferred and nonpreferred traffic on a typical link with 10% traffic overload. It is seen that the preferred lost traffic is near zero, whereas the nonpreferred lost traffic is much higher; this situation is maintained across a wide variation in the percentage of the preferred traffic load. Hence, bandwidth reservation protection is robust to traffic variations and provides significant dynamic protection of particular streams of traffic.

Bandwidth reservation is a crucial technique used in nonhierarchical networks to prevent "instability," which can severely reduce throughput in periods of congestion, perhaps by as much as 50% of the traffic-carrying capacity of a network [E.525]. The phenomenon of instability has an interesting mathematical solution to network flow equations, which has been presented in several studies [NAKAGOME73, KRUPP82, AKINPELU84]. These studies have shown that nonhierarchical networks exhibit two stable states, or bistability, under congestion and that networks can transition between

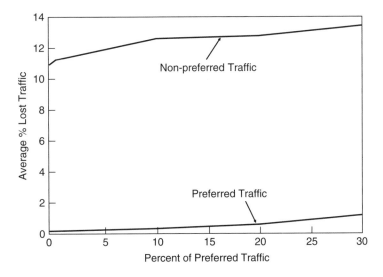

Figure 3.6 Dynamic bandwidth reservation performance under 10% overload.

these stable states in a network congestion condition that has been demonstrated in simulation studies. A simple explanation of how this bistable phenomenon arises is that under congestion, a network is often not able to complete a connection request on the primary shortest path, which consists in this example of a single link. If alternate routing is allowed, such as on longer, multiple-link paths, which are assumed in this example to consist of two links, then the connection request might be completed on a two-link path selected from among a large number of two-link path choices, only one of which needs sufficient idle bandwidth on both links to be used to route the connection. Because this two-link connection now occupies resources that could perhaps otherwise be used to complete two one-link connections, this is a less efficient use of network resources under congestion. In the event that a large fraction of all connections cannot complete on the direct link but instead occupy two-link paths, the total network throughput capacity is reduced by one-half because most connections take twice the resources needed. This is one stable state; i.e., most or all connections use two links. The other stable state is that most or all connections use one link, which is the desired condition.

Bandwidth reservation is used to prevent this unstable behavior by having the preferred traffic on a link be the direct traffic on the primary, shortest path, and the nonpreferred traffic, subjected to bandwidth reservation restrictions as described above, be the alternate-routed traffic on longer paths. In this way the alternate-routed traffic is inhibited from selecting longer alternate paths when sufficient idle trunk capacity is not available on all links of an alternate-routed connection, which is the likely condition under network and link congestion. Mathematically, studies of bistable network behavior have shown that bandwidth reservation used in this manner to favor primary shortest connections eliminates the bistability problem in nonhierarchical networks and allows such networks to maintain efficient utilization under congestion by favoring connections completed on the shortest path. For this reason, dynamic bandwidth reservation is applied universally in nonhierarchical TDM-based networks [E.529], and often in hierarchical networks [MUMMERT76]. As shown in this chapter and the case studies in Chapters 8 and 9, bandwidth reservation is an essential capability for a converged MPLS-based network.

Two case studies in Chapter 8 illustrate the possible pitfalls of excessive alternate routing and need for bandwidth reservation methods to guard against excessive alternate routing. One case involved a software problem that crippled the AT&T long-distance network on January 15, 1990, and a second that involved a new routing capability to avoid a voice enhancement capability in the network. These case studies are intended to illustrate possible pitfalls of excessive alternate routing and need for bandwidth reservation methods to guard against excessive alternate routing. In both cases cited, proper use of bandwidth reservation may well have helped alleviate the problems that occurred. As such, these case studies support the TQO protocol design principle that bandwidth reservation is critical to ensuring efficient and stable network performance.

There are differences in how and when bandwidth reservation is applied, however, such as whether the bandwidth reservation for connections routed on the primary path is in place at all times or whether it is dynamically triggered to be used only under network or link congestion. This is a complex network throughput trade-off issue because bandwidth reservation can lead to some loss in throughput under normal, low-congestion conditions. This loss in throughput arises when bandwidth is reserved for connections on the primary path, but these connection requests do not arrive and then the capacity is needlessly reserved when it might be used to complete other traffic, such as alternate-routed traffic that might otherwise be lost. However, under network congestion, the use of bandwidth reservation is critical to preventing network instability, as explained above [E.525].

It is beneficial for bandwidth reservation techniques to be included in IP-based and ATM-based routing methods in order to ensure the efficient use of network resources, especially under congestion conditions. Path selection methods such as optimized multipath for traffic engineering in IP-based MPLS networks [VILLAMIZAR99] or path selection in ATM-based PNNI networks [ATMFORUM-0055.002] give no guidance on the necessity for using bandwidth-reservation techniques. Such guidance is essential for acceptable network performance.

Alternative approaches are given for dynamically triggered bandwidth reservation techniques, where bandwidth reservation is triggered only under network congestion. Such methods are shown to be effective in striking a balance between protecting network resources under congestion and ensuring that resources are available for sharing when conditions permit. Section 3.6.1 illustrates the phenomenon of network instability through simulation studies, and the effectiveness of bandwidth reservation in eliminating the instability is demonstrated. Bandwidth reservation is also shown to be an effective technique to share bandwidth capacity among services on a primary path, where the reservation in this case is invoked to prefer link capacity on the primary path for one particular class of service as opposed to another class of service when network and link congestion are encountered. These two aspects of bandwidth reservation, i.e., for avoiding instability and for sharing bandwidth capacity among services, are illustrated further in the network modeling analysis in Section 3.6.

3.3.1 Per-VNET Bandwidth Allocation, Protection, and Reservation

Through the use of bandwidth allocation, reservation, and congestion control techniques, QoS resource management can provide good network performance under normal and abnormal operating conditions for all services sharing the integrated network. Such methods have been implemented and analyzed in practice for TDM-based networks [ASH98] and analyzed in detailed modeling studies for IP/MPLS-based networks in this chapter and have been the focus of several case studies presented in Chapters 8 and 9.

The per-VNET bandwidth allocation approach to QoS resource management is illustrated in Figure 3.7, where bandwidth is allocated to the individual VNETs (high-priority key services VNETs, normal-priority services VNETs, and best-effort low-priority services VNETs). This allocated bandwidth is protected by bandwidth

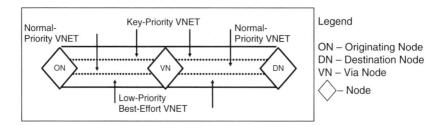

- ❏ distributed method applied on a per-virtual-network (per-VNET) basis
- ❏ ON allocates delta-bandwidth (DBW) to each VNET based on demand for VNET bandwidth increase
  - ❖ ON decides link-bandwidth-modification DEPTH threshold (D_i) based on
    - – bandwidth-in-progress (BWIP)
    - – routing priority (key, normal, best-effort)
    - – bandwidth allocation BWavg
    - – first/alternate choice path
  - ❖ ON launches a CRLSP bandwidth-modification message with explicit route, modify-flag, traffic parameters, & threshold D_i
- ❏ VNs keep local link state of idle link bandwidth (ILBW), including lightly loaded (LL), heavily loaded (HL), reserved (R), & busy (B)
- ❏ VNs compare link state to D_i threshold
- ❏ VNs send crankback/bandwidth-not-available message to ON if D_i threshold not met

Figure 3.7 Per-VNET bandwidth management.

reservation methods, as needed, but otherwise shared. Each ON monitors VNET bandwidth use on each VNET CRLSP and determines when the VNET CRLSP bandwidth needs to be increased or decreased. Bandwidth changes in VNET bandwidth capacity are determined by ONs based on an overall aggregated bandwidth demand for VNET capacity (not on a per-connection demand basis). Based on the aggregated bandwidth demand, these ONs make periodic discrete changes in bandwidth allocation, i.e., either increase or decrease bandwidth on the CRLSPs constituting the VNET bandwidth capacity. For example, if connection requests are made for VNET CRLSP bandwidth that exceeds the current CRLSP bandwidth allocation, the ON initiates a bandwidth modification request on the appropriate CRLSP(s). For example, this bandwidth modification request may entail increasing the current CRLSP bandwidth allocation by a discrete increment of bandwidth denoted here as delta-bandwidth (DBW). DBW is a large enough bandwidth change so that modification requests are made relatively infrequently. Also, the ON periodically monitors CRLSP bandwidth use, such as once each minute, and if bandwidth use falls below the current CRLSP allocation, the ON initiates a bandwidth modification request to decrease the CRLSP bandwidth allocation by a unit of bandwidth such as DBW.

In making a VNET bandwidth allocation modification, the ON determines the QoS resource management parameters, including the VNET priority (key, normal, or best-effort), VNET bandwidth in use, VNET bandwidth allocation thresholds, and whether the CRLSP is a first-choice CRLSP or alternate CRLSP. These parameters are used to access a VNET depth-of-search table to determine a DEPTH load state threshold (Di), or the "depth" to which network capacity can be allocated for the VNET bandwidth modification request. In using the DEPTH threshold to allocate VNET bandwidth capacity, the ON selects a first-choice CRLSP based on the routing table selection rules.

Path selection in this IP network illustration may use open shortest path first (OSPF) for intranetwork routing. In OSPF-based layer 3 routing, as illustrated in Figure 3.8, ON A determines a list of shortest paths by using, for example, Dijkstra's algorithm.

This path list could be determined based on administrative weights of each link, which are communicated to all nodes within the autonomous system (AS) domain. These administrative weights may be set, for example, to $[1 + \varepsilon \times \text{distance}]$, where ε is a factor giving a relatively smaller weight to the distance in comparison to the hop count. The ON selects a path from the list based on, for example, FXR, TDR, SDR, or EDR path selection, as discussed in Chapter 2.

For example, in using the first CRLSP A–B–E in Figure 3.8, ON A sends an MPLS label request message to VN B, which in turn forwards the label request message to DN E. VN B and DN E are passed in the explicit routing (ER) parameter contained in the label request message. Each node in the CRLSP reads the ER information and passes the label request message to the next node listed in the ER parameter. If the first path is congested at any of the links in the path, an MPLS notification message with a crankback parameter is returned to ON A, which can then attempt the next path. If FXR is used, then this path is the next path in the shortest path list, for example, path A–C–D–E. If TDR is used, then the next path is the next path in the routing table for the current time period. If SDR is used, OSPF implements a distributed method of flooding

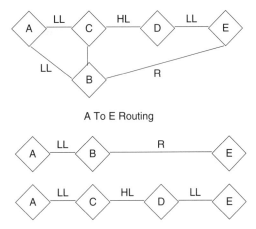

Figure 3.8 Label switched path selection for bandwidth modification request.

link status information, which is triggered either periodically and/or by crossing load state threshold values. This method of distributing link status information can be resource intensive and may not be any more efficient than simpler path selection methods such as EDR. If EDR is used, then the next path is the last successful path, and if that path is unsuccessful another alternate path is searched out according to the EDR path selection method.

Hence in using the selected CRLSP, the ON sends the explicit route, the requested traffic parameters (peak data rate, committed data rate, etc.), a DEPTH parameter, and a modify parameter in the MPLS setup message IE to each VN and the DN in the selected CRLSP. Whether or not bandwidth can be allocated to the bandwidth modification request on the first choice CRLSP is determined by each VN applying the QoS resource management rules. These rules entail that the VN determine the CRLSP link states, based on bandwidth use and bandwidth available, and compare the link load state to the DEPTH threshold Di sent in the MPLS signaling parameters, as explained further later in this section. If the first-choice CRLSP cannot admit the bandwidth change, a VN or DN returns control to the ON through the use of the crankback parameter in the MPLS release message IE. At that point the ON may then try an alternate CRLSP. Whether or not bandwidth can be allocated to the bandwidth modification request on the alternate path again is determined by the use of the DEPTH threshold compared to the CRLSP link load state at each VN. Priority queuing is used during the time the CRLSP is established, and at each link the queuing discipline is maintained such that the packets are given priority according to the VNET traffic priority.

Hence determination of the CRLSP link load states is necessary for QoS resource management to select network capacity on either the first-choice CRLSP or alternate CRLSPs. Four link load states are distinguished: lightly loaded (LL), heavily loaded (HL), reserved (R), and busy (B). Management of CRLSP capacity uses the link state model and the DEPTH model to determine if a bandwidth modification request can be accepted on a given CRLSP. The allowed DEPTH load state threshold Di determines if a bandwidth modification request can be accepted on a given link to an available bandwidth "depth." In setting up the bandwidth modification request, the ON encodes the DEPTH load state threshold allowed on each link in the DEPTH parameter Di, which is carried in the MPLS setup message IE. If a CRLSP link is encountered at a VN in which the idle link bandwidth and link load state are below the allowed DEPTH load state threshold Di, then the VN sends an MPLS release message IE with the crankback parameter to the ON, which can then route the bandwidth modification request to an alternate CRLSP choice. For example, in Figure 3.8, CRLSP A–B–E may be the first path tried where link A–B is in the LL state and link B–E is in the R state. If the DEPTH load state allowed is $Di = HL$ or better, then the CRLSP bandwidth modification request in the MPLS setup message IE is routed on link A–B but will not be admitted on link B–E, wherein the CRLSP bandwidth modification request will be cranked back in the MPLS release message IE to the originating node A to try alternate CRLSP A–C–D–E. Here the CRLSP bandwidth modification request succeeds, as all links have a state of HL or better.

3.3.1.1 Per-VNET Bandwidth Allocation/Reservation: Meshed Network Case

For purposes of bandwidth allocation reservation, two approaches are illustrated: one applicable to meshed network topologies and the other to sparse topologies. In meshed networks, a greater number of logical links result in less traffic carried per link, and functions such as bandwidth reservation need to be controlled more carefully than in a sparse network. In a sparse network the traffic is concentrated on much larger, and many fewer, logical links, and here bandwidth reservation does not have to be managed as carefully. Hence in the meshed network case, functions such as automatically triggering of bandwidth reservation on and off, dependent on the link/network congestion level, are beneficial to use. In the sparse network case, however, the complexity of such automatic triggering is not essential and bandwidth reservation may be permanently enabled without performance degradation.

This section discusses a meshed network alternative approach for bandwidth allocation/reservation and the following section discusses the sparse network case.

The DEPTH load state threshold is a function of bandwidth-in-progress, VNET priority, and bandwidth allocation thresholds, as shown in Table 3.1.

Note that BWIP, BWavg, and BWmax are specified per ON–DN pair and that the QoS resource management method provides for a key-priority VNET, a normal-priority VNET, and a best-effort VNET. Key services admitted by an ON on the key VNET are given higher priority routing treatment by allowing greater path selection DEPTH than normal services admitted on the normal VNET. Best-effort services admitted on the best-effort VNET are given lower priority routing treatment by allowing lesser path selection DEPTH than normal. The quantities $BWavg_i$ are computed periodically, such

Table 3.1 Determination of Depth-of-Search (DEPTH) Load State Threshold (Per-VNET Bandwidth Allocation, Meshed Network)

Load state allowed$_i$	Key-priority VNET	Normal-priority VNET		Best-effort priority VNET
		First-choice CRLSP	Alternate CRLSP	
R	If $BWIP_i \leq 2 \times BWmax_i$	If $BWIP_i \leq BWavg_i$	Not Allowed	Note 1
HL	If $BWIP_i \leq 2 \times BWmax_i$	If $BWIP_i \leq BWmax_i$	If $BWIP_i \leq BWavg_i$	Note 1
LL	All $BWIP_i$	All $BWIP_i$	All $BWIP_i$	Note 1

where
$BWIP_i$ = bandwidth in progress on VNET i
$BWavg_i$ = minimum guaranteed bandwidth required for VNET i to carry the average offered bandwidth load
$BWmax_i$ = the bandwidth required for VNET i to meet the traffic lost/delayed probability grade-of-service objective for CRLSP bandwidth allocation requests $= 1.1 \times BWavg_i$
Note 1 = CRLSPs for the best-effort priority VNET are allocated zero bandwidth; DiffServ queuing admits best-effort packets only if there is available bandwidth on a link.

as every week, w, and can be averaged exponentially over a several-week period, as follows:

$$BWavg_i(\text{w}) = .5 \times BWavg_i(\text{w-1}) + .5 \times [BWIPavg_i(\text{w}) + BWOVavg_i(\text{w})]$$

$BWIPavg_i$ = average bandwidth in progress across a load set period on VNET i

$BWOVavg_i$ = average bandwidth allocation request rejected (or overflow) across a load set period on VNET i

where all variables are specified per ON–DN pair and where $BWIP_i$ and $BWOV_i$ are averaged across various load set periods, such as morning, afternoon, and evening averages for weekday, Saturday, and Sunday, to obtain $BWIPavg_i$ and $BWOVavg_i$.

QoS resource management implements bandwidth reservation logic to favor connections routed on the first-choice CRLSP in situations of link congestion. If link congestion (or traffic lost/delayed) is detected, bandwidth reservation is immediately triggered and the reservation level N is set for the link according to the level of link congestion. In this manner bandwidth allocation requests attempting to alternate route over a congested link are subject to bandwidth reservation, and first-choice CRLSP requests are favored for that link. At the same time, the LL and HL link state thresholds are raised accordingly in order to accommodate the reserved bandwidth capacity N for the VNET. Figure 3.9 illustrates bandwidth allocation and the mechanisms by which bandwidth is protected through bandwidth reservation. Under normal bandwidth allocation demands, bandwidth is fully shared, but under overloaded bandwidth allocation demands, bandwidth is protected through the reservation mechanisms wherein each VNET can use its allocated bandwidth. Under failure, however, the reservation

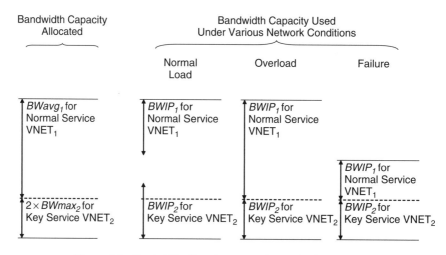

Figure 3.9 Bandwidth allocation, protection, and priority routing.

mechanisms operate to give the key VNET its allocated bandwidth before the normal-priority VNET gets its bandwidth allocation. As noted in Table 3.1, the best-effort, low-priority VNET is not allocated bandwidth nor is bandwidth reserved for the best-effort VNET. Further illustrations are given in Section 3.6 of the robustness of dynamic bandwidth reservation in protecting the preferred bandwidth requests across wide variations in traffic conditions.

The reservation level N (e.g., N may have one of four levels) is calculated for each link k based on the link traffic lost/delayed level of bandwidth allocation requests. The link traffic lost/delayed level is equal to the total requested but rejected (or overflow) link bandwidth allocation (measured in total bandwidth), divided by the total requested link bandwidth allocation, over the last periodic update interval, which is, for example, every 3 min. That is,

$BWOV_k =$ total requested bandwidth allocation rejected (or overflow) on link

$BWOF_k =$ total requested or offered bandwidth allocation on link k

$LLDL_k =$ link traffic lost/delayed level on link k

$\qquad = BWOV_k/BWOF_k$

If $LLDL_k$ exceeds a threshold value, the reservation level N is calculated accordingly. The reserved bandwidth and link states are calculated based on the total link bandwidth required on link k, $TRBW_k$, which is computed on-line, for example, every 1-min interval m, and approximated as follows:

$$TRBW_k(\mathrm{m}) = .5 \times TRBW_k(\mathrm{m}-1) + .5 \times [1.1 \times TBWIP_k(\mathrm{m}) + TBWOV_k(\mathrm{m})]$$

$TBWIP_k =$ sum of the bandwidth in progress ($BWIP_i$) for all VNETs i for bandwidth requests on their first-choice CRLSP over link k

$TBWOV_k =$ sum of bandwidth overflow ($BWOV_i$) for all VNETs i for bandwidth requests on their first choice CRLSP over link k

Therefore the reservation level and load state boundary thresholds are proportional to the estimated required bandwidth load, which means that the bandwidth reserved and the bandwidth required to constitute a lightly loaded link rise and fall with the bandwidth load, as, intuitively, they should.

3.3.1.2 *Per-VNET Bandwidth Allocation/Reservation: Sparse Network Case*

Here we discuss a sparse network alternative approach for bandwidth allocation/reservation. For the sparse network case of bandwidth reservation, a simpler method is illustrated that takes advantage of the concentration of traffic onto fewer, higher capacity backbone links. A small, fixed level of bandwidth reservation is used and permanently enabled on each link.

The DEPTH load state threshold again is a function of bandwidth-in-progress, VNET priority, and bandwidth allocation thresholds; however, only the reserved (R) and nonreserved (NR) states are used, as shown in Table 3.2.

The corresponding load state table for the sparse network case is shown in Table 3.3. Note that the reservation level is fixed and not dependent on any link lost/delayed level (*LLDL*) calculation or total required bandwidth (*TRBW*) calculation. Therefore *LLDL* and *TRBW* monitoring are not required in this candidate bandwidth allocation/protection method.

Table 3.2 Determination of Depth-of-Search (DEPTH) Load State Threshold (Per-VNET Bandwidth Allocation, Sparse Network)

Load state allowed$_i$	Key-priority VNET	Normal-priority VNET		Best-effort priority VNET
		First-choice CRLSP	Alternate CRLSP	
R	If $BWIP_i \leq 2 \times BWmax_i$	If $BWIP_i \leq BWavg_i$	Not allowed	Note 1
NR	If $2 \times BWmax_i < BWIP_i$	If $BWavg_i < BWIP_i$	If $BWavg_i < BWIP_i$	Note 1

where
$BWIP_i$ = bandwidth in progress on VNET i
$BWavg_i$ = minimum guaranteed bandwidth required for VNET i to carry the average offered bandwidth load
$BWmax_i$ = the bandwidth required for VNET i to meet the traffic lost/delayed probability grade-of-service objective for CRLSP bandwidth allocation requests $= 1.1 \times BWavg_i$
Note 1 = CRLSPs for the best effort priority VNET are allocated zero bandwidth; DiffServ queuing admits best-effort packets only if there is available bandwidth on a link.

Table 3.3 Determination of Link Load State (Sparse Network)

Link load state		Condition
Busy	B	$ILBW_k < DBW$
Reserved	R	$ILBW_k - RBWr_k < DBW$
Not reserved	NR	$DBW \leq ILBW_k - RBWr_k$

$ILBW_k$ = idle link bandwidth on link k
DBW = delta bandwidth requirement for a bandwidth allocation request
$RBWr_k$ = reserved bandwidth for link k $= .01 \times TLBW_k$
$TLBW_k$ = the total link bandwidth on link k

3.3.2 Per-Flow Bandwidth Allocation, Protection, and Reservation

Per-flow QoS resource management methods have been applied successfully in TDM-based networks, where bandwidth allocation is determined by edge nodes based on bandwidth demand for each connection request. Based on the bandwidth demand, these edge nodes make changes in bandwidth allocation using, for example, a per-flow CRLSP QoS resource management approach illustrated in this section. Again, the determination of the link load states is used for QoS resource management in order to select network capacity on either the first-choice path or alternate paths. Also the allowed DEPTH load state threshold determines if an individual connection request can be admitted on a given link to an available bandwidth "depth." In setting up each connection request, the ON encodes the DEPTH load state threshold allowed on each link in the connection-setup IE. If a link is encountered at a VN in which the idle link bandwidth and link load state are below the allowed DEPTH load state threshold, then the VN sends a crankback/bandwidth-not-available IE to the ON, which can then route the connection request to an alternate path choice. For example, in Figure 3.8, path A–B–E may be the first path tried where link A–B is in the LL state and link B–E is in the R state. If the DEPTH load state allowed is HL or better, then the connection request is routed on link A–B but will not be admitted on link B–E, wherein the connection request will be cranked back to the originating node A to try alternate path A–C–D–E. Here the connection request succeeds, as all links have a state of HL or better.

3.3.2.1 Per-Flow Bandwidth Allocation/Reservation: Meshed Network Case

Here again, two approaches are illustrated for bandwidth allocation reservation: one applicable to meshed network topologies and the other to sparse topologies. In meshed networks, a greater number of links result in less traffic carried per link, and functions such as bandwidth reservation need to be controlled more carefully than in a sparse network. In a sparse network the traffic is concentrated on much larger and many fewer links, and here bandwidth reservation does not have to be managed as carefully (such as automatically triggering bandwidth reservation on and off, dependent on the link/network congestion level).

This section discusses a meshed network alternative approach for bandwidth allocation/reservation, followed by the sparse network case.

The illustrative DEPTH load state threshold is a function of bandwidth-in-progress, service priority, and bandwidth allocation thresholds, as shown in Table 3.4. Note that all parameters are specified per ON–DN pair and that the QoS resource management method provides for key service and best-effort service. Key services are given higher priority routing treatment by allowing greater path selection DEPTH than normal services. Best-effort services are given lower priority routing treatment by allowing lesser

Table 3.4 Determination of Depth-of-Search (DEPTH) Load State Threshold (Per-Flow Bandwidth Allocation, Meshed Network)

Load state allowed$_i$	Key service	Normal service		Best-effort service
		First-choice path	Alternate path	
R	If $BWIP_i \leq 2 \times BWmax_i$	If $BWIP_i \leq BWavg_i$	Not allowed	Not allowed
HL	If $BWIP_i \leq 2 \times BWmax_i$	If $BWIP_i \leq BWmax_i$	If $BWIP_i \leq BWavg_i$	Not allowed
LL	All $BWIP_i$	All $BWIP_i$	All $BWIP_i$	All $BWIP_i$

$BWIP_i$ = bandwidth in progress on VNET i

$BWavg_i$ = minimum guaranteed bandwidth required for VNET i to carry the average offered bandwidth load

$BWmax_i$ = the bandwidth required for VNET i to meet the traffic lost/delayed probability grade-of-service objective

= $1.1 \times BWavg_i$

path selection DEPTH than normal. The quantities BWavg$_i$ are computed periodically, such as every week w, and can be averaged exponentially over a several-week period, as follows:

$$BWavg_i(\text{w}) = .5 \times BWavg_i(\text{w} - 1) + .5 \times [BWIPavg_i(\text{w}) + BWOVavg_i(\text{w})]$$

$BWIPavg_i$ = average bandwidth-in-progress across a load set period on VNET i

$BWOVavg_i$ = average bandwidth overflow across a load set period

where $BWIP_i$ and $BWOV_i$ are averaged across various load set periods, such as morning, afternoon, and evening averages for weekday, Saturday, and Sunday, to obtain $BWIPavg_i$ and $BWOVavg_i$. Illustrative values of the thresholds to determine link load states are given in Table 3.5.

The illustrative QoS resource management method implements bandwidth reservation logic to favor connections routed on the first-choice path in situations of link congestion. If link traffic lost/delayed is detected, bandwidth reservation is immediately triggered and the reservation level N is set for the link according to the level of link congestion. In this manner traffic attempting to alternate route over a congested link is subject to bandwidth reservation, and the first-choice path traffic is favored for that link. At the same time, the LL and HL link state thresholds are raised accordingly in order to accommodate the reserved bandwidth capacity for the VNET. The reservation level N (e.g., N may have one of four levels) is calculated for each link k based on the link traffic lost/delayed level and the estimated link traffic. The link traffic lost/delayed level is equal to the equivalent bandwidth overflow count divided

Table 3.5 Determination of Link Load State (Meshed Network)

Link load state		Condition
Busy	B	$ILBW_k < DBW$
Reserved	R	$ILBW_k \leq Rthr_k$
Heavily loaded	HL	$Rthr_k < ILBW_k \leq HLthr_k$
Lightly loaded	LL	$HLthr_k < ILBW_k$

$ILBW_k$ = idle link bandwidth on link k
DBW = delta bandwidth requirement for a bandwidth allocation request
$Rthr_k$ = reservation bandwidth threshold for link $k = N \times .05 \times TBW_k$ for bandwidth reservation level N
$HLthr_k$ = heavily loaded bandwidth threshold for link k $(Rthr_k + .05 \times TRBW_k)$
$TRBW_k$ = the total bandwidth required on link k to meet the traffic lost/delayed probability grade-of-service objective for bandwidth allocation requests on their first-choice CRLSP

by the equivalent bandwidth peg count over the last periodic update interval, which is typically 3 min. That is,

$$BWOV_k = \text{equivalent bandwidth overflow count on link k}$$

$$BWPC_k = \text{equivalent bandwidth peg count on link k}$$

$$LLDL_k = \text{link traffic lost/delayed level on link k}$$

$$= BWOV_k / BWPC_k$$

If $LLDL_k$ exceeds a threshold value, the reservation level N is calculated accordingly. The reserved bandwidth and link states are calculated based on the total link bandwidth required on link k, TBW_k, which is computed on-line, for example, every 1-min interval m, and approximated as follows:

$$TBW_k(m) = .5 \times TBW_k(m-1) + .5 \times [1.1 \times TBWIP_k(m) + TBWOV_k(m)]$$

$TBWIP_k$ = sum of the bandwidth in progress ($BWIP_i$) for all VNETs i for connections on their first-choice path over link k

$TBWOV_k$ = sum of bandwidth overflow ($BWOV_i$) for all VNETs i for connections on their first-choice path over link k

Therefore the reservation level and load state boundary thresholds are proportional to the estimated required bandwidth traffic load, which means that the bandwidth reserved and the bandwidth required to constitute a lightly loaded link rise and fall with the traffic load, as, intuitively, they should.

3.3.2.2 Per-Flow Bandwidth Allocation/Reservation: Sparse Network Case

Here we discuss a sparse network alternative approach for bandwidth allocation/reservation. For the sparse network case of bandwidth reservation, a simpler method is illustrated that takes advantage of the concentration of traffic onto fewer, higher capacity backbone links. A small, fixed level of bandwidth reservation is used on each link.

The DEPTH load state threshold again is a function of bandwidth-in-progress, VNET priority, and bandwidth allocation thresholds; however only the R and NR states are used, as shown in Table 3.6. The corresponding load state table for the sparse network case is shown in Table 3.7.

Note that reservation level is fixed and not dependent on any *LLDL* calculation or *TRBW* calculation. Therefore *LLDL* and *TRBW* monitoring is not required in this alternative approach to QoS resource management.

Table 3.6 Determination of Depth-of-Search (DEPTH) Load State Threshold (Per-Flow Bandwidth Allocation, Sparse Network)

Load state allowed$_i$	Key-priority VNET	Normal-priority VNET		Best-effort priority VNET
		First-choice path	Alternate path	
R	If $BWIP_i \leq 2 \times BWmax_i$	If $BWIP_i \leq BWavg_i$	Not allowed	Note 1
NR	If $2 \times BWmax_i < BWIP_i$	If $BWavg_i < BWIP_i$	If $BWavg_i < BWIP_i$	Note 1

$BWIP_i$ = bandwidth in progress on VNET i
$BWavg_i$ = minimum guaranteed bandwidth required for VNET i to carry the average offered bandwidth load
$BWmax_i$ = the bandwidth required for VNET i to meet the traffic lost/delayed probability grade-of-service objective
= $1.1 \times BWavg_i$
Note 1 = CRLSPs for the best-effort priority VNET are allocated zero bandwidth; DiffServ queuing admits best-effort packets only if there is available bandwidth on a link.

Table 3.7 Determination of Link Load State (Sparse Network)

Link load state		Condition
Busy	B	$ILBW_k < EQBW$
Reserved	R	$ILBW_k - RBWr_k < EQBW$
Not reserved	NR	$EQBW \leq ILBW_k - RBWr_k$

$ILBW_k$ = idle link bandwidth on link k
$EQBW$ = equivalent bandwidth requirement for a bandwidth allocation request
$RBWr_k$ = reserved bandwidth for link k = $.01 \times TLBW_k$
$TLBW$ = total link bandwidth on link k

3.4 **Queuing Mechanisms**

QoS resource management functions include class-of-service identification, routing table derivation, connection admission, bandwidth allocation, bandwidth protection, bandwidth reservation, priority routing, and priority queuing. This section discusses priority queuing as an illustrative traffic scheduling method and further assumes that a traffic shaper function is employed, such as a leaky-bucket model, to determine out-of-contract traffic behavior and appropriately mark packets for possible dropping under congestion. These scheduling and shaping mechanisms complement the connection admission mechanisms described in the previous sections to appropriately allocate bandwidth on links in the network.

Note that priority queuing is used as an illustrative scheduling mechanism, whereas other methods may be used. DiffServ does not require that a particular queuing mechanism be used to achieve EF, AF, etc. QoS. Therefore the queuing implementation used for DiffServ could be weighted fair queuing (WFQ), priority queuing (PQ), or another queuing mechanism, depending on the choice in the implementation. In the analysis, PQ is used for illustration; however, the same or comparable results would be obtained with WFQ or other queuing mechanisms.

See Appendix A for a review of queuing, scheduling, shaping, DiffServ, priority queuing, WFQ, and other QoS mechanisms.

In addition to the QoS bandwidth management procedure for bandwidth allocation requests, a QoS priority of service queuing capability is used during the time connections are established on each of the three VNETs. At each link, a queuing discipline is maintained such that the packets being served are given priority in the following order: key VNET services, normal VNET services, and best-effort VNET services. Following the MPLS CRLSP bandwidth allocation setup and the application of QoS resource management rules, the priority of service parameter and label parameter needs to be sent in each IP packet, as illustrated in Figure 3.10. The priority of service parameter may be included in the type of service (ToS), or differentiated services (DiffServ) [RFC2475], parameter already in the IP packet header. In the IP/MPLS case, the priority of service parameter is associated with the MPLS label appended to the IP

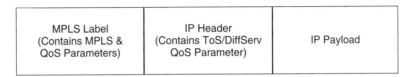

DiffServ-Differentiated Services
IP-Internet Protocol
MPLS-Multiprotocol Label Switching
QoS-Quality of Service
ToS-Type of Service

Figure 3.10 IP packet structure under MPLS packet switching.

packet [RFC3270], as described in Appendix A (see Figure A.1). In either case, from the priority of service parameters, the IP node can determine the QoS treatment based on the QoS resource management (priority queuing) rules for key VNET packets, normal VNET packets, and best effort VNET packets. In the IP/MPLS case, the MPLS label allows the IP/MPLS node to determine the next node to route the IP packet to, as well as the QoS treatment for the packet, which achieves a straightforward implementation of QoS resource management and MPLS routing.

3.5 Internetwork QoS Resource Management

In current practice, internetwork routing protocols in packet networks generally do not incorporate standardized path selection or per class-of-service QoS resource management. For example, in IP-based networks, BGP [RFC4271] is used for internetwork routing but does not incorporate per class-of-service resource allocation as described in this section. Also, MPLS techniques are still in progress for internetwork applications, such as path computation element (PCE) capability [PCE-ARCHITECTURE, PCE-REQUIREMENTS, PCE-PROTOCOL]. In the PCE architecture, path computation does not occur on the head-end (ingress) LSR, but on some other path computation entity that may not be physically located on the head-end LSR. The PCE capability supports applications within a single domain or within a group of domains, where a domain is a layer, IGP area, or AS with limited visibility from the head-end LSR. The protocol for communication between LSRs and PCEs, and between cooperating PCEs, will enable requests for path computation, including a full set of constraints and the ability to return multiple paths, as well as security, authentication, and confidentiality mechanisms. This includes both intradomain and interdomain TE LSPs, the generation of primary, protection, and recovery paths, as well as computations for (local/global) reoptimization and load balancing.

Extensions to internetwork routing methods discussed in this section therefore can be considered to extend the call/session routing and connection routing concepts to routing between networks. Internetwork routing can also apply class-of-service routing concepts described in Section 3.2 and increased routing flexibility for internetwork routing. Principles discussed in Section 3.2 for class-of-service derivation and policy-based routing table derivation also apply in the case of internetwork QoS resource management. As described in Chapter 2, internetwork routing works synergistically with multiple ingress/egress routing and alternate routing through transit networks. Internetwork routing can use link status information in combination with connection completion history to select paths and also use dynamic bandwidth reservation techniques, as discussed in Chapter 2 (Section 2.4). The case studies presented in Chapters 8 and 9 also illustrate internetwork class-of-service routing capabilities applied to IP/MPLS converged networks.

Internetwork routing can use the virtual network concept that enables service integration by allocating bandwidth for services and using dynamic bandwidth reservation controls. These virtual network concepts have been described in this chapter and can be extended directly to internetwork routing. For example, as illustrated in Figure 2.8 in Chapter 2 (Section 2.4), links connected to the originating network border nodes, such as links OBN1-DBN1, OBN2-DBN1, OBN1-VBN1, OBN1-VBN2, and OBN2-VBN2, can define VNET bandwidth allocation, protection, reservation, and routing methods. In that way, bandwidth can be fully shared among virtual networks in the absence of congestion. When a certain virtual network encounters congestion, bandwidth is reserved to ensure that the virtual network reaches its allocated bandwidth. Internetwork routing can employ class-of-service routing capabilities, including key service protection, directional flow control, link selection capability, automatically updated time-variable bandwidth allocation, and alternate routing capability through the use of overflow paths and control parameters such as internetwork routing load set periods. Link capability selection allows specific link characteristics, such as fiber transmission, to be preferentially selected. Thereby internetwork routing can improve performance and reduce the cost of the internetwork with flexible routing capabilities, such as described in Chapter 2.

Similar to intranetwork routing, internetwork routing may include the following steps for connection establishment:

- At the originating border node (OBN), the destination border node (DBN), SI, VNET, and QoS resource management information are determined through the number/name translation database and other service information available at the OBN.
- The DBN and QoS resource management information are used to access the appropriate VNET and routing table between the OBN and the DBN.
- The connection request is set up over the first available path in the routing table with the required transmission resource selected based on the QoS resource management data.

The rules for selecting the internetwork primary path and alternate paths for a connection can be governed by the availability of primary path bandwidth, node-to-node congestion, and link capability. The path sequence consists of the primary shortest path, lightly loaded alternate paths, heavily loaded alternate paths, and reserved alternate paths, where these load states are refined further by combining link load state information with path congestion state information. Internetwork alternate paths, which include nodes in the originating network and terminating network, are selected before alternate paths that include via-network nodes are selected. Greater path selection depth is allowed if congestion is detected to the destination network because more alternate path choices serve to reduce the congestion. During periods of no congestion, capacity not needed by one virtual network is made available to other virtual networks that are experiencing loads above their allocation.

The border node, for example, automatically computes the bandwidth allocations once a week and uses a different allocation for various load set periods, for example, each of 36 two-hour load set periods: 12 weekday, 12 Saturday, and 12 Sunday. The allocation of the bandwidth can be based on a rolling average of the traffic load for each of the virtual networks, to each destination node, in each of the load set periods. Under normal no-congestion network conditions, all virtual networks fully share all available capacity, but under network congestion link bandwidth is reserved to ensure that each virtual network gets the amount of bandwidth allotted. This dynamic bandwidth reservation during times of congestion results in network performance that is analogous to having the link bandwidth allocation between the two nodes dedicated for each VNET.

3.6 Modeling of TQO Methods

This section again uses the full-scale 135-node national network model developed in Chapter 2 to study various TQO scenarios and trade-offs. The 135-node national model is illustrated in Figure 2.9, the multiservice traffic demand model is summarized in Tables 2.1a–c, and the cost model is summarized in Table 2.2.

Generally the routing and capacity designs for the meshed logical topologies are optimized by using the DEFO algorithms presented in Chapter 6, while the routing and capacity designs for the sparse logical topologies are optimized by using the shortest path optimization and DEFO algorithms presented in Chapter 6.

3.6.1 Performance of Bandwidth Reservation Methods

As discussed in Section 3.3, dynamic bandwidth reservation can be used to favor one category of traffic over another category of traffic. A simple example of the use of this method is to reserve bandwidth in order to prefer traffic on the shorter primary paths over traffic using longer alternate paths. This is done most efficiently by using a method that reserves bandwidth only when congestion exists on links in the network. We now give illustrations of this method and compare the performance of a network in which bandwidth reservation is used under congestion to the case when bandwidth reservation is not used.

In the example, traffic is first routed on the shortest path and is then allowed to alternate route on longer paths if the primary path is not available. In the case where bandwidth reservation is used, 5% of the link bandwidth is reserved for traffic on the primary path when congestion is present on the link.

Table 3.8 illustrates the performance of bandwidth reservation methods for a high-day network load pattern. This is the case for multilink path routing being used on a per-flow basis in a sparse network topology.

Table 3.8 shows that performance improves when bandwidth reservation is used. The reason for the poor performance without bandwidth reservation is due to the lack of reserved capacity to favor traffic routed on the more direct primary paths under network congestion conditions. Without bandwidth reservation, nonhierarchical networks can exhibit unstable behavior in which essentially all connections are established on longer alternate paths as opposed to shorter primary paths, which reduces network throughput greatly and increases network congestion [AKINPELU84,

Table 3.8 Performance of Dynamic Bandwidth Reservation Methods for CRLSP Setup; Percentage Lost/Delayed Traffic under Overload (Per-Flow Multilink Path Routing in Sparse Network Topology; 135-Node Multiservice Network Model)

Overload factor	Without bandwidth reservation	With bandwidth reservation
7	11.94	3.86
8	22.85	9.66
10	37.74	24.78

Table 3.9 Performance of Dynamic Bandwidth Reservation Methods; Percentage Lost Traffic under 30% Overload (Per-Flow Two-Link SDR in Meshed Network Topology; 65-Node Network Model)

Hour	Without bandwidth reservation	With bandwidth reservation
2	12.19	0.22
3	22.38	0.18
5	18.90	0.24

KRUPP82, NAKAGOME73]. If the bandwidth reservation mechanism is added, then performance of the network is improved greatly.

Another example is given in Table 3.9, where two-link SDR is used in a meshed network topology. In this case, the average business day loads for a 65-node national network model were inflated uniformly by 30%. Table 3.9 gives the average hourly lost traffic due to loss of connection admissions in hours 2, 3, and 5, which correspond to the two early morning busy hours and the afternoon busy hour.

Again, the results of Table 3.9 show that performance improves dramatically when bandwidth reservation is used. A clear instability arises when bandwidth reservation is not used, because under congestion a network state in which virtually all traffic occupies two links instead of one link is predominant. When bandwidth reservation is used, flows are much more likely to be routed on a one-link path because the bandwidth reservation mechanism makes it less likely that a two-link path can be found in which both links have idle capacity in excess of the reservation level.

As discussed in Sections 3.3.1 and 3.3.2, in meshed networks such as the two-link SDR case illustrated in Table 3.9, it is most efficient to trigger bandwidth reservation under congestion rather than leaving bandwidth reservation enabled at all times without triggering. This is because reserved bandwidth can be underutilized if insufficient preferred traffic arrives to fully utilize the reserved bandwidth. Under normal traffic conditions, in which the engineered traffic levels would all be carried in the two-link

SDR design network, leaving reservation enabled at all times leads to nontrivial traffic loss, perhaps on the order of 1% for typical bandwidth reservation levels. While this may seem small, this traffic loss represents revenue loss that accumulates over the long run and is in fact unnecessary if reservation triggering is used. Alternatively, the engineered capacity can be increased to accommodate the inefficiency of nontriggered bandwidth reservation; however, this still represents a network cost.

The debate as to whether to trigger bandwidth reservation, such as a two-link SDR meshed network, led to a rather spirited (heated) debate in the RATS team in the design of voice network dynamic routing. Actually, it was a battle royal that went on for quite a long time and involved much detailed analysis. In the end, the triggered approach won out for the AT&T implementation of RTNR.

A performance comparison is given in Table 3.10 for a single link failure in a 135-node design averaged over 5 network busy hours, for the case without bandwidth reservation and with bandwidth reservation. Clearly the use of bandwidth reservation protects the performance of each virtual network class-of-service category.

3.6.2 Per-VNET vs Per-Flow Bandwidth Allocation

This section uses the 135-node model to compare the per-virtual network methods of QoS resource and the per-flow methods, as described in Section 3.3. These two cases can be seen in Figure 3.11, which illustrates the case of per-virtual network CRLSP bandwidth allocation and the case of per-flow CRLSP bandwidth allocation. Figure 3.11 compares the performance in terms of lost or delayed traffic under a focused overload scenario on the Oakbrook (OKBK), IL node (such as might occur, for example, with a radio call-in give-away offer). The size of the focused overload is

Table 3.10 Performance of Dynamic Bandwidth Reservation Methods; Percentage Lost/Delayed Traffic under 50% General Overload (Multilink STT-EDR; 135-Node Network Model)

Virtual network	Without bandwidth reservation	With bandwidth reservation
Business voice	2.42	0.00
Consumer voice	2.33	0.02
INTL-out	2.46	1.33
INTL-in (key)	2.56	0.00
Key voice	2.41	0.00
64-Kbps ISDN data	2.37	0.10
64-Kbps ISDN data (key)	2.04	0.00
384-Kbps ISDN data	12.87	0.00
VBR-RT voice	1.25	0.07
VBR-NRT MM	1.90	0.01
UBR MM	24.95	11.15

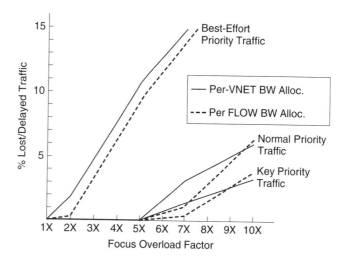

Figure 3.11 Performance under focused overload on OKBK node.

varied from the normal load (1× case) to a 10 times overload of the traffic to OKBK (10× case). Here a fixed routing (FXR) CRLSP bandwidth allocation is used for both the per-flow CRLSP bandwidth allocation case and the per-virtual network bandwidth allocation case. Results show that the per-flow and per-virtual network bandwidth allocation performance is similar; however, the improved performance of the key-priority traffic and normal-priority traffic in relation to the best-effort priority traffic is clearly evident.

The performance analyses for overloads and failures for the per-flow and per-virtual-network bandwidth allocation are now examined in which event-dependent routing with success-to-the-top path selection is used. Again the simulations include connection admission control with QoS resource management, in which we distinguish key services, normal services, and best-effort services as indicated in Tables 3.11–3.13. Table 3.11 gives performance results for a 30% general overload, Table 3.12 gives performance results for a six-times overload on a single network node, and Table 3.13 gives performance results for a single transport link failure. Performance analysis results show that the multilink STT-EDR per-flow bandwidth allocation and per-virtual network bandwidth allocation options perform similarly under overloads and failures.

3.6.3 Single-Area Flat Topology vs Multiarea Two-Level Hierarchical Flat Topology

We also investigate the performance of hierarchical network designs, which represent the topological configuration to be expected with multiarea [or multi-autonomous system (multi-AS) or multidomain] networks. Figure 2.13 shows the

Table 3.11 Performance of Per-Flow and Per-Virtual Network Bandwidth Allocation; Percentage Lost/Delayed Traffic under 30% General Overload (Single-Area Flat Network Topology; Multilink STT-EDR Routing; 135-Node Network Model)

Virtual network	Per-flow bandwidth allocation	Per-virtual network bandwidth allocation
Business voice	0.00	0.00
Consumer voice	0.00	0.00
INTL-out	0.00	0.00
INTL-in (key)	0.00	0.00
Key voice	0.00	0.00
64-SDS	0.00	0.00
64-Kbps ISDN data (key)	0.00	0.00
384-Kbps ISDN data	0.00	0.00
VBR-RT voice	0.00	0.00
VBR-NRT MM	0.00	0.00
UBR MM	4.15	3.94

Table 3.12 Performance of Per-Flow and Per-Virtual Network Bandwidth Allocation; Percentage Lost/Delayed Traffic under 6× Focused Overload on OKBK (Single-Area Flat Network Topology; Multilink STT-EDR Routing; 135-Node Network Model)

Virtual network	Per-flow bandwidth allocation	Per-virtual network bandwidth allocation
Business voice	0.00	0.01
Consumer voice	0.00	0.01
INTL-out	0.00	0.01
INTL-in (key)	0.00	0.00
Key voice	0.00	0.00
64-Kbps ISDN data	0.00	0.00
64-Kbps ISDN data (key)	0.00	0.00
384-Kbps ISDN data	0.00	0.00
VBR-RT voice	0.00	0.00
VBR-NRT MM	0.00	0.01
UBR MM	12.46	12.30

model considered, which consists of 135 edge nodes each homed onto 1 of 21 backbone nodes. Typically, the edge nodes may be grouped into separate areas and the backbone nodes into another area. Within each area a flat routing topology exists; however, between edge areas and the backbone area a hierarchical routing relationship exists. This routing hierarchy is modeled for both the per-flow and the per-virtual

Table 3.13 Performance of Per-Flow and Per-Virtual Network Bandwidth Allocation; Percentage Lost/Delayed Traffic under Failure on CHCG-NYCM Link (Single-Area Flat Network Topology; Multilink STT-EDR Routing; 135-Node Network Model)

Virtual network	Per-flow bandwidth allocation	Per-virtual network bandwidth allocation
Business voice	0.00	0.00
Consumer voice	0.00	0.00
INTL-out	0.00	0.00
INTL-in (key)	0.00	0.00
Key voice	0.00	0.00
64-Kbps ISDN data	0.00	0.00
64-Kbps ISDN data (key)	0.00	0.00
384-Kbps ISDN data	0.00	0.00
VBR-RT voice	0.00	0.00
VBR-NRT MM	0.00	0.00
UBR MM	0.17	0.17

Table 3.14 Performance of Multiarea Two-Level Hierarchical Network Topology; Percentage Lost/Delayed Traffic under 30% General Overload Per-Flow and Per-Virtual Network Bandwidth Allocation (Multilink STT-EDR Routing; 135-Node Network Model)

Virtual network	Per-flow bandwidth allocation	Per-virtual network bandwidth allocation
Business voice	0.00	0.00
Consumer voice	0.00	0.00
INTL-out	0.00	0.00
INTL-in (key)	0.00	0.00
Key voice	0.00	0.00
64 SDS	0.00	0.00
64-Kbps ISDN data (key)	0.00	0.00
384-Kbps ISDN data	0.00	0.00
VBR-RT voice	0.00	0.00
VBR-NRT MM	0.00	0.00
UBR MM	9.88	9.06

network bandwidth allocation alternatives, and the results are given in Tables 3.14 to 3.16 for the 30% general overload, six-times focused overload, and link failure examples, respectively. We can see that the performance of the hierarchical network case is substantially worse than the flat network model, which models a single area or autonomous system consisting of 135 nodes.

Table 3.15 Performance of Multiarea Two-Level Hierarchical Network Topology; Percentage Lost/Delayed Traffic under $6\times$ Focused Overload on OKBK Per-Flow and Per-Virtual Network Bandwidth Allocation (Multilink STT-EDR Routing; 135-Node Network Model)

Virtual network	Per-flow bandwidth allocation	Per-virtual network bandwidth allocation
Business voice	1.64	1.70
Consumer voice	2.27	2.22
INTL-out	1.11	0.89
INTL-in (key)	0.00	0.00
Key voice	0.00	0.00
64-Kbps ISDN data	0.40	0.27
64-Kbps ISDN data (key)	0.00	0.00
384-Kbps ISDN data	0.00	0.00
VBR-RT voice	0.94	0.93
VBR-NRT MM	1.85	1.80
UBR MM	12.86	12.88

Table 3.16 Performance of Multiarea Two-Level Hierarchical Network Topology; Percentage Lost/Delayed Traffic under Failure on CHCG-NYCM Link Per-Flow and Per-Virtual Network Bandwidth Allocation (Multilink STT-EDR Routing; 135-Node Network Model)

Virtual network	Per-flow bandwidth allocation	Per-virtual network bandwidth allocation
Business voice	0.00	0.00
Consumer voice	0.00	0.00
INTL-out	0.00	0.00
INTL-in (key)	0.00	0.00
Key voice	0.00	0.00
64-Kbps ISDN data	0.00	0.00
64-Kbps ISDN data (key)	0.00	0.00
384-Kbps ISDN data	0.00	0.00
VBR-RT voice	0.00	0.00
VBR-NRT MM	0.00	0.00
UBR MM	1.22	1.38

3.6.4 Need for MPLS and DiffServ

We illustrate the operation of MPLS and DiffServ in the multiservice network model with some examples. First suppose there is 10 Mbps of normal-priority traffic and

10 Mbps of best-effort priority traffic being carried in the network between node A and node B. Best-effort traffic is treated in the model as UBR traffic and is not allocated any bandwidth. Hence the best-effort traffic does not get any CRLSP bandwidth allocation and cannot be rejected by connection admission control (CAC) as a means to throttle back such traffic at the edge router. CAC is done for call/session-routed normal-priority and key-priority traffic, where such traffic could be denied bandwidth allocation. The only way that the best-effort traffic gets dropped/lost is to drop it at the queues; therefore, it is essential that traffic that is allocated bandwidth on the CRLSPs has higher priority at the queues than best-effort traffic. Therefore in the model the three classes of traffic get these DiffServ markings: best effort gets the best-effort (BE) DiffServ marking, which ensures that it will get best-effort priority queuing treatment. Normal-priority traffic gets the assured forwarding (AF) DiffServ marking, which is a middle-priority level of queuing treatment, and key-priority traffic gets the expedited forwarding (EF) DiffServ marking, which is the highest priority queuing level.

Now suppose that there is 30 Mbps of bandwidth available between A and B and that all normal-priority and best-effort traffic is getting through. Also suppose that the traffic for both normal-priority and best-effort traffic increases to 20 Mbps. The normal-priority traffic requests and gets a CRLSP bandwidth allocation increase to 20 Mbps on the A to B CRLSP. However, the best-effort traffic, because it has no bandwidth allocation and no CAC, is just sent into the network at 20 Mbps. Because there is only 30 Mbps of bandwidth available from A to B, the network must drop 10 Mbps of best-effort traffic in order to leave room for the 20 Mbps of normal-priority traffic. The way this is done in practice, and in the model, is through the queuing mechanisms governed by the DiffServ priority settings on each category of traffic. Through the DiffServ marking, the queuing mechanisms discard about 10 Mbps of best-effort traffic at the priority queues. If the DiffServ markings were not used, then normal-priority and best-effort traffic would compete equally on the first-in/first-out (FIFO) queues, and perhaps 15 Mbps of each would get through, which is not the desired situation.

Taking this example further, if normal-priority and best-effort traffic both increase to 40 Mbps, then normal-priority traffic tries to get a CRLSP bandwidth allocation increase to 40 Mbps. However, the most it can get is 30 Mbps, so 10 Mbps is denied through the CAC mechanism for normal-priority traffic in the MPLS constraint-based routing procedure. By having the DiffServ markings of AF on normal-priority traffic and BE on best-effort traffic, essentially all the best-effort traffic is dropped at the queues, as the normal-priority traffic is allocated and gets the full 30 Mbps of A to B bandwidth. If there were no DiffServ markings, then again perhaps 15 Mbps of both normal priority and best effort get through or, in this case, perhaps a greater amount of best-effort traffic is carried than normal-priority traffic, as 40 Mbps of best-effort traffic is sent into the network and only 30 Mbps of normal-priority traffic is sent into the network, and the FIFO queues will receive more best-effort pressure than normal-priority pressure.

Some general observations on the operation of MPLS and DiffServ in the multiservice TQO models include the following:

- In a multiservice network environment, with best-effort priority traffic, normal-priority traffic, and key-priority traffic sharing the same network, MPLS bandwidth allocation and DiffServ/priority queuing are both needed. Normal-priority and key-priority traffic use MPLS capabilities to receive bandwidth allocation while the best-effort traffic gets no bandwidth allocation. Under congestion (e.g., from overloads or failures), the DiffServ/priority queuing mechanisms push out best-effort priority traffic at the queues so that normal-priority and key-priority traffic can get through on the MPLS-allocated CRLSP bandwidth.
- In a multiservice network where normal-priority and key-priority traffic use MPLS to receive bandwidth allocation and there is no best-effort priority traffic, then the DiffServ/priority queuing becomes less important. This is because the MPLS bandwidth allocation and CAC mechanisms more or less assure that the queues will not overflow, and perhaps therefore DiffServ would not be needed as much.
- As bandwidth gets more plentiful, the point at which the MPLS and DiffServ mechanisms have a significant effect under traffic overload goes to a higher and higher threshold. For example, the models show that the overload factor at which congestion occurs gets larger as the bandwidth modules get larger (e.g., OC3 to OC12 to OC48 to OC192). However, the congestion point will always be reached with failures and/or large-enough overloads necessitating the MPLS/DiffServ mechanisms.

3.7 Summary and Conclusions

The conclusions reached in this chapter are as follows:

- Class-of-service routing is an important capability of converged TQO networks to define table-driven service elements and component application/network capabilities to avoid software development, network element development, and new network implementation for new service deployment
- Bandwidth reservation is critical to the stable and efficient performance of TQO methods in a network and to ensure the proper operation of multiservice bandwidth allocation, protection, and priority treatment.
- Per-VNET bandwidth allocation is essentially equivalent to per-flow bandwidth allocation in network performance and efficiency. Because of the much lower routing table management overhead requirements, as discussed and modeled in Chapter 4, per-VNET bandwidth allocation is preferred to per-flow allocation.
- QoS resource management is shown to be effective in achieving key service, normal service, and best-effort service differentiation.
- Both MPLS QoS and bandwidth management and DiffServ priority queuing management are important for ensuring that multiservice network performance objectives

are met under a range of network conditions. Both mechanisms operate together to ensure that QoS resource allocation mechanisms (bandwidth allocation, protection, and priority queuing) are achieved.

3.8 Applicability of Requirements

Bandwidth reservation, per-VNET bandwidth allocation, and QoS resource management are already in widespread use in TDM-based dynamic routing networks, as discussion in Chapter 1. These methods are extensible to IP/MPLS networks, as demonstrated in this chapter. Such methods are shown to provide robust and efficient networks and are applicable to both intranetwork and internetwork dynamic routing networks.

Based on these and other results presented in this book, we give service provider requirements for a standardized GTQO protocol, which includes generic service aspects, management aspects, and CAC aspects. These GTQO protocol requirements would then be used to drive the vendor implementations in the direction of network operator requirements and vendor interoperability. Service providers and their customers would benefit from these capabilities in terms of network performance and profitability, as demonstrated in this chapter and throughout this book. Service provider interest in adopting such TQO features then also leads to vendor profitability if their products support these features.

Chapter 4
Routing Table Management Methods and Requirements

4.1 Introduction

Routing table management typically entails the automatic generation of routing tables based on network topology and other information such as status. Routing table management information, such as topology update, status information, or routing recommendations, is used for purposes of applying the routing table design rules for determining path choices in the routing table. This information is exchanged between one node and another node, such as between the originating node (ON) and destination node (DN), for example, or between a node and a network element such as a TQO processor. This information is used to generate the routing table, and then the routing table is used to determine the path choices used in the selection of a path.

Link-state (LS) routing protocols use topology-state update mechanisms to build the topology database at each node, typically conveying the topology status through flooding of control messages containing link, node, and reachable address information between nodes. In the Private Network-Network Interface (PNNI) [ATMFORUM-0055.002] protocol developed by the ATM Forum, such mechanisms use the PNNI topology state element (PTSE); in the Open Shortest Path First (OSPF) protocol [RFC2328], they use the link-state advertisement (LSA). Topology information in PNNI is distributed in PTSEs, which are encapsulated in PNNI topology state packets (PTSPs) and periodically flooded to other nodes in the domain through all available links. Hello messages are used in LS protocols to establish and maintain link adjacencies.

This automatic generation function is enabled by the automatic exchange of link, node, and reachable address information among the network nodes. In order to achieve automatic update and synchronization of the topology database, which is essential for routing table management, IP- and ATM-based networks interpret Hello protocol mechanisms to identify links in the network and LSAs/PTSEs to achieve topology database synchronization of link, node, and reachable address information. Use of a single peer group/autonomous system for topology update leads to more efficient routing and easier administration and is best achieved by minimizing the use of topology state (LSA and PTSE) flooding for dynamic topology state information. A topology state element (TSE) has been standardized for TDM-based networks [E.361]. When this is available, then the HELLO and LSA/TSE/PTSE parameters will become the standard topology update method for interworking across IP-, ATM-, and TDM-based networks.

Congestion in LS protocols has caused many problems in the past [AT&T98, PAP-PALARDO01, CHOLEWKA99, JANDER01]. It can arise for many different reasons and can result in widespread loss of topology database information and overload in flooding of topology database information. In some instances of network overload, failure, and/or congestion, flooding mechanisms can overwhelm the routing control processors and bring the network down. Earlier work [CHOUDHURY01, CHOUDHURY03, RFC4222] presented analysis and simulation of congestion control and failure recovery for LS protocol networks.

A number of data network outages have been reported by service providers where recovery of the underlying LS protocols was inadequate. In the failure of a large frame relay network [AT&T98], an initial procedural error triggered two undetected software bugs, leading to a huge overload of control messages and loss of all topology-database information at every node. Analysis of the failure showed that a very large number of LS updates were sent to every node, causing general processor overload. As a result, the LS protocol was overwhelmed and unable to recover, and manual means had to be used to restart the network after a long outage. An event in a large ATM network, which used an OSPF-based LS protocol [PAPPALARDO01], caused an overload of control messages and a lengthy network outage resulted. Manual procedures were put in place to reduce flooding, thereby stabilizing the network. A PNNI-based outage has been reported [JANDER01] in which the root cause was "problems with the inter-switch PNNI code that coordinates the flow of traffic between switches." Based on these experiences, the LS protocols used were found to be vulnerable to loss of topology information, control overload to resynchronize databases, and other failure/overload scenarios.

Several vendors analyzed how quickly their LS protocol implementations recover from a total network failure scenario analogous to the event described in [AT&T98]. Results for each vendor-projected recovery time showed large variability; however, recovery times up to 5.5 h were estimated. Hence the expectation was that the recovery times for some vendor equipment are not adequate under a large failure scenario.

The failure experience, analysis, and simulation demonstrate that LS protocols, such as OSPF, may not be able to recover from large failures and overloads due to a control overload in performing routing table management. To address this problem, LS protocol extensions have been adopted in the IETF and ATM Forum for OSPF and PNNI [RFC4222, ATMFORUM-0200.000, ATMFORUM-0201.000], respectively, to prevent these protocols from going into congestion and to recover when congestion occurs. The adopted mechanisms include throttling of LS update flooding when congestion is detected, maintaining link adjacencies with prioritized processing of Hello and LS update acknowledgment messages, database backup, and database resynchronization.

It is assumed that the call/session routing protocol interworks with H.323 [H.323], ISDN user part (ISUP) [Q.761], and bearer-independent call control (BICC) [Q.1901] to accommodate setup and release of connection requests.

- Connection/bandwidth-allocation routing in support of bearer-path selection is assumed to employ OSPF/BGP path selection methods in combination with MPLS. MPLS employs a resource reservation protocol with traffic engineering extensions (RSVP-TE) [RFC3209] to establish constraint-based routing label switched paths (CRLSPs). Bandwidth allocation to CRLSPs is managed in support of QoS resource management, as discussed in Chapter 3.
- The MPLS CRLSP SETUP message carries the explicit route parameter specifying the via nodes (VNs) and destination node (DN) in the selected CRLSP and a parameter specifying the allowed bandwidth selection threshold on a link.
- The MPLS CRLSP RELEASE message is assumed to carry the crankback [MPLS-CRANKBACK] parameter specifying return of control of the connection/bandwidth-allocation request to the originating node for possible further alternate routing to establish additional CRLSPs.
- Call/session control routing is coordinated with connection/bandwidth allocation for bearer-path establishment, such as with the proposed vertical interface protocol [VERTICAL-INTERFACE].
- Reachability information is exchanged between all nodes. To provision a new IP address, the node serving that IP address is provisioned. The reachability information is flooded to all nodes in the network using the OSPF LSA flooding mechanism.
- The ON performs destination name/number translation, service processing, and all steps necessary to determine the routing table for the connection/bandwidth-allocation request across the IP network. The ON makes a connection/bandwidth-allocation request admission if bandwidth is available and places the connection/bandwidth-allocation request on a selected CRLSP.

IP-based networks employ an IP addressing method to identify node end points [RFC1518, STEVENS94]. A mechanism is available to translate E.164 addresses to IP addresses in an efficient manner. A protocol known as ENUM ("telephone number mapping") provides interworking between IP addressing and E.164 numbering/addressing in which a translation database is required, based on domain name system (DNS) technology, to convert E.164 addresses to IP addresses, SIP addresses, and other user resources [RFC3271]. With such a capability, IP nodes could make this translation of E.164 AESAs directly, thereby providing interworking with TDM- and ATM-based networks that use E.164 numbering and addressing. If this is the case, then E.164 addresses could become a standard addressing method for interworking across IP-, ATM-, and TDM-based networks.

As stated above, path selection in an IP-based network is assumed to employ OSPF/BGP in combination with the MPLS protocol that functions efficiently in combination with call/session control establishment of individual connections. In OSPF-based layer 3 routing, as illustrated in Figure 4.1, an ON N1 determines a list of shortest paths by using, for example, Dijsktra's algorithm.

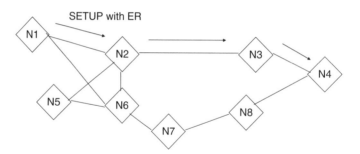

Figure 4.1 IP/MPLS routing example.

This path list could be determined based on administrative weights of each link, which are communicated to all nodes within the AS. These administrative weights may be set, for example, to $1 + \varepsilon \times$ distance, where ε is a factor giving a relatively smaller weight to the distance in comparison to the hop count. The ON selects a path from the list based on, for example, FXR, TDR, SDR, or EDR path selection, as described in Chapter 2. For example, to establish a CRLSP on the first path, the ON N1 sends an MPLS CRLSP SETUP message to VN N2, which in turn forwards the setup message to VN N3 and finally to DN N4. The VNs N2 and N3 and DN N4 are passed in the explicit route (ER) parameter contained in the MPLS CRLSP SETUP message. Each node in the path reads the ER information and passes the MPLS CRLSP SETUP message to the next node listed in the ER parameter. If the first-choice path is blocked at any of the links in the path, an MPLS CRLSP RELEASE message with crankback parameter is returned to the ON, which can then attempt the next path. If FXR is used, then this path is the next path in the shortest path list, for example, path N1-N6-N7-N8-N4. If TDR is used, then the next path is the next path in the routing table for the current time period. If SDR is used, OSPF implements a distributed method of flooding link status information, which is triggered either periodically and/or by crossing load state threshold values. As described in the beginning of this section, this method of distributing link status information can be resource intensive and indeed may not be any more efficient than simpler path selection methods such as EDR. If EDR is used, then the next path is the last successful path, and if that path is unsuccessful another alternate path is searched out according to the EDR path selection method.

Bandwidth-allocation control information is used to seize and modify bandwidth allocation on LSPs, to release bandwidth on LSPs, and for purposes of advancing the LSP choices in the routing table. Existing CRLSP setup and release messages, as described in [RFC3209], can be used with additional parameters to control CRLSP bandwidth modification, priority, DEPTH on a link, or CRLSP crankback [MPLS-CRANKBACK] to an ON for further alternate routing to search out additional bandwidth on alternate CRLSPs. Actual selection of a CRLSP is determined from the routing table, and CRLSP control information is used to establish the path choice. Forward information exchange is used in CRLSP setup and bandwidth modification and includes, for example, the following parameters:

- CRLSP SETUP-ER: The ER parameter in MPLS specifies each VN and the DN in the CRLSP and is used by each VN to determine the next node in the path.
- CRLSP SETUP-PRIORITY: The PRIORITY parameter is used by each VN to determine if the MPLS setup or modification request is admitted or rejected on that link.
- CRLSP SETUP-DEPTH: The DEPTH parameter is used by each VN to compare the load state on each CRLSP link to the allowed DEPTH threshold to determine if the MPLS setup or modification request is admitted or rejected on that link.
- CRLSP SETUP-MODIFY: The MODIFY parameter is used by each VN/DN to update the traffic parameters (e.g., committed data rate) on an existing CRLSP to determine if the MPLS modification request is admitted or rejected on each link in the CRLSP.

The PRIORITY, DEPTH, and MODIFY parameters are used in the MPLS SETUP message to control the bandwidth allocation, queuing priorities, and bandwidth modification on an existing CRLSP [RFC3214].

Backward information exchange is used to release a connection/bandwidth-allocation request on a link such as from a DN to a VN or from a VN to an ON and includes, for example, the following parameter:

- CRLSP RELEASE-CBK: The crankback parameter in the CRLSP RELEASE message is sent from the VN to ON or DN to ON and allows for possible further alternate routing at the ON to search out alternate CRLSPs for additional bandwidth.

A crankback parameter is available for the MPLS CRLSP RELEASE message [MPLS-CRANKBACK] to allow the ON to search out additional bandwidth on additional CRLSPs.

In order to achieve automatic update and synchronization of the topology database, which is essential for routing table design, IP-based networks already interpret Hello protocol mechanisms to identify links in the network. For topology database synchronization the OSPF LSA exchange is used to automatically provision nodes, links, and reachable addresses in the topology database. This information is exchanged between one node and another node, and in the case of OSPF a flooding mechanism of LSA information is used:

- HELLO: Provides for the identification of links between nodes in the network.
- LSA: Provides for the automatic updating of nodes, links, and reachable addresses in the topology database.

In summary, IP/MPLS-based networks already incorporate standard signaling for routing table management functions, which includes e ER, HELLO, and LSA capabilities. Additional requirements needed to support QoS resource management include the DEPTH parameter and MODIFY parameter in the MPLS CRLSP SETUP message, the crankback parameter in the MPLS CRLSP RELEASE message, and the support for QUERY, STATUS, and RECOM routing table design information exchange, as required in Section 4.5. Call/session control with the H.323 [H.323] and session initiation protocol [RFC2543] need to be coordinated with MPLS CRLSP connection/bandwidth-allocation control, as currently specified in ongoing work known as the "vertical interface protocol" [VERTICAL-INTERFACE].

4.3 Routing Table Management for ATM-Based Networks

PNNI is a standardized signaling and dynamic routing strategy for ATM networks adopted by the ATM Forum [ATMFORUM-0055.002]. PNNI provides interoperability among different vendor equipment and scaling to very large networks. Scaling is provided by a hierarchical peer group structure that allows the details of topology of a peer group to be flexibly hidden or revealed at various levels within the hierarchical structure. Peer group leaders represent nodes within a peer group for purposes of routing protocol exchanges at the next higher level. Border nodes handle inter-level interactions at connection setup. PNNI routing involves two components: (a) a topology distribution protocol and (b) path selection and crankback procedures. The topology distribution protocol floods information within a peer group. The peer group leader abstracts the information from within the peer group and floods the abstracted topology information to the next higher level in the hierarchy, including aggregated reachable address information. As the peer group leader learns information at the next higher level, it floods it to the lower level in the hierarchy, as appropriate. In this fashion, all nodes learn of network-wide reachability and topology.

PNNI path selection is source based in which the ON determines the high-level path through the network. The ON performs number translation, screening, service processing, and all steps necessary to determine the routing table for the connection/bandwidth-allocation request across the ATM network. The node places the selected path in the designated-transit-list (DTL) and passes the DTL to the next node in the SETUP message. The next node does not need to perform number translation on the called party number but just follows the path specified in the DTL. When a connection/bandwidth-allocation request is blocked due to network congestion, a PNNI crankback is sent to the first ATM node in the peer group. The first ATM node may then use the PNNI alternate routing after crankback capability to select another path for the connection/bandwidth-allocation request. If the network is flat, i.e., all nodes have the same peer group level, the ON controls the edge-to-edge path. If the network has more than one level of hierarchy, as the connection progresses from one peer group into another, the border node at the new peer group selects a path through that peer group to the next peer group downstream, as determined by the ON. This occurs recursively through the levels of hierarchy. If at any point the connection is blocked, e.g., when the selected path bandwidth is not available, then the connection is cranked back to the border node or ON for that level of the hierarchy and an alternate path is selected. The path selection algorithm is not stipulated in the PNNI specification, and each ON implementation can make its own path selection decision unilaterally. Because path selection is done at an ON, each ON makes path selection decisions based on its local topology database and specific algorithm. This means that different path selection algorithms from different vendors can interwork with each other.

In the routing example illustrated in Figure 4.1 now used to illustrate PNNI, an ON N1 determines a list of shortest paths by using, for example, Dijsktra's algorithm. This path list could be determined based on administrative weights of each link, which are communicated to all nodes within the peer group through the PTSE flooding mechanism. These administrative weights may be set, for example, to $1 + \varepsilon \times$ distance, where ε is a factor giving a relatively smaller weight to the distance in comparison to the hop count. The ON then selects a path from the list based on any of the methods described in Chapter 2, i.e., FXR, TDR, SDR, and EDR. For example, in using the first-choice path, the ON N1 sends a PNNI setup message to VN N2, which in turn forwards the PNNI setup message to VN N3 and finally to DN N4. The VNs N2 and N3 and DN N4 are passed in the DTL parameter contained in the PNNI setup message. Each node in the path reads the DTL information and passes the PNNI setup message to the next node listed in the DTL.

If the first path is blocked at any of the links in the path, overflows, or is excessively delayed at any of the queues in the path, a crankback message is returned to the ON, which can then attempt the next path. If FXR is used, then this path is the next path in the shortest path list, e.g., path N1-N6-N7-N8-N4. If TDR is used, then the next path is the next path in the routing table for the current time period. If SDR is used, PNNI implements a distributed method of flooding link status information, which is triggered either periodically and/or by crossing load state threshold values.

Connection/bandwidth-allocation control information is used in connection/bandwidth-allocation setup to seize bandwidth in links, to release bandwidth in links, and to advance path choices in the routing table. Existing connection/bandwidth-allocation setup and release messages [ATMFORUM-0148.001] can be used with additional parameters to control SVP bandwidth modification, priority, DEPTH on a link, or SVP crankback to an ON for further alternate routing. Actual selection of a path is determined from the routing table, and connection/bandwidth-allocation control information is used to establish the path choice. Forward information exchange is used in connection/bandwidth-allocation setup and includes, for example, the following parameters:

- SVC/SVP SETUP-DTL: The designated-transit-list (DTL) parameter in PNNI specifies each VN and the DN in the path and is used by each VN to determine the next node in the path.
- SVC/SVP SETUP-PRIORITY: The PRIORITY parameter is used by each VN to determine if the SVC/SVP setup or modification request is admitted or rejected on that link.
- SVC/SVP SETUP-DEPTH: The DEPTH parameter is used by each VN to compare the load state on the link to the allowed DEPTH to determine if the SVC connection/bandwidth-allocation request is admitted or rejected on that link.

- SVC/SVP MODIFY REQUEST-PRIORITY: The PRIORITY parameter is used by each VN to determine if the SVP modification request is admitted or rejected on that link.
- SVC/SVP MODIFY REQUEST-DEPTH: The DEPTH parameter is used by each VN to compare the load state on the link to the allowed DEPTH to determine if the SVP modification request is admitted or rejected on that link.

It is required that the PRIORITY and DEPTH parameters be carried in the SVC/SVP SETUP and SVC/SVP MODIFY REQUEST messages to control the bandwidth allocation and queuing priorities.

Backward information exchange is used to release a connection/bandwidth-allocation request on a link, such as from a DN to a VN or from a VN to an ON, and includes, for example, the following parameters:

- SVC/SVP RELEASE-CBK: The crankback parameter in the release message is sent from the VN to ON or DN to ON and allows for possible further alternate routing at the ON.
- SVC/SVP MODIFY REJECT-CBK: The crankback parameter in the modify reject message is sent from the VN to ON or DN to ON and allows for possible further alternate routing at the ON to search out additional bandwidth on alternate SVPs.

The SVC/SVP crankback parameter is already defined for PNNI-based signaling. It is also required in the SVC/SVP MODIFY REJECT message to allow the ON to search out additional bandwidth on additional SVC/SVPs.

In order to achieve automatic update and synchronization of the topology database, which is essential for routing table design, ATM-based networks already interpret Hello protocol mechanisms to identify links in the network. For topology database synchronization the PTSE exchange is used to automatically provision nodes, links, and reachable addresses in the topology database. This information is exchanged between one node and another node, and in the case of PNNI, a flooding mechanism of PTSE information is used:

- HELLO: Provides for the identification of links between nodes in the network.
- PTSE: Provides for the automatic updating of nodes, links, and reachable addresses in the topology database.

In summary, ATM-based networks already incorporate standard signaling and messaging directly applicable to routing implementation, which includes the DTL, crankback, priority, MODIFY, HELLO, and PTSE capabilities.

4.4 Routing Table Management for TDM-Based Networks

As discussed in Chapter 1 (see Table 1.2), TDM-based voice/ISDN networks have evolved several dynamic routing methods, which are widely deployed and include

TDR, SDR, and EDR implementations [ASH98]. TDM-based call/session and connection signaling protocols are described [Q.2761] for the signaling system 7 (SS7) ISUP-signaling protocol. We summarize the information exchange required between network elements to implement the TDM-based path selection methods, which include connection control information required for connection setup, routing table design information required for routing table generation, and topology update information required for the automatic update and synchronization of topology databases.

Routing table management information is used for purposes of applying the routing table design rules for determining path choices in the routing table. This information is exchanged between one node and another node, such as between the ON and DN, for example, or between a node and a network element such as a TQO processor. This information is used to generate the routing table, and then the routing table is used to determine the path choices used in the selection of a path. The following messages can be considered for this function:

- QUERY: Provides for an ON to DN or ON to TQO processor link and/or node status request.
- STATUS: Provides ON/VN/DN to TQO processor or DN to ON link and/or node status information.
- RECOM: Provides for a TQO processor to ON/VN/DN routing recommendation.

These information exchange messages are already deployed in nonstandard TDM-based implementations and need to be extended to standard TDM-based network environments.

In order to achieve automatic update and synchronization of the topology database, which is essential for routing table design, TDM-based networks need to interpret the Hello protocol mechanisms of ATM- and IP-based networks at the border nodes to identify links in the network, as discussed above for ATM-based networks. Also needed for topology database synchronization is a mechanism analogous to the PTSE exchange, as discussed above, which automatically provisions nodes, links, and reachable addresses in the topology database.

Path selection and QoS resource management control information is used in connection/bandwidth-allocation setup to seize bandwidth in links, to release bandwidth in links, and for purposes of advancing path choices in the routing table. Existing connection/bandwidth-allocation setup and release messages, as described in Recommendations Q.71, Q.761, and Q.2761, can be used with additional parameters to control path selection, priority, DEPTH on a link, or crankback to an ON for further alternate routing. Actual selection of a path is determined from the routing table, and connection/bandwidth-allocation control information is used to establish the path choice.

Forward information exchange is used in connection/bandwidth-allocation setup and includes, for example, the following parameters:

- CONNECTION SETUP-DTL/ER: The designated-transit-list/explicit-route (DTL/ER) parameter specifies each VN and the DN in the path and is used by each VN to determine the next node in the path.
- CONNECTION SETUP-PRIORITY: The PRIORITY parameter is used by each VN to determine if the setup request is admitted or rejected on that link.
- CONNECTION SETUP-DEPTH: The DEPTH parameter is used by each VN to compare the load state on the link to the allowed DEPTH to determine if the connection/bandwidth-allocation request is admitted or rejected on that link.

In SS7 ISUP these parameters could be carried in the initial address message (IAM).

Backward information exchange is used to release a connection/bandwidth-allocation on a link such as from a DN to a VN or from a VN to an ON and includes, for example, the following parameter:

- CONNECTION RELEASE-CBK: The crankback parameter in the release message is sent from the VN to ON or DN to ON and allows for possible further alternate routing at the ON.

In ISUP signaling this parameter could be carried in the RELEASE message.

4.5 Signaling and Information Exchange Requirements

Table 4.1 summarizes the required signaling and information exchange methods supported within each routing technology that are required to be supported across network types. Table 4.1 identifies the required information-exchange parameters, shown in nonbold type, to support the routing methods, and standards, shown in bold type, to support the information-exchange parameters.

These information-exchange parameters and methods are required for use within each network type and for interworking across network types. Therefore it is required that all information-exchange parameters identified in Table 4.1 be supported by the standards identified for each of the five network technologies. That is, it is required that standards be developed for all information-exchange parameters not currently supported, which are identified in Table 4.1 as references to sections of this chapter. This ensures information-exchange compatibility when interworking among the IP-, ATM-, and TDM-based network types, as denoted in the left three network technology columns. To support this information-exchange interworking across network types, it is further required that the information exchange at the interface be compatible across network types. Standardizing the required information routing methods and information-exchange parameters also supports the network technology cases in the right column of Table 4.1, in which PSTNs incorporate IP- or ATM-based technology.

Table 4.1 Required Signaling and Information-Exchange Parameters to Support Routing Methods (Required Standards in Bold and in Parenthesis; Section Numbers Refer to This Chapter)

Routing method		Network technology (standards source)			
		PSTN/TDM based (ITU-T standards)	ATM based (ATMF standards)	IP based (IETF standards)	PSTN/IP/ATM based (harmonized standards)
Call/session routing (number/name translation to routing address)		E.164-ADR, **(E.164, E.191, E.351, Section 4.5.1)**	E.164-AESA, CIC **(UNI, PNNI, AINI)**	E.164-AESA, IP-ADR, CIC **(Section 4.5.1)**	E.164-AESA, IP-ADR, CIC **(Section 4.5.1)**
Connection routing	Fixed routing	DTL/ER, CBK **(E.170, E.350, E.351, Section 4.5.2)**	DTL, CBK **(UNI, PNNI, AINI, BW-MODIFY)**	ER, CBK **(OSPF, BGP, MPLS)**	DTL/ER, CBK **(Section 4.5.2)**
	Time Dep. routing	DTL/ER, CBK **(E.170, E.350, E.351, Section 4.5.2)**	DTL, CBK **(Section 4.5.2)**	ER, CBK **(Section 4.5.2)**	DTL/ER, CBK **(Section 4.5.2)**
	State Dep. routing	DTL/ER, CBK **(E.170, E.350, E.351, Section 4.5.2)**	DTL, CBK **(UNI, PNNI, AINI, BW-MODIFY)**	ER, CBK **(OSPF, BGP, MPLS)**	DTL/ER, CBK **(Section 4.5.2)**
	Event Dep. routing	DTL/ER, CBK **(E.170, E.350, E.351, Section 4.5.2)**	DTL, CBK **(Section 4.5.2)**	ER, CBK **(Section 4.5.2)**	DTL/ER, CBK **(Section 4.5.2)**
QoS resource management	BW Alloc. and Protect.	QoS-PAR, TRAF-PAR, PRIORITY, DEPTH, MOD **(E.351, Section 4.5.3)**	QoS-PAR, TRAF-PAR, PRIORITY, DEPTH, MOD **(UNI, PNNI, AINI, BW-MODIFY)**	QoS-PAR, TRAF-PAR, PRIORITY, DEPTH, MOD **(OSPF, BGP, MPLS)**	QoS-PAR, TRAF-PAR, PRIORITY, DEPTH, MOD **(Section 4.5.3)**
	Priority routing	PRIORITY, DEPTH **(E.351, Section 4.5.3)**	PRIORITY, DEPTH **(UNI, PNNI, AINI, BW-MODIFY)**	PRIORITY, DEPTH **(OSPF, BGP, MPLS)**	PRIORITY, DEPTH **(Section 4.5.3)**

(Continued)

Table 4.1 Required Signaling and Information-Exchange Parameters to Support Routing Methods (Required Standards in Bold and in Parenthesis; Section Numbers Refer to This Chapter)—cont'd

Routing method		Network technology (standards source)			
		PSTN/TDM based (ITU-T standards)	ATM based (ATMF standards)	IP based (IETF standards)	PSTN/IP/ATM based (harmonized standards)
Routing table management	Priority queuing	N/A	DIFFSERV **(UNI, PNNI, AINI, BW-MODIFY)**	DIFFSERV **(DIFFSERV, OSPF, BGP, MPLS)**	DIFFSERV **(Section 4.5.3)**
	Topology update	HELLO, TSE **(E.351, Section 4.5.4)**	HELLO, PTSE **(UNI, PNNI, AINI, BW-MODIFY)**	HELLO, LSA **(OSPF, BGP, MPLS)**	HELLO, TSE **(Section 4.5.4)**
	Status update	RSE **(E.170, E.350, E.351, Section 4.5.4)**	PTSE **(UNI, PNNI, AINI, BW-MODIFY)**	LSA **(OSPF, BGP, MPLS)**	RSE **(Section 4.5.4)**
	Query for status	RQE **(E.170, E.350, E.351, Section 4.5.4)**	RQE **(Section 4.5.4)**	RQE **(Section 4.5.4)**	RQE **(Section 4.5.4)**
	Routing Recom.	RRE **(E.170, E.350, E.351, Section 4.5.4)**	RRE **(Section 4.5.4)**	RRE **(Section 4.5.4)**	RRE **(Section 4.5.4)**

We first discuss the routing methods identified by the rows of Table 4.1, followed by the harmonization of PSTN/IP/ATM-based information exchange, as identified by column 4 of Table 4.1, Sections 4.5.1 to 4.5.4 describe, respectively the call/session routing (number translation to routing address), connection routing, QoS resource management, and routing table management information-exchange parameters required in Table 4.1. Section 4.5.5 discusses the harmonization of routing methods standards for the two technology cases in the right column of Table 4.1 in which PSTNs incorporate IP- or ATM-based technology.

4.5.1 Call/Session Routing (Number Translation to Routing Address) Information-Exchange Parameters

As stated earlier, this book assumes the separation of call/session-control signaling for connection establishment from connection/bandwidth-allocation-control signaling for bearer-channel establishment. Call/session-control signaling protocols are described for SIP [RFC2543], for SS7 ISUP [Q.761], for BICC [Q.1901], for H.323 [H.323], and for the media gateway control (MEGACO) protocol [RFC2805, RFC3015]. Connection control signaling protocols include MPLS [RFC3209], ISUP [Q.761], PNNI [ATMFORUM-0055.002], UNI [ATMFORUM-0061.000], and SVP signaling [ATMFORUM-0127.000].

As discussed in Chapter 2, number/name translation should result in E.164 AESA addresses and/or IP addresses. It is required that provision be made for carrying E.164-AESA addresses and IP addresses in the connection-setup IE. In addition, it is required that a call/session identification code (CIC) be carried in the call/session-control and bearer-control connection-setup IEs in order to correlate the call/session-control setup with the bearer-control setup [ATMFORUM-0146.000]. Carrying these additional parameters in the SS7 ISUP connection-setup IEs is specified in the BICC protocol [Q.1901].

As shown in Table 4.1, it is required that provision be made for carrying E.164-AESA addresses and IP addresses in the connection-setup IE. In particular, it is required that E.164-AESA-address and IP-address elements be developed within IP- and PSTN/IP-based networks. It is required that number translation/routing methods supported by these parameters be developed for IP- and PSTN/IP-based networks. When this is the case, then E.164-AESA addresses and IP addresses will become the standard addressing method for interworking across IP-, ATM-, and TDM-based networks.

4.5.2   Connection Routing Information-Exchange Parameters

Connection/bandwidth-allocation control information is used to seize bandwidth on links in a path, to release bandwidth on links in a path, and for purposes of advancing path choices in the routing table. Existing connection/bandwidth-allocation setup and connection-release IEs, as described in [RFC3209, ATMFORUM-0055.002, ATMFORUM-0061.000, ATMFORUM-0148.001, Q.761], can be used with additional parameters to control CRLSP/SVC/SVP/CONNECTION path routing, PRIORITY, DEPTH bandwidth-allocation thresholds, and crankback to allow further alternate routing. Actual selection of a path is determined from the routing table, and connection/bandwidth-allocation control information is used to establish the path choice.

Source routing can be implemented through the use of connection/bandwidth-allocation control signaling methods employing the DTL or ER parameter in the connection-setup (CRLSP SETUP, SVC/SVP SETUP, IAM, MODIFY REQUEST) IE and the crankback (CBK) parameter in the connection-release (CRLSP RELEASE, DTL RELEASE, MODIFY REJECT, and CONNECTION RELEASE) IE. The DTL or ER parameter specifies all VNs and DN in a path, as determined by the ON, and the crankback parameter allows a VN to return control of the connection request to the ON for further alternate routing.

Forward information exchange is used in connection/bandwidth-allocation setup and includes, for example, the following parameter:

• Setup with designated-transit-list/explicit-route (DTL/ER) parameter: The ER parameter in MPLS and DTL parameter in PNNI specifies each VN and the DN in the path and is used by each VN to determine the next node in the path.

Backward information exchange is used to release a connection/bandwidth-allocation request on a link such as from a DN to a VN or from a VN to an ON, and the following parameter is required:

• Release with crankback parameter: The CBK parameter in the connection-release IE is sent from the VN to ON or DN to ON and allows for possible further alternate routing at the ON.

It is required that the CBK parameter be included in the connection release for TDM-based networks, the SVC/SVP release and SVC/SVP MODIFY REJECT IE for ATM-based networks, and MPLS CRLSP release IE for IP-based networks. This parameter is used to allow the ON to search out additional bandwidth on additional SVC/SVP/CRLSPs.

As shown in Table 4.1, it is required that the DTL/ER and CBK elements be developed within TDM-based networks, which will be compatible with the DTL element in ATM-based networks and the ER element in IP-based networks. It is required [E.350, E.351] that path-selection methods be developed supported by these parameters for TDM-based networks. Furthermore, it is required that TDR and EDR path-selection methods be developed supported by these parameters for ATM-, IP-, PSTN/ATM-, and PSTN/IP-based networks. When this is the case, then the DTL/ER and CBK parameters will become the standard path-selection method for interworking across TDM-, ATM-, and IP-based networks.

4.5.3 QoS Resource Management Information-Exchange Parameters

QoS resource management information is used to provide differentiated service priority in seizing bandwidth on links in a path and also in providing queuing resource priority. The following parameters are required:

• Setup with QoS parameters (QoS-PAR): The QoS-PAR include QoS thresholds such as transfer delay, delay variation, and packet loss. QoS-PAR are used by each VN to compare the link QoS performance to the requested QoS threshold to determine if the connection/bandwidth-allocation request is admitted or rejected on that link.

- Setup with traffic parameters (TRAF-PAR): The TRAF-PAR include traffic parameters such as average bit rate, maximum bit rate, and minimum bit rate. TRAF-PAR are used by each VN to compare the link traffic characteristics to the requested TRAF-PAR thresholds to determine if the connection/bandwidth-allocation request is admitted or rejected on that link.
- Setup with priority (PRIORITY) parameter: The PRIORITY parameter is used by each VN to determine if the connection/bandwidth-allocation request is admitted or rejected on that link.
- Setup with depth-of-search (DEPTH) parameter: The DEPTH parameter is used by each VN to compare the load state on the link to the allowed DEPTH to determine if the connection/bandwidth-allocation request is admitted or rejected on that link.
- Setup with modify (MOD) parameter: The MOD parameter is used by each VN to compare the requested modified traffic parameters on an existing SVP/CRLSP to determine if the modification request is admitted or rejected on that link.
- Differentiated services (DIFFSERV) parameter: The DIFFSERV parameter is used in IP- and ATM-based networks to support priority queuing. The DIFFSERV parameter is used at the queues associated with each link to designate the relative priority and management policy for each queue.

It is required that the QoS-PAR, TRAF-PAR, DTL/ER, PRIORITY, DEPTH, MOD, and DIFFSERV parameters be included in the MPLS CRLSP SETUP IE for IP-based networks, the SVC/SVP SETUP IE and SVP MODIFY REQUEST IE for ATM-based networks, and the initial address message (IAM) for TDM-based networks. These parameters are used to control the routing, bandwidth allocation, and routing/queuing priorities.

As shown in Table 4.1, it is required that the QoS-PAR and TRAF-PAR elements be developed within TDM-based networks to support bandwidth allocation and protection, which will be compatible with the QoS-PAR and TRAF-PAR elements in IP-based and ATM-based networks. In addition, it is required that the PRIORITY and DEPTH elements be developed within TDM-based networks, which will be compatible with the PRIORITY and DEPTH elements in ATM- and IP-based networks. Finally, it is required that the DIFFSERV element should be developed in ATM-based networks to support priority queuing. It is required that QoS-resource-management methods be developed and supported by these parameters for TDM-based networks. When this is the case, then the QoS-PAR, TRAF-PAR, PRIORITY, DEPTH, and DIFFSERV parameters will become the standard QoS-resource-management methods for interworking across IP-, ATM-, and TDM-based networks.

4.5.4 Routing Table Management Information-Exchange Parameters

Routing table management information is used for purposes of applying the routing table design rules for determining path choices in the routing table. This information is exchanged between one node and another node, such as between the ON and DN, for example, or between a node and a network element such as a TQO processor. This information is used to generate the routing table, and then the routing table is used to determine the path choices used in the selection of a path.

In order to achieve automatic update and synchronization of the topology database, which is essential for routing table design, IP- and ATM-based networks already interpret Hello protocol mechanisms to identify links in the network. For topology database synchronization the LSA is used in IP-based networks and PTSE exchange is used in ATM-based networks to automatically provision nodes, links, and reachable addresses in the topology database. Hence these parameters are required for this function:

• HELLO parameter: Provides for the identification of links between nodes in the network.
• TSE parameter: Provides for the automatic updating of nodes, links, and reachable addresses in the topology database.

These information exchange parameters are already deployed in IP- and ATM-based network implementations and are required to be extended to TDM-based network environments.

The following parameters are required for the status query and routing recommendation function:

• RQE parameter: Provides for an ON to DN or ON to TQO processor link and/or node status request.
• RSE parameter: Provides for a node to TQO processor or DN to ON link and/or node status information.
• RRE parameter: Provides for a TQO processor to node routing recommendation.

These information-exchange parameters are being standardized with Recommendation [E.350, E.351] and are required to be extended to ATM- and IP-based network environments.

As shown in Table 4.1, it is required that a TSE parameter be developed within TDM-based PSTN networks. It is required that topology update routing methods supported by these parameters be developed for PSTN/TDM-based networks. When this is the case, then the HELLO and TSE/LSA/PTSE parameters will become the standard topology update method for interworking across TDM-, ATM-, and IP-based networks.

As shown in Table 4.1, it is required that an RSE parameter be developed within TDM-based networks, which will be compatible with the LSA parameter in IP-based networks and the PTSE parameter in ATM-based networks. It is required [E.350, E.351] that status update routing methods supported by these parameters be developed for TDM-based networks. When this is the case, then the RSE/LSA/PTSE parameters will become the standard status update method for interworking across IP-, ATM-, and TDM-based networks.

As shown in Table 4.1, it is required that an RQE parameter be developed within IP-based, ATM-based, and PSTN/IP/ATM-based networks. It is required that query-for-status routing methods supported by these parameters be developed for IP-, ATM-, and PSTN/IP/ATM-based networks. When this is the case, then the RQE parameters will become the standard query for the status method for interworking across IP-, ATM-, and TDM-based networks.

As shown in Table 4.1, it is required that an RRE parameter be developed within IP-, ATM-, and PSTN/ATM-based networks. It is required that routing recommendation methods be developed supported by these parameters for IP-, ATM-, and PSTN/IP/ATM-based networks. When this is the case, then the RRE parameters will become the standard query for the status method for interworking across IP-, ATM-, and TDM-based networks.

4.5.5   Harmonization of Information-Exchange Standards

Harmonization of information-exchange standards is needed for the technology cases in the right column of Table 4.1. Achieving this will require contributions to standards bodies responsible for the impacted routing and information exchange signaling functions. Therefore, contributions are necessary to address needed number translation/routing functionality, which includes support for IP address parameters; needed routing table management information-exchange functionality, which includes query-for-status and routing-recommendation methods; and needed path selection information-exchange functionality.

4.5.6   Open Application Programming Interface (API)

Application programming interfaces are being developed to allow control of network elements through open interfaces available to individual applications. APIs allow applications to access and control network functions, including routing policy, as necessary, according to the specific application functions. The API parameters under application control, such as those specified in [PARLAY], are independent of the individual protocols supported within the network and therefore can provide a common language and framework across various network technologies, such as IP-, ATM-, and TDM-based technologies.

The signaling/information-exchange connectivity management parameters specified in this section, which need to be controlled through an applications interface, include QoS-PAR, TRAF-PAR, DTL/ER, PRIORITY, DEPTH, MOD, DIFFSERV, E.164-AESA, CIC, and perhaps others. The signaling/information-exchange routing policy parameters specified in this section, which need to be controlled through an applications interface, include TSE, RQE, RRE, and perhaps others. These parameters are required to be specified within the open API interface for routing functionality, and in this way applications will be able to access and control routing functionality within the network independent of the particular routing protocol(s) used in the network.

4.6 Examples of Call/Session Setups

We now illustrate the use of signaling/information-exchange messages described in the previous section, with typical examples of dynamic routing methods. Note that for simplicity paths are limited to one and two links; however, the procedures are general for multiple link paths.

4.6.1 Time-Dependent Routing Call/Session Setup

As discussed in Chapter 2, TDR uses a time-varying routing system to respond to network load variations. A sequence of paths is designed by the network design model, and crankback can be used when a link in a path is blocked at a via node to allow the originating node to advance to the next path. Figure 4.2 illustrates use of the SETUP and CRANKBACK messages in setting up a TDR call, as follows:

1. ON first tries direct link for call/session to; if bandwidth is available, ON reserves bandwidth and sends SETUP message to DN and completes call/session, if not ON proceeds to step 2.
2. ON finds next path in routing table; if no more paths in table ON proceeds to step 5; otherwise if idle bandwidth is on first link, ON reserves bandwidth and sends SETUP message to VN1; if no idle bandwidth is on first link ON returns to beginning of step 2; otherwise ON continues with step 3.
3. VN receives call/session SETUP and determines additional VNs and DN through the DTL/ER parameter in SETUP message; VN searches for idle bandwidth on the link to DN; if idle bandwidth is available, VN reserves bandwidth and sends SETUP message to next VN or DN and proceeds to step 4 when DN reached; if no idle

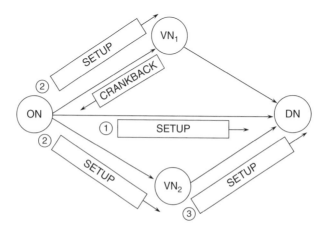

Figure 4.2 Use of signaling messages in TDR call/session setup.

bandwidth to next VN or DN, VN sends CRANKBACK message to ON and ON proceeds again with step 2.

4. DN receives call/session SETUP message, completes call/session setup, and ends call/session setup process.
5. ON blocks call/session setup and ends the call/session setup process.

4.6.2   Distributed Connection-by-Connection State-Dependent Routing (DC-SDR) Call/Session Setup

As discussed in Chapter 2, DC-SDR is a decentralized routing method with connection-by-connection updates based on real-time network status. For example, DC-SDR routing first selects the direct link between the ON and the DN. If no direct-link bandwidth is available, the ON checks the availability and load conditions of all of the paths to the DN on a per-call/session basis. If any of these paths are available, the call/session is set up over the least-loaded path. An available path is considered to be lightly loaded if the idle bandwidth on each link exceeds a threshold level. In order to determine all of the nodes in the network that satisfy this criterion, the ON sends a QUERY message to the DN (and some VNs in multilink paths) requesting the DN/VN to send a list of the nodes to which it has lightly loaded links. Upon receiving this list of nodes in the return STATUS message(s), the ON identifies any path(s) that currently has all lightly loaded links and therefore can be used for this call/session. Figure 4.3 illustrates the use of SETUP, QUERY, STATUS, and CRANKBACK messages in setting up a DC-SDR call/session, as follows:

1. ON first tries direct link for call/session to DN; if bandwidth is available ON reserves bandwidth and sends SETUP message to DN and completes call/session, if not ON proceeds to step 2.
2. ON sends QUERY message to DN and VNs on multilink paths request link status; DN and VNs return status information in STATUS message; ON finds most lightly loaded path to DN; if no such path is found ON proceeds to step 5, otherwise ON

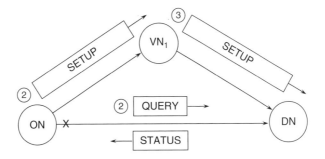

Figure 4.3   Use of signaling messages in DC-SDR call/session setup.

reserves bandwidth on first link in selected path and sends SETUP message to VNs and DN in path.

3. VN receives call/session SETUP message, determines further VNs and DN from DTL/ER parameter; VN reserves bandwidth on link and sends SETUP message to next VN or DN; process continues with step 4 when DN reached.

4. DN receives call/session SETUP message, completes call/session setup, and ends call/session setup process.

5. ON blocks call/session setup and ends the call/session setup process.

4.6.3 Centralized Periodic State-Dependent Routing (CP-SDR) Call/Session Setup

As discussed in Chapter 2, CP-SDR is a centralized real-time dynamic routing method with periodic updates based on periodic network status. CP-SDR provides periodic real-time routing decisions in the dynamic routing network. The CP-SDR method involves having an update of the idle bandwidth on each link sent via STATUS message to a TQO processor (TQOP) database every T (e.g., 10) seconds. Routing tables are determined from analysis of status data. Figure 4.4 illustrates the use of SETUP, QUERY, STATUS, and CRANKBACK messages in setting up a DP-SDR call/session, as follows:

1. All nodes send periodic STATUS messages to a central TQOP database containing the status of all connected links; ON first tries direct link for call/session to destination node; if bandwidth is available, ON reserves bandwidth and sends SETUP message to DN and completes call/session, if not ON proceeds to step 2.

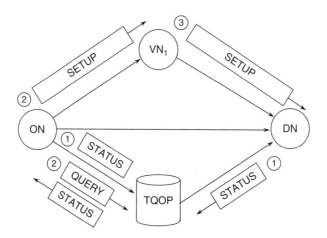

Figure 4.4 Use of signaling messages in DP-SDR call/session setup.

2. ON sends QUERY message to central TQOP database requesting the list of lightly loaded paths to DN; TQOP returns this information to ON in STATUS message; if no such path is found, ON proceeds to step 5; otherwise ON reserves bandwidth on first link in selected path and sends SETUP message to VNs and DN in path.
3. VN receives call/session SETUP message, determines further VNs and DN from DTL/ER parameter; VN reserves bandwidth on link and sends SETUP message to next VN or DN; process continues with step 4 when DN reached.
4. DN receives call/session SETUP message, completes call/session setup, and ends call/session setup process.
5. ON blocks call/session setup and ends the call/session setup process.

4.6.4   Event-Dependent Routing Call/Session Setup

As discussed in Chapter 2, EDR is a decentralized routing method based on a simplified decentralized learning method to achieve real-time dynamic routing. The direct link is used first if available, and a fixed alternate path is used until it is blocked. In this case a new alternate path is selected at random as the alternate path choice for the next call/session overflow from the direct link. Figure 4.5 illustrates use of the SETUP and CRANKBACK messages in setting up an EDR call/session, as follows:

1. ON first tries direct link for call/session to DN; if bandwidth is available, ON reserves bandwidth and sends SETUP message to DN and completes call/session, if not ON proceeds to step 2.
2. ON tries last successful path on previous call/session setup to DN; if no such path ON finds next path in route list; if no more paths in list ON proceeds to step 5; otherwise if idle bandwidth on first link, ON reserves bandwidth and sends SETUP

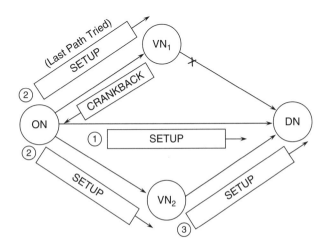

Figure 4.5   Use of signaling messages in EDR call/session setup.

message to VN1; if no idle bandwidth on first link ON returns to beginning of step 2; otherwise ON continues with step 3.

3. VN receives call/session SETUP and determines additional VNs and DN through the DTL/ER parameter in SETUP message; VN searches for idle bandwidth on the link to DN; if idle bandwidth is available, VN reserves bandwidth and sends SETUP message to next VN or DN and proceeds to step 4 when DN reached; if no idle bandwidth to next VN or DN, VN sends CRANKBACK message to ON and ON proceeds again with step 2.

4. DN receives call/session SETUP message, completes call/session setup, and ends call/session setup process.

5. ON blocks call/session setup and ends the call/session setup process.

4.7 Examples of Internetwork Routing

A network consisting of various subnetworks using different routing protocols is considered in this section. As illustrated in Figure 4.6, consider a network with four subnetworks denoted as networks A, B, C, and D, where each network uses a different routing protocol. In this example, network A is an ATM-based network that uses

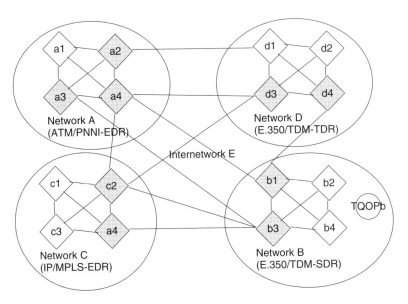

Figure 4.6 Example of an internetwork routing scenario (TQOPb denotes a TQO processor in network B for a centralized periodic SDR method. The set of shaded border nodes is Internetwork E for routing of connection/bandwidth-allocation requests among networks A, B, C, and D).

PNNI EDR path selection, network B is a TDM-based network that uses centralized periodic SDR path selection, network C is an IP-based network that uses MPLS EDR path selection, and network D is a TDM-based network that uses TDR path selection. Internetwork E is defined by the shaded border nodes in Figure 4.6 and is a virtual network where the interworking between networks A, B, C, and D is actually taking place.

4.7.1   Internetwork E Uses a Mixed Path Selection Method

Internetwork E can use various path selection methods in delivering connection/bandwidth-allocation requests among the subnetworks A, B, C, and D. For example, internetwork E can implement a mixed path selection method in which each node in internetwork E uses the path selection method implemented in its home subnetwork. Consider a connection/bandwidth-allocation request from node a1 in network A to node b4 in network B. Node a1 first routes the connection/bandwidth-allocation request to either node a3 or node a4 in network A and in doing so uses EDR path selection. In that regard node a1 first tries to route the connection/bandwidth-allocation request on the direct link a1–a4, and assuming that link a1–a4 bandwidth is unavailable then selects the current successful path a1–a3–a4 and routes the connection/bandwidth-allocation request to node a4 via node a3. In so doing node a1 and node a3 put the DTL/ER parameter (identifying ON a1, VN a3, and DN a4) and QoS-PAR, TRAF-PAR, PRIORITY, DEPTH, and DIFFSERV parameters in the connection/bandwidth-allocation request connection-setup IE.

Node a4 now proceeds to route the connection/bandwidth-allocation request to node b1 in subnetwork B using EDR path selection. In that regard node a4 first tries to route the connection/bandwidth-allocation request on the direct link a4–b1, and assuming that link a4–b1 bandwidth is unavailable then selects the current successful path a4–c2–b1 and routes the connection/bandwidth-allocation request to node b1 via node c2. In so doing node a4 and node c2 put the DTL/ER parameter (identifying ON a4, VN c2, and DN b1) and QoS-PAR, TRAF-PAR, PRIORITY, DEPTH, and DIFFSERV parameters in the connection/bandwidth-allocation request connection-setup IE.

If node c2 finds that link c2–b1 does not have sufficient available bandwidth, it returns control of the connection/bandwidth-allocation request to node a4 through use of a CBK parameter in the connection-release IE. If now node a4 finds that link d4–b1 has sufficient idle bandwidth capacity based on the RSE parameter in the status response IE from node b1, then node a4 could next try path a4–d3–d4–b1 to node b1. In that case node a4 routes the connection/bandwidth-allocation request to node d3 on link a4–d3, and node d3 is sent the DTL/ER parameter (identifying ON a4, VN d3, VN d4, and DN b1) and the PRIORITY and DEPTH parameters in the connection-setup IE. In that case node d3 tries to seize idle bandwidth on link d3–d4, and assuming that there is sufficient idle bandwidth routes the connection/bandwidth-allocation request to node d4 with the DTL/ER parameter (identifying ON a4, VN d3, VN d4, and DN b1) and the QoS-PAR, TRAF-PAR, PRIORITY, DEPTH, and DIFFSERV parameters in the connection-setup IE. Node d4 then routes the connection/bandwidth-allocation request on link d4–b1 to node b1, which has already been determined to have sufficient idle bandwidth capacity. If, on the other hand, there is insufficient idle d4–b1 bandwidth available, then node d3 returns control of the connection to node a4 through use of a CBK parameter in the connection-release IE. At that point node a4 may try another multilink path, such as a4–a3–b3–b1, using the same procedure as for the a4–d3–d4–b1 path.

Node b1 now proceeds to route the connection/bandwidth-allocation request to node b4 in network B using centralized periodic SDR path selection. In that regard node b1 first tries to route the connection/bandwidth-allocation request on the direct link b1–b4, and assuming that link b1–b4 bandwidth is unavailable then selects a two-link path b1–b2–b4, which is the currently recommended alternate path identified in the RRE parameter from the TQO processor (TQOPb) for network B. TQOPb bases its alternate routing recommendations on periodic (say every 10 s) link and traffic status information in the RSE parameters received from each node in network B. Based on the status information, TQOPb then selects the two-link path b1–b2–b4 and sends this alternate path recommendation in the RRE parameter to node b1 on a periodic basis (say every 10 s). Node b1 then routes the connection/bandwidth-allocation request to node b4 via node b2. In so doing node b1 and node b2 put the DTL/ER parameter (identifying ON b1, VN b2, and DN b4) and QoS-PAR, TRAF-PAR, PRIORITY, DEPTH, and DIFFSERV parameters in the connection/bandwidth-allocation request connection-setup IE.

A connection/bandwidth-allocation request from node b4 in network B to node a1 in network A would mostly be the same as the connection/bandwidth-allocation request from a1 to b4, except with all the steps listed above in reverse order. The difference would be in routing the connection/bandwidth-allocation request from node b1 in network B to node a4 in network A. In this case, based on the mixed path selection assumption in virtual network E, the b1 to a4 connection/bandwidth-allocation request would use centralized periodic SDR path selection, as node b1 is in network B, which uses centralized periodic SDR. In that regard node b1 first tries to route the connection/bandwidth-allocation request on the direct link b1–a4, and assuming that link b1–a4 bandwidth is unavailable then selects a two-link path b1–c2–a4, which is the currently recommended alternate path identified in the RRE parameter from the TQOPb for virtual network E. TQOPb bases its alternate routing recommendations on periodic (say every 10 s) link and traffic status information in the RSE parameters received from each node in virtual subnetwork E. Based on the status information, TQOPb then selects the two-link path b1–c2–a4 and sends this alternate path recommendation in the RRE parameter to node b1 on a periodic basis (say every 10 s). Node b1 then routes the connection/bandwidth-allocation request to node a4 via VN c2. In so doing node b1 and node c2 put the DTL/ER parameter (identifying ON b1, VN c2, and DN a4) and QoS-PAR, TRAF-PAR, PRIORITY, DEPTH, and DIFFSERV parameters in the connection/bandwidth-allocation request connection-setup IE.

If node c2 finds that link c2–a4 does not have sufficient available bandwidth, it returns control of the connection/bandwidth-allocation request to node b1 through use of a CBK parameter in the connection-release IE. If now node b1 finds that path b1–d4–d3–a4 has sufficient idle bandwidth capacity based on the RSE parameters in the status IEs to TQOPb, then node b1 could next try path b1–d4–d3–a4 to node a4. In that case node b1 routes the connection/bandwidth-allocation request to node d4 on link b1–d4 and node d4 is sent the DTL/ER parameter (identifying ON b1, VN d4, VN d3, and DN a4) and the QoS-PAR, TRAF-PAR, PRIORITY, DEPTH, and DIFF-SERV parameters in the connection-setup IE. In that case node d4 tries to seize idle bandwidth on link d4–d3, and assuming that there is sufficient idle bandwidth routes the connection/bandwidth-allocation request to node d3 with the DTL/ER parameter (identifying ON b1, VN d4, VN d3, and DN a4) and the QoS-PAR, TRAF-PAR, PRI-ORITY, DEPTH, and DIFFSERV parameters in the connection-setup IE. Node d3 then routes the connection/bandwidth-allocation request on link d3–a4 to node a4, which is expected based on status information in the RSE parameters to have sufficient idle bandwidth capacity. If, on the other hand, there is insufficient idle d3–a4 band-width available, then node d3 returns control of the connection to node b1 through use of a CBK parameter in the connection-release IE. At that point node b1 may try another multilink path, such as b1–b3–a3–a4, using the same procedure as for the b1–d4–d3–a4 path.

Allocation of end-to-end performance parameters across networks is addressed in Recommendation I.356, Section 9. An example is the allocation of the maximum transfer delay to individual network components of an end-to-end connection, such as national network portions and international portions.

4.7.2 Internetwork E Uses a Single Path Selection Method

Internetwork E may also use a single path selection method in delivering connection/bandwidth-allocation requests among the networks A, B, C, and D. For example, internetwork E can implement a path selection method in which each border node in internetwork E uses EDR. In this case the example connection/bandwidth-allocation request from node a1 in network A to node b4 in network B would be the same as described above. A connection/bandwidth-allocation request from node b4 in network B to node a1 in network A would be the same as the connection/bandwidth-allocation request from a1 to b4, except with all the steps listed above in reverse order. In this case, routing of the connection/bandwidth-allocation request from node b1 in network B to node a4 in network A would also use EDR in a similar manner to the a1 to b4 connection/bandwidth-allocation request described above.

4.8 Modeling of TQO Methods

This section again uses the full-scale national network model developed in Chapter 2 to study various TQO scenarios and trade-offs. The 135-node national model is illustrated in Figure 2.9, the multiservice traffic demand model is summarized in Table 2.1, and the cost model is summarized in Table 2.2.

Generally the routing and capacity designs for the meshed logical topologies are optimized by using the DEFO algorithms presented in Chapter 6, whereas the routing and capacity designs for the sparse logical topologies are optimized by using the shortest path optimization and DEFO algorithms presented in Chapter 6.

As shown, routing table management entails many different alternatives and trade-offs, such as the following:

- centralized routing table control versus distributed control
- preplanned routing table control versus on-line routing table control
- per-flow traffic management versus per-virtual network traffic management
- sparse logical topology versus meshed logical topology
- FXR versus TDR versus SDR versus EDR path selection
- multilink path selection versus two-link path selection
- path selection using local status information versus global status information
- global status dissemination alternatives, including status flooding, distributed query for status, and centralized status in a TQO processor

Here we evaluate the trade-offs in terms of the number of information elements and parameters exchanged, by type, under various TQO scenarios. This approach gives some indication of the processor and information exchange load required to support routing table management under various alternatives. In particular, we examine the following cases:

- Two-link DC-SDR
- Two-link STT-EDR
- Multilink CP-SDR
- Multilink DP-SDR
- Multilink DC-SDR
- Multilink STT-EDR

Tables 4.2 and 4.3 summarize comparative results for these cases, for the case of SDR path selection and STT path selection, respectively. The 135-node multiservice model was used for a simulation under a 30% general network overload in the network busy hour. The numbers in each table give the total messages of each type needed to do the indicated TQO functions, including flow setup, bandwidth allocation, crankback, and topology state flooding to update the topology database.

Tables 4.4 and 4.5 summarize comparative results for the cases of SDR path selection and STT path selection, respectively, in which the 135-node multiservice model was used for a simulation under a six-times focused overload on the OKBK node in the network busy hour.

Tables 4.6 and 4.7 summarize comparative results for the cases of SDR path selection and STT path selection, respectively, in which the 135-node multiservice model was used for a simulation under a facility failure on the CHCG-NYCM link in the network busy hour.

Table 4.2 Signaling and Information-Element (IE) Parameters Exchanged for Various TQO Methods with SDR Per-Flow Bandwidth Allocation; Number of Information Element Parameters Exchanged under 30% General Overload in Network Busy Hour (135-Node Multiservice Network Model)

TQO function	IE parameters	Two-link DC-SDR	Multilink CP-SDR	Multilink DP-SDR	Multilink DC-SDR
Call/session and connection routing	E.164-AESA, IP-ADR, CIC	21,511,629	21,511,629	21,511,629	21,511,629
QoS resource management	DTL/ER, QoS-PAR, TRAF-PAR, PRIORITY, DEPTH, MOD	24,009,586	21,511,629	21,511,629	21,511,629
Routing table management	CBK	287,288	0	0	0
	TSE		48,600	14,405,040	
	RSE	1,651,497			0
	RQE	1,651,497			0
	RRE		48,600		

Table 4.3 Signaling and Information-Element (IE) Parameters Exchanged for Various TQO Methods with STT-EDR Bandwidth Allocation; Number of Information Element Parameters Exchanged under 30% General Overload in Network Busy Hour (135-Node Multiservice Network Model)

TQO function	IE parameters	Two-link STT-EDR (per-flow bandwidth allocation)	Multilink STT-EDR (per-flow bandwidth allocation)	Multilink STT-EDR (per-virtual network bandwidth allocation)
Call/session and connection routing	E.164-AESA, IP-ADR, CIC	21,511,629	21,511,629	21,511,629
QoS resource management	DTL/ER, QoS-PAR, TRAF-PAR, PRIORITY, DEPTH, MOD	32,093,788	21,511,629	3,159,027
Routing table management	CBK TSE RSE RQE RRE	2,197,414	0	0

Table 4.4 Signaling and Information-Element (IE) Parameters Exchanged for Various TQO Methods with SDR Per-Flow Bandwidth Allocation; Number of Information Element Parameters Exchanged under 6× Focused Overload on OKBK in Network Busy Hour (135-Node Multiservice Network Model)

TQO function	IE parameters	Two-link DC-SDR	Multilink CP-SDR	Multilink DP-SDR	Multilink DC-SDR
Call/session and connection routing	E.164-AESA, IP-ADR, CIC	18,758,992	18,758,992	18,758,992	18,758,992
QoS resource management	DTL/ER, QoS-PAR, TRAF-PAR, PRIORITY, DEPTH, MOD	19,390,137	18,469,477	18,469,477	18,829,782
Routing table management	CBK	103,885	30,459	30,459	10,899
	TSE		48,600	14,405,040	
	RSE	1,072,869			1,507,684
	RQE	1,072,869			1,507,684
	RRE		48,600		

Table 4.5 Signaling and Information-Element (IE) Parameters Exchanged for Various TQO Methods with STT-EDR Bandwidth Allocation; Number of Information Element Parameters Exchanged under 6× Focused Overload on OKBK in Network Busy Hour (135-Node Multiservice Network Model)

TQO function	IE parameters	Two-link STT-EDR (per-flow bandwidth allocation)	Multilink STT-EDR (per-flow bandwidth allocation)	Multilink STT-EDR (per-virtual network bandwidth allocation)
Call/session and connection routing	E.164-AESA, IP-ADR, CIC	18,758,992	18,758,992	18,758,992
QoS resource management	DTL/ER, QoS-PAR, TRAF-PAR, PRIORITY, DEPTH, MOD	164,677,262	18,839,216	2,889,488
Routing table management	CBK TSE RSE RQE RRE	134,077,188	12,850	14,867

Table 4.6 Signaling and Information-Element (IE) Parameters Exchanged for Various TQO Methods with SDR Per-Flow Bandwidth Allocation; Number of Information Element Parameters Exchanged under Failure of CHCG-NYCM Link in Network Busy Hour (135-Node Multiservice Network Model)

TQO function	IE parameters	Two-link DC-SDR	Multilink CP-SDR	Multilink DP-SDR	Multilink DC-SDR
Call/session and connection routing	E.164-AESA, IP-ADR, CIC	16,547,302	16,547,302	16,547,302	16,547,302
QoS resource management	DTL/ER, QoS-PAR, TRAF-PAR, PRIORITY, DEPTH, MOD	16,735,827	16,561,929	16,561,929	16,561,929
Routing table management	CBK	7894	64,519	64,519	64,519
	TSE		48,600	14,405,040	
	RSE	277,796			1,653,869
	RQE	277,796			1,653,869
	RRE		48,600		

Table 4.7 Signaling and Information-Element (IE) Parameters Exchanged for Various TQO Methods with STT-EDR Bandwidth Allocation; Number of Information Element Parameters Exchanged under Failure of CHCG-NYCM Link in Network Busy Hour (135-Node Multiservice Network Model)

TQO function	IE parameters	Two-link STT-EDR (per-flow bandwidth allocation)	Multilink STT-EDR (per-flow bandwidth allocation)	Multilink STT-EDR (per-virtual network bandwidth allocation)
Call/session and connection routing	E.164-AESA, IP-ADR, CIC	16,547,302	16,547,302	16,547,302
QoS resource management	DTL/ER, QoS-PAR, TRAF-PAR, PRIORITY, DEPTH, MOD	16,770,061	16,652,418	2,790,003
Routing table management	CBK TSE RSE RQE RRE	22,685	64,519	13,957

Tables 4.8–4.10 summarize comparative results for the case of STT path selection, in the hierarchical network model shown in Figure 2.13, for the 30% general overload, the six-times focused overload, and the link failure scenarios, respectively. Both per-flow bandwidth allocation and per-virtual network bandwidth allocation cases are given.

Tables 4.2–4.10 illustrate the potential benefits of EDR methods in reducing routing table management overhead. Also, the per-flow bandwidth allocation is consuming far more LSP bandwidth allocation messages than per-VNET bandwidth allocation, while the traffic lost/delayed performance of the three methods is comparable.

Chapter 3 discussed EDR methods applied to QoS resource management, in which the connection bandwidth-allocation admission control for each link in the path is performed based on the local status of the link. That is, the ON selects any path for which the first link is allowed according to QoS resource management criteria. Each VN then checks the local link status of the links specified in the ER parameter against the PRIORITY and DEPTH parameters. If a subsequent link is not allowed, then a release with crankback is used to return to the ON, which may then select an alternate path. This use of this EDR path selection method, then, which entails the use of the release with crankback mechanism to search for an available path, is an alternative to SDR path selection alternatives, which may entail flooding of frequently changing link state parameters, such as available bandwidth.

A "least-loaded routing" strategy based on available bit rate on each link in a path is used in the SDR dynamic routing methods illustrated in the tables presented earlier and is a well-known, successful way to implement dynamic routing. Such SDR

Table 4.8 Signaling and Information-Element (IE) Parameters Exchanged for Various TQO Methods with STT-EDR Per-Virtual Network Bandwidth Allocation; Number of Information Element Parameters Exchanged under 30% General Overload in Network Busy Hour (135 Edge Node and 21 Backbone Node Hierarchical Multiservice Network Model)

TQO function	IE parameters	Multilink STT-EDR (per-flow bandwidth allocation)	Multilink STT-EDR (per-virtual network bandwidth allocation)
Call/session and connection routing	E.164-AESA, IP-ADR, CIC	21,511,629	21,511,629
QoS resource management	DTL/ER, QoS-PAR, TRAF-PAR, PRIORITY, DEPTH, MOD	21,511,629	3,161,371
Routing table management	CBK TSE RSE RQE RRE	0	0

Table 4.9 Signaling and Information-Element (IE) Parameters Exchanged for Various TQO Methods with STT-EDR Per-Virtual Network Bandwidth Allocation; Number of Information Element Parameters Exchanged under 6× Focused Overload on OKBK in Network Busy Hour (135 Edge Node and 21 Backbone Node Hierarchical Multiservice Network Model)

TQO function	IE parameters	Multilink STT-EDR (per-flow bandwidth allocation)	Multilink STT-EDR (per-virtual network bandwidth allocation)
Call/session and connection routing	E.164-AESA, IP-ADR, CIC	18,758,992	18,758,992
QoS resource management	DTL/ER, QoS-PAR, TRAF-PAR, PRIORITY, DEPTH, MOD	18,758,992	3,037,552
Routing table management	CBK TSE RSE RQE RRE	140,098	138,896

Table 4.10 Signaling and Information-Element (IE) Parameters Exchanged for Various TQO Methods with STT-EDR Per-Virtual Network Bandwidth Allocation; Number of Information Element (IE) Parameters Exchanged under Failure of CHCG-NYCM Link in Network Busy Hour (135 Edge Node and 21 Backbone Node Hierarchical Multiservice Network Model)

TQO function	IE parameters	Multilink STT-EDR (per-flow bandwidth allocation)	Multilink STT-EDR (per-virtual-network bandwidth allocation)
Call/session and connection routing	E.164-AESA, IP-ADR, CIC	16,547,302	16,547,302
QoS resource management	DTL/ER, QoS-PAR, TRAF-PAR, PRIORITY, DEPTH, MOD	16,712,295	2,809,705
Routing table management	CBK TSE RSE RQE RRE	165,603	41,539

methods have been used in several large-scale network applications in which efficient methods are used to disseminate the available link bandwidth status information, such as the query for status method using RQE and RRE parameters. However, there is a high overhead cost to obtain the available link bandwidth information when using flooding techniques, such as those which use the TSE parameter for link-state flooding. This is clearly evident in Tables 4.2–4.10. As a possible way around this, the EDR routing methods illustrated earlier do not require the dynamic flooding of available-bit-rate information. When EDR path selection with crankback is used in lieu of SDR path selection with link-state flooding, the reduction in the frequency of such link-state parameter flooding allows for larger area/peer group sizes. This is because link-state flooding can consume substantial processor and link resources in terms of message processing by the processors and link bandwidth consumed on the links. Crankback is then an alternative to the use of link-state-flooding algorithm for the ON to be able to determine which subsequent links in the path will be allowed.

4.9 Summary and Conclusions

The conclusions reached in this chapter are as follows:

- Per-VNET bandwidth allocation is preferred to per-flow allocation because of the much lower routing table management overhead requirements. Per-VNET bandwidth allocation is essentially equivalent to per-flow bandwidth allocation in network performance and efficiency, as discussed in Chapter 3.
- EDR TQO methods can lead to a large reduction in ALB flooding overhead without loss of network throughput performance. While SDR TQO methods typically use ALB flooding for TQO path selection, EDR TQO methods do not require ALB flooding. Rather, EDR TQO methods typically search out capacity by learning models, as in the STT method. ALB flooding can be very resource intensive, as it requires link bandwidth to carry LSAs, processor capacity to process LSAs, and the overhead can limit area/autonomous system size.
- EDR TQO methods lead to possible larger administrative areas as compared to SDR-based TQO methods because of lower routing table management overhead requirements. This can help achieve single-area flat topologies, which, as discussed in Chapter 3, exhibit better network performance and, as discussed in Chapter 6, greater design efficiencies in comparison with multiarea hierarchical topologies.

4.10 Applicability of Requirements

The benefits of per-VNET QoS resource management, sparse single-area flat topology, and multilink STT-EDR path selection methods lead to dramatically lower routing table management overhead, automatic provisioning expense reduction, and increased scalability. These results are reflected in the GTQO protocol for MPLS/GMPLS-based integrated voice/data dynamic routing networks. In particular, the GTQO protocol provides automatic provisioning of topology databases and fewer links to provision in sparse network topology, leading to operations expense and capital savings. Also, the GTQO protocol eliminates ALB flooding and allows larger/fewer areas, leading to dramatically improved network stability, performance, and scalability. The automatic exchange of link, node, and reachable address information across different network technologies has been standardized [E.361].

These and other results presented motivate the service provider requirements for the standardized GTQO protocol, which includes generic service aspects, management aspects, and CAC aspects. These GTQO protocol requirements should then be used to drive vendor implementations in the direction of network operator requirements and vendor interoperability.

EDR TQO path selection methods are already in widespread use in TDM-based dynamic routing networks, as discussed in Chapter 1. Such methods are not only simple and efficient, but have the distinct advantage of reducing the control overhead, leading to more scalable TQO solutions. Once again, vendors have yet to announce such TQO capabilities in their products, but the worldwide implementation of sophisticated TQO methods in TDM networks could provide some motivation for vendors to adopt these TQO requirements and capabilities, and their potential marketability. As demonstrated in this chapter and throughout this book, service providers and their customers would benefit from these capabilities in terms of network performance and profitability improvements. If vendors develop such TQO capabilities in their products, service provider interest in implementing such features also leads to vendor profitability.

Chapter 5

Traffic Engineering and QoS Optimization of GMPLS-Based Multilayer Dynamic Routing Networks

5.1 Introduction

GTQO protocol requirements are put forward in Chapter 10, which include GMPLS multilayer network dynamic routing capabilities. GTQO requirements are suggested for consideration by network architects and developers alike, and ultimately, I believe, such GTQO network directions will eventually emerge, and/or perhaps be reinvented. Reinvention by the right people and/or companies might perhaps give the best chance of implementation and deployment. Reinvention is surely possible, if not likely, in the long run. For example, the GMPLS-based GTQO capabilities discussed in this chapter have been reinvented, as they are at least a decade and a half old already. Let's take a closer look at that example.

First implemented during the 1980s, dynamic routing in voice networks provided considerable benefits in improved performance quality and reduced costs. As early as 1990, these benefits motivated the extension of dynamic routing to networks with dynamically rearrangeable transport capacity; that is the subject of [ASH90, ASH94] where the fully shared network (FSN) concept is described. FSN envisioned use of automatic control of optical cross-connects (OXCs) to achieve dynamic bandwidth allocation of transport and connection-switching capacity, where the envisioned benefits include robust network design, efficient capacity engineering, and automatic transport provisioning to achieve increased revenues and significant savings in capital and operations costs. The FSN concept builds on class-of-service dynamic routing capabilities by allowing automatic implementation of self-healing network strategies such as transport diversity, multiple homing, and transport restoration. Automatic control of OXCs allows rapid provisioning and rearrangement of internode transport capacity, access transport capacity, and connection switching capacity in much shorter time periods than is possible without FSN. An FSN design module is described [ASH94] that receives daily network traffic data, designs and allocates transport capacity based on traffic levels, calculates an efficient rearrangement strategy, interfaces with the connection switching nodes and OXCs through a control protocol, and automates the provisioning and control of transport and connection switching capacity within the FSN.

While highly promising in its perceived benefits, FSN proved difficult to implement for a variety of reasons. Chief among these reasons was that FSN technology crosses several network organizations and operations. Connection switching and transport are historically separate operational processes, maintained in separate organizations, with specialized tools, procedures, and personnel focused on each operation. Merging and converging these operations, tools, and personnel proved too big an obstacle to implement FSN. On the other hand, implementation of dynamic routing in connection switching networks, as discussed in Chapter 1, represented a monumental change across many different operational groups and was accomplished successfully by many service providers throughout the world, which showed that implementing technologies that fundamentally impact operational processes is not only possible, it was accomplished by numerous major service providers worldwide (see Table 1.2 in Chapter 1).

FSN was renamed GMPLS in recent years. It is good that the technology is emerging, by whatever name, because the benefits of these ideas are unchanged. See Appendix A for a review of GMPLS technology (see [FARREL05] for an excellent reference on the topic).

As outlined in Chapter 1, the problem statement for TQO design in this chapter includes the following:

- GMPLS LSP (logical link) routing and bandwidth allocation layer 2 design: Find an optimal GMPLS LSP dynamic routing and bandwidth allocation design and fast GMPLS LSP restoration strategy for arbitrary traffic loads and network topology that yield minimum cost capacity and maximum flow/revenue, with minimal control overhead, subject to meeting performance constraints.
- Physical fiber transport/layer 1 design: Find an optimal physical transport network design, bandwidth allocation strategy, and fast restoration procedure for arbitrary traffic loads and network topology that yield minimum cost capacity and maximum flow/revenue, with minimal control overhead, subject to meeting performance constraints.

This chapter describes and analyzes dynamic transport routing in light of GMPLS-based control capabilities to enable dynamic transport switching of dense wavelength division multiplexer (DWDM) light paths and layer 2 logical links through OXCs. GMPLS technology [RFC3945, FARREL04, FARREL05, L1VPN-FRAMEWORK, MLN-EVALUATION, MLN-REQUIREMENTS] offers a revolutionary new approach (first new multilayer dynamic routing revolution since FSN, at least) to integrated control of the layer 3 dynamic connection routing and layer 2 dynamic transport routing networks.

GMPLS-based dynamic transport routing offers advantages of simplicity of design and robustness to load variations and network failures. Dynamic transport routing can combine with dynamic connection routing to shift transport bandwidth among node pairs and services through use of flexible transport-switching technology. GMPLS-based dynamic transport routing can provide automatic link provisioning, diverse link routing, and rapid link restoration for improved transport capacity utilization and reliable performance under stress.

We present reliable transport routing models to achieve reliable network designs that meet predefined restoration service objectives for any transport link or node failure and that continue to provide connections to customers with essentially no perceived interruption of service. We show that robust routing techniques, such as dynamic connection routing, multiple ingress/egress routing, and logical link diversity routing, improve response to node or transport failures.

Cross-connect devices, such as OXCs, are able to switch transport channels, e.g., OC48 channels, onto different higher capacity transport links such as an individual DWDM channel on a fiber-optic cable. Transport paths can be rearranged at high speed using OXCs, typically within tens of milliseconds switching times. These OXCs can reconfigure logical transport capacity on demand, such as for peak-day traffic or emergency restoration of capacity under node or transport failure. Dynamic rearrangement of logical link capacity can involve reallocating both transport bandwidth and node terminations to different logical links. Real-time dynamic transport routing combined with real-time dynamic connection routing can be either distributed or centralized within the GMPLS network, and both approaches are addressed in this chapter.

Again using the 135-node national network model developed in Chapter 2, we give modeling results for GMPLS-based dynamic transport routing capacity design, performance under network failure, and performance under various network overload scenarios. These include dynamic transport routing capacity design and performance for network failures, general traffic overloads, unexpected overloads, and peak-day traffic loads. We conclude that GMPLS-based dynamic transport routing provides greater network throughput and, consequently, enhanced revenue, achieves efficient network design and capital savings, and greatly enhances network performance under failure and overload.

5.2   GMPLS-Based Dynamic Transport Routing Principles

Let's return to the TQO functional layer model discussed in Chapter 1 and review the layer 2 dynamic transport routing function enabled by GMPLS technology.

Figure 5.1 illustrates the four network layers considered in the TQO model being analyzed and designed. These layers correspond to the central network box in Figure 1.1 (Chapter 1). An additional layer considered in analysis and design is the TQO

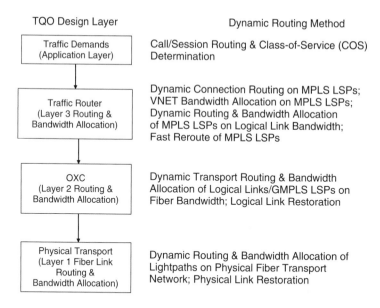

TQO Design Layer   Dynamic Routing Method

Traffic Demands
(Application Layer)   Call/Session Routing & Class-of-Service (COS)
                             Determination

Traffic Router   Dynamic Connection Routing on MPLS LSPs;
(Layer 3 Routing &   VNET Bandwidth Allocation on MPLS LSPs;
Bandwidth Allocation)   Dynamic Routing & Bandwidth Allocation
                             of MPLS LSPs on Logical Link Bandwidth;
                             Fast Reroute of MPLS LSPs

OXC   Dynamic Transport Routing & Bandwidth
(Layer 2 Routing &   Allocation of Logical Links/GMPLS LSPs on
Bandwidth Allocation)   Fiber Bandwidth; Logical Link Restoration

Physical Transport   Dynamic Routing & Bandwidth Allocation of
(Layer 1 Fiber Link   Lightpaths on Physical Fiber Transport
Routing &   Network; Physical Link Restoration
Bandwidth Allocation)

Figure 5.1 Dynamic connection routing (layer 3) and dynamic transport routing (layer 3).

operational/management layer, which is shown in the feedback loops around the central network box in Figure 1.1 (not shown in Figure 5.1). Each layer is explained briefly:

- Traffic/application layer: At this layer, call/session routing takes place, for example, using SIP [RFC3312]. Call/session routing involves the translation of a number or name to a routing address. Class of service of a call/session is also determined, which can include service identity, transport requirements, routing parameters, and link capabilities, as described in Chapter 3.
- MPLS LSPs/layer 3: Here dynamic routing of connections takes place in response to traffic demands in the form of calls/sessions. Calls/sessions fall within COSs, and COSs are assigned to VNETs (e.g., high-priority voice, normal-priority voice, VPN data, as illustrated in Figure 1.4); a VNET is allocated bandwidth on layer 2 logical links and the bandwidth allocation is managed to meet performance requirements. This mesh of MPLS LSPs forming the VNETs is carried in turn by GMPLS LSPs forming the layer 2 logical link network, and bandwidth allocated to VNETs can be shared with other VNETs when relatively idle, but is protected for exclusive use by traffic assigned to the particular VNET when necessary (accomplished through dynamic bandwidth reservation mechanisms explained in Chapter 3).
- Logical links/GMPLS LSPs/layer 2: Here dynamic routing of logical links takes place using GMPLS LSPs on the physical fiber transport network, where the GMPLS LSPs are allocated bandwidth on the physical fiber transport network so as to meet performance requirements. Fast restoration takes place at this layer should a logical link/GMPLS LSP fail.

- Physical fiber transport/layer 1: At this layer, light paths are routed and allocated bandwidth on the physical fiber transport network to meet performance requirements. GMPLS LSPs are used in a hierarchical fashion to provision high bandwidth "express links" between nodes, which appear as layer 1 physical links and are used to route layer 2 logical links. Fast restoration of physical links and express links takes place at this layer.
- Operational/management layer: Here the TQO operational/management functions are performed, which include traffic management (real-time performance monitoring, network control), capacity forecasting, daily and weekly performance monitoring, short-term network adjustment, and capacity design optimization.

Figure 5.1 therefore illustrates the concept of dynamic connection routing at layer 3 and dynamic transport routing at layer 2 from a generalized view of TQO layers and routing capabilities at each layer, with control at each layer enabled by GMPLS multilayer control. Figure 5.1 illustrates the relationship of the connection-level and transport-level dynamic routing methods used in the GMPLS-based dynamic transport routing network. Dynamic connection routing at layer 3, such as discussed in Chapter 2, is used to route connections comprising the underlying traffic demand. Traffic trunk capacity allocations are made for each VNET on the transport logical link capacity. For each connection the originating node analyzes the called number and determines the terminating node, class of service, and VNET. The originating node tries to set up the connection on the direct traffic trunk to the terminating node and, if unavailable, dynamic transport routing is used to rearrange the traffic trunk capacity as required to match the traffic demands and to achieve internode diversity, access diversity, and traffic trunk restoration following node, OXC, or fiber transport failures. The traffic trunk capacities are allocated by the traffic router to the logical link bandwidth and the logical link bandwidth allocated by the TQO processor to the fiber-link bandwidth, such that the bandwidth is used efficiently according to the level of traffic demand between the nodes.

At the application/traffic demand layer in the TQO hierarchy, call/session requests are routed using dynamic connection routing on the logical link network by connection routing logic. At the logical link demand layer in the TQO hierarchy, logical link transport demands are routed using OXC transport switching capabilities, which allow GMPLS-based dynamic transport routing to route transport demands in accordance with transport capacity demand based on traffic levels. Real-time logical link routing and real-time response to traffic congestion can be provided by OXC dynamic transport routing to improve network performance.

Now let's focus more on the relationship between the layer 1 physical transport link network and the layer 2 logical link network. An illustration of a physical transport link network is shown in Figure 5.2, and Figure 5.3 illustrates the mapping of layer 2 logical links onto the layer 1 physical transport link network of Figure 5.2. Some logical links overlay two or more physical fiber transport links. For example, in Figure 5.2, logical link AD traverses physical fiber transport links AB, BC, and CD.

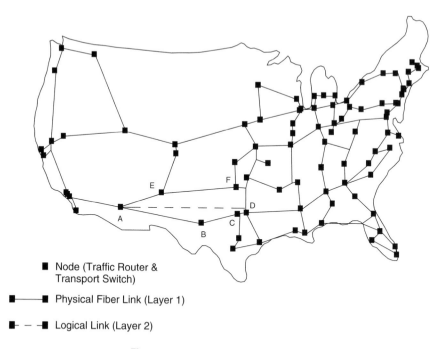

Figure 5.2 Transport network model.

GMPLS technology allows integrated control of the layer 2 logical link network and layer 1 physical transport link network and can realize the capabilities now described in connection with Figure 5.3.

Figure 5.3 further illustrates the difference between the physical transport network (layer 1) and the logical link network (layer 2). Logical links are, for example, GMPLS LSPs routed between network nodes under GMPLS control on the physical transport network. Logical links can be provisioned at given bandwidth capacities, such as OC3, OC12, OC48, and OC192, where the design capacity is dependent on the level of traffic demand between nodes.

Figure 5.3 indicates that a direct logical link is obtained by cross-connecting through a transport switching location under GMPLS control. Thus, the layer 2 logical link network is overlaid on a sparse layer 1 physical transport link network. A transport switching (cross-connect) device is traversed at each network node on a given logical link path, as illustrated in Figure 5.3. This is particularly promising when such a transport switching device has low cost.

Figure 5.4 illustrates layer 3/2 traffic/connection switching nodes (traffic router nodes) and layer 2/1 logical/physical link OXC transport switching nodes. Figure 5.4 illustrates the routing of the logical links in Figure 5.3 through the connection switching and transport switching nodes. As illustrated in Figure 5.4, the layer 2 logical links are multiplexed onto the higher capacity physical fiber links. Logical links are established by use of the OXC transport switching nodes.

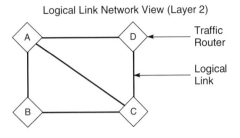

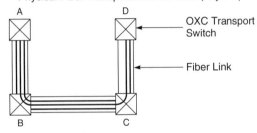

Figure 5.3   Logical links (layer 2) and physical transport network links (layer 1).

It is clear from Figures 5.2, 5.3, and 5.4 that in a logical link network constituted by GMPLS LSPs, many node pairs may have a "direct" logical link connection where none exists in the physical transport network. In this case a direct logical link is obtained by cross-connecting through a transport switching location, such as an OXC. This is distinct from the connection routing situation, in which a bearer connection is actually switched at an intermediate location. This distinction between transport switching (cross-connecting) and connection switching is a bit subtle, but it is fundamental to connection routing of calls/sessions and transport routing of logical links.

Figures 5.3 and 5.4 illustrate one of the logical inconsistencies encountered when we design the logical link network to be essentially separate from the physical transport link network. On the alternative path for connection setups from node B to nodes C through A, two logical links are involved: the logical link from B to A and the logical link from A to C. On this alternate path, connection switching is performed at node A to set up the B-to-C connection. However, observe from Figures 5.3 and 5.4 that the physical link path for this connection is, in fact, B to A to B to C, i.e., up and back from B to A (a phenomenon known as "backhauling") and then across from B to C. The sharing of capacity by various traffic loads in this way actually increases the efficiency of the network because the backhauled capacity to and from B and A is only used when no direct A-to-B or A-to-C traffic wants to use it. It is conceivable that under certain conditions, capacity could be put to more efficient use, which is studied in this chapter.

Hence a logical link connection is obtained by cross-connecting through transport switching devices, such as OXCs, which is distinct from call/session connection

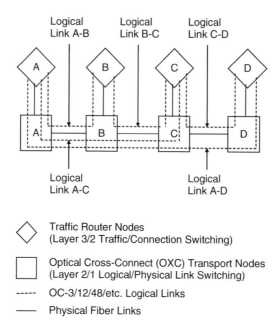

Figure 5.4 Logical network and physical network topology showing layer 3 connection switching and layer 2 logical link switching.

routing, where traffic routers switch a connection on the logical links at each node in the connection path. In this way, the logical link network is overlaid on a sparser physical transport link network.

In Chapter 2 we discussed a wide variety of dynamic connection routing methods. GMPLS-based dynamic transport routing methods incorporate dynamic path selection that seeks out and uses idle network capacity by using frequent, perhaps connection-by-connection, transport routing table update decisions. The trend in both connection routing and transport routing architecture is toward greater flexibility in resource allocation, which includes transport switching and connection switching resource allocation. A fixed transport routing architecture may have dynamic connection routing but fixed transport routing of logical link capacity. In a GMPLS-based dynamic transport routing architecture, however, we envision that the logical link capacities can be rearranged in real time. We now give examples of GMPLS dynamic transport routing.

5.3 GMPLS-Based Dynamic Transport Routing Examples

This section gives several illustrations of GMPLS-based dynamic transport routing. Indeed, some of the examples given are possible with a central TQO processor, or network management system, doing the transport network dynamic routing and management. However, using a central TQO processor would only make a case for reactive reprovisioning of the logical links over the physical transport network. Centralized control also may not be able to react in real time and could be a potential bottleneck for dynamic transport routing. GMPLS allows the intelligence for dynamic routing control to be distributed within the network and thereby GMPLS control is able to achieve more rapid, real-time dynamic transport routing. The downside of such distributed control is that during massive transport failures, for example, which require equally massive dynamic transport routing and repair events, there may be more contention for network resources in a distributed real-time GMPLS system, as multiple logical link reroute attempts are made without coordination.

In this section we give examples of seasonal and weekly rearrangement to illustrate dynamic traffic load patterns that would justify and benefit from logical link dynamic routing/rearrangement. However, these examples do not justify the need for real-time dynamic transport routing capability. Rather, examples are given in Section 5.6 of dynamic transport routing for peak Christmas day traffic, network failures due to a fiber cut, and an unexpected focused network overload due to a hurricane. These latter examples clearly illustrate how real-time dynamic transport routing is beneficially taking place within the network in a distributed manner rather than with a centralized tool. It needs to be pointed out that all of these distributed, real-time transport routing examples could perhaps also be done in a centralized fashion with a centralized management tool and possibly even gain incremental optimization benefits from centralized rather than distributed visibility. Once again, however, a centralized implementation has drawbacks of possible slowness, computational burden, and reliability. These distributed, GMPLS-based examples should reinforce and justify the utility of GMPLS-based real-time dynamic routing in the transport network.

As illustrated in Figure 5.5, the GMPLS-based dynamic transport routing network concept includes backbone routers (BRs), access routers (ARs), and OXCs. Access routers could route traffic, for example, from local connection switching nodes, customer premises equipment, and international connection switching nodes. Here a logical link transmission channel could consist, for example, of OC3-, OC12-, OC48-, or OCx-level bandwidth allocation. An OXC can cross-connect (or "transport switch") a logical link transmission channel within one terminating fiber wavelength channel in a DWDM system to a like channel within another fiber DWDM system. In the example illustrated, access routers connect to the OXC by means of transport links such as link AX1, and backbone routers connect to OXCs by means of physical transport links such as BX1. A number of backbone fiber/DWDM transport links interconnect the OXC network elements, such as links XX1 and XX2. Backbone logical links are terminated at each end by OXCs and are routed over fiber/DWDM spans on the physical transport network on the shortest physical paths. Inter-BR logical links are formed by cross-connecting the bandwidth channels through OXCs between a pair of backbone routers.

For example, the backbone logical link B1 from BR1 to BR2 is formed by connecting between BR1 and BR2 through fiber/DWDM links BX1, XX1, and BX2 by making appropriate cross-connects through OXC1, OXC2, and OXC3. Logical links have variable bandwidth capacity controlled by the GMPLS-based dynamic transport routing

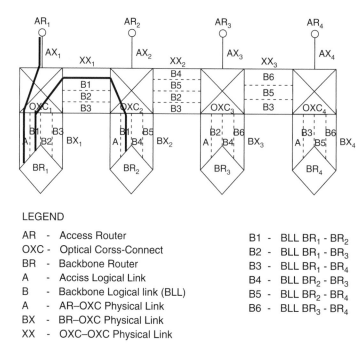

Figure 5.5 GMPLS-based dynamic transport routing network.

network. Access logical links are formed by cross-connecting between ARs and BRs, e.g., access router AR1 connected on fiber/DWDM links AX1 and BX1 through OXC1 to BR1 or, alternatively, access router AR1 connected on fiber/DWDM links AX1, XX1, and BX2 cross-connected through OXC1 and OXC2 to BR2. For additional network reliability, backbone routers and access routers may be dual homed to two OXCs, possibly in different building locations.

There are significant network design opportunities with GMPLS-based dynamic transport routing, and in the following sections we give examples of dynamic transport routing over different timescales. These examples illustrate the network efficiency and performance improvements possible with seasonal, weekly, daily, and real-time dynamic transport routing/rearrangement.

5.3.1 Seasonal Traffic Variations Example

An illustration of GMPLS-based dynamic transport routing for varying seasonal traffic demands is given in Figure 5.6. As seasonal demands shift, the dynamic transport network is better able to match demands to routed transport capacity, thus gaining efficiencies in transport requirements. Figure 5.6 illustrates how dynamic transport routing achieves network capacity reductions and shows how transport demand is routed according to varying seasonal requirements. As seasonal demands shift, the

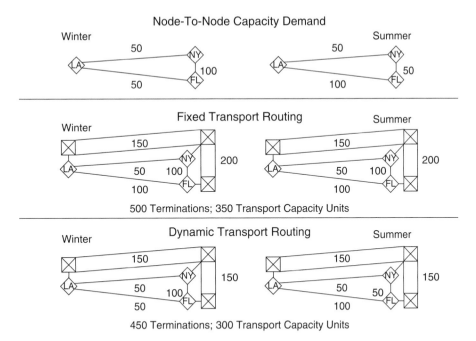

Figure 5.6 GMPLS-based dynamic transport routing vs fixed transport routing.

dynamic transport network is better able to match demands to routed transport capacity, thus gaining efficiencies in transport requirements. Figure 5.6 illustrates the variation of winter and summer capacity demands. With fixed transport routing, the maximum termination capacity and transport capacity are provided across the seasonal variations, because in a manual environment without dynamic transport routing it is not practical to disconnect and reconnect capacity on such short cycle times. When transport rearrangement is automated with GMPLS-based dynamic transport routing, however, the termination and transport design can be changed on a weekly, daily, or real-time basis to match the termination and transport design implementation with the actual network demands. Note that in the fixed transport network there is unused termination and transport capacity that cannot be used by any demands; sometimes this is called "trapped capacity" because it is available but cannot be accessed by any actual demand. In contrast, the dynamic transport network follows the capacity demand with flexible transport routing and, together with transport network design, reduces the trapped capacity.

Therefore, the variation of demands leads to capacity-sharing efficiencies, which in the example of Figure 5.6 reduce termination capacity requirements by 50-node terminations, or approximately 10% compared with the fixed transport network, and by 50 transport capacity requirements, or approximately 14%. Therefore, with GMPLS-based dynamic transport routing, capacity utilization can be made more efficient in comparison with fixed transport routing, because with dynamic transport network design the link sizes can be matched to the network load.

5.3.2 Week-to-Week Traffic Variations Example

With dynamic connection routing and dynamic transport routing design models, reserve capacity can be reduced in comparison with fixed transport routing. As described in Chapter 1, in-place capacity that exceeds the capacity required to exactly meet the design loads with the objective performance is called reserve capacity. Reserve capacity comes about because load uncertainties, such as forecast errors, tend to cause capacity buildup in excess of the network design that matches the forecast loads exactly. Reluctance to disconnect and rearrange traffic trunk and transport capacity contributes to this reserve capacity buildup. Typical ranges for reserve capacity are from 15 to 25 % or more of network cost. Models show that dynamic connection routing compared with fixed connection routing provides a potential 5 % reduction in reserve capacity while retaining a low level of short-term capacity design [ASH98].

With dynamic transport network design the logical link sizes can be matched to the network load. With GMPLS-based dynamic transport routing, the logical link capacity disconnect policy becomes, in effect, one in which logical link capacity is always disconnected when not needed for the current traffic loads. Models given in [FRANKS79] predict reserve capacity reductions of 10 % or more under this policy, and the modeling analysis results presented in Section 5.6 based on weekly dynamic transport design substantiate this conclusion.

Weekly design and rearrangement of logical link capacity can approach zero reserve capacity designs. Figures 5.7 and 5.8 illustrate the changing of routed transport capacity on a weekly basis between node pairs A–B, C–D, and B–E, as demands between these node pairs change on a weekly basis.

These transport routing and capacity changes are made automatically in the dynamic transport network, in which diverse transport routing of logical links A–B and C–D is maintained by the GMPLS-based dynamic transport routing network. Logical link diversity achieves additional network reliability.

5.3.3 Daily Traffic Variations Example

Daily design and rearrangement of transport link capacity can achieve performance improvements for similar reasons due to noncoincidence of transport capacity demands that can change daily. An example is given in Figures 5.9 and 5.10 for traffic noncoincidence experienced on peak days such as Christmas day. Figure 5.9 illustrates the normal business-day routing of access demands and inter-BR demands. On Christmas day, however, there are many busy nodes and many idle nodes. For example, node BR2 may be relatively idle on Christmas day (e.g., if it were a downtown business node), while BR1 may be very busy. Therefore, on Christmas day, BR2 demands to everywhere else in the network are reduced, and through dynamic

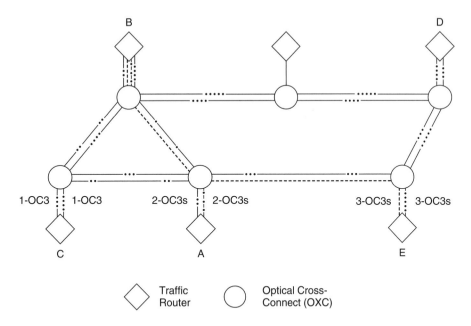

Figure 5.7   GMPLS-based dynamic transport routing network weekly arrangement (week 1 load pattern).

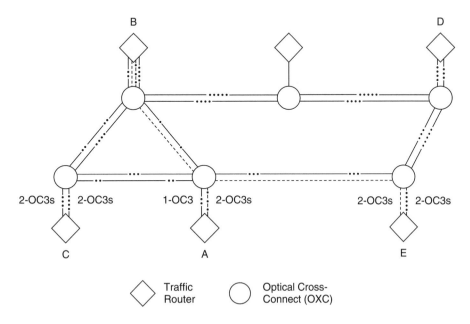

Figure 5.8   GMPLS-based dynamic transport routing network weekly arrangement (week 2 load pattern).

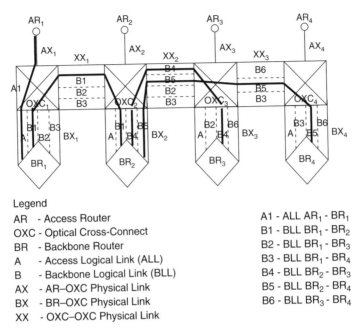

Legend
AR   - Access Router
OXC - Optical Cross-Connect
BR   - Backbone Router
A   - Access Logical Link (ALL)
B   - Backbone Logical Link (BLL)
AX   - AR–OXC Physical Link
BX   - BR–OXC Physical Link
XX   - OXC–OXC Physical Link

A1 - ALL AR_1 - BR_1
B1 - BLL BR_1 - BR_2
B2 - BLL BR_1 - BR_3
B3 - BLL BR_1 - BR_4
B4 - BLL BR_2 - BR_3
B5 - BLL BR_2 - BR_4
B6 - BLL BR_3 - BR_4

Figure 5.9   GMPLS-based dynamic transport routing peak-day design (before rearrangement).

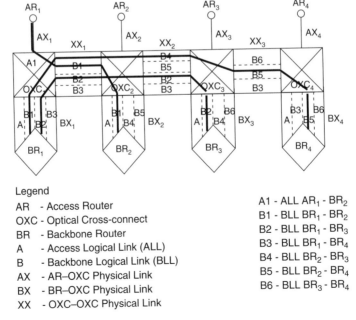

Legend
AR   - Access Router
OXC - Optical Cross-connect
BR   - Backbone Router
A   - Access Logical Link (ALL)
B   - Backbone Logical Link (BLL)
AX   - AR–OXC Physical Link
BX   - BR–OXC Physical Link
XX   - OXC–OXC Physical Link

A1 - ALL AR_1 - BR_2
B1 - BLL BR_1 - BR_2
B2 - BLL BR_1 - BR_3
B3 - BLL BR_1 - BR_4
B4 - BLL BR_2 - BR_3
B5 - BLL BR_2 - BR_4
B6 - BLL BR_3 - BR_4

Figure 5.10   GMPLS-based dynamic transport routing peak-day design (after rearrangement).

transport routing these transport capacity reductions can be made automatically. Similarly, BR1 demands are increased on Christmas day. Access demands such as those from AR1 can be redirected to freed-up termination capacity on BR2, as illustrated in Figure 5.10, which also frees up the termination capacity on BR1 to be used for inter-BR demand increases. By this kind of access demand and inter-BR demand rearrangement, based on noncoincident traffic shifts, more traffic to and from BR1 can be completed because inter-BR logical link capacity is increased, now using freed-up transport capacity from the reduction in the transport capacity needed by BR2. On a peak day such as Christmas day, the busy nodes are often limited by inter-BR logical link capacity; this rearrangement reduces or eliminates this bottleneck, as is illustrated in the Christmas day dynamic transport network design example in Section 5.6.5.

The balancing of access and inter-BR capacity throughout the network can lead to robustness to unexpected load surges. This load-balancing design is illustrated in Section 5.6.4 with an example based on a hurricane-caused focused overload in the northeastern United States. Dynamic transport and connection switching capacity rearrangements based on instantaneous reaction to unforeseen events such as earthquakes could be made in the dynamic transport network.

5.3.4 Real-Time Traffic Variations Example

With GMPLS-based dynamic transport routing, the ultimate GMPLS application is that logical transport bandwidth is shifted in real time at layer 2 among node pairs and services through the use of fast dynamic cross-connect devices. One approach to real-time GMPLS bandwidth allocation that is modeled in several scenarios in the following section (network failure and unexpected overload scenarios) is now described.

For real-time bandwidth allocation of dynamic transport routing networks, the simplest case is that the layer 2 logical links are directly overlaid on the layer 1 physical fiber links. Connections are routed dynamically within the network by connection switching and OXC transport switching bandwidth on every logical/fiber transport link. As a result, the bandwidth allocation procedure is relatively simple in that the traffic demands of the various node pairs are aggregated directly to the one logical/fiber transport link and then each logical/fiber transport link is sized to carry the total traffic demand from all node pairs that use the logical/fiber transport link. However, this approach involves a large amount of OXC transport switching for each connection and may not scale well or even be a feasible approach. Another approach is to do real-time bandwidth allocation to the MPLS LSPs controlling the layer 3 VNET bandwidth allocation. This approach would still require layer 3 connection switching on the logical links comprising the "direct" MPLS LSPs. An alternative real-time bandwidth allocation procedure is now described to avoid much of this layer 2 transport switching and layer 3 connection switching and approach the limiting GMPLS real-time bandwidth allocation model described.

Logical link bandwidth allocation at layer 2 also creates direct logical links, again using GMPLS to do real-time bandwidth allocation to the direct logical links. This

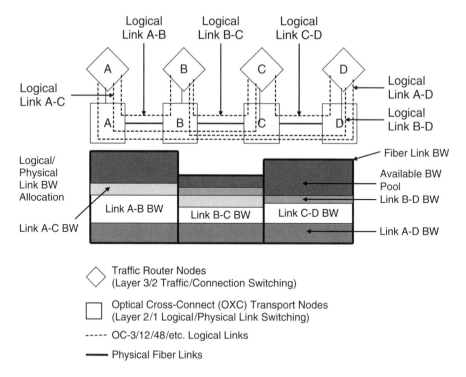

Figure 5.11 GMPLS real-time bandwidth allocation model.

approach saves layer 3 connection switching and layer 2 logical link transport switching and approaches the limiting GMPLS real-time bandwidth allocation scenario where logical/fiber links overlay each other, as described above. Figure 5.11 illustrates the real-time GMPLS bandwidth allocation model. It is assumed that the three physical fiber links in this example all have different bandwidth capacity. Logical link bandwidth is allocated to the direct logical links in accordance with traffic demands, and normally not all logical link bandwidth is assigned; thus, there is a pool of unassigned bandwidth. In cases of traffic overload for a given node pair, the node first sets up connections on the direct logical link that connects the node pair. If the direct logical link bandwidth is exhausted, the direct logical link bandwidth is increased by using the available pool of bandwidth, and the connection is set up on the direct logical link. That is, if there is available bandwidth in the bandwidth pool, then the bandwidth is allocated to the direct logical link and is used to set up the connection. In a similar manner, in the event that bandwidth is underutilized on the direct logical link, excess bandwidth is released to the available pool of bandwidth and then becomes available for assignment to other direct logical links between other node pairs. That is, if the logical link bandwidth is sufficiently underutilized, the bandwidth is returned to the available pool of layer 1 fiber-link bandwidth. The network nodes make these direct logical link additions and reductions of network resources on a dynamic basis through analysis of the traffic demand collected at the individual nodes.

In this real-time dynamic transport routing approach, we allow logical link bandwidth between the various nodes to be adjusted dynamically, in near real time. GMPLS-based dynamic transport routing capability enables dynamic bandwidth allocation of the logical link capacities on demand, in a distributed manner, such as for emergency restoration of capacity under node or transport failure. This capability also appears desirable for use in relatively slow rearrangement of capacity, such as for busy-hour traffic, weekend traffic, peak-day traffic, and weekly redesign of logical link capacities. At various times the demands for connection switching and transport capacity by the various node pairs and services that ride on the same optical fibers will differ. In a dynamic transport network, if a given demand for logical link capacity between a certain node pair decreases and a second goes up, we allow the logical link capacity to be reassigned to the second node pair. The ability to rearrange logical link capacity dynamically and automatically results in cost savings. Large segments of bandwidth can be provided on fiber routes, and then the transport capacity can be allocated at will with the dynamic routing/rearrangement mechanism enabled by GMPLS control. This ability for simplified capacity management is discussed further in Chapter 6, where analysis models illustrate the design simplicity and capacity utilization efficiency enabled by a GMPLS-controlled dynamic transport routing network.

GMPLS-based dynamic transport routing can provide dynamic restoration of failed capacity, such as that due to fiber cuts, onto spare or backup transport capacity. GMPLS-based dynamic transport routing provides a self-healing network capability to ensure a networkwide path selection and immediate adaptation to failure.

FASTAR [CHAO91], for example, implements centralized automatic control of transport switching devices to restore service quickly following a transport failure. As illustrated in Figure 5.12, a fiber cut can disrupt large logical link capacities, and dynamic transport restoration can restore logical link transport capacity quickly. GMPLS-based dynamic transport routing provides a self-healing network capability to ensure a networkwide path selection and immediate adaptation to failure. As illustrated in Figure 5.12, a fiber cut near the Nashville node severed 8.576 Gbps of logical link/VNET capacity in the connection switching network (private-line logical link capacity was also affected), and after dynamic transport restoration a total of 3.84 Gbps of logical link/VNET capacity was still out of service in the connection switching network. In the example, dynamic transport restoration is implemented by centralized automatic control of transport cross-connect devices to restore service quickly following a transport failure, such as caused by a cable cut.

Traffic connection loss rate is shown at 5-min intervals, corresponding to the network traffic data received every 5 min. At time 0 (the fiber cut), many connections are instantly disconnected and customers begin redialing to restore their connections. Dynamic connection routing is able to complete these redialed connections on idle network logical link/VNET capacity. However, connections can be completed only up to a certain point because a large amount of logical link/VNET bandwidth capacity has been temporarily lost. Traffic loss rate therefore builds up after a few minutes

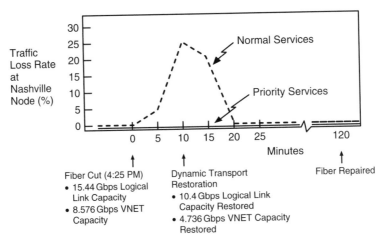

Figure 5.12 Fiber cut example with dynamic connection routing (layer 3) and dynamic transport routing.

as available logical link/VNET capacity is filled by redialed/reestablished connections and additional redialed and/or new connections cannot be completed. However, at the same time dynamic transport routing is restoring the logical link (VNET and private-line) capacity on backup physical transport capacity, which causes the traffic loss rate to start to fall again. Over the duration of this event, more than 12,000 connections were lost in the connection switching network, almost all of them originating or terminating at the Nashville node, and it is noteworthy that the traffic loss rate in the network returned to zero after the 4.736 Gbps of logical link/VNET capacity was restored, even though there was still 3.84 Gbps of logical link/VNET capacity still out of service.

Dynamic connection routing was able to find paths on which to complete traffic even though there was far less logical link/VNET capacity than normal even after the dynamic transport restoration. Hence dynamic connection routing in combination with dynamic transport restoration provides a self-healing network capability, and even though the cable was repaired 2 h after the cable cut, degradation of service was minimal. In this example, dynamic connection routing also provided priority routing for selected customers and services, as described in Chapter 3, which permits priority connections to be routed in preference to other connections, and traffic loss rate of the priority services is essentially zero throughout the whole event.

Over the duration of an event, connections are lost until sufficient capacity is restored for the network to return to zero traffic loss rate. That is, both dynamic transport routing and dynamic connection routing are able to find available paths on which to restore the failed connections. This improved network performance provides additional service revenues as formerly lost connections are completed, and it improves service quality to the customer.

These examples illustrate that implementation of GMPLS-based dynamic transport routing provides better network performance at reduced cost. These benefits are similar to those achieved by dynamic connection routing, and, as shown, the combination of dynamic connection and transport routing provides synergistic reinforcement to achieve these network improvements. Dynamic transport routing allows significant reductions in network capital costs with more efficient network design, as described in Section 6.3.2 and illustrated in Section 6.4.6 of Chapter 6. Automated logical link provisioning and rearrangement lead to operations expense savings.

5.4 Distributed Real-Time Dynamic Transport Routing Algorithm Design

This section gives an example of real-time dynamic transport routing algorithm design. This example is a real-time, distributed algorithm, in contrast to a centralized, periodic rearrangement algorithm, and other possible models. We note that there are many approaches to combining layer 2 and layer 3 dynamic routing with GMPLS-based control; this is one possible approach that is used in the models presented in Section 5.6.

It is assumed in the approach that TQO traffic, transport, and topology data are exchanged between traffic router/OXC nodes. For example, path computation element (PCE) capabilities described in [PCE-ARCHITECTURE, PCE-REQUIREMENTS, PCE-PROTOCOL] enable traffic router/OXC nodes, together with the full traffic engineering database (TEDB) with visibility to the traffic/topology within the network domain, to execute the algorithms described in this section on this TEDB in a distributed manner. These algorithms can also be implemented in a centralized manner, of course, again using the PCE concepts and protocols or a centralized TQO processor. Related proposals on virtual network topology and PCE capability can be found in [SHIOMOTO05].

This dynamic transport routing model can distinguish access logical links (ALLs), backbone logical links (BLLs), and physical fiber links (see Figures 5.9 and 5.10). MPLS LSPs constitute the ALLs and the VNETs within the BLL network. $BWavg_i$ is the minimum guaranteed bandwidth required for VNET i to carry the average offered bandwidth load (see Chapter 3, Section 3.3.1, Figure 3.3). In the following model, the routing and bandwidth allocation methods are provided for the MPLS LSPs, ALLs, BLLs, and $BWavg_i$ design values within the GMPLS network.

Traffic router nodes can do the following:

- obtain real-time traffic data
- smooth and update the current node-to-node traffic estimates
- compute ALL and BLL bandwidth requirements based on traffic estimates
- compute $BWavg$ bandwidth allocation on ALLs and BLLs
- route ALL and BLL bandwidth allocations on physical fiber links
- route ALL and BLL capacity on diverse routes through the transport network

- execute a real-time transport rearrangement sequence to minimize cross-connect activities in traffic routers and OXCs
- populate the traffic/connection routing, transport routing, and cross-connect data structures in the traffic routers and OXCs to implement the real-time transport network rearrangement

Logical link rerouting is done with a "make before break" procedure (also known as a "bridge and roll" procedure) to eliminate any discontinuity of service in progress. The rerouting of ALL capacity also requires that routing tables be rearranged appropriately so that prefixes terminating on one router before an ALL reroute are distributed to the new router after the reroute. Here, the real-time dynamic transport routing design must meet network performance objectives for the estimated traffic loads with minimum cost and provide a robust design, with no interruption of service, for any unforeseen load patterns and network failures.

The mathematical models given in this section are used to estimate traffic, size BLL capacity, reallocate ALL capacity between overloaded and underloaded traffic routers, compute diverse BLL capacity requirements, and rearrange network capacity. Figure 5.13 illustrates the real-time dynamic transport routing algorithm; further details of the model steps are now given.

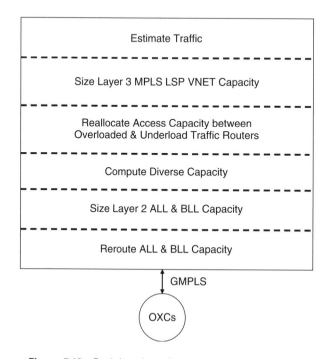

Figure 5.13 Real-time dynamic transport routing algorithm.

5.4.1 Estimate Traffic

Based on real-time traffic data, the traffic routers compute running estimates of (a) average daily loads and (b) statistical variation of the load patterns. With these data the design model estimates the load patterns and traffic variation parameters for the next few minutes interval.

5.4.2 Size Layer 3 MPLS LSP VNET Capacity

Layer 3 MPLS LSP VNET capacity requirements can be determined, for example, by the VTFO, TLFO, or DEFO models discussed in Chapter 6. The VTFO model is most practical for real-time applications, as it is a simple procedure that can be executed quickly and efficiently. Bandwidth is allocated for every VNET on the MPLS LSP capacity. Bandwidth allocations for individual VNETs, denoted as $BWavg_i$ for VNET i, are shared among VNETs under normal network conditions but are dedicated to VNET i under congestion. The originating traffic router collects traffic data in real time and determines the level of traffic demand to each destination in the network for each VNET i. Based on these estimated demands and available capacity in the network, the traffic router allocates the VNET i capacity requirements on the layer 3 MPLS LSP links. $BWavg_i$ is the minimum guaranteed bandwidth for a VNET. If a VNET is meeting its traffic loss probability objective, other VNETs are free to share the $BWavg_i$ bandwidth allocated to that VNET, if needed. The quantity $BWavg_{ki}$ is calculated for VNET i on link k as follows:

$$BWavg_{ki} = d_k \times D_{ki}/[\Sigma (n = 1, M)D_{kn}]$$

d_k = MPLS LSP capacity for traffic router pair k
D_{ki} = offered traffic load for traffic router pair k for VNET i.

Here, VNETs n are numbered 1 to M.

5.4.3 Reallocate Access Capacity between Overloaded and Underloaded Traffic Routers

If the total interrouter termination capacity available on a traffic router is exceeded by the estimated interrouter capacity demand, then additional interrouter termination capacity is generated for the traffic router by rehoming (rerouting) ALL capacity to underloaded traffic routers that have spare termination capacity. This ALL rerouting frees terminations on the overloaded traffic routers, which can then be used to satisfy the interrouter BLL demand. Traffic router termination capacity is sized to meet network demands up to a specified level of overload above the current traffic estimates in order to achieve robustness to traffic load variations in the current network loading. After ALL terminations are rerouted to underloaded traffic routers, router-to-router traffic loads are adjusted according to the number of ALL terminations moved and through use of a Kruithof iteration procedure [KRUITHOF37]. The Kruithof method is illustrated in Chapter 6. After the router-to-router traffic levels are adjusted, the layer 3 MPLS LSP capacity requirements are recomputed.

5.4.4 Compute Diverse Capacity

The logical link/VNET sizing model provides for diverse sizing of the layer 3 MPLS LSP capacity in order to achieve a traffic restoration level (TRL) objective under network failure. As discussed in the following section, the TRL objective specifies that for single fiber transport link or traffic router failures, the BLL capacity of the network is sized to carry at least a certain minimum percentage of the design traffic load, denoted as the TRL objective. For example, if the TRL objective is 0.5, this means that following any single fiber cut in the transport network, at least 50% of the design traffic is still carried after the failure. The model used for the traffic restoration level design of layer 3 MPLS LSP links is as follows.

TRL is the traffic restoration level objective

T_k is the minimum ALL/BLL capacity required for traffic router pair k to meet the TRL objective

The required level of surviving MPLS LSP capacity after a fiber transport failure is given such that a minimum of $T_k/2$ of the LSP capacity is routed, if possible, over each of two diverse physical paths, while ensuring that MPLS LSP modularity conditions (if any) are met. A further constraint is that the total MPLS LSP capacity d_k must be greater than or equal to T_k. If that is possible it ensures that a failure of either diverse path allows enough MPLS LSP capacity to survive to meet the TRL objective. Diverse MPLS LSP capacity is allocated and, if possible, the $T_k/2$ diverse BLL capacity is realized on the diverse path. Similarly, the diverse ALL capacity required to be split between traffic router nodes to achieve TRL objectives for traffic router failure is calculated in the same way. This same procedure is followed whether the ALL capacity is brought into one building location or routed diversely into multiple OXC building locations.

5.4.5 Size Layer 2 ALL and BLL Capacity

The real-time dynamic transport routing network is composed of OXCs and fiber links between them. To design candidate layer 2 ALLs/BLLs, we first find all the shortest paths between OXCs on the fiber network and then break each shortest path into unique segments beginning and ending on an OXC; these segments are then the candidate ALLs/BLLs. Diverse ALL/BLL paths through the fiber link network are designed by first constructing a "violations matrix" for each logical link. This matrix describes the degree of physical overlap between any pair of ALLs/BLLs. The set of candidate ALLs/BLLs defines a connectivity among the OXCs. We also have the underlying fiber link topology for all the ALLs/BLLs, and from physical routing information we can compute span violations between all ALLs/BLLs. We use a span-diverse model to find a set of candidate span-diverse shortest paths between all OXCs [BHADARI97]. This method allows for both traffic router and span violations with a weighted penalty function. Each ALL/BLL capacity requirement is split on two or more diverse transport paths so that typically the diverse capacity $(T_k/2)$ is routed on the longer path. For example, in Figure 5.2, the BLL capacity between traffic router A and traffic router B is split between transport path AB and transport path AE–EF–FD–DC–CB, in which the diverse capacity is routed on the AE–EF–FD–DC–CB path and the remaining BLL capacity is routed on the AB path.

An express (logical) link is a "through link" and if there is sufficient demand, for example, between OXC A and OXC D in Figure 5.2, provisioning of express link AD may be justified. Then the BLL path between OXCs A and F can route over express link AD and BLL DF. With this transport routing we bypass OXCs B and C by cross-connecting through the OXC at these traffic routers, thus saving traffic router terminations. We use an iterative greedy heuristic to eliminate candidate express links, where each candidate express link is tested by flowing the BLL demand. If the express link is justified by the capacity demand, it is left for further consideration in the next iteration, otherwise it is eliminated. Subsequent iterations flow demands and eliminate candidate express links where not justified.

In the iterative procedure we find a minimum cost alternative path for each partially filled express link that minimizes OXC terminations. For a given express link, its minimum cost alternate path is the concatenation of two or more shorter express or ALLs/BLLs. Topologically, the minimum cost alternate path comprises the same underlying physical fiber links as the shortest path. We then move traffic off partially filled express links onto its minimum cost alternate path, starting with the longest express link and rounding the ALL/BLL flow down to a multiple of full OC3s. The "overflow" ALL/BLL demand is split off and routed onto the corresponding minimum cost alternate path. This procedure is repeated for each express link in the greedy ordered list and must terminate on BLLs. Backbone link capacity is then rounded up to the next OC3 module of capacity. In this algorithm, ALL/BLL capacity requirements are determined to achieve sufficient capacity to meet network demands up to a specified level of overload.

5.4.6   Reroute ALL and BLL Capacity

Once the bandwidth allocation design is completed for the estimated traffic, a combinatorics optimization method computes the logical link rerouting that minimizes OXC cross-connect activities by first recognizing common route segments between existing and target logical link topologies and then finding the cross-connect actions that maximally reuse these common segments. In the model, we compute a sequence of BLL disconnect and connect orders so as to always maintain the maximum capacity connected throughout the network rearrangement. The traffic router node executes real-time logical link reroutes using GMPLS to execute make before break logical link reroutes so as to maintain continuity of service within the dynamic transport network.

5.5 Reliable Transport Network Design

Frank Ianna, retired president of AT&T Network Services, was one of AT&T's foremost advocates of network reliability. He was right, of course, that network reliability is at the top of everyone's list of absolute "MUST MEET" requirements, yours and mine included. No one wants service interruptions, delays, or poor transmission—network reliability is paramount and people will pay more to receive it. Frank gave many talks I attended where he repeated the same message concerning network reliability. His "Network Requirements" slide showed a lengthy list of network requirements, where the first three were "network reliability." He joked each time that if you couldn't meet all the requirements at least meet any two of the top three!

All network designers should be champions of reliability, as is Frank Ianna, and every effort should be made to build reliability into the network design. GMPLS capabilities offer a golden opportunity to make dramatic improvements in that regard. In this section we discuss some of these reliable transport network design approaches.

In the event of link, node, or other network failure, the network design needs to provide sufficient surviving capacity to meet the required performance levels. For example, if a major fiber link fails, it could have a catastrophic effect on the network because traffic for many node pairs could not use the failed link. Similarly, if one of the nodes fails, it could isolate a whole geographic area until the node is restored to service.

With these two kinds of major failures in mind, we present reliable transport routing models to achieve reliable network design so as to provide service for predefined restoration objectives for any transport link or node failure in the network and continue to provide connections to customers with essentially no perceived interruption of service. This approach tries to integrate capabilities in both the layer 3 connection routing and the layer 2 transport routing network to make the network robust or insensitive to failure. The basic aims of these models are to provide link diversity and protective capacity augmentation where needed so that specific "network robustness" objectives, such as traffic restoration level objectives, are met under failure events. This means that the network is designed so that it carries at least the TRL fraction of traffic under the failure event. For example, a traffic restoration level objective of 70% means that under any single transport link failure in the transport network, at least 70% of the original traffic for any affected node pair is still carried after the failure; for the unaffected node pairs, the traffic is carried at the normal performance grade-of-service objectives. These design models provide designs that address the network response immediately after a network event. It is also desirable to have transport restoration respond after the occurrence of the network event to bring service back to normal. Transport restoration is also addressed in this chapter.

Reliable network performance objectives may require, for example, the network to carry 50% of its busy-hour load on each link within 5 min after a major network failure in order to eliminate isolations among node pairs. Such performance may be provided through traffic restoration techniques, which include link diversity, traffic restoration capacity, and dynamic connection routing. Reliable network performance objectives might also require a further reduction of connection lost/delayed level to less than 5% within, say, 1 min or less to limit the duration of degraded service. This is possible through transport restoration methods that utilize transport nodes along with real-time distributed transport restoration control described in Section 5.4. A further objective may be to restore at least 50% of severed traffic trunks in affected links within this time period.

The transport restoration process restores capacity for "switched services" as well as "dedicated services" (also known as "private-line services") in the event of logical transport link failures. In the real-time transport routing algorithm presented in Section 5.4, it is envisioned that transport restoration is conducted by using all available restoration capacity and currently idle transport capacity. Optimization of the total cost of transport restoration capacity is possible through a design that increases sharing opportunities of the restoration capacity among different failure scenarios. Real-time transport restoration may also require the use of dedicated restoration capacity for each link and, thus, a lesser opportunity for sharing the restoration capacity. For the purpose of this analysis, we assume that all network transport may be protected with an objective level of restoration capacity. Transport restoration level (TPRL) is the term used to specify the minimal percentage of capacity on each transport logical link that is restorable. A transport restoration level is implemented in the analysis model by restoring each affected link in a failure to a specified level. Here, we further distinguish between transport restoration levels for switched services and dedicated services and designate them by TPRLs and TPRLd, respectively.

We now describe logical transport routing design models for survivable networks. Before we describe the models, let's discuss the concept of link diversity using the example of the four-node network in Figures 5.3 and 5.4. The physical transport network is depicted at the bottom of Figure 5.3 and the corresponding logical transport (traffic) network at the top. For example, the direct logical link for connecting nodes A and D may ride the path A–B–C–D in the physical transport network. There is no logical link between nodes B and D, which means that there is no direct traffic trunk capacity from node B to D. A single physical transport link failure may affect more than one logical link. For example, in Figures 5.3 and 5.4, the failure of the physical transport link B–C affects logical links A–B, A–C, and B–C. Logical link diversity refers to a logical link design in which direct capacity for a logical link is split on two or more different physical transport paths. For example, in Figure 5.2, the direct logical link capacity for the link A–D may be split onto the two physical transport paths A–B–C–D and a physically diverse path A–E–F–D. A link diversity policy, say, of 70/30 corresponds to the fact that no more than 70% of the direct logical link (traffic trunk) capacity is routed on a single physical transport link for the different transport paths for that logical link. The advantage of logical link diversity is that if a physical transport link fails, the traffic for a particular node pair can still use the direct logical link capacity that survived on the physical transport path not on the failed link.

We now present models for transport routing design for physical transport link failure and node failure.

5.5.1 Transport Link Design Models

We assume that we have two distinct transport paths for direct logical link capacity for each node pair. In the model, traffic demand is converted to virtual trunk demand such as based on direct and overflow logical transport capacity, as also illustrated in Chapter 6 (see Figure 6.10 for a discussion of the optimal traffic split between direct and overflow paths). Let v be the virtual trunk requirement for the traffic demand for a particular node pair. Let d be the virtual trunk capacity to be put on the primary physical transport path and s be the virtual trunk capacity to be put on the alternate physical transport paths for the direct logical link of the given node pair. Let b be the number of virtual trunks required for this traffic link in the absence of link diversity, as determined by the network design model. Let t be the traffic restoration level (TRL) objective under a link failure scenario. Let Δb be the link capacity augmentation that may be needed for this logical link.

The goal in a failure event is to carry a portion tv of the total virtual trunk demand for the affected node pairs. Thus, if $tv \leq \Delta b/2$, we set $\Delta b = 0$ (no augmentation) with $d = b - tv$ and $s = tv$. In this way, if either transport path fails, we can carry at least tv of the virtual trunk demand and meet the traffic restoration level requirement. On the other hand, if $tv > b/2$, then we want

$$(b + \Delta b)/2 = tv$$

which implies

$$\Delta b = 2tv - b$$

In this case, we set $d = s = (b + \Delta b)/2$. This procedure is repeated for every demand pair in the network. The incremental cost of the network is the cost of trunk augmentation and routing the direct logical link capacity for each node pair, if any, on two transport paths.

This procedure can be extended to the general case of k distinct physical transport paths. So, for k distinct physical transport paths, if

$$tv \leq (k - 1)b/k$$

then $\Delta b = 0$ with $d = b - tv$ on the first physical transport path and $tv/(k - 1)$ on each of the other $(k - 1)$ transport paths. If

$$tv > (k - 1)b/k$$

then

$$\Delta b = ktv - (k-1)/b$$

with each of the k transport paths having $(b+\Delta b)/k$ trunks.

A transport link model is illustrated in Figure 5.14, where each transport logical link cross section is assumed on the average to contain certain fractions of switched services (N) and dedicated services (M) transport bandwidth capacity. A portion of the switched services and dedicated services transport bandwidth capacity is further presumed to be restorable in real time, such as with MPLS fast reroute tunnels [RFC4090], or perhaps with SONET ring transport arrangements (lowercase n and m values).

Capacity that is not restored in real time is restored with transport restoration, e.g., under control of a TQO processor, to a specified TPRL value. The lower part of Figure 5.14 demonstrates the interaction between switched services and dedicated services transport bandwidth capacity in the restoration process. The restoration process is assumed to restore the first unit of transport capacity (e.g., OC3) after x seconds, with y seconds to restore each additional unit of transport capacity. The actual x and y restoration time constants depend on many factors, such as TQO processor capabilities

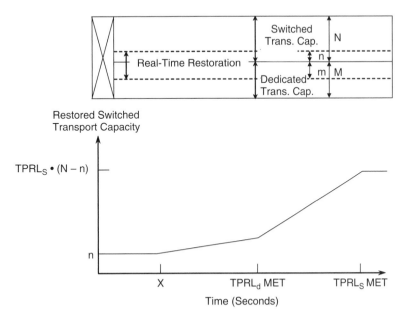

TPRL_S = Transport Restoration Level For Switched Transport Capacity
TPRL_d = Transport Restoration Level For Dedicated Transport Capacity

Figure 5.14 Transport restoration model.

and communication protocol; however, these are independent of the reliable network design principles being discussed. MPLS fast reroute and SONET ring restoration can occur in about 50–200 ms, and such real-time restoration is included in the model. A prioritization method is assumed, whereby transport links that carry higher priority dedicated services are restored first. Because switched services and dedicated services transport bandwidth capacity is often mixed at the transport logical link level, some switched services capacity is also restored.

Different levels of transport restoration may also be assigned for the dedicated services (TPRLd) and switched services (TPRLs) transport bandwidth. Once again, the dedicated transport bandwidth refers to transport capacity used by dedicated services (or private-line services), while switched transport bandwidth refers to capacity used by switched services with calls/sessions set up by connection switching network elements. Each type of bandwidth demand is then restored to the corresponding level of restoration. Figure 5.14 also shows how the restoration level for switched services transport bandwidth varies as a function of time. Some level of bandwidth capacity is restored in real time (n). After x seconds, transport restoration is initiated with one unit of transport capacity being restored in each y seconds, with a smaller fraction of each transport capacity unit being allocated to switched services traffic. The switched services portion in each transport capacity unit subsequently increases to a larger fraction after dedicated traffic is restored to its designated level TPRLd. Transport restoration stops after both the TPRLd and TPRLs objectives are met.

5.5.2 Node Design Models

Node failure restoration design incorporates the concept of dual homing, as discussed in Chapter 2 in connection with multiple ingress/egress routing (see Figure 2.8). With single homing, the traffic from a particular geographical area normally goes to the single node nearest to it in order to carry the ingress and egress traffic. For example, in Figure 5.15 the traffic from the served area A1 enters the network through node B; similarly, the served area A2 traffic enters the network through node C. Now, if node B fails, then area A1 gets isolated. To protect against such an event, areas A1 and A2 are homed to more than one node—to nodes B and C in this case (Figure 5.15, bottom). This is the concept of dual homing, in which we address the issue of designing a reliable network when one of the nodes may fail.

For every node to be protected, we assign a dual-homed node. Before failure, we assume that any load from a node to the protected node and its dual-homed node is equally divided; i.e., if the original traffic load between area A1 and node A is $a1$, and between area A2 and the dual-homed node, C, is $a2$, then we assume that under normal network conditions, the load between nodes A and B is $(a1 + a2)/2$, and the same for the load between nodes A and C. We refer to this concept as balanced load. Then, under a failure event such as a node B failure, we carry load equal to $(a1 + a2)/2$ between nodes A and C (see Figure 5.15, bottom). We call this design objective a 50% traffic restoration level objective in a manner very analogous to the

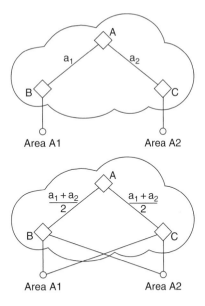

Figure 5.15 Illustration of dual homing.

link failure event. As we can see from the bottom of Figure 5.15, this restoration level of traffic from or to area A1 is then still carried.

In the node restoration design model, the node pairs that are going to be considered for the node failure design scenarios are determined. Next, the dual-homing nodes are determined for each traffic demand and the balanced-load traffic is routed accordingly. For each node pair, one of the nodes is assumed to fail. Then this node cannot have any incoming or outgoing traffic and, also, cannot be a via node for any traffic between other node pairs. Using these constraints, we solve an optimization model that minimizes the incremental augmentation cost to carry the resulting traffic demand pattern in the network. Then, we reverse the roles of the nodes for this pair and solve the optimization model again with these constraints. This design process is repeated for every pair of candidate nodes for each node failure scenario.

5.6 Modeling of TQO Methods

In this section we give modeling results for GMPLS-based dynamic transport routing capacity design, performance under network failure, and performance under various network overload scenarios. We again use the full-scale national network model developed in Chapter 2 to study various TQO scenarios and trade-offs. The 135-node national model is illustrated in Figure 2.9, the multiservice traffic demand model is summarized in Table 2.1, and the cost model is summarized in Table 2.2.

Generally the routing and capacity designs for the meshed logical topologies are optimized by using the DEFO algorithms presented in Chapter 6, while the routing and capacity designs for the sparse logical topologies are optimized by using the shortest path optimization and DEFO algorithms presented in Chapter 6. The network capacity design algorithms for GMPLS dynamic transport routing networks modeled in this chapter are discussed in Section 6.3.2 in Chapter 6.

5.6.1 GMPLS-Based Dynamic Transport Routing Capacity Design

In this example we illustrate dynamic transport routing design for traffic loads with week-to-week traffic variation. Design models used in this analysis are detailed in Chapter 6 (in particular, in Section 6.3.2). GMPLS-based dynamic transport routing network design allows more efficient use of node capacity and transport capacity and can lead to a reduction of network reserve capacity while improving network performance. Table 5.1 illustrates a comparative design of the 135-node national intercity network model's normalized logical-link capacity requirements for the base case without dynamic transport routing and the network requirements with dynamic transport routing network design. When week-to-week seasonal traffic variations are taken into account, the dynamic transport routing design can provide a reduction in network reserve capacity. As shown in Table 5.1, the traffic trunk savings always exceed 10%, which translates into a significant reduction in capital expenditures.

As illustrated in Chapter 6, dynamic transport routing network design also achieves higher fiber link fill rates, which reduces transport costs further. The GMPLS-based dynamic transport routing network implements automated inter-BR and access logical-link diversity, logical-link restoration, and node backup restoration to enhance the network survivability over a wide range of network failure conditions. We now illustrate dynamic transport routing network performance under design for normal traffic loads, fiber transport failure events, unpredictable traffic load patterns, and peak-day traffic load patterns.

Table 5.1 GMPLS-Based Dynamic Transport Routing Capacity Savings with Week-to-Week Seasonal Traffic Variations (Normalized Capacity Cost)

Forecast period	Capacity of fixed transport routing design	Capacity of dynamic transport routing design	Capacity savings (%)
Year 1	1.000	0.873	12.7
Year 2	1.048	0.919	12.3
Year 3	1.087	0.968	11.0
Year 4	1.138	1.019	10.4

5.6.2 Performance for Network Failures

Simulations are performed for the fixed transport and dynamic transport network performance for a fiber cut in Newark, New Jersey, in which approximately 8.96 Gbps of traffic trunk capacity was lost. The results are shown in Table 5.2. Here, a threshold of 50% or more node-pair traffic loss rate is used to identify node pairs that are essentially isolated; hence, the rearrangeable transport network design eliminates all isolations during this network failure event.

An analysis is also performed for the network performance after transport restoration, in which the fixed and dynamic transport network designs are simulated after 29% of the lost trunks are restored. The results are shown in Table 5.3. Again, the dynamic transport network design eliminates all network isolations, some of which still exist in the base-fixed transport routing network after traffic trunk restoration.

From this analysis we conclude that the combination of dynamic connection routing, logical-link diversity design, and transport restoration provides synergistic network survivability benefits. Dynamic transport network design automates and maintains logical-link diversity, as well as access network diversity in an efficient manner, and provides automatic transport restoration after failure.

A network reliability example is given for dual-homing transport demands on various OXC transport nodes. In one example, an OXC failure at the Littleton, Massachusetts, node is analyzed, in which we use the full-scale transport network model illustrated in Figure 5.2, and the results are given in Table 5.4. Because transport

Table 5.2 Network Performance for Fiber Cut in Newark, NJ

	Traffic lost/delayed (%)	Number of node pairs with lost/delayed >50%
Fixed transport routing	14.4	963
Dynamic transport routing	4.2	0

Table 5.3 Network Performance for Fiber Cut in Newark, NJ (after Transport Logical-Link Restoration)

	Traffic lost/delayed (%)	Number of node pairs with lost/delayed >50%
Fixed transport routing	7.0	106
Dynamic transport routing	0.6	0

Table 5.4 Dynamic Transport Network Performance under OXC Failure

	Traffic lost/delayed (%)	Number of node pairs with lost/delayed >50%
Fixed transport routing	4.1	231
Dynamic transport routing, dual homing	1.3	0
Dynamic transport routing, dual homing, load balancing, logical-link restoration	0.6	0

demands are diversely routed between nodes and dual-homed between access nodes and OXC devices, this provides additional network robustness and resilience to traffic node and transport node failures. When the network is designed for load balancing between access and internode demands and when traffic trunk restoration is performed, the performance of the GMPLS-based dynamic transport routing network is further improved.

Figure 5.16 illustrates a typical instance of network design with traffic restoration level objectives and transport restoration level objectives, as compared with the base network with no TRL or TPRL design objectives. In the example, a fiber link failure occurs in the model network f seconds after the beginning of the simulation, severing a large amount of transport capacity in the network and cutting off thousands of

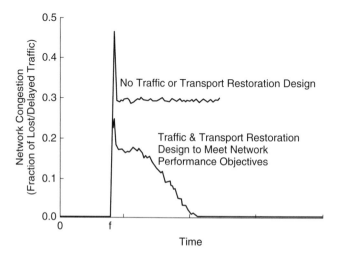

Figure 5.16 Network performance for link failure with traffic and transport restoration design.

existing connections. Therefore, in the simulation results shown in Figure 5.16, we see a large jump in the traffic loss rate at the instant of the cut. A transient flurry of reattempts follows as cut-off customers redial and reestablish their connections. This connection restoration process is aided by the traffic restoration level design, which provides link diversity and protective transport capacity to meet the TRL objectives immediately following a failure. This TRL design, together with the ability of dynamic connection routing to find surviving capacity wherever it exists, quickly reduces the transient traffic loss rate level, which then remains roughly constant for about x seconds until the transport restoration process begins. At x seconds after the link failure, the transport restoration process begins to restore capacity that was lost due to the failure. The traffic loss rate then continues to drop during that period when transport restoration takes place until it reaches essentially a level of zero traffic loss rate. Figure 5.16 illustrates the comparison between network performances with and without the traffic and transport restoration design techniques presented in this chapter.

This traffic restoration level design allows for varying levels of diversity on different links to ensure a minimum level of performance. Robust routing techniques such as dynamic connection routing, multiple ingress/egress routing, and logical link diversity routing further improve response to node or transport failures. Transport restoration is necessary to reduce network traffic loss rate to low levels. Given, for example, a 50% traffic restoration level design, it is observed that this combined with transport restoration of 50% of the failed transport capacity in affected links is sufficient to restore the traffic to low traffic loss rate levels. Therefore, the combination of traffic restoration level design and transport restoration level design is seen both to be cost effective and to provide fast and reliable performance. The traffic restoration level design eliminates isolations between node pairs, and the transport restoration level is used to reduce the duration of poor service in the network. Traffic restoration techniques combined with transport restoration techniques provide the network with independent means to achieve reliability against multiple failures and other unexpected events and are essential elements of reliable network design.

5.6.3 Performance for General Traffic Overloads

The 135-node national network model is designed for dynamic transport routing with normal engineered traffic loads using the DEFO model described in Chapter 6 and results in a 15% savings in reserve trunk capacity over the fixed transport routing model. In addition to this large savings in network capacity, the network performance under a 10% general network overload of all traffic demands results in the performance comparison illustrated in Table 5.5. Hence, GMPLS-based dynamic transport routing network designs achieve significant capital savings while also achieving superior network performance.

Table 5.5 Network Performance for 10% Traffic Overload

	Traffic lost/delayed (%)	Node pair maximum lost/delayed (%)
Fixed transport routing	0.11	17.3
Dynamic transport routing	0	0

Table 5.6 Network Performance for Unexpected Traffic Overload (Focused Overload in Northeastern United States Caused by Hurricane)

	Traffic lost/delayed (%)	Node pair maximum lost/delayed (%)
Fixed transport routing	0.43	22.7
Dynamic transport routing	0.28	13.3

5.6.4 Performance for Unexpected Overloads

Dynamic transport routing network design provides load balancing of node traffic load and transport logical-link capacity so that sufficient reserve capacity is provided throughout the network to meet unexpected demands on the network. The advantage of such design is illustrated in Table 5.6, which compares the simulated network traffic loss for the fixed transport routing network design and dynamic transport routing network design during a hurricane-caused focused traffic overload in the northeastern United States. Such unexpected focused overloads are not unusual in any network, and the additional robustness provided by GMPLS-based dynamic transport routing network design to the unexpected traffic overload patterns is clear from these results.

Another illustration of the benefits of load balancing is given in Figure 5.17, in which a 25% traffic overload is focused on a node in Jackson, Mississippi.

Because the dynamic transport network is load balanced between access demands and inter-BR demands, this provides additional network robustness and resilience to unexpected traffic overloads, even though the GMPLS-based dynamic transport routing network in this model has more than 15% less capacity than the fixed transport routing network. In this example, transport rearrangement triggered by traffic loss is allowed in the dynamic transport network. That is, as soon as node-pair traffic loss is detected, additional logical-link capacity is added to the affected links by cross-connecting spare node-termination capacity and spare logical-link capacity, which has been freed up as a result of the more efficient dynamic transport network design. As can be seen from Figure 5.17, this greatly improves the network response to the overload.

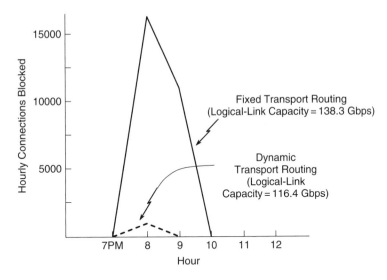

Figure 5.17 Dynamic transport routing performance for 25% overload on Jackson, Mississippi, node.

Table 5.7 Network Performance for Christmas Day Traffic Overload

Hour of day	Fixed transport network traffic lost/delayed (%)	Dynamic transport network traffic lost/delayed (%)
9:00 to 10:00 AM	17.2	0
10:00 to 11:00 AM	22.2	0
11:00 to 12:00 AM	29.7	0

5.6.5 Performance for Peak-Day Traffic Loads

A dynamic transport network design is performed for the Christmas traffic loads, and simulations are performed for the base network and rearrangeable transport network design for the Christmas day traffic. Results for the inter-BR traffic loss rate are summarized in Table 5.7. Clearly, the dynamic transport network design eliminates the inter-BR network traffic loss, although the access node to BR traffic loss may still exist but is not quantified in the model. In addition to increased revenue, customer perception of network quality is also improved for these peak-day situations.

5.7 Summary and Conclusions

In this chapter we presented and analyzed dynamic transport network architectures. GMPLS-based dynamic transport routing is a routing and bandwidth allocation method, which combines dynamic connection routing with dynamic transport routing and for which we describe associated network design methods. We present a number of analysis, design, and simulation models related to dynamic transport network architectures. We find that networks benefit dramatically in reliability, efficiency, and performance as the ability to flexibly route transport bandwidth is increased, and can also simplify network management and design.

Full-scale network analysis models are used to measure the performance of the network for dynamic transport routing network design in comparison with the fixed transport network design under a variety of network conditions, including normal daily load patterns; unpredictable traffic load patterns, such as caused by a hurricane; known traffic overload patterns, such as occur on Christmas day; and network failure conditions, such as a large fiber cut. Based on the results from these models, the conclusions reached in this chapter are as follows:

- GMPLS-based dynamic transport routing (a) provides greater network throughput and, consequently, enhanced revenue; (b) achieves efficient network design and capital savings (as discussed further in Chapter 6); (c) enhances network performance under failure, which results from interbackbone-router and access logical-link diversity in combination with the dynamic connection routing and transport restoration of logical links; and (d) improves network performance in comparison with fixed transport routing for all network conditions simulated, which include abnormal and unpredictable traffic load patterns.
- Traffic and transport restoration level design allows for link diversity to ensure a minimum level of performance under failure.
- Network reliability is achieved by robust traffic/transport routing techniques, which include dynamic connection routing, multiple ingress/egress routing, and logical link diversity routing, and these techniques dramatically improve response to node or transport failures.

5.8 Applicability of Requirements

Some of the dynamic transport routing capabilities described in this chapter have been implemented as nonstandard, vendor-proprietary capabilities in some service provider networks. This is the case, for example, for automatic transport restoration, such as with MPLS fast reroute, SONET rings, and TQO processor (e.g., FASTAR) capability described in Section 5.3. However, full dynamic transport routing capability as described in this chapter has not, to the author's knowledge, been implemented as yet in any service provider network. This is particularly the case for any GMPLS-based implementations.

There are, however, proposals for standardization of such capabilities, such as the virtual network topology proposals and path computation element capability described in [SHIOMOTO05]. These proposals may eventually be specified in standards, such as in the IETF working groups building the GMPLS protocol suite and the PCE capabilities described in Chapter 10.

Highly desirable GMPLS-based TQO capabilities will integrate both MPLS traffic/connection routing and GMPLS transport routing capabilities in network devices. For the same reasons that FSN ran into difficulty, however, integration of such capabilities may be hard for vendors to achieve because they do not typically make both transport and traffic devices, although some vendors may do this in the future. Nevertheless, there are MPLS vendors who can control GMPLS transport networks as an overlay model and optical vendors who support dynamic transport routing using GMPLS. PCE support for such capabilities is probably some way off for MPLS or GMPLS networks. As demonstrated in this chapter and throughout this book, service providers and their customers would benefit from these capabilities in terms of network reliability, performance, and profitability improvements. While vendors have yet to develop such GMPLS-based TQO capabilities in their products, the service provider interest in adopting such TQO features leads to vendor profitability if these features are offered in their products.

Chapter 6

Optimization Methods for Routing Design and Capacity Management

6.1 Introduction

In this chapter we review analysis, design, and optimization methods for TQO and point the reader to further development in the book and references for relevant theory and further details. As outlined in Chapter 1, the problem statement for TQO design in this chapter includes the following:

- Maximum flow/revenue dynamic routing/TQO design: Given traffic loads and network topology/capacity, find the maximum flow/revenue dynamic routing/TQO design.
- Minimum cost capacity design: Given traffic loads and node locations, find the minimum cost link topology, link capacity, and dynamic routing/TQO design, subject to meeting performance constraints.

We discuss optimization methods and principles for routing design optimization, including (a) shortest path optimization models and (b) discrete event simulation models, which capture complex routing behavior. We also discuss optimization methods and principles for capacity design optimization, including (a) discrete event flow optimization (DEFO) models, (b) traffic load flow optimization (TLFO) models, (c) virtual trunk flow optimization (VTFO) models, and (d) dynamic transport routing capacity design models. We discuss the impacts of traffic variations on network design, including minute-to-minute, hour-to-hour, day-to-day, and forecast uncertainty/reserve capacity design impacts.

All of these techniques have been applied extensively in real network operational scenarios over a very long period of time. Truitt's link optimization model [TRU-ITT54] was introduced over 50 years ago and has been used extensively ever since in applications worldwide. The DEFO model has been used for nearly two decades to design AT&T's operational RTNR network and has been applied extensively in architecture studies, such as the case studies presented in Chapters 8 and 9. Also, the TLFO model has been used to design AT&T's operational DNHR network for over 2 decades as well.

Here we highlight the principal optimization techniques used throughout the book and presented in this chapter for routing design optimization and capacity design optimization. Good books on optimization techniques include [GIRARD90, PIORO89, PIORO04]:

- Routing design optimization: Multilink shortest path routing (MSPR) and two-link EDR/SDR techniques are analyzed and designed using simulation modeling techniques presented in Section 6.2.1 and shortest path optimization presented in Section 6.2.2. Simulation analysis is applied in Chapters 2–6 to design MSPR and two-link routing algorithms based on SDR link status information and EDR approaches that use learning models. Simulation models are used in the case studies (Chapters 8 and 9) of integrated voice/data dynamic routing design, including optimization of routing design parameters, such as the triggering mechanism for automatic bandwidth reservation, and the algorithm for increasing and decreasing VNET bandwidth allocation.
- Capacity design optimization: Capacity design is done primarily using the DEFO technique described in Section 6.3.2. Very complex routing networks have been designed by the DEFO model, including all routing methods in Chapters 2–6 and case studies presented in Chapters 8 and 9. Sparse and meshed topologies, as well as hierarchical and flat topologies, are designed by the DEFO model. Examples of DEFO capacity designs are given, which include (a) per-VNET versus per-flow network capacity design, (b) integrated versus separate voice/ISDN and data network capacity designs, (c) MSPR versus two-link network capacity design, (d) single-area flat versus two-level hierarchical network capacity design, (e) EDR versus SDR network capacity design, and (f) dynamic transport routing versus fixed transport routing network capacity design.

Many other optimization techniques used for routing and capacity design optimization are not illustrated in detail, such as multicommodity flow linear programming, Erlang fixed point computation, Truitt's link optimization method, VTFO capacity design, and TLFO capacity design. The latter three techniques are surveyed in this chapter. As mentioned above, there are many good books devoted to network optimization techniques, and I unabashedly recommend [ASH98] for an excellent and rather exhaustive treatment of such design, analysis, and optimization techniques.

A question often asked is "how close to optimum are the solutions yielded by these optimization methods?" The truthful answer is *we don't know* because it is quite impossible to obtain the optimal solution to these design problems. However, there is much evidence based on practical experience with the methods and designs, as well as reasons pointed out later in the chapter, that the solutions presented yield excellent designs that are likely "close" to optimum, but we can't prove that. We can show that certain properties of the algorithms are necessary conditions for optimality in a mathematical sense.

However, the true routing design optimization and capacity design optimization problems addressed in this chapter are so complex that no one knows how to compute the optimal solution; the problems are far, far too complex! Network design complexity is completely intractable from an exact mathematical solution point of view and is on the order of the complexity of DNA, the human brain, and the observable universe! All solutions to these problems are approximations, as no one has the optimum solution except God, and anyone who pretends to have the optimal solutions is merely displaying his "falutin" fakery (to quote Dick Hamming, a well-known Bell Labs scientist and inventor of Hamming codes).

We use the 135-node model to illustrate the use of the DEFO model for per-flow multiservice network design and per-VNET design and to provide comparisons of these designs. We also study multilink versus two-link network designs, single-area flat topologies versus two-level hierarchical topology design, EDR versus SDR network design, and GMPLS-based dynamic transport routing versus fixed transport routing network design.

The conclusions reached are that (a) DEFO models enable design of networks with very complex routing behavior, (b) sparse versus mesh topology leads to capital cost advantages and operation simplicity, (c) voice/data integration provides capital cost advantages and operational simplicity, (d) multilink routing methods exhibit greater design efficiencies compared to two-link routing methods, (e) single-area flat topologies exhibit greater design efficiencies compared to multiarea hierarchical topologies, (f) EDR methods exhibit comparable design efficiencies to SDR, and (g) GMPLS-based dynamic transport routing achieves capital savings by concentrating capacity on fewer, high-capacity physical fiber links.

6.2 Routing Design and Optimization Methods

Different approaches to routing design and optimization are used for the many different types of routing analyzed in our modeling studies. Sparse network topologies with relatively low connectivity of layer 2 logical links lend themselves to shortest path optimization techniques. We call these types of routing approaches multilink shortest path routing approaches, and many different versions of MSPR are designed and analyzed, including MSPR based on SDR link status information methods, and EDR approaches that use learning models to find the best shortest paths through the network, such as the STT approach to learning good alternate shortest paths.

Simulation models are used for MSPR SDR and EDR routing designs analyzed in Chapters 2–6. A detailed case study of integrated voice/data MSPR EDR design is presented in Chapter 9, in which multiple alternate MSPR path routing based on EDR techniques is designed and optimized. There it is shown how routing design parameters are optimized by using simulation models, such as (a) level of reserved capacity varied from 0 to 10% of link capacity, (b) number of allowed primary and alternate paths; the number is varied from 2 to 10 paths, and (c) the algorithm for increasing and decreasing VNET bandwidth allocation, where various models are studied and compared.

Meshed network topologies with relatively high connectivity of layer 2 logical links lend themselves to one- and two-link path optimization techniques. We call these types of routing approaches two-link approaches. Many different versions of two-link routing are designed and analyzed, including SDR link status information methods, such as LLR, and EDR approaches that use learning models to find the best shortest paths through the network, such as STT. Simulation models are also used for two-link SDR and EDR routing designs analyzed in Chapters 2–6. A detailed case study of two-link SDR design is presented in Chapter 8, where it is shown how routing design parameters are optimized by using simulation models, such as (a) the number of link occupancy states, including three-, four-, five-, and six-state models, and (b) the triggering mechanism for automatic bandwidth reservation.

Constrained shortest path routing optimization models consider path hops, distance, available link bandwidth state information, and other criteria to find the optimum path through a network. Typical applications of shortest path optimization include finding LLR paths in the MSPR models based on SDR techniques. Chapters 2–6 evaluate MSPR algorithms based on SDR techniques such as LLR.

In the following sections we discuss discrete event simulation models and shortest path optimization models.

6.2.1 Discrete Event Simulation Models

Discrete event simulation modeling is a well-established technique for routing design, capacity design, and performance analysis, and such models are a versatile method used to study and optimize TQO design and performance. Discrete event simulation models can accurately capture nonlinear and complex network behavior and are used for network design and optimization. For example, DEFO design models are extremely flexible and successful in the design of very complex routing and bandwidth allocation algorithms and as a basis for network capacity design methods, for the case studies presented in Chapters 8 and 9, and for capacity design of multiservice GTQO networks, as described in Chapter 10.

Simulation models, on the other hand, can have long run times, especially for packet-based network models that attempt to model all the protocol steps and details. Simulation models, however, can capture packet network dynamics in an efficient way, without modeling all the protocol details. See in particular the simulation models presented in Chapter 9 for the optimization of integrated voice/data MPLS-based network designs, where queuing behavior is approximated by bufferless queuing models [BONALD02] and other techniques.

Another issue with simulation models is their ability to achieve sufficient accuracy, for example, in trying to estimate rare-event probabilities such as extremely small packet loss rates such as 10^{-9}. However, in Section 6.3.2 we show how to evaluate the confidence interval of such parameters by evaluating the binomial distribution, for example, for the 90th percentile confidence interval. As an example, suppose that network traffic is such that 1 million connection requests arrive in a single busy-hour period, and we wish to design the network to achieve 1% average traffic loss probability (TLP) or less. If the network is designed based on the simulated results to yield at most .00995 probability of lost/delayed traffic, i.e., at most 9950 connection requests are lost/delayed out of 1 million connection requests, then we can be more than 90% sure that the network has a maximum traffic loss probability of .01. For a specific node pair where 2000 connection requests arrive in a single busy-hour period, suppose we wish to design the node pair to achieve 1% average TLP or less. If the network capacity is designed in the simulation model to yield at most .0075 probability of lost/delayed traffic for the node pair, i.e., at most 15 connection requests are lost/delayed out of 2000 connection requests in the simulation model, then we can be more than 90% sure that the node pair has a maximum TLP of .01. Such methods are used to ensure that design objectives are met, taking into consideration the sampling errors of discrete event simulation models.

We now explain the main elements of constructing a discrete event simulation model. To begin with, such a model has a simulated clock that controls the time at which events are executed. Individual events, such as the arrival of voice connection requests or data flow connection requests, are put on an event list, and at the simulated time of their arrival they are routed on the simulated links in the model using the exact routing logic of the routing method being studied. Poisson arrivals are often used, for example, to model originating traffic connections, together with an exponential holding time distribution having a given mean. However, any arrival distribution or holding time distribution could be simulated as well.

As an example of a typical routing logic, a connection request is first routed on the direct simulated link (or primary shortest path if the direct link does not exist), and if the direct link/shortest path is busy, the connection is routed on the next path in the routing table. Bandwidth reservation is applied in selecting capacity on each link. If any of the simulated links on the alternate path are busy, the connection request is then routed on the next path in the routing table. In the simulation, if a link in a path is busy, this condition results in a simulated crankback signaling message that notifies the originating node that the path is congested and alternate paths might be tried, if allowed by the particular routing algorithm. If a connection finds an idle path, the simulated link capacity is made busy, the connection holding time is determined according to the exponential holding time distribution (other distributions can easily be modeled in simulations), and the end time of the connection is noted in the event list for a later disconnect event at the simulated time the connection is disconnected. At the simulated disconnect time, the simulated link capacity occupied by the connection is made idle once again, and the connections-in-progress counter for the affected node pair is decremented. Hence the simulation model can model complex network routing logic very accurately, thereby giving accurate estimates of network performance for such logic.

Complex queuing behavior also can be readily modeled in the simulation for packet-based networks. Statistical data are gathered in the simulation, such as the number of arriving call/session requests, lost connection requests, connections in progress, and crankback events. Simulation models can also be used to validate analytical models such as the ones presented in [ASH98]. However, connection-by-connection simulations can go far beyond the ability of analytical models to represent complex network behavior.

Simulation models must correctly predict actual network behavior, otherwise such models cannot be used to predict future behavior. This important point is called "model calibration and validation." In model calibration, predicted data of the model are compared to actual observed data, and in a properly calibrated model predicted and actual data match up. The basic principle of model calibration/validation is that if a model is not calibrated and validated against actual behavior, it cannot be used to predict future behavior. Of course, this is of critical importance when using simulation models to design future network architectures.

Simulation models used have been so calibrated and validated against actual network data wherever possible. For example, simulation models used in the case studies presented in Chapters 8 and 9 have been validated against actual network data. That is, when the models are used to simulate actual networks, such as the RTNR and RINR networks, actual RTNR/RINR network data are available to be compared to simulation model data. The simulation model must then be calibrated to match actual network data, and once that is done, the simulation model is validated properly.

A good illustration of a properly calibrated/validated model, in this case for a hydrologic model rather than a network model, is given [DONIGIAN02] for a Connecticut watershed model. This is a nice study and clearly illustrates the principles of model calibration and validation. It shows that observed watershed data, which are readily available, accurately match model-predicted data in several Connecticut rivers and that the model is therefore properly calibrated and validated. The article makes the important point that:

> Model calibration and validation are necessary and critical steps in any model application. For most all watershed models, calibration is an iterative procedure of parameter evaluation and refinement, as a result of comparing simulated and observed values of interest. Model validation is in reality an extension of the calibration process. Its purpose is to assure that the calibrated model properly assesses all the variables and conditions which can affect model results, and demonstrate the ability to predict field observations for periods separate from the calibration effort.

I've been building models for over 40 years and have been responsible through the RATS team for the design of AT&T's voice and data networks using models I've developed along with my colleagues of these networks. AT&T would never accept the predictions of my models, upon which billions of dollars of revenue depend, unless the models accurately predicted current and future behavior. Model calibration and validation are of critical importance.

6.2.2   Shortest Path Routing Design Models

The Bellman–Ford method [BELLMAN57], Dijkstra's method [DIJKSTRA59], and Floyd–Warshall algorithm [FLOYD62, WARSHALL62, CORMEN90], for example, are often used for shortest path optimization. Dijkstra's algorithm solves the single source problem and, without worsening the run time, can compute the shortest paths from a given node in a graph to all other nodes. The Bellman–Ford algorithm also solves the single source problem, and the Floyd–Warshall algorithm solves for the shortest paths for all node pairs. Algorithms are available for finding the k-shortest paths between node pairs, shortest paths considering multiple criteria, and many other variations of this classical shortest path optimization problem. A large number of books are devoted to such optimization methods [e.g., BERTSEKAS92, CORMEN90, MINOUX86, PIORO04].

To illustrate the Bellman–Ford algorithm, let C_{ij} represent the cost of the minimum cost path from node i to node j. If node i and node k have a direct link with link cost (administrative weight) c_{ik}, the minimum cost path between nodes i and j can be obtained by solving Bellman's equation:

$$C_{ij} = \min(k)(c_{ik} + C_{kj})\quad\quad\quad\quad (1)$$

One can solve for the C_{ij} by initially setting

$$C_{ij} = c_{ij} \text{ if nodes } i \text{ and } j \text{ are connected}$$
$$C_{ij} = \text{infinity if nodes } i \text{ and } j \text{ are not connected}$$

and then iteratively solving Eq. (1) until the C_{ij} values converge.

Shortest path optimization may use a topology database that includes, for example, the link cost and available bandwidth on each link. From the topology database, a node could determine a list of shortest paths to another node by using Bellman–Ford's or Dijkstra's algorithm based on the link costs (or administrative weights), which are communicated to all nodes within the routing domain through the routing protocol. These link costs may be set, for example, to $[1 + \varepsilon \times \text{distance}]$, where ε is a factor giving a relatively smaller weight to the distance in comparison to the hop count. Alternatively, the available bandwidth on the link can be used to determine the link cost; some combination of link distance, available bandwidth, or other criteria could also be used.

6.2.3   Hierarchical Routing Design Models

Hierarchical FXR models are designed by applying hierarchical path constraints, as described in Chapter 2 (Section 2.3.1). Hierarchical FXR limits path choices and can lead to inefficient network designs compared to nonhierarchical (flat) network MSPR approaches. If we choose shortest paths based on cost and relax the routing constraints

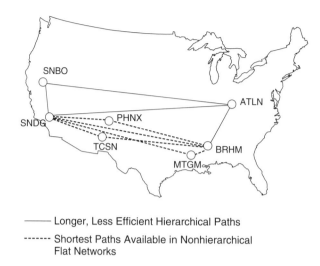

——— Longer, Less Efficient Hierarchical Paths

------- Shortest Paths Available in Nonhierarchical
Flat Networks

Figure 6.1 Shortest path routing and hierarchical routing.

dictated by a hierarchical network structure, i.e., use a flat network structure, a more efficient network results. Figure 6.1 illustrates the selection of shortest paths between two network nodes, SNDG and BRHM. Figure 6.1 shows the actual routing used in the five-level hierarchical FXR network, which was implemented for decades in the Bell System network prior to its replacement by dynamic routing. Longer paths, such as SNDG–SNBO–ATLN–BRHM, which did arise in the hierarchical FXR network through hierarchical path selection, are less efficient than shortest path selection, such as SNDG–PHNX–BRHM, SNDG–TCSN–BRHM, or SNDG–MTGM–BRHM. The latter paths are indeed allowed and used in a nonhierarchical, flat network, such as implemented currently with dynamic routing. Routing on the least costly, most direct, or shortest paths is often more efficient than routing over longer hierarchical paths.

As described in Chapter 1 (Section 1.6.2), this five-level hierarchy was replaced by DNHR during the 1980s and later by RTNR during the 1990s. A detailed description of the design of hierarchical routing networks, and hierarchical network capacity design methods, is given in [ASH98].

6.3 Capacity Design and Optimization Methods

This section describes capacity design optimization techniques, including DEFO, TLFO, VTFO, and dynamic transport routing capacity design models, and illustrates how they are applied to various dynamic network designs. Capacity design is done using the simulation-based DEFO technique for the modeling/analysis studies presented, including FXR, MSPR-SDR, MSPR-EDR, two-link-SDR, two-link-EDR, and dynamic transport routing network design. Sparse and meshed topologies, as well as hierarchical and flat topologies, are designed by the DEFO model. Capacity design of dynamic transport routing networks is done using a relatively simple procedure in which the traffic demands are aggregated to the transport links and each transport link is sized to carry the total traffic demand. Several examples of these capacity design procedures are given in Section 6.4, which include the following:

- Per-VNET versus per-flow network capacity design
- Integrated versus separate voice/ISDN and data network capacity designs
- MSPR versus two-link network capacity design
- Single-area flat versus two-level hierarchical network capacity design
- EDR versus SDR network capacity design
- Dynamic transport routing versus fixed transport routing network capacity design

Before describing the capacity design models, we first discuss the impacts of traffic variations on network design, including minute-to-minute, hour-to-hour, day-to-day, and forecast uncertainty/reserve capacity design impacts.

6.3.1   Capacity Design Cost Impacts for Traffic Load Variations

Fundamental Telephonia–BellHead beliefs are that networks should be carefully engineered to carry the expected traffic—Bellheads have sophisticated theories to do careful engineering, and some of these theories are presented in this chapter. However, Geekia NetHeads are unfailingly scornful of BellHeads' careful engineering and are forever chanting "capacity is free, just put in an infinite amount and stop worrying!" BellHeads retort that those who think that capacity is free aren't the ones paying for it and that 100 years of careful traffic engineering have proven successful and wise and have paid off big time! Recently, another version of this same argument has crept into the trade press under the heading "Mr. QoS versus Mr. Bandwidth" [BORTHICK05].

While we don't resolve the argument here, Geekians will be happy to observe that all of the design methods discussed here are shown to be applicable to networks that incorporate their revered and ingenious protocols: SIP, MPLS, DiffServ, DSTE, RSVP, NSIS, and others. Telephonians (and practicing Telephonicians) will recognize that their time-honored and highly successful network design principles, optimization techniques, engineering criteria, and performance goals are included in the GTQO protocol requirements. While not everyone will be dancing in the aisles over that compromise, I expect a good turnout for the celebration in any case.

Networks are subject to overloads and failures, no matter how "infinite" we try to make the bandwidth or how sophisticated we design the control technology. Parkinson's law applies to all networks—available bandwidth will fill up—and Murphy's law applies to all networks—something will go wrong. These laws apply no matter what. Everyone has experienced communication network overloads and failures, and overload/failure events are typical and unavoidable in all types of networks, no matter what the technology, size, etc. TQO protocol optimization and capacity design optimization are essential components in making networks perform well and meet design objectives.

Therefore, we declare that the infinite bandwidth argument is invalid and not used. Besides, it's against the law, Parkinson's and Murphy's laws, that is. Telcos paying for capacity don't do this anyway. So pay attention to the techniques presented in this chapter, they *are* used. Before presenting the capacity management optimization principles and design models, let's first review the capacity design cost impacts of applying those principles and models for various traffic load variations.

Capacity management must provide sufficient capacity to carry the expected traffic variations, such as those detailed in Table 1.1 in Chapter 1, so as to meet end-to-end traffic performance objectives, such as loss/delayed probability objective levels. Here the term loss/delayed probability refers to the denial or nonadmission of a call/session or connection request, or packet loss/delay within the queuing functions, based, for example, on the lack of available resources, such as link bandwidth, queuing resources, call processing resources, application server resources, and media server resources. Traffic load variations lead in direct measure to capacity increments and can be categorized as (a) minute-to-minute instantaneous variations and associated busy-hour traffic load capacity, (b) hour-to-hour variations and associated "hour-to-hour ("multihour") capacity," (c) day-to-day variations and associated "day-to-day capacity," and (d) week-to-week variations and associated "reserve capacity." As noted in Table 1.1, Chapter 1, capacity management excludes nonrecurring traffic such as caused by overloads (focused or general overloads) or failures. The process of dealing with such nonrecurring traffic events in network design is described further in Chapter 7.

Nonalternate routing networks and FXR networks, along with associated capacity design techniques, lead to capacity requirements that can be reduced by improved routing techniques. Upper limits on capacity savings that can be achieved with improved routing techniques and associated capacity design are given in Figure 6.2. Experience has shown that practical capacity design techniques are available to achieve much of the projected upper bounds on savings, on the order of 30–50% of the network cost is possible, as illustrated in Figure 6.2. The following sections discuss each of the minute-to-minute, hour-to-hour, day-to-day, and week-to-week traffic variation impacts on capacity design.

6.3.1.1 Impacts of Within-the-Hour Minute-to-Minute Traffic Variations

Design methods within the capacity management procedure account for the mean and variance of the within-the-hour variations of the offered and overflow loads. For example, classical methods [e.g., WILKINSON56, WILKINSON58, HILL76] are used to size links for these two parameters of load. Nonhierarchical shortest path routing can provide savings in network design compared to hierarchical path routing.

Routing methods such as hierarchical FXR limit path choices and often provide less efficient designs as a result of the more limited routing flexibility. If we choose paths based on cost and relax constraints, such as a hierarchical network structure, a more efficient network results. Thereby additional benefits can be provided in

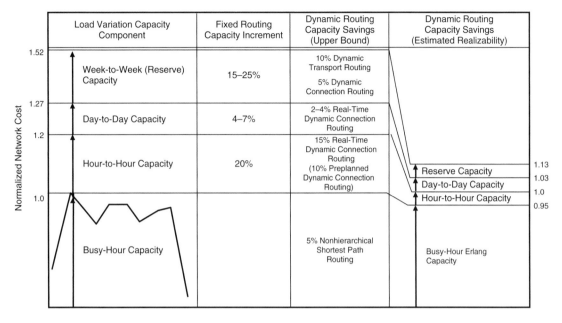

Figure 6.2 Estimated capacity savings with optimized capacity design for load variation components.

network design by allowing a more flexible routing plan that is not restricted to hierarchical routes but allows the selection of the shortest nonhierarchical paths. Figure 6.1 illustrates the selection of shortest paths between two network nodes, SNDG and BRHM. Longer paths, such as SNDG–SNBO–ATLN–BRHM, which might arise through hierarchical path selection, are less efficient than shortest path selection, such as SNDG–PHNX–BRHM, SNDG–TCSN–BRHM, and SNDG–MTGM–BRHM. There are really two components to the shortest path selection savings. One component results from eliminating link splintering. Splintering occurs, for example, when more than one node is required to satisfy a traffic load within a given area, such as a metropolitan area. Multiple links to a distant node could result, thus dividing the load among links that are less efficient than a single large link. A second component of shortest path selection savings arises from path cost. Routing on the least costly, most direct, or shortest paths is often more efficient than routing over longer hierarchical paths.

Capacity design impacts of using nonhierarchical (flat network) shortest paths versus hierarchical paths can lead to cost savings on the order of 5% of network cost in typical applications. More details on this analysis can be found in [ASH98].

6.3.1.2 Impacts of Hour-to-Hour Traffic Variations

Multihour dynamic routing network design accounts for the hour-to-hour variations of the load, and as illustrated in Figure 6.2, hour-to-hour capacity can vary up to 20%

or more of network capacity. Hour-to-hour capacity can be reduced by multihour dynamic routing design models such as the DEFO, TLFO, and VTFO optimization models described in this chapter.

Dynamic routing design improves network utilization relative to fixed routing design because fixed routing cannot respond flexibly to traffic load variations that arise from business/residential traffic patterns, time zones, seasonal variations, and other causes. Dynamic routing design increases network utilization efficiency by varying routing tables in accordance with traffic patterns and designing capacity accordingly. A simple illustration of this principle is shown in Figure 6.3, where there is afternoon peak load demand between nodes A and B but a morning peak load demand between nodes A and C and nodes C and B.

Here a simple dynamic routing design is to provide capacity only between nodes A and C and nodes C and B but no capacity between nodes A and B. Then the A–C and C–B morning peak loads route directly over this capacity in the morning, and the A–B afternoon peak load uses this same capacity by routing this traffic on the A–C–B path in the afternoon. A fixed routing network design provides capacity for the peak period for each node pair, thus providing capacity between nodes A and B, as well as between nodes A and C and nodes C and B.

The effect of multihour network design is illustrated by a national intercity network design model illustrated in Figure 6.4. Here it is shown that about 20% of the network's cost can be attributed to designing for time-varying loads, as also portrayed in Figure 6.2.

As illustrated in Figure 6.4, the 17 hourly networks are obtained by using each hourly traffic load, and ignoring the other hourly loads, to size a network that perfectly matches that hour's load. Each hourly network represents the hourly traffic load capacity cost portrayed in Figure 6.4. The 17 hourly networks show that three network

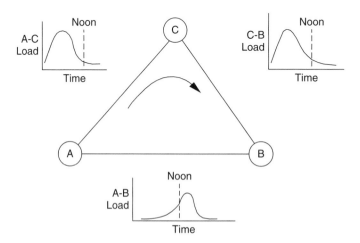

Figure 6.3 Multihour network design.

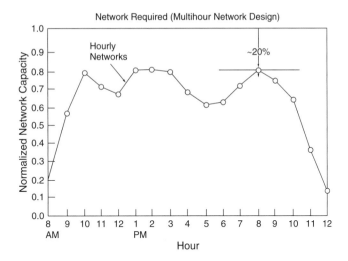

Figure 6.4   Hourly versus multihour network design.

busy periods are visible, where we see morning, afternoon, and evening busy periods, and the noon-hour drop in load and the early evening drop as the business day ends and residential traffic demand increases in the evening. The hourly network curve separates the capacity provided in the multihour network design into two components: below the curve is the capacity needed in each hour to meet the load and above the curve is the capacity that is available but is not needed in that hour. This additional capacity exceeds 20% of the total network capacity through all hours of the day, which represents the multihour capacity cost referred to in Figure 6.2. This gap represents the additional capacity required by the network to meet noncoincident traffic loads.

Capacity design impacts of multihour dynamic routing network design versus FXR network design can lead to cost savings on the order of 10–15% of network cost in typical applications. As illustrated in Figure 6.2, the 10% cost savings is related to preplanned (or TDR) implementations of dynamic routing, whereas the 15% cost savings is related to real-time (or SDR or EDR) implementations of dynamic routing. More details on this analysis can be found in [ASH98].

6.3.1.3   *Impacts of Day-to-Day Traffic Variations*

It is known that some daily variations are systematic. For example, in voice networks, morning busy hours are usually higher than afternoon and evening busy hours, and Monday morning traffic is usually higher than Friday morning. For data networks, evening busy hours are usually higher than daytime busy hours. Traffic levels are very similar in voice and data networks from one day to the next; however, given day-to-day load variations, the exact traffic levels differ for any given day. This load variation can be characterized in network design by a stochastic model for the daily variation, which results in additional capacity called day-to-day capacity. Day-to-day capacity is needed to meet the average traffic lost/delayed probability objective when the load varies according to the stochastic model. Day-to-day capacity is nonzero due to the nonlinearities in link traffic loss and/or link queuing delay levels as a function of load. When the load on a link fluctuates about a mean value, because of day-to-day variation, the mean traffic lost/delayed rate is higher than the traffic lost/delayed rate produced by the mean load. Therefore, additional capacity is provided to maintain the traffic lost/delayed probability grade-of-service objective in the presence of day-to-day load variation. As illustrated in Figure 6.2, typical day-to-day capacity required is 4–7% of the network cost for medium to high day-to-day variations, respectively.

In network capacity design, a traffic load model is typically assumed where the loads vary according to a day-to-day variation model, characterized, for example, by a gamma distribution with one of three levels of variance [WILKINSON58]. This is in accordance with realistic voice and data traffic load variation, which exhibit an actual realized load with a random fluctuation from day to day. Studies have established that this source of uncertainty requires the network to be augmented in order to maintain the required performance objectives. Accommodating day-to-day variations in the network design procedure can use an equivalent load technique that models each node pair in the network as an equivalent link designed to meet the performance objectives. For example, using standard day-to-day variation design models [HILL76, WILKINSON58], the link bandwidth N is determined for the mean load R with its specified level of day-to-day variation, which meets the performance objectives. Then holding fixed the calculated equivalent bandwidth capacity N, we calculate a larger equivalent load Re that would require the same equivalent bandwidth N but assuming that the equivalent load Re has no day-to-day variation. The equivalent traffic load Re is then used in place of R, as it produces the same equivalent bandwidth as the original load R but in the absence of day-to-day variation.

This simplified approach has been used in large-scale capacity network design applications and, as illustrated in Figure 6.2, provides on the order of 2–4% cost savings for medium to high day-to-day variations, respectively. More details on design techniques and cost impacts related to day-to-day traffic variations can be found in [ASH98].

6.3.1.4 Impacts of Week-to-Week Traffic Variations

Reserve capacity, such as day-to-day capacity, comes about because load uncertainties—in this case forecast errors—tend to cause capacity buildup in excess of the network design that exactly matches the forecast loads. Reluctance to disconnect and rearrange link and transport capacity contributes to this reserve capacity buildup. At a minimum, the currently measured mean load is used to adjust routing and capacity design, as needed. In addition, the forecast-error variance component is used in some models to build in so-called protective capacity. Reserve or protective capacity can provide a cushion against overloads and failures, and generally benefits network performance. However, provision for reserve capacity is not usually built into the capacity management design process, but arises because of sound adminis-trative procedures. These procedures attempt to minimize total cost, including both network capital costs and operations costs. As illustrated in Figure 6.2, studies have shown that reserve capacity in some networks is in the range of 15 to 25% or more of network cost [FRANKS79]. This is described further in Chapter 5 and in the modeling studies presented in Section 6.4.

Network designs are made based on measured traffic loads and estimated traffic loads that are subject to error. In network capacity design we use forecast traffic loads because the network capacity must be in place before the loads occur. Errors in the forecast traffic reflect uncertainty about the actual loads that will occur, and as such the design needs to provide sufficient capacity to meet the expected load on the network in light of these expected errors. Studies have established that this source of uncertainty requires the network to be augmented in order to maintain the traffic lost/delayed probability grade-of-service objectives [FRANKS79].

The capacity management process accommodates the random forecast errors in the procedures. When some realized node-to-node performance levels are not met, additional capacity and/or routing changes are provided to restore the network per-formance to the objective level. Capacity is often not disconnected in the capacity management process even when load forecast errors are such that this would be possible without performance degradation. Capacity management, then, is based on the forecast traffic loads and the link capacity already in place. Consideration of the in-service link capacity entails a transport routing policy that could consider (a) fixed transport routing, in which transport is not rearranged, and (b) dynamic transport routing, as discussed in Chapter 5, which allows flexible logical network rearrange-ment, including some logical network capacity disconnects.

The logical capacity disconnect policy may leave capacity in place even though it is not called for by the network capacity design. In-place capacity that is in excess of the capacity required to exactly meet the design loads with the objective performance is called reserve capacity. There are economic and service implications of the capacity management strategy. Insufficient capacity means that occasionally link capacity must be connected on short notice if the network load requires it. This is short-term capacity management, and the details of this operational process are discussed in Chapter 7. There is a trade-off between reserve capacity and short-term capacity management. [FRANKS79] analyzes a model that shows the level of reserve capacity to be in the range of 6–25% when forecast error, measurement error, and other effects are present. In fixed transport routing networks, if links are found to be overloaded when actual loads are larger than forecasted values, additional link capacity is provided to restore the objective performance levels, and, as a result, the process leaves the network with reserve capacity even when the forecast error is unbiased.

On occasion, the planned design underprovides link capacity at some point in the network, again because of forecast errors, and short-term capacity management is required to correct these forecast errors and restore objective service performance levels. This is also discussed further in Chapter 7.

Operational studies in fixed transport routing networks have measured 20–25% for network reserve capacity. In fact, I continue to monitor AT&T's RTNR network on a daily basis, and based on the model now presented in Figure 6.5 estimate average reserve capacity on the order of 15–20%. Quite coincidentally, this daily analysis of the RTNR network comes out in a report appropriately called the "Ash Report." As illustrated in Figure 6.5, the procedure I use entails comparing the RTNR capacity in place with an optimal capacity design for the current traffic loads. For this optimal RTNR capacity design, I use the DEFO model presented in Section 6.3.2.

The model illustrated in Figure 6.5 is used to study network design of a network on the basis of forecast loads, in which the network design accounts for both the current network and the forecast loads in capacity management. Capacity management can make short-term capacity additions if network performance for the realized traffic loads becomes unacceptable and cannot be corrected by routing adjustments. Capacity management tries to minimize reserve capacity while maintaining the design performance objectives and an acceptable level of short-term capacity additions. Capacity management uses the traffic forecast, which is subject to error, to determine the forecast network capacity, which takes into account the existing network capacity so as to minimize rearrangements when implementing the forecast capacity needs. If necessary, short-term capacity additions are made to restore network performance when design objectives are not met, as shown in the model.

With fixed connection routing and fixed transport routing, link capacity augments called for by the design model for the forecast network are implemented, and when the network design calls for reduced bandwidth capacity on a link, a disconnect policy is invoked to decide whether link capacity should be disconnected. This disconnect policy reflects a degree of reluctance to disconnect link capacity so as to ensure that disconnected link capacity is not needed a short time later if traffic loads grow. With

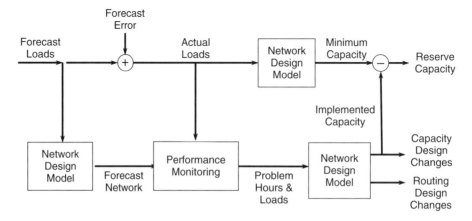

Figure 6.5 Design model illustrating forecast error and reserve capacity trade-off.

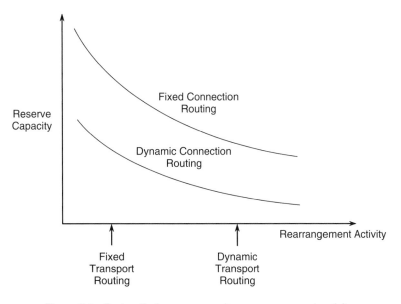

Figure 6.6 Trade-off of reserve capacity vs rearrangement activity.

dynamic connection routing and fixed transport routing, a reduction in reserve capacity is possible while retaining a low level of short-term capacity management. With dynamic connection routing and dynamic transport routing, an additional reduction in reserve capacity is achieved, as illustrated in Figure 6.6. With dynamic transport routing design, reserve capacity can be reduced in comparison with fixed transport routing because with dynamic transport network design the link sizes can be better matched to the network load. In addition to dynamic transport routing, methods such as the Kalman filter [PACK82], which provides more accurate traffic forecasts, can help reduce the level of reserve capacity.

By accessing available reserve capacity, dynamic connection routing provides an additional 5% reduction in reserve capacity compared to fixed traffic routing. Models to illustrate this are presented in [ASH98]. Reserve capacity can be reduced through dynamic transport routing on the order of 10% of network capacity compared to fixed transport routing, as illustrated in the modeling analysis presented in Section 6.4. This 10–15% potential reduction in reserve capacity cost has also been illustrated in Figure 6.2.

6.3.2 Capacity Design and Optimization Models

We now discuss four capacity design models—DEFO, TLFO, VTFO, dynamic transport network design models—and illustrate how they are applied to various dynamic network designs. For each model we discuss the following steps: initialization, routing design, capacity design, and parameter update.

As mentioned in the introduction, capacity design is done using the DEFO technique for most routing models considered in this book: FXR, MSPR-SDR, MSPR-EDR, two-link-SDR, two-link-EDR, and dynamic transport routing network design. DEFO models optimize the routing of discrete event flows and the associated link capacities and are able to capture very complex routing behavior through a simulation model embedded in the algorithm. Sparse and meshed topologies, as well as hierarchical and flat topologies, are designed by the DEFO model.

The capacity design of dynamic transport routing networks is simplified by assuming that the layer 2 logical links are directly overlaid on the layer 1 physical fiber links. Connections are routed dynamically within such a network by doing both connection switching and OXC transport bandwidth switching for every connection request on every logical/fiber transport link. As a result, the capacity design procedure is to aggregate the traffic demands directly to each logical/fiber transport link and then size each logical/fiber transport link to carry the total traffic.

6.3.2.1 Discrete Event Flow Optimization Models

DEFO models are used for fixed and dynamic connection/transport routing network design. These models optimize the routing of discrete event flows, as measured in units of individual connection requests, and the associated link capacities. Figure 6.7 illustrates steps of the DEFO model.

The event generator converts traffic demands to discrete connection-request events. This can use a Poisson process or more complex traffic processes, such as self-similar traffic. The discrete event model provides routing logic according to the particular

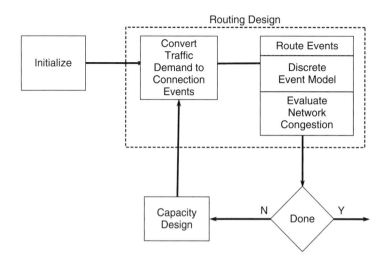

Figure 6.7 Discrete event flow optimization (DEFO) model.

routing method and routes the connection-request events according to the routing table logic. DEFO models use embedded simulation models for path selection and routing table management to route discrete-event demands on the link capacities, and the link capacities are then optimized to meet the required flow. We generate initial link capacity requirements based on the traffic load matrix input to the model. Based on design experience with the model, an initial node-termination capacity is estimated based on a maximum design occupancy in the node busy hour of 0.93, and the total network occupancy (total traffic demand/total link capacity) in the network busy hour is adjusted to fall within the range of 0.84 to 0.89. Network performance is evaluated as an output of the discrete event model, and any needed link capacity adjustments are determined. Capacity is allocated to individual links in accordance with the Kruithof allocation method [KRUITHOF37], which distributes link capacity in proportion to the overall demand between nodes, as now described.

Kruithof's technique is used to estimate the node-to-node capacity requirements p_{ij} from the originating node i to the terminating node j under the condition that the total node link capacity requirements may be established by adding the entries in the matrix $p = [p_{ij}]$. Assume that a matrix $q = [q_{ij}]$, representing the node-to-node link capacity requirements for a previous iteration, is known. Also, the total link capacity requirements b_i at each node i and the total link capacity requirements d_j at each node j are estimated as

$$b_i = a_i/\gamma$$
$$d_j = a_j/\gamma$$

where a_i is the total traffic at node i, a_j is the total traffic at node j, and γ is the average traffic-carrying capacity per unit of bandwidth, or node design occupancy, which is typically on the order of 0.8. The terms p_{ij} can be obtained as follow:

$$fac_i = b_i/(\Sigma(j)q_{ij})$$
$$fac_j = d_j/(\Sigma(i)q_{ij})$$
$$E_{ij} = (fac_i + fac_j)/2$$
$$p_{ij} = q_{ij} \times E_{ij}$$

After these equations are solved iteratively, the converged steady-state values of p_{ij} are obtained.

The DEFO model can generate connection-request events according, for example, to a Poisson arrival distribution and exponential holding times, or with more general arrival streams and arbitrary holding time distributions, because such models can readily be implemented in the discrete routing table simulation model. Connection-request events are generated in accordance with the traffic load matrix input to the model. These events are routed on the selected path according to the routing table rules, as modeled by the routing table simulation, which determines the selected path for each connection request event and flows the event onto the network capacity.

The output from the routing design is the fraction of traffic lost and delayed in each time period. From this traffic performance, the capacity design determines the new link capacity requirements of each node and each link to meet the design performance level. From the estimate of lost and delayed traffic at each node in each time period, an occupancy calculation determines additional node link capacity requirements for an updated link capacity estimate. Such a link capacity determination is made based on the amount of lost/delayed traffic. The total lost/delayed traffic Δa is estimated at each of the nodes, and an estimated link capacity increase ΔT for each node is calculated by the relationship

$$\Delta T = \Delta a / \gamma$$

where again γ is the average traffic-carrying capacity per unit of bandwidth. Thus, the ΔT for each node is distributed to each link according to the Kruithof estimation method described earlier. Because the Kruithof allocation method [KRUITHOF37] distributes link capacity in proportion to the overall demand between nodes and in accordance with link cost, overall network cost is minimized. Sizing individual links in this way ensures an efficient level of utilization on each link in the network to optimally divide the load between the direct link and the overflow network. Once the links have been resized, the network is reevaluated to see if the performance objectives are met; if not, another iteration of the model is performed.

We evaluate the confidence interval of the engineered lost/delayed traffic in the model. For this analysis, we evaluate the binomial distribution for the 90th percentile confidence interval. Suppose that for a traffic load of A in which connection requests arrive over the designated time period of stationary traffic behavior, there are on average m lost connection requests out of n attempts. This means that there is an average observed traffic loss probability (TLP) of

$$\text{TLP} = m/n$$

where, for example, TLP = .01 for a 1% average traffic loss probability. Now, we want to find the value of the 90th percentile traffic loss probability p such that

$$E(n, m, p) = \Sigma(r = m, n) C_{rm} p^r q^{n-r} \geq .90$$

where

$$C_{rm} = n!/(n-r)!r!$$

is the binomial coefficient and

$$q = 1 - p$$

Then the value p represents the 90th percentile TLP confidence interval. That is, there is a 90% chance that the observed traffic loss probability will be less than or equal to the value p. Methods given in [WEINTRAUB63] are used to numerically evaluate these expressions.

As an example application of this method to the DEFO model, suppose that network traffic is such that 1 million connection requests arrive in a single busy-hour period, and we wish to design the network to achieve 1% average TLP or less. If the network is designed in the DEFO model to yield at most .00995 probability of lost/delayed traffic, i.e., at most 9950 connection requests are lost/delayed out of 1 million connection requests in the DEFO model, then we can be more than 90% sure that the network has a maximum traffic loss probability of .01. For a specific node pair where 2000 connection requests arrive in a single busy-hour period, suppose we wish to design the node pair to achieve 1% average TLP or less. If the network capacity is designed in the DEFO model to yield at most .0075 probability of lost/delayed traffic for the node pair, i.e., at most 15 connection requests are lost/delayed out of 2000 connection requests in the DEFO model, then we can be more than 90% sure that the node pair has a maximum TLP of .01. These methods are used to ensure that the traffic loss probability design objectives are met, taking into consideration the sampling errors of the discrete event model.

6.3.2.2 Discussion of DEFO Model

The greatest advantage of the DEFO model is its ability to capture very complex routing behavior through the equivalent of a simulation model provided in software in the routing design module. By this means, very complex routing networks have been designed by the model, which include all of the routing methods discussed in Chapter 2, TDR, SDR, and EDR methods, the multiservice QoS resource allocation models discussed in Chapter 3, and the complex multiservice dynamic routing design case studies presented in Chapters 8 and 9. Recall that the capacity design of VNET architectures considers all VNETs at once in an integrated network design, in which all the complex dynamic functions are considered together, including per-VNET dynamic routing, per-VNET dynamic bandwidth allocation, bandwidth sharing, bandwidth reservation, and per-VNET queuing. In short, the integrated VNET design takes into account the complex dynamics, and efficiencies, of statistical multiplexing in packet networks where bandwidth is maximally shared. This full sharing approach avoids the network inefficiencies that would result from designing separate VNETs, one at a time, in which bandwidth is not shared and statistical multiplexing is not realized. All of these dynamics must be considered at once in the capacity design while meeting multidimensional performance objectives.

We could put on our "falutin" hat, as Dick Hamming joked, and pretend to formulate and solve the "exact" mixed integer programming, NP-hard formulation of the optimization problem. Nonsense I say, one cannot even write down all the complexity in a mathematical optimization formulation, let alone solve such a problem. This is not to say that mathematical analysis cannot give great insight, but only within a more focused and limited analysis. As one example, I would point to the work by Franks [FRANKS79] described in Section 6.3.1, which used an elegantly simple model to produce "trunk provisioning operating characteristics" (TPOC) curves. The TPOC curves showed the important dynamics of reserve capacity and reluctance to disconnect trunks in an elegant way. Work by Kaufman [KAUFMAN81] and Roberts [ROBERTS81] yielded the well-known "Kaufman–Roberts formula," which describes the blocking probability of a link on which traffic with different bit rates is multiplexed. This is also a beautiful piece of work. Finally, Meier-Hellstern [MEIER-HELLSTERN89] analyzed the Markov-modulated Poisson process (MMPP), and the interrupted Poisson process to model the peaked overflow traffic is a wonderful piece of analysis that accurately solved a classical problem of finding the individual traffic characteristics (mean and variance) of multiple traffic streams offered to a trunk group. However, these great pieces of analysis solve only a piece of a very big, magnificent puzzle posed by network design.

In my humble opinion ("IMHO"), as we Geekia NetHeads say so often in the IETF, the most effective, practical, and implementable approach to dimensioning such complex networks, which is otherwise a completely intractable, hopelessly complex network design problem, is the DEFO method. And while making big claims, I'd add that the DEFO model is general enough to include all TQO models yet to be determined (IMHO).

Multicommodity flow linear programming (LP) optimization models are used widely, for example, in the capacity design of TDR networks [ASH98]. Such multicommodity flow LP models are used to optimize network capacity for traffic load variations, as discussed in this section for the TLFO and VTFO models. It is interesting to note, however, that such LP models are not necessary for the capacity design of meshed two-link SDR or EDR networks using the DEFO model. In addition, no LP is needed for any of the capacity design models in the case of sparse MSPR networks.

For the MSPR case, the reason that no LP optimization is needed is that all traffic in the network capacity design for the engineered traffic loads follows a single shortest path. That is, no alternate paths are needed or beneficial in the capacity design, as links in the sparse network topology typically have high capacity and very low traffic loss probability performance. Therefore, traffic does not overflow (get blocked) on the primary MSPR path. Because all traffic routes on a single shortest path, all the traffic variations are accommodated by sizing the single shortest path properly. Think of a road that is big enough to carry all the cars during all times of the day. Even though traffic varies widely during the day, no one has to seek an alternate route, as all cars get through just fine on the primary route. This is not to say that when traffic exceeds the design level or when there is a "road failure" (e.g., a crash on the primary route) that causes disruption then alternate routes on the road network (and the MSPR network) are definitely in order.

For the two-link-SDR and two-link-EDR cases, the reason that no LP optimization is needed is that the DEFO method finds optimal alternate routes by modeling the path selection optimization in the DEFO simulation model built into DEFO capacity design.

In the meshed network design for the engineered traffic loads, many alternate paths are needed and beneficial in the capacity design, as links in the meshed network topology typically have much smaller capacity and relatively high traffic overflow (blocking) probability performance compared to sparse MSPR capacity designs. Therefore traffic does overflow (get blocked) on the direct one-link path, if it exists, but optimal alternate routes are found by the DEFO algorithm to automatically accommodate all the traffic variations in an optimal fashion. In our road network analogy, the primary route is thin and normally congests, and many people need to seek an alternate route where they can get through. However, a big traffic helicopter in the sky lets each driver know the optimum alternate route.

How good are the DEFO solutions? Hey, that's a good question, but no precise answer can be given. DEFO models are compared [ASH98] to other design models, such as the TLFO and VTFO models presented next, and typically outperform these models by several percentage points in network cost. This is a significant gain for a relatively small price of increased computational effort. As discussed in the introduction, no comparison can be made to a truly optimal solution, as such a solution is impossible to obtain.

So we must resort to arm waving to make any claim about optimality. We could quote "Weber's theorem," based on Joe Weber's classical simulation studies during the early 1960s [WEBER62, WEBER63], which showed, supposedly, that "all good network designs had about the same cost." That is, Weber concluded from his studies that the optimal network design, and ones close to the optimal design, form a very flat region is the "network design cost space," if you will. In coming up with this "theorem," Joe produced many different network designs that were all "good designs" and had about the same cost. From that one deduces "Weber's theorem," that "all good network designs are optimal." Nice try, but no cigar, not true: "Weber's conjecture" would certainly have been a better catch phrase. The problem with Weber's theorem became clear a couple of decades later when the design models presented in this section, i.e., DEFO, TLFO, and VTFO models, produced networks significantly lower in cost than the network designs produced in Weber's analysis. Comparing apples to apples, these algorithms yielded network designs lower by 20% or more in total network cost. Some of the effects missed by Weber were the large potential savings due to hour-to-hour traffic variation effects, as discussed in Section 6.3.1. So much for arm waving based on Weber's theorem.

However, this line of reasoning does make an important point, which is that the designs produced by DEFO, TLFO, and VTFO methods produce far better network designs than any methods that came before. And these are not just theoretical, academic claims, the network designs based on DEFO, TLFO, and VTFO techniques have been deployed in very large-scale operational networks. As we pointed out in the introduction, those networks just have to work right—they are real networks with real customers with real services. Because DEFO models outperform TLFO and VTFO models, presented in the following sections, by several percentage points in network cost, DEFO models are put on top of the heap of network design models. We know of no better model for designing these complex networks, which is our answer to the question posed earlier: "how good are the DEFO solutions?"

6.3.2.3 Example Application of DEFO Model

A flow diagram of the DEFO model, in which the multilink STT-EDR logical blocks described in Chapter 2 are implemented, is illustrated in Figure 6.8. In this section we give a capacity design example of the use of this particular model, which is also based on the case study presented in Chapter 9.

A hub-and-spoke, two-layer network topology is designed in this example by the DEFO model, where the spoke nodes are homed to the nearest hub node. The hub nodes are selected based on nodes with the largest overall traffic load. An initial link topology is then established as follows. A link is automatically established between the spoke node and the nearest hub node with a minimum OC48 capacity. Candidate links are initially established between all the hub nodes, i.e., the hub nodes are fully interconnected by candidate links, which can be later eliminated in the DEFO model. Other candidate links (e.g., between spoke nodes or between spoke and nonhome-hub nodes) are established if at least 67% of an OC48 module is required based on the direct node-to-node traffic demand. Traffic is then routed on shortest paths, where the shortest primary and alternate paths are determined by the Bellman–Ford algorithm, described in Section 6.2.2. Links are then eliminated (except spoke-to-home-hub links)

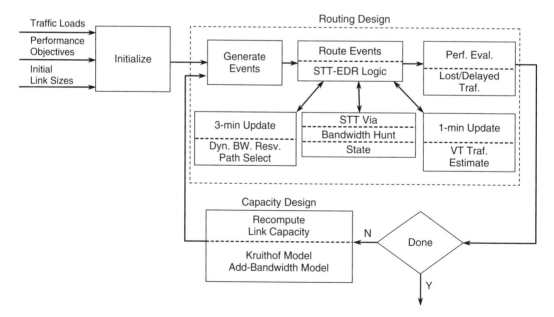

Figure 6.8 Discrete event flow optimization model with multilink success-to-the-top event-dependent routing.

if less than 67% of an OC48 module is required based on the routed link traffic demand. Traffic is then routed again over this reduced link topology, and links are sized to 80% occupancy based on the routed link traffic demand. Finally, the link capacities are rounded up to the nearest OC48 module size to yield the initial link topology.

The DEFO model then generates connection-request events according to a Poisson arrival distribution and exponential holding times (more general arrival streams and arbitrary holding time distributions could also be simulated, as such models can readily be implemented in the DEFO model). Connection-request events are generated in accordance with the traffic load matrix input to the model. These events are routed on the selected path according to the routing table rules described later in this section, which are modeled in detail by the routing table simulation. The simulation logic flows the event onto the network capacity over the selected path for each connection event, denotes the beginning and ending time of the event in the event list, and logs detailed information on the event, including VNET and statistical bandwidth information.

The output from the routing design step is the fraction of traffic lost and delayed. From this traffic performance, the capacity design determines the new link capacity requirements of each link to meet the design performance level. From the estimate of lost and delayed traffic, an occupancy calculation determines additional link capacity requirements for an updated link capacity estimate. The total lost traffic Δa is estimated on each link, and an estimated link capacity increase ΔT is calculated by the relationship $\Delta T = \Delta a / .8$. Links sizes are increased by ΔT and then rounded upward to the nearest OC48 module. Once the links have been resized, the network is reevaluated to see if the performance objectives are met; if not, another iteration of the model is performed.

We evaluate the 90th percentile confidence interval of the engineered traffic loss probability using the binomial distribution. For example, suppose 1 million connections arrive in a single busy-hour period and we wish to design the network to achieve 1% average traffic lost/delayed or less, with 90% confidence. In that case the network is designed in the DEFO model to yield at most .00995 probability of traffic lost/delayed, i.e., at most 9950 connections are lost out of 1 million connections in the DEFO model. If that is achieved in the DEFO design, then we can be more than 90% sure that the network has a maximum traffic lost/delayed probability of .01. Suppose for another node pair where 2000 connections arrive in a single busy-hour period we wish to design the node pair to achieve 1% average traffic lost/delayed probability or less, with 90% confidence. If the network capacity is designed in the DEFO model to yield at most .0075 probability of traffic lost/delayed for the node pair, i.e., at most 15 connections are lost out of 2000 connections in the DEFO model, then we can be more than 90% sure that the node pair has a maximum traffic lost/delayed probability of .01. These methods are used to ensure that the traffic lost/delayed probability design objectives are met, taking into consideration the sampling errors of the discrete event model.

Details of the actual network designs in this example are presented in the case study in Chapter 9.

6.3.2.4 Traffic Load Flow Optimization Models

TLFO models are used for fixed and dynamic connection/transport routing network design. These models optimize the routing of traffic flows and the associated link capacities. Such models typically use analytical expressions to represent often non-linear network behavior and to capture the routing of traffic loads over the network model. Approximations/heuristics are often used in such models, and for dynamic routing network design, the solution can involve a large-scale, multicommodity flow LP optimization problem. Various types of TLFO models are distinguished as to how flow is assigned to links, paths, and routes. In fixed network design, traffic flow is assigned to direct links and overflow from the direct links is routed to alternate paths through the network, as described in the Truitt link flow optimization model presented in the next section. In dynamic routing network design, TLFO models can be path based, in which traffic flow is assigned directly to individual paths, or route based, in which traffic flow is assigned to candidate routes.

As applied to fixed and dynamic routing networks, TLFO models do network design based on shortest path selection and LP traffic flow optimization. An example of a traffic load flow optimization model is illustrated in Figure 6.9. There are two versions of this model: path-TLFO and route-TLFO models, and in both cases an LP optimization model is incorporated in the capacity design module. In the path-TLFO approach, the large-scale, multicommodity, multitime-period LP optimization model assigns traffic demands directly to individual paths and incorporates upper-bound flow constraints on each path in order to force a feasible solution that reflects the

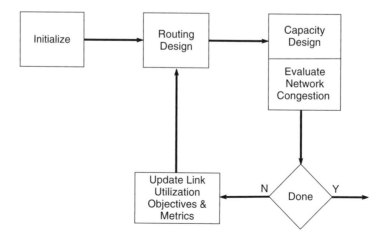

Figure 6.9 Traffic load flow optimization (TLFO) model.

dynamics of alternate path selection. Recall that shortest least-cost path routing gives connections access to paths in order of cost, such that connections access all the bandwidth capacity on the primary direct path between nodes prior to attempting more expensive overflow paths. However, the order of path selection is not known at the outset in the path-TLFO approach. The upper bound constraints and LP model are solved iteratively to determine this path order, along with the optimal, feasible flow assignment and capacity requirements.

In the route-TLFO approach, on the other hand, candidate routes are constructed for each node pair in advance of performing the LP optimization, with specific path selection rules. For example, a route-TLFO model might construct a number of candidate routes for each node pair assuming multilink or two-link path routing with crankback and originating node control capabilities incorporated in the routing table. In this case, a proportion of the traffic flow can be computed for each path and link in the route, as the order of path selection is predetermined prior to solving the LP optimization model. The LP optimization model then selects the optimal routes from among the candidates available, over the multiple time periods of the traffic demand, in order to minimize the network cost.

In both the path-TLFO and the route-TLFO approaches, the LP flow optimization model strives to share link capacity to the greatest extent possible with the variation of loads in the network. This is done by equalizing the loads on links throughout the busy periods of the network traffic demands, such that each link is used to the maximum extent possible in all time periods.

In both the path-TLFO and the route-TLFO approaches, the routing design step finds the shortest paths between nodes in the network. In the path-TLFO model, the routing design step also computes the upper bounds on the flow assigned to each path. In the route-TLFO model, paths are combined into candidate routes, and the proportion of flow on each path and link is determined. In both cases, the candidate paths/routes and constraints (upper bounds on path flows or path/link flow proportions) are fed to the LP flow optimization model, which then assigns traffic flow to the candidate paths/routes.

The capacity design step takes the routing design resulting from the LP optimization and solves a fixed-point traffic flow model to determine the capacity of each link in the network. This model determines the flow on each link and sizes the link to meet the performance level design objectives used in the routing design step. Once the links have been sized, the cost of the network is evaluated and compared to the last iteration.

If the network cost is still decreasing, the update module then performs the following steps: (a) computes the slope of the capacity versus load curve on each link, which reflects the incremental link cost, and updates the link "length" using this incremental cost as a weighting factor and (b) recomputes a new estimate of the optimal link utilization (or, equivalently, the overflow probability) using the Truitt method described in the next section.

The new link lengths and utilization estimates are fed to the routing design, which again constructs path/route choices from the shortest paths, and so on. Minimizing incremental network costs helps convert a nonlinear optimization problem to an LP optimization problem. Yaged [YAGED71, YAGED73] and Knepley [KNEPLEY73] take advantage of this approach in their network design models. This approach also favors large efficient links, which carry traffic at higher utilization efficiency than smaller links. Selecting an efficient link utilization level (or, equivalently, a probability of lost/delayed traffic) on each link in the network is basic to the route/path-TLFO model. The link utilization optimization model [TRUITT54], as described in the next section, is used in the TLFO model to optimally divide the load between the direct link and the overflow network. It is worth pointing out that Yaged's methods were the basis for transport network design in the AT&T network for many years; Knepley's approach was used to design the defense network known as AUTOVON; and Truitt's model has been used worldwide since he invented it back in the 1950s.

Girard [GIRARD90] analyzed the TLFO model in some mathematical detail and showed that the "link length" based on incremental cost was, in fact, a necessary condition for optimality. A great amount of additional detail on the route-TLFO model and path-TLFO model is presented in [ASH98], where detailed, step-by-step, numerical examples are given of the implementation and use of these models.

This model produced excellent designs and outperformed by a very large measure the capacity design models that preceded it. We spoke about the comparisons among DEFO, TLFO, VTFO, and Weber's designs in the previous section. The path-TLFO model, which was also known as the "unified algorithm," was used for decades of operation in AT&T's DNHR and RTNR network implementations, which are described in Chapter 1. These are very large-scale network implementations where operational models *must* operate efficiently and correctly—*nothing can be left to chance*—and indeed that has been achieved. The proof is in the pudding.

6.3.2.5 Link Flow Optimization Model

Link flow optimization models, or "Truitt-triangle" models [TRUITT54], as they are sometimes called, are widely used for fixed hierarchical network design, on a world-wide basis. Such models are also fundamentally embedded in the TLFO models just discussed and in the VTFO model presented in the next section.

As illustrated in Figure 6.10, link capacity design requires a trade-off of the traffic load carried on the link and traffic that must route on alternate paths.

High link occupancy implies more efficient capacity utilization; however, high occupancy leads to link congestion and the resulting need for some traffic that cannot be routed on the direct link to overflow to alternate paths. However, alternate paths usually entail longer, more costly paths. A good balance can be struck by using Truitt's method between link capacity design and alternate path utilization.

Figure 6.10 illustrates a network where traffic is offered on link A–B connecting node A and node B. Some of the traffic can be carried on link A–B; however, when the capacity of link A–B is exceeded, some of the traffic must be carried on alternate paths or be lost. The objective is to determine the direct A–B link capacity and alternate routing path flow such that all the traffic is carried at minimum cost. A simple

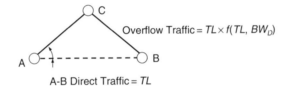

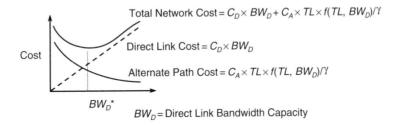

Figure 6.10   Trade-off between direct link cost/capacity and alternate path cost/capacity.

optimization procedure is used to determine the best proportion of traffic to carry on the direct A–B link and how much traffic to alternate route to other paths in the network. As the direct link capacity is increased, the direct link cost increases while the alternate path cost decreases as more direct capacity is added because the overflow load decreases and therefore the cost of carrying the overflow load decreases. An optimum, or minimum, cost condition is achieved when the direct A–B link capacity is increased to the point where the cost per incremental unit of bandwidth capacity to carry traffic on the direct link is just equal to the cost per unit of bandwidth capacity to carry traffic on the alternate network. This is a design principle used in many design models, be they sparse or meshed networks, fixed hierarchical routing networks, or dynamic nonhierarchical routing networks. We see this model incorporated several times in the optimization techniques presented in this chapter.

The following quantities are defined in Figure 6.10:

TL = A–B traffic load to be carried on direct link or alternate path
C_D = direct link cost per unit of bandwidth on direct link
C_A = alternate path cost per unit of bandwidth on alternate path
BW_D = direct link bandwidth capacity
γ = traffic load carried per unit of bandwidth capacity on alternate path
$f(TL, BW_D)$ = link traffic loss probability for offered traffic load TL and link capacity BW_D

Here the function f is a nonlinear (convex) function of both the TL and the BW_D variables. In the classical application of Truitt's method [TRUITT54], function f is the

Erlang B formula. Then

$$\text{Total cost} = \text{direct link cost} + \text{alternate path cost}$$
$$\text{Direct link cost} = C_D \times BW_D$$
$$\text{Alternate path cost} = C_A \times TL \times f(TL, BW_D)\gamma$$

and, as shown in Figure 6.10,

$$\text{Total cost} = C_D \times BW_D + C_A \times TL \times f(TL, BW_D)/\gamma$$

The optimum direct link capacity that minimizes total cost is BW_D.

It is interesting to note that this link capacity optimization (Truitt) model is not necessary for capacity design of sparse MSPR networks, but is applicable and widely used for the design of meshed networks, e.g., hierarchical, two-link SDR or EDR networks. For the sparse network MSPR case, the reason that no Truitt model is needed is that all the engineered traffic in the engineered network follows a single shortest path. No alternate paths are needed or beneficial in the capacity design, as links in the sparse network topology typically have high capacity and very low traffic loss probability (TLP) performance. Therefore, traffic does not overflow (get blocked) on the primary MSPR path, i.e., TLP is essentially zero, and no optimization of the link TLP is required.

For the meshed network design, many alternate paths are needed and beneficial in the capacity design, as links in the meshed network topology typically have much smaller capacity and relatively high TLP performance compared to sparse MSPR capacity designs. That is, the engineered traffic in the engineered network typically is routed on several paths, where the primary path overflows traffic to several alternate paths. Therefore, traffic does overflow (get blocked) on the direct (often 1-link) path, and the Truitt model is needed to optimize the direct link capacity and TLP level. This is the basic mechanism in fixed hierarchical routing network capacity design, as well as in TLFO and VTFO capacity design.

Further in-depth coverage of link optimization techniques can be found in [ASH98], including Wilkinson's equivalent random method for peaked overflow traffic [WILKINSON56, WILKINSON58], the Nyquist and Rapp approximations, and Neal–Wilkinson theory for accounting for day-to-day load variations [HILL76].

6.3.2.6 Virtual Trunk Flow Optimization Models

VTFO models are used for fixed and dynamic connection/transport network design. These models optimize the routing of "virtual trunk (VT)" flows, as measured in units of VT bandwidth demands such as T1, OC1, and OC12. For application to network capacity design, VTFO models use mathematical equations at the outset to convert

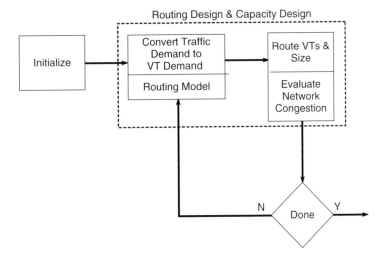

Figure 6.11 Virtual trunk flow optimization (VTFO) model.

traffic demands to VT capacity demands, and the VT capacity demands are then routed and optimized. Figure 6.11 illustrates the VTFO steps.

In the "convert traffic demand" step, traffic demands are converted directly to VT demands, and this model typically assumes an underlying traffic/connection routing structure to perform this calculation. For example, the Truitt method described in the previous section, and as also used in the TLFO network design method described earlier, is used in the VTFO model to directly convert traffic demand to VT demand. In contrast to the TLFO use of the Truitt model, in this VTFO application of the model we obtain an equivalent VT demand, by hour, as opposed to an optimum link utilization objective. Here the node-to-node traffic demands are converted to node-to-node VT demands by using the Truitt approach to optimally divide the traffic load between the direct link and the overflow network, as illustrated in Figure 6.10, by using the link capacity optimization procedure given in the previous section. This approach is used to optimally divide the load between the shortest path and the overflow network, to obtain an equivalent VT demand, by time period. We first calculate the direct path capacity according to the optimal sizing procedure, which yields an efficient direct path utilization level and the direct path bandwidth demands. The alternate path bandwidth demand is determined readily according to the overflow from the direct path by assuming a constant occupancy level γ (e.g., .8) for the overflow bandwidth demand. Furthermore, this VT calculation determines the proportion of direct VT flow and alternate-routed VT flow for later use in the LP optimization model.

In the "route VTs" step, a large-scale, multicommodity, multitime-period LP flow optimization model is solved to optimally route the hourly node-to-node VT demands on the shortest, least-cost paths. In this LP model, the direct path flows are constrained by the proportion of direct/alternate VT flow determined in the initial "convert VT demand" step, as described above. Once VT flows are routed by the LP model, the links are sized for the resulting flow assignment. Once the links have been sized, the performance of the network is evaluated; if the performance objectives are not met, further modification is made to capacity requirements. Network performance is checked by flowing the traffic loads over the resulting capacity design using a fixed-point model and, if necessary, another iteration of the VTFO model is performed.

More details of the VTFO model algorithm, as well as example applications, are presented in [ASH98]. In particular, information is presented on the solution of the large-scale, multicommodity flow, multitime-period LP using a variety of solution techniques for that optimization problem.

6.3.2.7 Dynamic Transport Routing Capacity Design Models

For capacity design of dynamic transport routing networks, described in Chapter 5, the simplest case is that the layer 2 logical links are directly overlaid on the layer 1 physical fiber links. Connections are routed dynamically within the network by connection switching and OXC transport bandwidth switching on every logical/fiber transport link. As a result, the capacity design procedure is relatively simple in that the traffic demands of the various node pairs are aggregated directly to the one logical/fiber transport link and then each logical/fiber transport link is sized to carry the total traffic demand from all node pairs that use the logical/fiber transport link.

This situation is illustrated in Figure 6.12, where the three layer 2 logical links overlay the three layer 1 physical fiber links. The traffic between the six node pairs in Figure 6.12 is aggregated onto these three logical/fiber transport links, which correspond topologically to the three physical fiber links, and then each logical/fiber link is sized to carry the total traffic demand from all node pairs that use the logical/fiber link.

As illustrated in Figure 6.13, one subtlety of the design procedure is deciding what performance objectives (e.g., traffic lost/delayed probability objective) to use for sizing the logical/fiber links. The difficulty is that many node pairs send traffic over the same logical/fiber link, and each of these node pairs has a different number of logical/fiber links in its path. This means that for each traffic load, a different level of performance, e.g., traffic lost/delayed probability, on a given logical/fiber link is needed to ensure, say, a 1% level of TLP end to end. With many kinds of traffic present on the link, we are guaranteed an acceptable TLP objective if we identify the path through each logical/fiber link that requires the largest number of links, n, and size the link to a $1/n$ TLP objective. In Figure 6.13, link L1 has a largest number n equal to 6, and link L2 has a largest number n equal to 4. If the end-to-end TLP objective is 1%, then the link-TLP objectives are determined as given in Figure 6.13. As shown in network modeling studies in the next section, the dynamic transport routing network sized in this simple manner still achieves significant efficiencies.

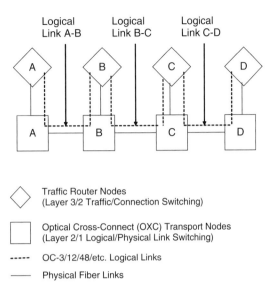

Figure 6.12   Dynamic transport routing model—logical/fiber links overlay physical fiber links.

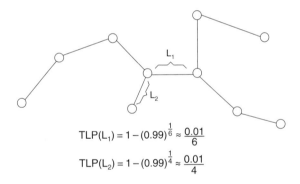

Figure 6.13   Dynamic transport routing network design model calculation of traffic loss probability.

6.4   Modeling of TQO Methods

This section again uses the full-scale 135-node national network model developed in Chapter 2 to study various TQO scenarios and trade-offs. The 135-node national network model is illustrated in Figure 2.9, the multiservice traffic demand model is summarized in Table 2.1, and the cost model is summarized in Table 2.2.

Generally the routing and capacity designs for the meshed logical topologies are optimized by using the DEFO algorithms presented in the previous section, while the routing and capacity desins for the sparse logical topologies are optimized by using the shortest path optimization and DEFO algorithms presented in the previous section. The network capacity design algorithms for GMPLS dynamic transport routing networks modeled in this chapter are discussed in the previous section.

6.4.1 Per-VNET vs Per-Flow Network Design

Here we illustrate the use of the DEFO model to design for a per-flow multiservice network TQO strategy and a per-VNET TQO strategy and to provide comparisons of these designs. The per-flow and per-VNET designs for the flat 135-node model are summarized in Table 6.1.

As shown in Table 6.1, the per-VNET design compared to the per-flow design yields the following results:

- the per-flow design has .996 of the total termination capacity of the per-VNET design
- the per-flow design has .991 of the total transport capacity of the per-VNET design
- the per-flow design has .970 of the total network cost of the per-VNET design

These results indicate that the per-VNET design and per-flow design are quite comparable in terms of capacity requirements and design cost. Chapter 3 showed that the performance of these two designs was also quite comparable under a range of network scenarios.

6.4.2 Integrated vs Separate Voice/ISDN and Data Network Designs

The comparative designs for separate and integrated network designs under multilink STT-EDR, with per-flow QoS resource management, are given in Table 6.2 for the following cases:

- voice/ISDN-only traffic (VNETs 1–8 in Table 2.1)
- data-only traffic (VNETs 9–11 in Table 2.1)
- integrated voice/ISDN and data design (VNETs 1–11 in Table 2.1)

As shown in Table 6.2, the separate voice/ISDN and data designs compared to the integrated design yield the following results:

- the integrated design has .937 of the total termination capacity as the separate voice/ISDN and data network designs
- the integrated design has .963 of the total transport capacity as the separate voice/ISDN and data network designs
- the integrated design has .947 of the total cost as the separate voice/ISDN and data network designs

Table 6.1 Design Comparison of Per-VNET and Per-Flow Bandwidth Allocation; Multilink STT-EDR Connection Routing; Sparse Single-Area Flat Topology (135-Node Multiservice Network Model; DEFO Design Model)

Network design parameters		Per-VNET bandwidth allocation design	Per-flow bandwidth allocation design
Number of links	OC3 links	583	482
	OC12 links	294	389
	OC48 links	104	111
	Total links	981	982
Termination capacity (equivalent DS0s, millions)	OC3 links	3.16	2.30
	OC12 links	6.07	6.64
	OC48 links	7.30	7.50
	Total	16.5	16.4
Transport capacity (equivalent DS0-miles, millions)	OC3 links	1536.3	1185.5
	OC12 links	3876.0	4105.4
	OC48 links	3952.9	3994.5
	Total	9365.2	9285.3
Termination cost ($ millions)	OC3 links	61.0	44.4
	OC12 links	58.5	64.0
	OC48 links	28.6	29.4
	Total	148.1	137.7
Transport cost ($ millions)	OC3 links	299.6	229.8
	OC12 links	621.3	659.6
	OC48 links	237.3	240.0
	Total	1158.1	1129.5
Total cost ($ millions)	OC3 links	360.6	274.2
	OC12 links	679.8	723.6
	OC48 links	265.8	269.5
	Total	1306.2	1267.2
Routing analysis (network busy hour)	Average links/connection	1.84	1.86
	# Node pairs 1 link/connection	982	982
	# Node pairs 2 links/connection	3698	3698
	# Node pairs 3 links/connection	4365	4365

Table 6.2 Comparison of Voice/ISDN-Only Design (VNETs 1–8), Data-Only Design (VNETs 9–11), and Integrated Voice/ISDN and Data Design (VNETs 1–11); Multilink STT-EDR Connection Routing; Per-Flow Bandwidth Allocation; Sparse Single-Area Flat Topology (135-Node Multiservice Network Model; DEFO Design Model)

Network design parameters		Voice/ISDN-only design	Data-only design	Integrated voice/ISDN and data design
Number of links	OC3 links	92	393	482
	OC12 links	159	294	389
	OC48 links	3	109	111
	Total links	254	796	982
Termination capacity	OC3 links	0.36	1.87	2.30
(equivalent DS0s,	OC12 links	2.76	4.99	6.64
millions)	OC48 links	0.20	7.34	7.50
	Total	3.31	14.2	16.4
Transport capacity	OC3 links	380.1	937.7	1185.5
(equivalent	OC12 links	1284.4	3025.8	4105.4
DS0-miles, millions)	OC48 links	160.0	3853.4	3994.5
	Total	1824.5	7816.9	9285.3
Termination cost	OC3 links	6.92	36.0	44.4
($ millions)	OC12 links	26.6	48.1	64.0
	OC48 links	0.78	28.7	29.4
	Total	34.2	112.8	137.7
Transport cost	OC3 links	70.0	182.2	229.8
($ millions)	OC12 links	211.1	486.8	659.6
	OC48 links	9.33	231.9	240.0
	Total	290.4	900.9	1129.5
Total cost	OC3 links	76.9	218.3	274.2
($ millions)	OC12 links	237.7	534.9	723.6
	OC48 links	101.2	260.6	269.5
	Total	324.7	1013.8	1267.2
Routing analysis (network busy hour)	Average links/connection	2.32	1.96	1.86
	# Node pairs 1 link/connection	254	796	982
	# Node pairs 2 links/connection	2895	3350	3698
	# Node pairs 3 links/connection	5806	4899	4365
	# Node pairs 4 links/connection	90	0	0

These results indicate that the integrated design is somewhat more efficient in design due to the economy of scale of the higher capacity network elements, as reflected in the cost model given in Table 2.2.

The comparative designs for separate and integrated network designs under two-link STT-EDR connection routing with per-flow QoS resource management are given in Table 6.3 for the following cases:

- voice/ISDN-only traffic (VNETs 1–8 in Table 2.1)
- data-only traffic (VNETs 9–11 in Table 2.1)
- integrated voice/ISDN and data design (VNETs 1–11 in Table 2.1)

Table 6.3 shows that the separate voice/ISDN and data designs compared to the integrated design yield the following results:

- the integrated design has .948 of the total termination capacity as the separate voice/ISDN and data network designs
- the integrated design has .956 of the total transport capacity as the separate voice/ISDN and data network designs
- the integrated design has .804 of the total cost as the separate voice/ISDN and data designs

These results indicate that the integrated design is somewhat more efficient in design termination and transport capacity. It is about 20% more efficient in cost due to the economy of scale of the higher capacity network elements, as reflected in the cost model given in Table 2.2.

The comparative designs for separate and integrated network designs under two-link DC-SDR connection routing with per-flow QoS resource management are given in Table 6.4 for the following cases:

- voice/ISDN-only traffic (VNETs 1–8 in Table 2.1)
- data-only traffic (VNETs 9–11 in Table 2.1)
- integrated voice/ISDN and data design (VNETs 1–11 in Table 2.1)

We see from these results that the separate voice/ISDN and data designs compared to the integrated design yield the following comparisons:

- the integrated design has .951 of the total termination capacity as the separate voice/ISDN and data network designs
- the integrated design has .958 of the total transport capacity as the separate voice/ISDN and data network designs
- the integrated design has .806 of the total cost as the separate voice/ISDN and data network designs

These results indicate that the integrated design is somewhat more efficient in design termination and transport capacity. It is about 20% more efficient in cost due

Table 6.3 Comparison of Voice/ISDN-Only Design (VNETs 1–8), Data-Only Design (VNETs 9–11), and Integrated Voice/ISDN and Data Design (VNETs 1–11); Two-Link STT-EDR Connection Routing; Per-Flow Bandwidth Allocation; Sparse Single-Area Flat Topology (135-Node Multiservice Network Model; DEFO Design Model)

Network design parameters		Voice/ISDN-only design	Data-only design	Integrated voice/ISDN and data design
Number of links	OC3 links	170	61	47
	OC12 links	169	92	100
	OC48 links	0	186	192
	Total links	339	339	339
Termination capacity (equivalent DS0s, millions)	OC3 links	0.65	0.35	0.28
	OC12 links	3.85	2.02	2.22
	OC48 links	0.0	20.1	23.1
	Total	4.50	22.5	25.6
Transport capacity (equivalent DS0-miles, millions)	OC3 links	1031.0	611.4	501.0
	OC12 links	982.4	3401.0	3600.2
	OC48 links	0.0	6133.9	7529.4
	Total	2013.4	10,146.3	11,630.6
Termination cost ($ millions)	OC3 links	12.6	6.84	5.44
	OC12 links	37.1	19.5	21.4
	OC48 links	0.0	78.8	90.6
	Total	49.7	105.1	117.4
Transport cost ($ millions)	OC3 links	186.7	110.4	90.4
	OC12 links	173.7	522.0	553.1
	OC48 links	0.0	392.5	477.5
	Total	360.4	1024.9	1120.9
Total cost ($ millions)	OC3 links	199.3	117.2	95.8
	OC12 links	210.8	541.5	574.4
	OC48 links	0.0	471.3	568.1
	Total	410.1	1130.0	1238.4
Routing analysis (network busy hour)	Average links/connection	2.77	2.77	2.77
	# Node pairs 1 link/connection	340	340	340
	# Node pairs 2 links/connection	3249	3249	3249
	# Node pairs 3 links/connection	8487	8487	8487
	# Node pairs 4 links/connection	14	14	14

Table 6.4 Comparison of Voice/ISDN-Only Design (VNETs 1–8), Data-Only Design (VNETs 9–11), and Integrated Voice/ISDN and Data Design (VNETs 1–11); Two-Link DC-SDR Connection Routing; Per-Flow Bandwidth Allocation; Sparse Single-Area Flat Topology (135-Node Multiservice Network Model; DEFO Design Model)

Network design parameters		Voice/ISDN-only design	Data-only design	Integrated voice/ISDN and data design
Number of links	OC3 links	170	63	48
	OC12 links	169	90	99
	OC48 links	0	186	192
	Total links	339	339	339
Termination capacity	OC3 links	0.65	0.37	0.29
(equivalent DS0s,	OC12 links	3.83	2.00	2.20
millions)	OC48 links	0.0	20.1	23.17
	Total	4.48	22.5	25.66
Transport capacity	OC3 links	1029.7	638.3	501.2
(equivalent	OC12 links	976.0	3356.8	3599.6
DS0-miles, millions)	OC48 links	0.0	6133.8	7528.9
	Total	2005.7	10,128.9	11,629.8
Termination cost	OC3 links	12.5	7.12	5.60
($ millions)	OC12 links	36.9	19.3	21.2
	OC48 links	0.0	78.8	90.7
	Total	49.4	105.2	117.5
Transport cost	OC3 links	186.4	115.2	90.5
($ millions)	OC12 links	172.6	515.2	552.9
	OC48 links	0.0	392.5	477.6
	Total	359.0	1023.0	1238.5
Total cost	OC3 links	199.0	122.4	96.1
($ millions)	OC12 links	209.5	534.5	574.1
	OC48 links	0.0	471.3	568.3
	Total	408.4	1128.1	1238.5
Routing analysis	Average links/connection	2.77	2.77	2.77
(network busy hour)	# Node pairs 1 link/connection	340	340	340
	# Node pairs 2 links/connection	3249	3249	3249
	# Node pairs 3 links/connection	8487	8487	8487
	# Node pairs 4 links/connection	14	14	14

to the economy of scale of the higher capacity network elements, as reflected in the cost model given in Table 2.2.

6.4.3 Multilink vs Two-Link Network Design

We see from the results in Tables 6.2 and 6.3 that the multilink EDR network design compared to two-link EDR design yields the following results:

- the voice/ISDN-only multilink-EDR design has .735 of the total termination capacity of the two-link design
- the voice/ISDN-only multilink-EDR design has .906 of the total transport capacity of the two-link design
- the voice/ISDN-only multilink-EDR design has .792 of the total cost of the two-link design
- the data-only multilink-EDR design has .631 of the total termination capacity of the two-link design
- the data-only multilink-EDR design has .770 of the total transport capacity of the two-link design
- the data-only multilink-EDR design has .897 of the total cost of the two-link design
- the integrated multilink-EDR design has .640 of the total termination capacity of the two-link design
- the integrated multilink-EDR design has .798 of the total transport capacity of the two-link design
- the integrated multilink-EDR design has 1.023 of the total cost of the two-link design

These results show that multilink designs are generally more efficient than two-link designs in transport and termination capacity and have lower cost for the separate designs and comparable cost for the integrated design.

6.4.4 Single-Area Flat vs Two-Level Hierarchical Network Design

Table 6.5 illustrates use of the DEFO model to design for a per-flow two-level hierarchical multiservice network design and a two-level hierarchical per-VNET design and provides comparisons of these designs. Recall that the hierarchical model, illustrated in Figure 3.7 in Chapter 3, consists of 135 edge nodes and 21 backbone nodes. The edge nodes are homed onto the backbone nodes in a hierarchical relationship. The per-flow and per-VNET designs for the hierarchical 135 edge node and 21 backbone node model are summarized in Table 6.5.

We see from the results in Table 6.5 that the hierarchical per-VNET design compared to the hierarchical per-flow design yields the following comparisons:

- the hierarchical per-flow design has .956 of the total termination capacity of the hierarchical per-VNET design

Table 6.5 Design Comparison of Per-VNET and Per-Flow Bandwidth Allocation; Multilink STT-EDR Connection Routing; 135 Edge Node and 21 Backbone Node Sparse Multiarea Two-Level Hierarchical Topology (Multiservice Network Model; DEFO Design Model)

Network design parameters		Per-VNET bandwidth allocation design	Per-flow bandwidth allocation design
Number of links	OC3 links	60	40
	OC12 links	97	113
	OC48 links	186	187
	Total links	343	340
Termination capacity (equivalent DS0s, millions)	OC3 links	0.36	0.21
	OC12 links	2.09	2.18
	OC48 links	19.62	18.72
	Total	22.08	21.12
Transport capacity (equivalent DS0-miles, millions)	OC3 links	654.4	377.2
	OC12 links	3462.2	3608.0
	OC48 links	5870.9	5923.6
	Total	9987.5	9908.8
Termination cost ($ millions)	OC3 links	70.0	4.1
	OC12 links	20.2	21.0
	OC48 links	76.8	73.3
	Total	104.0	98.5
Transport cost ($ millions)	OC3 links	118.0	68.0
	OC12 links	531.6	554.0
	OC48 links	376.7	377.1
	Total	1026.3	991.2
Total cost ($ millions)	OC3 links	125.0	72.2
	OC12 links	551.8	575.0
	OC48 links	453.5	450.4
	Total	1130.3	1097.6
Routing analysis (network busy hour)	Average links/connection	2.90	2.77
	# Node pairs 1 link/connection	344	340
	# Node pairs 2 links/connection	2706	3249
	# Node pairs 3 links/connection	6703	8487
	# Node pairs 4 links/connection	2158	14
	# Node pairs 5 links/connection	179	0

- the hierarchical per-flow design has .992 of the total transport capacity of the hierarchical per-VNET design
- the hierarchical per-flow design has .971 of the total network cost of the hierarchical per-VNET design

These results indicate that the hierarchical per-VNET design and hierarchical per-flow designs are quite comparable in terms of capacity requirements and design cost. Chapter 3 showed that the performance of these two designs was also quite comparable under a range of network scenarios.

By comparing Tables 6.1 and 6.5, we can find the relative capacity of the single-area flat network design and the multiple-area, two-level hierarchical network design (per-flow case):

- the single-area flat design has .776 of the total termination capacity of the multiarea two-level hierarchical design
- the single-area flat design has .937 of the total transport capacity of the multiarea two-level hierarchical design
- the single-area flat design has 1.154 of the total network cost of the multiarea two-level hierarchical design

In this model, single-area flat designs have less total termination and transport capacity as multiarea hierarchical designs and are therefore more efficient in engineered capacity. However, the hierarchical designs appear to be less expensive than the flat designs. This is because of the larger percentage of OC48 links in the hierarchical designs, which is also considerably sparser than the flat design and therefore the traffic loads are concentrated onto fewer, larger, links. As discussed in Chapter 2, there is an economy of scale built into the cost model, which affords the higher capacity links (e.g., OC48 as compared to OC3) a considerably lower per unit of bandwidth cost, and therefore a lower overall network cost is achieved as a consequence. However, the performance analysis results discussed in Chapter 3 show that the flat designs perform better than the hierarchical designs under the overload and failure scenarios that were modeled. This also is a consequence of the sparser hierarchical network and lesser availability of alternate paths for more robust network performance.

6.4.5 EDR vs SDR Network Design

Next we examine the meshed network designs for the two-link STT-EDR network and the two-link DC-SDR network, which were discussed in the modeling studies presented in Chapter 2. Designs for the two-link STT-EDR and two-link DC-SDR connection routing networks, with per-flow QoS resource management, are given in Table 6.6, which again are obtained using the DEFO model to design the 135-node national network model.

Table 6.6 Design Comparison of Two-Link STT-EDR and Two-Link DC-SDR Connection Routing; Per-Flow Bandwidth Allocation; Meshed Single-Area Flat Topology (135 Edge Node Multiservice Network Model; DEFO Design Model)

Network design parameters		Two-link STT-EDR design	Two-link DC-SDR design
Number of links	OC3 links	47	48
	OC12 links	100	99
	OC48 links	192	192
	Total links	339	339
Termination capacity (equivalent DS0s, millions)	OC3 links	0.28	0.29
	OC12 links	2.22	2.20
	OC48 links	23.14	23.17
	Total	25.64	25.66
Transport capacity (equivalent DS0-miles, millions)	OC3 links	501.0	501.2
	OC12 links	3600.2	3599.6
	OC48 links	7529.4	7528.9
	Total	11,630.6	11,629.8
Termination cost ($ millions)	OC3 links	5.44	5.60
	OC12 links	21.4	21.2
	OC48 links	90.6	90.7
	Total	117.4	117.5
Transport cost ($ millions)	OC3 links	90.4	90.5
	OC12 links	553.1	552.9
	OC48 links	477.5	477.6
	Total	1120.9	1121.0
Total cost ($ millions)	OC3 links	95.8	96.1
	OC12 links	574.4	574.1
	OC48 links	568.1	568.3
	Total	1238.4	1238.5
Routing analysis (network busy hour)	Average links/connection	2.77	2.77
	# Node pairs 1 link/connection	340	340
	# Node pairs 2 links/connection	3249	3249
	# Node pairs 3 links/connection	8487	8487
	# Node pairs 4 links/connection	14	14

We see from the results given in Table 6.6. that the EDR network design compared to the SDR design yields the following comparisons:

- the EDR design has .999 of the total termination capacity of the SDR design
- the EDR design has 1.000 of the total transport capacity of the SDR design
- the EDR design has .999 of the total network cost of the SDR design

We note that the designs are very comparable to each other and have essentially the same total network design costs. This suggests that there is not a significant advantage for employing link-state information in these network designs, and given the high overhead in flooding link-state information, EDR methods are preferred.

6.4.6 Dynamic Transport Routing vs Fixed Transport Routing Network Design

Finally we examine the design comparisons of dynamic transport routing compared with the fixed transport routing. In the model we assume multilink STT-EDR connection routing with per-flow QoS resource management and once again use the DEFO design model for the flat 135-node network model. The results are summarized in Table 6.7.

As shown in Table 6.7, the fixed transport network design compared to the dynamic transport design yields the following results:

- the dynamic transport design has 1.097 of the total termination capacity of the fixed transport network design
- the dynamic transport design has 1.048 of the total transport capacity of the fixed transport network design
- the dynamic transport design has .516 of the total network cost of the fixed transport network design

These results indicate that the dynamic transport design has more termination capacity and transport capacity than the fixed transport network design, but substantially lower cost. The larger capacity comes about because of the larger fiber backbone link bandwidth granularity compared to the logical link granularity in the fixed transport routing case. The lower cost of the dynamic transport network comes about, however, because of the economies of scale of the higher capacity transport and termination elements, as reflected in Table 2.2. Chapter 5 showed the superior performance of the dynamic transport rating design under a range of network scenarios.

Table 6.7 Design Comparison of Fixed Transport Routing and Dynamic Transport Routing; Multilink STT-EDR Connection Routing; Per-Flow Bandwidth Allocation; Sparse Single-Area Flat Topology (135-Node Multiservice Network Model; DEFO Design Model)

Network design parameters		Fixed transport routing design	Dynamic transport routing design
Number of links	OC3 links	482	0
	OC12 links	389	0
	OC48 links	111	173
	Total links	982	173
Termination capacity (equivalent DS0s, millions)	OC3 links	2.30	0
	OC12 links	6.64	0
	OC48 links	7.50	18.0
	Total	16.4	18.0
Transport capacity (equivalent DS0-miles, millions)	OC3 links	1185.5	0
	OC12 links	4105.4	0
	OC48 links	3994.5	9731.0
	Total	9285.3	9731.0
Termination cost ($ millions)	OC3 links	44.4	0
	OC12 links	64.0	0
	OC48 links	29.4	70.6
	Total	137.7	70.6
Transport cost ($ millions)	OC3 links	229.8	0
	OC12 links	659.6	0
	OC48 links	240.0	584.2
	Total	1129.5	584.2
Total cost ($ millions)	OC3 links	274.2	0
	OC12 links	723.6	0
	OC48 links	269.5	654.8
	Total	1267.2	654.8
Routing analysis (network busy hour)	Average links/connection	1.86	2.49
	# Node pairs 1 link/connection	982	173
	# Node pairs 2 links/connection	3698	2371
	# Node pairs 3 links/connection	4365	6085
	# Node pairs 4 links/connection	0	416

6.5 Summary and Conclusions

The conclusions reached in this chapter are as follows:

- DEFO design models are shown to be able to capture very complex network behavior through the equivalent of a simulation model provided in software, for example, in the routing design module. By this means, very complex networks have been designed by the model, which include all of the routing methods discussed in Chapter 2 (FXR, TDR, SDR, and EDR methods), the multiservice QoS resource allocation models discussed in Chapter 3, and all the case studies discussed in Chapter 8.
- Sparse topology options, such as obtained with the multilink STT-EDR, DC-SDR, and DP-SDR routing options, lead to capital cost advantages and, more importantly, to operational simplicity and expense cost reduction. Capital cost savings are subject to the particular connection/transport switching and transport cost assumptions. Operational issues are detailed further in Chapter 7.
- Voice and data integration provides capital cost advantages, achieves operational simplicity and expense cost reduction, and leads to more efficient networks when voice traffic migrates to VoIP and uses voice compression technology.
- Multilink routing methods exhibit greater design efficiencies in comparison with two-link routing methods. As discussed and modeled in Chapter 3, multilink topologies exhibit better network performance under overloads in comparison with two-link routing topologies; however, the two-link topologies do better under failure scenarios.
- Single-area flat topologies exhibit greater design efficiencies in termination and transport capacity, but higher cost, and, as discussed and modeled in Chapter 3, better network performance in comparison with multiarea hierarchical topologies. As illustrated in Chapter 4, larger administrative areas can be achieved through the use of EDR-based TQO methods as compared to SDR-based TQO methods.
- EDR methods exhibit comparable design efficiencies to SDR. This suggests that there is not a significant advantage for employing link-state information in these network designs, especially given the high overhead in flooding link-state information in SDR methods.
- Dynamic transport routing achieves capital savings by concentrating capacity on fewer, high-capacity physical fiber links and, as discussed in Chapter 5, achieves higher network throughput and enhanced revenue by their ability to flexibly allocate bandwidth on the logical links serving the access and internode traffic.

6.6 Applicability of Requirements

DEFO modeling capabilities described in this chapter are already in use for capacity management in TDM-based dynamic routing networks and have been used extensively in network architecture studies, as illustrated in the case studies presented in

Chapters 8 and 9. In addition, the building blocks and principles of efficient capacity design, as discussed in this chapter, have all been implemented in both TDM-based and IP-based network design and management.

As shown in this chapter, of particular benefit are designs based on STT-EDR TQO routing, voice/data integration, multilink path routing, sparse, flat topologies, and multilayer dynamic connection/connection/transport routing networks. Service providers and their customers would benefit from these capabilities in terms of network performance and profitability improvements. Vendors can profit from service provider interest in adopting such TQO features by tailoring their products accordingly.

Chapter 7
Traffic Engineering and QoS Optimization Operational Requirements

7.1 Introduction

Figure 7.1 illustrates the TQO model first introduced in Chapter 1 for network routing and network management/design in converged voice/data networks. TQO functions include traffic management, capacity management, and network planning. Figure 7.1 illustrates these functions as interacting feedback loops around the network. The input driving the network is a noisy traffic load, consisting of predictable average demand components added to unknown forecast error and other load variation components. The feedback controls function to regulate the service provided by the network through traffic management controls, capacity adjustments, and routing adjustments.

These are classical functions applicable to any network and have been applied successfully in both data networks and voice networks.

In the beginning of the Internet, the emphasis on "network management" in data networks was on defining and implementing protocols that achieved interoperation of the functional areas of data network management. "Network management" in voice networks encompasses all of the activities necessary to identify conditions that may adversely affect network performance and service to the customer, and the application of network controls to minimize their impact.

Taken together, TQO traffic management and capacity management aspects in both data and voice networks include the following functions:

- performance management—collect and analyze real-time network status and performance data; monitor packets dropped, timeouts, collisions, CRC errors, etc.; focus on how smoothly the network is running and whether it can handle the workload it currently has; detect abnormal network conditions, investigate and identify reasons for abnormal network conditions, initiate corrective action and/or control, coordinate with other network management centers (e.g., maintenance) on matters that affect service

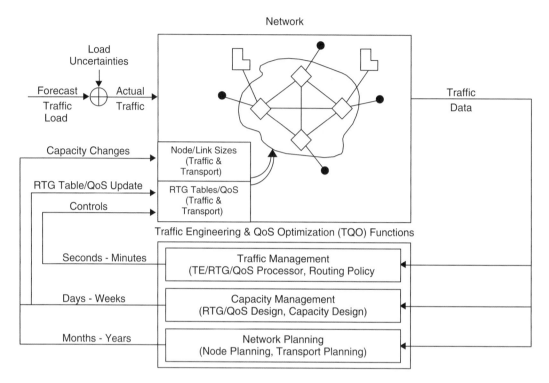

Figure 7.1 TQO model for voice, data, and converged networks.

- fault management—deal with problems and emergencies in the network, such as router failures and power losses; entails both reactive and proactive network fault management
- capacity management—gather statistics on equipment and facility use; analyze trends to justify network upgrades and/or bandwidth increases
- configuration management—track device settings, inventory, configuration, provisioning, and makes adjustments as needed

Traffic management, which includes both performance management and fault management functions listed earlier, provides monitoring of network performance through collection and display of real-time traffic and performance data and allows traffic management controls such as code blocks, connection request gapping, and reroute controls to be inserted when circumstances warrant. Capacity management includes capacity forecasting, daily and weekly performance monitoring, and short-term network adjustment. Forecasting operates over a multiyear forecast interval and drives network capacity expansion. Daily and weekly performance monitoring identify any service problems in the network. If service problems are detected, short-term network adjustment can include routing table updates and, if necessary, short-term capacity additions to alleviate service problems. Updated routing tables are sent to the nodes either directly or via an automated routing update system. Short-term capacity additions are the exception, and most capacity changes are normally forecasted, planned, scheduled, and managed over a period of months or a year or more. Network design embedded in capacity management includes routing design and capacity design. Network planning includes longer term node planning and transport network planning, which operates over a horizon of months to years to plan and implement new node and transport capacity.

We focus on the steps involved in traffic management of a (G)MPLS network implementing TQO functions, capacity forecasting, daily and weekly performance monitoring, and short-term network adjustment. For each of these three topics, we illustrate the steps involved with examples.

Monitoring of traffic and performance data is a critical issue for traffic management, capacity forecasting, daily and weekly performance monitoring, and short-term network adjustment. Capabilities for traffic and performance data monitoring have been somewhat lacking in IP-based networks [FELDMAN00, GUNNAR04], which is in sharp contrast to TDM-based networks where such TQO monitoring data have been developed to a sophisticated standard over a period of time [ASH98].

It has been stated [GUNNAR04] that "despite the importance of knowing the traffic matrix, the support in routers for measuring traffic matrices is poor and operators are often forced to estimate the traffic matrix from other available data, typically link load measurements and routing configurations." Several techniques for traffic matrix estimation are described, including gravity (also known as "tomogravity") models [ZIPF46, KOWALSKI95, ROUGHAN02, FELDMAN01, ZHANG03], Kruithof's project method [KRUITHOF37, KRUPP79], and others. Direct measurement of traffic matrices has been proposed in IETF [LAI03], but so far has been rejected.

The discussions in this chapter intend to point out the kind and frequency of TQO traffic and performance data required to support each function.

In regard to traffic forecasting, the competitive structure of the access and core networks within the global Internet means that traffic forecasting may be more challenging as the volume of traffic produced depends on the tariff or pricing strategy that can change quickly. For example, a variety of wireless services pricing models put forward by competitors made the demand harder to predict. There are also cross-services impacts, such as when various VoIP services came on-line; these services impacted traditional PSTN traffic demand. However, such econometric and competitive factors have been incorporated in the decentralized (among service providers) forecasting and planning in the telecom world, and such approaches must be extended to the decentralized global Internet structure. The fact that an end-to-end connection may span several domains operated by different administrations makes QoS delivery a challenging issue. But that property has applied since day 1 in all voice and data networking, wherein a large number of independent, interconnected network operators must together operate the "global network" in a coherent way. A centralized administrative model is discussed in this chapter that is applicable within a given administrative domain, and such centralized, per-domain approaches are used today across multiple, decentralized, interconnected domains. This model can be extended in an analogous way to the multioperator global Internet, wherein a federated approach is still necessary for security and national autonomy.

Network management controls, such as traditional connection-gapping controls, are being applied in MPLS-based packet data networks. As pointed out in Chapter 5 regarding GMPLS and its predecessor, fully shared network (FSN), good ideas stay around and may be either temporarily forgotten and/or go unnoticed, but continue to be proposed and/or reinvented, and eventually get implemented. Such is the case as networks converge to integrated GMPLS-based TQO voice/data dynamic routing networks: eventually the good ideas will see the light of day.

We illustrate an MPLS network operational implementation in Section 7.7 by taking an example from AT&T's MPLS operations/network management architecture.

7.2 Traffic Management

This section concentrates on the surveillance and control of the MPLS-based TQO network. It also discusses the interactions of traffic managers with other work centers responsible for MPLS-based TQO network operation. Traffic management functions should be performed at a centralized work center and be supported by centralized traffic management operations functions (TMOF), perhaps embedded in a centralized TQO processor (here denoted TMOF-TQOP). A functional block diagram of TMOF-TQOP is illustrated in Figure 7.2.

7.2.1 Real-Time Performance Monitoring

The surveillance of the MPLS-based TQO network should be performed through monitoring the node pairs with the highest traffic loss/delayed performance, preferably on a geographical display, which is normally monitored at all times. This display should be used in the auto-update mode, which means that every 5 min, for example, TMOF-TQOP automatically updates the exceptions shown on the map itself and displays the node pairs with the highest traffic loss/delayed performance. TMOF-TQOP also should have displays that show the node pairs with the highest traffic loss/delayed percent within threshold values.

Traffic managers are most concerned with what connection requests can be rerouted and therefore want to know the location of the heaviest concentrations of lost connection routing attempts. For that purpose, traffic loss/delayed percentages can be misleading. From a service revenue standpoint, the difference between 1 and 10% traffic lost/delayed on a node pair may favor concentration on the 1% traffic lost/delayed situation because there are more connection requests to reroute. TMOF-TQOP should also display all the exceptions that there are with the auto threshold display, which displays everything exceeding the present threshold, e.g., either 1% traffic loss/delayed or 1 or more lost connection requests, in 5 min. In the latter case, this display then shows the total lost connection requests and not just the highest pairs.

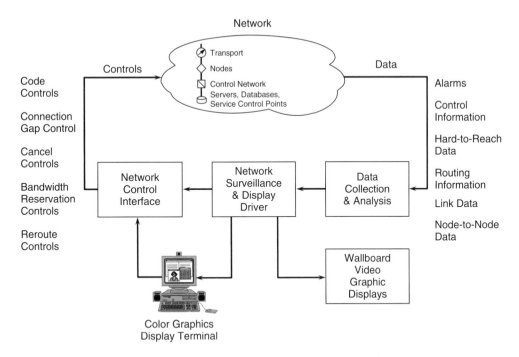

Figure 7.2 Traffic management operations functions within TQO processor.

For peak-day operation, or operation on a high day (such as Christmas day or the Monday after Thanksgiving), traffic managers should work back and forth between the auto threshold display and the highest lost-connection-count pair display. They can spend most of their time with the auto threshold display, where they can see all traffic that is being lost/delayed. Then, when traffic managers want to concentrate on clearing out some particular congestion problem, they can look at the highest lost-connection-count pair display, an additional feature of which is that it allows the traffic manager to see the effectiveness of controls.

The traffic manager can recognize certain patterns from surveillance data. For example, a focused overload on a particular city/node, such as caused by a flooding situation discussed later in the chapter. The typical traffic pattern under a focused overload is that most locations show heavy traffic loss/delayed into and out of the focus-overload node. Under such circumstances, the display should show the traffic loss/delayed percentage for any node pair in the MPLS-based TQO network that exceeds 1% traffic loss/delayed.

A node failure pattern is clearly evident to traffic managers with the TMOF-TQOP display of node pairs with the highest traffic lost/delayed performance. Transport failures should also show distinct patterns on these displays, but the resulting display pattern depends on the failure itself.

7.2.2 Network Control

The MPLS-based TQO network needs automatic controls built into the node processing and also requires automatic and manual controls that can be activated from TMOF-TQOP. We first describe the required controls and what they do, and then we discuss how the traffic managers work with these controls. Two protective automatic traffic management controls are required in the MPLS-based TQO network: dynamic overload control (DOC), which responds to node congestion, and dynamic bandwidth reservation (DBR), which responds to link congestion. DOC and DBR should be selective in the sense that they control traffic destined for hard-to-reach points in the network more stringently than other traffic. Hard-to-reach traffic is identified by call/session routing prefix as the fraction of call/sessions attempts not completed and can be controlled by aggregated address blocks or for a particular address.

The complexity of MPLS/TQO networks makes it necessary to place more emphasis on fully automatic controls that are reliable and robust and do not depend on manual administration. DOC and DBR should respond automatically within the node software. For DBR, the automatic response can be coupled, for example, with two bandwidth reservation threshold levels, represented by the amount of idle bandwidth on a link. DBR bandwidth reservation levels should be automatic functions of the link size.

DOC and DBR are not strictly link dependent but should also depend on the node pair to which a controlled connection request belongs. A connection request offered to an overloaded via node should either be canceled at the originating node or be advanced to an alternate via node, depending on the destination of the connection. DBR should differentiate between primary (shortest) path and alternate path connection requests.

DOC and DBR should also use a simplified method of obtaining hard-to-reach control selectivity. In the MPLS TQO network, hard-to-reach codes can be detected by the terminating node, which then communicates them to the originating nodes and via nodes. Because the terminating node is the exit point from the MPLS network, the originating node should treat a hard-to-reach code detected by a terminating node as hard to reach on all links.

DOC should normally be permanently enabled on all links. DBR should automatically be enabled by an originating node on all links when that originating node senses general network congestion. DBR is particularly important in the MPLS TQO network because it minimizes the use of less efficient alternate path connections and maximizes useful network throughput during overloads. The automatic enabling mechanism for DBR ensures its proper activation without manual intervention. DOC and DBR should automatically determine whether to subject a controlled connection request to a cancel or skip control. In the cancel mode, affected connection requests are blocked from the network, whereas in the skip mode such connection requests skip over the controlled link to an alternate link. DOC and DBR should be completely automatic controls. Capabilities such as automatic enabling of DBR, the automatic skip/cancel mechanism, and the DBR one-link/multilink traffic differentiation adapt these controls to the TQO network and make them robust and powerful automatic controls.

Code blocking controls block connection requests to a particular destination code. These controls are particularly useful in the case of focused overloads, especially if the connection requests are blocked at or near their origination. Code blocking controls need not block all connections unless the destination node is completely disabled, such as through a natural disaster or equipment failure. Nodes equipped with code-blocking controls can typically control a percentage of the connection requests to a particular code. The controlled E.164 name (dialed number code), for example, may be NPA, NXX, NPA-NXX, or NPA-NXX-XXXX, when in the latter case one specific customer is the target of a focused overload.

A connection-gapping control, illustrated in Figure 7.3, is typically used by network managers in a focused connection request overload, such as sometimes occurs with radio call-in give-away contests.

Connection gapping allows one connection request for a controlled code or set of codes to be accepted into the network, by each node, once every x seconds, and connection requests arriving after the accepted connection request are rejected for the next x seconds. In this way, connection gapping throttles the connection requests and prevents the overload of the network to a particular focal point.

An expansive control is also required. Reroute controls should be able to modify routes by inserting additional paths at the beginning, middle, or end of a path sequence. Such reroutes should be inserted manually or automatically through TMOF-TQOP. When a reroute is active on a node pair, DBR should be prevented on that node pair from going into the cancel mode, where if the traffic loss/delayed is heavy enough on a particular node pair it triggers the DBR cancel mode. Hence, if a reroute is active, connection requests should have a chance to use the reroute paths and not be lost/delayed prematurely by the DBR cancel mode.

In the MPLS TQO network, a display should be used to graphically represent the controls in effect. Depending on the control in place, either a certain shape or a certain color should tell traffic managers which control is implemented. Traffic managers should be able to tell if a particular control at a node is the only control on that node. Different symbols should be used for the node depending on the controls that are in effect.

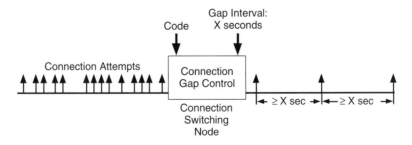

Figure 7.3 Connection gap control.

7.2.3   Work Center Functions

7.2.3.1   Automatic Controls

The MPLS TQO network requires automatic controls, as described earlier, and if there is spare capacity, traffic managers can decide to reroute connection requests. In a focused overload scenario, the links are normally fully utilized, and there is often no network capacity available for reroutes. The DBR control is normally active at the time of a focused overload, and in order to favor connection requests originating from the focused overload node, traffic managers sometimes must disable the DBR control manually at the focused overload node. This action then gives preference to connection requests originating from the focused overload node. Thereby, the focused overload node achieves a much better completion rate of outgoing connection requests than will the other nodes at completing connections into the focused overload node. This control results in using the link capacity more efficiently.

Traffic managers should be able to manually enable or inhibit DBR and also inhibit the cancel mechanism for both DBR and DOC. Traffic managers should monitor DOC controls very closely because they can indicate connection switching congestion or node failure. Therefore, DOC activations should be investigated much more thoroughly and more quickly than DBR activations, which are frequently triggered by normal heavy traffic.

7.2.3.2   Code Controls

Code controls are used to cancel connection requests for very hard-to-reach codes. Code controls are used when connection requests cannot complete to a point in the network or there is isolation. For example, traffic managers should use code controls for a focused overload situation, such as caused by an earthquake, in which there can also be isolation. Normal hard-to-reach traffic caused by heavy traffic volumes will be blocked by the DBR control, as described earlier.

Traffic managers should use data on hard-to-reach codes in certain situations for problem analysis. For example, if there is a problem in a particular area, one of the first things traffic managers should look at are hard-to-reach data to see if they can identify one code or many codes that are hard to reach and if they are from one location or several locations.

7.2.3.3   Reroute Controls

Traffic managers should sometimes use manual reroute even when an automatic reroute capability is available. Reroutes are used primarily for transport failures or heavy traffic surges, such as traffic on heavier than normal days, where the surge is above the normal capabilities of the network to handle the load. Those are the two prime reasons for rerouting. However, traffic managers should normally not use reroute controls into a disaster area.

7.2.3.4   Peak-Day Control

Peak-day routing in the MPLS TQO network should involve using the primary (shortest) path (CRLSP) as the only path not subject to DBR controls and the remaining available paths as alternate paths all subject to DBR controls. The effectiveness of the additional alternate paths and reroute capabilities depends very much on the peak day itself. The greater the peak-day traffic, the less effective the alternate paths are. That is, on higher peak days, such as Christmas and Mother's Day, the network is filled with connections mostly on the primary shortest paths. On lower peak days, such as Thanksgiving, Easter, or Father's Day, the use of alternate paths and rerouting capabilities are more effective. This is because the peaks, although they are high and have an abnormal traffic pattern, are not as high as on Christmas or Mother's Day. So on these days there is additional capacity to complete connection requests on the alternate paths. Reroute paths are normally most available in the early morning and late evening of a peak-day traffic pattern. Depending on the peak day, at times there is also a lull in traffic in the afternoon, and TMOF-TQOP should normally be able to find reroute paths that are available during the lull period.

7.2.4   Traffic Management on Peak Days

A typical peak-day routing method uses the primary shortest path between node pairs as the only path not subject to DBR controls, followed by alternate paths protected by DBR. This method is more effective during lighter peak days such as Thanksgiving, Easter, and Father's Day. With the lighter loads, when the network is not fully saturated, there is a much better chance of using the alternate paths. However, when we enter peak-day busy hours, with a peak load over most of the network, the completion of connection requests occurs primarily on the shortest path because of the effect of bandwidth reservation. At other times, the alternate paths are very effective in completing connection requests.

7.2.5   Interfaces to Other Work Centers

The main interaction traffic managers have is with capacity managers. Traffic managers notify capacity managers of conditions in the network that are affecting data that they use in making decisions as to whether to add capacity. Examples are transport failures and node failures that would distort traffic data. A node congestion signal can trigger DOC; DOC cancels all traffic destined to a node while the node congestion is active. All connection requests to the failed node are reflected as overflow connection requests for the duration of the node congestion condition. This can be a considerable amount of canceled traffic, which distorts the traffic counts.

The capacity manager notifies traffic managers of the new link capacity requirements that they are trying to get installed but that are delayed. Traffic managers can then expect to see congestion on a daily basis or several times a week until the capacity is added. This type of information is passed back and forth on a weekly or perhaps daily basis.

7.3 Capacity Management: Forecasting

This section concentrates on the forecasting of node-to-node traffic loads and the sizing of the MPLS network. It also discusses the interactions of network forecasters with other work centers responsible for MPLS TQO network operations.

Network forecasting functions should be performed from a capacity administration center and supported by network forecasting operations functions (NFOF) integrated into the TQOP. Here we denote these as NFOF-TQOP functions. A functional block diagram of NFOF-TQOP is illustrated in Figure 7.4. The following two sections discuss the steps involved in each functional block.

7.3.1 Load Forecasting

7.3.1.1 Configuration Database Functions

As illustrated in Figure 7.4, the configuration database is used in the forecasting function, and within this database are defined various specific components of the network itself, for example: backbone nodes, access nodes, transport points of presence, buildings, manholes, microwave towers, and other facilities.

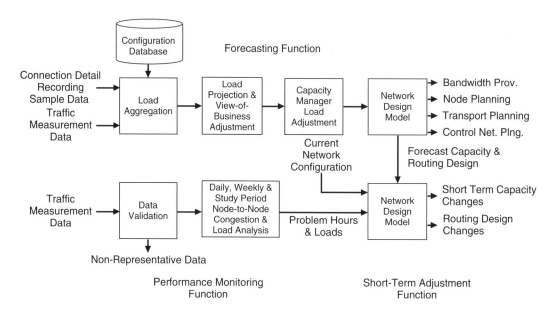

Figure 7.4 Capacity management functions.

Forecasters maintain configuration data for designing and forecasting the MPLS TQO network. Included in data for each backbone node and access node, for example, are the number/name translation capabilities, equipment type, type of signaling, homing arrangement, internetwork routing capabilities, operator service routing capabilities, and billing/recording capabilities. When a forecast cycle is started, which is normally each month, the first step is to extract the relevant pieces of information from the configuration database that are necessary to drive network forecasting operations functions in NFOF-TQOP. One of the information items should indicate the date of the forecast view, which corresponds to the date when the configuration files were frozen and therefore reflects the network structure at the time the forecast is generated.

7.3.1.2   Load Aggregation, Basing, and Projection Functions

NFOF-TQOP should process data from a centralized message database, which represents a record of all connection requests placed on the network, over four study periods within each year, e.g., March, May, August, and November, each a 20-day study period. Because a message database can be voluminous, a sampling method can be used to reduce the data volume processed, e.g., a 5% sample of recorded connections for 20 days. Forecasters can then equate that 5%, 20-day sample to one average business day. The load information then consists of messages and traffic load by study period. In the load aggregation step, NFOF-TQOP may apply factors to equate the traffic load volume obtained from recorded traffic load to the actual traffic load.

The next step in load forecasting is to aggregate all of the access-node-to-access-node loads up to the backbone node-pair level. This produces the backbone-node-to-backbone-node traffic item sets. These node-to-node traffic item sets are then routed to the candidate links. NFOF-TQOP should then project those aggregated loads into the future, using smoothing techniques to compare the current measured data with previously projected data and to determine an optimal estimate of the base and projected loads. The result is the initially projected loads that are ready for forecaster adjustments and business/econometric adjustments.

7.3.1.3   Load Adjustment Cycle and View of Business
Adjustment Cycle

Once NFOF-TQOP smoothes and projects data, forecasters can then enter a load adjustment cycle. This should be an on-line process that has the capability to go into the projected load file for all the forecast periods for all the years and apply forecaster-established thresholds to those loads. For example, if the forecaster requests to see any projected load that has deviated more than 15% from what it was projected to be in the last forecast cycle, a load analysis module in NFOF-TQOP should search through all the node pairs that the forecaster is responsible for, sort out the ones that exceed the thresholds, and show them on a display. The forecaster then has the option to change the projected loads or accept them.

After the adjustment cycle is complete and the forecasters have adjusted the loads to account for missing data, erroneous data, more accurate current data, or specifically planned events that cause a change in load, forecasters should then apply the view of the business adjustments. Up to this point, the projection of loads has been based on projection models and network structure changes, as well as the base study period billing data. The view of the business adjustment is intended to adjust the future network loads to compensate for the effects of competition, rate changes, and econometric factors on the growth rate. This econometric adjustment process tries to encompass those factors in an adjustment that is applied to the traffic growth rates. Growth rate adjustments should be made for each business, residence, and service category, as econometric effects vary according to service category.

7.3.2 Network Design

Given the MPLS node-pair traffic loads, adjusted by the forecasters, and also adjusted for econometric projections, the network design model should then be executed by NFOF-TQOP based on those traffic loads. The node-to-node loads are estimated for each hourly traffic load, including the load variability. Once the information has been processed in the design model, NFOF-TQOP should output the forecast report. Once the design model has run for a forecast cycle, the forecast file and routing information should be sent downstream to the provisioning systems, planning systems, and capacity management system, and the capacity manager takes over from there as far as implementing the routing and the link capacity called for in the forecast.

7.3.3 Work Center Functions

Capacity management and forecasting operations functions should be centralized in NFOF-TQOP. Work should be divided on a geographic basis so that forecasters and capacity managers for a region can work with specific work centers within the region. These work centers include node planning and implementation organizations and transport planning and implementation organizations. Their primary interface should be with the system that is responsible for issuing the orders to augment link capacity. Another interface is with the routing organization that processes the routing information coming out of NFOF-TQOP.

NFOF-TQOP should be automated to the maximum extent possible, and by combining the forecasting job and the capacity management job into one centralized operation, additional efficiencies will be achieved. These operations require people who are able to understand and deal with complex network behavior. Other work center functions can usefully be centralized, e.g., node planning, transport planning, equipment ordering, and inventory control. With centralized equipment ordering and inventory control, for example, all equipment required for the network can be bulk ordered and distributed. This leads to a much more efficient use of inventory.

7.3.4   Interfaces to Other Work Centers

The forecasting process essentially drives all the downstream construction and planning processes for an entire network operation. Therefore, network forecasters work cooperatively with node planners, transport planners, traffic managers, and capacity managers. With an MPLS TQO network, forecasting, capacity management, and traffic management must work together closely. One way to ensure close working relationships is by having centralized work centers.

7.4   Capacity Management: Daily and Weekly Performance Monitoring

In this section we concentrate on the analysis of node-to-node capacity management data and the design of the MPLS TQO network. Capacity management becomes mandatory at times, such as when node-to-node traffic data show that congestion problems exist in the network or when it is time to implement a new forecast. We discuss the interactions of capacity managers with other work centers responsible for MPLS network operation. Capacity management functions should be performed from a capacity administration center and should be supported by the capacity management operations functions (CMOF) embedded, for example, in the TQOP (denoted here as the CMOF-TQOP). A functional block diagram of the CMOF-TQOP is illustrated within the lower three blocks of Figure 7.4. The following sections discuss the processes in each functional block.

7.4.1   Daily Congestion Analysis Functions

A daily congestion summary should be used to give a breakdown of the highest to the lowest node-pair congestion that occurred the preceding day. This is an exception-reporting function, in which there should be an ability to change the display threshold. For example, the capacity manager can request to see only node pairs whose congestion level is greater than 10%. Capacity managers investigate to find out whether they should exclude these data and, if so, for what reason. One reason for excluding data is to keep nonrepresentative data from downstream processing if such data are associated with an abnormal network condition. This would prevent designing the network for this type of nonrecurring network condition. In order to find out what the network condition was that may have caused nonrepresentative data, capacity managers consult with the traffic managers. If, for example, traffic managers indicate that data are associated with an abnormal network condition, such as a focused overload, say, due to a flooding condition the night before, then capacity managers may elect to exclude data.

7.4.2 Study-Week Congestion Analysis Functions

The CMOF-TQOP functions should also support weekly congestion analysis. This should normally occur after capacity managers form the weekly average using the previous week's data. Study-week data should then be used in the downstream processing to develop the study-period average traffic and congestion levels. Weekly congestion data are displayed basically the same way as daily congestion data and give the node pairs that had congestion for the week. This study-week congestion analysis function gives another opportunity to review data to see if there is a need to exclude any weekly data.

7.4.3 Study-Period Congestion Analysis Functions

Once each week, the study-period average should be formed using the most current 4 weeks of data. The study-period congestion summary gives an idea of the congestion during the most current study period, in which node pairs that experienced average business day average traffic lost/delayed greater than 1% are identified. If congestion is found for a particular node pair in a particular hour, the design model may be exercised to solve the congestion problem. In order to determine whether they should run the design model for that problem hour, capacity managers should first look at study-period congestion detail data. For the node pair in question they should look at the 24 h of data to see if there are any other hours for that node pair that should be investigated. Capacity managers should also determine if there is pending capacity addition for the problem node pair.

7.5 Capacity Management: Short-Term Network Adjustment

7.5.1 Network Design Functions

There are several features that should be available in the design model. First, capacity managers should be able to select a routing change option. With this option, the design model should make routing table changes to utilize the network capacity that is in place to minimize congestion. The design model should also design the network to the specified performance grade-of-service objectives. If it cannot meet the objectives with the network capacity in place, it specifies how much capacity to add to which links in order to meet the performance objectives. The routing table update implementation should be automatic from the CMOF-TQOP all the way through to the network nodes. An evaluator option of the design model should be available to determine the carried traffic per link, or link utilization, for every link in the network for the busiest hour.

7.5.2   Work Center Functions

Capacity managers should have an equal share of MPLS network links that they are responsible for administering. Each capacity manager therefore deals primarily with one network region. Capacity managers also need to work with transport planners so that the transport capacity planned for the links under the capacity manager's responsibility is monitored by the capacity manager. If, on a short-term basis, capacity has to be added to the network, capacity managers find out from the transport planner whether the transport capacity is available. CMOF-TQOP should be highly automated, and the time the capacity manager spends working with CMOF-TQOP system displays should be small compared with other daily responsibilities. One of the most time-consuming work functions is following up on the capacity orders to determine status. If capacity orders are delayed, the capacity manager is responsible for making sure that the capacity is added to the network as soon as possible. With the normal amount of ongoing network activity, that is the most time-consuming part of the work center function.

7.5.3   Interfaces to Other Work Centers

The capacity manager needs to work with the forecasters to learn of network activity that will affect the MPLS TQO network. For example, one concern is new nodes coming into the network. Capacity managers should interact quite frequently with traffic managers to learn of network conditions such as cable cuts, floods, or disasters. Capacity managers detect such activities the next day in traffic data; the network problem stands out immediately. Before they exclude data, however, capacity managers need to talk with the traffic managers to find out specifically what the problem was in the network. In some cases, capacity managers will share information with traffic managers about events in the network that traffic managers may not be aware of. For example, capacity managers may be able to see failure events in traffic data, and they can share this type of information with the traffic managers. Other information capacity managers might share with traffic managers relates to peak days. Capacity managers are able the next morning to give the traffic managers the actual reports and information of the load and congestion experienced in the network.

Capacity managers also work with the data collection work center. For example, if the data collection work center misses collecting data from a particular node for a particular day, capacity managers should discuss this with that work center to try to get data back into CMOF-TQOP. For example, if data are missed one night on a particular node, the node should be available to be repolled to pull data into CMOF-TQOP.

Capacity managers frequently communicate with the routing work centers because normally there is much ongoing activity with routing administration. For example, capacity managers work with the routing work centers to set up the standard numbering/naming plans so that routing tables are updated properly. Capacity managers also work with the work centers doing the capacity order activity on the links for which they are responsible. Capacity managers should try to raise the priority on capacity orders if there is a congestion condition, and often a single congestion condition may cause multiple activities in the MPLS TQO network.

7.6 Comparison of Off-Line (FXR/TDR) versus On-Line (SDR/EDR) TQO Methods

With an on-line (SDR/EDR-based) MPLS TQO network, as compared to an off-line (FXR/TDR-based) network, several improvements occur in TQO functions. Within FXR/TDR-based networks, TMOF-TQOP should automatically put in reroutes to solve congestion problems by looking everywhere in the network for additional available capacity and adding additional alternate paths to the existing preplanned paths. With SDR/EDR-based networks, in contrast, this automatic rerouting function is replaced by real-time examination of all admissible routing choices.

Hence an important simplification introduced with SDR/EDR-based TQO networks is that routing tables need not be calculated by the design model because these are computed in real time by the node or TQOP. This leads to simplifications in that the routing tables computed in FXR/TDR-based networks are no longer needed. Hence simplifications are introduced into the administration of network routing. With FXR/TDR, routing tables must be periodically reoptimized and downloaded into nodes via the CMOF-TQOP process. Reoptimizing and changing the routing tables in the FXR/TDR-based network represent an automated yet large administrative effort involving perhaps millions of records. This function is simplified in SDR/EDR-based networks, as the routing is generated automatically within the network. Also, because SDR/EDR-based TQO protocols adapt to network conditions, less network churn and short-term capacity additions are required. This is one of the operational advantages of SDR/EDR-based MPLS TQO networks, i.e., to automatically adapt so as to move the traffic load to where capacity is available in the network.

7.7 MPLS Operations Architecture Example

In this section, we illustrate the design of AT&T's MPLS operations architecture. As illustrated in Figure 7.5, the guiding design principles of this architecture are converged network operations systems and automated operational processes. Design principles used to implement converged network systems include (a) modular platform design where each module deploys a single platform to perform the intended functions (e.g., one fault management platform, one performance management platform, one configuration management platform), (b) shared databases of record with a common data model and a single database, and (c) policy-based configuration to simplify the MPLS network configuration design.

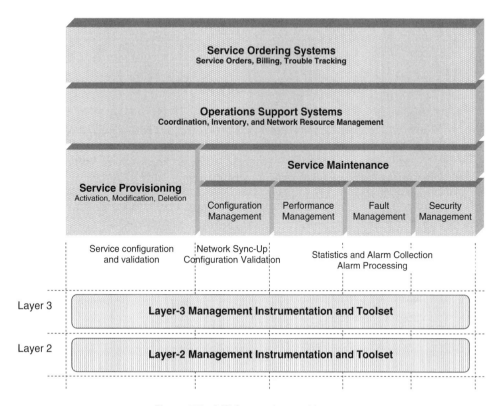

Figure 7.5 MPLS operations architecture.

Fully automated operation may be impossible to achieve in practice; however, each operational step is automated to the extent possible. For example, this strategy leads to the following automated network management approach:

- rule-based domain-specific and cross-domain correlation applied to layer 2 and layer 3 MPLS domains, where rules are developed based on operational experience
- event correlation performed as close to the domain as possible
- self-healing via autocorrective actions, such as using $1 \times N$ backup for automatic reroute during failure
- autotesting, autodiagnose, and autorepair functions invoked from multiple functional areas, such as using MPLS ping to autotest interfaces, detect problems, and initiate repair

We now illustrate these MPLS operations architecture functions:

- connectivity to managed assets within customer networks
- modeling VPN topologies across the service provider network

- fault management
- performance management

7.7.1 Connectivity to Managed Assets

The operations organization must have connectivity to all managed assets within the network. Managed assets that lie within customer VPNs are invisible to the core network, and therefore connectivity is required from the operations center into the managed assets within customer VPNs, while securing the customer's VPN from unauthorized access originating from outside the customer's VPN. Assets that might need to be managed and that lie within the scope of the customer's VPN include the PE-CE links, as well as customer-premises equipment such as the customer edge router.

7.7.2 Modeling of VPN Topologies

With VPNs and traffic engineering, the virtual topology of the customer network needs to be modeled and should provide information defined across the physical network topology as follows:

- relationship between PE-CE network interfaces to customer VPNs
- connectivity topology among customer sites that lie within the same VPN (e.g., full mesh, partial mesh)
- connectivity topology spanning multiple VPNs (i.e., extranet)

Such information can be used to determine whether a problem is service affecting. For example, a VPN-based topology model is useful in determining which VPNs and customers are affected corresponding to a PE router being unreachable from the network core.

7.7.3 Fault Management

Fault management monitors the operational status of network elements, protocols, and services within the network domain. Fault monitoring is done at the element level, path level, and service level. These aspects of fault information are not independent of each other. For example, an LDP session being down could cause a path to become unavailable or congested and/or could also impact a service to become unavailable. One root cause of the LDP session down could therefore cause multiple network events to be generated; one for the LDP down event, one for an unavailable path between a specific source and destination, and one for a service impact alert. To achieve end-to-end automated operations, correlation is needed to group all three related fault conditions into one network event. The correlated network event will be able to identify the root cause of the related events and its level of service impacts (e.g., percentage or number of packets dropped) so a single trouble ticket can be generated with service impact information. The service impact information can be used to identify the severity of the network event, as well as to assist in the priority of the service restoration.

Correlation is a powerful tool to drastically reduce the number of trouble tickets generated by fault monitoring. Reduction of the number of trouble tickets is necessary to improve the troubleshooting time as well as time to repair (or service restoration). To assist in fault correlation, a few basic rules are used:

- container-based rule—group all the traps from ports on the same bay into one report.
- link-topology-based rule—group the traps from both the far end and the near end that are physically connected into one report.
- protocol-based rule—group the alarms from higher protocol layers under a subtitle as secondary alarms and report the lower protocol layer alarms as primary ones. For example, group SONET section failure traps (layer 1 trap) with link down traps (layer 2 trap) with LDP session traps (layer 3 trap).
- cross-event rule—group alarms resulting from a sequence of events that relates to each other, such as the case that a slot failed, the function switched to the standby slot, which became active, the failed slot becomes standby. Another example of correlating the fault monitoring events is as follows: (a) node sffca81ck has been restarted, (b) node sffca81ck CPU utilization exceeds 81%, and (c) node sffca81ck CPU utilization exceeds 77%.

Maintenance process automation is modeled in these seven steps:

- Fault identification
- Network event analysis, including correlation
- Create tickets
- Pick tickets
- Isolate trouble, including diagnosis
- Restore and repair network, including remote restore and repair
- Test and turn up

When a fault condition in the MPLS network occurs, traps/alarms are sent to the fault management system for monitoring. An interesting challenge is to reduce the number of alarms generated for a single event, as a network event (a trap) could indicate a logical failure (e.g., an LDP session down or MPLS VRF down). A hard failure (e.g., a link down) often triggers multiple logical channel failures and thus many traps will be generated and sent within a very short time interval. Network event correlation is needed to filter or to suppress the related traps and to identify the root cause of the event. A ticket can be generated automatically when a root cause of an event is found. Once a ticket is generated, autotesting can be performed based on the ticket information to isolate the network problem. Once a root cause of a network problem is diagnosed, restoration or repair can be done automatically or, in some cases, manually (e.g., by changing a router card). Once the service is restored, another test will be done before service is turned up for operation.

7.7.4 Performance Management

Performance management in the AT&T implementation includes service level, element level, and traffic flow monitoring.

Service level monitoring measures the customer's experience across the network to identify potential violations of SLAs ahead of the customer identifying such impairments. This function requires the deployment of monitoring systems across the network and requires a good understanding of what is the representative sample of customer traffic traversing the network. Both passive monitoring and active probing technologies are used to quantify the customer experience in terms of specific criteria, such as latency/delay, packet loss, and packet jitter, corresponding to the representative customer traffic. In large-scale, MPLS-based VPN networks, such monitoring needs to be representative of the customer experience within the context of the customer VPN. Building a VPN-specific monitoring solution requires being able to address scalability in terms of the increasing size of the customer's VPN and an increase in the number of VPNs across the network.

Element level monitoring tracks the utilization of individual active network assets with the intention of identifying utilization trends that might point to root causes associated with potential overutilization of that element. This provides a low-level perspective of how individual network assets behave in response to customer traffic traversing the network. Additional requirements include monitoring logical elements, such as traffic engineering tunnels, and new MPLS parameters, such as the number of routes within a VPN.

Traffic flow monitoring quantifies traffic flows across key network boundaries, such as to/from the Internet, between a customer VPN and the core network, and within the network to understand if network resources are being utilized per network design. This requires monitoring instrumentation that can efficiently examine the embedded contents of MPLS-labeled packets.

7.7.5 MPLS MIB Architecture

The simple network management protocol (SNMP), along with management information bases (MIBs) containing configurable parameter data, traffic data, and other management information, is now widely used for data network management. To support network operations, various MPLS MIB modules are used, including the LDP MIB [RFC3815], LSR MIB [RFC3813], and TE MIB [RFC3812] in the core network and the VPN MIB [RFC4382], FTN MIB [RFC3814], BGP MIB [RFC4273], and IF MIB [RFC2863] at the network edge. The LDP MIB [RFC3815] is used to manage LDP sessions between different LDP peers. The LSR MIB [RFC3813] monitors the label switching behavior of LSRs and is used to manage LSPs, particularly for troubleshoot-ing and isolation of impairments indicated through monitoring with the LDP MIB [RFC3815]. MPLS traffic engineering tunnels are managed by the TE MIB [RFC4812]. The VPN MIB [RFC4382] contains instrumentation to manage MPLS/BGP VPNs and has tables to model VRF table entries and the interfaces associated with these VRFs. The ingress LER performs the mapping between incoming prefixes and outgoing LSPs, and this mapping is managed by the FTN MIB [RFC3814]. The BGP MIB [RFC4273] is used to manage MP-BGP sessions. The IF MIB [RFC2863] is used for the manage-ment and monitoring of physical and logical interfaces, such as operational status, utilization, and error counters.

7.7.6 MPLS OAM Operational Experience

AT&T has beneficially applied automated operations to its operational implementation. A few examples are given in this section to illustrate automated processes, OSSs, network, and services, and we summarize the operational benefits derived.

Figure 7.6 illustrates the automated, converged, fault platform, called the com-mon fault platform, which implements automated fault-management operations. The common fault platform houses layers 1, 2, and 3 fault records, and business rules are used to perform cross-domain correlation to associate related faults into a consolidated fault record for further process automation. The process automation module is a

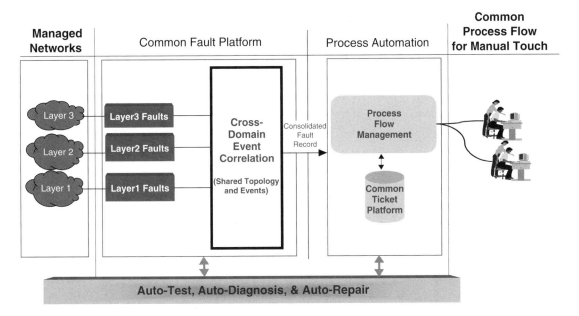

Figure 7.6 Common fault platform.

centralized, rule-based, expert system, where field-based rules managers can build new rules as well as edit, activate, and deactivate existing rules for process flow automation. The rules are used to monitor equipment alarms and detect when field technician intervention is necessary. When the process automation module determines that a rule can be applied to an alarm, it processes the alarm and may request further information on the alarm by sending commands to the associated network element. The process automation module evaluates the fault record and performs initial process automation, such as autodiagnose, autotest, and autorepair. Based on results of the initial process automation, rules are used to determine whether a ticket needs to be generated.

The process automation module can automatically create and refer out tickets through a work management system. If a ticket is to be created, the process flow assembles the required information and sends it to the common ticket module for ticket generation. In order to achieve automated operation, the common ticket module automatically moves the ticket through to resolution. Driven by ticket events, and as the ticket moves through its life cycle, additional process automation steps can be

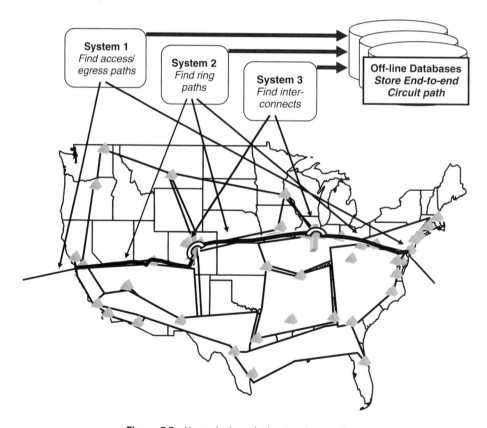

Figure 7.7 Yesterday's optical network operations.

taken to reduce the manual work. If the ticket cannot be completed by the automated steps and needs manual intervention, the technician will manually work the ticket. Upon completion of the manual work, the ticket is put back into the automated steps. When the fault changes state, the common fault platform sends an update message to the process flow automation module to update the consolidated fault record and the ticket status.

As an example, when the common fault platform receives traps from network elements, it does rule-based, cross-domain event correlation and defines a network event. This network event is sent to the process automation module, which then adds another layer of correlation to include process information, such as customer complaints and/or results from work center trouble identification, troubleshooting, and diagnostics. The process automation module then does automatic testing, generates the trouble ticket, and automates the process steps so as to reduce or eliminate the manual work in resolving the problem and closing the trouble ticket.

Figures 7.7 and 7.8 illustrate the application of operations automation to the optical core network. Figure 7.7 illustrates yesterday's operations, which managed SONET rings connected by digital cross-connects or manual patch panels. Transport bandwidth provisioning involved finding available capacity across a series of rings and interconnects using several OSSs, where all data about paths are kept in off-line databases. In contrast, Figure 7.8 illustrates migration to automated operations of the

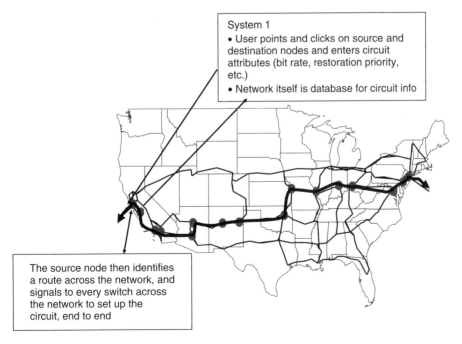

System 1
• User points and clicks on source and destination nodes and enters circuit attributes (bit rate, restoration priority, etc.)
• Network itself is database for circuit info

The source node then identifies a route across the network, and signals to every switch across the network to set up the circuit, end to end

Figure 7.8 Operational migration to automated intelligent optical network.

intelligent optical core network. In this migration, the network consists of intelligent nodes, each with a complete map of all available routes to any destination, and one system initiates the end-to-end transport bandwidth provisioning, which is derived and routed automatically by the intelligent network elements.

7.8 Summary and Conclusions

As discussed in this chapter, the benefits of implementing automated MPLS operations, including traffic management and capacity management, are as follows:

- expense savings through automated operations
- capital savings through efficient capacity management techniques
- increased network throughput and revenues with TQO implementation and operation, and automatic traffic management controls (e.g., DOC, DBR, automatic alternate routing)

  Conclusions reached in this chapter include the following:

- Monitoring of traffic and performance data is required for traffic management, capacity forecasting, daily and weekly performance monitoring, and short-term network adjustment.
- Traffic management is required to provide monitoring of network performance through collection and display of real-time traffic and performance data and to allow traffic management controls such as code blocks, connection request gapping, and reroute controls to be inserted when circumstances warrant.
- Capacity management is required for capacity forecasting, daily and weekly performance monitoring, and short-term network adjustment.
- Forecasting is required to operate over a multiyear forecast interval and drive network capacity expansion.
- Daily and weekly performance monitoring is required to identify any service problems in the network. If service problems are detected, short-term network adjustment can include routing table updates and, if necessary, short-term capacity additions to alleviate service problems.
- Short-term capacity additions are required as needed in exceptional cases; most capacity changes are normally forecasted, planned, scheduled, and managed over a period of months or a year or more.

7.9 Applicability of Requirements

All of the TQO operational requirements in this chapter are already in use in deployed packet-based and TDM-based dynamic routing networks, and the benefits listed in the previous section are being realized. In fact, these methods are generally necessary and applicable to any network, particularly to MPLS-based and GMPLS-based integrated voice/data dynamic routing networks. The success of these TQO operational methods in various network applications provides some basis for service providers to deploy these capabilities more widely. While vendors have announced many of these operational capabilities in their products, vendors can profit from service provider interest in adopting such TQO features by tailoring their products accordingly.

Chapter 8
Case Studies 1: Traffic Engineering and QoS Optimization for Operational Integrated Voice/Data Dynamic Routing Networks

8.1 Introduction

This chapter describes case studies of TQO protocol design for integrated voice/data dynamic routing networks. First we review the TQO design principles used for voice, data, and integrated voice/data network design. We then present case studies for TQO protocol design: (a) circuit-switched integrated voice/data dynamic routing networks, for both single intradomain and internetwork routing cases, and (b) MPLS/GMPLS-based integrated voice/data dynamic routing networks. We also discuss two case studies where designs went astray, but at the same time provided valuable lessons for future designs.

These case studies reflect the studies, planning, and implementation of TQO in a large service provider's (AT&T's) network over several decades. They show the connection between the solutions espoused by the Geekia NetHeads and the time-honored principles held dear by the Telephonia BellHeads. As discussed in Chapter 1, comprehensive studies by the RATS team led to AT&T's conception, evaluation, and eventual migration of its worldwide voice/ISDN network to real-time, adaptive TQO/dynamic routing. This migration took place through the 1980s and 1990s, and the implementation continues into the 2000s. These breakthrough technologies are widely implemented by service providers throughout the world (see Table 1.2 in Chapter 1) and are still very much in operation. Such TQO/dynamic routing capabilities revolutionized the reliability, performance, traffic handling efficiency, and revenue generation capabilities of these networks.

The case studies presented in this chapter graphically illustrate the lessons learned by the migration to these TQO technologies. There is much to be learned from this highly successful effort, and IMHO Geekia NetHeads and Telephonia BellHeads should pay close attention to the lessons taught in this chapter. All too often, unfortunately, NetHeads and BellHeads seem unwilling to study these lessons, let alone apply them. Geekia dwellers often seem of the opinion that TDM voice networks use tin cans connected by strings, and Telephonia dwellers often think that the Internet runs on patches and hacks, but have no clue as to the workings and sophistication of Internet protocols. NetHeads may immediately reject any "lessons" that smack of TDM or Telephonia, such as did a Cisco VP NetHead whose summary of such lessons was "to the BellHeads, everything looks like a telephone call." There is a bit more to be learned from these experiences than what the Cisco VP NetHead took in. Telephonia BellHeads, on the other hand, endlessly lecture the NetHeads on the absolute necessity to adhere to the axioms espoused in their ITU recommendations, which belabor abstract (and sometimes abstruse) topics having to do, for example, with layer network architecture principles and such. Stern warnings are issued frequently that any violation of these laws may result in chaos, if not complete disaster.

It's time to change these (NIH?) hang-ups and seek a compromise with a motivational carrot. GTQO requirements presented in Chapter 10 are in part the outcome of the case studies discussed in the chapter. The Geekians' piece of the carrot is that their protocols are incorporated in the GTQO requirements, and the Telephonians' piece of the carrot is that their design principles are incorporated in the GTQO requirements. Problem solved! In fact, the RATS team proved that NetHead–RATS and BellHead–RATS can indeed work well together, despite the gap, and reach consensus on TQO architecture directions that incorporate the best ideas of both worlds.

TQO protocol design and optimization, the basic issues addressed in these case studies, seek to find an optimal TQO protocol for arbitrary traffic loads and network topology, which yields minimum-cost capacity and maximum-flow/revenue, with minimal control overhead, subject to meeting performance constraints. In the first two case studies, we illustrate the design and optimization of large-scale, state-dependent TQO protocols: real-time network routing/class of service (RTNR/COS) and real-time internetwork routing/class of service (RINR/COS). RTNR/COS and RINR/COS are state-dependent TQO protocols used in practice in very large-scale applications implemented in the AT&T integrated voice/data dynamic routing network in 1991 and 1995, respectively. These TQO protocols have integrated a number of voice and ISDN data services onto VNETs, where the VNETs constitute a converged, shared network with sophisticated bandwidth allocation/management capabilities and two levels of traffic priority (high and normal). These two case studies capture the conception and theoretical analysis studies that accompanied the deployment of RTNR/COS and RINR/COS.

The third and fourth case studies illustrate where alternate routing may have contributed to network congestion. These examples are intended to illustrate possible pitfalls of excessive alternate routing and the need for careful consideration of protection techniques, primarily the need for bandwidth reservation methods in these examples, to guard against excessive alternate routing. One case involved a software problem that crippled the AT&T long-distance network on January 15, 1990, and a second that involved a new routing capability to avoid a voice enhancement capability in the network. In both cases cited, proper use of bandwidth reservation may well have helped alleviate the problems that occurred.

In these case studies we use discrete event simulation models to illustrate the design and optimization of RTNR/COS and RINR/COS. The simulation model is used to illustrate (a) the selection of RTNR/COS and RINR/COS from among a large number of TQO alternatives and (b) the optimization of the RTNR/COS and RINR/COS protocols by evaluating the performance as a function of various design parameters. These parameters include the number of link occupancy states, link state occupancy thresholds, triggering mechanism for congestion detection, and others. Generally the routing and capacity designs for the meshed logical topologies are optimized by using the DEFO algorithms presented in Chapter 6.

8.2 Case Study: TQO Protocol Design of Circuit-Switched Integrated Voice/Data Dynamic Routing Network

TQO in the form of dynamic routing protocols has been in operation in circuit-switched TDM networks since 1984, when dynamic nonhierarchical routing (DNHR, a TDR method) cut over into operation in the AT&T network. This was followed by many other such TQO implementations worldwide, and the current status of dynamic routing/TQO implementations is given in Table 1.2 in Chapter 1, along with a brief overview of dynamic routing/TQO in circuit-switched networks.

In this section we use discrete event simulation models to illustrate the design and optimization of RTNR/COS, a large-scale, state-dependent TQO protocol. As depicted in Table 1.2 in Chapter 1, RTNR/COS replaced DNHR and is a distributed connection-by-connection state-dependent routing (DC-SDR) method, implemented in the AT&T voice network in 1991. This TQO protocol allows the integration of voice and ISDN data services onto VNETs carried on an integrated shared network and incorporates sophisticated VNET bandwidth allocation/management capabilities as well as two levels of traffic priority: high and normal. RTNR/COS has been enormously successful and is still very much in operation, and will likely remain so for many years to come.

We first illustrate the principles of circuit-switched, integrated, voice/data TQO protocols, using RTNR/COS as an example, and then illustrate the analysis used to optimize the TQO protocol design. Even though we use a particular protocol to illustrate the principles, these are generic principles that must be addressed in any such TQO protocol design. These principles are not limited to voice networks, but apply to any voice, data, or integrated voice/data network TQO protocol design. We will see them appear again in the subsequent case studies presented in this chapter.

8.2.1 Principles of TQO Protocol Design for Integrated Voice/Data Dynamic Routing Networks

RTNR/COS is used to illustrate the principles incorporated in the TQO protocol design of integrated voice/data dynamic routing networks:

- class-of-service (COS) routing capabilities for service flexibility and multiservice VNET bandwidth allocation
- CAC, source-based path selection, crankback, for bandwidth allocation to COSs/VNETs
- load state mapping, bandwidth reservation techniques for stable performance and bandwidth sharing
- dynamic connection routing, priority routing for efficient utilization and reduced routing overhead
- meet performance objectives for integrated COSs

We begin with an overview and then discuss details of each principle of TQO protocol design.

RTNR/COS first selects the direct link if capacity is available, and if not available then selects the least-loaded two-link alternate path from among all possible two-link paths. The available bandwidth capacity or occupancy of each link is mapped into a discrete number of link states, and the link-state occupancy information signaling between network nodes to enable selection of the least-loaded two-link path. Furthermore, a small amount of link capacity called the bandwidth-reservation level R is reserved on each link. A connection on the direct link is allowed to access all capacity, including the reserved capacity R. However, the reserve capacity R cannot be used on an alternate two-link path. That is, if less than R units of bandwidth capacity are available on either link of a two-link alternate path, a connection cannot use that path. This bandwidth reservation mechanism favors direct one-link paths under network congestion conditions. Without reservation, nonhierarchical networks can exhibit unstable behavior in which essentially all connections are established on two-link as opposed to one-link paths, which reduces network throughput greatly and increases network congestion greatly [AKINPELU84, KRUPP82, NAKAGOME73].

8.2.1.1 Class-of-Service Routing

The class-of-service capabilities of RTNR/COS entail identifying the COS parameters, which include:

- service identity (SI)
- transport capability (TC)
- virtual network (VNET)
- link capability (LC)
- QoS and traffic threshold parameters

The SI describes the actual service associated with the connection. The TC represents the bearer-level transport protocol and bandwidth required by services mapped to a given VNET. The VNET describes the bandwidth allocation and routing table parameters to be used by the service. The LC describes the link hardware capabilities, such as fiber, radio, satellite, and digital circuit multiplexing equipment (DCME), that the connection should require, prefer, or avoid. The combination of SI, TC, VNET, and LC constitutes the class of service, which together with the network node number is used to access routing table data.

COS determination begins with translation at the originating node of the called number to determine the routing address of the destination node. If multiple ingress/egress routing is used, multiple destination node addresses are derived for the connection.

Data derived from information such as link characteristics, Q.931 message information elements, information interchange digits, and network control point routing information are used to derive the class of service for the connection. This is now illustrated for SI, TC, VNET, and LC derivation.

To derive the SI, the type of origin, type of destination, signaling service type, and dialed number/name service type are used. The type of origin can be derived normally from the type of incoming link to the connected network domain, connecting to a directly connected (also known as nodal) customer equipment location, a switched access local exchange carrier, or an international carrier location. Similarly, based on the dialed numbering plan, the type of destination network is derived and can be a directly connected (nodal) customer location if a private numbering plan is used (e.g., within a virtual private network), a switched access customer location if a North American Numbering Plan (NANP) number is used to the destination, or an international customer location if the international E.164 numbering plan is used. Signaling service type is derived based on bearer capability within signaling messages, information digits in dialed digit codes, numbering plan, or other signaling information and can indicate long-distance service (LDS), virtual private network (VPN) service, ISDN switched digital service (SDS), and other service types. Finally, dialed number service type is derived based on special dialed number codes such as 800 numbers or 900 numbers and can indicate 800 (FreePhone) service, 900 (Mass-Announcement) service, and other service types. Type of origin, type of destination, signaling service type, and dialed number service type are then all used to derive the SI. An SI mapping table maps these four inputs to derive the SI, and this policy-based routing table is changeable by administrative updates, in which new service information can be defined without software modifications to the node processing.

An LDS SI, for example, is derived from the following information:

1. The type of origination network is a switched access local exchange carrier because the connection originates from a local exchange carrier node.
2. The type of destination network is a switched access local exchange carrier based on the NANP dialed number.

3. The signaling service type is long-distance service based on the numbering plan (NANP).
4. The dialed number service type is not used to distinguish long-distance service SI.

An 800 (FreePhone) service SI, for example, is derived from similar information, except that the dialed number service type is based on the 800 dialed "FreePhone" number to distinguish the 800 service SI.

A VPN service SI, for example, is derived from similar information, except that the signaling service type is based on the originating customer having access to VPN intelligent network (IN)-based services to derive the VPN service SI.

A TC is assigned to each SI in a table, and an SI/TC-to-VNET mapping table is used to derive the VNET. Table 2.1 in Chapter 2 illustrates the VNET mapping table. VNETs have associated with them various routing parameters, including service priority (key service or normal service).

Routing rules are then applied to map the derived SI, TC, VNET, and LC to the routing table and associated parameters. LC selection allows connections to be routed on links that have the particular characteristics required by these connections. A connection can require, prefer, or avoid a set of link characteristics, such as fiber transmission, radio transmission, satellite transmission, or compressed voice transmission. LC requirements for the connection can be determined by the SI of the connection or by other information derived from the signaling message or from the routing number. The routing logic allows the connection to skip those links that have undesired characteristics and to seek a best match for the requirements of the connection.

Prior to the COS routing innovation, it was frequently the case that new service introduction required new software development, hardware development, and deployment of a new network. In sharp contrast, however, COS routing tables are changeable by administrative updates and require no software development to implement new services within the COS framework. Such capabilities have been used many times within the COS routing framework to administratively define new services, with no software or network element hardware development required. That is, the voice and ISDN services are provided on an integrated dynamic routing network and require no new network development or hardware deployment to define and implement new services. As such, COS routing is a breakthrough technology and a component of the GTQO protocol described in Chapter 10.

8.2.1.2 *Connection Admission Control (CAC), Source-Based Path Selection, Crankback*

Nodes using RTNR/COS first select the direct link between originating node (ON) and destination node (DN). When no direct link is available, the ON checks the availability and load conditions of all of the two-link paths to the DN on a per connection basis. If any of these two-link paths are available, the connection is set up over the least-loaded two-link path. Traffic loads are dynamically balanced across links throughout the network to maximize the throughput of the network.

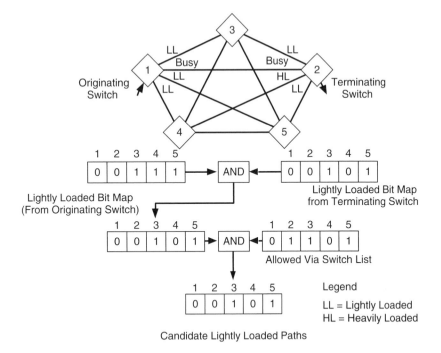

Figure 8.1   Determining least-loaded paths.

As illustrated in Figure 8.1, an available two-link path from ON to DN goes through a via node (VN) to which both ON and DN have idle link capacity, i.e., neither link is busy. An available two-link path is considered to be lightly loaded if the idle capacity on both links exceeds a threshold level. In order to determine all of the nodes in the network that satisfy this criterion, the ON sends a message to the DN over the signaling network, requesting DN to send a list of the nodes to which it has lightly loaded links. Upon receiving this list of nodes from DN, the ON compares this list with its own list of nodes to which it has lightly loaded links. Any node that appears in both lists currently has lightly loaded links to both ON and DN and therefore can be used as the VN for a two-link connection for this connection. In Figure 8.1 there are two lightly loaded paths found between ON and DN.

The node identifiers used in the node list sent by DN must be recognized by the ON. Each node in the network is assigned a unique network node number (NNN); these NNNs are used as node identifiers. In the example depicted in Figure 8.1, there are five nodes in a network that have been arbitrarily assigned NNNs. With these NNN assignments, a list of nodes can be represented by a bit map that has a 1-bit entry for each NNN in the network. In Figure 8.1, a "1" entry is made in the bit map for each NNN having a lightly loaded link to DN. ON also maintains its own bit map listing each NNN having a lightly loaded link to ON. Using bit maps makes it very easy and efficient for the ON to find all lightly loaded two-link paths. The ON simply ANDs the bit map it receives from DN, which lists all of the lightly loaded links out of DN, with its own bit map to produce a new bit map that identifies all the VNs with lightly loaded links to both ON and DN. Bit maps also are a very compact way to store a list of nodes. This is an important consideration, as the list is sent in a signaling message. In the simplest case, only 16 bytes of data are needed for a network with 128 nodes.

Because some of the available two-link paths may not provide good voice transmission quality, network administrators can restrict path selection to the two-link paths that provide good transmission quality through use of another bit map, the allowed VN list, which specifies the acceptable VNs from ON to DN. As illustrated in Figure 8.1, ANDing this bit map with the bit map containing the VNs of all of the available two-link paths removes the VNs of paths with unacceptable transmission quality. When two or more available paths have the same load status, as in Figure 8.1 where two lightly loaded paths are found, the ON randomly picks one of these paths to use for the connection. To pick a path for this particular connection to DN, the ON starts a circular search through the bit map list of paths with the same load status, beginning with the entry immediately following the VN it last used for a connection to DN.

Requesting link status on a per connection basis ensures that the current network conditions are known for selecting a two-link path for the connection. However, sending a request message and waiting for the response add to the setup time for the connection. This additional connection setup delay can be avoided. When the ON does not find any available direct link capacity to DN, it requests the current list of nodes to which DN has idle capacity. Rather than waiting for a response from DN to set up the connection, the ON can select a two-link path using the most recently received status response from DN. When the new status response is received, the ON stores it away for use the next time it needs to select a two-link path to DN. Because the status of the idle link capacity is not as current using this method, the two-link path selected has a greater probability of lost traffic. When this happens, the VN uses a crankback signaling message to return the connection to the ON. The ON must then wait for the status response from DN and pick a new VN for the connection using this up-to-date information. With these methods, RTNR/COS uniformly and substantially reduces connection setup delay in comparison to other dynamic routing strategies.

8.2.1.3 Load State Mapping, Bandwidth Reservation

In order to dynamically balance traffic loads across the network, it is necessary to know the actual load conditions of links throughout the network and use two-link paths that have the least loaded links. RTNR/COS uses six discrete load states for links: lightly loaded 1 (LL1), LL2, LL3, heavily loaded (HL), reserved, and all busy. The idle capacity on a link is compared with the load state thresholds for the link to determine the load condition of the link. This determination is made every time capacity on the link is either seized or released. The DN identifies both the nodes to which it has idle link capacity, and the load condition of the links to each of these nodes, in the reply message sent to the ON. The DN does this by sending multiple bit map lists in this reply message; a bit map list of the nodes to which it has an LL1 link, a bit map list of the nodes to which it has an LL2 (or less loaded) link, and so on. The ON maintains similar bit map lists of the nodes to which it has idle capacity, ordered by the load condition of the links to these nodes. The ON first compares the list of nodes to which it has an LL1 link with the list of nodes to which the DN has an LL1 link to determine if any node appears in both lists. If not, the ON successively compares the other load status lists to find the VN with the least-loaded available links.

In an RTNR/COS network, connections for a particular *COS-i* are assumed to consume an average bandwidth equal to *r-i*, using a single unit of capacity denoted as one virtual link (VT). For example, each VT would have *r-i* equal to 64 Kbps of bandwidth for voice connections or 64-Kbps switched digital service connections, *r-i* equal to 384 Kbps of bandwidth for 384-Kbps switched digital service connections, and would have *r-i* equal to 1536 Kbps of bandwidth for each 1536-switched digital service connection. The load state thresholds used for a particular link are based on the current estimates of four quantities maintained by node ON, for each *COS-i*, and for each node DN:

- connections in progress, *CIP-i*, which is the number of active connections from ON to DN for a particular *COS-i* (measured on-line by the node and includes connections completed on both direct and two-link connections)
- node-to-node traffic loss probability level, *NN-i*, which is the rate of traffic loss for connections from ON to DN for *COS-i* (estimated on-line by the node)
- offered traffic load, *TL-i*, to each of the other nodes in the network (this approximation is based on *CIP-i* and *NN-i*, measured over the last several minutes)
- *VTtraf-i*, which is the number of VTs required to meet the grade-of-service (*GOS-i*) objective for the current *TL-i* from ON to DN for *COS-i* (estimated on-line by the node and can exceed the total direct link capacity between ON and DN, meaning that capacity from two-link alternate paths is needed to meet the *GOS-i* objective for the current offered traffic load)

The load state thresholds for the lightly loaded and heavily loaded states are set to fixed percentages of the *VTtraf-i* estimate. As such, the load state thresholds rise as the *VTtraf-i* estimate to that node increases. Higher load state thresholds reduce the chances that the link is used for two-link connections for connections to or from other nodes; this enables the link to carry more direct traffic and therefore better handle the traffic load between the nodes connected by the link. The reserved state threshold is based on the reservation level *R-i* calculated on each link, which in turn is based on the traffic loss probability level *NN-i*, as shown in Table 8.1.

If the number lost connections to DN exceeds the *NN-i* threshold, which is computed each periodic update interval, then the node immediately triggers that next level of

Table 8.1 Link Reservation Level

NN-i_k *blk. threshold*	*Reservation level*	R-i_k *(VTs)*
[0, .01]	0	0
[.01, .05]	1	$.05 \times VTtraf\text{-}i_k$
[.05, .15]	2	$.1 \times VTtraf\text{-}i_k$
[.15, .5]	3	$.15 \times VTtraf\text{-}i_k$
[.5, .1]	4	$.2 \times VTtraf\text{-}i_k$

bandwidth reservation. For example, if the current bandwidth reservation level is level 0, as given in Table 8.1, and if the number of lost connections reaches the number needed for bandwidth reservation level 1, then level 1 is triggered immediately. In this way reservation protection is applied immediately following a load surge or facility failure, which aids greatly in improving the node and network response to load variation and failure.

Then the reserved virtual link capacity *Rtraf-i* are at most *R-i*, as defined earlier, and are bounded above by *VTtraf-i* − *CIP-i* as follows:

$$Rtraf\text{-}i = \min[R\text{-}i, \ \max(0, \ VTtraf\text{-}i - CIP\text{-}i)]$$

Figure 8.2 summarizes these mechanisms for RTNR/COS bandwidth reservation. (The significance of the *VTeng-i* variables in Figure 8.2 is discussed later in this section.) Each node continuously checks the traffic loss rate for connection attempts to each of the other nodes in the network. If the ON finds that the *GOS-i* objective for its connection attempts to DN is not met, where the *GOS-i* objective is taken as .01

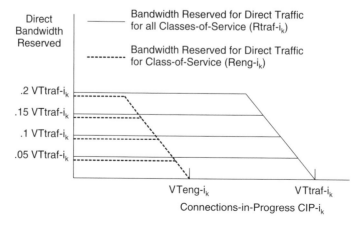

Figure 8.2 Operation of RTNR/COS bandwidth reservation.

for illustration in Figure 8.2, the ON sets *Rtraf-i*. As shown in Figure 8.2, the higher the node-to-node traffic loss probability, the greater the bandwidth reserved *Rtraf-i* for direct traffic versus alternate routed traffic. *Rtraf-i* is set to the difference between the *VTtraf-i* estimate and the current *CIP-i* to DN, with an upper bound equal to *R-i*, given in Table 8.1. This difference is the number of additional connections from the ON to DN that need to be completed to reach the current *VTtraf-i* estimate. The ON adjusts *Rtraf-i* as the number of completed connections to DN (*CIP-i*) changes. Every time the ON completes a new connection attempt to DN, either over the direct link or a two-link path, the ON checks to see whether the reserved state threshold should be decremented for the link to DN. Likewise, when a connection to DN disconnects, the ON checks to see if the *Rtraf-i* threshold should be incremented. By following these actions, the ON turns the reservation control for this link off and on as the number of connections in progress to DN oscillates around the *VTtraf-i* estimate.

To derive link load states, each node ON determines the total bandwidth *BWtraf* needed to meet the combined traffic load from ON to DN for all *N COS-i*, as follows:

$$BWtraf = \Sigma(i = 1, \ N)[VTtraf\text{-}i \ \times \ r\text{-}i]$$

Also, node ON determines the total reserved bandwidth for *N* COSs, as follows:

$$RBWtraf = \Sigma(i = 1, \ N)[Rtraf\text{-}i \times r\text{-}i]$$

If the idle link bandwidth for the link from ON to DN is ILBW, then the link load states are given as shown in Table 8.2.

Therefore the reservation level and state boundary thresholds are proportional to the estimated offered-traffic-load level, which means that the bandwidth reserved and the idle bandwidth required to constitute a lightly loaded link rise and fall with the traffic load, as intuitively it should. Under normal nontraffic-loss network conditions, all COSs fully share all available capacity. As discussed earlier, when traffic loss occurs for *COS-i*, RTNR/COS bandwidth reservation is activated to prohibit alternate routed traffic from seizing direct link capacity designed for *COS-i*. This is accomplished by

Table 8.2 Link Load States

Idle link bandwidth	State
$ILBW < r\text{-}i$	Busy
$r\text{-}i \le ILBW \le RBWtraf$	Reserved
$RBWtraf < ILBW \le .05 \times BWtraf + RBWtraf$	HL
$.05 \times BWtraf + RBWtraf < ILBW \le .1 \times BWtraf + RBWtraf$	LL3
$.1 \times BWtraf + RBWtraf < ILBW \le .2 \times BWtraf + RBWtraf$	LL2
$.2 \times BWtraf + RBWtraf < ILBW$	LL1

setting the reserved state threshold equal to the total bandwidth reserved, *RBWtraf* for this link, and placing the link in the reserved state when the idle bandwidth on the link is less than this reserved state threshold. As bandwidth on the link become idle when old connections disconnect, the link capacity is reserved for new connection attempts between the ON and the DN. The lightly loaded and heavily loaded state thresholds for the link are adjusted upward from their base values by the amount of the reserved state threshold as given in Table 8.2. Once the ON finds that the *GOS-i* objective for its connection attempts to DN is again being met, the reserved state threshold for the link between these two nodes is reset to zero, and the lightly loaded and heavily loaded state thresholds are adjusted accordingly.

8.2.1.4 Dynamic Connection Routing, Priority Routing

The rules for selecting primary (direct) and alternate (via) paths for a connection are depicted in Table 8.3.

The path selection is governed by the availability of direct link capacity, total node traffic loss rate *TN-i*, and node-to-node traffic loss rate *NN-i*. The path sequence consists of the direct link, if it exists, lightly loaded 1 via paths, lightly loaded 2 via paths, lightly loaded 3 via paths, heavily loaded via paths, and reserved via paths. Two thresholds, *DEPTHhl-i* and *DEPTHr-i*, are defined that govern the "controlled use" of the heavily loaded and reserved via paths, as follows. If $CIP\text{-}i < DEPTHhl\text{-}i \times VTtraf\text{-}i$, then connections to DN for *COS-i* can be routed using heavily loaded via paths. Also if $CIP\text{-}i < DEPTHr\text{-}i \times VTtraf\text{-}i$, then connections to DN for *COS-i* can use reserved via paths. Hence the factors *DEPTHhl-i* and *DEPTHr-i* are factors controlling the depth of selection for a via path on a given connection.

In general, greater path selection depth is allowed if traffic loss is detected to DN, as more alternate route choices serve to reduce the traffic loss to DN. This greater selection depth is inhibited, however, if the total node traffic loss rates reach a high level, indicating that a general overload condition is obtained, in which case it is more advantageous to reduce alternate routing. Also, if there is no direct link capacity or the node-to-node traffic is small, say with *VTtraf-i* less than 15 VTs, then the selection depth again is increased, as bandwidth reservation becomes ineffective

Table 8.3 RTNR/COS Path Selection

Path state	Selection order
Primary/direct	1
Alternate/via lightly loaded 1	2
Alternate/via lightly loaded 2	3
Alternate/via lightly loaded 3	4
Alternate/via heavily loaded	5 (controlled use)
Alternate/via reserved	6 (controlled use)

or even impossible, and greater dependence on alternate routing is needed to meet network traffic loss probability objectives. The use of heavily loaded and reserved links for two-link connections is relaxed for connections between two nodes that are not connected by a direct link or when the link capacity is reduced greatly by a network failure event, such as a fiber cut. In this manner the traffic loss rate performance can be controlled by the depth of access to via paths in the heavily loaded and reserved state.

These mechanisms are illustrated in Figure 8.3, where we focus on the controlled use of heavily loaded paths. The objective of accessing heavily loaded via paths is to increase completions from the ON to DN such that the required link capacity *VTtraf-i* needed to meet the *GOS-i* objective is provided. As shown in Figure 8.3, lightly loaded RTNR/COS paths can always be selected. However, heavily loaded RTNR/COS paths are selected only under the conditions that (a) an *NN-i* traffic loss rate in excess of the *GOS-i* objective of .01 is detected and (b) *CIP-i* is less than *VTtraf-i*. When *CIP-i* exceeds *VTtraf-i*, then heavily loaded paths should not be required to meet the *GOS-i* objective, and thereby heavily loaded capacity can be used by other traffic still in need of additional capacity. By controlling the use of heavily loaded two-link connections, the completion rate for connections between nodes that have not been meeting their *GOS-i* objective is improved, while possibly increasing the traffic loss rate for connections between pairs of nodes that are within their *GOS-i* objective. Links in the reserved state are normally used only for direct traffic, but may be used for via routing when higher priority connections are placed under heavy network congestion.

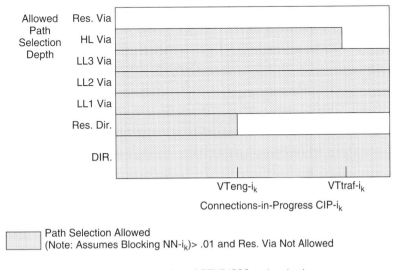

Figure 8.3   Operation of RTNR/COS path selection.

8.2.1.5 Meet Performance Objectives for Integrated COSs

RTNR/COS is used to implement a dynamic COS network and therefore is used for voice services, 64-, 384-, and 1536-Kbps switched digital data services, and other COSs. Because RTNR/COS maintains traffic loss rates, $VTtraf\text{-}i$ estimates, and current connections-in-progress counts $CIP\text{-}i$ for each $COS\text{-}i$ and controls the use of direct and two-link paths based on these measurements, it is able to meet different traffic loss probability objectives and load levels for different COSs. For example, COSs with different transmission capabilities, e.g., voice and 384-Kbps switched digital services, can have different traffic loss probability objectives, as can COSs that require the same transmission capabilities, e.g., domestic voice and international voice services. In this way, RTNR/COS maximizes the performance of a dynamic COS network in meeting traffic loss rate and connection throughput objectives for all COSs.

We illustrate in Figure 8.4 the dynamic COS routing strategy, which includes the following steps for connection establishment:

- at the ON, the COS (SI, TC, VNET, LC) and DN are identified
- the COS and DN information is used to select the corresponding routing pattern data, which includes path sequence selection, reservation levels, load state thresholds, and traffic measurements
- an appropriate path is selected through execution of path selection logic and possible exchange of network status bit maps, and the connection is established on the selected path

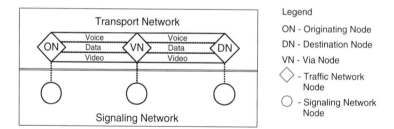

Step 1: Identify class-of-service (service identity, transport capability, routing pattern, link capability), virtual network, & destination node

Step 2: Determine routing pattern data for virtual network (path sequence selection, reservation levels, load state thresholds, bandwidth allocation, traffic measurements)

Step 3: Dynamically select available path capacity (determine network status, execute path selection logic, route call)

Figure 8.4 Dynamic class-of-service routing.

As illustrated in Figure 8.4, the various COSs share bandwidth on the network links. For this purpose the dynamic COS network capacity is designed to handle the combined forecasted traffic loads for many COSs. The network capacity design process allots a certain bandwidth, in units of the number of direct VTs, between ON and DN to *VNET-i*, which is referred to as *VTeng-i*. *VTeng-i* is the minimum guaranteed bandwidth for *VNET-i*, but if *COS-i* is meeting its *GOS-i* traffic loss probability objective, other COSs are free to share the *VTeng-i* bandwidth allotted to *COS-i*. The quantities *VTeng-i* are chosen in the network engineering process such that their sum over all COSs sharing the bandwidth of the direct link is equal to the total bandwidth on the link, as do the three *VTeng-i* segments illustrated in Figure 8.4.

The ON uses the quantities *VTtraf-i*, *CIP-i*, *NN-i*, and *VTeng-i* to dynamically allocate link bandwidth to COSs. Under normal nontraffic loss network conditions, all COSs fully share all available capacity. Because of this, the network has the flexibility to carry a traffic overload between two nodes for one COS if the traffic load for other COSs is sufficiently below their engineered levels. An extreme traffic overload between two nodes for one COS may cause connections for other COSs to be lost, in which case bandwidth is reserved to ensure that each COS gets the amount of bandwidth allotted by the network engineering process. This reservation during times of overload results in network performance that is analogous to having bandwidth between the two nodes dedicated for each COS.

Figure 8.2 illustrates the reservation of direct link bandwidth. When traffic loss occurs for *COS-i*, RTNR/COS bandwidth reservation is enabled to prohibit alternate routed traffic and traffic from other COSs from seizing direct link capacity designed for *COS-i*. Here the reserved direct VTs for *COS-i*, *Reng-i*, are given by

$$Reng\text{-}i = \min[R\text{-}i, \ \max(0, VTeng\text{-}i - CIP\text{-}i)]$$

As shown in Figure 8.2, when the ON detects that the current traffic loss rate level *NN-i* for connections for *COS-i* exceeds the *GOS-i* objective, bandwidth reservation is triggered for direct traffic for *COS-i*, and the reserved bandwidth on the direct link for any COS is at most *VTeng-i* − *CIP-i*.

As shown in Figure 8.3, sharing of bandwidth on the direct link is implemented by allowing connections for *COS-i* to always seize a VT on the direct link if *CIP-i* is below the level *VTeng-i*. However, if *CIP-i* is equal to or greater than *VTeng-i*, then connections for *COS-i* can seize virtual link capacity on the direct link only when the idle bandwidth on the link is greater than the bandwidth reserved by other COSs that are not meeting their traffic loss probability objectives. That is, if

$$CIP\text{-}i \geq VTeng\text{-}i$$

and the idle link bandwidth *ILBW* is greater than a reserved bandwidth threshold

$$ILBW \geq r\text{-}i + RBWeng$$

then we select a VT on the direct link. Here the total reserved bandwidth *RBWeng* for *N* COSs is the sum of the reserved direct bandwidth given by

$$RBWeng = \Sigma(i = 1, N)[Reng\text{-}i \times r\text{-}i]$$

Hence traffic for other COSs is restricted from seizing direct link capacity being reserved for *COS-i* to meet its *VTeng-i* engineered bandwidth allocation. In this manner each COS is assured a minimal level of network throughput determined by the network engineering process. When *CIP-i* exceeds *VTeng-i*, the engineered capacity allotted for *COS-i* is used up and connections can then be routed to unreserved direct link capacity or to available via paths, as shown in Figure 8.3. Finally, when *CIP-i* exceeds the *VTtraf-i*, then reservation is no longer needed to meet the *GOS-i* objective for *COS-i*, and VTs are shared by all traffic, including alternate routed traffic.

8.2.2 Optimization of TQO Protocol

RTNR/COS was selected after extensive study of a wide range of TQO methods, including extensive simulation comparisons of TDR, EDR, and SDR methods. Much of the comparative simulation analysis is reported in [ASH98]. In this section, the simulation model is used to illustrate the design trade-offs of the RTNR/COS protocol by optimizing the performance as a function of various design parameters, which include the number of link occupancy states, link state occupancy thresholds, triggering mechanism for congestion detection, and others.

Various RTNR/COS parameters not reported here, such as DEPTH of search strategies, bandwidth reservation levels, and other parameters, are also optimized through discrete event simulation models, typically using the 135-node network and VNET traffic models, as used in this chapter. Optimization of a bandwidth reservation level is studied for the MPLS/GMPLS TQO design case study in Chapter 9. There it is found that a reservation level in the range of 3–5% of link capacity provides the best overall performance to avoid instability from alternate routing while keeping efficiency near the optimum level possible (see Tables 9.15 and 9.16 in Chapter 9). Those results are consistent with independent studies of optimal reservation levels for other dynamic routing algorithms, such as RTNR/COS and RINR/COS considered in this chapter.

We now examine the optimum level of RTNR/COS state aggregation, or "granularity" of the state information, in which we consider several cases in the simulation study. This example illustrates a typical trade-off study approach for TQO parameter optimization in which several alternates are hypothesized, simulated performance is examined across a full range of scenarios, and then the best alternative is selected.

We first study RTNR/COS protocol performance as a function of the number of link occupancy states, including three-, four-, five-, and six-state models, which are illustrated in Figure 8.5. An example of a six-state model is given at the top of Figure 8.5. The six states are maximum lightly loaded (LL3), medium lightly loaded (LL2), minimum lightly loaded (LL1), heavily loaded (HL), reserved (R), and busy (B).

• 6-State Model

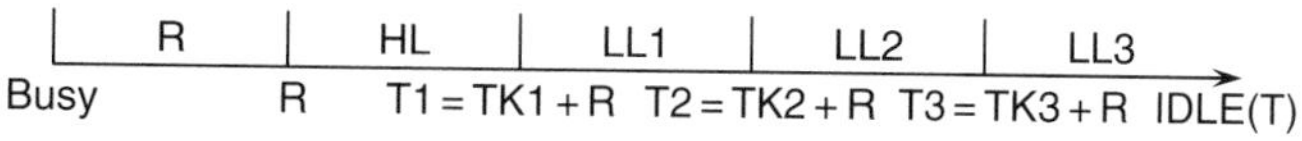

Automatic Bandwidth Reservation	
NN BLK, %	R (Bandwidth)
≤1	0
1–5	TK1
5–15	2×TK1
>15	3×TK1

Load Status Threshold			
	Bandw.	Min	Max
TK1	0.5×T	2	10
TK2	2×TK1	11	20
TK3	4×TK1	21	40

• 5-State Model: No LL3 State
• 4-State Model: No LL3 and LL2 States
• 3-State Model: No LL3, LL2, and Reserved States

Legend: R (Reserved), LL (Lightly Loaded), & HL (Heavily Loaded)

Figure 8.5   RTNR/COS three-, four-, five-, and six-state link models.

Table 8.4   Network Traffic Loss Rate Performance under High-Day Network Load for Three-, Four-, and Six-State RTNR/COS Models (% Traffic Loss Rate, 65-Node Network)

Hour	RTNR/COS (three states)	RTNR/COS (four states)	RTNR/COS (six states)
2	12.19	.47	.22
3	22.38	.58	.18
5	18.90	.44	.24
8	.00	.00	.00
15	.00	.31	.08
Average	12.05	.39	.16
Maximum	51.35	23.03	11.85
99%	41.24	7.20	2.87
90%	28.53	1.29	.07

Illustrative values of the thresholds that define these six states are given in Figure 8.5. Five-, four-, and three-state models are defined that omit the LL3 state, the LL2 state, and the R state, respectively.

Table 8.4 illustrates the performance of the RTNR/COS link-state models for a high-day network load pattern, based on the simulation model analysis. Table 8.4 gives the average hourly traffic loss rate in hours 2, 3, 5, 8, and 15, which correspond to the two early morning busy hours, the afternoon busy hour, the evening busy hour, and the weekend (Sunday night) busy hour, respectively. Also given at the bottom of Table 8.4 is the average traffic loss rate over these five load set periods, the average traffic loss rate over the five load set periods for the node pair with the highest average traffic loss rate, the node pair that had the 99th percentile highest average traffic loss rate, and the node pair that had the 90th percentile highest average traffic loss rate.

We can see from the results of Table 8.4 that RTNR/COS performance improves as more link states are used. The performance of the RTNR/COS three-state model is far worse than the performance of the other RTNR/COS models. The reason for this poor performance is due to the lack of reserved bandwidth capacity to favor direct one-link paths under network congestion conditions. As discussed earlier and in Chapter 3, without reservation, nonhierarchical networks can exhibit unstable behavior in which essentially many connections are established on two-link as opposed to one-link paths, which as shown in Table 8.4 greatly reduces network throughput and increases network traffic loss rate. If we add the reserved link state, as in the four- and six-state models, performance of the RTNR/COS network is improved greatly.

These results dramatically illustrate the necessity of employing bandwidth reservation principles in TQO protocol design. This illustration, among others throughout the book, justifies inclusion of bandwidth reservation in the GTQO protocol described in Chapter 10.

Results for high-day conditions with the 103-node simulation model are given in Table 8.5, and comparison of the four-, five-, and six-state models shows that network performance is monotonically improved as more states are added, as would be expected. However, additional simulation studies show that having more than six states does not measurably improve performance.

Sensitivities of the results to various parameters were investigated, which included link state thresholds, the amount of reserved capacity R, the triggering mechanism for congestion detection, and others. We now discuss results for the triggering mechanism for automatic bandwidth reservation as one example; details of other examples can be found in [ASH98].

Table 8.6 demonstrates the effect of an automatic bandwidth reservation-triggering mechanism using a 60-s update interval and the connections lost. The method based on connections lost provides a weighted, real-time estimate of node-to-node and total node traffic loss rate, which is updated on a connection-by-connection basis. That is, the node-to-node traffic loss rate is estimated as $b(i) = (1 - \alpha) \times r(i) + \alpha \times b(i-1)$, where $b(i)$ is the real-time traffic loss rate estimate for a given node pair based on the ith connection attempt, α is a number between zero and 1 that represents the weight assigned to previous values of the traffic loss rate estimate, and $r(i)$ is defined

Table 8.5 Network Traffic Loss Rate Performance under High-Day Network Load for Three-, Five-, and Six-State RTNR/COS Models (% Traffic Loss Rate, 103-Node Network)

Hour	RTNR/COS (four states)	RTNR/COS (five states)	RTNR/COS (six states)
2	.16	.03	.02
3	1.03	.80	.76
5	.82	.50	.45
15	.00	.00	.00
Average	.54	.36	.34
Maximum	19.25	15.36	15.02
99%	7.72	5.45	4.73
90%	1.57	.61	.52

Table 8.6 Effect of Triggering Mechanism on RTNR/COS Network Traffic Loss Rate Performance (High Day, % Traffic Loss Rate)

Hour	Lost connection based	Time based (60 s)
2	.05	.02
3	1.10	.76
5	.90	.45
15	.00	.00
Average	.56	.34
Maximum	18.71	15.02
99%	8.22	4.73
90%	0.73	0.52

to be 1 if connection i is lost and zero if it is not lost. This real-time traffic loss rate estimate is then used to trigger bandwidth reservation R. Several values of parameter α were tested, as were variations of the definition of $r(i)$. One variation defined $r(i)$ as the average traffic loss rate over a short, fixed time interval such as 15 s. However, the results of many simulations show that automatic bandwidth reservation based on the real-time traffic loss rate estimate is not as effective as that based on the 60-s update interval. The reason is that automatic bandwidth reservation based on the real-time traffic loss rate estimate is overly sensitive in triggering bandwidth reservation to turn on and too slow to remove it, and consequently bandwidth is overreserved. Therefore, automatic bandwidth reservation with a 60-s node-to-node traffic loss rate update time appears most promising.

We have presented a case study that illustrates the protocol design and optimization of RTNR/COS, a representative voice/ISDN network TQO protocol. This case study illustrates the principles of class-of-service derivation, determining network status, determining link load states, allocating traffic to primary and alternate paths, and achieving objectives for integrated network services. What has been learned are these key take-away's:

- COS routing provides a means to avoid software development, hardware development, and new network deployment for each new service
- quantization of network status can have a significant effect on network performance
- derivation of network status can be accomplished efficiently
- bandwidth reservation is critical to ensuring efficient and stable network performance
- alternate routing use and control are essential to ensuring efficient and stable network performance
- service objectives can be achieved for individual network services on an integrated voice/data dynamic TQO network

We apply these principles now to the case study of TQO design of RINR/COS and then illustrate with two case studies how violation of these principles can have a possibly severe detrimental effect on network performance. In Chapter 9 we present the final case study with the application of these principles to the case study of TQO protocol design for integrated voice/data IP/MPLS–GMPLS-based networks.

8.3 Case Study: TQO Protocol Design of Circuit-Switched, Internetwork, Integrated Voice/Data Dynamic Routing Networks

As illustrated in Figure 8.6, RINR/COS routing extends RTNR/COS concepts to distributed real-time dynamic routing, for example, between a national network and all connecting international carrier networks, all connecting local exchange carrier networks, and all connecting customer networks. Like RTNR/COS, RINR/COS uses a virtual network concept that enables service integration by allocating bandwidth for services and using real-time bandwidth reservation controls. Therefore, links can be fully shared among VNETs in the absence of congestion. When a certain VNET encounters traffic loss, bandwidth reservation is triggered on links to ensure that the VNET reaches its allocated bandwidth. RINR/COS provides class-of-service routing capabilities, including key service protection, directional flow control, link capability selection, automatically updated time-variable bandwidth allocation, VTeng, and greatly expanded transit routing capability through the use of overflow paths and control parameters such as RINR/COS load set periods. Link capability selection allows specific link hardware characteristics, such as fiber transmission, to be selected preferentially. As in the case of RTNR/COS, RINR/COS improves performance and reduces the cost of the internetwork routing by applying these TQO protocol design principles.

Figure 8.6 illustrates how RINR/COS extends RTNR/COS capabilities to dynamic internetwork routing in the international application, on the links between originating

Real-Time Network Routing/
Class-of-Service (RTNR/COS)

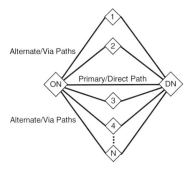

Real-Time Internetwork Routing/
Class-of-Service (RINR/COS)

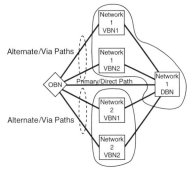

λ Try Primary/Direct Path First; if Busy, Select
  Best Alternate Path Based on Real-time
  Network Status
λ Routing Changes in Real Time
λ Network-Wide Path Selection
λ Originating Node Queries Destination Node
  for Network Status
λ Primary/direct Traffic Protected by Bandwidth
  Reservation During Periods of Congestion

λ Try Primary/direct Path First; if Busy,
  Select Alternate Path Based on Real-time
  Link Status & Call History
λ Routing Changes in Real Time
λ Network-Wide Path Selection
λ Originating Node Uses Real-Time Link
  Status & Call History
λ Primary/Direct Traffic Protected by
  Bandwidth Reservation During Periods of
  Congestion

Figure 8.6 Extending real-time network routing/class of service (RTNR/COS) to real-time internetwork routing/class of service (RINR/COS).

border node (OBN), and destination border node (DBN). With RINR/COS, international connections are routed first to a primary/direct path, if it exists and is available, to a list of alternate/via paths through via border nodes (VBNs) in the same network (VBN1 and VBN2 in network 1), and finally to a list of alternate paths through VBNs in other networks, such as those in network 2. Therefore, the RINR/COS paths are divided into three types: the primary/direct path, alternate paths in the same network, and alternate (or transit) paths through other networks. Alternate paths use links to VBNs to get to the DBN.

RINR/COS tries to find an available alternate path based on load state and connection completion performance in which the OBN uses its link busy/idle status to the VBN, in combination with the connection completion performance from the VBN to the DBN, in order to find the least-loaded, most available path to route the connection over. For each path, a load state and a completion state are tracked. The load state indicates whether links from the OBN to the DBN are lightly loaded, heavily loaded, reserved, or busy. The completion state indicates whether a path is achieving above-average completion, average completion, or below-average completion. The selection of an alternate/via path is based on the load state and completion state. Alternate paths in the same network and in a transit third network are each considered separately. Within a category of alternate/via paths, selection is based on the load state and completion state. During times of congestion, the link to a DBN may be in a reserved state, in which case the remaining capacity is reserved for traffic to the DBN. During periods of no congestion, capacity not needed by one VNET is made available to other VNETs that are experiencing loads above their allocation.

RINR/COS uses four discrete load states for links: lightly loaded, heavily loaded, reserved, and busy. The idle capacity in a link is compared with the load state thresholds for the link to determine its load condition. This determination is made every time a flow on the link is either set up or released. The load state thresholds used for a particular link are based on the current estimates of the same four quantities as maintained by RTNR/COS for *OBN-j* for each *VNET-i* and for each *DBN-k* that can include one or an aggregation of a number of DBNs:

- connections-in-progress *CIP-i*, which is the number of active connections from *OBN-j* to *DBN-k* for a particular *VNET-i*
- node-to-node traffic loss rate *NN-i* for connections from *OBN-j* to *DBN-k* for a particular *VNET-i*
- offered traffic load *TL-i* to each of the other DBNs in the network, which is based on the number of connections-in-progress *CIP-i* and the traffic loss rate to each DBN measured over the last several minutes
- *VTtraf-i*, which is the virtual capacity required to meet the traffic loss probability grade-of-service (*GOS-i*) objective for the current offered traffic load *TL-i* from *OBN-j* to *DBN-k* for a particular *VNET-i*.

Load state thresholds for the lightly loaded and heavily loaded states are set to fixed percentages of the *VTtraf-i_k* estimate. As such, load state thresholds rise as the *VTtraf-i* estimate to that node increases. Higher load state thresholds reduce the chances that the link is used for alternate path connections for connections to other nodes; this enables the link to carry more direct traffic and therefore better handle the traffic load between the nodes connected by the link. The reserved state threshold is based on the reservation level *R-i* calculated on each link, which in turn is based on the node-to-area traffic loss rate level.

As mentioned previously, the completion rate is tracked on the various via paths by taking account of the signaling message information relating either successful completion or noncompletion of a connection through a VBN. A noncompletion, or failure, is scored for the connection if a signaling release message is received from the far end after the connection seizes capacity on a link, indicating a network incompletion cause value. If no such signaling release message is received after the connection seizes a link, then the connection is scored as a success. There is no completion count for a connection that does not seize a link. Each OBN keeps a connection completion history of the success or failure of the last 10 connections using a particular alternate/via path, and it drops the oldest record and adds the connection completion for the newest connection on that path. Based on the number of connection completions relative to the total number of connections, a completion state is computed using the completion rate thresholds, which are now discussed.

The completion state is dynamic in that the connection completions are tracked continuously, and if a path suddenly experiences a greater number of connection non-completions, connections are routed over the path whose completion rate represents the highest rate of connection completions.

The completion rate for each path is the number of completed connections out of the last 10 connections recorded, where a high completion rate threshold and a low completion rate threshold are defined. Every 3 min, the average completion rate is computed and the thresholds are determined. On a per-connection basis, the connection completion rate is compared with the appropriate threshold to select the route. From the completion states, connections are normally routed on the first path that experiences no recent failure or a high completion state with a lightly loaded egress link. A path experiencing no recent failure is one that, within a prescribed interval (say 300 s), has had no connection failures on it. If such a path does not exist, then a path having an average completion state with a lightly loaded egress link is selected, followed by a path having a low completion state with a lightly loaded egress link. If no path with a lightly loaded egress link is available, and if the search depth permits the use of a heavily loaded egress link, the paths with heavily loaded egress links are searched in the order of no recent failure, high completion, average completion, and low completion. If no such paths are available, paths with reserved egress links are searched in the same order, based on the connection completion state, if the search depth permits the use of a reserved egress link.

The rules for selecting primary/direct and alternate/via paths for a connection are governed by the availability of primary/direct path capacity and node-to-node traffic loss rate. The path sequence consists of the primary/direct path, if it exists, lightly loaded alternate paths, heavily loaded alternate paths, and reserved alternate paths. In general, greater path selection depth is allowed if traffic loss is detected to DBN-k because more alternate path choices serve to reduce the traffic loss rate to DBN-k. The use of heavily loaded and reserved links for alternate path connections is relaxed for connections between two nodes that are not connected by a primary/direct path. In this manner the traffic loss rate performance can be controlled by the depth of access to alternate paths in the heavily loaded and reserved states. Links in the reserved state are normally used only for primary/direct traffic but may be used for alternate routing when higher priority connections are placed under heavy network congestion.

RINR/COS implements class-of-service routing, which is similar to RTNR/COS routing and includes the following steps for connection establishment:

- class of service (service identity, transport capability, VNET, and link capability) and DBN are identified
- class of service and DBN information is used to select the corresponding VNET data (path sequence selection, reservation levels, load state thresholds, bandwidth allocation, and traffic measurements)
- path is selected through execution of path selection logic and the connection is established on the selected path

The various VNETs share bandwidth on the network links. On a weekly basis, the OBN allocates primary/direct bandwidth on the link between the OBN and the DBN to *VNET-i*, which is referred to as *VTeng-i*. The OBN automatically computes the *VTeng-i* bandwidth allocations once a week. A different allocation is used for each of 36 two-hour load set periods: 12 weekday, 12 Saturday, and 12 Sunday. The allocation of the bandwidth is based on a rolling average of the traffic load for each of the VNETs, to each DBN, in each of the 36 load set periods. *VTeng-i* is based on average traffic levels and is the minimum guaranteed bandwidth for *VNET-i*, but if *VNET-i* is meeting its *GOS-i* traffic loss probability objective, other VNETs are free to share the *VTeng-i* bandwidth allotted to it.

Node *OBN-j* uses the quantities *VTtraf-i, CIP-i, NNi*, and *VTeng-i* to dynamically allocate link bandwidth to VNETs. Under normal nontraffic-loss network conditions, all VNETs fully share all available capacity. Because of this, the network has the flexibility to carry a traffic overload between two nodes for one VNET if the traffic loads for other VNETs are sufficiently below their design levels. An extreme traffic overload between two nodes for one VNET may cause connections for other VNETs to be lost, in which case link capacity is reserved to ensure that each VNET gets the amount of bandwidth allotted. This reservation during times of overload results in network performance that is analogous to having link capacity between the two nodes dedicated for each VNET.

As shown in Figure 8.7, sharing of bandwidth on the direct link is implemented by allowing connections on *VNET-i* to always seize capacity on the primary/direct path if the connections in progress *CIP-i* are below the level *VTeng-i*. However, if *CIP-i* is equal to or greater than *VTeng-i*, connections on *VNET-i* can seize capacity on the primary/direct path only when the idle-link bandwidth (ILBW) on the path is greater

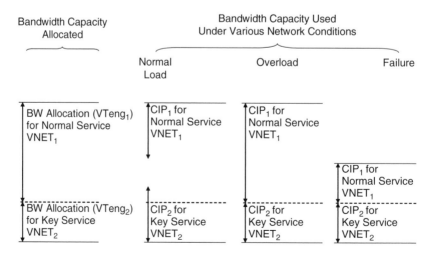

Figure 8.7 Bandwidth allocation, protection, and priority routing.

than the bandwidth reserved by other VNETs that are not meeting their traffic loss probability objectives.

As in RTNR/COS, key services in RINR/COS are given preferential treatment on the primary/direct path, on which the reserved bandwidth *RBWeng* is kept separately for key VNETs, as well as for all VNETs. For key VNETs, if *CIP-i* < *VTeng-i*, then an idle VT on the direct engineered path can always be seized. An additional restriction, however, is imposed in selecting primary/direct path capacity for connections for normal services. That is, if *CIP-i* < *VTeng-i*, then we select a VT on the primary/direct path only if

$$ILBW \geq r\text{-}i + RBWeng \text{(key VNETs)}$$

This additional restriction allows preferential treatment for key services, especially under network failures in which there is insufficient capacity to complete all connections, which is illustrated in Figure 8.7.

For key services, connections can be routed on heavily loaded paths if

$$CIP\text{-}i < \max(VT\min\text{-}i, DEPTHHL\text{-}i \times VTeng\text{-}i)$$

and on reserved paths if

$$CIP\text{-}i < \max(VT\min\text{-}i, DEPTHR\text{-}i \times VTeng\text{-}i)$$

where *DEPTHHL-i* and *DEPTHR-i* are fixed lower bounds on the depth factors *DEPTHhl-i* and *DEPTHr-i* and *VT*min-*i* is a fixed lower bound on key service search depth. Here again, key services are given preferential treatment, but only up to a maximum level of key service traffic. This choking mechanism for selecting via path capacity is necessary to limit the total capacity actually allocated to key service traffic.

In general, greater search depth is allowed if traffic loss is detected from an OBN to a DBN because more alternate path choices serve to reduce the traffic loss rate. If there is no primary/direct path capacity or the node-to-area traffic is small, say with *VTtraf-i* less than 15 VTs, then the search depth is again increased because bandwidth reservation becomes ineffective or even impossible and greater dependence on alternate routing is needed to meet network traffic loss probability objectives. The key service protection mechanism provides an effective network capability for service protection. A constraint is that key service traffic should be a relatively small fraction (preferably less than 20%) of total network traffic. As in RTNR/COS, the provisioning of COS routing logic for new services can be flexibly supported via the RINR/COS administrative process, without node software development, new hardware development, or new network implementation.

Link capability (LC) selection allows connections to be routed on specific transmission bandwidth that has the particular characteristics required by these connections.

In general, a connection can require, prefer, or avoid a set of transmission characteristics such as fiber optic or radio transmission, satellite or terrestrial transmission, or compressed or uncompressed transmission. The LC selection requirements for the connection can be determined by the service identity (SI) of the connection. The LC selection logic allows the connection to skip links that have undesired characteristics and to seek a best match for the requirements of the connection. For any SI, a set of LC selection preferences may be specified. If an LC is required for a connection, then any link that does not have that characteristic is skipped. If a characteristic is preferred, links with that characteristic are used first. Links without the preferred characteristic will be used next, but only if no links with the preferred characteristic are available. For example, if the absence of satellite is required, then only links with Satellite = No are used. If we prefer the absence of satellite, then links with Satellite = No are used first and then links with Satellite = Yes.

The simulation model is used to compare network performance under hierarchical (HIER) routing, which was the prior method of operation, and RINR/COS, which replaced hierarchical routing. A full-scale network model of the Pacific Rim network is used for the study. The model is simulated for a variety of traffic conditions to include average-day traffic, Chinese New Year and Christmas day peak traffic, and network failure scenarios. Under the Chinese New Year peak traffic condition, the network is very heavily congested and network capacity is used to nearly its maximum extent. As illustrated in Table 8.7, the RINR/COS strategy makes a substantial improvement in network performance across all service categories, and across a wide variation in key service traffic, compared with the previous HIER network.

The actual performance of the international RINR/COS network during a Chinese New Year traffic overload agreed well with these simulation model predictions and confirmed the improved performance of RINR/COS. Table 8.8 compares the performance of international traffic between the United States and China during the Chinese New Year celebration for (a) HIER international routing plus HIER domestic routing without multiple ingress/egress routing (MIER), (b) HIER plus RTNR/MIER, and (c) RINR/COS plus RTNR/MIER. Results represent actual performance measurements over the period during which the international routing methods were upgraded to RTNR/MIER and then to RINR/COS. Over this period, traffic levels generally increased.

Table 8.7 Network Traffic Loss Rate Performance Comparison for DNHR and RTNR Multiple Ingress–Egress Routing (MIER) Chinese New Year (February 3–5, 1991; February 14–16, 1992)

Day of Chinese New Year	DNHR (1991)	RTNR/MIER (1992)
Day 1	73.2	31.6
Day 2	44.6	6.0
Day 3	6.0	.0
Average traffic loss rate	53.6	19.3

Table 8.8 Chinese New Year Estimated Traffic Loss Rate Performance

Virtual network	HIER + RTNR/MIER	RINR/COS + RTNR/MIER
Out voice	34.5	.3
In voice	35.5	3.2
Out key	35.5	.0
Overall	35.2	2.5

Table 8.9 Network Traffic Loss Rate Performance Comparison for Chinese New Year: HIER + HIER, HIER + RTNR/MIER, and RINR/COS + RTNR/MIER

Virtual network	HIER (1991)	HIER + RTNR/MIER (1992)	RINR/COS + RTNR/MIER (1996)
Voice	73.2	31.6	.7
Key voice	—	—	.0
Average	73.2	31.6	.7

We see from these results the considerable improvement in the network performance following the introduction of RTNR/MIER and then RINR/COS for Chinese New Year traffic. The predicted performance for HIER plus RTNR/MIER, as given in Table 8.8, is comparable to actual HIER plus RTNR/MIER performance, as shown in Table 8.9. It is also clear that key service protection provides essentially zero traffic loss rate, even under the most severe overload conditions in the network. Hence, as routing flexibility increased, network performance substantially improved for the benefit of customers and increased profitability of the network.

We have presented a case study that illustrates the protocol design and optimization of RINR/COS, a representative voice/ISDN internetwork TQO protocol. Once again, this case study illustrates TQO protocol design principles of class-of-service derivation, determining network status, determining link load states, allocating traffic to primary and alternate paths, and achieving objectives for integrated network services. Several of the important conclusions from the first case study are reinforced for internetwork TQO protocol design:

- COS routing provides a means to avoid software development, hardware development, and new network deployment for each new service
- quantification of network status can have a significant effect on network performance
- derivation of network status can be efficiently accomplished
- bandwidth reservation is critical to ensuring efficient and stable network performance

- alternate routing use and control are essential to ensuring efficient and stable network performance
- service objectives can be achieved for individual network services on an integrated voice/data dynamic TQO network

We now present two case studies that show how violation of these TQO protocol design principles can have a possibly severe detrimental effect on network performance.

8.4 Case Studies: Examples of Alternate Routing Contributing to Network Congestion

Here we illustrate two examples of where alternate routing and lack of bandwidth reservation may have contributed to network congestion. These examples are intended to illustrate possible pitfalls of excessive alternate routing and the need for careful consideration of protection techniques, primarily the need for bandwidth reservation methods in these examples, to guard against excessive alternate routing.

A software problem crippled the AT&T long-distance network on January 15, 1990, when a software problem in the signaling network prevented millions of connections from being completed. The problem affected all 114 of AT&T's 4ESS nodes and resulted in the loss of about half of the long-distance, international, software-defined network and toll-free 800 connections on AT&T's voice/ISDN network. The software error was corrected and full service was restored after about 9 h: the disruption began at 2:25 PM EST and was not resolved until about 11:30 PM. The problem, which began in a New York City node, quickly spread through AT&T's signaling network, causing nodes throughout the network to shut down. A software upgrade designed to restore service more quickly and improve network reliability was loaded into the 4ESS nodes and caused the disruption.

The problem began when a piece of equipment in the New York node developed problems, which caused the New York node to send a congestion control message to all the other nodes it is linked with that it was not accepting additional traffic during the recovery from the problem. After the successful recovery, the New York node went back in service and began processing connections. With the new software, the reappearance of traffic from the New York node is supposed to tell other nodes (say node B) that the NY node is working again. Node B then resets its internal logic to indicate that NY is back in service. The problem occurred when node B got a second connection-attempt message from NY while it was in the process of resetting its internal logic. The second signaling message confused the software (a bug in the program), which tried to execute an instruction that didn't make any sense, so node B shut itself down to avoid spreading the problem. Unfortunately, node B then sent a message to other nodes that it was out of service and wasn't accepting additional traffic. Once node B reset itself and began operating again, it sent out connection processing messages via the signaling link, which caused identical failures around the network as other nodes got second messages from node B while they were in the process of resetting their internal logic to indicate that node B was working again. It was a chain reaction: any node that was connected to B was put into the same condition. The event just repeated itself in every node over and over again. If the nodes hadn't gotten a second message while resetting, there would have been no problem. If the messages had been received farther apart, it would not have triggered the problem. AT&T solved the problem by reducing the messaging load on the signaling network, which allowed the nodes to reset themselves properly and the network to stabilize.

At the time of the failure, DNHR logic was being used in the network, just prior to the replacement of DNHR by RTNR. DNHR logic could use several alternate routing paths, called "engineered paths," which were not protected by bandwidth reservation techniques. As shown in Chapter 3, bandwidth reservation is essential under congestion to curtail alternate routing to favor use of primary/direct paths rather than alternate paths. It is possible, although not verified, that excessive use of engineered paths could have contributed to excessive alternate routing connection attempts, which in turn resulted in nodes resetting themselves, as described earlier, during this highly unusual failure condition. A network management control called "selective trunk reservation" [ASH98] could have been used to initiate bandwidth reservation on engineered DNHR paths and would have significantly curtailed alternate routing during the incident. Unfortunately, this control was not initiated during the failure so it is unclear if this control would have helped stabilize the network.

A second example involves link selection capability routing (LSCR), which was developed in the mid-1990s. LSCR allowed avoidance of a network voice enhancement feature called "TrueVoice" because certain analog data connections (e.g., fax) could be degraded by the TrueVoice enhancement algorithms. Links were selectively implemented in the network that did not have the TrueVoice feature, and the LSCR routing algorithm automatically selected these links for connections designed to avoid the feature. In particular, bandwidth reservation and protection from unstable network behavior (as described in Chapter 3) were not used for the TrueVoice avoidance connections because these were initially a very small subset of all connections. That is, TrueVoice avoidance connections had full access, without bandwidth reservation being imposed, to all direct and alternate path capacity that provided the TrueVoice avoidance capability. Over time, however, the level of TrueVoice avoidance traffic grew to a point where some transient congestion and unstable behavior could be caused by overusing alternate two-link paths in the network. This phenomenon is described in Chapter 3 and is illustrated in this chapter with the case study of RTNR/COS TQO protocol design. Soon thereafter, TrueVoice was retired in the network and the LSCR avoidance feature became unnecessary.

We have given two case studies that illustrate how violation of TQO protocol design principles can have a possibly severe detrimental effect on network performance. One case involved a software problem that crippled the AT&T long-distance network on January 15, 1990, and a second that involved a new routing capability to avoid a voice enhancement capability in the network. In particular, two design principles came into focus in these examples:

- bandwidth reservation is critical to ensuring efficient and stable network performance
- alternate routing use and control are essential to ensuring efficient and stable network performance

These examples are intended to illustrate possible pitfalls of excessive alternate routing and the need for bandwidth reservation methods to guard against excessive alternate routing. In both cases cited, proper use of bandwidth reservation may well have helped alleviate the problems that occurred. As such, these case studies provide learning for us all, i.e., none of us is a know it all, not the Geekians nor the Telephonians, even though at times we both claim to be.

In Chapter 9 we present the case study of TQO protocol design for integrated voice/data IP/MPLS-GMPLS-based networks. Here again we illustrate the application of the TQO protocol design principles to this case study as with the case studies presented in this chapter.

8.5 Applicability of Requirements

Sophisticated, on-line, TQO routing methods are widely deployed in TDM networks, such as RTNR/COS and RINR/COS discussed in the first two case studies. The GTQO protocol described in Chapter 10 incorporates capabilities learned from the case studies in this chapter, as follows:

- COS routing capabilities for service flexibility and multiservice VNET bandwidth allocation
- CAC, source-based path selection, crankback, for bandwidth allocation to COSs/VNETs
- load state mapping, bandwidth reservation techniques for stable performance, and bandwidth sharing
- dynamic connection routing, priority routing for efficient utilization, and reduced routing overhead
- meet performance objectives for integrated COSs

As illustrated in the case studies, there is an opportunity for increased profitability and performance through application of the TQO design principles and GTQO protocol. These and other results presented support the service provider requirements for the GTQO protocol, which should be used to drive standards and vendor implementations in the direction of network operator requirements and vendor interoperability.

Service providers and their customers would benefit from these capabilities in terms of service quality, automation, network reliability, and performance. Vendors would benefit by service provider adoption of these features, if developed in their products. That sounds like a win–win scenario to me.

Chapter 9

Case Studies 2: Traffic Engineering and QoS Optimization for Operational Integrated Voice/Data Dynamic Routing Networks

9.1 Introduction

This chapter continues with the case studies presented in Chapter 8 of TQO protocol design of integrated voice/data dynamic routing protocols. In Chapter 8 we presented four case studies for TQO protocol design: (a) circuit-switched integrated voice/data dynamic routing networks for intradomain routing, (b) circuit-switched integrated voice/data dynamic routing networks for internetwork routing, and (c) two case studies of designs that went astray, but at the same time provided valuable lessons for future designs. In this chapter we present a case study of MPLS/GMPLS-based integrated voice/data dynamic routing networks.

In this final case study, we develop a 71-node national network model and multiservice traffic demand model for the TQO protocol design in an MPLS/GMPLS-based integrated voice/data dynamic routing network. We again use discrete event simulation models to illustrate the design and optimization of this large-scale, state-dependent TQO protocol, which allows the integration of a number of voice and data VNETs, called DiffServ-aware MPLS TE (DSTE) class types (CTs) in this technology, on an integrated shared packet network, with sophisticated bandwidth allocation/management capabilities. The routing and capacity designs for the meshed logical topologies are optimized by using the DEFO algorithm, while the routing and capacity designs for the sparse logical topologies are optimized by using the shortest path optimization and DEFO algorithms presented in Chapter 6. A 5 CT traffic model is developed and three levels of traffic priority—high, normal, and best-effort—are designated for each CT. First we illustrate the selection of an EDR-based path selection protocol from among a large set of candidates. Then, five options are defined for the TQO bandwidth management protocol, which are compared in the case study. These options include various connection admission control (CAC), bandwidth allocation/management, and queuing approaches.

The modeling and simulation analysis shows a 10–15% reduction in loss/delay for voice traffic and up to a 5–20% reduction in loss/delay for data traffic for the preferred MPLS/GMPLS-based option compared to the other options. Routing design parameters are optimized for the preferred option by using the simulation models, and these parameters include (a) level of reserved capacity (varied from 0 to 10% of link capacity), (b) number of allowed primary and alternate paths (varied from 2 to 10 paths), and (c) algorithm for increasing and decreasing VNET bandwidth allocation, where various models are studied and compared.

GTQO requirements presented in Chapter 10 are in part the outcome of the case study discussed in this chapter. Geekian protocols—MPLS, DiffServ, DSTE, RSVP, NSIS, and others—are central to the GTQO protocol requirements, and Telephonian networking principles—bandwidth reservation, alternate routing, capacity design, and others—are included as well based on the results of these case studies, operational experience, and analysis presented throughout the book. Dancing in the aisles starts again here!

We illustrate the application of the TQO protocol design principles to the case study in this chapter as with the previous case studies presented in Chapter 8:

- COS routing capabilities for service flexibility and multiservice VNET bandwidth allocation
- CAC, source-based path selection, crankback, for bandwidth allocation to COSs/VNETs
- load state mapping, bandwidth reservation techniques for stable performance, and bandwidth sharing
- dynamic connection routing, priority routing, EDR path selection for efficient utilization, and reduced routing overhead
- queuing priority mechanisms for COS differentiation
- meet performance objectives for integrated COSs

I think you'll find this final case study very interesting, and once we're through with that let's wrap up the book in Chapter 10 with the summary, conclusions, GTQO protocol requirements, and the long-awaited Geekia/Telephonia unification treaty.

9.2 Case Study: TQO Protocol Design of MPLS/GMPLS-Based Integrated Voice/Data Dynamic Routing Network

Packet-switched data networks typically use link-state, or shortest-path-first (SPF), distributed-database routing protocols and, as discussed in Chapter 1, are classified as DP-SDR protocols. Networks are rapidly evolving to carry all voice/data services on converged, packet-switched, IP/MPLS-based networks, driven in part by the extremely rapid growth of IP-based data services. Here a converged, multiservice network refers to one in which various class types (CTs) share the transmission, connection/transport switching, management, and other resources of the network. Note that CTs are equivalent to VNETs in the previous case studies. As mentioned in the introduction, CTs are defined in DiffServ-aware MPLS TE (DSTE) technology, and we chose to use the Geekia-originated jargon in this case study because DSTE is quite central to the analysis in this case study. Geekian jargon is good anyway; Geekians just love to make up clever acronyms, especially for their IETF working groups (SPEERMINT, CRISP, SIEVE, MAGMA, DIME, SIPPING, SIMPLE, FORCES, BEHAVE, etc.). There is no end to their creativity.

As with VNETs, CTs can include various groupings/aggregations of services, including CBR voice, VoIP, high-priority VoIP, VBR data, and best-effort data. There are quantitative performance objectives that CTs need to meet, such as end-to-end traffic loss rate, delay, and delay-jitter objectives. These objectives are achieved through a combination of TQO, traffic management, and capacity management capabilities.

The TQO methods based on the EDR and SDR dynamic routing protocols illustrated in Figure 9.1 are shown in this case study to be extensible to integrated voice/data TQO networks, particularly to IP/MPLS technology. In the integrated voice/data TQO protocol design and optimization, we illustrate the trade-offs between these various approaches and show that (a) aggregated per-CT network bandwidth allocation compares favorably with per-flow allocation and (b) EDR methods perform just as well or better than SDR methods with flooding, which means that EDR path selection has the potential to enhance network scalability significantly.

The principles and lessons from the case studies presented in Chapter 8 are applied to this case study, and, in particular, the conclusions and results of this case study are directly applied to the GTQO protocol requirements presented in Chapter 10. Vendors have yet to announce such GTQO capabilities in their products, however. Current practice often involves overprovisioning of IP networks, thereby avoiding the need for more efficient TQO capabilities, but with concomitant low utilization and efficiency [ODLYZKO03]. Consistent with Odlyzko's analysis, Meddeb [MEDDEB05] concludes that in order to support QoS in IP networks, "average network utilization should be kept low, typically less than 30 percent, while for ATM and frame relay up to 80 percent utilization can be reached ... despite some IP QoS features including DiffServ and RSVP." There is therefore an opportunity for increased profitability and performance in IP/MPLS-based networks through application of these TQO principles

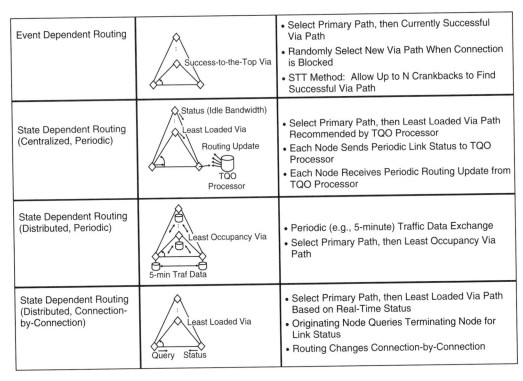

Figure 9.1 EDR and SDR dynamic path selection methods.

and methods, as in the GTQO protocol described in Chapter 10 based on these case studies.

There is not an extensive literature on this emerging topic as yet, which is still under development. Awduche [AWDUCHE99, RFC3272] gives excellent overviews of TQO approaches for IP-based networks and also provides traffic engineering requirements [RFC2702]. Crawley [RFC2386] and Xiao [XIAO99] provide good background and context for TQO in the Internet. A few early implementations of off-line, network management-based TQO approaches have been published, such as in the Global Crossing network [XIAO00a], Level3 network [LEVEL3-TE], and Cable & Wireless network [CABLE-WIRELESS-TE]. Some studies have proposed more elaborate TQO approaches in IP networks [APOSTOLOPOULOS99, ELWALID01, MA98, XIAO00b], as well as in ATM networks [AHMADI92].

In this final, grand-finale case study, we develop a large-scale, 71-node, integrated voice/data IP/MPLS network model and multiservice traffic demand model for the TQO protocol design. We again use discrete event simulation models to illustrate the design and optimization of this large-scale, state-dependent TQO protocol on an integrated shared packet network, with sophisticated bandwidth allocation/management capabilities. These discrete event simulation models accurately capture nonlinear and complex behavior to optimize the TQO protocol from among a wide range of candidate TQO methods. A 5 DSTE-CT traffic model is developed, and three levels of traffic priority—high, normal, and best-effort—are designated for each CT.

First we review the work in Chapter 2 to determine an optimal path selection method for IP/MPLS-based, integrated voice/data, dynamic routing/TQO protocols. We illustrate the selection of an STT-EDR protocol from among a large set of candidates based on extensive comparisons of TDR, EDR, and SDR methods. Then, five options are defined for the TQO bandwidth management and QoS optimization protocol, which are compared in the case study. These options include various admission control, bandwidth allocation/management, and queuing approaches. We find that a DSTE protocol and maximum allocation with reservation (MAR) bandwidth allocation model perform best from among many candidate methods. This DSTE/MAR approach also incorporates the STT-EDR path selection protocol.

We then use the simulation model to optimize the performance of the DSTE/MAR/STT-EDR protocol within the design trade-offs, which include the level of reserved capacity, the number of allowed alternate paths, and the algorithm for increasing and decreasing the CT bandwidth allocation. The modeling and simulation analysis shows a 10–15% reduction in loss/delay for voice traffic and up to a 5–20% reduction in loss/delay for data traffic for the preferred MPLS/GMPLS-based option compared to the other options.

The GTQO protocol requirements in Chapter 10 are based largely on the results and conclusions of this case study, and also on the TQO design principles used in the case studies in Chapter 8 and this chapter.

9.3   Optimization of TQO Path Selection Protocol

In Chapter 2 we use discrete event simulation models to optimize the integrated voice/data TQO path selection protocol from among a wide range of candidates, including TDR, EDR, and SDR methods. An STT-EDR path selection protocol is selected from this initial optimization study, and we then use the simulation model to optimize the performance of the STT-EDR protocol within the design trade-offs. The integrated voice/data TQO path selection protocol is optimized for these design trade-offs, among others:

- logical topology (sparse, mesh)
- connection routing method (two-link, multilink, SDR, EDR, etc.)
- bandwidth allocation method (aggregated/per CT, per flow)
- QoS (number of queues, high/normal/best-effort priority treatment, etc.)

Generally the meshed logical topologies typical of TDM-based networks are optimized by one- and two-link routing, while the sparse logical topologies typical of packet-switched networks are optimized by multilink shortest-path routing. Comparative analysis of the candidate integrated voice/data TQO protocols leads to the following conclusions:

- EDR connection routing methods exhibit comparable design efficiencies to SDR routing methods.
- Sparse topology designs with multilink shortest-path routing (MSPR) provide better connection/transport switching and transport design efficiencies in comparison to mesh designs with two-link routing.
- Per-CT bandwidth allocation exhibits comparable design efficiencies to per-flow bandwidth allocation.

Figure 9.2 illustrates an integrated voice/data TQO model in which bandwidth is allocated on an aggregated basis to the individual CTs. In the model, CTs have different priorities, including high-priority, normal-priority, and best-effort priority services CTs. Bandwidth allocated to each CT is protected by bandwidth reservation methods, as needed, but bandwidth is otherwise shared among CTs. Each ON monitors CT bandwidth use on each CT LSP, which is enabled by MPLS technology [RFC3031],

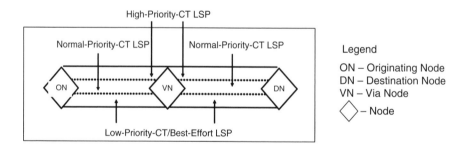

- ❏ distributed bandwidth allocation method applied on a per-class-type (CT) LSP basis
- ❏ ON allocates bandwidth to each CT LSP based on demand
  - ❖ ON decides CT LSP bandwidth increase based on
    - − link bandwidth-in-progress (BWIP)
    - − routing priority (high, normal, best-effort)
    - − link bandwidth allocation for CT (link bandwidth constraint BC)
    - − link reserved bandwidth RBW
  - ❖ ON periodically decreases CT LSP bandwidth allocation based on bandwidth use
- ❏ nodes keep local link state of idle link bandwidth (ILBW), including available bandwidth (ABW) and reserved bandwidth (RBW) states
- ❏ VNs send crankback message to ON if DSTE-MAR bandwidth allocation rules not met

Figure 9.2 Per-class type (CT) LSP bandwidth management.

and determines when the CT LSP bandwidth needs to be increased or decreased. In Figure 9.2, changes in CT bandwidth capacity are determined by ONs based on an overall aggregated bandwidth demand for CT capacity (not on a per-connection/per-flow demand basis). Based on the aggregated bandwidth demand, ONs make periodic discrete changes in bandwidth allocation, i.e., either increase or decrease bandwidth on the LSPs constituting the CT bandwidth capacity. For example, if connection requests are made for a CT LSP bandwidth that exceeds the current LSP bandwidth allocation, the ON initiates a bandwidth modification request on the appropriate LSP(s), which may entail increasing the current LSP bandwidth allocation by a discrete increment of bandwidth denoted here as delta bandwidth (*DBW*). *DBW*, for example, could be the additional amount needed by the current connection request. In any case, *DBW* is a large enough bandwidth change so that CT bandwidth modification requests are made relatively infrequently. The bandwidth admission control for each link in the path is performed based on the status of the link using the bandwidth allocation procedure described later in this section, where we further describe the role of the different parameters such as reserved bandwidth RBW shown in Figure 9.2 in the admission control procedure. Also, the ON periodically monitors LSP bandwidth use, such as once each minute, and if bandwidth use falls below the current LSP allocation, the ON initiates a bandwidth modification request to decrease the LSP bandwidth allocation, e.g., down to the current level of bandwidth utilization.

In making a CT bandwidth allocation modification, the ON determines the CT priority (high, normal, or best-effort), CT bandwidth in use, and CT bandwidth allocation thresholds. These parameters are used to determine whether network capacity can be allocated for the CT bandwidth modification request. In the simulation models, path selection takes different forms for the following cases:

- Two-link STT-EDR: Paths are limited to one or two links, with STT-EDR path selection and a meshed network design model.
- Two-link DC-SDR: Paths are limited to one or two links, with DC-SDR path selection and a meshed network design model.
- Multilink STT-EDR: Shortest paths of an arbitrary number of links can be used, with STT-EDR path selection and a sparse network design model.
- Multilink DC-SDR: Shortest paths of an arbitrary number of links can be used, with DC-SDR path selection and a sparse network design model.
- Multilink DP-SDR: Shortest paths of an arbitrary number of links can be used, with DP-SDR path selection and a sparse network design model.

Figure 9.3 illustrates the operation of STT-EDR path selection and admission control combined with per-CT bandwidth allocation. ON A monitors CT bandwidth use on each CT LSP and determines when the CT LSP bandwidth needs to be increased or decreased. Based on the bandwidth demand, ON A makes periodic discrete changes in bandwidth allocation, i.e., either increase or decrease bandwidth on the LSPs constituting the CT bandwidth capacity. If connection requests are made for CT LSP bandwidth that exceeds the current LSP bandwidth allocation, ON A initiates

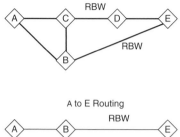

Example of STT-EDR routing method:
1. if node A to node E bandwidth needs to be modified (say increased by DBW) primary LSP-p (e.g., LSP A-B-E) is tried first
2. available bandwidth tested locally on each link in LSP-p, if bandwidth not available (e.g., link BE is in reserved RBW state & this CT is above its bandwidth allocation), crankback to node A
3. if DBW is not available on one or more links of LSP-p, then the currently successful LSP-s (e.g., LSP A-C-D-E) is tried next
4. if DBW is not available on one or more links of LSP-s, then a new LSP is searched by trying additional candidate paths until a new successful LSP-n is found or the candidate paths are exhausted
5. LSP-n is then marked as the currently successful path for the next time bandwidth needs to be modified

Figure 9.3 STT-EDR path selection and per-CT bandwidth allocation.

a bandwidth modification request on the appropriate LSP(s). The STT-EDR TQO algorithm used is adaptive and distributed in nature and uses learning models to find good paths.

For example, in Figure 9.3 if the LSR-A to LSR-E bandwidth needs to be modified, say increased by *DBW*, the primary LSP-p (A–B–E) is tried first. The bandwidth admission control for each link in the path is performed based on the status of the link using the bandwidth allocation procedure described later in this section, where we further describe the role of the reserved bandwidth RBW shown in Figure 9.3 in the admission control procedure. If the first choice LSP cannot admit the bandwidth change, node A may then try an alternate LSP. If *DBW* is not available on one or more links of LSP-p, then the currently successful LSP-s A–C–D–E (the "STT path") is tried next. If *DBW* is not available on one or more links of LSP-s, then a new LSP is searched by trying additional candidate paths (not shown) until a new successful LSP-n is found or the candidate paths are exhausted. LSP-n is then marked as the currently successful path for the next time bandwidth needs to be modified. *DBW*, for example, can be set to the additional amount of bandwidth required by the connection request. Also, ON A periodically monitors LSP bandwidth use, such as once each minute, and if bandwidth use falls below the current LSP allocation, the ON initiates a bandwidth modification request to decrease the LSP bandwidth allocation down to the currently used bandwidth level. In the models discussed next, the per-CT bandwidth allocation and admission control method compares favorably with the per-flow method, and the STT-EDR path selection method compares favorably with the SDR methods.

In the model of DP-SDR, the status updates with link-status flooding occur every 10 s. Note that the multilink DP-SDR performance results should also be comparable to the performance of multilink CP-SDR, in which status updates and path selection updates are made every 10 s, respectively, to and from a TQO processor. With the SDR methods, the available link bandwidth information in the topology database is used to generate the shortest, least-congested paths. In routing a connection, the ON checks the equivalent bandwidth and available load state on the first-choice path, then on the currently successful alternate path (EDR) or least-loaded shortest path (SDR), and then sequentially on all other candidate alternate paths. Each VN checks the equivalent bandwidth and available load state and uses crankback to the ON if the equivalent bandwidth or allowed load-state threshold are not met.

Based on a 135-node model, performance comparisons are presented in Table 9.1 for the various integrated voice/data TQO methods, including two-link and multilink EDR and SDR approaches, and a baseline case of no TQO or bandwidth allocation methods is applied. Table 9.1 gives performance results for a six-times overload on a single network node at Oakbrook, IL (OKBK). The numbers in Table 9.1 indicate the percentage of traffic lost in the admission control, in which case all paths have insufficient capacity, plus the percentage of traffic delayed in the queues. Note that on high rate links, traffic delayed in the queues will almost always be dropped/lost, as shown in the case of a "bufferless" model [BONALD02]. The performance analysis results show that the multilink options in sparse topologies perform somewhat better under overloads than the two-link options in meshed topologies because of greater sharing of network capacity. Under failure, the two-link options perform better for many of the CT categories than the multilink options because they have a richer

Table 9.1 Performance Comparison for Various TQO Methods for 6× Focused Overload on OKBK (% Lost/Delayed Traffic)

Class type	Mesh two-link STT-EDR	Mesh two-link DC-SDR	Sparse multilink STT-EDR	Sparse multilink DC-SDR	Sparse multilink DP-SDR	No TQO methods applied
Normal-priority voice	5.93	2.86	0.00	0.12	0.14	10.81
High-priority voice	0.81	1.77	0.00	0.00	0.00	8.47
Normal-priority data	7.12	3.49	0.00	2.75	3.18	12.88
High-priority data	0.00	0.00	0.00	0.00	0.00	0.46
Best-effort data	14.07	14.68	12.46	12.39	12.32	9.75

choice of alternate routing paths and are much more highly connected than the multilink networks. Loss of a link in a sparely connected multilink network can have more serious consequences than in more highly connected logical networks. The performance results illustrate that capacity sharing of different traffic class types, when combined with TQO and priority queuing, leads to efficient use of bandwidth with minimal traffic delay and loss impact, even under overload and failure scenarios.

The EDR and SDR path selection methods are quite comparable for the two-link, meshed-topology network scenarios. However, the EDR path selection method performs somewhat better than the SDR options in the multilink, sparse-topology case. In addition, the DC-SDR path selection option performs somewhat better than the DP-SDR option in the multilink case, which is a result of the 10-s-old status information causing misdirected paths in some cases. Hence, it can be concluded that frequently updated, available-link-bandwidth state information does not necessarily improve performance in all cases, and that if available-link-bandwidth state information is used, it is sometimes better that it is very recent status information.

Some of the conclusions from the performance comparisons for integrated voice/data TQO path selection protocol optimization are as follows:

- TQO methods result in network performance that is always better and usually substantially better than when no TQO methods are applied.
- Sparse-topology multilink-routing networks provide better overall performance under overload than meshed-topology networks, but performance under failure may favor the two-link meshed-topology options with more alternate routing choices.
- EDR TQO methods exhibit comparable or better network performance compared to SDR methods.
- State information as used by the SDR options (such as with link-state flooding) provides essentially equivalent performance to the EDR options, which typically use distributed routing with crankback and no flooding.
- Single-area flat topologies exhibit better network performance in comparison with multiarea hierarchical topologies.
- Bandwidth reservation is critical to the stable and efficient performance of TQO methods in a network and to ensure the proper operation of integrated voice/data bandwidth allocation, protection, and priority treatment.
- Per-CT bandwidth allocation is essentially equivalent to per-flow bandwidth allocation in network performance and efficiency. Because of the much lower routing table management overhead, per-CT bandwidth allocation is preferred to per-flow allocation.
- CAC with MPLS bandwidth management and DiffServ queuing priority [RFC2475] are important for ensuring that integrated voice/data network performance objectives are met under a range of network conditions. Both mechanisms operate together to enable bandwidth allocation, protection, and priority queuing.

Regarding the final point, in an integrated voice/data TQO network where high-priority, normal-priority, and best-effort traffic share the same network, under congestion the DiffServ priority-queuing mechanisms push out the best-effort priority traffic at the queues so that the normal-priority and high-priority traffic can get through on the MPLS-allocated LSP bandwidth.

Table 9.2 gives a comparison of the control overhead performance of (a) DP-SDR with topology state flooding and per-flow bandwidth allocation, (b) STT-EDR with per-flow bandwidth allocation, and (c) STT-EDR with per-CT bandwidth allocation. The numbers in Table 9.2 give the total messages of each type needed to do the indicated TQO functions, including flow setup, bandwidth allocation, crankback, and topology state flooding to update the topology database. The DP-SDR method does available-link-bandwidth flooding to update the topology database while the EDR method does not. In the simulation there is a six-times focused overload on the Oakbrook node. Clearly the DP-SDR/flooding method is consuming more message resources, particularly LSA flooding messages, than the STT-EDR method. Also, the per-flow bandwidth allocation is consuming far more LSP bandwidth allocation messages than per-CT bandwidth allocation, while the traffic lost/delayed performance of the three methods is comparable.

Some of the conclusions from the comparisons of routing table management overhead are as follows:

- Per-CT bandwidth allocation is preferred to per-flow allocation because of the much lower routing table management overhead. Per-CT bandwidth allocation is essentially equivalent to per-flow bandwidth allocation in network performance and efficiency.
- EDR methods provide a large reduction in flooding overhead without loss of network throughput performance. Flooding is very resource intensive, as it requires link bandwidth to carry topology state messages, processor capacity to process topology state messages, and the overhead limits autonomous system size. EDR methods therefore can help increase network scalability.

Table 9.2 Routing Table Management Overhead; SDR/Flooding/Per-Flow, EDR/Per-Flow, EDR/Per-CT (6× Focused Overload on OKBK)

DR function	Message type	DP-SDR flooding (per-flow bandwidth allocation)	STT-EDR (per-flow bandwidth allocation)	STT-EDR (per-CT bandwidth allocation)
Flow routing	Flow setup	18,758,992	18,758,992	18,758,992
LSP routing, bandwidth allocation, queue management	LSP bandwidth allocation	18,469,477	18,839,216	2,889,488
	Crankback	30,459	12,850	14,867
Topology database update	LSA	14,405,040		

STT-EDR path selection, which entails the use of the crankback mechanism to search for an available path, is in sharp contrast to SDR path selection, which may entail flooding of frequently changing link state parameters such as available-link-bandwidth. With EDR path selection, the reduction in the frequency of such link-state parameter flooding allows for increased scalability. This is because link-state flooding can consume substantial processor and link resources, in terms of message processing by the processors and link bandwidth consumed by messages on the links.

Figure 9.4 compares the performance of per-CT LSP bandwidth allocation and per-flow LSP bandwidth allocation and shows the lost or delayed traffic under a focused overload scenario on the Oakbrook, IL, node (such a scenario might occur, for example, with a radio call-in give-away offer). The size of the focused overload is varied from the normal load (1× case) to a 10-times overload of the traffic to Oakbrook (10× case). The results show that the per-flow and per-CT bandwidth allocation performance is similar; however, the improved performance of the high-priority traffic and normal-priority traffic in relation to the best-effort priority traffic is clearly evident.

In summary, integrated voice/data, IP/MPLS-based TQO protocol design, and optimization have been illustrated in this case study. These designs are based on results of discrete event analysis models, which illustrate the trade-offs between various TQO approaches and parameter selection. In the protocol design study, the per-CT bandwidth allocation method compares favorably with the per-flow method. Furthermore, we find that the fully distributed STT-EDR method of LSP bandwidth allocation performs just as well or better than the SDR methods with flooding, which means that STT-EDR path selection has the potential to enhance network scalability significantly.

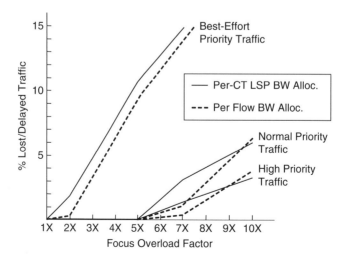

Figure 9.4 Performance under focused overload on OKBK node.

9.4 Optimization of TQO Bandwidth Management Protocol

In this section we present a simulation modeling and analysis study of the optimization of the integrated voice/data TQO bandwidth management protocol for this case study. Networks that carry real-time traffic, such as VoIP, need a CAC mechanism to reject connections when additional connections would adversely affect connections already in progress. Without QoS CAC, all VoIP connections on congested links may suffer seriously degraded quality, as shown later in the case study.

The integrated voice/data TQO bandwidth management protocol must satisfy the following requirements:

- Meet performance objectives.
- Provide a cost-effective solution for QoS that does not rely on overprovisioning.
- Give emergency service connections (e.g., GETS/ETS/E911) higher priority of completion. Emergency connections should be admitted up to a specified limit and may be allowed to degrade the QoS of connections in progress up to a performance limit, but the quality of emergency connections themselves should be maintained during high levels of network use.
- Operate across routing areas and autonomous systems boundaries.
- Interwork with partner service providers.
- Account for all traffic in allocating network bandwidth, support codecs with different bandwidth requirements, and account for header compression when used.

In the following sections we describe (a) the integrated voice/data TQO bandwidth management protocol options considered in the simulation analysis, (b) the traffic model, network design model, and simulation model used in the analysis, (c) results of the analysis, and (d) conclusions of the case study.

9.4.1 TQO Bandwidth Management Protocol Options

A basic premise of the integrated voice/data TQO bandwidth management protocol is that a properly engineered core network employing DiffServ will provide good quality voice service if the bandwidth required by the voice traffic stays within its allocation. Therefore, the integrated voice/data TQO bandwidth management protocol function is to assure that the amount of real-time traffic (e.g., VoIP) does not exceed the available bandwidth. One of the objectives of the integrated voice/data TQO bandwidth management protocol is to admit new connections only when the new connections will not adversely affect connections in progress.

A key aspect of the integrated voice/data TQO bandwidth management protocol options is the degree of resource coordination at the interface between the application layer and the IP/MPLS network layer. We considered three basic approaches: direct coordination, indirect coordination, and no coordination. Direct coordination means that signaling of a connection in the application layer would trigger control plane communication between the application layer and the IP/MPLS network layer to allocate resources. As such, direct coordination would accurately communicate real-time bandwidth demand to the IP/MPLS network layer, which could react instantaneously in its resource and bandwidth allocation. However, direct coordination would have a higher level of control plane overhead than other approaches as a result. Indirect coordination means no control plane communication between the application layer and the IP/MPLS network layer. Rather, the application and IP/MPLS layers are indirectly coordinated by the operations support system (OSS) configuring resource allocation based on forecast demands. With indirect coordination, therefore, the IP/MPLS layer would not be able to react to instantaneous deviations from the forecast traffic levels. However, control plane overhead would be lower than for indirect coordination. No coordination means no direct or indirect communication between the application layer and the IP/MPLS layer. This approach provides no ability to allocate resources according to traffic demands, but would have the least control plane overhead as a result.

In the direct coordination option studied in the simulation modeling analysis, the application layer requests bandwidth on a per-connection basis from the network layer and expects a confirmation of the ability of the network to fulfill that reservation. The IP/MPLS layer, however, allocates resources on a per-aggregate set of connections basis rather than on a per-connection basis. Aggregation within the network layer makes this direct coordination approach more scalable than per-connection resource allocation within the network layer. The latter approach was eliminated in the analysis, based on scalability limitations, and was not evaluated in the simulation study. A direct coordination approach in which the application layer requests bandwidth on a per-aggregate set of connections was also eliminated in the analysis, based on application layer complexity limitations, and was not evaluated in the simulation study.

In the indirect coordination options studied in the simulation modeling analysis, traffic forecasts are provided by the OSS and used for off-line capacity management, which includes adjusting queue bandwidth allocations, adjusting MPLS LSP bandwidth allocations, and determining the LSP primary routes and alternates routes. Packets are marked in the DiffServ code point (DSCP) field of the IP headers and in the EXP/COS field of the MPLS labels according to predefined rules. There is no control plane signaling between the application and IP/MPLS network layers. Indirect coordination based on real-time performance monitoring was not defined in detail and eliminated in the analysis and hence was not evaluated in the simulation study.

We now describe the options that were evaluated extensively within the modeling and simulation analysis study.

9.4.1.1 Option A (Direct Coordination): MSE CAC, DSTE/MAR, DiffServ/Five Queues

Referring to Figure 9.5, the basic elements considered in all the integrated voice/data TQO bandwidth management protocol options are the application layer gateway (GW), the multiservice edge (MSE) routers, and the call/session control agent (CCA). The

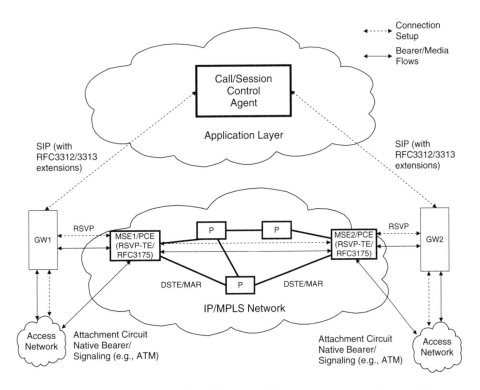

Figure 9.5 Integrated voice/data TQO bandwidth management protocol (option A).

GW implements the session initiation protocol (SIP) with preconditions (RFC 3312), allowing the integration of resource management with SIP. This allows the GW to determine whether the network has sufficient bandwidth before completing the establishment of a session initiated using SIP. One of the factors in determining whether to admit a connection is learning the IP address, port, and session parameters (such as codec bandwidth requirements) from the connection end point. An offer/answer exchange carried in SIP messages allows the initiating GW to determine this information. The GW receiving the offer does not alert the user or otherwise proceed with session establishment until both ends know that the preconditions are met.

As illustrated in Figure 9.5, option A uses direct coordination per connection. To determine whether there is sufficient bandwidth to complete a connection, the originating and destination GWs each send for each connection a resource reservation protocol (RSVP) bandwidth request to the network MSE router to which it is connected. The bandwidth request takes into account header compression, where applicable. The originating GW combines local CAC information from the MSE router with remote CAC information obtained via SIP resource management with preconditions [RFC3312], as described earlier.

The MSE then (a) determines whether there is enough bandwidth on the route between the originating and destination GWs to accommodate the connection,

(b) communicates the accept/reject decision to the GW on a connection-by-connection basis, and (c) optimizes network resources by dynamically adjusting bandwidth allocations. If a tunnel is operating near capacity, the network may dynamically adjust the tunnel size within a set of parameters. That is, the MSE maintains the per-CT tunnel capacity based on aggregated RSVP requests and responds on a connection-by-connection basis based on the available capacity. The MSE can periodically adjust the tunnel capacity upward, when needed, and periodically adjust the tunnel capacity downward, when spare capacity exists in the tunnel.

In option A, the OSS provisions DSTE [RFC3564] tunnels between the MSEs based on the traffic forecast and current network utilization. These guaranteed bandwidth DSTE tunnels are created using RSVP-TE [RFC3209] and apply the DSTE/MAR [RFC4124, RFC4126] bandwidth constraints model to determine tunnel bandwidth allocation. These DSTE tunnels are engineered and provisioned by the OSS based on the forecasted traffic load and, when needed, the tunnels for the different CTs can take different paths.

A Path Computation Element (PCE) [PCE-ARCH, PCE-REQUIREMENTS, PCE-PROTOCOL] provides bandwidth management and explicit alternate routing, as well as interarea/inter-AS/interservice-provider traffic engineering. The DSTE tunnels can also be protected against failure by using MPLS Fast Reroute.

The MSE routers support RSVP aggregation for scalability [RFC3175] using aggregation mechanisms that deviate somewhat from RFC 3175 [DSTE-AGGREGATION]. That is, the GW sends a PATH message to the MSE router every time it receives a SIP connection setup message with an IP media address that can be reached through the DSTE tunnel. The RSVP aggregator in the MSE router keeps a running total of bandwidth usage on the DSTE tunnel, adding the bandwidth requirements during connection setup and subtracting during connection teardown. The aggregator responds with an RESV message saying whether there is sufficient bandwidth for the connection from that originating MSE to the destination MSE. The destination GW also sends a PATH message to its MSE router to check whether there is enough bandwidth on the DSTE tunnel from the destination MSE to the originating MSE. The aggregate bandwidth usage on the DSTE tunnel is also available to the DSTE MAR algorithm. If the aggregate bandwidth usage exceeds some threshold, then the MSE will send a PATH message through the tunnel to the other end, requesting bandwidth (perhaps enough for several additional connections). If the size of the DSTE tunnel cannot be increased on the primary and alternate LSPs, then when the DSTE tunnel bandwidth is exhausted, the aggregator will send RSVP messages denying the reservation, and the GW will reject those connections. When DSTE tunnels are underutilized, the bandwidth of the tunnel will be reduced periodically to some appropriate level.

Option A assumes five separate queues in the core implemented with DiffServ based on EXP/COS bits. These queues include two expedited forwarding (EF) priority queues [RFC3246], with the highest priority assigned to emergency traffic (GETS/ETS/E911) and the second priority assigned to normal-priority real time (e.g., VoIP) traffic. Two separate assured forwarding (AF) queues [RFC2597] are assumed for premium private data and premium public data traffic, and a separate best-effort queue is assumed for the best-effort traffic. Several DSTE tunnels may share the same physical link, and therefore share the same queue.

9.4.1.2 Option B (Indirect Coordination): GW CAC, DSTE/MAM, DiffServ/Five Queues

Option B involves indirect coordination of capacity requirements over per-CT DSTE maximum allocation model (MAM) [RFC4125] tunnels in the IP/MPLS network. In option B, each GW manages virtual link capacity to other GWs, which are sized to the forecasted traffic load, and rejects connections when the virtual link capacity is used up. RSVP-TE is used to create and support bandwidth-aware DSTE tunnels. An OSS does off-line tunnel management and creates guaranteed bandwidth tunnels between the MSE routers by allocating bandwidth to the DSTE/MAM tunnels and determining the LSP routing between the MSE routers. The OSS also provides a PCE equivalent function for interarea, inter-AS, or interservice-provider LSP bandwidth management. DiffServ is applied based on the EXP/COS bits and is assumed to have five queues in the core to accommodate GETS/ETS priority queuing, as described earlier under option A. The OSS creates virtual link capacity between each GW–GW pair and allocates bandwidth based on the forecasted traffic load to support those virtual links. Each GW must keep a running total bandwidth of all connections on the virtual links connecting GW–GW pairs. When a new connection would cause the aggregate bandwidth allocation of a virtual link to be exceeded, taking account of header compression where applicable, it is lost. The OSS periodically reallocates virtual link bandwidth to the GWs. The GW implements SIP with preconditions [RFC3312], and the GW CAC parameters are controlled by OSS traffic management.

9.4.1.3 Option C (Indirect Coordination): GW CAC, No DSTE, DiffServ/Three Queues

Option C involves indirect coordination like option B, but this option only uses Diff-Serv in the IP/MPLS network, not DSTE/MAM tunnels. The OSS creates virtual link capacity between each GW–GW pair and allocates bandwidth based on the fore-casted traffic load to support those virtual links. Each GW must keep a running total bandwidth of all connections on the virtual links connecting GW–GW pairs. When a new connection would cause the aggregate bandwidth allocation of a GW to be exceeded, it must be rejected. Option C assumes off-line queue management and has a PCE equivalent function to provide bandwidth management for interarea, inter-AS, or interservice-provider traffic. DiffServ is applied based on the EXP/COS bits, but option C assumes only three queues in the core and does not provide priority queuing to GETS/ETS connections. Each GW manages virtual links to the other GWs and rejects connections when those virtual links are full, taking account of header compression where applicable. The OSS periodically reallocates virtual link bandwidth to the GWs.

The GW implements SIP with preconditions [RFC3312], and the GW CAC parameters are controlled by OSS traffic management.

9.4.1.4 Option D (No Coordination): No CAC, No DSTE, DiffServ/Three Queues

Option D involves no coordination between the application layer and the IP/MPLS layer. It relies on DiffServ, with no CAC functions. Option D assumes only three queues in the core; it does not provide priority queuing to GETS/ETS connections and aggregates the premium private and premium public data in the same queue.

9.4.1.5 Option E (No Coordination): No CAC, No DSTE, No DiffServ/One Queue

Option E corresponds to the case in which there is no CAC and no differentiation among different classes of service with regard to queuing in the network (i.e., one queue, no DiffServ).

Table 9.3 summarizes the technical characteristics of the TQO options that were evaluated extensively.

Table 9.3 Summary of Integrated Voice/Data TQO Options

Option	Connection admission control (CAC)	DiffServ-aware MPLS traffic engineering (DSTE) bandwidth management	DiffServ queues (priority queues for voice)
A—MSE CAC, DSTE/MAR, DiffServ/5 Queues	Network Layer Multiservice Edge Router (MSE)	Maximum Allocation with Reservation (MAR)	5 (2)
B—GW CAC, DSTE/MAM, DiffServ/5 Queues	Application Layer Gateway (GW)	Maximum Allocation Model (MAM)	5 (2)
C—GW CAC, No DSTE, DiffServ/3 Queues	Application Layer Gateway (GW)	No	3 (1)
D—No CAC, no DSTE, DiffServ/3 Queues	No	No	3 (1)
E—No CAC, No DSTE, 1 Queue	No	No	1 (None)

9.4.2 Traffic, Network Design, and Simulation Model Description

This section describes the voice and data traffic model, network design model, and simulation model developed to evaluate the performance of the integrated voice/data TQO options in detail.

9.4.2.1 Traffic Model Description

A 71-node national network model and multiservice traffic demand model are used to study the integrated voice/data TQO options. The 71-node model is illustrated in Figure 9.6, which shows 71 MSE locations, of which 18 are also hub router ("SNRC") locations, and the fiber transport network routing.

A five CT traffic model was developed and is summarized in Table 9.4. Each VoIP connection for CT1 and CT2 is assumed to have a constant bit rate of 86.8 Kbps, which includes a G.711 voice payload (20-ms packets) of 160 bytes, RTP/UDP/IP headers of 40 bytes, PPP header with 4-byte FCS of 9 bytes, and MPLS labels of 8 bytes. Based

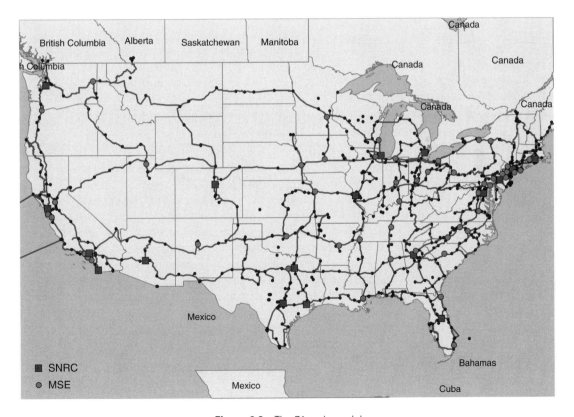

Figure 9.6 The 71-node model.

Table 9.4 Traffic Model: Class Types and Traffic Levels

CT1: high-priority VoIP (GETS/ETS/E911)
   High-priority EF
   0.1% of voice traffic
   0.03% of total traffic

CT2: normal-priority VoIP
   Normal-priority EF
   99.9% of voice traffic
   29.5% of total traffic

CT3: premium private data
   Normal-priority AF
   5% of data traffic
   3.5% of total traffic

CT4: premium public data
   Normal-priority AF
   45% of data traffic
   31.7% of total traffic

CT5: best-effort data
   Best-effort priority
   50% of data traffic
   35.2% of total traffic

on measured traffic, each data traffic flow for CT3, CT4, and CT5 is assumed to have a 768-Kbps mean and a uniform variability up to a maximum of 1536 Kbps. Table 9.4 indicates the total traffic levels for each CT, as well as the priority of the traffic in each CT. One of three levels of traffic priority—high, normal, and best-effort—are designated for each CT, as illustrated in Table 9.4.

All traffic loads are projected to 2008. Five load set periods are available for CT1 and CT2 voice traffic, which include the business day morning, afternoon, and evening busy periods, as well as the weekend morning and evening busy periods. The voice traffic is busiest at the business day morning period. A single time period is available for the data traffic used in the model. However, a separate, more aggregated set of hourly data traffic measurements were analyzed and indicate that the data traffic has an evening busy period on both business day and weekend. That is, voice traffic and data traffic exhibit noncoincidence, which could lead to network design efficiencies in taking advantage of the noncoincident traffic patterns when an integrated voice and data IP/MPLS network is designed.

In total, the voice traffic loads projected in the model amount to 122 Gbps in the busy hour, and the data traffic loads to 276 Gbps. That is, voice loads account for 29.5% of the total traffic in the model. Furthermore, voice traffic varies up to 91% of the total traffic on individual links, as illustrated in Table 9.5, and up to 95% of the total traffic on individual nodes, as illustrated in Table 9.6.

Table 9.5 Traffic Model: Links with >80% Voice Traffic

ALBQNMMA—DNVRCOMA (81%)
ATLNGATL—CLMASCTL (84%)
CMBRMA01—SYRCNYSU (85%)
DLLSTXTL—FTWOTXED (82%)
GRCYNYGC—NYCMNY54 (80%)
HMSQNJHS—PHLAPASL (91%)
HSTNTX01—NWORLAMA (81%)

Table 9.6 Traffic Model: Nodes with >60% and >80% Voice Traffic

Hub router/MSE nodes with >60% voice traffic
    HSTNTX01 (63%)
    ORLDFLMA (63%)
    PHNXAZMA (68%)

MSE nodes with >80% voice traffic

BLTMMDCH (85%)	BRHMALMT (86%)
CLMASCTL (92%)	DNWDGAAT (83%)
FTLDFLOV (89%)	GRCYNYGC (89%)
HMSQNJHS (95%)	JCVLFLCL (87%)
LSVLKYCS (82%)	NWORLAMA (89%)
OMAHNENW (84%)	PITBPADG (81%)
RCMDVAGR (82%)	SBNDIN05 (83%)
SHOKCA02 (89%)	SPKNWA01 (85%)
SYRCNYSU (93%)	

9.4.2.2 *Network Design Model Description*

A DEFO network design model is used to design the 71-node MSE network. As described in Chapter 6, DEFO models optimize the routing of discrete event flows, as measured in units of individual connection requests, and the associated link capacities. A network simulation model is incorporated directly in the network design and optimization method. Nonlinear and complex behavior can be modeled accurately, and meeting performance objectives can be assured. However, DEFO methods can be computationally intensive.

Figure 9.7 illustrates the steps of the DEFO network design model. We first give an overview and then describe the details of the model. We generate initial link capacity requirements based on the traffic load matrix input to the model. Within the "routing design" step, the event generator converts traffic demands to discrete connection-request events. The discrete event simulation model in this routing design step provides the routing logic corresponding to the particular routing method being

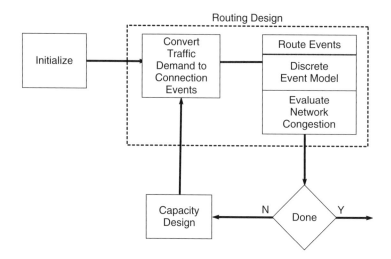

Figure 9.7 Discrete event flow optimization (DEFO) model.

used and routes the connection-request events according to the routing table logic. That is, these discrete-event demands are routed on the link capacities, and the link capacities are then optimized to meet the required flow. Network performance is evaluated as an output of the discrete event simulation model, and any needed link capacity adjustments are determined in the "capacity design" step.

A hub and spoke, two-layer network topology is designed by the DEFO model, where the spoke MSE nodes are homed to the nearest hub MSE node. The hub MSE nodes are selected based on (a) existing hub router node locations or (b) MSE nodes with the largest overall traffic load. Two cases were considered for the number of hub nodes: (a) the existing 18 hub router nodes and (b) the existing 18 hub router nodes plus 7 other largest MSE nodes.

An initial link topology is then established as follows. A link is automatically established between the spoke node and the nearest hub node with a minimum OC48 capacity. Candidate links are initially established between all the hub nodes, i.e., the hub nodes are fully interconnected by candidate links, which can be later eliminated in the DEFO model. Other candidate links (e.g., between spoke nodes or between spoke and nonhome-hub nodes) are established if at least 67% of an OC48 module is required based on the direct node-to-node traffic demand. Traffic is then routed on shortest paths, where the shortest primary and alternate paths are determined by the Bellman–Ford algorithm, described later in this section. Links are then eliminated (except spoke-to-home-hub links) if less than 67% of an OC48 module is required based on the routed link traffic demand. Traffic is then routed again over this reduced link topology, and links are sized to 80% occupancy based on the routed link traffic demand. Finally, the link capacities are rounded up to the nearest OC48 module size to yield the initial link topology.

The DEFO model then generates connection-request events according to a Poisson arrival distribution and exponential holding times (more general arrival streams and arbitrary holding time distributions could also be simulated, as such models can readily be implemented in the discrete event simulation model). Connection-request events are generated in accordance with the traffic load matrix input to the model. These events are routed on the selected path according to the routing table rules described later in this section, which are modeled in detail by the routing table simulation. The simulation logic flows the event onto the network capacity over the selected path for each connection event, denotes the beginning and ending time of the event in the event list, and logs detailed information on the event, including CT and statistical bandwidth information.

The output from the routing design step is the fraction of traffic lost and delayed. From this traffic performance, the capacity design determines the new link capacity requirements of each link to meet the design performance level. From the estimate of lost and delayed traffic, an occupancy calculation determines additional link capacity requirements for an updated link capacity estimate. The total lost traffic Δa is estimated on each link, and an estimated link capacity increase ΔT is calculated by the relationship

$$\Delta T = \Delta a / \gamma$$

where γ is the average traffic-carrying capacity per unit of bandwidth (e.g., $\gamma = 0.8$ network-wide is a typical approximation). Link sizes are increased by ΔT and then rounded upward to the nearest OC48 module. Once the links have been resized, the network is reevaluated to see if the performance objectives are met; if not, another iteration of the model is performed.

We evaluate in the model the confidence interval of the engineered traffic loss probability. For this analysis, we evaluate the binomial distribution for the 90th percentile confidence interval. Suppose that for a traffic load of A in which connections arrive over the designated time period of stationary traffic behavior, there are, on average, m lost connections out of n attempts. This means that there is an average observed traffic lost/delayed probability (*TLDP*) of

$$TLDP = m/n$$

where, for example, $TLDP = .01$ for a 1% average traffic lost/delayed probability. Now, we want to find the value of the 90th percentile traffic lost/delayed probability p such that

$$E(n, m, p) = \Sigma(r = m, n)\ C_{rn}p^r q^{n-r} \geq .90$$

where

$$C_{rn} = n!/(n - r)!r!$$

is the binomial coefficient, and

$$q = 1 - p$$

Then the value p represents the 90th percentile traffic lost/delayed probability confidence interval. That is, there is a 90% chance that the observed traffic lost/delayed probability will be less than or equal to the value p. Methods given in [WEINTRAUB63] are used to numerically evaluate these expressions.

As an example application of these methods to the DEFO model, suppose that network traffic is such that 1 million connections arrive in a single busy-hour period, and we wish to design the network to achieve 1% average traffic lost/delayed or less. If the network is designed in the DEFO model to yield at most .00995 probability of traffic lost/delayed, i.e., at most 9950 connections are lost out of 1 million connections in the DEFO model, then we can be more than 90% sure that the network has a maximum traffic lost/delayed probability of .01. For a specific node pair where 2000 connections arrive in a single busy-hour period, suppose we wish to design the node pair to achieve 1% average traffic lost/delayed probability or less. If the network capacity is designed in the DEFO model to yield at most .0075 probability of traffic lost/delayed for the node pair, i.e., at most 15 connections are lost out of 2000 connections in the DEFO model, then we can be more than 90% sure that the node pair has a maximum traffic lost/delayed probability of .01. These methods are used to ensure that the traffic lost/delayed probability design objectives are met, taking into consideration the sampling errors of the discrete event model.

The greatest advantage of the DEFO model is its ability to capture very complex routing behavior through the equivalent of a simulation model provided in software in the routing design module. By this means, very complex routing networks have been designed by the model, which include all of the routing methods embedded in the TQO options considered in the case study. Complex traffic processes, such as self-similar traffic, can also be modeled with DEFO methods. A flow diagram of the DEFO model is illustrated in Figure 9.8, in which the logical blocks of the STT-EDR routing logic incorporated in option A are implemented. This STT-EDR routing logic is described further in the next section.

Both meshed and sparse network designs are generated for the 71 MSE network. Note that the simulation study included larger and smaller networks in the range of 18 to 140 nodes, and the simulation results were not very sensitive to the number of nodes. Also, as shown in results to be presented shortly, the simulations were not very sensitive to the number of hub nodes or to whether the network had a sparse or meshed topology so the simulation results are valid over a range of the number of nodes, connectivity, and topology.

These meshed and sparse designs are constructed using the DEFO model described earlier. In the sparse design, there are 18 hub MSE nodes, which correspond to the 18 hub MSE routers in the network model. The 53 spoke MSE nodes are singly homed to the nearest hub node. In all, there are 86 links in the sparse model with 53 links from spoke nodes to hub nodes and 33 interhub-node links, which correspond to the

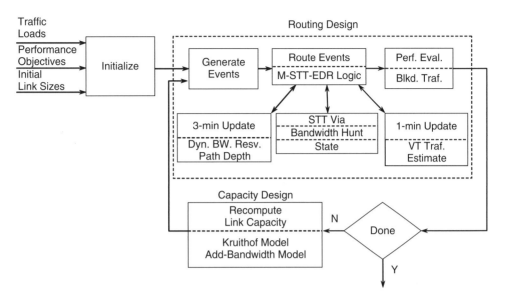

Figure 9.8 Discrete event flow optimization model with multilink success-to-the-top event-dependent routing (STT-EDR).

current interhub-router links in the network model. All links are sized to a multiple of OC48 bandwidth capacity based on the traffic load projected on the link. Multilink shortest path routing is used as described further later in this section, and the network designs meet the performance objectives under the engineered load.

In the meshed design, on the other hand, there are 25 hub MSE nodes upon which the other 46 spoke MSE nodes are multiply homed, with at least one link to the nearest hub node and any other links that are justified based on projected traffic levels. In addition, links between spoke nodes are allowed if justified based on projected traffic levels. In all, there are 122 links in the meshed design.

9.4.2.3 Simulation Model Description

We describe the simulated routing logic for option A, which is the most general of the options considered; other options have subsets of the logical functions described here. In the simulation model of option A, a connection is first routed on the primary (shortest) path, and if the primary path is busy, the connection is routed on an alternate path in the routing table. In the simulation, if a link in a path is busy, this condition results in a simulated crankback signaling message that notifies the originating node that the path is congested and alternate paths might be tried. If a connection finds an idle path, the simulated link capacity is made busy, the connection holding time is determined according to the exponential holding time distribution, and the end time of the connection is noted in the event list for a later disconnect event at the simulated time the connection is disconnected. At the simulated disconnect time, the simulated link capacity occupied by the connection is made idle once again. Bandwidth allocation to the primary and alternate LSPs uses the MAR bandwidth allocation procedure, as described later in this section. As also described later in this section, the queuing behaviors for the CT traffic priorities are also modeled in the simulation.

We now describe further details of the option A STT-EDR simulation model, which include the path selection algorithm, bandwidth allocation model, connection admission control procedure, priority queuing mechanism, bufferless queuing model, and bandwidth allocation algorithm.

Path selection uses a topology database that includes available bandwidth on each link. From the topology database, the originating node determines a list of shortest paths by using the Bellman–Ford algorithm. This path list is determined based on administrative weights of each link, which are communicated to all nodes within the routing domain. These administrative weights are set to $[1 + \varepsilon \times \text{distance}]$, where ε is a factor giving a relatively smaller weight to the distance in comparison to the hop count. Many variations of these administrative weighting factors were studied at length in order to select the model giving the best overall performance. It should also be noted that with TE capabilities to select explicit routes, many other criteria (e.g., transport routing, transport technology) could be considered in selecting primary and alternate routes.

To illustrate the Bellman–Ford algorithm, let Cij represent the cost of the minimum cost path from node i to node j. If node i and node k have a direct link with link cost (administrative weight) cik, the minimum cost path between node i and j can be obtained by solving Bellman's equation:

$$Cij = \min(k) \ (cik + Ckj) \tag{1}$$

One can solve for the Cij by initially setting

$$Cij = cij \text{ if nodes } i \text{ and } j \text{ are connected}$$

$$Cij = \text{infinity if nodes } i \text{ and } j \text{ are not connected}$$

and then iteratively solving Eq. (1) until the Cij values converge.

Option A incorporates EDR path selection in which the routing tables are updated locally on the basis of whether connections succeed or fail on a given path choice. In the EDR learning approach, if the primary shortest path is congested, the first alternate path is selected on the basis of last successful alternate path tried, which is tried again until congested, at which time another path is selected at random and tried on the next connection request. A successful path thus rises to the top as the first alternate path. This STT-EDR path selection procedure uses a simplified decentralized learning method to achieve flexible adaptive routing.

An example of STT-EDR path selection is shown in Figure 9.3. The primary LSP-p is used first if sufficient resources are available; if not, a currently successful alternate LSP-s is used until it is congested (i.e., sufficient resources are not available, such as bandwidth not available on one or more links). In the case that LSP-s is congested, a new alternate LSP-n is selected at random as the alternate path choice for the next connection request overflow from the primary path. The current alternate path choice is maintained as long as a connection can be established successfully on the path. Hence the routing table is constructed with the information determined during connection setup, and no additional information, such as that obtained through flooding topology information, is required by the ON.

Figure 9.3 illustrates STT-EDR path selection in the case that bandwidth of a path needs to be increased by a bandwidth amount *DBW*. In using the first LSP A–B–E to accomplish the bandwidth change, originating node A sends an RSVP-TE MPLS "modify" message to VN B, which in turn forwards the message to destination node E. Nodes B and E are passed in the explicit-routing parameter contained in the modify message. Each node in the LSP reads the explicit-routing information and passes the setup message to the next node listed in the explicit-routing parameter. The bandwidth admission control for each link in the path is performed based on the status of the link using the MAR bandwidth allocation procedure described later in this section, where we further describe the role of the reserved bandwidth RBW shown in Figure 9.3 in the admission control procedure. If the first-choice LSP cannot admit the bandwidth change, node A may then try an alternate LSP. The second path tried is the last successful path LSP-s A–C–D–E (the "STT path"); if that path is unsuccessful, another alternate path is searched out from the alternate path list.

Option A incorporates the MAR bandwidth constraint model [RFC4126] incorporated within DSTE [RFC4124]. We now describe the details of DSTE/MAR operation. Whether or not bandwidth can be allocated to the bandwidth modification request on an LSP is determined based on the LSP link load state at each node. Three link load states are distinguished in MAR: available bandwidth (*ABW*), reserved bandwidth (*RBW*), and bandwidth not available (*BNA*). Given a bandwidth request $= DBW$, link k is in the

$$ABW \text{ state if } ILBW_k \geq RBW_k + DBW$$

$$RBW \text{ state if } ILBW_k < RBW_k + DBW$$

$$BNA \text{ state if } ILBW_k < DBW$$

where $ILBW_k$ is idle link bandwidth on link k and RBW_k is reservation bandwidth threshold for link k.

Management of LSP capacity uses this link state model, and the allowed load state algorithm now described to determine if a bandwidth modification request can be accepted on a given LSP. In the allowed load state algorithm, a small amount of reserved bandwidth RBW_k governs the admission control on link k. Associated with each CTc on link k are the allocated bandwidth constraints BCc_k to govern bandwidth allocation and protection. The reservation bandwidth on a link, RBW_k, can be accessed when a given CTc has bandwidth-in-use $BWIPc_k$ below its allocated bandwidth constraint BCc_k. However, if $BWIPc_k$ exceeds its allocated bandwidth constraint BCc_k, then the reservation bandwidth RBW_k cannot be accessed. In this way, bandwidth can be fully shared among CTs if available, but is otherwise protected by bandwidth reservation methods. Therefore, bandwidth can be accessed for a bandwidth request $= DBW$ for CTc on a given link k based on the following rules.

For an LSP on a high-priority or normal-priority CTc:

$$\text{If } BWIPc_k \leq BCc: \text{ admit if } DBW \leq ILBW_k$$
$$\text{If } BWIPc_k > BCc: \text{ admit if } DBW \leq ILBW_k - RBW_k;$$

or, equivalently,

$$\text{If } DBW \leq ILBWc_k, \text{ admit the LSP}$$

where

$$ILBWc_k = \text{idle link bandwidth on link } k \text{ for } CTc$$
$$= ILBW_k - delta0/1(CTc_k) \times RBW_k$$
$$delta0/1(CTc_k) = 0 \text{ if } BWIPc_k < BCc_k$$
$$delta0/1(CTc_k) = 1 \text{ if } BWIPc_k \geq BCc_k$$

For an LSP on a best-effort priority CTc:

$$\text{allocated bandwidth } BCc = 0;$$

DiffServ queuing serves best-effort packets only if there is available link bandwidth.

In setting the bandwidth constraints for CTc_k, for a normal priority CTc, the bandwidth constraints BCc_k on link k are set by allocating the maximum link bandwidth $LINK\_BW_k$ in proportion to the forecast or measured traffic load bandwidth $TRAF\_LOAD\_BWc_k$ for CTc on link k. That is:

$$PROPORTIONAL\_BWc_k$$
$$= TRAF\_LOAD\_BWc_k/[\Sigma(c) \{TRAF\_LOAD\_BWc_k, c = 0, MaxCT\text{-}1\}]$$
$$\times LINK\_BW_k$$

For normal priority CTc:

$$BCc_k = PROPORTIONAL\_BWc_k$$

For a high-priority CT, the bandwidth constraint BCc_k is set to a multiple of the proportional bandwidth. That is, for high-priority CTc:

$$BCc_k = FACTOR \times PROPORTIONAL\_BWc_k$$

where $FACTOR$ is set to a multiple of the proportional bandwidth (e.g., $FACTOR = 2$ or 3 is typical). This results in some overallocation ("overbooking") of the link bandwidth and gives priority to the high-priority CTs. Normally the bandwidth allocated to high-priority CTs, i.e., CT1 in our model, should be a relatively small fraction of the total link bandwidth, a maximum of 10–15% being a reasonable guideline. Given the traffic levels provided in Table 9.4, high-priority CT1 traffic could be at most 0.1% of the total link bandwidth on any given link.

As stated earlier, the bandwidth allocated to a best-effort priority CTc is set to zero. That is, for best-effort priority CTc:

$$BCc_k = 0$$

In the DSTE/MAM bandwidth constraints model [RFC4125], as used in TQO option B, the bandwidth constraints for each CT are set to a multiple of the proportional bandwidth allocation:

Normal priority CTs: $BCc_k = FACTOR1 \times PROPORTIONAL\_BW_k$,

High priority CTs: $BCc_k = FACTOR2 \times PROPORTIONAL\_BW_k$

Best-effort priority CTs: $BCc_k = 0$

Simulations show that for MAM (e.g., in option B), the sum of BCc should exceed the total link bandwidth for better efficiency, as follows:

1. For normal priority CTs, the BCc values need to be overallocated (overbooked) to get reasonable performance. It was found that overallocating by 100%, i.e., setting $FACTOR1 = 2$, gave reasonable performance.
2. For high-priority CTs, the BCc values need to be overallocated by a larger multiple $FACTOR2 > FACTOR1$ in MAM, which gives better performance.

Each CT is restricted in MAM to its allocated bandwidth constraint BCc_k, which is the maximum level of bandwidth allocated to each CT on each link. The rather large amount of overallocation in MAM improves efficiency but somewhat defeats the "bandwidth protection/isolation" needed with a bandwidth constraints model, as one CT can now invade the bandwidth allocated to another CT.

In the no-DSTE options C, D, and E, no reservation or protection of CT bandwidth is applied, and bandwidth allocation requests are admitted if bandwidth is available.

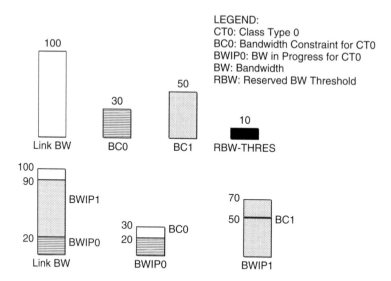

Figure 9.9 Illustration of DSTE MAR operation: Bandwidth allocation and bandwidth constraints for class type 0 and class type 1.

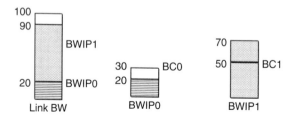

Bandwidth increase request = 5 = DBW arrives for Class Type 0 (CT0):
accept for CT0 since BWIP0 < BC0 and DBW (= 5) < ILBW (= 10)

Bandwidth increase request = 5 = DBW arrives for Class Type 1 (CT1):
reject for CT1 since BWIP1 > BC1 and
DBW (= 5) > ILBW − RBW = 10 − 10 = 0

Figure 9.10 Illustration of DSTE MAR operation: Request for bandwidth increase on class type 0 and class type 1.

We give a simple example of the MAR bandwidth allocation algorithm, as illustrated in Figures 9.9 and 9.10. As shown in Figure 9.9, assume that there are two class types: CT0, CT1, and a particular link with

$$LINK\_BW = 100$$

with the allocated bandwidth constraints set as follows:

$$BC0 = 30$$

$$BC1 = 50$$

These bandwidth constraints are based on the forecast traffic loads, as discussed earlier. Either CT is allowed to exceed its bandwidth constraint BCc as long as there is at least RBW units of spare bandwidth remaining. Assume $RBW = 10$. So under overload, if

$$BWIP0 = 20$$

$$BWIP1 = 70$$

then for this loading

$$ILBW = 100 - 20 - 70 = 10$$

As illustrated in Figure 9.10, CT0 can take the additional bandwidth (up to 10 units) if the demand arrives, as it is below its BC value. CT1, however, can no longer increase its bandwidth on the link, as it is above its BC value and there is only $RBW = 10$ units of idle bandwidth left on the link. If best-effort traffic is present, it can always seize whatever idle bandwidth is available on the link at the moment, but is subject to being lost at the queues in favor of the higher priority traffic.

   As shown in Figure 9.10, a request arrives to increase bandwidth for CT1 by 5 units of bandwidth (i.e., $DBW = 5$). We need to decide whether to admit this request or not. Since for CT1

$$BWIP1 > BC1 \ (70 > 50), \ \text{and}$$

$$DBW > ILBW - RBW \ (\text{i.e.}, 5 > 10 - 10)$$

the bandwidth request is rejected by the bandwidth allocation rules given earlier. Now let's say a request arrives to increase bandwidth for CT0 by 5 units of bandwidth (i.e., $DBW = 5$). We need to decide whether to admit this request or not. Since for CT0

$$BWIP0 < BC0 \ (20 < 30), \ \text{and}$$

$$DBW < ILBW \ (\text{i.e.}, 5 < 10)$$

The example illustrates that with the current state of the link and the current CT loading, CT1 can no longer increase its bandwidth on the link, as it is above its BC1 value and there is only $RBW = 10$ units of spare bandwidth left on the link. However, CT0 can take the additional bandwidth (up to 10 units) if the demand arrives, as it is below its BC0 value.

The algorithm for bandwidth additions and deletions to LSPs is as follows. The bandwidth constraint parameters defined in the MAR algorithm [RFC4126] do not change based on traffic conditions. In particular, these parameters defined in [RFC4126], as described earlier, are configured and do not change until reconfigured: $LINK\_BW_k$, BCc_k, and RBW_k. However, the reserved bandwidth variables change based on traffic: $BWIPc_k$, $ILBW_k$, and $ILBWc_k$. In the simulation, the $BWIPc_k$ and bandwidth allocated to each DSTE/MAR tunnel is dynamically changed based on traffic: it is increased when the traffic demand increases (using RSVP aggregation) and it is decreased periodically when the traffic demand decreases. Furthermore, if tunnel bandwidth cannot be increased on the primary path, an alternate LSP path is tried. When LSP tunnel bandwidth needs to be increased to accommodate a given connection request, the bandwidth is increased by the amount of the needed additional bandwidth, if possible. The tunnel bandwidth rises quickly to the currently needed maximum bandwidth level, wherein no further requests are made to increase bandwidth, as departing flows leave some amount of available or spare bandwidth in the tunnel to use for new requests. Tunnel bandwidth is reduced periodically (e.g., every 60 s) down to the level of the actually utilized bandwidth. Many other approaches were tried to increasing and decreasing tunnel bandwidth, such as increasing by more than currently needed bandwidth, or decreasing by only a fraction of the spare bandwidth; these approaches are discussed shortly.

Priority EF queuing for CT1 and CT2 VoIP traffic and AF queuing for CT3 and CT4 data traffic are maintained such that the packets are given priority according to the CT traffic priority. The queuing model assumes three levels of priority: high, normal, and best effort. CT1 (high-priority VoIP, for GETS/ETS/E911) and CT2 (normal-priority VoIP) use two priority queues with an EF DiffServ per-hop behavior. CT1 is given a higher priority EF queue than CT2. CT3 and CT4 (premium private and premium public data, respectively) are given a normal-priority AF per-hop behavior. CT5 is given a best-effort per-hop behavior, which is the lowest priority queue. All five queues have static bandwidth allocation limits applied based on the level of forecast traffic on each link, such that the bandwidth limits will not be exceeded under normal conditions, allowing for some traffic overload. Furthermore, a bufferless queuing model is assumed in that once the bandwidth on the link is exceeded, packets are counted as lost/delayed. This bufferless model is a good approximation when the link bandwidth is large [BONALD02], which is the case in this model in that a minimum OC48 link size is assumed.

Figure 9.11 illustrates the bandwidth allocation of the LSPs established for the five CTs and also shows an example assignment of the EXP/COS bits to control the DiffServ per-hop behaviors.

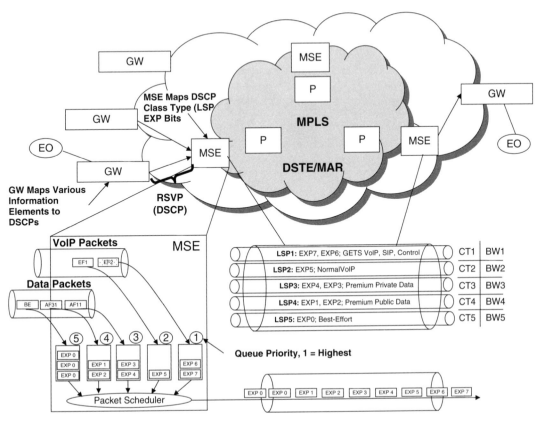

Figure 9.11 Illustration of class type LSP bandwidth allocation and assignment of DiffServ EXP/COS bits.

9.5 Modeling Results

A large number of simulation comparisons were performed, including overload scenarios, failure scenarios, TQO versus no TQO, and different assumptions on the number of queues in the IP/MPLS network. We also illustrate the optimization of various parameters in TQO option A, including the level of reserved capacity RBW_k, the number of allowed primary and alternate paths, and the algorithm for increasing and decreasing CT bandwidth allocation.

Table 9.7 shows the performance results of simulating each of four TQO options using a mesh network design with multiple link failures. The entries in the white area of Table 9.7 indicate the percentage lost or delayed packets averaged over the whole network. The entries in the shaded area of Table 9.7 indicate the percentage of connections lost by the CAC mechanism. Option A exhibits the best performance not only for VoIP traffic, but for premium data traffic as well. Options B and C exhibit comparable performance, and both perform better than option E (no CAC).

Table 9.7 Simulation Modeling Performance Comparison: Multiple Link Failures

Class type	A *MSE CAC* *DSTE/MAR* *5 queues*	B *GW CAC* *DSTE/MAM* *5 queues*	C *GW CAC* *no DSTE* *3 queues*	E *No CAC* *no DSTE* *1 queue*
Normal-Priority Voice	0.06	0.93	0.97	7.39
GETS/ETS Priority Voice	0.00	0.00	0.00	7.01
Premium Private Data	0.00	5.74	6.52	11.15
Premium Public Data	0.00	6.73	6.52	11.75
Best-Effort Data	18.98	21.18	21.00	9.76

Model Assumptions:
- 71-MSE Simulation Model, Meshed Design
- Multiple Link Failures
- Results are in Total Network % Lost/Delayed Packets
  (Shaded = CAC Blocking; White = Queuing Loss)

Observations:
- A provides best performance (virtually all loss in best-effort data)
- B & C exhibit comparable performance; both perform better than E
- E voice degradation applies to all calls; does not meet GETS/ETS QoS objectives

    Table 9.8 shows the results of simulating each of five options using a meshed network design with focused overload (three times overload on Chicago). The entries in the white area of Table 9.8 indicate the percentage lost or delayed packets averaged over the whole network. The entries in the shaded area of Table 9.8 indicate the percentage of connections lost by the CAC mechanism. Again, option A exhibits the best performance not only for VoIP traffic, but for premium data traffic as well. Virtually all of the queuing loss is experienced by best-effort data packets. Only 0.13% of connections are lost using option A, and there is no queuing loss for admitted VoIP connections. On the other hand, options B and C experience substantial (almost equal) lost connections, but the CAC mechanism prevents queuing loss for admitted connections. Options D and E, which do not have any CAC mechanism, suffer more than 8% average queuing loss, which means all VoIP connections in the affected region will suffer severely degraded quality, and the data traffic will also suffer heavy packet losses.

    Table 9.9 shows the results of simulating each of four options using a meshed network design with focused overload (three times overload on Chicago). In this scenario there is a 50% overbooking of the voice tunnel bandwidth and bandwidth limits on the queues. The entries in the white area of Table 9.9 indicate the percentage lost or delayed packets averaged over the whole network. The entries in the shaded area of Table 9.9 indicate the percentage of connections lost by the CAC mechanism.

Table 9.8 Simulation Modeling Results: Focused Overload

Class type	A *MSE CAC* *DSTE/MAR* *5 queues*	B *GW CAC* *DSTE/MAM* *5 queues*	C *GW CAC* *no DSTE* *3 queues*	D *No CAC* *no DSTE* *3 queues*	E *No CAC* *no DSTE* *1 queue*
Normal-Priority Voice	0.13	13.06	13.04	8.79	8.08
GETS/ETS Priority Voice	0.00	0.00	0.00	8.79	9.42
Premium Private Data	0.01	0.77	2.44	2.17	13.81
Premium Public Data	0.00	1.99	2.44	2.17	16.20
Best-Effort Data	32.86	29.48	28.94	28.741	13.37

Model Assumptions:
- 71-MSE Simulation Model, Meshed Design
- $3\times$ Overload on CHCG
- Results are in Total Network % Lost/Delayed Packets
  (Shaded = CAC Blocking; White = Queuing Loss)

Observations:
- A provides best performance (virtually all loss in best-effort data)
- B/C not robust to traffic variations, exhibit comparable performance
- D/E voice degradation applies to all calls; do not meet GETS/ETS QoS objectives

Again, option A exhibits the best performance not only for VoIP traffic, but for premium data traffic as well. Virtually all of the queuing loss is experienced by best-effort data packets. Only 0.05% of connections are lost using option A, and there is no queuing loss for admitted VoIP connections. Overbooking improves the voice throughput for all the options, as expected, especially for option D. Once again, options B and C experience substantial (almost equal) lost connections, but the CAC mechanism prevents queuing loss for admitted connections. Option D, which does not have any CAC mechanism, suffers 1% average queuing loss, which means all VoIP connections in the affected region will suffer severely degraded quality, and the data traffic will also suffer heavy packet losses.

Table 9.10 shows the results of simulating option A using a meshed network design with three times focused overloads on Phoenix, Arizona, Houston, Texas, Baltimore, Maryland, and New Orleans, Louisiana. The entries in the white area of Table 9.10 indicate the percentage lost or delayed packets averaged over the whole network. The entries in the shaded area of Table 9.10 indicate the percentage of connections lost by the CAC mechanism plus the percentage of lost/delayed packets by the queuing mechanisms (the percentage of queuing loss alone is shown in parentheses). These simulations indicate that both CAC-rejected connections and queuing loss/delay can occur in many scenarios; these illustrate a few examples. The main point of these results is that with five queues (two EF queues, with higher priority for GETS/ETS

Table 9.9 Simulation Modeling Results: Focused Overload with Overbooking of Voice Traffic

Class type	A *MSE CAC* *DSTE/MAR* *5 queues*	B *GW CAC* *DSTE/MAM* *5 queues*	C *GW CAC* *no DSTE* *3 queues*	D *No CAC* *no DSTE* *3 queues*
Normal-Priority Voice	0.05	9.12	9.11	1.00
GETS/ETS Priority Voice	0.00	0.00	0.00	1.00
Premium Private Data	0.00	0.98	2.75	3.43
Premium Public Data	0.00	2.28	2.75	3.43
Best-Effort Data	33.74	29.48	30.77	32.45

Model Assumptions:
- 71-MSE Simulation Model, Meshed Design
- $3\times$ Overload on CHCG
- Overbooking of bandwidth for voice
- Results are in Total Network % Lost/Delayed Packets
  (Shaded = CAC Blocking; White = Queuing Loss)

Observations:
- A provides best performance (virtually all loss in best-effort data)
- Overbooking improves throughput of B, C, and especially D
- Still little difference between B and C
- D voice degradation applies to all calls; does not meet GETS/ETS QoS objectives

traffic), GETS/ETS traffic can achieve its QoS objectives. However, if a second priority EF queue is not provided, then GETS/ETS traffic will get the same queuing loss as normal voice traffic, and the GETS/ETS performance objectives would not be met.

Table 9.11 shows the results of simulating each of four options using a meshed network design with a combination of multiple link failures and a focused overload (two times overload on Chicago). The entries in the white area of Table 9.11 indicate the percentage lost or delayed packets averaged over the whole network. The entries in the shaded area of Table 9.11 indicate the percentage of connections lost by the CAC mechanism. Again, option A exhibits the best performance not only for VoIP traffic, but for premium data traffic as well. Virtually all of the queuing loss is experienced by best-effort data packets. Only 0.18% of connections are lost using option A, and there is no queuing loss for admitted VoIP connections. Once again, options B and C experience substantial (almost equal) lost connections, but the CAC mechanism prevents queuing loss for admitted connections. Option E, which does not have any CAC mechanism, has the poorest performance and suffers more than 12% average queuing loss, which means all VoIP connections in the affected region

Table 9.10 Simulation Modeling Results: Focused Overload Scenarios for Option A

Class type	A MSE CAC DSTE/MAR 5 queues (focus on PHNXAZ)	A MSE CAC DSTE/MAR 5 queues (focus on HSTNTX)	A MSE CAC DSTE/MAR 5 queues (focus on BLTMMD)	A MSE CAC DSTE/MAR 5 queues (focus on NWORLA)
Normal-Priority Voice	1.61 (0.59)	4.05 (3.04)	4.74 (3.49)	5.40 (3.57)
GETS/ETS Priority Voice	0.00	0.00	0.00	0.00
Premium Private Data	4.45	7.73	1.96	1.11
Premium Public Data	3.63	8.23	1.97	1.53
Best-Effort Data	7.64	6.37	1.88	1.31

Model Assumptions:
• 71-MSE Simulation Model, Meshed Design
• Focused Overload on node indicated
• Results are in Total Network % Lost/Delayed Packets
  (Shaded = Total CAC Blocking & Queuing Loss (Queuing Loss); White = Queuing Loss)

Observations:
• Both CAC blocking & queuing loss occur in many scenarios, these are a few examples
• 5 queues allow GETS/ETS to achieve QoS objectives
• 4 queues will not allow GETS/ETS to achieve QoS objectives

will suffer severely degraded quality, and the data traffic will also suffer heavy packet losses.

Table 9.12 shows the performance results of simulating each of four TQO options using a sparse network design with multiple link failures. The entries in the white area of Table 9.12 indicate the percentage lost or delayed packets averaged over the whole network. The entries in the shaded area of Table 9.12 indicate the percentage of connections lost by the CAC mechanism. Option A exhibits the best performance not only for VoIP traffic, but for premium data traffic as well. Options B and C exhibit comparable performance and both perform better than option E (no CAC). There is virtually no difference in voice performance relative to the meshed design (Table 9.7) and only a small difference in data performance. These results demonstrate that the relative performance of the various options is robust to changes in the network topology.

Table 9.11 Simulation Modeling Results: Multiple Link Failures and Focused Overload

Class type	A MSE CAC DSTE/MAR 5 queues	B GW CAC DSTE/MAM 5 queues	C GW CAC no DSTE 3 queues	E No CAC no DSTE 1 queue
Normal-Priority Voice	0.18	7.20	7.20	12.11
GETS/ETS Priority Voice	0.00	0.00	0.00	12.70
Premium Private Data	4.76	13.22	15.27	19.99
Premium Public Data	5.85	15.57	15.27	20.99
Best-Effort Data	35.70	28.68	28.89	16.94

Model Assumptions:
- 71-MSE Simulation Model, Meshed Design
- Multiple Link Failures & Overload at CHCG
- Results are in Total Network % Lost/Delayed Packets
  (Shaded = CAC Blocking; White = Queuing Loss)

Observations:
- A provides best performance; some loss for premium data but virtually none for voice
- B and C outperform E
- D voice degradation applies to all calls; does not meet GETS/ETS QoS objectives

   Table 9.13 shows the results of simulating each of four options using a sparse network design *i*th focused overload (three times overload on Chicago). The entries in the white area of Table 9.13 indicate the percentage lost or delayed packets averaged over the whole network. The entries in the shaded area of Table 9.13 indicate the percentage of connections lost by the CAC mechanism. Again, option A exhibits the best performance not only for VoIP traffic, but for premium data traffic as well. Virtually all of the queuing loss is experienced by best-effort data packets. Only 0.50% of connections are lost using option A and there is no queuing loss for admitted VoIP connections. On the other hand, options B and C experience substantial (almost equal) lost connections, but the CAC mechanism prevents queuing loss for admitted connections. Option E, which does not have any CAC mechanism, suffers more than 12% average queuing loss, which means all VoIP connections in the affected region will suffer severely degraded quality, and the data traffic will also suffer heavy packet losses. These results exhibit somewhat higher loss levels relative to the meshed design (Table 9.8). However, these results again demonstrate that

Table 9.12 Simulation Modeling Performance Comparison: Multiple Link Failures (Sparse Design)

Class type	A MSE CAC DSTE/MAR 5 queues	B GW CAC DSTE/MAM 5 queues	C GW CAC no DSTE 3 queues	E No CAC no DSTE 1 queue
Normal-Priority Voice	0.12	0.93	0.97	7.42
GETS/ETS Priority Voice	0.00	0.00	0.00	6.36
Premium Private Data	1.12	1.93	2.52	8.60
Premium Public Data	1.77	2.84	2.52	10.44
Best-Effort Data	22.88	23.88	23.49	9.62

Model Assumptions:
- 71-MSE Simulation Model, Sparse Design
- Multiple Link Failures
- Results are in Total Network % Lost/Delayed Packets
  (Shaded = CAC Blocking; White = Queuing Loss)

Observations:
- No difference in voice throughput relative to meshed design
- Small difference in data loss
- B & C outperform E
- E voice degradation applies to all calls; does not meet GETS/ETS QoS objectives

the relative performance of the various options is robust to changes in the network topology.

Table 9.14 shows the results of simulating each of four options using a sparse network design with a combination of multiple link failures and a focused overload (two times overload on Chicago). The entries in the white area of Table 9.14 indicate the percentage lost or delayed packets averaged over the whole network. The entries in the shaded area of Table 9.14 indicate the percentage of connections lost by the CAC mechanism. Again, option A exhibits the best performance not only for VoIP traffic, but for premium data traffic as well. Virtually all of the queuing loss is experienced by best-effort data packets. Only 0.28% of connections are lost using option A, and there is no queuing loss for admitted VoIP connections. Once again, options B and C experience substantial (almost equal) lost connections, but the CAC mechanism prevents queuing loss for admitted connections. Option E, which does not have any CAC mechanism, has the poorest performance and suffers more than

Table 9.13 Simulation Modeling Results: Focused Overload (Sparse Design)

Class type	A MSE CAC DSTE/MAR 5 queues	B GW CAC DSTE/MAM 5 queues	C GW CAC no DSTE 3 queues	E No CAC no DSTE 1 queue
Normal-Priority Voice	0.50	15.81	15.81	12.16
GETS/ETS Priority Voice	0.00	0.00	0.00	11.68
Premium Private Data	0.76	0.66	0.30	18.28
Premium Public Data	0.75	1.02	0.30	18.77
Best-Effort Data	44.82	39.78	40.98	17.75

Model Assumptions:
- 71-MSE Simulation Model, Sparse Design
- $3\times$ Overload on CHCG
- Results are in Total Network % Lost/Delayed Packets
  (Shaded = CAC Blocking; White = Queuing Loss)

Observations:
- Higher loss levels relative to meshed design
- A provides best performance (virtually all loss in best-effort data)
- B/C not robust to traffic variations, exhibit comparable performance
- E voice degradation applies to all calls; does not meet GETS/ETS QoS objectives

11% average queuing loss, which means all VoIP connections in the affected region will suffer severely degraded quality, and the data traffic will also suffer heavy packet losses. There is virtually no difference in voice and data performance relative to the meshed design (Table 9.11), and the results once again demonstrate that the relative performance of the various options is robust to changes in the network topology.

We now illustrate the optimization of the integrated voice/data TQO option A for the following parameters:

- Level of reserved capacity: RBW_k is varied from 0 to 10% of link capacity
- Number of allowed primary and alternate paths: the number is varied from 2 to 10 paths
- Algorithm for increasing and decreasing CT bandwidth allocation: various models are studied, as described later in this section

Tables 9.15 and 9.16 illustrate the results for the level of reserved capacity RBW_k, as this level is varied from 0 to 10% of link capacity, for the meshed network design, with the focused overload scenario (three times overload on Chicago) and multiple

Table 9.14 Simulation Modeling Results: Multiple Link Failures and Focused Overload (Sparse Design)

Class type	A *MSE CAC* *DSTE/MAR* *5 queues*	B *GW CAC* *DSTE/MAM* *5 queues*	C *GW CAC* *no DSTE* *3 queues*	E *No CAC* *no DSTE* *1 queue*
Normal-Priority Voice	0.28	7.20	7.20	11.34
GETS/ETS Priority Voice	0.00	0.00	0.00	11.20
Premium Private Data	4.69	6.74	9.81	14.57
Premium Public Data	7.35	10.17	9.81	17.11
Best-Effort Data	30.01	29.50	29.61	15.87

Model Assumptions:
- 71-MSE Simulation Model, Meshed Design
- Multiple Link Failures & Overload at CHCG
- Overbooking of bandwidth for voice
- Results are in Total Network % Lost/Delayed Packets
  (Shaded = CAC Blocking; White = Queuing Loss)

Observations:
- Virtually no difference relative to meshed design
- A provides best performance (virtually all loss in best-effort data)
- B & C exhibit comparable performance; both perform better than E
- E voice degradation applies to all calls; does not meet GETS/ETS QoS objectives

link failures scenario, respectively. The results indicate that a reservation level in the range of 3–5% of link capacity provides the best overall performance.

Tables 9.17 and 9.18 illustrate the results for the number of allowed primary and alternate paths, as this level is varied from 1 to 10, for the meshed network design, with the focused overload scenario (three times overload on Chicago) and multiple link failures scenario, respectively. The results indicate that six or more primary and alternate paths provide the best overall performance.

Tables 9.19 and 9.20 illustrate the results for the algorithm for increasing and decreasing CT bandwidth allocation, for the meshed network design, with the focused overload scenario (three times overload on Chicago) and multiple link failures scenario, respectively. In the simulation, the bandwidth allocated to each DSTE/MAR tunnel is dynamically changed based on traffic: it is increased as needed when the traffic demand increases above the currently allocated level (using RSVP aggregation) and it is decreased periodically when the traffic demand decreases. Furthermore, if tunnel bandwidth cannot be increased on a primary path, an alternate LSP path is tried. When LSP tunnel bandwidth needs to be increased to accommodate a given connection request, the bandwidth is increased by a multiple (denoted as the MULTUP parameter) of the amount of the needed additional bandwidth, if possible.

Table 9.15 Simulation Modeling Results: Focused Overload with Variable Level of Bandwidth Reservation

Class type	Option A MSE CAC, DSTE/MAR, 5 queues (reservation level—% of link bandwidth)					
	0.0	**0.5**	**1.0**	**3.0**	**5.0**	**10.0**
Normal-Priority Voice	0.22	0.13	0.08	0.04	0.04	0.06
GETS/ETS Priority Voice	0.00	0.00	0.00	0.00	0.00	0.00
Premium Private Data	0.01	0.01	0.01	0.00	0.00	0.00
Premium Public Data	0.00	0.00	0.00	0.00	0.00	0.00
Best-Effort Data	33.15	32.86	33.10	32.44	32.80	32.47

Model Assumptions:
- 71-MSE Simulation Model, Meshed Design
- $3\times$ Overload on CHCG
- Results are in Total Network % Lost/Delayed Packets
  (Shaded = CAC Blocking; White = Queuing Loss)

Observations:
- Reservation level of 3–5% of link bandwidth provides best performance

For example, if an increase in bandwidth to accommodate a single connection is needed, then if MULTUP is set to 4, the tunnel bandwidth will be increased sufficiently to accommodate four additional connections. The tunnel bandwidth quickly rises to the currently needed maximum bandwidth level, wherein no further requests are made to increase bandwidth, as departing flows leave a constant amount of available or spare bandwidth in the tunnel to use for new requests. Tunnel bandwidth is reduced periodically (e.g., every 60 s) by a multiplicative factor (denoted as the XDOWN parameter) times the difference between the allocated tunnel bandwidth and the current level of the actually utilized bandwidth (i.e., the current level of spare bandwidth). The number of times tunnel bandwidth is increased and decreased is also counted over a simulated hour, and recorded in the tables.

Results indicate that MULTUP = 1 and XDOWN = .5 provide the best overall performance.

Tables 9.21 and 9.22 illustrate the results for the algorithm for increasing and decreasing CT bandwidth allocation, for the meshed network design, with the focused overload scenario (three times overload on Chicago) and multiple link failures scenario, respectively. In these simulations the time period for the periodic reduction in tunnel bandwidth is varied over 15, 30, 60, 120, and 300 s. In each of these cases the MULTUP parameter is held at 1 and the XDOWN parameter is held at .5. The

Table 9.16 Simulation Modeling Results: Multiple Link Failures with Variable Level of Bandwidth Reservation

Class type	Option A MSE CAC, DSTE/MAR, 5 queues (reservation level—% of link bandwidth)					
	0.0	0.5	1.0	3.0	5.0	10.0
Normal-Priority Voice	0.08	0.07	0.06	0.06	0.06	0.06
GETS/ETS Priority Voice	0.00	0.00	0.00	0.00	0.00	0.00
Premium Private Data	0.00	0.00	0.00	0.00	0.00	0.00
Premium Public Data	0.00	0.00	0.00	0.00	0.00	0.00
Best-Effort Data	20.00	18.99	19.52	19.19	18.82	18.34

Model Assumptions:
- 71-MSE Simulation Model, Meshed Design
- Multiple Link Failures
- Results are in Total Network % Lost/Delayed Packets (Shaded = CAC Blocking; White = Queuing Loss)

Observations:
- Reservation level of $\geq 1\%$ of link bandwidth provides best performance

number of times tunnel bandwidth is increased and decreased is also counted over a simulated hour, and recorded in the tables.

Results indicate that the number of bandwidth increases and decreases is a strong function of the time period for the periodic reduction in tunnel bandwidth, whereas the network lost/delayed traffic performance is not a strong function of this parameter. Therefore the parameter can be chosen to minimize the tunnel bandwidth changes in order to maximize scalability. However, an upper limit of 5 min is reasonable in order for the bandwidth allocation to react quickly to fast traffic demand changes, which can occur, for example, under a radio-call-in focused overload, a TV commercial break, or other often-observed traffic surges. Overall it appears that setting this time period to 120 or 300 s provides good performance in terms of minimizing the bandwidth management change frequency, while still providing reasonable responsiveness to changes in bandwidth demand.

9.6 Summary and Conclusions

The modeling and simulation analysis in this case study shows that CAC can provide significant performance improvement over no-CAC. For example, scenarios modeled show up to 10–15% reduction in loss/delay for voice traffic for option A, but less

Table 9.17 Simulation Modeling Results: Focused Overload with Variable Number of Primary and Alternate Paths

Class type	Option A MSE CAC, DSTE/MAR, 5 queues (number of primary & alternate paths)						
	1	2	4	5	6	8	10
Normal-Priority Voice	0.50	0.21	0.15	0.09	0.10	0.13	0.13
GETS/ETS Priority Voice	0.00	0.00	0.00	0.00	0.00	0.00	0.00
Premium Private Data	1.95	0.52	0.18	0.11	0.01	0.01	0.01
Premium Public Data	3.74	1.85	0.67	0.41	0.00	0.00	0.00
Best-Effort Data	33.09	31.30	32.69	33.04	33.73	32.86	32.86

Model Assumptions:
- 71-MSE Simulation Model, Meshed Design
- 3× Overload on CHCG
- Results are in Total Network % Lost/Delayed Packets
  (Shaded = CAC Blocking; White = Queuing Loss)

Observations:
- 6 or more primary & alternate paths provide best performance

improvement for options B and C. Results also show up to 5–20% reduction in lost/delayed premium data traffic for option A, but less improvement for options B and C. The analysis revealed that there would be unacceptable voice quality for no-CAC options D and E.

CAC also enables emergency services (GETS/ETS/E911) performance objectives to be achieved, which are not achieved with no-CAC options. It was found that a separate emergency-services queue is needed to assure emergency-services performance for scenarios where the normal-priority VoIP queue congests.

We found that results are not sensitive to the connectivity of the network design in that both meshed and sparse designs give similar results.

We conclude that option A is more robust than other options to wide changes of traffic patterns as well as failure scenarios. Options B and C provide inferior voice performance relative to option A and are not as robust to traffic changes as option A. We also found that option B does not give performance advantages over option C. Option D provides some differentiation for voice, but has a risk of degraded performance for all voice traffic if the EF priority queue congests and provides no additional priority/protection for emergency-services traffic.

The overall conclusion is that integrated voice/data TQO option A performs best, options B and C provide some improvement, and options D and E provide unacceptable performance.

Table 9.18 Simulation Modeling Results: Multiple Link Failures with Variable Number of Primary and Alternate Paths

Class type	Option A MSE CAC, DSTE/MAR, 5 queues (number of primary & alternate paths)						
	1	**2**	**4**	**5**	**6**	**8**	**10**
Normal-Priority Voice	0.15	0.10	0.06	0.06	0.07	0.07	0.07
GETS/ETS Priority Voice	0.00	0.00	0.00	0.00	0.00	0.00	0.00
Premium Private Data	5.76	2.13	0.00	0.00	0.00	0.00	0.00
Premium Public Data	6.85	3.22	0.00	0.00	0.00	0.00	0.00
Best-Effort Data	21.11	22.12	18.93	19.58	18.99	18.99	18.99

Model Assumptions:
- 71-MSE Simulation Model, Meshed Design
- Multiple Link Failures
- Results are in Total Network % Lost/Delayed Packets
  (Shaded = CAC Blocking; White = Queuing Loss)

Observations:
- 4 or more primary & alternate paths provide the best performance

We investigated various parameters in order to optimize the performance of option A. We found that the following parameters provided the best overall performance:

- reservation level in the range of 3–5% of link capacity
- five or more primary and alternate paths
- tunnel bandwidth allocation increase factor MULTUP = 1 and decrease factor XDOWN = .5
- time period for periodic reduction in tunnel bandwidth of 120 s or more provides good performance and reasonable responsiveness to changes in bandwidth demand

In Chapter 10 we present the GTQO protocol requirements based in large part on the case studies in this chapter and Chapter 8 of TQO protocol design for integrated voice/data IP/MPLS–GMPLS-based networks. These case studies have applied the TQO protocol design principles developed in the book, as follows:

- COS routing capabilities for service flexibility and multiservice CT bandwidth allocation
- CAC, source-based path selection, crankback, for bandwidth allocation to COSs/CTs

Table 9.19 Simulation Modeling Results: Focused Overload with Variable MULTUP and XDOWN Parameters for Bandwidth Management

Class type	Option A MSE CAC, DSTE/MAR, 5 queues (bandwidth management parameters: MULTUP, XDOWN)						
	1.0, 1.0	2.0, 1.0	4.0, 1.0	1.0, 0.0	1.0, 0.25	1.0, 0.5	1.0, 0.75
Normal-Priority Voice	0.12	9.58	11.13	0.04	0.08	0.06	0.09
GETS/ETS Priority Voice	0.00	0.00	0.00	0.00	0.00	0.00	0.00
Premium Private Data	0.01	1.00	0.97	0.00	0.01	0.01	0.02
Premium Public Data	0.00	2.37	2.35	0.00	0.00	0.00	0.00
Best-Effort Data	32.86	30.59	30.09	35.38	33.86	33.37	33.80
No. of BW Increases (MIL)	3.38	0.006	0.003	0.10	1.38	2.20	2.82
No. of BW Decreases (MIL)	0.34	0.09	0.09	0.00	0.15	0.14	0.14

Model Assumptions:
- 71-MSE Simulation Model, Meshed Design
- 3× Overload on CHCG
- Results are in Total Network% Lost/Delayed Packets
  (Light Shading = CAC Blocking; White = Queuing Loss; Dark Shading = Bandwidth Increases/Decreases)

Observations:
- MULTUP = 1.0 & XDOWN = 0.5 provides best performance

- load state mapping, bandwidth reservation techniques for stable performance, and bandwidth sharing
- dynamic connection routing, priority routing for efficient utilization, and reduced routing overhead
- meet performance objectives for integrated COSs

Based on the results and conclusions of the case study, option A, and the analysis and findings throughout the book, the GTQO protocol for MPLS/GMPLS-based dynamic routing networks is applicable to core networks, access networks, and inter-network applications and incorporates the following capabilities:

- class-of-service routing to define service elements in terms of component application/network capabilities to avoid software development or network element development for new service deployment
- per-CT (versus per-flow) QoS resource management, bandwidth allocation, dynamic bandwidth reservation, and DSTE methods for multiservice networking and lower routing table management overhead

Table 9.20 Simulation Modeling Results: Multiple Link Failures with Variable MULTUP and XDOWN Parameters for Bandwidth Management

Class type	Option A MSE CAC, DSTE/MAR, 5 queues (bandwidth management parameters: MULTUP, XDOWN)						
	1.0, 1.0	2.0, 1.0	4.0, 1.0	1.0, 0.0	1.0, 0.25	1.0, 0.5	1.0, 0.75
Normal-Priority Voice	0.06	0.93	0.92	0.03	0.05	0.06	0.07
GETS/ETS Priority Voice	0.00	0.00	0.00	0.00	0.00	0.00	0.00
Premium Private Data	0.00	5.71	5.66	0.14	0.00	0.00	0.00
Premium Public Data	0.00	6.78	6.81	0.12	0.00	0.00	0.00
Best-Effort Data	18.98	21.05	21.17	19.15	20.22	19.84	19.41
No. of BW Increases (MIL)	3.47	0.001	0.00	0.20	1.46	2.19	2.91
No. of BW Decreases (MIL)	0.35	0.09	0.09	0.00	0.14	0.14	0.14

Model Assumptions:
- 71-MSE Simulation Model, Meshed Design
- Multiple Link Failures
- Results are in Total Network % Lost/Delayed Packets
  (Light Shading = CAC Blocking; White = Queuing Loss; Dark Shading = Bandwidth Increases/Decreases)

Observation:
- MULTUP = 1.0 & XDOWN = 0.5 provides best performance

- MPLS-based explicit routing and alternate routing
- STT-EDR path selection methods for better performance and lower overhead
- MPLS/DiffServ functionality for packet scheduling and priority queuing
- separate emergency-services queue to assure emergency-services performance when normal-priority queue congests
- sparse, single-area flat topology (while retaining edge-core architecture) and multi-link routing for better performance and design efficiency
- GMPLS-based dynamic transport routing, FRR, and transport restoration, for better reliability, performance, and design efficiency
- traffic and performance monitoring for traffic management and capacity management; traffic management controls including code blocks, connection request gapping, and reroute controls
- DEFO models for capacity design of multiservice GTQO networks to capture complex routing and network behavior

These MPLS/GMPLS-based GTQO methods ensure stable/efficient performance of GTQO networks in managing resources and differentiating key service, normal service, and best-effort service.

Table 9.21 Simulation Modeling Results: Focused Overload with Variable Time Period for Periodic Reduction in Tunnel Bandwidth

Class type	Option A MSE CAC, DSTE/MAR, 5 queues (time period for periodic reduction in tunnel bandwidth, seconds)				
	15	30	60	120	300
Normal-Priority Voice	0.04	0.04	0.05	0.06	0.06
GETS/ETS Priority Voice	0.00	0.00	0.00	0.00	0.00
Premium Private Data	0.00	0.01	0.02	0.00	0.00
Premium Public Data	0.00	0.00	0.00	0.02	0.00
Best-Effort Data	32.38	32.66	33.76	33.47	33.65
No. of BW Increases (MIL)	4.25	3.02	2.14	1.49	0.92
No. of BW Decreases (MIL)	0.54	0.28	0.15	0.08	0.03

Model Assumptions:
- 71-MSE Simulation Model, Meshed Design
- 3× Overload on CHCG
- Results are in Total Network % Lost/Delayed Packets
  (Light Shading = CAC Blocking; White = Queuing Loss; Dark Shading = Bandwidth Increases/Decreases)

Observations:
- Time period for periodic change in tunnel bandwidth of 120 seconds or more provides best performance

Various extensions to IETF standards are in progress to realize the GTQO protocol requirements, including end-to-end QoS signaling needs, PCE capabilities, and RSVP aggregation extensions. These extensions are all detailed in Chapter 10.

9.7 Applicability of Requirements

As illustrated in this final case study, there is an opportunity for increased profitability and performance in MPLS/GMPLS-based networks through application of the GTQO protocol. These and other results presented support the service provider requirements for the GTQO protocol, which should then be used to drive standards and vendor implementations in the direction of network operator requirements and vendor inter-operability. Sophisticated, on-line, TQO routing methods are widely deployed in TDM

Table 9.22 Simulation Modeling Results: Multiple Link Failures with
Variable Time Period for Periodic Reduction in Tunnel Bandwidth

Class type	Option A MSE CAC, DSTE/MAR, 5 queues (time period for periodic reduction in tunnel bandwidth, seconds)				
	15	30	60	120	300
Normal-Priority Voice	0.06	0.06	0.05	0.05	0.04
GETS/ETS Priority Voice	0.00	0.00	0.00	0.00	0.00
Premium Private Data	0.00	0.00	0.00	0.00	0.00
Premium Public Data	0.00	0.00	0.00	0.00	0.00
Best-Effort Data	19.67	18.23	18.42	18.78	0.00
No. of BW Increases (MIL)	4.16	3.07	2.21	1.58	1.00
No. of BW Decreases (MIL)	0.50	0.27	0.14	0.07	0.03

Model Assumptions:
- 71-MSE Simulation Model, Meshed Design
- Multiple Link Failures
- Results are in Total Network % Lost/Delayed Packets
  (Light Shading = CAC Blocking; White = Queuing Loss; Dark Shading = Bandwidth Increases/Decreases)

Observations:
- Time period for periodic change in tunnel bandwidth of 120 seconds or more provides best performance

networks, such as discussed in the first two case studies, but have yet to be extended to IP/MPLS-based TQO, as illustrated in the final case study.

Vendors have yet to announce such GTQO capabilities in their products. Understandably, vendors prioritize features to develop based on marketing analysis and salability of their products and select features that have the broadest applicability and market potential, according to their projections. Service providers and their customers clearly would benefit from these capabilities, and service provider interest in adopting such GTQO features leads to vendor profitability also. The worldwide successful implementation of sophisticated TQO methods in TDM networks should be an incentive for vendors to pay close attention to these GTQO requirements and capabilities in MPLS networks and their potential marketability.

So, dear reader, let us now conclude our saga of the "war of two worlds" between the Geekia NetHeads and Telephonia BellHeads and speak of a truce. Let the guns be silent and let a joyful, peaceful quiet prevail over these worlds now.

Chapter 10

Summary, Conclusions, and Generic Traffic Engineering and QoS Optimization Requirements

10.1 Introduction

This chapter summarizes the results of studies presented in this book, and based on the results of these studies, operational experience, and established practice, a generic TQO (GTQO) protocol is described for network evolution to IP-based, MPLS/GMPLS-enabled technologies. The GTQO requirements and capabilities then form the basis for standards extensions, protocol development, and implementation of GTQO methods in packet-based, integrated voice/data dynamic routing networks. IP/MPLS/GMPLS standards extensions needed to accommodate the GTQO protocol requirements and capabilities are summarized.

Some of the most important, and perhaps least known, conclusions of the analysis models are as follows:

- EDR path selection is preferred to SDR path selection and could dramatically reduce IGP flooding needed and thereby increase IGP scalability,
- aggregated per-VNET bandwidth allocation is preferred to per-flow bandwidth allocation,
- GMPLS-based dynamic transport routing provides greater network reliability, throughput, revenue, and capital savings, and
- DEFO design models are extremely flexible and successful in the design of complex routing algorithms and as a basis for network capacity design methods.

The GTQO requirements apply to both access and core network architectures and include end-to-end QoS signaling, class-of-service routing, per-VNET QoS resource management, dynamic bandwidth reservation, DSTE/MAR bandwidth allocation,

STT-EDR path selection, DiffServ queuing priority, and GMPLS-based dynamic transport routing.

Clearly the GTQO protocol is one of many possibilities, and we also present several other TQO approaches that may well be deployed in some form, including (a) distributed VNET-based TQO approaches, some analogous to the GTQO approach and flow-aware networking, (b) centralized TQO approaches, such as TQO processor (TQOP), resource and admission control function (RACF), intelligent routing service control point (IRSCP), DiffServ bandwidth broker, and network-aware resource broker (NARB), and (c) competitive and cooperative game theoretic models.

Various IP/MPLS/GMPLS standards extensions needed to accommodate the GTQO requirements and capabilities are discussed, which include end-to-end QoS signaling, CAC priority, DSTE/MAR, PCE capability, RSVP aggregation over DSTE LSP tunnels, header compression over MPLS, MPLS crankback, protection/restoration mechanisms, and OSPF congestion control.

10.2 TQO Modeling and Analysis

In Chapters 2–6 and Chapters 8 and 9 we use network models to illustrate the traffic engineering methods developed in this book. A full-scale 135-node national network model is used together with a multiservice voice/data traffic demand model to study various TQO scenarios and trade-offs. A 71-node model is developed in Chapter 9 for a case study of TQO protocol design for MPLS/GMPLS-based integrated voice/data dynamic routing networks. Typical data and voice traffic loads are used to model the various network alternatives. Most of the traffic load volume in the two models represents data services, although real-time (e.g., VoIP) services constitute a substantial portion of the total traffic. An underlying assumption in the models is that PSTN legacy services, such as 64-Kbps voice and ISDN services currently offered on service provider networks, are migrated and emulated on the converged IP/MPLS network. This assumption is consistent with the NGN concept [CARUGI05] that proposes to have PSTN services emulated on the NGN architecture. The cost model represents typical connection/transport switching and transport costs and illustrates the economies of scale for costs of high capacity network elements.

Many different alternatives and trade-offs are examined in the analysis models, including:

- centralized routing table control versus distributed control
- off-line, preplanned (e.g., TDR-based) routing table control versus on-line routing table control (e.g., SDR or EDR based)
- per-flow traffic management versus per-VNET (or per-traffic-trunk) traffic management
- sparse logical topology versus meshed logical topology
- FXR versus TDR versus SDR versus EDR path selection

- multilink path selection versus two-link path selection
- path selection using local status information versus global status information
- global status dissemination alternatives, including status flooding, distributed query for status, and centralized status in a TQO processor

Table 10.1 summarizes the comparisons and observations, based on the modeling, in each of these alternatives and trade-offs (further details of these results are contained in Chapters 2–6, as indicated at the top of Table 10.1).

Table 10.1 Trade-Off Categories and Comparisons (Based on Modeling in Chapters 2–6)

Trade-off category	Traffic management performance comparisons (Chapters 2 and 3)	Routing table management comparisons (Chapter 4)	Capacity management comparisons (Chapters 5 and 6)
TQO methods applied vs no TQO methods applied	TQO methods considerably improve performance	Control load comparable	Comparable design efficiency
Centralized vs distributed routing table control	Distributed control performance somewhat better (more up-to-date status information)	Control load comparable on per-node basis	Comparable design efficiency
Off-line/preplanned (TDR) vs on-line (SDR, EDR) routing table control	On-line control somewhat better performance	TDR and EDR control load less than SDR	SDR and EDR comparable design efficiency; both better than TDR
FXR vs TDR vs SDR vs EDR path selection	EDR/SDR performance better than TDR better than FXR	FXR/TDR/EDR have lower control load than SDR	EDR/SDR design efficiency better than TDR better than FXR
Multilink path selection vs two-link path selection	Multilink path selection better under overload; two-link path selection better under failure; two-link path selection lower call/session set-up delay	Multilink path selection control load generally less than two-link path selection	Multilink design efficiency better than two link
Sparse logical topology vs meshed logical topology	Sparse topology better under overload; meshed topology better under failure	Sparse topology control load generally less than meshed topology	Sparse topology design efficiency somewhat better than meshed

(Continued)

Table 10.1 Trade-Off Categories and Comparisons (Based on Modeling in Chapters 2–6)—cont'd

Trade-off category	Traffic management performance comparisons (Chapters 2 and 3)	Routing table management comparisons (Chapter 4)	Capacity management comparisons (Chapters 5 and 6)
Single-area flat topology vs multiarea hierarchical topology	Single-area performance better than multiarea	SDR case: multiarea control load less than single-area control load EDR case: total control load comparable	Single-area topology design efficiency somewhat better than multiarea
Local status information vs global status information	Local status performance somewhat better than global (more up-to-date information)	Local status control load less than global status control load	Comparable design efficiency
Status dissemination: status flooding vs distributed query-for-status vs centralized status in TQOP	Distributed query-for-status somewhat better than status flooding and centralized status (more up-to-date information)	Centralized TQOP and distributed query-for-status comparable on per-node basis; status flooding considerably higher control load	Comparable design efficiency
Per-flow traffic management vs per-virtual-network (per-traffic-trunk) traffic management	Comparable performance	Per-virtual-network control load less than per-flow control load	Per-flow design efficiency somewhat better than per-virtual-network
Integrated voice and data network vs separate voice and data networks	Integrated network performance better than separate network performance	Total control load comparable	Integrated network design efficiency better than separate network

10.3 Summary and Conclusions Reached

Following is a summary of the main conclusions reached in this book, based primarily on the modeling and analysis presented in each chapter. Chapter 1 describes the evolution of TQO methods in data and voice networks and presents a general model for

TQO functions, which include traffic management and capacity management functions responding to traffic demands on the network. It describes a traffic-variations model that these TQO functions are responding to. In Chapter 2, we present models for call/session routing, which entails number/name translation to a routing address associated with service requests and compare various connection routing methods. In Chapter 3, we examine QoS resource management methods in detail and illustrate per-flow versus per-VNET resource management and the realization of multiservice integration with priority routing services.

In Chapter 4, we identify and discuss routing table management approaches, which include TQO signaling and information exchange requirements needed for interworking across network types. In Chapter 5 we describe methods for dynamic transport routing, which is enabled by the capabilities of GMPLS and OXC transport switching devices, to dynamically rearrange transport network capacity. In Chapter 6 we describe principles for TQO capacity optimization and management, and in Chapter 7 we present TQO operational requirements. In Chapters 8 and 9 we present three case studies for TQO protocol design in operational networks: (a) circuit-switched integrated voice/ISDN dynamic routing networks for intranetwork applications, (b) circuit-switched integrated voice/ISDN dynamic routing networks for internetwork applications, and (c) MPLS/GMPLS-based integrated voice/data dynamic routing networks. We also discuss two case studies in Chapter 8 where TQO designs went astray, but at the same time provided valuable lessons for future designs.

10.3.1 Chapter 1: Summary and Conclusions on TQO Models

Chapter 1 begins with a general model for TQO functions at each network layer, as well as traffic management and capacity management operational functions. Network layers include the traffic/application layer, connection/MPLS LSP layer, logical link/GMPLS LSP layer, and physical network layer. We formulate the TQO design problem addressed at each layer and outline the solution approach, where the latter includes an analysis of TQO design and operational experience, as well as design/analysis studies. The analysis of TQO design and operational experience traces the evolution and benefits of TQO methods using ARPANET to illustrate TQO evolution in data networks and the AT&T network to illustrate TQO evolution in voice networks. TQO design principles are identified that emerged along with the TQO evolution. We present the key results and conclusions of the GTQO design based on TQO design/operational experience in voice and data networks, modeling and analysis studies, and detailed case studies.

10.3.2 Chapter 2: Summary and Conclusions on Call/Session Routing and Connections Routing Methods

In Chapter 2, we present models for call/session routing, which entails number/name translation to a routing address associated with service requests, and also compare various connection (bearer-path) routing methods. We introduce a full-scale, 135-node national network model and a multiservice traffic demand model, which is used throughout the book to study various TQO scenarios and trade-offs in TQO optimization. The model is used in Chapter 2 to illustrate TQO network design, including integrated voice and data designs based on MPLS technology. Various performance analyses are presented for network overloads and failures, which illustrate the benefits of TQO on network performance. These models provide in-depth studies of the trade-offs between various TQO approaches, including (a) fixed routing, time-dependent routing, state-dependent routing, and event-dependent routing path selection methods, (b) two-link and multilink path selection methods, (c) resource management and connection admission control methods, (d) service priority differentiation of key services, normal services, and best-effort services, and (e) single-area flat topologies versus multiarea hierarchical topologies.

Performance comparisons are presented for various TQO methods and a baseline case of no TQO methods applied. The TQO modeling conclusions include the following:

- In all cases of the TQO methods being applied, network performance is always better and usually substantially better than when no TQO methods are applied.
- Sparse-topology multilink-routing networks provide better overall performance under overload than meshed-topology networks, but performance under failure may favor the two-link STT-EDR or DC-SDR meshed-topology options with more alternate routing choices.
- Single-area flat topologies exhibit better network performance and, as discussed and modeled in Chapter 6, greater design efficiencies in comparison with multiarea hierarchical topologies. As illustrated in Chapter 4, larger administrative areas can be achieved through use of EDR-based TQO methods as compared to SDR-based TQO methods.
- EDR TQO path selection methods exhibit comparable or better network performance compared to SDR methods.
  a. EDR TQO methods are shown to be an important class of TQO algorithms. EDR TQO methods are distinct from the TDR and SDR TQO methods in how the paths (e.g., MPLS LSPs) are selected. In the SDR TQO case, the available link bandwidth, based on LSA flooding of ALB information, is typically used to compute the path. In the EDR TQO case, the ALB information is not needed to compute the path, therefore the ALB flooding does not need to take place (reducing the overhead).
  b. EDR TQO algorithms are adaptive and distributed in nature and typically use learning models to find good paths in a network. For example, in an STT-EDR TQO method, if the LSR-A to LSR-B bandwidth needs to be modified, say increased by DBW, the primary LSP-p is tried first. If DBW is not available on one or more links of LSP-p, then the currently successful LSP-s is tried next. If DBW is not available on one or more links of LSP-s, then a new LSP is searched by trying additional candidate paths until a new successful LSP-n is found or the

candidate paths are exhausted. LSP-n is then marked as the currently successful path for the next time bandwidth needs to be modified. The performance of distributed EDR TQO methods is shown to be equal to or better than SDR methods, centralized or distributed.

   c. While SDR TQO models typically use ALB flooding for TQO path selection, EDR TQO methods do not require ALB flooding. Rather, EDR TQO methods typically search out capacity by learning models, as in the STT method given above. ALB flooding can be very resource intensive, as it requires link bandwidth to carry LSAs, processor capacity to process LSAs, and the overhead can limit area/AS size. Modeling results show EDR TQO methods can lead to a large reduction in ALB flooding overhead without loss of network throughput performance (as shown in Chapter 4).

   d. State information as used by the SDR options (such as with link-state flooding) provides essentially equivalent performance to the EDR options, which typically used distributed routing with crankback and no flooding.

   e. Various path selection methods can interwork with each other in the same network, as required for multivendor network operation.

- Internetwork routing methods extend the intranetwork call/session routing and connection routing concepts, such as flexible path selection and per-class-of-service bandwidth selection, to routing between networks.

10.3.3 Chapter 3: Summary and Conclusions on TQO Protocol Design for MPLS-Based Dynamic Routing Networks

In Chapter 3, we examine QoS resource management methods in detail and illustrate per-flow versus per-VNET resource management and the realization of multiservice integration with priority routing services. QoS resource management (sometimes called QoS routing) functions include class-of-service identification, routing table derivation, connection admission control, bandwidth allocation, bandwidth protection, bandwidth reservation, priority routing, priority queuing, and other related resource management functions. QoS resource management methods applied successfully in circuit-switched networks are extended to packet-switched, (G)MPLS-based networks, and GTQO requirements are identified for application to intranetwork, access, and internetwork applications. Class-of-service routing provides a means to define network services through table-driven concepts rather than software development and new network deployment. Whereas the historical model of new service development always led to a "stovepipe" approach with specialized software development to implement the service and hardware development to build a new network and network elements, class-of-service routing defines service and network capabilities in tables within the network nodes. That is, definition of new services capabilities are table driven and require no software development or network element development. Bandwidth allocation control in the GTQO method is based on estimated bandwidth needs, bandwidth use, and status of links in the VNET. It is shown that dynamic bandwidth reservation, a network capability that enables preferential treatment for "preferred" traffic over "nonpreferred" traffic, is an essential GTQO capability for a converged MPLS-based network.

We again use the full-scale national network model to analyze a wide variety of MPLS-based QoS resource management methods in which bandwidth is allocated to each of several VNETs and VNETs are assigned a priority corresponding to either high-priority key services, normal-priority services, or best-effort low-priority services. The conclusions reached include the following:

- Class-of-service routing defines service elements in terms of component application and network capabilities, which can then be specified and provisioned in tables within the network nodes. This table-driven approach to new service deployment requires no software development or network element development, avoids the historical stovepipe approach to deploying new services in separate networks, and is fully consistent with converged TQO network evolution and deployment.
- Bandwidth reservation is critical to the stable and efficient performance of TQO methods in a network and to ensure the proper operation of multiservice bandwidth allocation, protection, and priority treatment.
- Per-VNET bandwidth allocation is essentially equivalent to per-flow bandwidth allocation in network performance and efficiency. Because of the much lower routing table management overhead requirements, as discussed and modeled in Chapter 4, per-VNET bandwidth allocation is preferred to per-flow allocation.
- QoS resource management is shown to be effective in achieving high-priority (key) service, normal-service, and best-effort service differentiation.
- Both MPLS QoS and bandwidth management and DiffServ priority queuing management are important for ensuring that multiservice network performance objectives are met under a range of network conditions. Both mechanisms operate together to ensure that QoS resource allocation mechanisms (bandwidth allocation, protection, and priority queuing) are achieved.

10.3.4 Chapter 4: Summary and Conclusions on Routing Table Management Methods and Requirements

In Chapter 4, we identify and discuss routing table management approaches and provide information exchange requirements needed for interworking across network types. Routing table management entails the automatic generation of routing tables based on information such as topology update, status update, and routing recommendations. This information is used for purposes of applying the routing table design rules to determine path choices in the routing table. Link-state (LS) routing protocols such as OSPF use topology-state update mechanisms to build the topology database at each node, typically conveying the topology status through flooding of control messages containing link, node, and reachable-address information between nodes. Congestion in LS protocols has caused many problems in the past, can arise for many different reasons, and can result in widespread loss of topology database information and overload in flooding of topology database information. These and other routing table management information exchange issues are examined in this chapter.

We again use the full-scale 135-node national network model to study various TQO scenarios and routing table management alternatives and trade-offs, such as (a) centralized routing table control versus distributed control, (b) preplanned routing table control versus on-line routing table control, (c) per-flow traffic management versus per-VNET traffic management, (d) sparse logical topology versus meshed logical topology, (e) fixed routing versus time-dependent routing versus event-dependent routing path selection, (f) multilink path selection versus two-link path selection, (g) path selection using local status information versus global status information, and (h) global status dissemination alternatives, including status flooding, distributed query for status, and centralized status in a TQO processor. The conclusions reached include the following:

- Per-VNET bandwidth allocation is preferred to per-flow allocation because of the much lower routing table management overhead requirements. Per-VNET bandwidth allocation is essentially equivalent to per-flow bandwidth allocation in network performance and efficiency, as discussed in Chapter 3.
- EDR TQO methods can lead to a large reduction in ALB flooding overhead without loss of network throughput performance. While SDR TQO methods typically use ALB flooding for TQO path selection, EDR TQO methods do not require ALB flooding. Rather, EDR TQO methods typically search out capacity by learning models, as in the STT method. ALB flooding can be very resource intensive, as it requires link bandwidth to carry LSAs, processor capacity to process LSAs, and the overhead can limit area/AS size.
- EDR TQO methods lead to possible larger administrative areas as compared to SDR-based TQO methods because of lower routing table management overhead requirements. This can help achieve single-area flat topologies, which, as discussed in Chapter 3, exhibit better network performance and, as discussed in Chapter 6, greater design efficiencies in comparison with multiarea hierarchical topologies.

Hence results show that per-VNET QoS resource management, sparse, single-area flat topology (while retaining edge-core architecture), multilink routing, and STT-EDR path selection methods lead to dramatically lower routing table management overhead. These results are reflected in the GTQO protocol requirements. In particular, the GTQO protocol provides automatic provisioning of topology databases and fewer links to provision in sparse network topology, leading to operations expense and capital savings. Also, the GTQO protocol eliminates available-link-bandwidth flooding and allows larger/fewer areas, leading to dramatically improved network stability, performance, and scalability.

10.3.5 Chapter 5: Summary and Conclusions on TQO Protocol Design of GMPLS-Based Multilayer Dynamic Routing Networks

In Chapter 5 we describe methods for dynamic transport routing, which is enabled by the capabilities of GMPLS and OXC devices, to dynamically rearrange transport network capacity. GTQO protocol requirements for GMPLS-based dynamic routing networks are developed, and it is shown that the GMPLS capabilities have actually been reinvented. As early as 1990, dynamic routing benefits in improved performance quality and reduced costs motivated the extension of dynamic routing to networks with rearrangeable transport capacity, which was then called the fully shared network (FSN) concept. Like GMPLS, FSN envisioned use of automatic control of OXCs to achieve dynamic bandwidth allocation of transport and connection/transport switching capacity, where the realized benefits include robust network design, efficient capacity engineering, and automatic transport provisioning to achieve increased revenues and significant savings in capital and operations costs. Therefore GMPLS technology, very analogous to FSN, offers a revolutionary new approach (first new multi-layer dynamic routing revolution since FSN, at least) to integrated control of the layer 3 dynamic connection routing and layer 2 dynamic transport routing networks. GMPLS-based control capabilities enable dynamic transport routing to combine with dynamic connection routing to shift transport bandwidth among node pairs and services through use of flexible transport switching technology and switching of DWDM light paths and layer 2 logical links through OXCs. This allows simplicity of design and robustness to load variations and network failures and provides automatic link provisioning, diverse link routing, and rapid link restoration for improved transport capacity utilization and performance under stress.

Again using the 135-node national network model, we give modeling results for GMPLS-based dynamic transport routing capacity design, performance under network failures, general traffic overloads, unexpected overloads, and peak-day traffic loads. We conclude that GMPLS-based dynamic transport routing provides greater network throughput and, consequently, enhanced revenue, achieves efficient network design and capital savings, and greatly enhances network performance under failure and overload, as follows:

- GMPLS-based dynamic transport routing provides greater network throughput and, consequently, enhanced revenue, and at the same time capital savings should result, as discussed in Chapter 6.
  a. Dynamic transport routing network design enhances network performance under failure, which arises from automatic interbackbone-router and access logical-link diversity in combination with the dynamic connection routing and transport restoration of logical links.
  b. Dynamic transport routing network design improves network performance in comparison with fixed transport routing for all network conditions simulated, which include abnormal and unpredictable traffic load patterns.

- Traffic and transport restoration level design allows for link diversity to ensure a minimum level of performance under failure.
- Robust routing techniques, which include dynamic connection routing, multiple ingress/egress routing, and logical link diversity routing, improve response to node or transport failures.

10.3.6 Chapter 6: Summary and Conclusions on Optimization Methods for Routing Design and Capacity Management

In Chapter 6 we discuss optimization methods and principles for routing design optimization, including (a) shortest path optimization models and (b) discrete event simulation models, which capture complex routing behavior. We also discuss optimization methods and principles for capacity design optimization, including (a) DEFO models, (b) TLFO models, (c) VTFO models, and (d) dynamic transport routing capacity design models. We discuss the impacts of traffic variations on network design, including minute-to-minute, hour-to-hour, day-to-day, and forecast uncertainty/reserve capacity design impacts. All of these techniques have been applied extensively in real network operational scenarios over a very long period of time. Truitt's link capacity design model was introduced over 50 years ago and has been used in many network design applications ever since. More recently, but already in operation for nearly two decades, the DEFO model has been used to design AT&T's operational voice/ISDN network and has been applied extensively in architecture studies, such as the case studies presented in Chapters 8 and 9.

We again use the full-scale 135-node national network model to study various TQO scenarios and trade-offs. We illustrate the use of the DEFO model for per-flow multiservice network design and per-VNET design and to provide comparisons of these designs. We also study multilink versus two-link network designs, single-area flat topologies versus two-level hierarchical topology design, event-dependent routing versus state-dependent routing design, and GMPLS-based dynamic transport routing versus fixed transport routing network design. The conclusions reached include the following:

- DEFO design models are shown to be able to capture very complex routing behavior through the equivalent of a simulation model provided in software in the routing design module. By this means, very complex routing networks have been designed by the model, which include all of the routing methods discussed in Chapter 2 (FXR, TDR, SDR, and EDR methods) and the multiservice QoS resource allocation models discussed in Chapter 3.
- Sparse topology options, which incorporate multilink dynamic routing options, lead to capital cost advantages and, more importantly, to operation simplicity and cost reduction. Capital cost savings are subject to the particular connection/transport switching and transport cost assumptions. Operational issues are detailed further in Chapter 7.

- Voice and data integration can provide capital cost advantages and, more importantly, can achieve operational simplicity and cost reduction; if IP-telephony takes hold and a significant portion of voice calls/sessions use voice compression technology, this could lead to more efficient networks.
- Multilink routing methods exhibit greater design efficiencies in comparison with two-link routing methods. As discussed and modeled in Chapter 3, multilink topologies exhibit better network performance under overloads in comparison with two-link routing topologies; however, the two-link topologies do better under failure scenarios.
- Single-area flat topologies exhibit greater design efficiencies in termination and transport capacity, but higher cost and, as discussed and modeled in Chapter 3, better network performance in comparison with multiarea hierarchical topologies. As illustrated in Chapter 4, larger administrative areas can be achieved through the use of EDR-based TQO methods as compared to SDR-based TQO methods.
- EDR methods exhibit comparable design efficiencies to SDR. This suggests that there is not a significant advantage for employing link-state information in these network designs, especially given the high overhead in flooding link-state information in SDR methods.
- Dynamic transport routing achieves capital savings by concentrating capacity on fewer, high-capacity physical fiber links and, as discussed in Chapter 5, achieves higher network throughput and enhanced revenue by their ability to flexibly allocate bandwidth on the logical links serving the access and internode traffic.

10.3.7 Chapter 7: Summary and Conclusions on TQO Operational Requirements

In Chapter 7 we present TQO operational requirements for traffic management and capacity management functions in both data and voice networks, as follows: (a) performance management, which collects and analyzes real-time network status and performance data, detects abnormal network conditions, investigates and identifies the reasons for abnormal network conditions, initiates corrective action, and coordinates with other network management centers on matters that affect service; (b) fault management, which deals with problems and emergencies in the network, such as router failures and power losses; (c) capacity management, which gathers statistics on equipment and facility use and analyzes trends to justify network upgrades and/or bandwidth increases; (d) configuration management, which tracks device settings, inventory, configuration, provisioning, and makes adjustments as needed; (e) issuing reports of abnormal network situations, actions taken and results obtained; and (f) providing advance planning for known or predictable network situations. Traffic management corrective action includes controls such as code blocks, connection request gapping, and reroute controls to be activated when circumstances warrant.

Capacity management includes capacity forecasting, daily and weekly performance monitoring, and short-term network adjustment. We illustrate the steps involved in these functions with examples. In particular, we illustrate an MPLS network management implementation by taking an example from AT&T's MPLS operations architecture.

The conclusions reached on operational requirements include the following:

- Monitoring of traffic and performance data is required for traffic management, capacity forecasting, daily and weekly performance monitoring, and short-term network adjustment.
- Traffic management is required to provide monitoring of network performance through collection and display of real-time traffic and performance data and allow traffic management controls such as code blocks, connection request gapping, and reroute controls to be inserted when circumstances warrant.
- Capacity management is required for capacity forecasting, daily and weekly performance monitoring, and short-term network adjustment.
- Forecasting is required to operate over a multiyear forecast interval and drive network capacity expansion.
- Daily and weekly performance monitoring is required to identify any service problems in the network. If service problems are detected, short-term network adjustment can include routing table updates and, if necessary, short-term capacity additions to alleviate service problems. Updated routing tables are sent to the nodes either directly or via an automated routing update system.
- Short-term capacity additions are required as needed, but only as an exception, whereas most capacity changes are normally forecasted, planned, scheduled, and managed over a period of months or a year or more.
- Network design, which includes routing design and capacity design, is required within the capacity management function.
- Network planning is required for longer term node planning and transport network planning and operates over a horizon of months to years to plan and implement new node and transport capacity.

10.3.8 Chapters 8 and 9: Summary and Conclusions on Case Studies of TQO for Operational Integrated Voice/Data Dynamic Routing Networks

In Chapters 8 and 9 we present three case studies for TQO protocol design in operational networks: (a) circuit-switched integrated voice/ISDN dynamic routing networks for intranetwork applications, (b) circuit-switched integrated voice/ISDN dynamic routing networks for internetwork applications, and (c) MPLS/GMPLS-based integrated voice/data dynamic routing networks. We also discuss two case studies in Chapter 8 where TQO designs went astray, but at the same time provided valuable lessons for future designs. These case studies reflect the studies, planning, and implementation of TQO in a large service provider's (AT&T's) network over several decades. TQO protocol design and optimization, as illustrated in the case studies, seek to find an optimal TQO protocol for arbitrary traffic loads and network topology, which yields minimum cost capacity and maximum flow/revenue. Chapters 8 and 9 illustrate the use of numerous optimization methods to solve this problem.

In the first two case studies presented in Chapter 8, we illustrate the design and optimization of large-scale, state-dependent TQO protocols: real-time network routing/class of service (RTNR/COS) and real-time internetwork routing/class of service (RINR/COS). In these case studies we use the DEFO model to illustrate the design and optimization of RTNR/COS and RINR/COS and the conception and theoretical analysis studies that preceded the development and deployment of RTNR/COS and RINR/COS. As such, these case studies provide a learning experience for emerging networks, i.e., for converged IP/MPLS networks, which are the subject of the final (fifth) case study.

The third and fourth case studies presented in Chapter 8 illustrate where alternate routing may have contributed to network congestion. These examples are intended to illustrate possible pitfalls of excessive alternate routing and need for protection techniques, primarily the need for bandwidth reservation methods to guard against excessive alternate routing. One case involved a software problem that crippled the AT&T long-distance network on January 15, 1990, and a second that involved a new routing capability to avoid a voice enhancement capability in the network. In both cases cited, proper use of bandwidth reservation may well have helped alleviate the problems that occurred.

In the final case study, presented in Chapter 9, we develop a 71-node national network model and multiservice traffic demand model for the TQO protocol design in an MPLS/GMPLS-based integrated voice/data dynamic routing network. We again use the DEFO model to illustrate the design and optimization of this large-scale, state-dependent TQO protocol, which allows the integration of a number of voice and data services, called DSTE class types (CTs) in this technology, on an integrated shared packet network, with sophisticated bandwidth allocation/management capabilities. A 5 CT traffic model is developed and three levels of traffic priority—high, normal, and best effort—are designated for each VNET. We illustrate the selection of an EDR-based path selection protocol from among a large set of candidates and define five options for the TQO bandwidth management protocol, which include various admission control, bandwidth allocation/management, and queuing approaches. The modeling and simulation analysis shows a 10–15% reduction in loss/delay for voice traffic and up to 5–20% reduction in lost/delayed data traffic for the preferred MPLS/GMPLS-based option compared to the other options.

These case studies provide an important basis for the GTQO protocol requirements, as described in the following sections, which are also based on the modeling analysis studies and operational experience.

10.4   GTQO Protocol for MPLS/GMPLS-Based Integrated Voice/Data Dynamic Routing Networks

GTQO protocol requirements and methods are described in this section for consideration in network evolution. These requirements are based on:

- results of analysis models presented in the book, which illustrate the trade-offs between various TQO approaches,
- TQO operational experience, as discussed in Chapter 1, and
- results of case studies presented in Chapters 8 and 9, which apply TQO protocol design principles.

10.4.1   GTQO Protocol Requirements

The GTQO protocol must support all access technologies, protocols, and services, while meeting end-to-end performance objectives with a cost-effective solution. It must be applicable to both access and backbone networks, for example, to slow speed access networks and to broadband DSL, cable, and fiber access networks. Some access technologies already have TQO protocol specifications in place, such as the broadband remote access server (BRAS) technology applicable to DSL access and the Dynamic Quality of Service Specification (DQOS) for cable access networks. The GTQO protocol model must operate across routing areas, ASs, and service provider boundaries. Emergency services must be given higher priority in the GTQO protocol and must also provide the functionality to deny new connections and to terminate existing lower-precedence connections in networks that serve different levels of users and communications, such as in military networks [ASSURED-SERVICES-RQMTS, ASSURED-SERVICES-ARCH].

Following are the GTQO protocol requirements that must be supported by the GTQO capabilities and standards extensions described in the following sections:

- support all access technologies (e.g., wireless, cable, DSL, fiber) and access protocols (e.g., BRAS, DQOS)
- support legacy services and QoS requirements
- meet end-to-end performance objectives
- be backward compatible with non-GTQO-enabled networks
- give emergency services higher priority of completion; allow emergency connections to degrade QoS of connections in progress; maintain quality of emergency connections during network stress
- operate across routing areas, ASs, and service provider boundaries
- accommodate different bandwidth requirements for individual flows (e.g., to account for various codecs, header compression); account for all traffic in allocating network bandwidth
- meet scalability requirements in terms of maximum number of calls/sessions

Based on these requirements, the GTQO protocol capabilities that meet the requirements are now described.

10.4.2 GTQO Capabilities to Meet Requirements

The GTQO protocol for flows, connections, and transport in MPLS-based and GMPLS-based dynamic routing networks incorporates distributed, on-line processing, aggregated, per-VNET (versus per-flow) bandwidth allocation, and dynamic transport routing capabilities. These required GTQO capabilities apply to both access and core network architectures:

- end-to-end QoS signaling to achieve end-to-end QoS performance requirements through multiple Internet domains,
- class-of-service routing to define service elements in terms of component application/network capabilities to avoid software development or network element development for new service deployment,
- per-VNET QoS resource management, bandwidth allocation, dynamic bandwidth reservation, and DSTE methods for multiservice networking and lower routing table management overhead,
- MPLS-based explicit routing to achieve STT-EDR path selection methods for better performance and lower control overhead,
- MPLS/DiffServ functionality for packet scheduling and priority queuing,
- separate emergency-services queue to assure emergency-services performance when normal-priority queue congests
- sparse, single-area flat topology (while retaining edge-core architecture) and multi-link routing for better performance and design efficiency,
- GMPLS-based dynamic transport routing, traffic, and transport restoration, for better reliability, performance, and design efficiency,
- traffic/performance monitoring for traffic management and capacity management, and traffic management controls such as code blocks, connection request gapping, and reroute controls, and
- DEFO models for capacity design of multiservice GTQO networks to capture complex routing behavior and design.

GTQO requires the ability to achieve end-to-end QoS through multiple Internet domains, which is ensured through end-to-end QoS signaling. For example, the originating node initiates an end-to-end, interdomain QoS signaling message containing the QoS parameters, such as QoS class, QoS performance objectives, traffic parameters, reservation priority, and others. The QoS message may cross multiple domains, perhaps supporting different QoS models, and each node on the data path checks the availability of resources and ability to meet the specified performance requirements. If an intermediate node cannot accommodate the request, it indicates this is a return signaling message and the reservation is denied. If no intermediate node has denied the reservation, the QoS message is forwarded to the next domain, and eventually to the destination node. End-to-end QoS signaling is described further in Section 10.6.5, under the discussion of standards extensions needed to meet the GTQO requirements.

Class-of-service routing defines a table-driven approach to new service deployment and ensures flexibility to define new services without software development or network element development. Class-of-service routing is discussed in detail in Chapter 3.

GTQO capabilities ensure stable/efficient performance of GTQO networks in managing resources and differentiating key service, normal service, and best-effort service. Figure 10.1 illustrates per-VNET bandwidth allocation and management methods, where bandwidth is allocated to the individual VNETs and managed as illustrated. Allocated VNET bandwidth is protected by bandwidth reservation methods, as needed, but otherwise shared. Each ON monitors VNET bandwidth use and determines when VNET LSP bandwidth needs to be increased or decreased. Bandwidth changes in VNET bandwidth capacity are determined by ONs based on an overall aggregated bandwidth demand for VNET capacity and make periodic discrete changes in bandwidth allocation. Per-VNET bandwidth allocation and management are discussed in detail in Chapter 3.

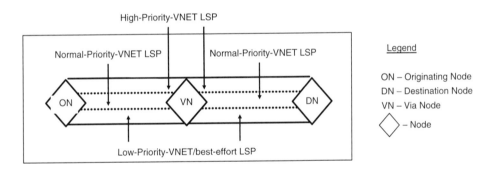

- ❏   distributed bandwidth allocation method applied on a per-VNET LSP basis
- ❏   ON allocates bandwidth to each VNET LSP based on demand
  - ❖   ON decides VNET LSP bandwidth increase based on
    - –   link bandwidth-in-progress (BWIP)
    - –   routing priority (high, normal, best-effort)
    - –   link bandwidth allocation for VNET (link bandwidth constraint BC)
    - –   link reserved bandwidth RBW
  - ❖   ON periodically decreases VNET LSP bandwidth allocation based on bandwidth use
- ❏   nodes keep local link state of idle link bandwidth (ILBW), including available bandwidth (ABW) and reserved bandwidth (RBW) states
- ❏   VNs send crankback message to ON if DSTE-MAR bandwidth allocation rules not met

Figure 10.1   Per-VNET bandwidth allocation and management.

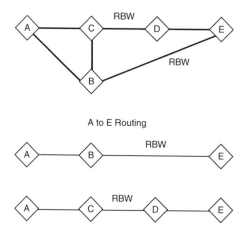

Example of Option A (STT-EDR) routing method:
1. if node A to node E bandwidth needs to be modified (say increased by DBW) primary LSP-p (e.g., LSP A-B-E) is tried first
2. available bandwidth tested locally on each link in LSP-p, if bandwidth not available (e.g., link BE is in reserved bandwidth (RBW) state & this CT is above its bandwidth allocation), crankback to node A
3. if DBW is not available on one or more links of LSP-p, then the currently successful LSP-s (e.g., LSP A-C-D-E) is tried next
4. if DBW is not available on one or more links of LSP-s, then a new LSP is searched by trying additional candidate paths until a new successful LSP-n is found or the candidate paths are exhausted
5. LSP-n is then marked as the currently successful path for the next time bandwidth needs to be modified

Figure 10.2 GTQO multilink STT-EDR path selection in a sparse network topology.

Figure 10.2 illustrates the multilink STT-EDR path selection method within a sparse, single-area topology. The multilink STT-EDR method is distributed and reduces control signaling requirements and flooding needs dramatically, thereby increasing scalability. STT-EDR path selection and spare topologies are discussed in Chapters 2 and 3, and the control signaling implications are discussed in Chapter 4.

Figure 10.3 illustrates the monitoring of network traffic and performance data to support GTQO traffic management and capacity management functions. Figure 10.4 illustrates the GTQO traffic management functions, and Figure 10.5 illustrates the GTQO capacity management functions. These functions are discussed in detail in Chapter 7.

Figure 10.6 illustrates the DEFO design model applicable to GTQO capacity management design functions. The greatest advantage of the DEFO model is its ability to capture very complex routing behavior through the equivalent of a simulation model provided in a design algorithm. The DEFO model is discussed in detail in Chapter 7.

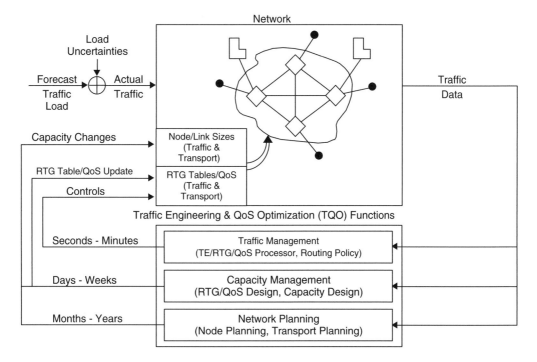

Figure 10.3   Monitoring traffic and performance data to support GTQO traffic management and capacity management functions.

10.4.3   GTQO Protocol Description

Figure 10.7 illustrates the GTQO protocol model. The end points are IP/PBXs, individual-usage SIP/RTP end devices, hard and soft SIP phones, IADs, and so on, and traffic enters and leaves the core via possibly bandwidth-constrained access networks. The basic elements in the GTQO protocol model are the gateways (GW), multiservice edge (MSE) routers, provider (P) routers, and the call/session control agent. The GW functionality may be implemented in a customer edge (CE) device or it could be a stand-alone network element. In Figure 10.7, the GWs are assumed to handle both signaling and bearer control. However, other configurations might use distributed soft switches where separate media gateways are managed by a media gateway controller (in this configuration, signaling and bearer control are fully decoupled). The GW implements SIP with preconditions [RFC3312], allowing the integration of resource management with SIP. This allows the GW to determine whether the network has sufficient bandwidth before completing the establishment of a session initiated using SIP. One of the factors in determining whether to admit a connection is learning the IP address, port, and session parameters (such as codec bandwidth requirements). An offer/answer exchange carried in SIP messages allows the initiating GW to determine

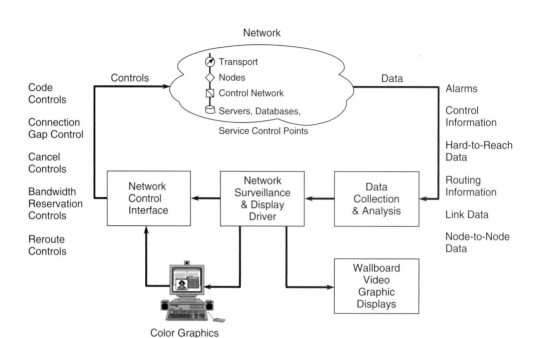

Figure 10.4   GTQO traffic management operations functions.

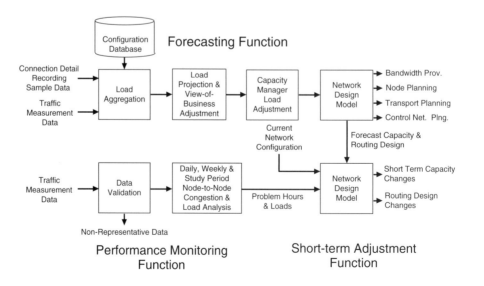

Figure 10.5   GTQO capacity management functions.

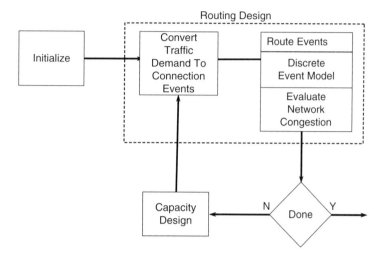

Figure 10.6 DEFO model to support GTQO capacity management.

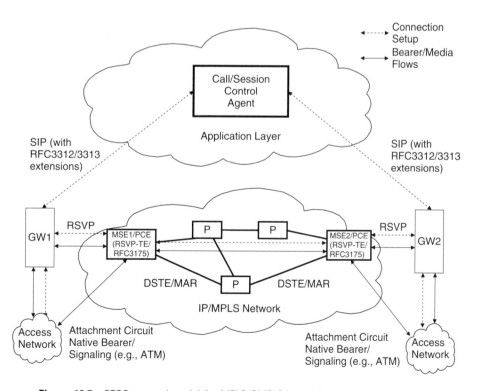

Figure 10.7 GTQO protocol model for MPLS/GMPLS-based dynamic routing networks.

this information. The GW receiving the offer does not alert the user or otherwise proceed with session establishment until both ends know that the preconditions are met.

Figure 10.7 illustrates the GTQO protocol model capability to determine whether there is sufficient bandwidth to complete a connection, where the originating and terminating GWs each send for each connection an RSVP bandwidth request to the network MSE router to which it is connected. The bandwidth request takes into account header compression, where applicable. The originating GW combines local TQO information from the MSE router with remote TQO information obtained via SIP resource management [RFC3312], as described earlier.

The MSE then (a) determines whether there is enough bandwidth on the route between the originating and destination GWs to accommodate the connection, (b) communicates the accept/reject decision to the GW on a connection-by-connection basis, and (c) optimizes network resources by dynamically adjusting bandwidth allocations. As illustrated in Figure 10.7, MPLS DSTE/MAR LSP tunnels are established between MSEs. If a DSTE/MAR LSP tunnel is operating near capacity, the network may dynamically adjust the LSP tunnel size within a set of parameters. That is, the MSE maintains the per-VNET LSP tunnel capacity based on aggregated RSVP requests and responds on a connection-by-connection basis based on the available capacity. The MSE can periodically adjust the LSP tunnel capacity upward, when needed, and periodically adjust the LSP tunnel capacity downward, when spare capacity exists in the LSP tunnel. A "make before break" mechanism can be used to adjust LSP tunnel capacity to avoid any service interruption.

In the GTQO protocol model, an operations support system (OSS) provisions the DSTE LSP tunnels [RFC3564] between the MSEs based on the traffic forecast and current network utilization. These guaranteed bandwidth DSTE LSP tunnels are created using RSVP-TE [RFC3209] and apply the DSTE/MAR bandwidth constraints model [RFC4126] to determine LSP tunnel bandwidth allocation. These DSTE LSP tunnels are engineered and provisioned by the OSS based on the forecasted traffic load and, when needed, the LSP tunnels for the different VNETs, also known in DSTE terminology as class types (CTs), can take different paths. A PCE [PCE-ARCHITECTURE, PCE-REQUIREMENTS, PCE-PROTOCOL] provides bandwidth management and explicit alternate routing, as well as interarea/inter-AS/interservice-provider TE path computation. The DSTE LSP tunnels can also be protected against failure by using MPLS fast reroute.

The MSE routers support RSVP aggregation for scalability [RFC3175] using aggregation mechanisms that deviate somewhat from RFC 3175. That is, the GW sends a PATH message to the MSE router every time it receives a SIP connection setup message with an IP media address that can be reached through the DSTE LSP tunnel. The RSVP aggregator in the MSE router keeps a running total of bandwidth usage on the DSTE LSP tunnel, adding the bandwidth requirements during connection setup and subtracting during connection teardown. The aggregator responds with an RESV message saying whether there is sufficient bandwidth for the connection from that originating MSE to the destination MSE. The destination GW also sends a PATH message to its MSE router to check whether there is enough bandwidth on the DSTE LSP tunnel from the destination MSE to the originating MSE. The aggregate bandwidth usage on the DSTE LSP tunnel is also available to the DSTE MAR algorithm. If the aggregate bandwidth usage exceeds some threshold, then the MSE sends a PATH message through the LSP tunnel to the other end, requesting bandwidth (perhaps enough for several additional connections). If the size of the DSTE LSP tunnel cannot be increased on the primary and alternate LSPs, then when the DSTE LSP tunnel bandwidth is exhausted, the aggregator will send an RSVP message denying the reservation, and the GW will reject those connections. When DSTE LSP tunnels are underutilized, the bandwidth of the LSP tunnel will be reduced periodically to an appropriate level.

Dynamic LSP tunnel bandwidth adjustment is one approach to bandwidth management, and there are of course many other approaches. For example, a less complex approach might be to traffic engineer MPLS-TE LSP tunnels based on traffic history and then periodically perform TQO load leveling by distributing the load across parallel LSP tunnels. Such alternative approaches are analyzed in Chapter 9 and are shown to be less efficient and robust compared with the dynamic LSP tunnel bandwidth approach.

The GTQO protocol model assumes separate queues in the core implemented with DiffServ based on CoS/EXP bits. These queues include two expedited forwarding (EF) priority queues, with the highest priority assigned to emergency traffic and the second priority assigned to normal-priority real-time traffic. Several assured forwarding (AF) queues are assumed for various data traffic, e.g., premium private data traffic, premium public data traffic, and a separate best-effort queue is assumed for the best-effort traffic. Several DSTE LSP tunnels may share the same physical link, and therefore share the same queue. We note that not all vendors support multiple strict-priority queues, and it may be preferable to avoid a proliferation of queues in the core elements, both because of vendor limitations and to simplify core configurations. An alternative is to have a single AF queue (including best-effort traffic) with class-based WRED so that there is differential dropping within the queue.

Table 10.2 summarizes the technology components supported by the GTQO protocol model.

10.5 Comparative Analysis of GTQO Protocol Model and Alternative Models

The GTQO protocol requirements and capabilities form the basis for standards extensions, development, and implementation of GTQO methods in packet-based, integrated voice/data dynamic routing networks. Both Geekian and Telephonian views are taken into account in the GTQO model, as we fully recognize that both sets of ideas are always right. Clearly the optimal GTQO approach presented in this book is not the one and only solution. To the contrary, we present here several other excellent solution approaches that may well be deployed in some form. This, of course, is rather obvious, for example, many TQO approaches have been deployed in voice networks.

Table 10.2 Technology Components Supported by the GTQO Model

Layer	Technology components
Application layer	• SIP with preconditions [RFC3312]; SIP resource priority header [RFC4412] • Issue RSVP bandwidth request for connection admission control [RFC2205]
IP/MPLS/GMPLS network layers	• End-to-end QoS signaling [QOS-SIG-NTLP, QOS-SIG-NSLP, QOS-SIG-QSPEC, QOS-SIG-Y1541-QOSM]; • MPLS [RFC3031]; GMPLS [RFC3945]; RSVP [RFC1633, RFC2205-2216] • DiffServ [RFC2475]; MPLS support of DiffServ [RFC3270] • 2 EF queues to support high-priority and normal-priority real-time connections; multiple AF queues to support premium data services; BE queue to support best-effort data services [RFC2597, RFC2598] • Create bandwidth guarantee LSP tunnel, DSTE MAR [RFC4126, RFC3564] • Bandwidth-aware MPLS LSP tunnels [RFC3209] • QoS CAC decision • Aggregate bandwidth requests, RSVP aggregation [RFC3175, DSTE-AGGREGATION] • PCE functionality for interarea, inter-AS, inter-SP [PCE-ARCHITECTURE, PCE-REQUIREMENTS, PCE-PROTOCOL] • Map 5-tuple to DSTE LSP tunnel
Operations/management layer	• Track utilization and performance • Provisioning GW and MSE/backbone routers • Determine bandwidth allocation between GWs • Determine bandwidth allocation between MSEs • Queue allocation on GW/backbone routers • Managing DSTE LSP tunnels in IP/MPLS/GMPLS network • PCE support • Provide real-time monitoring and active control

We can expect (and hope, in fact) that the same happens with integrated voice/data MPLS-based networks in the future.

In the following, we summarize and reference:

• distributed VNET-based TQO approaches employing CAC mechanisms, which are analogous to the GTQO approach,

- distributed TQO approaches employing no CAC mechanism, such as flow-aware networking,
- centralized TQO approaches, such as TQO processor (TQOP), resource and admission control function (RACF), intelligent routing service control point (IRSCP), DiffServ bandwidth broker, and network-aware resource broker (NARB), and
- competitive and cooperative game theoretic models.

10.5.1 Distributed TQO Approaches

In this section we summarize distributed TQO approaches. Note that IntServ and DiffServ are distributed TQO mechanisms standardized in the IETF and described in Appendix A (the DiffServ bandwidth broker concept, also developed in IETF, is described in the next section on centralized TQO approaches).

10.5.1.1 Distributed VNET-Based TQO Approaches with CAC

The next-generation network is expected to offer a number of different classes of service (or QoS classes) to end users, where the classes of service are supported by VNET bandwidth allocation methods. VNET-based TQO approaches provide virtual partitioning of network resources, including bandwidth and buffer space, where different VNETs have customized treatment of the aggregate traffic within that QoS class. To get service differentiation it is necessary to add bandwidth allocation and CAC functionality. With those additional control mechanisms in place, QoS/GoS performance objectives can be met at the flow level by appropriately designing (a) class-of-service routing, (b) VNET topology and capacity, (c) CAC and constraint-based routing, (d) packet-level shaping, scheduling, and queuing, and (e) bandwidth allocation and reservation mechanisms. The advantage of the distributed TQO and VNET bandwidth allocation approach is scalability and robustness to network failure, but may in some instances sacrifice a small bit of optimality, compared to centralized approaches, as a trade-off. The GTQO protocol is in fact one such distributed VNET-based approach.

The approach put forward by Leon-Garcia and Mason [LEON-GARCIA03, LEON-GARCIA05] is functionally similar to the VNET approach described here. However, the implementation is different, where a clever approach is incorporated using MPLS label stacking (hierarchical LSPs), as described in Appendix A. This alternative constructs VNETs by concatenating virtual links rather than using a collection of end-to-end MPLS LSP tunnels or traffic trunks. The granularity at which bandwidth is managed affects the performance and the implementation complexity. The MPLS LSP-based, per-VNET approach in the GTQO protocol is preferable to per-flow bandwidth management, as the per-VNET approach is much less complex to implement and the performance of the two approaches is comparable. The further aggregation proposed by Leon-Garcia may well provide additional scalability advantages. The TEQUILA work [TRIMINTZIOS01] proposes a related approach, and its functionality includes a distributed dynamic route management and dynamic resource management architecture.

10.5.1.2 Flow-Aware Networking (Distributed TQO Approach without CAC)

Flow-aware networking [BONALD02] is one TQO approach that does not directly employ a CAC mechanism. A conventional router routes each incoming packet, applies class-based QoS, and places the packet in the appropriate outgoing queue. A flow-aware router, on the other hand, classifies the 5-tuples in the IP header and uses a hashing function to uniquely identify the flow. Each flow is assigned a flow state that identifies the QoS treatment while the flow is in progress; a flow state is terminated if no further matching packet arrives within, say, 10 s of the last packet. QoS is applied at the flow level with a per-flow scheduler to allow scheduling of flows independently of each other. The advantages in considering traffic in terms of flows rather than individual packets are (a) congestion control and QoS guarantees, (b) traffic control, and (c) per-flow pricing strategies. In flow-aware networking, packets are routed as whole flows, i.e., streams of related packets, rather than as individual packets as in current IP/MPLS networks.

The detailed per-flow data obtained in flow-aware networking, such as flow length, rate, delay variation, and other parameters, enable a number of new network benefits. The advantage of flow-aware networking is that per-flow reservations are not required, and the solution may be more scalable in that respect. However, identifying and classifying flows and retaining flow state are large computational tasks and are done in hardware/firmware in current implementations.

10.5.2 Centralized TQO Approaches

Various centralized TQO approaches have been proposed, such as a TQOP, RACF, IRSCP, DiffServ bandwidth broker, and NARB. While centralized TQO approaches may, in some cases, have some incremental benefit in terms of solution optimality, they usually pay a price in terms of network reliability and scalability. Reliability is impacted by centralizing critical functions, and possibly having a single point of failure. Scalability is impacted by have a large computational burden placed in a single processing entity.

10.5.2.1 TQO Processor (TQOP)

In Chapter 2, we considered a CP-SDR approach employing a centralized (per domain) TQOP. We found that distributed TQO approaches had a number of performance and reliability advantages over the centralized approach. However, centralized TQO approaches have been highly successful in the TDM voice network realm (see discussion of DCR and Table 1.2 in Chapter 1). Centralized TQO solutions may also emerge with implementations of centralized PCE capabilities in MPLS/GMPLS networks [PCE-ARCHITECTURE, PCE-REQUIREMENTS, PCE-PROTOCOL]. Note, however, that PCE functionality can be distributed or centralized.

10.5.2.2   *Resource and Admission Control Function (RACF)*

Within the NGN architecture [Y.2001, Y.2011], the RACF acts as the arbitrator for QoS [Y.1291] resource negotiation and reservation based on user profiles, SLAs, policy rules, service priority, and resource availability within access and core transport. RACF is a centralized TQO concept that includes the following attributes and functions:

- supports resource and admission control across multiple administrative domains
- supports a variety of applications that require QoS control
- supports different CPE intelligence and capability
- controls transport resources, verifies resource availability, and reserves resources
- supports different access and core transport technologies (e.g., xDSL, UMTS, CDMA2000, Cable, LAN, WLAN, Ethernet, MPLS, IP, ATM)
- arbitrates resource negotiation between service control functions and transport functions in the access and core networks
- provides abstract view of transport network infrastructure details (e.g., topology, connectivity, resource utilization, QoS mechanisms, control mechanisms) to service control functions
- interacts with transport functions to control packet filtering, traffic classification, marking, policing, priority handling, bandwidth reservation/allocation, network address/port translation, and firewall
- supports QoS signaling [TRQ-QOS-SIG] and CAC based on estimated path performance and QoS objectives
- performs policy-based resource control to enforce policy decisions
- supports both relative QoS control and absolute QoS control
- supports QoS differentiation

10.5.2.3   *Intelligent Routing Service Control Point (IRSCP)*

The IRSCP [CAESAR05, FEAMSTER04] is a logically centralized control point where control state and logic are kept to control the network elements. IRSCP simplifies network operation and enables new services. IRSCP addresses the problems of adding value-added services to data networks, i.e., (a) the distributed network control plane across the individual network elements, such as routers, and (b) changing or customizing this functionality and working within or around the constraints imposed by the existing network equipment and protocol standards. To enable backwards compatibility with the installed base of network equipment, the IRSCP communicates with the network elements using standard protocols, such as BGP. IRSCP uses BGP to send and receive routes for any defined address family, such as IPv4 or VPN, and set route attributes to drive the routers' decisions, such as for path selection, QoS policies, data collection, and traffic filtering. IRSCP realization may consist of a number of distributed components such as route servers, i.e., it can be physically decentralized while still being logically centralized.

10.5.2.4 DiffServ Bandwidth Broker

The goal of DiffServ is controlled sharing of bandwidth, which can be done by agents called bandwidth brokers. The DiffServ bandwidth broker concept [RFC2638] envisions a centralized (per-domain) entity that arbitrates and reserves bandwidth resources within and between DiffServ domains. An end-to-end path may traverse multiple domains and ISPs, resulting in the need for SLAs between ISPs to ensure that performance objectives are met. Bandwidth brokers have some knowledge of priorities and policies and allocate bandwidth with respect to those policies. Bandwidth brokers are configured with these policies, keep track of the current allocation of marked traffic, and interpret new requests to mark traffic in light of the policies and current allocation. A bandwidth broker has a policy database that keeps the information on who can do what when and a method of using that database to authenticate requesters. The bandwidth broker concept is not defined precisely in terms of detailed functional requirements and architecture specification.

10.5.2.5 Network-Aware Resource Broker (NARB)

The NARB [LEHMAN06] is a centralized concept to enable routing, path computation, and signaling in a GMPLS-based dynamic transport network. It has been implemented in the so-called Dynamic Resource Allocation in GMPLS Optical Networks (DRAGON) concept based on GMPLS-controlled dynamic bandwidth allocation. One justification made by the authors for implementing NARB is that interdomain routing, path computation, and signaling are beyond what is defined in standards and the capability of current vendor equipment. The NARB therefore enables these functions across a heterogeneous mix of network technologies and vendor equipment. NARB features and capabilities are functionally similar to those being specified in the PCE concept [PCE-ARCHITECTURE, PCE-REQUIREMENTS, PCE-PROTOCOL], which is described in the next section on standards extensions.

10.5.3 Competitive and Cooperative Game Theoretic Models

Achieving end-to-end QoS in the Internet is challenging because it is composed of interconnected but independent administrative domains (ASs), which precludes an entirely centralized QoS solution across all domains. Rather, the control of resources in large-scale telecommunication networks ultimately requires a decentralized control architecture. For example, a distributed multidomain architecture is required employing DiffServ/MPLS and SLAs, linking these administrative domains. Linking these domains together also requires a suitable signaling and control architecture. Adaptive routing and admission control have proven to be an effective means of increasing network efficiency and service quality in the face of variable and uncertain traffic demand and network failures. The presence of distributed adaptive algorithms introduces game-theoretic aspects associated with the competition for network resources and fairness issues. Cooperative and noncooperative game theory provides a useful framework for the synthesis and evaluation of network control schemes.

There is an explosive growth in the number of players in the telecommunications marketplace, including public carriers, information providers, and Internet service providers (ISPs), where ISPs are playing the role of broker between the public carriers and end users. There is a need for models to describe the interplay among resource allocation, QoS, and pricing schemes, and game theoretic concepts and decision theory are important in modeling market behavior and devising effective resource allocation and pricing mechanisms. A market managed network approach to end-to-end QoS resource management employs pricing schemes to provide a tight dynamic coupling between network congestion state and the price paid for access to a given level of QoS. Pricing is closely related to the provision of adequate QoS to heterogeneous users. By adopting an appropriate pricing policy and selecting prices optimally, a service provider can offer the necessary incentives to users so that they select the service most suitable to their needs. DaSilva [DaSILVA00] provides a good survey of pricing concepts for broadband networks and suggests that pricing for Internet QoS is an open problem that must be addressed prior to wide-scale deployment of QoS in the Internet. Pricing must consider both the choice of pricing policy, i.e., the factors employed to price a given call/session or traffic flow, and the setting of prices, i.e., selecting the optimal prices that result in the desired behavior by users.

Andrew Odlyzko [ODLYZKO99] introduces the "Paris Metro Pricing" (PMP) concept wherein he suggests that appropriate pricing mechanisms in the Internet could regulate flow, and therefore QoS. PMP recognizes that the principle of peak traffic pricing, such as used on the Paris metro during peak traffic periods to regulate demand, could be considered for any market mechanism, particularly the Internet. The PMP concept provides differentiated services in the Internet by partitioning the network into several logically separate channels. Each channel would treat all packets equally on a best-effort basis—there would be no formal guarantees of QoS—and would differ only in the prices paid for using them. Channels with higher prices would attract less traffic, thereby providing better service. Price would be the primary tool of traffic management. PMP is a simple differentiated services solution and is designed to accommodate user preferences at the cost of sacrificing some of the utilization efficiency of the network.

Frank Kelly [KELLY98] makes theoretical progress in the area of pricing and rate control for elastic traffic and models a single network service provider and a set of users. He demonstrates that it is possible to achieve fair and efficient decentralized resource allocation and that equilibrium is reached such that there is no incentive for either users or provider to depart from the equilibrium price and rate vector. La and Ananthram [LA00] show that the proportionally fair and socially optimum allocation (Pareto optimality) can be achieved with information available at the end systems, which facilitates implementation in the Internet. He and Walrand [HE02] and Semret *et al.* [SEMRET00] report research on models of the current multiple AS Internet architecture as three types of players: end users who buy best-effort services from ISPs who act as retailers and large carriers who sell bandwidth to ISPs and can be thought of as wholesalers. Studies of the dynamic behavior of such market-managed networks employing DiffServ and dynamic SLAs have found that control strategies exist that result in stable operating points; however, they also find cases of instability. There are various other proposals advanced for providing end-to-end QoS with competitive and cooperative game theoretic-based models, although these are still in an embryonic stage. See, for example, [DZIONG96a, DZIONG96b, GIBBENS99, ODLYZKO03, YAICHE00].

10.6 Needed Standards Extensions and Technologies to Meet GTQO Protocol Requirements

Let us return now to Geekia and Telephonia and recall how they develop network standards on those planets. In Geekia they hold IETF meetings where hoards of bearded geeks flop on the floors, glued to their computers, and ravage the cookies and food whenever possible. While in Telephonia they hold ITU meetings where everyone dresses formally, sits politely, and speaks in turn, but where participants may quietly stab each other in the back if slightly provoked.

In some places, such as AT&T before the breakup of the Bell System in 1984, the architecture and development units were in the same "vertically integrated" corporation. In that environment, systems engineers gave architecture requirements to development engineers in the same company, and the architecture became reality. Such things no longer exist. The reality is that vendors are both network architects and developers and basically tell the service-provider/system engineers what architecture they need and what is actually available to purchase. This is not always what the systems engineers have in mind. But there is an avenue to realizing system engineers' requirements, that is, through the standards process. Vendors are usually obligated to implement and offer standards-based solutions to service providers.

I became involved in external standards starting in the early 1990s and made good progress in TE/routing standardization in the ITU-T Routing Question in Study Group 2 (Network Operations). In particular, a series of 7 TE/routing standards [E.360.x] laid the groundwork for vendor requirements for TE/routing. This was all well and good on Telephonia, but wait! After the emergence of the worldwide revolution of Internet/IP-based technology in the mid-1990s, I also pursued standardization efforts in the IETF, initially in the TEWG and MPLS working groups. The initial thrust was to bring the [E.360.x] concepts into the IETF standardization effort and influence emerging TE, MPLS, routing, and other IETF standards. But I immediately found there is much to be learned regarding IETF culture on Geekia. A well-known and well-respected IETFer gave me my first lesson on the mailing list, with a stern lecture to the effect that "this is not the way we do things in the IETF and in the Internet" (a search still brings up this email lecture from Curtis Villamizar).

Many lessons followed on IETF's deeply ingrained counterphilosophies, where [E.360.x]-based concepts were seemingly at odds with time-honored and inviolate Geekian principles and directions. And while the [E.360.x]-based RFCs never came to fruition, several TE-related RFCs along the way introduced some of the basic [E.360.x] concepts. These are discussed in this section, but the work is not done yet. Various standards extensions and technologies are needed to accommodate the GTQO protocol requirements and capabilities. Table 10.2 summarizes the standards extensions needed, which include the following:

- multiprotocol label switching (MPLS) [RFC3031]
- generalized multiprotocol label switching (GMPLS) [RFC3945]
- resource reservation protocol (RSVP) [RFC2205]
- differentiated services (DiffServ) [RFC2475]
- MPLS-based QoS standards [RFC3270]
- DiffServ-aware MPLS traffic engineering (DSTE) mechanisms [RFC3564, RFC4124]
- maximum allocation with reservation (MAR) bandwidth constraints model for DSTE application [RFC4126, PRIORITY1, PRIORITY2]
- path computation element (PCE) capability for interarea, inter-AS, and interservice provider optimal, diverse, and MPLS fast reroute (FRR) path computation [PCE-ARCHITECTURE, PCE-REQUIREMENTS, PCE-PROTOCOL]
- RSVP aggregation extensions over DSTE LSP tunnels [DSTE-AGGREGATION]
- header compression over MPLS [RFC4247, HC-OVER-MPLS-PROTOCOL]
- QoS signaling protocol and signaling of QoS parameters [QOS-SIG-NTLP, QOS-SIG-NSLP, QOS-SIG-QSPEC, QOS-SIG-Y1541-QOSM]
- admission control priority service classes [PRIORITY3, PRIORITY4]
- service priority signaling requirements [TRQ-QOS-SIG, PRIORITY5]
- ETS/GETS support in IP networks [ETS1, ETS2, ETS3]
- SIP resource priority header (RPH) [RFC4412]
- crankback routing extensions for alternate routing during MPLS LSP setup or modification [CRANKBACK]
- protection/restoration mechanisms to support fast restoration capabilities [GMPLS-RECOVERY-SPEC, GMPLS-RECOVERY-PROTOCOL]
- OSPF congestion control mechanisms [RFC4222]
- assured services requirements and architecture [ASSURED-SERVICES-RQMTS, ASSURED-SERVICES-ARCH]
- MPLS proxy admission control [MPLS-PROXY1, MPLS-PROXY2]
- PseudoWire (PW) [RFC3985]
- session initiation protocol (SIP) [RFC3261]
- IP multimedia subsystem (IMS) [3GPP-TS.22.228]
- broadband remote access server (BRAS) [DSLFORUM-TR-059]
- dynamic quality of service (DQOS) [CABLELABS-DQOS-05]
- session border controller (SBC) [CAMARILLO05]

IP/MPLS/GMPLS standards and technologies are discussed in some detail in Appendix A, including MPLS, GMPLS, RSVP, IntServ, DiffServ, and MPLS-based QoS standards. The other standards and technologies in this list are discussed in the following sections.

10.6.1 DiffServ-Aware MPLS Traffic Engineering (DSTE)

DSTE combines the QoS capabilities of DiffServ with the TE capabilities of MPLS to allocate bandwidth and control QoS for various VNETs (classes of service, also called "class types" in DSTE). Class types include, for example, high- and normal-priority VoIP, premium private data, and premium public data. DSTE uses admission control to allocate bandwidth to each class type and also provides bandwidth protection/QoS without relying on overengineering. Various "bandwidth constraints models" control bandwidth allocation/protection within the DSTE framework. DSTE provides hard QoS for each class type without relying on overengineering and also maximizes the amount of traffic that can be transported on a given set of resources.

DSTE CAC admits flows based on bandwidth availability, priority, and QoS requirements. DSTE provides MPLS LSP setup based on explicit constraint-based routing and traffic parameter/bandwidth requirements. DSTE assigns DiffServ priority to each class type, e.g., a high-priority EF class might be assigned to high-priority VoIP (GETS/ETS/E911) and a normal-priority EF class might be assigned to normal-priority VoIP. [RFC3564] details DSTE requirements, and DSTE protocol extensions have been issued [RFC4124]. As mentioned earlier, DSTE bandwidth constraint models control bandwidth allocation/protection to each class type. Three bandwidth constraints models have been made experimental RFCs, as follows:

- "maximum allocation model" (MAM) [RFC4125] allocates a maximum bandwidth level to each class type on each link, and bandwidth is protected from use by other class types
- "maximum allocation with reservation" (MAR) [RFC4126] allocates bandwidth to each class type on each link and uses dynamic bandwidth reservation to protect bandwidth under congestion, but allows bandwidth sharing in absence of congestion
- "Russian dolls model" (RDM) [RFC4127] allocates bandwidth progressively to each class type, but requires LSP preemption to work well

Implementation experience will decide which of the DSTE bandwidth constraints models will move toward Standards Track RFCs.

Analysis of the RDM approach [RFC4128] shows that it can perform poorly when preemption is not enabled. The MAR and MAM bandwidth constraints models are extensively analyzed in modeling and simulation studies discussed in detail in Chapter 9. It is demonstrated that the MAR bandwidth constraints model performs well in comparison to the MAM bandwidth constraints model and is therefore included in the GTQO protocol model.

10.6.2 Path Computation Element (PCE)

PCE capabilities support TE in MPLS and GMPLS networks. The PCE working group in the IETF is currently specifying:

- a PCE-based architecture for the computation of paths for MPLS and GMPLS TE LSPs [PCE-ARCHITECTURE],
- a protocol for communication between LSRs and PCEs, and between cooperating PCEs, to enable LSRs to make path computation requests to PCEs, including a full set of constraints [PCE-REQUIREMENTS, PCE-PROTOCOL], and
- requirements for extensions to existing routing and signaling protocols (e.g., RSVP-TE, OSPF-TE) in support of PCE discovery and signaling of interdomain paths.

PCE is included in the GTQO protocol model. In the PCE architecture, path computation does not occur on the head-end (ingress) LSR, but on some other path computation entity that may not be physically located on the head-end LSR. The PCE capability supports applications within a single domain or within a group of domains, where a domain is a layer, IGP area, or AS with limited visibility from the head-end LSR.

The protocol for communication between LSRs (termed path computation clients, or PCCs) and PCEs, and between cooperating PCEs, enables requests for path computation, including a full set of constraints and an ability to return multiple paths, as well as security, authentication, and confidentiality mechanisms. This includes both intradomain and interdomain TE LSPs and the generation of primary, protection, and recovery paths, as well as computations for local/global reoptimization and load balancing.

10.6.3 RSVP Aggregation Extensions over DSTE Tunnels

[DSTE-AGGREGATION] specifies the aggregation of RSVP end-to-end reservations over MPLS TE or DSTE LSP tunnels, based on modified [RFC3175] procedures. This approach can be used to implement CAC for a very large number of flows in a scalable manner, as the core routers are unaware of the end-to-end RSVP reservations and are only aware of the MPLS TE LSP tunnels.

IntServ [RFC1633] provides a means for the delivery of end-to-end QoS to applications over heterogeneous networks. RSVP [RFC2205] can be used by applications to request resources from the network, and the network responds by explicitly admitting or rejecting these RSVP requests, where applications signal resource requirements by using IntServ parameters [RFC2211, RFC2212]. DiffServ [RFC2475] supports differentiated treatment of packets, and in contrast to the per-flow orientation of IntServ and RSVP, DiffServ networks classify packets into one of a small number of aggregated classes based on the DSCP in the packet's IP header, and at each DiffServ router, packets are subjected to a PHB invoked by the DSCP. DiffServ eliminates the need for per-flow state and per-flow processing and therefore scales well to large networks. However, DiffServ does not include any mechanism for communication between applications and the network. Significant benefits can be achieved by combining IntServ and DiffServ [RFC2998] to support dynamic provisioning and topology aware admission control, including aggregated RSVP reservations, per flow RSVP, or a TQO processor. [RFC3175] describes an architecture where multiple end-to-end RSVP reservations share the same ingress router (aggregator) and the same egress router (deaggregator) at the edges of an aggregation region and can be mapped onto a single aggregate reservation within the aggregation region. MPLS TE [RFC3209] enables TE LSP tunnels to carry arbitrary aggregates of traffic. MPLS TE uses constraint-based routing to compute the path for an TE LSP tunnel. Then, CAC is performed during the establishment of TE LSP tunnels to ensure they are granted their requested resources. With DSTE, separate DSTE LSP tunnels can be used to carry different DiffServ classes of traffic and different resource constraints can be enforced for these different classes.

TE LSP tunnels have much in common with the aggregate RSVP reservations used in [RFC3175]:

- a TE LSP tunnel is subject to CAC and thus is effectively an aggregate bandwidth reservation
- packet scheduling relies exclusively on DiffServ classification and PHBs
- both TE LSP tunnels and aggregate RSVP reservations are controlled at the edge of the aggregation core
- both TE LSP tunnels and aggregate RSVP reservations are signaled using RSVP

[DSTE-AGGREGATION] provides a specification for performing aggregation of end-to-end RSVP reservations over MPLS TE LSP tunnels. The main change over the procedures defined in [RFC3175] is to reassign responsibilities from the deaggregator to the aggregator (i.e., the LSP tunnel head end). With [RFC3175], mapping end-to-end reservations to aggregate reservations and resizing the aggregate reservations are assigned to the deaggregator. [LSP-HIER] defines how to aggregate MPLS TE LSPs by creating a hierarchy of such LSPs. This involves nesting of end-to-end LSPs into an aggregate LSP in the core by using the MPLS label stack construct. [DSTE-AGGREGATION] capitalizes on the similarities between nesting of TE LSPs over TE LSP tunnels and RSVP aggregation over TE LSP tunnels and reuses the procedures of [LSP-HIER].

[DSTE-AGGREGATION] combines the benefits of [RFC3175] with the benefits of MPLS, including the following:

- CAC can be provided over any segment of the end-to-end path
- core routers are unaware of end-to-end RSVP reservations and only maintain aggregate TE LSP tunnels
- packet scheduling relies exclusively on DiffServ classification and PHBs
- aggregate reservations can use constraint-based routing
- aggregate reservations can be protected against failure with MPLS fast reroute

10.6.4   Header Compression over MPLS

Header compression techniques can reduce RTP/UDP/IP headers by up to 90%, which can greatly improve efficiency for services such as VoIP where headers contribute significant overhead. Work is in progress in the IETF to allow header compression to be done over MPLS LSPs, which will provide benefits to service providers as they migrate legacy TDM voice traffic to VoIP over the MPLS core network. Header compression over MPLS avoids link-by-link decompression/recompression cycles and thus is significantly more efficient than current techniques. Requirements for header compression over MPLS are complete [RFC4247], and the protocol extensions work [HC-OVER-MPLS-PROTOCOL] is in progress.

10.6.5   QoS Signaling Protocol

For signaling of individual flows, the IETF Next Steps in Signaling (NSIS) working group is progressing QoS signaling. NSIS QoS signaling addresses the shortcomings of the RSVP protocol and defines a two-layer QoS signaling model:

- NSIS QoS signaling layer protocol (QoS-NSLP) [QOS-SIG-NSLP]
- NSIS transport layer protocol (NTLP) [QOS-SIG-NTLP]

Furthermore, [QOS-SIG-NSLP] defines a QoS specification (QSPEC) object, which contains the QoS parameters required by a QoS model (QOSM). A QOSM specifies the QoS parameters and procedures that govern the resource management functions in a QoS-aware router. Multiple QOSMs can be supported by the QoS-NSLP, and the QoS-NSLP allows stacking of QSPEC parameters to accommodate different QOSMs being used in different domains. As such, NSIS provides a mechanism for interdomain QoS signaling and interworking.

The QSPEC parameters defined in [QOS-SIG-QSPEC] include, among others:

1. TRAFFIC DESCRIPTION Parameters:
   - <Token Bucket> Parameters
   - <Bandwidth> Parameter
2. CONSTRAINTS Parameters:
   - <PHB Class> Parameter
   - <Y.1541 QoS Class> Parameter
   - <DSTE Class Type> Parameter
   - <Admission Priority> Parameter
   - <Preemption Priority> & <Defending Priority> Parameters
   - <Path Latency> Parameter
   - Etc.

The definition of various QOSMs is in progress, as follows:

- QOSMs that implement IntServ and DiffServ functionality, by default
- "NSIS QOSM for Networks Using Y.1541 QoS Classes" [QOS-SIG-Y1541-QOSM], based on ITU-T Recommendations [Y.1541] "Network Performance Objectives for IP-Based Services: and [TRQ-QOS-SIG] "Signaling Requirements for IP-QoS"

- "NSIS QOSM for Networks Using Resource Management in Diffserv (RMD)"
- "3GPP QOSM"

The ability to achieve end-to-end QoS through multiple Internet domains is also an important requirement. In the GTQO approach, end-to-end QoS signaling is used to ensure end-to-end QoS, and we give an example of using NSIS QoS signaling and the Y.1541-QOSM to achieve this.

The QoS originating node (ON) initiates an end-to-end, interdomain QoS RESERVE message containing the QoS parameters, including, for example, <Y.1541 QoS Class>, <Token Bucket>, <Reservation Priority>, <Path Latency>, and perhaps other parameters for the flow. The RESERVE message may cross multiple domains perhaps supporting different QOSMs. At the ingress edge node of the local-QOSM domain, the end-to-end, interdomain RESERVE message triggers the generation of local QoS parameters derived from the RESERVE message, consistent with the local QOSM. The local parameters and QOSM are used for QoS processing in the local-QOSM domain, and then the original RESERVE message sent by the ON is used for QoS processing at the QoS destination node (DN).

Each node on the data path checks the availability of resources and accumulating the delay, delay variation, and loss ratio parameters. If an intermediate node cannot accommodate the new request, it indicates this by marking a single bit, and the reservation is denied. If no intermediate node has denied the reservation, the ON RESERVE message is forwarded to the next domain. If any node cannot meet the requirements designated by the ON RESERVE message to support a QoS parameter, e.g., it cannot support the accumulation of end-to-end delay with the <Path Latency> parameter, the node sets a flag that will deny the reservation. Also, parameter negotiation can be done, for example, by setting the <Y.1541 QoS Class> to a lower class than specified in the ON RESERVE message. When the available <Y.1541 QoS Class> must be reduced from the desired <Y.1541 QoS Class>, say, because the delay objective has been exceeded, then there is an incentive to respond to the ON with an available value for delay in the <Path Latency> parameter. For example, if the available <Path Latency> is 150 ms (still useful for many applications) and the desired QoS is 100 ms (according to the desired <Y.1541 QoS Class> Class 0), then the response would be that Class 0 cannot be achieved and Class 1 is available (with its 400-ms objective). In addition, the response includes an available <Path Latency> = 150 ms, making acceptance of the available <Y.1541 QoS Class> more likely.

10.6.6 Crankback Routing for MPLS LSP Setup or Modification

In a distributed, constraint-based routing environment, the information used to compute a path may be out of date. This means that MPLS and GMPLS TE LSP setup requests may be lost by links or nodes without sufficient resources. Crankback is a method whereby setup failure information is returned from the point of failure to allow new setup attempts to be made avoiding the congested resources. Crankback can also be applied to LSP recovery to indicate the location of the failed link or node. [CRANKBACK] specifies crankback signaling extensions for use in MPLS signaling using RSVP-TE as defined in [RFC3209] and GMPLS signaling as defined in [RFC3473]. These extensions allow LSP setup requests to be retried on an alternate path that detours around congested links or nodes. This offers significant improvements in the successful setup and recovery ratios for LSPs, especially in situations where a large number of setup requests are triggered at the same time.

10.6.7 OSPF Congestion Control

[RFC4222] addresses congestion control in IP networks that use OSPF routing. Congestion in data network routing protocols can arise for many different reasons. There is evidence based on previous failures experienced by service providers that link-state protocols such as OSPF may not be able to recover from large failures that can result in overload in flooding of topology database information. In some instances of network overload, failure, and/or congestion, redundancy of the flooding mechanism can overwhelm the routing control processors and bring the network down. To prevent this, OSPF extensions have been adopted to (a) prioritize treatment of HELLO and LSA acknowledgement packets, (b) reduce the rate of flooding of LSAs, and (c) maintain link adjacencies. Many vendors have already implemented some of the basic principles of the RFC. There is related work that specifies routing congestion control extensions in the PNNI protocol developed by the ATM forum [ATMFORUM-0200.000, ATMFORUM-0201.000].

10.6.8 PseudoWire

[RFC3985] addresses PseudoWire technology, which encapsulates any service in a common IP/MPLS format that preserves the service's features and end-to-end OAM&P. PseudoWires decouple services from the underlying infrastructure that carries them and applies at both the packet and transport layers. PseudoWires provide unified management and standards-based support of legacy protocols on IP/MPLS/Ethernet-based networks. The technology encompasses network access, edge, and core functions; is usable by any operator, cable MSO, interexchange carrier, and wireless operator; saves capital expense and operating expense by moving ATM, frame relay, and Ethernet services over the IP/MPLS core; and improves packet services transport efficiency through aggregation and multiplexing.

10.6.9 Session Initiation Protocol (SIP)

SIP [RFC3261] is an essential application-layer signaling protocol for creating, modifying, and terminating sessions that transport multimedia conferences, telephone calls/sessions, and multimedia distribution. SIP has emerged as crucial technology for controlling communications in IP-based NGNs. SIP INVITE messages allow users to negotiate compatible media types, support user mobility by proxying and redirecting requests to the user's current location, and register user location. SIP is independent of lower-layer transport protocol; users communicate via multicast, mesh of unicast relations, or a combination of both.

10.6.10   IP Multimedia Subsystem (IMS)

IMS [3GPP-TS.22.228] enables fixed/mobile convergence and builds on SIP. IMS delivers IP applications over wired, wireless, packet-switched/circuit-switched access technologies. It employs an open architecture to create services more efficiently by distributed systems, possibly owned by different parties, versus a single service-provider-controlled infrastructure. Key elements of IMS include the call session control function (CSCF), which acts as a centralized routing engine, policy manager, and policy enforcement point for delivering applications to various end points. The home subscriber server (HSS) creates a master subscriber database for identity profiles, billing, and permissions data.

10.6.11   Broadband Remote Access Server (BRAS)

BRAS [DSLFORUM-TR-059] supports multiple dynamic services over a DSL infrastructure and is considered a stepping stone to FTTX. BRAS defines three traffic-forwarding streams, EF, AF, and BE SLA levels, and introduces an application service provider (ASP) interface to a service provider's regional access network.

10.6.12   Dynamic Quality of Service (DQOS)

DQOS [CABLELABS-DQOS-05] supports a communication protocol to enable QoS signaling for voice and real-time multimedia services over a cable infrastructure. The DQOS protocol uses SIP with extensions for management of network resources and dynamic QoS mechanisms.

10.6.13   Session Border Controller (SBC)

SBC technology [CAMARILLO05] provides control of real-time session traffic at the signaling, call/session-control, and packet layers between network segments and elements, including NATs and firewalls.

10.7 Benefits of GTQO Protocol for MPLS/GMPLS-Based Dynamic Routing Networks

The benefits of the GTQO protocol for MPLS/GMPLS-based integrated voice/data dynamic routing networks are as follows:

- class-of-service routing saves software, hardware, and new network development for new service deployment (Chapters 3 and 8)
- STT-EDR path selection and per-VNET bandwidth allocation reduce IGP flooding and control overhead dramatically, thereby increasing scalability (Chapters 2, 3, and 4)
- GMPLS-based dynamic transport routing increases network reliability, throughput, revenue, and capital savings (Chapters 5 and 6)
- DEFO design models able to handle very complex routing/bandwidth allocation algorithms for capacity design (Chapter 6)
- lower operations and capital cost on the order of 30–50% of network cost (Chapters 6 and 7)
- improved performance and increased network throughput (Chapters 2, 3, 8, and 9)
- simplified and automated network operations/management (Chapters 5 and 7)

Simplified network operations and management come about because of the following impacts of the GTQO methods:

- distributed control (Chapter 2)
- eliminate ALB flooding (Chapter 4)
- larger/fewer routing areas (Chapter 4)
- automatic provisioning of topology database (Chapters 3 and 7)
- fewer links/sparse network to provision (Chapters 2, 4, and 7)

So GTQO represents a possible "great step forward" for converged MPLS/GMPLS networks. That is, unless another technology revolution comes along to trump the current revolution, such as optical, TDM burst-switched photons over fibers, no packets, just photons, everywhere. Simple, and we're ready with a solution for that one too.

10.8 Applicability of Requirements

Dear reader, I set the stage in Chapter 1 for the "war of the worlds" that encompasses Geekia and Telephonia, and these worlds have been at war for about 40 years. This book focuses on a truce and the convergence of these two disparate worlds, and the GTQO approach bridges the gap between the NetHeads and the BellHeads in TQO space. The GTQO protocol for converged MPLS/GMPLS networks is applicable to core networks, access networks, and internetwork applications. It is based on the analysis and findings in the book, particularly on the results of the case studies presented in Chapters 8 and 9, as well as operational experience. As illustrated in the final case study, there is an opportunity for increased profitability and performance in MPLS/GMPLS networks, which supports service provider requirements. These requirements should drive standards extensions, vendor implementations, and interoperability.

We take our final lesson from the first two case studies: sophisticated, on-line, TQO methods have succeeded and are widely deployed in Telephonian-type networks, but have yet to be extended to IP/MPLS-based Geekian-type networks, as suggested by the final case study. Telephonian TQO was launched in 1984, 2 years before the IETF even had their first meeting. So Geekians! Hear Ye! Hear Ye! Telephonians are winning!

It's somewhat like the fable of the tortoise and the hare. The slow teletortoise had a very big head start ($\sim$90 years or so head start), but the speedy hairygeek, even with its very late start, quickly zoomed ahead of the teletortoise. But wait, the hairygeek fell asleep along the way and didn't finish the race, not yet anyway. So Geekians, pay attention, get up and get going! The teletortoise is still "running," albeit slowly, and making steady progress; and don't forget, slow and steady wins the race.

So, dear reader, we conclude now the "war of two worlds" between the Geekia NetHeads and Telephonia BellHeads. We speak now of truce and bridging the gap, and that result is the motivation and hopefully the lasting value of this book. We've seen how NetHead beliefs, which led to the astounding breakthroughs that gave us the Internet, and how BellHead beliefs, which fueled 100 years of crown-jewel technological innovation and yielded the greatest machine ever devised, can all be applied to bridge the gap. Both the TQO design principles, as illustrated and applied throughout the book, and the GTQO requirements, as derived from these design principles, reflect the lessons and wisdom of both worlds. NetHead philosophy and BellHead thinking are deeply embedded, and from thence comes the expectation that both Geekia and Telephonia will adopt a convergence treaty based on these important lessons. That represents an expected outcome, as well as a great step forward for converged networks in general.

I think I'm qualified to set such a treaty and try to bridge the gap. As I admitted long ago in this book, I'm the "consummate BellHead," as one colleague put it, and another colleague said that when you look up "BellHead" in the dictionary, there's a picture of me right there. But he also added, "it's really good to be the best at what you do!" But also keep in mind that I'm at least 50% NetHead as well. I've been working toward full Geekian NetHead status for more than 20 years, and have participated in IETF for more than half of its entire life.

So as the ranking converged Geekian/Telephonian NetHead/BellHead, I conclude the book and project that the hairygeek and teletortoise will tie at the finish line, both will sign the treaty, and both will declare victory.

With that, shall we call the new united world UT(Q)Opia, with a silent Q?

Appendix A
Traffic Engineering and QoS Optimization Technology Overview

A.1 Introduction

This appendix reviews some of the key TQO technologies: MPLS, GMPLS, QoS mechanisms, IntServ, RSVP, DiffServ, and MPLS-based QoS mechanisms. This is intended as a quick refresher and/or a brief introduction for those unfamiliar with these technologies. Ample references are provided for more detailed coverage of these important topics. A focus of this book is on TQO protocol design for MPLS- and GMPLS-based networks, where MPLS and GMPLS are used at the MPLS LSP and GMPLS LSP design layers, respectively. MPLS and GMPLS are revolutionary new network control capabilities designed and standardized in the IETF. Networks are rapidly evolving toward converged MPLS/GMPLS-based technologies, and in this book we give detailed case studies and examples of MPLS/GMPLS network design and optimization.

A.2 Multiprotocol Label Switching (MPLS)

In this section we give an overview of MPLS technology and begin with a brief history on the evolution of MPLS and then summarize some of the benefits and technical details. Work on MPLS is carried out in the IETF under the auspices of the MPLS working group. The charter of the IETF MPLS working group and a list of working documents and RFCs that have been issued are listed on the MPLS home page at http://ietf.org/html.charters/mpls-charter.html.

MPLS groups packets to be forwarded in the same manner into forwarding equivalence classes (FECs) and labels are used to mark the packets to identify the forwarding path. The assignment of a packet to an FEC is done once, at the entry point to the network. MPLS capable label switching routers (LSRs) then use the label to make packet forwarding decisions. MPLS packets are able to carry a number of labels in a last-in first-out stack, which is highly useful where two levels of routing are taking place across transit routing domains, such as in widely deployed MPLS virtual private networks (VPNs). A sequence of LSRs defines a label switched path (LSP), which can be hop by hop where each node independently decides the next hop, and explicitly routed where the ingress node specifies the path to be taken. MPLS is able to work with any data link technology, connection oriented and connectionless.

In the mid-1990s, Internet service providers were often using an overlay model to run IP over ATM, but this posed scalability problems. Vendors started to develop means to take advantage of both high-speed ATM switching and lower-cost (but then slower) IP routing, with developments such as:

- "IP switching"—Ipsilon (1996) [NEWMAN98]
- "Tag switching"—Cisco (1996) [REKHTER97]
- "Aggregate route-based IP switching (ARIS)"—IBM [VISWANATHAN98]
- "IP navigator"—Cascade/Ascend/Lucent
- "Cell switched router (CSR)"—Toshiba (1995) [RFC2098]
- "IPSOFACTO"—[ACHARYA97]

These solutions attempted to improve the throughput and delay performance of IP by using standard routing protocols to create "paths" between end points. Packets would follow a particular path based on the packet characteristics, wherein ATM switches would switch the packets along the path. Tag switching is considered by some to be the "prestandard" implementation of the MPLS architecture.

These mid-1990s initiatives led to the development of MPLS in the IETF, starting in March 1997: "multiprotocol" because it can be transported over many different link layer protocols; "label" because the protocols are transported with a label changed at each hop; "switching" because labels are of local significance. By 2001, the IETF MPLS working group issued the first set of proposed standards for MPLS, and many more RFCs have been issued since then (the RFCs are listed on the MPLS home page at http://ietf.org/html.charters/mpls-charter.html).

Because today's IP-based routers perform at comparable speeds to ATM switches, this negates the original motivation for MPLS. However, MPLS provides important new networking capabilities, such as QoS, traffic engineering, fast reroute, and VPNs [RFC4364]. AT&T was one of the early implementers of an MPLS-based service, with the highly successful development of IP-enabled frame relay, which implements an RFC 4364-style MPLS-VPN solution.

Now we turn to the technical details of MPLS. In conventional packet networks, such as those that use IP and OSPF routing [RFC2328], a packet travels from one router to the next and each router makes an independent forwarding decision for that packet. Each router analyzes the packet's header and independently chooses a next hop for the packet based on the packet header and routing algorithm. The router periodically runs a network layer routing algorithm, such as OSPF, and the results are stored in the routing table for rapid lookup. For example, in conventional IP forwarding, a router will map an address prefix X in its routing tables based on the "longest match" for each packet's destination address. As the packet traverses the network, each hop in turn reexamines the packet and assigns it to a next hop.

The integration of layer 3 datagram forwarding and layer 2 transport switching uses label lookups to allow more efficient packet classification, and a flurry of vendor-specific approaches appeared between 1994 and 1997, as listed above. Because these approaches were proprietary and not interoperable, the IETF formed the MPLS working group to address routing scalability, provision of more flexible routing services, improved performance, and simplified integration of layer 3 routing and packet/connection switching technologies, with the overall goal of providing a standard label-swapping architecture [RFC3031].

In MPLS [RFC3031], the ingress router first classifies the packet into an FEC based on header information and then maps the FEC to a next hop based on the routing algorithm. The assignment of a packet to an FEC is done just once, and the FEC to which the packet is assigned is encoded as a 4-byte fixed length value known as a "label." The MPLS label formats, also known as a "shim" header, are illustrated in Figure A.1. When a packet is forwarded to its next hop, the label is sent along with it. At subsequent hops, there is no further analysis of the packet's network layer header. Rather, the label is used as an index into a table, which specifies the next hop and a new label. The old label is replaced with the new label, called "label swapping" and the packet is forwarded to its next hop. MPLS is able to be transported over any link

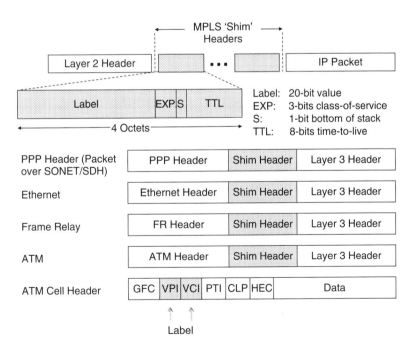

Figure A.1   MPLS "shim" header formats.

layer protocol, including IP, ATM, FR, and Ethernet, as also illustrated in Figure A.1, and hence the "multiprotocol" terminology is used. We make a clear distinction here between "multiprotocol," meaning MPLS over any link layer (layer 2) technology, and "multiprotocol," meaning anything over MPLS, which is sometimes used to also include PseudoWire technology carrying encapsulated ATM, frame relay, and Ethernet packets over an MPLS network. A router that supports MPLS is known as a "label switching router" or LSR.

Each MPLS packet has a shim header that is encapsulated between the link layer and the network layer. A virtual path identifier/virtual channel identifier (VPI/VCI) pair is a label used in ATM networks to identify bandwidth channels (or circuits). Note that even though ATM uses the VPI/VCI as the MPLS label, an MPLS shim header is still used. Conversely, even though a frame relay frame carries a shim header, the label is present in the data link connection identifier (DLCI). As illustrated in Figure A.1, the MPLS header contains a label, TTL field, class-of-service (CoS) field, and stack indicator. Note that the CoS field is also known as the EXP bits field, as these three bits were originally designated as EXPerimental bits. MPLS defines a fundamental separation between the grouping of packets that are to be forwarded in the same manner (i.e., the FECs), and the labels used to mark the packets. At any one node, all packets within the same FEC could be mapped onto the same locally significant label, given that they have the same requirements. The assignment of a particular packet to an FEC is done once, at the entry point to the network. MPLS-capable LSRs then use only the label and CoS field to make packet forwarding and classification decisions. Label merging is possible where multiple incoming labels are to receive the same FEC.

MPLS packets are able to carry a number of labels, organized in a last-in first-out stack [RFC3032]. This can be highly useful in a number of applications, such as where two levels of routing are taking place across transit routing domains or where an MPLS-based VPN is implemented [RFC4364]. Regardless of the existence of the hierarchy, in all instances the forwarding of a packet is based on the label at the top of the stack. In order for a packet to travel through a tunnel, the node at the transmitting side of the tunnel pushes a label relating to the tunnel onto the stack and sends the packet to the next hop in the tunnel. An ordering of LSRs defines an LSP. Two options are defined for the selection of a route for a particular forwarding class. Hop-by-hop routing defines a process where each node independently decides the next hop of the route. Explicit routing is where a single node, most often the ingress node of a path, specifies the route to be taken in terms of the LSRs in the path. Explicit routing may be used to implement TE algorithms to balance the traffic load.

There are two approaches to label path control. Independent path control means that LSRs are able to create label bindings and distribute these bindings to their peers independently. This is useful when bindings relate to information distributed by routing protocols such as OSPF. In this case, MPLS distributes labels using the label distribution protocol (LDP) [RFC3036], where paths relate to certain routes. Ordered path control is used to ensure that a particular traffic class follows a path with a specified set of QoS properties. In this case, labels are distributed as part of the reservation protocol RSVP-TE [RFC3209], which allocates labels to packets of a specific flow or to an aggregated set of flows [RFC3175]. Within the MPLS architecture, label distribution binding decisions are generally made by the downstream node, which then distributes the bindings in the upstream direction. This implies that the receiving node allocates the label. However, there are also instances where upstream allocation may also be useful. In terms of the approach to state maintenance used within MPLS, a soft state mechanism is employed, implying that labels will require refreshing in order to avoid time-outs. Approaches to this include the MPLS peer keep-alive mechanism and the time-out mechanisms inherent within routing and reservation protocols (in instances where they are used to carry out label distribution).

MPLS forwarding has a number of advantages over conventional network forwarding:

- can be done by traffic routers capable of label swapping but not capable of analyzing network layer headers; how an FEC is assigned can be complicated but does not affect label swapping
- an ingress router may use any information it has to determine the FEC, e.g., the port on which the packet arrives (conventional forwarding can only consider information that travels with the packet in the packet header)
- a packet can be labeled differently based on the ingress router, and forwarding decisions can then depend on the ingress router (cannot be done with conventional forwarding, as the ingress router identity does not travel with the packet)
- a packet can be forced to follow an explicit path rather than being chosen by the routing algorithm to support TE
- class of service can be inferred from the label, and routers may then apply different scheduling and discard disciplines to different packets

A.3 Generalized Multiprotocol Label Switching (GMPLS)

GMPLS is an extension of MPLS to include the packet layer as well as the transport layer, with its optical network elements. As with MPLS, the GMPLS standard focuses on both routing and signaling parts of the control plane. By providing a common control plane for packet and transport layers, GMPLS enables end-to-end, dynamic bandwidth provisioning, optical transport networks, and thereby is a key enabler of intelligent optical networking.

Work on GMPLS is carried in the IETF under the auspices of the CCAMP working group and, to some extent, the L1VPN working group. The charter of the IETF CCAMP working group and a list of working documents and RFCs that have been issued are listed on the CCAMP home page at http://ietf.org/html.charters/ccampcharter.html. The charter of the IETF L1VPN working group and a list of working documents and RFCs that have been issued are listed on the L1VPN home page at http://ietf.org/html.charters/l1vpn-charter.html.

GMPLS [RFC3945, FARREL04, FARREL05, L1VPN-FRAMEWORK, MLN-EVALUATION, MLN-REQUIREMENTS] differs from MPLS in that it supports multiple types of transport switching, including TDM, lambda, and fiber (port) switching. Support for additional transport switching types requires GMPLS to extend MPLS, which includes how labels are requested and communicated, how errors are propagated, and other extensions. Interfaces on LSRs can be subdivided into the following classes:

- Packet Switch Capable (PSC): interfaces that recognize packet boundaries and can forward data based on the packet header. Examples include interfaces on routers that forward data based on the IP header and the MPLS label.
- Layer 2 Switch Capable (L2SC): interfaces that recognize frame/cell boundaries and can switch data based on the frame/cell header. Examples include Ethernet bridges that switch data based on the content of the MAC header and ATM-LSRs that forward data based on the ATM VPI/VCI.
- Time-Division Multiplex Capable (TDM): interfaces that switch data based on the time slot in a repeating cycle. Examples include SONET/SDH cross-connects, terminal multiplexers, or add-drop multiplexers.
- Lambda Switch Capable (LSC): interfaces that switch data based on the wavelength. Examples include optical cross-connects (OXCs) that can operate at the individual wavelength level.
- Fiber-Switch Capable (FSC): interfaces that switch data based on the real-world physical spaces. Examples include an OXC that can operate at the single or multiple fiber level.

In MPLS, LSRs recognize either packet/cell boundaries and are able to process packet/cell headers. With GMPLS, non-PSC LSRs recognize neither packet nor cell boundaries and therefore cannot forward data based on the information carried in either packet or cell headers. Instead, GMPLS non-PSC LSRs include devices where the transport switching decision, in addition to packet switching decisions, is based on time slots, wavelengths, or physical ports. However, note that GMPLS PSC LSRs do recognize packet and cell boundaries and therefore can forward data based on the information carried in either packet or cell headers.

A bandwidth channel, or circuit, can be established only between, or through, interfaces of the same type. Depending on the particular technology being used for each interface, different channel names can be used, e.g., SDH circuit, optical trail, and light path. In GMPLS, all these channels are LSPs. The concept of nested LSP (LSP within LSP) in MPLS facilitates building a forwarding hierarchy of LSPs. This hierarchy of LSPs can occur on the same interface or between interfaces. For example, a hierarchy can be built if an interface is capable of multiplexing several LSPs from the same technology, e.g., a lower order SONET/SDH LSP (e.g., VT2/VC-12) nested in a higher order SONET/SDH LSP (e.g., STS-3c/VC-4). The nesting can also occur between interface types, e.g., at the top of the hierarchy are FSC interfaces, followed by LSC interfaces, followed by TDM interfaces, followed by L2SC interfaces, and followed by PSC interfaces. This way, an LSP that starts and ends on a PSC interface can be nested into an LSP that starts and ends on an L2SC interface, which in turn can be nested into an LSP that starts and ends on a TDM interface, which in turn can be nested into an LSP that starts and ends on an LSC interface, which in turn can be nested into an LSP that starts and ends on an FSC interface.

MPLS defines the establishment of LSPs that span only PSC or L2SC interfaces; GMPLS extends this control plane to support each of the five classes of interfaces defined above. GMPLS is based on extensions to MPLS-TE [RFC2702]. In order to facilitate constraint-based routing of LSPs, nodes need more information about the links in the network than standard intranetwork routing protocols provide. These TE attributes are distributed using the transport mechanisms in routing protocols such as OSPF (e.g., flooding) and are taken into consideration by the LSP routing algorithm. GMPLS extends routing protocols and algorithms to carry TE link information and extends signaling protocols to carry explicit routes.

Transport technologies supported by GMPLS can have a very large number of parallel links between two adjacent nodes. For scalability purposes, multiple data links can be combined to form a single TE link, and the management of TE links can be done using the out-of-band link management protocol (LMP) [RFC4202]. LMP runs between adjacent nodes and provides mechanisms to maintain control channel connectivity, verify the physical connectivity of the data links, correlate link information, suppress downstream alarms, and localize link failures for protection/restoration purposes. Traditional IP routing requires that each link connecting two adjacent nodes must be configured and advertised. Having such a large number of parallel links does not scale well, for example, link state routing information must be flooded throughout the network.

GMPLS adapts the MPLS control plane to address this issue with the concept of link bundling and automated configuration and control with LMP. In some cases a combination of <TE link identifier, label> is sufficient to unambiguously identify the appropriate resource used by an LSP. In other cases, a combination of <TE link identifier, label> is not sufficient, for example, a TE link between a pair of SONET/SDH cross-connects, where this TE link is composed of several fibers. In this case the label is a TDM time slot; moreover, this time slot is significant only within a particular fiber. Thus, when signaling an LSP over such a TE link, one needs to specify not just the identity of the link, but also the identity of a particular fiber within that TE link, as well as a particular label (time slot) within that fiber. Such cases are handled by using the link bundling construct, which is described in [RFC4201]. Link bundling addresses the issues of configuration and scalability of advertisement.

GMPLS extends MPLS to control TDM, LSC, and FSC layers, as follows:

- an MPLS LSP can include a mix of links with heterogeneous label encoding (e.g., links between routers, links between routers and ATM-LSRs, and links between ATM-LSRs). GMPLS extends this by including links where the label is encoded as a time slot, a wavelength, or a position in physical space.
- an MPLS LSP that carries IP has to start and end on a router. GMPLS extends this by requiring an LSP to start and end on similar types of interfaces.

- the type of a link-layer protocol transported by a GMPLS LSP is extended to allow such payloads as SONET/SDH, G.709, 1Gb or 10Gb Ethernet, etc.
- MPLS LSPs are unidirectional, GMPLS supports the establishment of bidirectional LSPs.

Note that both MPLS and GMPLS bandwidth allocation can be performed only in discrete units, which is a function of the lower layer technology. That is, bandwidth can only be assigned in units that the physical medium can handle, and in PSC routers this is usually bytes per second; sometimes 1000s of bytes per second. At the transport layer, one could assign bandwidth, for example, in fractions of a wavelength, which could have some advantages on end-system equipment.

A.4 QoS Mechanisms

In this section we discuss QoS mechanisms, including IntServ, DiffServ, and MPLS combined with DiffServ. We will not attempt to review queuing theory basics, as the topic is vast and there are many excellent books, papers, and other references on the topic. Some of my favorite books on the topic include [COOPER72, KLEINROCK75, KLEINROCK76]. You should also consult [ASH98] for some applications of queuing theory to teletraffic-related topics, such as derivation of the Erlang B formula, Neal-Wilkinson theory, and other topics.

QoS is usually associated with hard, quantifiable metrics related to bandwidth, delay, jitter, etc. To achieve QoS requires the definition of service classes, signaling, and connection admission control (CAC). QoS mechanisms include (a) conditioning (policing, shaping, or dropping), (b) queue management, e.g., random early detection (RED), (c) queue scheduling, e.g., weighted fair queuing (WFQ), and (d) link-layer mechanisms.

A.4.1   Traffic Shaping and Policing Algorithms

Traffic shaping controls network traffic in order to optimize or guarantee performance, low latency, and/or bandwidth. Traffic shaping entails packet classification, queue disciplines, enforcing policies, congestion management, QoS, and fairness. It provides a mechanism to control the volume of traffic being sent into the network and the rate at which the traffic is being sent. For this reason, traffic shaping is implemented at the network edges to control the traffic entering the network. It also may be necessary to identify traffic flows that allow the traffic-shaping mechanism to shape them differently. Traffic shaping works by smoothing, or debursting, traffic flows by smoothing the peaks and troughs of data transmission. A before-and-after example of how traffic shaping works is as follows. Before traffic shaping: 10 packets in one second, 0 packets in the next second, 10 packets in the next second, 0 packets the next second. After traffic shaping: 1 packet per 0.2 s.

Shaping removes jitter at the expense of some latency. Two predominant methods for shaping traffic are the leaky bucket and token bucket mechanisms. Both of these algorithms have different properties and are used for different purposes. The leaky bucket imposes a hard limit on the data transmission rate, whereas the token bucket allows a certain amount of burstiness while imposing a limit on the average data transmission rate.

In contrast to traffic shaping, traffic policing is a method of marking/dropping packets in excess of the committed traffic rate and burst size. Policing may be performed at network ingress or logical policing points. We give an example of traffic policing.

A.4.1.1 Leaky-Bucket Algorithm

The leaky-bucket algorithm is used to control the rate at which traffic is sent to the network and provides a mechanism by which bursty traffic can be shaped to present a steady stream of traffic to the network, as opposed to traffic with erratic bursts of low-volume and high-volume flows. An analogy for the leaky bucket is a scenario in which four lanes of automobile traffic converge into a single lane. A regulated admission interval into the single lane of traffic flow helps the traffic move. The benefit of this approach is that traffic flow into the major arteries (the network) is predictable and controlled. The major liability is that when the volume of traffic is vastly greater than the bucket size, in conjunction with the drainage-time interval, traffic backs up in the bucket beyond bucket capacity and is discarded.

The algorithm is as follows:

- arriving packets are placed in a bucket with a hole in the bottom
- the bucket can queue at most b bytes
- a packet that arrives when the bucket is full is discarded
- packets drain through the hole in the bucket into the network at a constant rate of r bytes per second, thus smoothing traffic bursts

The size b of the bucket is limited by the available memory of the system.

The leaky bucket may use available network resources efficiently when traffic volume is low and network bandwidth is available. The leaky-bucket mechanism does not allow individual flows to burst up to port speed, effectively consuming network resources at times when there would not be resource contention in the network. The token bucket implementation does, however, accommodate traffic flows with bursty characteristics. The leaky-bucket and token-bucket implementations can be combined to provide maximum efficiency and control of the traffic flows into a network.

A.4.1.2 Token-Bucket Algorithm

The token bucket is similar in some respects to the leaky bucket, but the primary difference is that the token bucket allows bursty traffic to continue transmitting while there are tokens in the bucket, up to a user-configurable threshold. It thereby accommodates traffic flows with bursty characteristics. The token bucket mechanism dictates that traffic can be transmitted based on the presence of tokens in the bucket. Tokens each represent a given number of bytes, and when tokens are present a flow is allowed to transmit traffic up to its peak burst rate if there are adequate tokens in the bucket and if the burst threshold is configured appropriately.

The algorithm is as follows (*assume each token = 1 byte*):

- a token is added to the bucket every $1/r$ seconds
- the bucket can hold at the most b tokens
- if a token arrives when the bucket is full, it is discarded
- when a packet of n bytes arrives, n tokens are removed from the bucket, and the packet is sent to the network
- if fewer than n tokens are available, no tokens are removed from the bucket, and the packet is considered to be nonconformant

The algorithm allows bursts of up to b bytes, but over the long run the output of conformant packets is limited to the constant rate, r. Nonconformant packets can be treated in various ways:

- dropped
- queued for subsequent transmission when sufficient tokens are in the bucket
- transmitted but marked as nonconformant and possibly to be dropped subsequently if the network is overloaded

Policing checks conformance to a configured (or signaled) traffic profile. As illustrated in Figure A.2, a token bucket algorithm enforces behavior such that in-profile traffic is injected into the network and out-of-profile traffic may be marked, delayed, or discarded. The treatment of a series of packets leaving the shaping queue depends on the size of the packet and the number of bytes remaining in the conform bucket. These packets are policed based on the following rules. Tokens are updated in the conform bucket at the token arrival rate r. If the number of bytes in the conform bucket b is greater than or equal to the packet bytes p, the packet conforms and the conform action is taken on the packet. If the packet conforms, p bytes are removed from the conform bucket and the conform action is completed for the packet. If the number of bytes in the conform bucket b is fewer than p, the exceed action is taken.

For example, if the token bucket is configured with the average rate r of 1000 bytes/second and the normal burst size is 1000 bytes, if the initial token bucket starts full at 1000 bytes, and a 450-byte packet arrives, the packet conforms because enough bytes are available in the conform token bucket. The conform action (send)

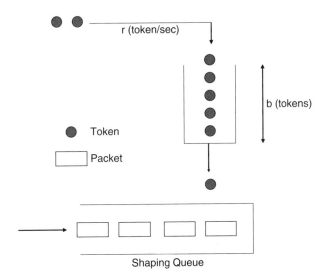

Figure A.2   Token bucket algorithm.

is taken by the packet and 450 bytes are removed from the token bucket (leaving 550 bytes). If the next packet arrives 0.25 s later, 250 bytes are added to the token bucket (0.25*1000), leaving 800 bytes in the token bucket. If the next packet is 900 bytes, the packet exceeds and the exceed action (drop) is taken. No bytes are taken from the token bucket.

A.4.2   Queue Management and Scheduling

Queue management and queue scheduling can improve on traditional FIFO queuing, which provides no service differentiation and can lead to network performance problems. QoS requires routers to support some form of queue scheduling and management to prioritize packets and control queue depth to minimize congestion. Queue management is important to prevent full queues, which are problematic because (a) new connections cannot get through, called lock-out, (b) it can lead to all packets from existing flows being dropped, resulting in across-the-board TCP slow starts (called congestive collapse), and (c) it causes inability to handle bursts of traffic.

Approaches to queue management include random early detection (RED) [RFC2309]. As illustrated in Figure A.3, RED monitors average queue length (*AvgLen*) and drops arriving packets with increasing probability as *AvgLen* increases. No action is taken if *AvgLen* < *MinTH*; however, all packets are dropped if *AvgLen* > *MaxTH*. Variants of RED include flow RED (FRED), which implements per-flow RED queues, and weighted RED (WRED), which provides per-class RED queues. RED is somewhat heavy handed in its sometimes overcontrol and should be used with caution.

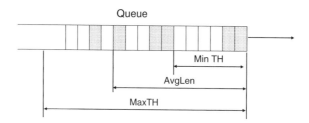

Figure A.3 Queue management using random early detection.

Queue scheduling decides which packet to send out next and is used to manage bandwidth. There are different approaches to queue scheduling, as there are no standard mechanisms. Most router implementations provide some sort of priority queuing mechanism. Fair queuing objectives are to provide fair access to bandwidth and other resources and ensure that no one flow receives more than its fair share of resources. Fair queuing assumes that queues are serviced in a bit-by-bit round robin fashion in which one bit is transmitted from each queue (in actuality bits are not interleaved from different queues). As illustrated in Figure A.4, the scheduler computes when the packet would have left the router using bit-by-bit round robin as follows:

$$P(i) = \text{packet length of flow } i$$
$$S(i) = \text{when router begins sending packet}$$
$$F(i) = \text{when router finishes sending packet}$$
$$A(i) = \text{when packet arrives at router}$$

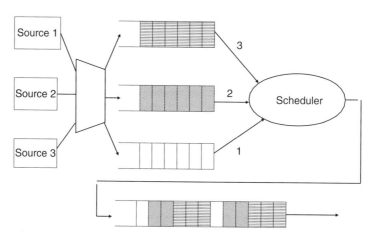

Figure A.4 Weighted fair queuing (WFQ).

Therefore,

$$F(i) = S(i) + P(i) \text{ or}$$
$$F(i) = MAX(F(i-1), A(i)) + P(i)$$

Each $F(i)$ (time stamp) is computed for each packet and the one with the smallest $F(i)$ value is transmitted.

Fair queuing assumes equal service for all flows, wherein each flow gets $1/N$th of bandwidth for N flows. That is, each flow has a weight $= 1$. WFQ enables more than a fair share of bandwidth to be provided to a given flow based on a "weight" assigned to the flow. In WFQ, the bandwidth allocation is in proportion to the sum S of the weights of the flow sources. For example, if a flow has weight of 4 and $S = 8$, then the flow gets $4/8$ or 50% of the bandwidth. WFQ is work conserving in that a router will always transmit packets if they are present in the queue, i.e., the link is never idle as long as packets have arrived. In the example illustrated in Figure A.4, the WFQ scheduler orders packets for departure based on the weights assigned to each source. Source #1 gets 50%, source #2 get 33%, and source #3 gets 16.67% of the bandwidth. WFQ provides flow protection and can be used to bound delay.

Voice requires low latency and jitter, and queuing strategies are augmented with strict priority queues for voice. However, voice must be a small percentage of traffic or other queues will get "starved," i.e., they will not be served adequately and drop packets.

Link efficiency mechanisms address the problem that big packets can get in the way of small voice packets on slow speed links. To address this, big packets can be fragmented and interleaved with voice packets, which is known as link fragment interleaving ([RFC1990] for PPP links, FRF.12 for Frame Relay PVCs). Of course, segmentation and reassembly create additional processing overhead.

A.5 Integrated Services (IntServ)

IntServ QoS mechanisms modify the basic IP model to support real-time and best-effort flows, in which a flow can be host to host or application to application. IntServ is achieved by performing admission control and installing per-flow state along the path. IntServ uses a setup protocol, the resource reservation protocol (RSVP), so that applications can signal their QoS requirements into the network [RFC1633, RFC2205-2216]. IntServ/RSVP signaling maintains per-flow state in the core network, and thereby IntServ scalability has posed several challenges; however, these have been addressed by mechanisms discussed later in this section.

In the IntServ architecture, three classes of service are used based on an application's delay requirements:

- guaranteed-service class, which provides for delay-bounded service agreements
- controlled-load service class, which provides for a form of statistical delay service agreement (nominal mean delay) that will not be violated more often than in an unloaded network

- best-effort service, which is further partitioned into three categories: interactive burst (e.g., Web), interactive bulk (e.g., FTP), and asynchronous (e.g., email)

Guaranteed service and controlled load classes are based on quantitative service requirements and both require signaling and admission control in network nodes. These services can be provided either per flow or per flow aggregate, depending on flow concentration at different points in the network. Best-effort service, on the other hand, does not require signaling. Guaranteed service is particularly well suited to the support of real-time, delay-intolerant applications. However, critical, tolerant applications and some adaptive applications can generally be efficiently supported by controlled load services. Other adaptive and elastic applications are accommodated in the best-effort service class. Because IntServ leaves the existing best-effort service class mostly unchanged (except for a further subdivision of the class), it does not involve any change to existing applications.

A.6 Resource Reservation Protocol (RSVP)

RSVP [RFC1633, RFC2205-2216] provides traffic control by supporting the following functions: (a) admission control, which determines if a QoS request can be granted, (b) packet classifier, which maps packets to a service class by looking at the contents of the IP header, and (c) packet scheduling, which forwards packets based on service class using queuing mechanisms such as WFQ. Admission control is supported by RSVP PATH messages, which mark a path and deliver the path QoS information to the receiver, and RESV messages, which flow upstream to the sender and mark the QoS state. RSVP uses a "soft state" mechanism, in which PATH and RESV refresh messages flow periodically to refresh the flow state in each router.

Any continuing work on RSVP is carried in the IETF under the auspices of the TSVWG working group. The charter of the IETF TSVWG working group and a list of working documents and RFCs that have been issued are listed on the TSVWG home page at http://ietf.org/html.charters/tsvwg-charter.html.

RSVP is based on the concept of a session, which is composed of at least one data flow defined in relation to the 5-tuple source address, source port, destination address, destination port, and protocol id. PATH messages are sent periodically toward the destination and establish a path state per flow in the routers. RESV messages are periodically sent toward the sources and establish the required reservations along the path followed by the data packets. The style of reservation in RSVP is receiver oriented, as receivers initiate the requests for resources to be reserved. Teardown messages (PATHTEAR and RESVTEAR) are used for immediate release of the path state and reservations. Teardown requests can be initiated by a sender or receiver, or any intermediate RSVP router upon state time-out or service preemption.

A lifetime L is associated with each reserved resource, and the timer is reset each time an RESV message confirms the use of the resource. If the timer expires, the resource is freed. This principle of resource management based on timers is called soft state. Soft state is also applied to the path state in the routers; in this case, the timer is reset upon reception of a PATH message. By default, L is 2 min 37.5 s [RFC2205]. Because RSVP messages are delivered unreliably and acknowledgements are not used, RSVP uses the soft state protocol mechanism to ensure reliable state information in the routers.

Although it is recognized that the support of per-flow guarantees in the core of the Internet poses severe scalability problems, various enhancements have allowed RSVP to be far more scalable than the original design. These include RSVP aggregation mechanisms [RFC3175] and refresh reduction mechanisms [RFC2961]. With RSVP aggregation, hosts generate normal end-to-end RSVP messages, which are ignored in the aggregated region, where routers generate aggregate RSVP messages creating single aggregate reservations from ingress to egress. The aggregate reservation should equal the sum of all the RSVP flows, and a policy dictates how often aggregated RSVP messages flow. In order to reduce RSVP overhead with refresh reduction, a bundle message reduces overall message handling load, an identifier identifies an unchanged message more readily, a message acknowledge supports reliable message delivery, and a summary refresh message enables refreshing state without the transmission of whole refresh messages.

A.7 Differentiated Services (DiffServ)

DiffServ mechanisms use edge-based packet-marking, local per-class forwarding behaviors, and resource management to support multiple service levels over an IP-based network. DiffServ terminology is as follows:

- Per hop behavior (PHB): the DiffServ treatment (scheduling/dropping) applied by a router to all the packets that are to experience the same DiffServ service
- Differentiated services code point (DSCP): the value in the IP header indicating which PHB is to be applied to the packet
- Behavior aggregate (BA): the set of all packets that has the same DSCP (and thus that will receive the same PHB)
- Ordered aggregate (OA): the set of BAs that has an ordering constraint and must go into the same queue
- PHB scheduling class (PSC): the set of PHBs applied to an OA, which uses the same queue

DSCPs in the packet header indicate how packets should be serviced at each hop and are marked at the ingress based on analysis of the packet. Intermediate routers service the packets based on the DSCPs. The DiffServ architecture specifies the DSCP format for each PHB. DiffServ is designed to be simpler and more scalable than RSVP/IntServ, as no signaling or per-flow state needs to be maintained in the core network. DiffServ requires no change to applications and is efficient for core routers, as just a few bits indicate the forwarding treatment and the complex classification work is done at the network edge. Furthermore, the network transport can be IP, ATM, frame relay, MPLS, or a mixture. Different packet handling services and mappings are possible, for example, the service class indicator (e.g., premium and best-effort) can indicate congestion control priority where low-priority packets are discarded first.

The DSCP was formerly the IPv4 type of service (TOS) field and IPv6 traffic class field. Six bits of the TOS byte are allocated to the DSCP, and two bits are allocated to the explicit congestion notification (ECN) [RFC2474]. DiffServ PHBs defined to date are as follows:

- Default: best effort
- Expedited forwarding (EF): low delay, latency, jitter service [RFC3246]
- Assured forwarding (AF): four "relative" classes of service [RFC2597]
- Class selectors: backwards compatible with IP precedence

As illustrated in Figure A.5, routers at the edge of the DiffServ domain classify flows and mark packets with the DSCP. Edge route also measures traffic, compares to a traffic profile, and performs traffic conditioning (shape/drop as needed). Routers in the core of a DiffServ domain identify the PHB and implement PHB functionality by queue management/scheduling techniques.

By recognizing that most of the data flows generated by different applications can be ultimately classified into a few general categories (i.e., traffic classes), the DiffServ architecture provides simple and scalable service differentiation. It does this by discriminating and treating the data flows according to their traffic class, thus providing a logical separation of the traffic in the different classes. DiffServ achieves scalability and flexibility by following a hierarchical model for network resource management:

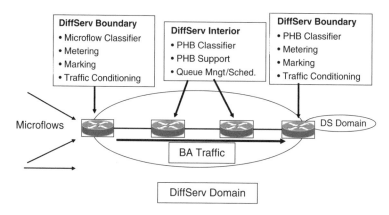

Figure A.5 DiffServ processing.

- Interdomain resource management: service levels, and hence traffic contracts, are agreed at each boundary point between a customer [RFC2208] and a provider for the traffic entering the provider network;
- Intradomain resource management: the service provider is solely responsible for the configuration and provisioning of resources and policies within its network.

Therefore DiffServ is based on local service agreements at customer/provider boundaries, and end-to-end services are built by concatenating such local agreements at each domain boundary along the route to the final destination. Service providers build services with a combination of traffic classes and traffic conditioning to ensure that traffic characteristics conform to a traffic profile and that traffic contracts are respected, and billing. Provisioning and partitioning of both boundary and interior resources are the responsibility of the service provider and, as such, outside the scope of DiffServ. DiffServ does not impose either the number of traffic classes or its characteristics on a service provider, and although traffic classes are nominally supported by interior routers, DiffServ does not impose any requirement on interior resources and functionalities. Traffic conditioning (metering, marking, shaping, or dropping) in the interior of a network is left to the discretion of the service providers.

The net result of the DiffServ approach is that per-flow state is avoided within the network, as individual flows are aggregated in classes. Compared with IntServ, traffic classes in DiffServ are accessible without signaling, which means they are readily available to applications without any setup delay. Consequently, traffic classes can provide qualitative or relative services to applications but not quantitative requirements. The only functionality imposed by DiffServ on interior routers is packet classification. This classification is simplified from that in RSVP because it is based on a single IP header field containing the DSCP rather than multiple fields from different headers. This has the potential of allowing functions performed on every packet, such as traffic policing or shaping, to be done at the boundaries of domains, so forwarding is the main operation performed within the network.

Simultaneously providing several services with differing qualities within the same network is a difficult task. Despite its apparent simplicity, DiffServ does not make this task any simpler. Instead, in DiffServ it was decided to keep the operating mode of the network simple by pushing as much complexity as possible onto network provisioning and configuration. Provisioning requires knowledge of traffic patterns and volumes traversing each node of the network, which also requires a good knowledge of network topology and routing. Provisioning is performed on a much slower timescale than the timescales at which traffic dynamics and network dynamics (e.g., route changes) occur, which means it is impossible to guarantee that overloading of resources will be avoided. This is caused by two factors:

- Packets can be bound to any destination and thus may be routed toward any border router in the domain; in the worst case, a substantial proportion of the entering packets might all exit the domain through the same border router.
- Route changes can suddenly shift vast amounts of traffic from one router to another.

Therefore, even with capacity overprovisioned at both interior and border routers, traffic and network dynamics can cause congestion and violation of service agreements. In addition, capacity overprovisioning results in a very poor statistical multiplexing gain and is therefore inefficient and expensive. Bandwidth is a class property shared by all the flows in the class, and the bandwidth received by an individual flow depends on the number of competing flows in the class as well as the fairness of their respective responses to traffic conditions in the class. Therefore, to receive some quantitative bandwidth guarantees, a flow must reserve its share of bandwidth along the data path, which involves some form of end-to-end signaling and admission control among logical entities called DiffServ bandwidth brokers (TQO processors). This end-to-end signaling should also track network dynamics (i.e., route changes) to enforce the guarantees, which can prove very complex.

However, delay and error rates are class properties that apply to every flow of a class. This is because in every router visited, all the packets sent in a given class share the queue devoted to that class. Consequently, as long as each router manages its queues to maintain a relative relationship between the delay and/or error rate of different classes, relative service agreements can be guaranteed without any signaling. However, if quantitative delay or error rate bounds are required, end-to-end signaling and admission control are also required. End-to-end signaling and admission control would increase the complexity of the DiffServ architecture. The idea of dynamically negotiable service agreements has also been suggested as a way of improving resource usage in the network [RFC2475]. Such dynamic service-level agreements would require complex signaling, as the changes might affect the agreements a provider has with several neighboring networks.

Therefore in its simplest and most general form, DiffServ can efficiently provide pure relative service agreements on delay and error rates among classes. However, unless complex signaling and admission control are introduced in the DiffServ architecture or robustness is sacrificed to some extent, guarantees on bandwidth, as well as quantitative bounds on delay and error rates, cannot be provided. It should be noted that from a complexity point of view, a DiffServ scenario with dynamic provisioning and admission control is very close to an IntServ scenario with flow aggregation. The difference is that precise delay and error rate bounds might not be computed with DiffServ, as the delays and error rates introduced by each router in the domain may not be available to the DiffServ bandwidth broker/TQO processor.

DiffServ alone, therefore, does not represent the ultimate solution for QoS support for all types of applications, and combining DiffServ and IntServ capabilities could combine their individual advantages and mitigate some of their individual drawbacks. Figure A.6 illustrates an approach to the integration of DiffServ and IntServ [RFC2998]. RSVP messages flow end to end, which are ignored by DiffServ routers in the core of the network. Edge routers in this configuration perform both IntServ and DiffServ QoS mechanisms, while backbone routers only perform DiffServ QoS functions. An IntServ flow is tunneled through the core DiffServ domain in this configuration.

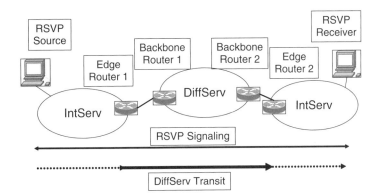

Figure A.6 Integration of IntServ and DiffServ.

As detailed in [RFC2998], significant benefits can be achieved by combining IntServ and DiffServ to support dynamic provisioning and topology-aware admission control, including aggregated RSVP reservations, per flow RSVP, or a DiffServ bandwidth broker/TQO processor. The advantage of using aggregated RSVP reservations is that it offers dynamic, topology-aware admission control over the DiffServ region without the scalability burden of per-flow reservations and the associated level of RSVP signaling in the DiffServ core. [RFC3175] describes an architecture where multiple end-to-end RSVP reservations share the same ingress router (aggregator) and the same egress router (deaggregator) at the edges of an aggregation region and can be mapped onto a single aggregate reservation within the aggregation region. This considerably reduces the amount of reservation state that needs to be maintained by routers within the aggregation region. Furthermore, traffic belonging to aggregate reservations is classified in the data path purely using DiffServ marking.

A.8 MPLS-Based QoS Mechanisms

The DSCP field is not directly visible to an MPLS LSR, as the LSR forwards packets based only on the MPLS header and the DSCP is contained in the IP header. As such, information on DiffServ QoS treatment is made visible to the LSR using the CoS/EXP field and/or label in the MPLS header, as illustrated in Figure A.1 and explained in the following paragraphs.

DiffServ routers forward packets to the next hop and egress interface based only on the destination IP address, which is independent of the packet's DiffServ PHB treatment. As discussed above, packet scheduling is based only on the DSCP. In contrast, MPLS routers that also implement DiffServ make a forwarding and scheduling decision based on the label and DiffServ information conveyed in the MPLS header in one of two ways:

- E-LSP, where the queuing treatment and drop priority are inferred from the CoS/EXP field
- L-LSP, where the queuing treatment is inferred from the label and the drop priority is inferred from the CoS/EXP field

Therefore the MPLS CoS/EXP field enables different service classes to be offered for individual labels. E-LSPs can be set up with existing, non-DiffServ-aware signaling (LDP, RSVP). The CoS/EXP bits to PHB mapping is configured on every router. However, L-LSPs require extensions to LDP and RSVP to bind the queuing treatment to the MPLS label [RFC3270]. For more fine-grained QoS treatment, a separate label can be used for each class where, in this instance, the label would represent both the forwarding and the service classes.

In Chapters 3, 4, and 6 we analyze the benefits of per-flow QoS support versus aggregated per-VNET QoS support in terms of network performance, control load overhead, and capacity design implications, respectively. We conclude that the incremental benefits of per-flow QoS support, in terms of small or no improvement in performance and/or capacity design efficiencies, are not worth the significant additional control processing load such an approach would entail. Many more details on these trade-offs are given in Chapters 3, 4, and 6 on those topics.

Glossary

2-STT-EDR	2-link Success To the Top Event Dependent Routing
2-DC-SDR	2-link Distributed Connection-by-connection State Dependent Routing
3GPP	3rd Generation Partnership Project
4ESS	Number 4 Electronic Switching System
ABW	Available BandWidth
ADR	AddRess
AESA	ATM End-System Address
AF	Assured Forwarding
AFI	Authority and Format Identifier
AINI	ATM Inter-Network Interface
ALBQNM	ALBuQuerque, New Mexico
ALL	Access Logical Link
ALLOC	ALLOCation
AN	Access Node
API	Application Programming Interface
AR	Access Router
ARIS	Aggregate Route-based IP Switching
ALBYNY	ALBanY, New York
ANHMCA	ANaHeiM, California
ARPANET	Advanced Research Projects Agency NETwork
AS	Autonomous System
ATLNGA	ATLaNta, GeorgiA
ATM	Asynchronous Transfer Mode
ATMF	ATM Forum
AvgLen	Average Length
B	Busy
BA	Behavior Aggregate
BANDW	BANDWidth
BB	BackBone
BBN	Bolt, Beranek and Newman
BC	Bandwidth Constraint
BE	Best Effort
BEHAVE	Behavior Engineering for Hindrance AVoidancE
BGP	Border Gateway Protocol
BICC	Bearer Independent Call Control
BLK	BLocKed, or BLocKing
BLL	Backbone Logical Link
BLTMMD	BaLTiMore, MarylanD
BNA	Bandwidth Not Available

BR	Backbone Router
BRAS	Broadband Remote Access Server
BRHMAL	BiRmingHam, Alabama
BW	BandWidth
BWavg	BandWidth average
BWIP	BandWidth In Progress
BWIPavg	BandWidth In Progress average
BWmax	BandWidth maximum
BWOF	BandWidth OFfered
BWOV	BandWidth OVerflow
BWOVavg	BandWidth OVerflow average
BWPC	BandWidth Peg Count
BWtraf	BandWidth traffic
BX	Backbone router to optical cross connect (OXC) link
CAC	Connection Admission Control
CAP	CAPacity
CBK	CRanKback
CBR	Constant Bit Rate
CCA	Call/session Control Agent
CCAMP	Common Control And Measurement Plane
CCS	Common-Channel Signaling
CDMA	Code Division Multiple Access
CE	Customer Edge (router)
CGH	Chung-Graham-Huang
CHCGIL	ChiCaGo, Illinois
CHT	CHina Telecom
CIC	Call/session Identification Code
CIDR	Classless Inter-Domain Routing
CIP	Connections In Progress
CLMASC	CoLuMbiA, South Carolina
CLP	Cell Loss Priority
CMBRMA	CaMBRidge, MAssachusetts
CMOF	Capacity Management Operations Functions
COS	Class Of Service
CPE	Customer Provider Equipment
CP-SDR	Centralized Periodic–State Dependent Routing
CPU	Central Processing Unit
CRC	Cyclic Redundancy Check
CRISP	Cross Registry Information Service Protocol
CRLSP	Constraint-based Routing Label Switched Path
CSCF	Call Session Control Function
CSPF	Constrained Shortest Path First
CSR	Cell Switched Router
CST	Central Standard Time
CT	Class Type
CVS	Constant bit rate Voice Service
DAR	Dynamic Alternative Routing
DARPA	Defense Advanced Research Projects Agency
DBN	Destination Border Node

DBR	Dynamic Bandwidth Reservation
DBW	Delta BandWidth
DCC	Data Country Code
DCME	Digital Circuit Multiplexing Equipment
DC-SDR	Distributed Connection-by-connection–State Dependent Routing
DCR	Dynamically Controlled Routing
DCS	Digital Cross-connect System
DDD	Direct Distance Dialing
DEFO	Discrete Event Flow Optimization
DEPTHHL	DEPTH Heavily Loaded
DEPTHR	DEPTH Reserved
DIFFSERV	DIFFerentiated SERVices
DIME	DIameter Maintenance and Extensions
DLCI	Data Link Connection Identifier
DLLSTX	DaLLas, TeXas
DN	Destination Node
DNHR	Dynamic NonHierarchical Routing
DNS	Domain Name System
DNVRCO	DeNVeR, Colorado
DOC	Dynamic Overload Control
DP-SDR	Distributed Periodic–State Dependent Routing
DQOS	Dynamic Quality Of Service
DS	DiffServ
DS3	Digital Signal level 3
DSCP	DiffServ Control Point
DSL	Digital Subscriber Line
DSP	Domain Specific Part
DSTE	DiffServ-aware MPLS Traffic Engineering
DTL	Designated Transit List
DWDM	Dense Wavelength Division Multiplexing
DYN	DYNamic
ECN	Explicit Congestion Notification
EDR	Event Dependent Routing
EF	Expedited Forwarding
EGP	Exterior Gateway Protocol
E-LSP	EXP Label Switched Path
EMAIL	Electronic MAIL
ENUM	Electronic NUMbering
EQBW	EQuivalent BandWidth
EQUIV	EQUIValent
ER	Explicit Route
EST	Eastern Standard Time
ETS	Emergency Telecommunications Service
EVAL	EVALuation
EXP	EXPerimental
FASTAR	FAST Automatic Restoration
FCS	Frame Check Sequence
FEC	Forwarding Equivalence Class
FIFO	First In First Out

FL	FLorida
FORCES	FORwarding and Control Element Separation
FR	Frame Relay
FRED	Flow Random Early Detection
FRHD	FReeHolD, New Jersey
FRF	Frame Relay Forum
FRR	Fast ReRoute
FSC	Fiber Switch Capable
FSN	Fully Shared Network
FTLDFL	ForT LauDerdale, Florida
FTN	Forward equivalence class To Next hop label forwarding entry
FTP	File Transfer Protocol
FTS	Federal Telecommunications System
FTTX	Fiber To The X (Curb, Premises, etc.)
FTWOTX	ForT WOrth, TeXas
FXR	FiXed Routing
Gbps	Gigabits per second
GETS	Government Emergency Telecommunications Service
GFC	Generic Flow Control
GMPLS	Generalized MultiProtocol Label Switching
GOS	Grade Of Service
GRCYNY	GaRden CitY, New York
GTQO	Generic Traffic engineering and QoS Optimization
GOS	Grade-Of-Service
GMPLS	Generalized MultiProtocol Label Switching
GSDN	Global Software-Defined Network
GW	GateWay
HC	Header Compression
HEC	Header Error Control
HIER	HIERarchical
HL	Heavily Loaded
HLthr	Heavily Loaded threshold
HMSQNJ	HaMilton SQuare, New Jersey
HOSTID	HOST IDentification
HPR	High Performance Routing
HSS	Home Subscriber Server
HSTNTX	HouSToN, TeXas
HTR	Hard To Reach
HTTP	HyperText Transfer Protocol
IAD	Integrated Access Device
IAM	Initial Address Message
ICD	International Code Designator
IDI	Initial Domain Identifier
IDP	Initial Domain Part
IE	Information Element
IETF	Internet Engineering Task Force
IF	InterFace
IGP	Interior Gateway Protocol
ILBW	Idle-Link BandWidth

IMHO	In My Humble Opinion
IMS	IP Multimedia Subsystem
IN	Intelligent Network
INTL	INTernationaL
IntServ	Integrated Services
IP	Internet Protocol
IPv4	Internet Protocol version 4
IPv6	Internet Protocol version 6
IRSCP	Intelligent Routing Service Control Point
ISDN	Integrated Services Digital Network
ISP	Internet Service Provider
ISUP	Integrated Services digital network User Part
ITU-T	International Telecommunications Union–Telecommunications (standardization sector)
JCVLFL	JaCksonViLle, Florida
Kbps	Kilobits per second
L1VPN	Layer 1 Virtual Private Network
L2SC	Layer 2 Switch Capable
LA	Los Angeles
LAN	Local Area Network
LC	Link Capability
LDP	Label Distribution Protocol
LDS	Long Distance Service
LER	Label Edge Router
LL	Lightly Loaded
LLDL	Link Lost/Delayed Level
L-LSP	Label–Label Switched Path
LLR	Least Loaded Routing
LMP	Link Management Protocol
LP	Linear Program
LS	Link State
LSA	Link State Advertisement
LSC	Lambda Switch Capable
LSCR	Link Selection Capability Routing
LSP	Label Switched Path
LSR	Label Switching Router
LSVLKY	LouiSViLle, KentuckY
MAGMA	Multicast and Anycast Group Membership
MAM	Maximum Allocation Model
MAR	Maximum Allocation with Reservation
MaxCT	Maximum Class Type
MaxTH	Maximum THreshold
Mbps	Megabits per second
MBS	Maximum Burst Size
MCI	Microwave Communications Incorporated
MFA	MPLS Frame Relay ATM (Forum)
MIB	Management Information Base
MIER	Multiple Ingress/Egress Routing
MinTH	Minimum THreshold

MIR	Multiple Intelligent Routing
MLN	Multi-Layer Network
MMPP	Markov Modulated Poisson Process
MOD	MODify
MP-BGP	MultiProtocol Border Gateway Protocol
MPLS	MultiProtocol Label Switching
MPR	Minimum Packet Rate
ms	millisecond
MSE	Multi-Service Edge
MSO	Multi-Service Operator
MSPR	Multilink Shortest Path Routing
M-STT-EDR	Multilink Success To the Top Event Dependent Routing
MTGMAL	MonTGoMery, ALabama
NANP	North American Numbering Plan
NARB	Network Aware Resource Broker
NAT	Network Address Translator
NCC	Network Control Center
NET	NETwork
NETID	NETwork IDentification
NFOF	Network Forecasting Operations Functions
NGN	Next Generation Network
NIH	Not Invented Here
NN	Node to Node
NNN	Network Node Number
NPA	Numbering Plan Area
NR	Non-Reserved
NRA	Network Routing Address
NRT	Non Real Time
NSIS	Next Steps In Signaling
NSLP	NSIS Signaling Layer Protocol
NTLP	NSIS Transport Layer Protocol
NTT	Nippon Telegraph and Telephone (Company)
NWORLA	NeW ORleans, LouisiAna
NY	New York
NYCMNY	New York City Main, New York
OA	Ordered Aggregate
OAM	Operations, Administration, and Maintenance
OAM&P	Operations, Administration, Maintenance, and Provisioning
OBN	Originating Border Node
OC	Optical Carrier
OKBKIL	OaKBrooK, ILlinois
OKLDCA	OaKLanD, CaliforniA
OMAHNE	OMAHa, NEbraska
ON	Originating Node
ORLDFL	ORLanDo, FLorida
OSPF	Open Shortest Path First
OSS	Operations Support System
OXC	Optical cross Connect
P	Provider (router)

PAR	PARameter
PBX	Private Branch eXchange
PCC	Path Computation Client
PCE	Path Computation Element
PDV	Packet Delay Variation
PE	Provider Edge (router)
PERF	PERFormance
PHB	Per-Hop Behavior
PHLAPA	PHiLAdelphia, PennsylvAnia
PHNXAZ	PHoeNiX, AriZona
PIB	Policy Information Base
PITBPA	PiTtsBurg, PennsylvaniA
PLNG	PLaNninG
PLR	Packet Loss Ratio
PMP	Paris Metro Pricing
PNNI	Private Network–Network Interface
PPP	Point-to-Point Protocol
PPR	Peak Packet Rate
PQ	Priority Queuing
PSC	Packet Switch Capable, or PHB Scheduling Class
PSTN	Public Switched Telephone Network
PTD	Packet Transfer Delay
PTI	Payload Type Indication
PTSE	PNNI Topology State Element
PTSP	PNNI Topology State Packet
PVC	Permanent Virtual Circuit
PW	Pseudo-Wire
QoS	Quality of Service
QOSM	QoS Model
QSPEC	QoS SPECification
R	Reserved (state)
RACF	Resource and Admission Control Function
RATS	Routing/Addressing Traffic-engineering Strategy
RBW	Reserved BandWidth
RBWeng	Reserved BandWidth engineered
RBWtraf	Reserved BandWidth traffic
RCMDVA	RiChMonD, VirginiA
RDM	Russian Doll Model
RECOM	RECOMmendation
RED	Random Early Detection
Reng	Reserved engineered
RESV	RESerVe, or RESerVation
RESVTEAR	RESerVe TEAR
RFC	Request For Comments
RINR	Real-time Inter-Network Routing
RMD	Resource Management with DiffServ
RPH	Resource Priority Header
RQE	Routing Query Element
RQMTS	ReQuireMenTS

RRE	Routing Recommendation Element
RSE	Routing Status Element
RSVP	Resource ReserVation Protocol
RSVP-TE	Resource ReserVation Protocol–Traffic Engineering
RT	Real Time
RTG	RouTinG
Rthr	Reservation bandwidth threshold
RTNR	Real-Time Network Routing
RTP	Real-time Transport Protocol
Rtraf	Reserved traffic
S	Sequence (bit)
SBC	Session Border Controller
SBNDIN	SouthBeND, INdiana
SCP	Service Control Point
SDH	Synchronous Digital Hierarchy
SCRM	SaCRaMento, California
SDI	Switched Digital International
SDP	Session Description Protocol
SDR	State Dependent Routing
SDS	Switched Digital Service
SHOKCA	SHerman OaKs, CAlifornia
SI	Service Identity
SIEVE	Sieve Mail Filtering Language
SIG	SIGnaling
SIMPLE	SIP for Instant Messaging and Presence Leveraging Extensions
SIP	Session Initiation Protocol
SIPPING	Session Initiation Protocol Proposal INvestiGation
SLA	Service Level Agreement
SLKCUT	Salt LaKe City, UTah
SNBOCA	SaN BernadinO, CAlifornia
SNDGCA	SaN DieGo, CAlifornia
SNFCCA	SaN FranCisco, CAlifornia
SNMP	Simple Network Management Protocol
SNRC	Service Node Routing Complex
SONET	Synchronous Optical NETwork
SP	Service Provider
SPEERMINT	Session PEERing for Multimedia INTerconnect
SPF	Shortest Path First
SPKNWA	SPoKaNe, WAshington
SPR	Sustainable Packet Rate
SS7	Signaling System number 7
STR	State and Time dependent Routing
STS	Synchronous Transport Signal
STT	Success To the Top
STT-EDR	Success To the Top–Event Dependent Routing
SVC	Switched Virtual Circuit
SVP	Switched Virtual Path
SYRCNY	SYRaCuse, New York

SW	SWitching
T1	Transmission level 1
TBWIP	Total BandWidth In Progress
TBW	Total BandWidth
TBWOV	Total BandWidth OVerflow
TC	Transport Capability
TCP	Transmission Control Protocol
TCSNAZ	TuCSoN, AriZona
TDM	Time Division Multiplexing
TDR	Time Dependent Routing
TE	Traffic Engineering
TEDB	Traffic Engineering Data Base
Telco	Telephone company
Telecom	Telecommunications
TEWG	Traffic Engineering Working Group
TK	TrunK
TL	Traffic Load
TLBW	Total Link BandWidth
TLDP	Total Lost/Delayed Probability
TLFO	Traffic Load Flow Optimization
TLP	Traffic Loss Probability
Tmax	Time maximum
TMOF	Traffic Management Operations Functions
ToS	Type of Service
TPOC	Trunk Provisioning Operating Characteristics
TPRL	TransPort Restoration Level
TPRLd	TransPort Restoration Level dedicated services
TPRLs	TransPort Restoration Level switched services
TQO	Traffic Engineering and QoS Optimization
TQOP	TQO Processor
TRAF	TRAFfic
TRANS	TRANSmission, or TRANSport
TRBW	Total Required BandWidth
TRL	Traffic Restoration Level
TSE	Topology State Element
TSVWG	TranSport Working Group
TTL	Time To Live
UBR	Unassigned Bit Rate
UC	University of California
UDP	User Datagram Protocol
UMTS	Universal Mobile Telecommunications System
UNI	User Network Interface
VBN	Via Border Node
VBR	Variable Bit Rate
VC	Virtual Channel
VCI	Virtual Channel Identifier
VN	Via Node
VNET	Virtual NETwork
VoIP	Voice over Internet Protocol

VP	Virtual Path
VPI	Virtual Path Identifier
VPN	Virtual Private Network
VRF	Virtual Routing and Forwarding table
VT	Virtual Trunk
VTeng	Virtual Trunk engineered
VTFO	Virtual Trunk Flow Optimization
VTmin	Virtual Trunk minimum
VTtraf	Vritual Trunk traffic
WFQ	Weighted Fair Queuing
WHPLNY	WHite PLains, New York
WIN	Worldwide International Network (routing)
WLAN	Wireless Local Area Network
WRED	Weighted Random Early Detection
WWW	World Wide Web

References and Bibliography

References

[3GPP-TS.22.228] "Service Requirements for the IP Multimedia Core Network Subsystem; Stage 1," 3GPP TS 22.228.

[ACHARYA97] Acharya, A., *et al.*, "A Framework for IP Switching over Fast ATM Cell Transport (IPSOFACTO)," Conference on Broadband Networking Technology, Vol. 3233, Chapter 36, Dallas, TX, November 1997.

[AHMADI92] Ahmadi, H., *et al.*, "Dynamic Routing and Call Control in High-Speed Integrated Networks," Proceedings of ITC-13, Copenhagen, 1992.

[AKINPELU84] Akinpelu, J. M., "The Overload Performance of Engineered Networks with Nonhierarchical and Hierarchical Routing," Bell System Technical Journal, Vol. 63, 1984.

[APOSTOLOPOULOS99] Apostolopoulos, G., "Intra-Domain QoS Routing in IP Networks: A Feasibility and Cost/Benefit Analysis," IEEE Network Magazine, September 1999.

[ASH03] Ash, J., "Performance Evaluation of QoS Routing Methods for IP-Based Networks," Computer Communications, May 2003.

[ASH04] Ash, G. R., and Chemouil, P., "20 Years of Dynamic Routing in Circuit-Switched Networks: Looking Backward to the Future," IEEE Communications Magazine, October 2004.

[ASH81] Ash G. R., *et al.*, "Design and Optimization of Networks with Dynamic Routing," Bell System Technical Journal, Vol. 80, Number 8, 1981.

[ASH81a] Ash, G. R., Kafker, A. H., and Krishnan, K. R., "Servicing and Real-Time Control of Networks with Dynamic Routing," Bell System Technical Journal, Vol. 60, No. 8, October 1981.

[ASH83] Ash, G. R., Kafker, A. H., and Krishnan, K. R., "Intercity Dynamic Routing Architecture and Feasibility," Proceedings of the Tenth International Teletraffic Congress, Montreal, Canada, June 1983.

[ASH85] Ash, G. R., "Use of a Trunk Status Map for Real-Time DNHR," Proceedings of the Eleventh International Teletraffic Congress, Kyoto, Japan, September 1985.

[ASH87] Ash, G. R., "Traffic Network Routing, Control, and Design for the ISDN Era," Fifth ITC Specialists Seminar: Traffic Engineering for ISDN Design and Planning, Lake Como, Italy, May 1987.

[ASH88] Ash, G. R., Blake, B. M., and Schwartz, S. D., "Integrated Network Routing and Design," Proceedings of the Twelfth International Teletraffic Congress, Torino, Italy, June 1988.

[ASH89] Ash G. R, *et al.*, "Robust Design and Planning of a Worldwide Intelligent Network," IEEE Journal on Selected Areas in Communications, Vol. 7, No. 8, 1989.

[ASH89a] Ash, G. R., and Oberer, E., "Dynamic Routing in the AT&T Network—Improved Service Quality at Lower Cost," Proceedings of the IEEE Global Telecommunications Conference, Dallas, Texas, November 1989.

[ASH90] Ash, G. R., and Schwartz, S. D., "Traffic Control Architectures for Integrated Broadband Networks," International Journal of Digital and Analog Communication Systems, Vol. 3, Number 2, April–June 1990.

[ASH91] Ash G. R, et al., "Real-Time Network Routing in a Dynamic Class-of-Service Network," Proceedings of International Teletraffic Congress, ITC 13, Copenhagen, Denmark, 1991.

[ASH92] Ash, G. R., Chen, J.-S., Frey, A. E., Huang, B. D., Lee, C.-K., and McDonald, G., "Real-Time Network Routing in the AT&T Network—Improved Service Quality at Reduced Cost," Proceedings of the IEEE Global Telecommunications Conference, Orlando, Florida, December 1992.

[ASH94] Ash, G. R., Chan, K. K., and Labourdette, J.-F., "Analysis and Design of Fully Shared Networks," Proceedings of International Teletraffic Congress, ITC 14, Antibes, France, 1994.

[ASH94a] Ash, G. R., and Huang, B. D., "Comparative Evaluation of Dynamic Routing Strategies for a Worldwide Intelligent Network," Proceedings of the 14th International Teletraffic Congress, Antibes, France, June 1994.

[ASH98] Ash, G. R., *Dynamic Routing in Telecommunications Networks*, McGraw-Hill, 1998.

[ASH99] Ash, G. R., Chen, J., Fishman, S. D., and Maunder, A., "Routing Evolution in Multiservice Integrated Voice/Data Networks," International Teletraffic Congress ITC-16, Edinburgh, Scotland, June 1999.

[ASSURED-SERVICES-RQMTS] Pierce, M., and Choi, D., "Requirements for Assured Service Capabilities in Voice over IP," IETF work in progress.

[ASSURED-SERVICES-ARCH] Pierce, M., and Choi, D., "Architecture for Assured Service Capabilities in Voice over IP," IETF work in progress.

[ATMFORUM-0025.001] ATM Forum Technical Committee, "Specification of the ATM Inter-Network Interface (AINI) ATM Inter-Network Interface (AINI) Specification Version 1.1," af-cs-0025.001, September 2002.

[ATMFORUM-0055.002] ATM Forum Technical Committee, "Private Network-Network Interface Specification Version 1.1 (PNNI 1.1)," af-pnni-0055.002, April 2002.

[ATMFORUM-0061.000] ATM Forum Technical Committee, "ATM User-Network Interface (UNI) Signaling Specification Version 4.0," af-sig-0061.000, July 1996.

[ATMFORUM-0127.000] ATM Forum Technical Committee, "PNNI SPVC Addendum Version 1.0," af-cs-0127.000, July 1999.

[ATMFORUM-0146.000] ATM Forum Technical Committee, "Operation of the Bearer Independent Call Control (BICC) Protocol with SIG 4.0/PNNI 1.0-AINI," af-cs-vmoa-0146.000, July 2000.

[ATMFORUM-0148.001] ATM Forum Technical Committee, "Modification of Traffic Parameters for an Active Connection Signalling Specification (PNNI, AINI, and UNI) Version 2.0," af-cs-0148.001, May 2001.

[ATMFORUM-0200.000] ATM Forum Technical Committee, "PNNI Routing Congestion Control, Version 1.0," af-cs-0200.000, June 2004.

[ATMFORUM-0201.000] ATM Forum Technical Committee, "PNNI Routing Resynchronization Control, Version 1.0," af-cs-0201.000, June 2004.

[AT&T98] "AT&T announces cause of frame-relay network outage," AT&T Press Release, April 22, 1998.

[AWDUCHE99] Awduche, D., "MPLS and Traffic Engineering in IP Networks," IEEE Communications Magazine, December 1999.

[BELLMAN57] Bellman, R. E., *Dynamic Programming*, Princeton University Press, 1957.

[BERSEKAS92] Bertsekas, D., and Gallager, R., *Data Networks*, Prentice-Hall, 1992.

[BHADARI97] Bhandari, R., "Optimal Physical Diversity Algorithms and Survivable Networks," Proceedings of IEEE Symposium on Computers and Communications, ISCC'97, Alexandria, Egypt, July 1997.

[BLACK34] Black, H. S., "Stabilized Feedback Amplifiers," Bell Syst. Tech. J., 1934.

[BODE40] Bode, H. W., "Feedback Amplifier Design," Bell System Tech. J., Vol. 19, p. 42, 1940.

[BOLOTIN99] Bolotin, V., *et al.*, "IP Traffic Characterization for Planning and Control, Teletraffic Engineering in a Competitive World," P. Key and D. Smith (Eds.), Elsevier, Amsterdam, 1999.

[BONALD02] Bonald, T., Oueslanti-Boulahia, S., and Roberts, J. W., "IP Traffic and QoS Control: The Need for a Flow-Aware Architecture," World Telecommunications Congress, Paris, France, September 2002.

[BORTHICK05] Borthick, S. L., "Mr. QoS versus Mr. Bandwidth," Business Communications Review, September 2005.

[BURKE61] Burke, P. J., "Blocking Probabilities Associated with Directional Reservation," unpublished memorandum, 1961.

[CABLE-WIRELESS-TE] Liljenstolpe, C., "An Approach to IP Network Traffic Engineering (Cable & Wireless)," IETF work in progress.

[CABLELABS-DQOS-05] "PacketCable Dynamic Quality of Service Specification," CableLabs Specification PKT-SP-DQOS-I12-050812, August 2005.

[CAMARILLO05] Camarillo, G., *et al.*, "Functionality of Existing Session Border Controller (SBC)," Internet-Draft, February 2005.

[CAMERON82] Cameron, W. H., Regnier, J., Galloy, P., and Savoie, A. M., "Dynamic Routing for Intercity Telephone Networks," Proceedings of the Tenth International Teletraffic Congress, Montreal, Canada, June 1983.

[CARON88] Caron, F., "Results of the Telecom Canada High Performance Routing Trial," Proceedings of the Twelfth International Teletraffic Congress, Torino, Italy, June 1988.

[CARUGI05] Carugi, M., *et al.*, "Introduction to the ITU-T NGN Focus Group Release 1: Target Environment, Services, and Capabilities," IEEE Communications Magazine, November 2005.

[CAESAR05] Caesar, M., *et al.*, "Design and Implementation of a Routing Control Platform," Proc. NSDI, May 2005.

[CHAO91] Chao, C.-W., *et al.*, "FASTAR: A Robust System for Fast DS3 Restoration," Proceedings of GLOBECOM 1991, Phoenix, Arizona, December 1991, pp. 1396–1400.

[CHEMOUIL86] Chemouil, P., Filipiak, J., and Gauthier, P., "Analysis and Control of Traffic Routing in Circuit-Switched Networks," Computer Networks and ISDN Systems, Vol. 11, No. 3, March 1986.

[CHOUDHURY01] Choudhury, G., Maunder, A. S., and Sapozhnikova, V., "Faster Link-State IGP Convergence and Improved Network Scalability and Stability," LCN 2001, Tampa, Florida, November 14–16, 2001.

[CHOUDHURY03] Choudhury, G., Ash, G., Manral, V., Maunder, A., and Sapozhnikova, V., "Prioritized Treatment of Specific OSPF Packets and Congestion Avoidance: Algorithms and Simulations," AT&T Technical Report, August 2003.

[CHOLEWKA99] Cholewka, K., "MCI Outage Has Domino Effect," Inter@ctive Week, August 20, 1999.

[COOPER72] Cooper, R. B., *Introduction to Queueing Theory*, Macmillan, New York; Collier-Macmillan Limited, London, 1972.

[CORMEN90] Cormen, T. H., *et al.*, *Introduction to Algorithms*, MIT Press and McGraw-Hill, 1990.

[CRANKBACK] Farrel, A., *et al.*, "Crankback Signaling Extensions for MPLS Signaling," IETF work in progress.

[DaSILVA00] DaSilva, L. A., "Pricing for QoS-Enabled Networks: A Survey," IEEE Communications Surveys, Second Quarter 2000.

[DiBENEDETTO89] DiBenedetto A., *et al.*, "Dynamic Routing of the Italcable Telephone Traffic: Experience and Perspectives," Proceedings Globecom 1989, Dallas, TX, 1989.

[DIJKSTRA59] Dijkstra, E. W., "A Note on Two Problems in Connection with Graphs, Numerical Mathematics," Vol. 1, 1959, pp. 269–271.

[DONIGIAN02] Donigian, A. S., Jr., "Watershed Model Calibration and Validation: The HSPF Experience," AQUA TERRA Consultants, September 2002.

[DSLFORUM-TR-059] Anschutz, T., "DSL Evolution: Architecture Requirements for the Support of QoS-Enabled IP Services," DSLForum TR-059, September 2003.

[DSTE-AGGREGATION] LeFaucheur, F., *et al.*, "Aggregation of RSVP Reservations over MPLS TE/DS-TE Tunnels," IETF work in progress.

[DZIONG97] Dziong, Z., Juda, M., and Mason, L., "A Framework for Bandwidth Management in ATM Networks: Aggregate Equivalent Bandwidth Estimation Approach," IEEE ACM Transactions, February 1997.

[DZIONG96a] Dziong, Z., and Mason, L. G., "Fair-Efficient Call Admission for Broadband Networks: A Game Theoretic Framework" Vol. 4, No. 1, IEEE/ACM Transactions on Networking, February 1996.

[DZIONG96b] Dziong, Z., Zhang, J., and Mason, L. G. "Virtual Network Design: An Economic Approach," ITC Specialists Seminar on Control in Communications, Lund, Sweden, October 1996.

[E.164] ITU-T Recommendation, "The International Telecommunications Numbering Plan."

[E.170] ITU-T Recommendation, "Traffic Routing Principles," Geneva, 1988, Rev. 1992, Rev. 1997.

[E.191] ITU-T Recommendation, "B-ISDN Numbering and Addressing," October 1996.

[E.350] ITU-T Recommendation, "Dynamic Routing Interworking," Geneva, 1988, Rev. 1992.

[E.351] ITU-T Recommendation, "Routing of Multimedia Connections across TDM-, ATM-, and IP-Based Network," March 2000.

[E.353] ITU-T Recommendation, "Routing of Calls when Using International Network Routing Addresses," February 2001.

[E.360.X] ITU-T Recommendations, "QoS Routing and Related Traffic Engineering Methods for Multiservice TDM-, ATM-, and IP-Based Networks," May 2002.

[E.361] ITU-T Recommendation, "QoS Routing Support for Interworking of QoS Service Classes across Routing Technologies," May 2003.

[E.525] ITU-T Recommendation, "Designing Networks to Control Grade of Service," May 1992.

[E.529] ITU-T Recommendation, "Network Dimensioning Using End-to-End GoS Objectives," May 1997.

[E.716] ITU-T Recommendation, "User Demand Modeling in Broadband-ISDN," October 1996.

[ELWALID01] Elwalid, A., *et al.*, "MATE: MPLS Adaptive Traffic Engineering," Proceedings INFOCOM'01, April 2001.

[ETS1] Dolly, M., Nguyen, A., "Proposed Issue: Technical Report in Support of Emergency Telecommunications Service in IP Networks," ATIS/PTSC Contribution T1S1.7/2003-732, November 2004.

[ETS2] Dolly, M., (Ed.), "Output Baseline Text: Support of ETS in IP Networks," ATIS/PTSC Contribution T1S1.7/2003-663, November 2004.

[ETS3] "ETS Technical Report," T1S1.7 Editing Group, ATIS/PTSC Contribution T1S1.7/2003-629 R1, November 2004.

[FARREL04] Farrel, A., *The Internet and Its Protocols*, Morgan Kaufmann, 2004.

[FARREL05] Farrel, A., and Bryskin, I., *GMPLS: Architecture and Applications*, Morgan Kaufmann, 2005.

[FEAMSTER04] Feamster, N., *et al.*, "The Case for Separating Routing from Routers," ACM SIGCOMM workshop on Future Directions in Network Architecture (FDNA), August 2004.

[FELDMAN00] Feldman, A., *et al.*, "Netscope: Traffic Engineering for IP Networks," IEEE Network Magazine, March 2000.

[FELDMAN01] Feldman, A., *et al.*, "Deriving Traffic Demands for Operational IP Networks: Methodology and Experience," ACM Transactions on Networking, June 2001.

[FELDMAN99] Feldman, A., *et al.*, "Dynamic of IP Traffic: A Study of the Role of Variability and the Impact of Control," Proceedings of the ACM SIGCOMM, September 1999.

[FIELD83] Field, F. A., "The Benefits of Dynamic Nonhierarchical Routing in Metropolitan Traffic Networks," Proceedings of the Tenth International Teletraffic Congress, Montreal, Canada, June 1983.

[FLOYD62] Floyd, R. W., "Algorithm 97: Shortest Path," Communications of the ACM, June 1962.

[FRANKS79] Franks, R. L., *et al.*, "A Model Relating Measurements and Forecast Errors to the Provisioning of Direct Final Trunk Groups," Bell System Technical Journal, Vol. 58, No. 2, February 1979.

[FRF.12] Frame Relay Forum, "Frame Relay Fragmentation Implementation Agreement," December 1997.

[GAUTHIER87] Gauthier, P., Chemouil, P., and Klein, M., "STAR: A System to Test Adaptive Routing in France," Proceedings of the IEEE Global Telecommunications Conference, Tokyo, Japan, 1987.

[GIBBENS86] Gibbens, R. J. "Some Aspects of Dynamic Routing in Circuit-Switched Telecommunications Networks," Statistics Laboratory, University of Cambridge, January 1986.

[GIBBENS88] Gibbens R. J, *et al.*, "Dynamic Alternative Routing: Modeling and Behavior," Proc. of Int'l Teletraffic Congress, ITC 12, Turin, Italy, 1988.

[GIBBENS99] Gibbens, R. J., and Kelly, F. P., "Resource pricing and the evolution of congestion control," Automatica 35, 1999.

[GIRARD90] Girard, A., *Routing and Dimensioning in Circuit-Switched Networks*, Addison-Wesley, Reading, MA, 1990.

[GMPLS-RECOVERY-SPEC] Lang, J. P., *et al.*, "Generalized Multi-Protocol Label Switching (GMPLS) Recovery Functional Specification," IETF work in progress.

[GMPLS-RECOVERY-PROTOCOL] Lang, J. P., *et al.*, "RSVP-TE Extensions in Support of End-to-End Generalized Multi-Protocol Label Switching (GMPLS)-Based Recovery," IETF work in progress.

[GUNNAR04] Gunnar, A., *et al*, "Traffic Matrix Estimation on a Large IP Backbone—A Comparison on Real Data," ACM Internet Measurement Conference, Taormina, Sicily, Italy, October 2004.

[H.323] ITU-T Recommendation, "Visual Telephone Systems and Equipment for Local Area Networks Which Provide a Non-Guaranteed Quality of Service," November 1996.

[HC-OVER-MPLS-PROTOCOL] Ash, J., *et al.*, "Protocol Extensions for Header Compression over MPLS," IETF work in progress.

[HE02] He, L., and Walrand, J., "Dynamic Provisioning of Service Level Agreements between Interconnected Networks," Conference on Stochastic Networks, Stanford, June 2002.

[HEIDARI06] Heidari, F., Mason, L., and Mannor, S., "Comparative Evaluation of Learning and Load Sharing Algorithms," to appear.

[HEYMAN00] Heyman, D. P., and Mang, X., "Why Modeling Broadband Traffic Is Difficult, and Potential Ways of Doing It," Fifth INFORMS Telecommunications Conference, Boca Raton, FL, March 2000.

[HEYMAN99] Heyman, D. P., "Estimation of MMPP Models of IP Traffic," unpublished work.

[HILL76] Hill, D. W., and Neal, S. R., "The Traffic Capacity of a Probability Engineered Trunk Group," Bell System Technical Journal, Vol. 55, No. 7, September 1976.

[JANDER01] Jander, M., "In Qwest Outage, ATM Takes Some Heat," Light Reading, April 6, 2001.

[KAUFMAN81] Kaufman, J. S., "Blocking in a Shared Resource Environment," IEEE Transactions on Communications, Vol. 29, 1981, pp. 1474–1481.

[KELLY91] Kelly, F., "Effective Bandwidths at Multi-Class Queues," Queueing Systems 9, 1991.

[KELLY98] Kelly, F. P., et al., "Rate Control in Communication Networks: Shadow Prices, Proportional Fairness and Stability," Operations Research Society, Vol. 49, 1998.

[KLEINROCK75] Kleinrock, L. I., Queueing Systems, Vol. I: Theory, John Wiley & Sons, New York, 1975.

[KLEINROCK76] Kleinrock, L. I., Queueing Systems, Vol. II: Computer Applications, John Wiley & Sons, New York, 1976.

[KNEPLEY73] Knepley, J. E., "Minimum Cost Design for Circuit Switched Networks," Technical Note Numbers 36–73, Defense Communications Engineering Center, System Engineering Facility, Reston, Virginia, July 1973.

[KOWALSKI95] Kowalski, J., and Warfield, B., "Modeling Traffic Demand between Nodes in a Telecommunications Network," Australian Telecommunications and Networks Conference, Sydney, Australia, December 1995.

[KRISHNAN88] Krishnan, K. R., and Ott, T. J., "State-Dependent Routing for Telephone Traffic: Theory and Results," Proceedings of the 25th Conference on Decision and Control, Athens, Greece, December 1988.

[KRUITHOF37] Kruithof, J., "Telefoonverkeersrekening, De Ingenieur," Vol. 52, No. 8, February 1937.

[KRUPP79] Krupp, R. S., "Properties of Kruithof's Projection Method," Bell System Technical Journal, Vol. 58, No. 2, February 1979.

[KRUPP82] Krupp, R. S., "Stabilization of Alternate Routing Networks," IEEE International Communications Conference, Philadelphia, Pennsylvania, 1982.

[KUO95] Kuo, B., Automatic Control Systems, Prentice Hall, 1995.

[LA00] La, R. J., and Ananthram, V., "Charge-Sensitive TCP and Rate Control in the Internet," Proceedings IEEE INFOCOM'00, March 2000.

[LAI03] Lai, W., et al., "Requirements for Internet Traffic Engineering Measurement," IETF work in progress.

[LANGLOIS91] Langlois, F., and Regnier, J., "Dynamic Congestion Control in Circuit-Switched Telecommunications Networks," Proceedings of the Thirteenth International Teletraffic Congress, Copenhagen, Denmark, June 1991.

[LEHMAN06] Lehman, T., et al., "DRAGON: A Framework for Service Provisioning in Heterogeneous Grid Networks," IEEE Communications Magazine, March 2006.

[LELAND94] Leland, W., et al., "On the Self-Similar Nature of Ethernet Traffic," IEEE/ACM Transactions on Networking, February 1994.

[LEON-GARCIA03] Leon-Garcia, A., and Mason, L. G., "Virtual Network Resource Management for Next Generation Networks," Communications Magazine, July 2003.

[LEON-GARCIA05] Leon-Garcia, A., and Mason, L. G., "Virtual Network Approach to Scalable IP Service Deployment and Efficient Resource Management," October 2005.

[LEVEL3-TE] Springer, V., et al., "Level3 MPLS Protocol Architecture," IETF work in progress.

[LSP-HIER] Kompella, K., et al., "LSP Hierarchy with Generalized MPLS TE," IETF work in progress.

[L1VPN-FRAMEWORK] Takeda, T., "Framework and Requirements for Layer 1 Virtual Private Networks," IETF work in progress.

[MA98] Ma, Q., "Quality of Service Routing in Integrated Services Networks," Ph.D. Thesis, Carnegie Mellon, 1998

[MASE89] Mase, A., and Yamamoto, H., "Advanced Traffic Control Methods for Network Management," IEEE Journal on Selected Areas in Communication, Vol. 7, No. 8, 1989.

[McQUILLAN80] McQuillan, J., et al., "The New Routing Algorithm for the Internet," IEEE Transactions on Communications, May 1980.

[MEDDEB05] Meddeb, A., "Why Ethernet WAN Transport?" IEEE Communications Magazine, November 2005.

[MEIER-HELLSTERN89] Meier-Hellstern, K. S., "The Analysis of a Queue Arising in Overflow Models," IEEE Trans. Commun., Vol. 37, No. 4, pp. 367–372, April 1989.

[MINOUX86] Minoux, M., Mathematical Programming: Theory and Algorithms, Wiley, 1986.

[MITRA91] Mitra D., and Seery J. B., "Comparative Evaluations of Randomized and Dynamic Routing Strategies for Circuit-Switched Networks," IEEE Transactions on Communications, pp. 102–116, January 1991.

[MLN-EVALUATION] Le Roux, J. L., et al., "Evaluation of Existing GMPLS Protocols Against Multi Layer and Multi Region Networks (MLN/MRN)," IETF work in progress.

[MLN-REQUIREMENTS] Shiomoto, K., et al., "Requirements for GMPLS-Based Multi-Region and Multi-Layer Networks (MRN/MLN)," IETF work in progress.

[MPLS-CRANKBACK] Farrel, A., et al., "Crankback Signaling Extensions for MPLS and GMPLS RSVP-TE," IETF work in progress.

[MPLS-PROXY1] Phelan, T., and Bhargava, A., "MPLS Proxy Admission Control Protocol Definition," MPLS and Frame Relay Alliance, MPLS/FR 6.0.0, October 2004.

[MPLS-PROXY2] Phelan, T., "MPLS Proxy Admission Control Protocol," MPLS and Frame Relay Alliance, MPLS/FR 7.0.0, October 2004.

[MUMMERT76] Mummert, V. S., "Network Management and Its Implementation on the No. 4ESS," International Switching Symposium, Japan, 1976.

[NAKAGOME73] sNakagome, Y., and Mori, H., "Flexible Routing in the Global Communication Network," Proceedings of the Seventh International Teletraffic Congress, Stockholm, Sweden, 1973.

[NEWMAN98] Newman, P., et al., "IP Switching: ATM under IP," IEEE/ACM Transactions on Networking, Vol. 6, No. 2, April 1998.

[NYQUIST32] Nyquist, H., "Regeneration Theory," Bell Syst. Tech. J., 1932.

[ODLYZKO03] Odlyzko, A., "Data Networks Are Lightly Utilized, and Will Stay That Way," The Review of Network Economics, Vol. 2, No. 3, September 2003

[ODLYZKO99] Odlyzko, A., "Paris Metro Pricing for the Internet," Proc. ACM Conference on Electronic Commerce (EC'99), ACM, 1999.

[OSBORNE30] Osborne, H. S., "A General Switching Plan for Telephone Toll Services," Transactions of the AIEE, Vol. 49, October 1930, pp. 1549–1557.

[PACK82] Pack, C. D., and Whitaker, B. A., "Kalman Filter Models for Network Forecasting," Bell System Technical Journal, Vol. 61, No. 1, January 1982.

[PAPPALARDO01] Pappalardo, D., "AT&T, Customers Grapple with ATM Net Outage," Network World, February 26, 2001.

[PARLAY] "Parlay API Specification 1.2," September 1999.

[PCE-ARCHITECTURE] Farrel, A., Ash, J., and Vasseur, JP, "Path Computation Element (PCE) Architecture," IETF work in progress.

[PCE-PROTOCOL] Vasseur, J. P., *et al.*, "Path Computation Element (PCE) Communication Protocol (PCEP)—Version 1," IETF work in progress.

[PCE-REQUIREMENTS] Ash, J., *et al.*, "PCE Communication Protocol Generic Requirements," IETF work in progress.

[PILLIOD52] Pilliod, J. J., "Fundamental Plans for Toll Telephone Plant," Bell System Technical Journal, Vol. 31, No. 5, September 1952, pp. 832–850.

[PIORO89] Pioro, M., "Design Methods for Non-Hierarchical Circuit Switched Networks with Advanced Routing," Warsaw University of Technology Publications, 1989.

[PIORO04] Pioro, M., and Medhi, D., *Routing, Flow, and Capacity Design in Communication and Computer Networks*, Morgan Kaufmann, 2004.

[PRIORITY1] Tarapore, P. S., *et al.*, "Mechanisms for IP Priority Services and Standards Implications," ATIS/PRQC Contribution T1A1/2003-127 R1, May 2004.

[PRIORITY2] Tarapore, P. S., "Priority Considerations for Next Generation Networks," ITU-T NGN Focus Group Contribution FGNGN-ID-00154, September 2004.

[PRIORITY3] "User Plane Priority Levels for IP Networks and Services," ATIS/PRQC Technical Report, November 2004.

[PRIORITY4] Tarapore, P. S., *et al.*, "Control Plane Traffic Priority Considerations in IP Networks," ATIS/PRQC Contribution T1A1/2003-180, July 2004.

[PRIORITY5] Dolly, M., *et al.*, "Discussion on Associating Control Signaling Messages with Media Priority Levels," ATIS/PTSC Contribution T1S1.7/2003-577, October 2004.

[Q.71] ITU-T Recommendation, "ISDN Circuit Mode Switched Bearer Services."

[Q.761] ITU-T Recommendation, "Functional Description of the ISDN User Part of Signalling System No. 7," 1993.

[Q.1901] ITU-T Recommendation, "Bearer Independent Call Control Protocol," February 2000.

[Q.2761] ITU-T Recommendation, "Broadband Integrated Services Digital Network (B-ISDN) Functional Description of the B-ISDN User Part (B-ISUP) of Signaling System Number 7."

[QOS-SIG-NSLP] Van den Bosch, S., *et al.*, "NSLP for Quality-of-Service Signaling," IETF work in progress.

[QOS-SIG-NTLP] Hancock, R., *et al.*, "NSIS Transport Layer Protocol," IETF work in progress.

[QOS-SIG-QSPEC] Ash, J., *et al.*, "QoS-NSLP QSPEC Template," IETF work in progress.

[QOS-SIG-Y1541-QOSM] Ash, G. R., *et al.*, "Y.1541-QOSM–Y.1541 QoS Model for Networks Using Y.1541 QoS Classes," IETF work in progress.

[REGNIER90] Regnier J., and Cameron, W. H., "State-Dependent Dynamic Traffic Management for Telephone Networks," IEEE Communications Magazine, Vol. 28, No. 10, 1990.

[REKHTER97] Rekhter, Y., *et al.*, "Tag Switching Architecture Overview," Proceedings of the IEEE 1997, Vol. 85, No. 12, 1997.

[ROUGHAN02] Roughan, M., *et al.*, "Experience in Modeling Backbone Traffic Variability: Models, Metrics, Measurements, and Meaning," Proceedings of ACM SIGCOMM Internet Measurement Workshop, Marseille, France, November 2002.

[ROBERTS81] Roberts, J. W., "A Service System with Heterogeneous User Requirement," Performance of Data Communications Systems and Their Applications," G. Pujolle (Ed.), Amsterdam, North-Holland, 1981, pp. 423–431.

[RFC768] Postel, J., "User Datagram Protocol," RFC 768, August 1980.

[RFC793] DARPA, "Transmission Control Protocol," September 1981.

[RFC882] Mockapetris, P., "Domain Names: Concepts and Facilities," RFC 882, November 1983.

[RFC883] Mockapetris, P., "Domain Names: Implementation and Specification," RFC 882, November 1983.

[RFC1157] Case, J., *et al.*, "A Simple Network Management Protocol (SNMP)," RFC 1157, May 1990.

[RFC1518] Rekhter, Y., and Li, T., "An Architecture for IP Address Allocation with CIDR," RFC 1518, September 1993.

[RFC1519] Fuller, V., *et al.*, "Classless Inter-Domain Routing (CIDR): An Address Assignment and Aggregation Strategy," RFC 1519, September 1993.

[RFC1633] Braden, R., *et al.*, "Integrated Services in the Internet Architecture: An Overview," RFC 1633, June 1994.

[RFC1812] Baker, F., *et al.*, "Requirements for IP Version 4 Routers," RFC 1812, June 1995.

[RFC1990] Sklower, K., *et al.*, "The PPP Multilink Protocol (MP)," RFC 1990, August 1996.

[RFC2098] Katsube, Y., *et al.*, "Toshiba's Router Architecture Extensions for ATM: Overview," RFC 2098, February 1997.

[RFC2205] Braden, R., *et al.*, "Resource ReSerVation Protocol (RSVP)—Version 1 Functional Specification," RFC 2205, September 1997.

[RFC2206] Baker, F., *et al.*, "RSVP Management Information Base Using SMIv2," RFC 2206, September 1997.

[RFC2207] Berger, L., and O'Malley, T., "RSVP Extensions for IPSEC Data Flows," RFC 2207, September 1997.

[RFC2208] Mankin, A., *et al.*, "Resource ReSerVation Protocol (RSVP) Version 1 Applicability Statement—Some Guidelines on Deployments," RFC 2208, September 1997.

[RFC2209] Braden, R., and Zhang, L., "Resource ReSerVation Protocol (RSVP) Version 1 Message Processing Rules," RFC 2209, September 1997.

[RFC2210] Wroclawski, J., "The Use of RSVP with IETF Integrated Services," RFC2210, September 1997.

[RFC2211] Wroclawski, J., "Specification of the Controlled-Load Network Element Service," RFC 2211, September 1997.

[RFC2212] Shenker, S., *et al.*, "Specification of Guaranteed Quality of Service," RFC 2212, September 1997.

[RFC2213] Baker, F., *et al.*, "Integrated Services Management Information Base Using SMIv2," RFC 2213, September 1997.

[RFC2214] Baker, F., *et al.*, "Integrated Services Management Information Base Guaranteed Service Extensions Using SMIv2," RFC 2214, September 1997.

[RFC2215] Shenker, S., and Wroclawski, J., "General Characterization Parameters for Integrated Service Network Elements," RFC 2215, September 1997.

[RFC2328] Moy, J., "OSPF Version 2," RFC 2328, April 1998.

[RFC2386] Crawley, E., *et al.*, "A Framework for QoS-Based Routing in the Internet," RFC 2386, August 1998.

[RFC2474] Nichols, K., *et al.*, "Definition of the Differentiated Services Field (DS Field) in the IPv4 and IPv6 Headers," RFC 2474, December 1998.

[RFC2475] Blake, S., *et al.*, "An Architecture for Differentiated Services," December 1998.

[RFC2597] Heinanen, J., *et al.*, "Assured Forwarding PHB Group," RFC 2597, June 1999.

[RFC2638] Nichols, K., Jacobson, V., and Zhang, L., "A Two-Bit Differentiated Services Architecture for the Internet," RFC 2638, July 1999.

[RFC2702] Awduche, D., *et al.*, "Requirements for Traffic Engineering over MPLS," RFC 2702, September 1999.

[RFC2805] Greene, N., *et al.*, "Media Gateway Control Protocol Architecture and Requirements," April 2000.

[RFC2863] McCloghrie, K., *et al.*, "The Interfaces Group MIB Using SMIv2," RFC 2863, June 2000.

[RFC2961] Berger, L., *et al.*, "RSVP Refresh Overhead Reduction Extensions," RFC 2961, April 2001.

[RFC2998] Bernet, Y., *et al.*, "A Framework for Integrated Services Operation over Diffserv Networks," RFC 2998, November 2000.

[RFC3015] Cuervo, F., *et al.*, "Megaco Protocol Version 1.0," RFC 3015, November 2000.

[RFC3031] Rosen, E., *et al.*, "Multiprotocol Label Switching Architecture," RFC 3031, January 2001.

[RFC3032] Rosen, E., *et al.* "MPLS Label Stack Encoding," RFC 3032, January 2001.

[RFC3036] Andersson, L., *et al.*, "LDP Specification," RFC 3036, January 2001.

[RFC3175] Baker, F., *et al.*, "Aggregation of RSVP for IPv4 and IPv6 Reservations," RFC 3175, September 2001.

[RFC3209] Awduche, D., *et al.*, "RSVP-TE: Extensions to RSVP for LSP Tunnels," RFC 3209, December 2001.

[RFC3214] Ash, J., "LSP Modification Using CR-LDP," RFC 3214, January 2002.

[RFC3246] Davie, B., "An Expedited Forwarding PHB," RFC 3246, March 2002.

[RFC3261] Rosenberg, J., *et al.*, "SIP: Session Initiation Protocol," RFC 3261, June 2002.

[RFC3270] Le Faucheur, F., *et al.*, MPLS Support of Differentiated Services, May 2002.

[RFC3271] Faltstrom, P., and Mealling, M., "The E.164 to Uniform Resource Identifiers (URI) Dynamic Delegation Discovery System (DDDS) Application (ENUM)," RFC 3271, April 2004.

[RFC3272] Awduche, D., *et al.*, "Overview and Principles of Internet Traffic Engineering," RFC 3272, May 2002.

[RFC3312] Camarillo, G., *et al.*, "Integration of Resource Management and Session Initiation Protocol (SIP)," RFC 3312, October 2002.

[RFC3473] L. Berger, *et al.*, "Generalized MPLS Signaling: RSVP-TE Extensions," RFC 3473, January 2003.

[RFC3564] LeFaucher, F., *et al.*, "Requirements for Support of Differentiated Services-Aware MPLS Traffic Engineering," RFC 3564, July 2003.

[RFC3630] Katz, D., *et al.*, "Traffic Engineering (TE) Extensions to OSPF Version 2," RFC 3630, September 2003.

[RFC3784] Smit, H., and Li, T., "Intermediate System to Intermediate System (IS-IS) Extensions for Traffic Engineering (TE)," RFC 3784, June 2004.

[RFC3812] Srinivasan, C., *et al.*, "Multiprotocol Label Switching (MPLS) Traffic Engineering Management Information Base," RFC 3812, June 2004.

[RFC3813] Srinivasan, C., *et al.*, "Multiprotocol Label Switching (MPLS) Label Switching Router (LSR) Management Information Base," RFC 3813, June 2004.

[RFC3814] Nadeau, T., *et al.*, "Multiprotocol Label Switching (MPLS) Forwarding Equivalence Class to Next Hop Label Forwarding Entry (FEC-To-NHLFE) Management Information Base," RFC 3814, June 2004.

[RFC3815] Cucchiara, I. J., *et al.*, "Definitions of Managed Objects for the Multiprotocol Label Switching, Label Distribution Protocol (LDP)," RFC 3815, June 2004.

[RFC3945] Mannie, E., *et al.*, "Generalized Multi-Protocol Label Switching (GMPLS) Architecture," RFC 3945, October 2004.

[RFC3985] Bryant, S., and Pate, P., "Pseudo Wire Emulation Edge-to-Edge (PWE3) Architecture," March 2005.

[RFC4080] Hancock, R., *et al.*, "Next Steps in Signaling (NSIS): Framework," RFC 4080, June 2005.

[RFC4090] Pan, P., *et al.*, "Fast Reroute Extensions to RSVP-TE for LSP Tunnels," RFC 4090, May 2005.

[RFC4124] Le Faucheur, F., *et al.*, "Protocol Extensions for Support of Diff-Serv-Aware MPLS Traffic Engineering," RFC 4124, June 2005.

[RFC4125] LeFaucher, F., and Lai, W., "Maximum Allocation Bandwidth Constraints Model for Diff-Serv-Aware MPLS Traffic Engineering," RFC 4125, June 2005.

[RFC4126] Ash, J., "Max Allocation with Reservation Bandwidth Constraints Model for DiffServ-Aware MPLS Traffic Engineering and Performance Comparisons," June 2005.

[RFC4127] LeFaucher, F., "Russian Dolls Bandwidth Constraints Model for Diffserv-Aware MPLS Traffic Engineering," RFC 4127, June 2005.

[RFC4128] Lai, W., "Bandwidth Constraints Models for Differentiated Services (Diffserv)-Aware MPLS Traffic Engineering: Performance Evaluation," RFC 4128, June 2005.

[RFC4201] Kompella, K., Rekhter, Y., and Berger, L., "Link Bundling in MPLS Traffic Engineering (TE)," RFC 4201, October 2005.

[RFC4202] Lang, J., "Link Management Protocol (LMP)," RFC 2404, October 2005.

[RFC4222] Choudhury, G., *et al.*, "Prioritized Treatment of Specific OSPF Packets and Congestion Avoidance," RFC 4222, October 2005.

[RFC4247] Ash, J., *et al.*, "Requirements for Header Compression over MPLS," RFC 4247, November 2005.

[RFC4271] Rekhter, Y., *et al.*, "A Border Gateway Protocol 4 (BGP-4)," RFC 4271, January 2006.

[RFC4273] Haas, J., and Hares, S., "Definitions of Managed Objects for the Fourth Version of Border Gateway Protocol (BGP-4)," RFC 4273, January 2006.

[RFC4364] Rosen, E., and Rekhter, Y., "BGP/MPLS VPNs," RFC 4364, February 2006.

[RFC4379] Kompella, K., *et al.*, "Detecting MPLS Data Plane Failures," RFC 4379, February 2006.

[RFC4382] Nadeau, T., *et al.*, "MPLS/BGP Virtual Private Network Management Information Base Using SMIv2," RFC 4382, February 2006.

[RFC4412] Schulzrinne, H., and Polk, J., "Communications Resource Priority for the Session Initiation Protocol (SIP)," RFC 4412, February 2006.

[SEMRET00] Semret, N., Liao, R. R.-F., Campbell, A. T., and Lazar, A. A., "Pricing, Provisioning and Peering: Dynamic Markets for Differentiated Internet Services and Implications for Network Interconnections," IEEE JSAC, Vol. 18, No. 12, December 2000.

[SHIOMOTO05] Shiomoto, K., *et al.*, "Requirements for GMPLS-Based Multi-Region Networks (MRN)," IETF work in progress.

[SIKORA98] Sikora, J., and Teitelbaum, B., "Differentiated Services for Internet2," Internet2: Joint Applications/Engineering QoS Workshop, Santa Clara, CA, May 1998.

[STACEY87] Stacey, R. R., and Songhurst D. J., "Dynamic Alternative Routing in the British Telecom Trunk Network," Proceedings ISS 1987, Phoenix, AZ, 1987.

[STEENSTRUP95] Steenstrup, M. (Ed.), *Routing in Communications Networks*, Prentice-Hall, 1995.

[STEINBERG96] Steinberg, S. G., "Netheads vs. Bellheads," Wired Magazine, October 1996.

[STEVENS94] Stevens, W. R., *TCP/IP Illustrated, Volume 1, The Protocols*, Addison-Wesley, 1994.

[TRQ-QOS-SIG] ITU-T Recommendation, "Signaling Requirements for IP-QoS," January 2004.

[TRIMINTZIOS01] Trimintzios, *et al.*, "A Management and Control Architecture for Providing IP Differentiated Services in MPLS-Based Networks," May 2001.

[TRUITT54] Truitt, C. J., "Traffic Engineering Techniques for Determining Trunk Requirements in Alternate Routed Networks," Bell System Technical Journal, Vol. 31, No. 2, March 1954.

[VERTICAL-INTERFACE] Dolly, M., et al., "Discussion on Associating of Control Signaling Messages with Media Priority Levels," T1S1.7 and PRQC, October 2004.

[VILLAMIZAR99] Villamizar, C., "MPLS Optimized Multipath," IETF work in progress.

[VISWANATHAN98] Viswanathan, A., et al., "Aggregate Route-Based IP Switching (ARIS)," IBM Technical Report TR29.2353, February 1998.

[WARSHALL62] Warshall, S., "A Theorem on Boolean Matrices," Journal of the ACM, January 1962.

[WATANABE87] Watanabe, Y., and Mori, H., "Dynamic Routing Schemes for International ISDNs," Proceedings of the Fifth ITC Specialists Seminar: Traffic Engineering for ISDN Design and Planning, Lake Como, Italy, May 1987.

[WEBER62] Weber, J. H., "Some Traffic Characteristics of Communication Networks with Automatic Alternate Routing," Bell System Technical Journal, Vol. 41, 1962, pp. 769–796.

[WEBER64] Weber, J. H., "A Simulation Study of Routing and Control in Communications Networks," Bell System Technical Journal, Vol. 43, 1964, pp. 2639–2676.

[WEINTRAUB63] Weintraub, S., Tables of Cumulative Binomial Probability Distribution for Small Values of p, Collier-Macmillan Limited, London, 1963.

[WILKINSON56] Wilkinson, R. I., "Theories of Toll Traffic Engineering in the U.S.A.," Bell System Technical Journal, Vol. 35, No. 6, March 1956.

[WILKINSON58] Wilkinson, R. I., "A Study of Load and Service Variations in Toll Alternate Route Systems," Proceedings of the Second International Teletraffic Congress, The Hague, Netherlands, July 1958, Document No. 29.

[XIAO99] Xiao, X., et al., "Internet QoS: A Big Picture," IEEE Network, March/April 1999.

[XIAO00a] Xiao, X., et al., "Traffic Engineering with MPLS in the Internet," IEEE Network, March 2000.

[XIAO00b] Xiao, X., "Providing Quality of Service in the Internet," Ph.D. Thesis, Michigan State University, 2000.

[Y.1291] ITU-T Recommendation, "An Architectural Framework for Support of Quality of Service (QoS) in Packet Networks."

[Y.1540] ITU-T Recommendation, "Internet Protocol Data Communication Service—IP Packet Transfer and Availability Performance Parameters," December 2002.

[Y.1541] ITU-T Recommendation, "Network Performance Objectives for IP-Based Services," May 2002.

[Y.2001] ITU-T Recommendation, "General Overview of NGN."

[Y.2011] ITU-T Recommendation, "General Principles and General Reference Model for Next Generation Networks."

[YAGED71] Yaged, B., Jr., "Long Range Planning for Communications Networks," Ph.D. Thesis, Polytechnic Institute of Brooklyn, 1971.

[YAICHE00] Yaiche, H., Mazumdar, R., and Rosenberg, C., "A Game Theoretic Framework for Bandwidth Allocation and Pricing in Broadband Networks," IEEE/ACM Transactions on Networking, Vol. 8, No. 5, October 2000.

[YAGED73] Yaged, B., "Minimum Cost Design for Circuit Switched Networks," Vol. 3, 1973, pp. 193–224.

[ZHANG03] Zhang, Y., et al., "Fast Accurate Computation of Large-Scale IP Traffic Matrices from Link Loads," Proceedings of ACM Sigmetrics, 2003.

[ZIPF46] Zipf, G. K., "Some Determinates of the Circulation of Information," American Journal of Psychology, Vol. 59, 1946.

Bibliography

Apostolopoulos, G., "On the Cost and Performance Trade-Offs of Quality of Service Routing," Ph.D. Thesis, University of Maryland, 1999.

Apostolopoulos, G., *et al.*, "Implementation and Performance Measurements of QoS Routing Extensions to OSPF," Proceedings of INFOCOM'99, April 1999.

Armitage, G., *Quality of Service in IP Networks: Foundations for a Multi-Service Internet*, Macmillan, April 2000.

Ash, G. R., *et al.*, "Routing Evolution in Multiservice Integrated Voice/Data Networks," Proceeding of ITC-16, Edinburgh, June 1999.

Ash, G. R., "Performance Evaluation of QoS-Routing Methods for IP-Based Multiservice Networks," Computer Communications Magazine, July 2003.

Chaudhary, V. P., Krishnan, K. R., and Pack, C. D., "Implementing Dynamic Routing in the Local Telephone Companies of the USA," Proc. of Int'l Teletraffic Congress, ITC 13, Copenhagen, Denmark, 1991.

Chemouil, P., Lebourges, M., and Gauthier, P., "Performance Evaluation of Adaptive Traffic Routing in a Metropolitan Network: A Case Study," Proceedings Globecom 1989, Dallas, TX, 1989.

Crovella, M. E., "Self-Similarity in WWW Traffic: Evidence and Possible Causes," IEEE Transactions on Networking, December 1997.

Dantzig, G. B., *Linear Programming and Extensions*, Princeton University Press, 1963.

Doverspike, *et al.*, "Future Transport Network Architectures," IEEE Communications Magazine, August 1999.

Davie, B. S., and Rekhter, Y., *MPLS: Technology and Applications*, Morgan Kaufmann, May 2000.

Dziong, Z., Pioro, M., and Krner, U., "State-Dependent Routing in Circuit-Switched Networks: A Maximum Reward Approach," Proc. of International Teletraffic Congress, ITC 12, Turin, Italy, 1988.

[E.352] ITU-T Recommendation, "Routing Guidelines for Efficient Routing Methods."

[E.412] ITU-T Recommendation, "Network Management Controls."

[E.490] ITU-T Recommendation, "Traffic Measurement and Evaluation: General Survey," June 1992.

[E.600] ITU-T Recommendation, "Terms and Definitions of Traffic Engineering," March 1993.

[E.651] ITU-T Recommendation, "Reference Connections for Traffic Engineering of IP Access Networks."

[E.716] ITU-T Recommendation, "User Demand Modeling in Broadband-ISDN," October 1996.

[E.734] ITU-T Recommendation, "Methods for Allocation and Dimensioning Intelligent Network (IN) Resources," October 1996.

[E.735] ITU-T Recommendation, "Framework for Traffic Control and Dimensioning in B-ISDN," May 1997.

[E.736] ITU-T Recommendation, "Methods for Cell Level Traffic Control in the B-ISDN," May 1997.

[E.737] ITU-T Recommendation, "Dimensioning Methods for B-ISDN," May 1997.

[E.745] ITU-T Recommendation, "Cell Level Measurement Requirements for the B-ISDN," March 2000.

[E.800] ITU-T Recommendation, "Terms and Definitions Related to Quality of Service and Network Performance Including Dependability," August 1994.

Feldman, A., Rexford, J., and Caceres, R., "Efficient Policies for Carrying Web Traffic over Flow-Switched Networks," IEEE/ACM Transactions on Networking, December 1998.

Ferguson, P., and Huston, G., *Quality of Service: Delivering QoS on the Internet and in Corporate Networks*, John Wiley & Sons, 1998.

Filipiak J., *Modelling and Control of Dynamic Flows in Networks*, Springer Verlag, 1988.

Floyd, S., and Jacobson, V., "Random Early Detection Gateways for Congestion Avoidance," IEEE/ACM Transactions on Networking, August 1993.

Forestier, J. P., "A Decentralized Approach for Real-Time Adaptive Control of Telecommunications Network," Proceedings Networks 1980, Paris, France, 1980.

Fortz, B., and Thorup, M., "Internet Traffic Engineering by Optimizing OSPF Weights," Proceedings of IEEE INFOCOM, March 2000.

Fortz, B., Rexford, J., and Thorup, M., "Traffic Engineering with Traditional IP Routing Protocols," IEEE Communications Magazine, October 2002.

Ghani, N., Duxit, S., and Wang, T., "On IP-over-WDM Integration," IEEE Communications Magazine, March 2000.

Ghanwani, A., *et al.*, "Traffic Engineering Standards in IP Networks Using MPLS," IEEE Communications Magazine, December 1999.

Gimpelson, L. A., "Network Management: Design and Control of Communications Networks," Electrical Communications, Vol. 49, No. 1, 1974

Girard, A., *Routing and Dimensioning in Circuit-Switched Networks*, Addison Wesley, 1990.

Gojmerac, I., "Routing and Traffic Engineering for Future IP Networks," COST 279 Meeting, Rome, Italy, 2004

Grandjean, C., "Call Routing Strategies in Telecommunications Networks," Proceedings of International Teletraffic Congress, ITC 5, New York, 1967.

Granel, E., *et al.*, "A Comparative Study of Several Dynamic Routing Algorithms with Adaptive Pre-Selection and Selection Phase," Proceedings of International Teletraffic Congress, ITC 13, Copenhagen, Denmark, 1991.

Huitema, C., *Routing in the Internet*, Prentice Hall, 1995.

Halabi, B., *Internet Routing Architectures*, Cisco Press, 1997.

[H.225.0] ITU-T Recommendation, "Media Stream Packetization and Synchronization on Non-Guaranteed Quality of Service LANs," November 1996.

[H.245] ITU-T Recommendation, "Control Protocol for Multimedia Communication," March 1996.

Hennion, B., "Feedback Methods for Calls Allocation on the Crossed Traffic Routing," Proceedings of International Teletraffic Congress, ITC 9, Torremolinos, Spain, 1979.

Heyman, D. P., and Lakshman, T. V., "What are the Implications of Long-Range Dependence for VBR-Video Traffic Engineering," IEEE Transactions on Networking, June 1996.

Huston, G., Cerf, V. G., and Chapin, L., *Internet Performance Survival Guide: QoS Strategies for Multi-Service Networks*, John Wiley & Sons, February 2000.

[I.211] ITU-T Recommendation, "B-ISDN Service Aspects," March 1993.

[I.324] ITU-T Recommendation, "ISDN Network Architecture," 1991.

[I.327] ITU-T Recommendation, "B-ISDN Functional Architecture," March 1993.

[I.356] ITU-T Recommendation, "B-ISDN ATM Layer Cell Transfer Performance," October 1996.

ITU/UNDP, "Seminar on Intelligent Routing Strategies Including Network Management Aspects," Zruc, Czechoslovakia, 1986.

Juttner, A., Szentesi, A., Harmatos, J., Pioro, M., and Gajowniczek, P., "On Solvability of an OSPF Routing Problem," 15th Nordic Teletraffic Seminar, Lund, 2000.

Karmarkar, N. K., "A New Polynomial Time Algorithm for Linear Programming,"Combinatorica, Vol. 4, No. 4, 1984, pp. 373–395.

Karmarkar, N. K., and Ramakrishnan, K. G., "Implementation and Computational Results of the Karmarkar Algorithm for Linear Programming, Using an Iterative Method for Computing Projections," 13th International Symposium on Mathematical Programming, Tokyo, Japan, 1988.

Kilkki, K., *Differentiated Services for the Internet*, Macmillan, 1999.

Kobayashi, H., *Modeling and Analysis*, Addison-Wesley, 1978.

Krishnamurthy, B., and Rexford, J., *Web Protocols and Practice*, Addison-Wesley, 2001.

Krupp, R. S., "Stabilization of Alternate Routing Networks," IEEE International Communications Conference, Philadelphia, PA, 1982.

Kurose, J. F., and Ross, K. W., *Computer Networking, A Top-Down Approach Featuring the Internet*, Addison-Wesley, 2000.

Li, T., "MPLS and the Evolving Internet Architecture," IEEE Communications Magazine, December 1999.

Ma, Q., and Steenkiste, P., "On Path Selection for Traffic with Bandwidth Guarantees," Proceedings of IEEE International Conference on Network Protocols, October 1997.

Ma, Q., and Steenkiste, P., "Quality-of-Service Routing for Traffic with Performance Guarantees," Proceedings of IFIP Fifth International Workshop on Quality of Service, May 1997.

Ma, Q., and Steenkiste, P., "Routing Traffic with Quality-of-Service Guarantees," Proceedings of Workshop on Network and Operating Systems Support for Digital Audio and Video, July 1998.

Ma, Q., and Steenkiste, P., "Supporting Dynamic Inter-Class Resource Sharing: A Multi-Class QoS Routing Algorithm," Proceedings of IEEE INFOCOM'99, March 1999.

Ma, T., and Shi, B., "Bringing Quality Control to IP QoS," Network Magazine, November 2000.

Mason, L. G., and Girard, A., "Control Techniques and Performance Models for Circuit-Switched Networks," Proceedings of CDC 1982, Orlando, FL, 1982.

Mason, L. G., "Equilibrium Flows, Routing Patterns and Algorithms for Store-and-Forward Networks," North-Holland, Large Scale Systems, Vol. 8, 1985.

McDysan, D., *QoS and Traffic Management in IP and ATM Networks*, McGraw-Hill, 1999.

Metz, C., *IP Switching: Protocols and Architecture*, McGraw-Hill, 1998.

Moy, J., *OSPF: Anatomy of an Internet Routing Protocol*, Addison Wesley, 1999.

Narendra, K. S., Wright, E. A., and Mason, L. G., "Application of Learning Automata to Telephone Traffic Routing and Control," IEEE Transactions on Systems, Man and Cybernetics, Vol. SMC-7, No. 11, November 1977.

Odlyzko, A., "The Economics of the Internet: Utility, Utilization, Pricing, and Quality of Service," http://www.dtc.umn.edu/~odlyzko/doc/networks.html.

Park, K., and Willinger, W., *Self-Similar Network Traffic and Performance Evaluation*, John Wiley & Sons, August 2000.

[Q.765.5] ITU-T Recommendation, "Application Transport Mechanism: Bearer Independent Call Control (BICC)," December 1999.

[Q.2931] ITU-T Recommendation, "Broadband Integrated Services Digital Network (B-ISDN): Digital Subscriber Signalling System No. 2 (DSS 2): User-Network Interface (UNI) Layer 3 Specification for Basic Call/Connection Control," February 1995.

Oueslati, S., and Roberts, J. W., "Application of Trunk Reservation to Elastic Flow Routing," Proceedings of IFIP Networking 2000, Paris, France, 2000.

[RFC1889] Schulzrinne, H., Casner, S., Frederick, R., and Jacobson, V., "RTP: A Transport Protocol for Real-Time Applications," RFC 1889, January 1996.

[RFC1940] Estrin, D., Li, T., Rekhter, Y., Varadhan, K., and Zappala, D., "Source Demand Routing: Packet Format and Forwarding Specification (Version 1)," RFC 1940, May 1996.

[RFC1992] Castineyra, I., Chiappa, N., and Steenstrup, M., "The Nimrod Routing Architecture," RFC 1992, August 1996.

[RFC2722] Brownlee, N., and Ruth, G., "Traffic Flow Measurement: Architecture," RFC 2722, October 1999.

Roberts, J. W., "Traffic Theory and the Internet," IEEE Communications Magazine, January 2001.

Sahinoglu, Z., and Tekinay, S., "On Multimedia Networks: Self-Similar Traffic and Network Performance," IEEE Communication Magazine, January 1999.

Schwefel, H.-P., and Lipsky, L., "Performance Results for Analytic Models of Traffic in Telecommunication Systems, Based on Multiple ON-OFF Sources with Self-Similar Behavior," 16th International Teletraffic Congress, Edinburgh, June 1999.

Special Issue: Advanced Traffic Control Methods for Circuit-Switched Telecommunications Networks, IEEE Communications Magazine, Vol. 28, No. 10, 1990.

Special Issue: Dynamic Routing in Telecommunications Networks, IEEE Communications Magazine, Vol. 33, No. 7, 1995.

Strand, J., Chiu, A., and Tkach, R., "Issues for Routing in the Optical Layer," IEEE Communications Magazine, February 2001.

Swallow, G., "MPLS Advantages for Traffic Engineering," IEEE Communications Magazine, December 1999.

Szybicki, E., and Bean, A. E., "Advanced Traffic Routing in Local Telephone Network: Performance of Proposed Call Routing Algorithms," Proceedings of International Teletraffic Congress, ITC 9, Torremolinos, Spain, 1979.

Wilkinson, R. I., "Some Comparisons of Load and Loss Data with Current Teletraffic Theory," Bell System Technical Journal, Vol. 50, October 1971, pp. 2807–2834.

Yates, J. M., Rumsewicz, M. P., and Lacey, J. P. R., "Wavelength Converters in Dynamically-Reconfigurable WDM Networks," IEEE Communications Society Survey Paper, 1999.

Index